THESES
IN
ENGLISH LITERATURE
1894-1970

THESES
IN
ENGLISH LITERATURE
1894-1970

Compiled and Edited
by
PATSY C. HOWARD
Abilene Christian College

THE PIERIAN PRESS
Ann Arbor, Michigan
1973

Library of Congress Catalog Card Number 78-172776
ISBN 0-87650-021-1

THE PIERIAN PRESS
P.O. Box 1808
Ann Arbor, MI. 48106

To My Mother

LILLIAN BELLE HOWARD

and in Memory of My Late Father

JAMES CLIFFORD HOWARD

FOREWORD

This bibliography of unpublished baccalaureate and masters' theses is
drawn primarily from listings made by the compiler who personally collected
the material at many southwestern, southern and eastern colleges and
universities during the summer of 1970. The collection is necessarily
incomplete. It serves as the beginning of a series whose goal is to make
a complete, easily-accessible listing of theses in literature throughout
the world.

The purposes of this compilation are: 1) to indicate which fields of
research have received noticeable attention; 2) to indicate those areas
of research generally unexplored by graduate students; and 3) to provide
convenient bibliographies on highly specialized topics for those students
presently engaged in bibliographic scholarship.

The entries in this volume are arranged alphabetically by the most
commonly used name for each English writer. Under each classification the
theses and essays are alphabetized by thesis author. Each title is numbered,
and cross references, if any, are indicated by these numbers. A cumulative
thesis author index as well as a limited subject index is provided at the
end of the bibliography. A list of participating institutions is also
provided immediately following this Foreword.

As to the form taken by the bibliography, the editor feels it is the
most useful one in view of the thesis series far-reaching scope. Along with
the usually accepted abbreviations, we decided to shorten State (St),
College (Coll) and University (Univ). The designation of the degree was
also abbreviated: MA for Master of Arts, M Phil for Master of Philosophy,
M Ed for Master of Education, MS for Master of Science, M Litt for Master of
Literature, MFA for Master of Fine Arts, BA for Bachelor of Arts, B Litt for
Bachelor of Literature and BS for Bachelor of Science.

In this first volume the basis for the selection of the bibliographic
entries has been one of availability. The response from librarians has
been overwhelming. Those contacted have been very gracious and most enthusiastic. The compiler wishes to thank the numerous reference librarians,
department heads and personal friends for their contributions to this work.
Contributions from the following are gratefully acknowledged:

Charles Adams, Sister Albina-Marie, C M Baker, Cheryl Bandy, Patty Barker,
Verne and Robert Barker, Carolynne Barnes, Harry Bergholz, Paula Bernard,
Edmund Bojarski, Laura Boyer, Luther Brown, Randy Brown, Charles E Butler,
John K Cameron, Myrtle Carroll, Beverly Anne Carter, Richard R Chamberlin,
Marcy Chambers, Antoinette Ciolli, Dorothy H Claybourne, William Cook Jr,
Kathleen Creech, Joyce A Crenshaw, Barna Csuros, J H Deardoff, Billy H and
Peggy Dennard, Frieda Dickson, Sister Laura Dillon, Elva Love Dobson,
Don Donham, Evelyn Ehrlich, C M Ellis, Charlotte Engelhardt, George Ewing,
Teri Falls, Obion W Feagin, Sue Findley, Ezra C Fitch, Kathyrn Forbes,
Thomas Frazier, A C Garvin, Dennis Gibson, Paula Gillen, Eleanor Goehring,
Sara Lou Goff, Martha Graham, Beth Granichen, Rebecca Green, S B Gribble,
Bob and Sue Griggs, Arthur Goldzweig, Bernadette Gualtieri, Willie D Halsell,
Helen Haney, Jill Hardin, Trena Harlan, Mary Harlow, Betty Hartbank,
Lois Harzfeld, Dorothy Heicke, Millicent Hering, Ruth V Hewlett,
Dorothy Hiecke, Ann T Hinckley, Beryl Hoskin, Monty Howard, William Humble,
Sharon Humphrey, I Isaacson, Dick and Kaye Ivey, Jennifer Jacques,
Katharine Jaffe, Jacqueline Jenkins, Jane Ann Jenkins, Ruth Johnson,
Barbara Jones, Martha Jones, Margaret A Joseph, Minnie S Kallam,
Margaret J Keefe, Charles H Kemp, Eura LaDelle Key, Edith Keys, Floreine Kibler,
Margaret J Kyle, Evelyn Lightfoot, Bob and Judy McCourt, Kathleen McCourt,
John MacEachern, Mary A McKenzie, Edmund Maloney, Sister Mary Marguerite,

Larry May, Floyd S Merritt, William Messenger, Eleanor Mitchell,
Dorothy Moore, Margaret Moseley, Judith Mowery, A M Mumper, Janet H Murphy,
M G Nelson, the C B Nichols, Debbie Nunnally, Roberto Pasqualato, Angela Paulo
Sandy Pinsker, Sara and Franz Pittman, Mary Lynn Potts, Helen J Poulton,
James Pula, Linda Rabon, Dianne Rabun, Frances D Rhome, Ann Rose, Roylyn Rose,
Charity M Roth, Deborah Rudloff, Anna Loe Russell, Shirley Sailors, Orlan Sawe
Sara Sawey, Elizabeth B Scott, Rita Scott, P O Selby, John H Sharpe,
Donald Siefker, Henry L Simmons, Charles Small, Lee Smith, Margaret Smith,
Dolores Smittle, Mildred D Southwick, W A Stanton, Elizabeth Steele,
Alice Steger, Marion Stein, Jocelyn E Stevens, John Stevens, Joan Stewart,
Diana Svien, Ken Swearingen, Bruce Teets, Juanita Terry, Dan R Thorson,
Elaine M Tieman, Anne L Turner, the late W E "Bill" Tyler, Margaret D Uridge,
Dean Waddell, Arnold S Wajenberg, Mary Lou and Wayne Walden, Jim Walker,
Pearl Walker, James F Warfield, Billie White, Nancy A Whitman, Marvin E Wiggin
Geneva Williams, Robert Williams, Harold Williamson, Henry W Wingate,
Marian H Withington and Anne Womeldorf.

The following bibliographies have been most helpful: Elton F Henley's
A Checklist of Masters' Theses in the United States on William Wordsworth;
Paul F Friesner's *Bibliography of Masters' Theses at Fort Hays Kansas
State College 1930-1962*; Clyde H Cantrell and Walton R Patrick's *Southern
Literary Culture: A Bibliography of Masters' and Doctors' Theses*; Edmund A
and Henry T Bojarski's *Joseph Conrad: A Bibliography of Masters' Theses
and Doctoral Dissertations*; Robert F Stephens' *A Bibliography of Masters'
Theses Concerning Edmund Spenser*; S J Sackett's *Masters' Theses in
Literature (1964-1966)*.

A special thank you for the professional typing of Mrs Barbara Aycock,
as well as for her unbelievable patience with an often changed manuscript.

PATSY C HOWARD
Abilene Christian College

LIST OF INSTITUTIONS

ALABAMA

Auburn University (Auburn); Birmingham-Southern College (Birmingham); University of Alabama (University)

ARIZONA

Arizona State University (Tempe); Northern Arizona University (Flagstaff); University of Arizona (Tucson)

ARKANSAS

Arkansas State College (Conway); Henderson State College (Arkadelphia); University of Arkansas (Fayetteville)

CALIFORNIA

California State College at Long Beach (Long Beach); Claremont Graduate School (Claremont); Dominican College of San Rafael (San Rafael); Fresno State College (Fresno); Mills College (Oakland); Occidental College (Los Angeles); Sacramento State College (Sacramento); San Diego State College (San Diego); San Francisco College for Women (San Francisco); San Jose State College (San Jose); Stanford University (Palo Alto); University of California at Berkeley (Berkeley); University of California at Davis (Davis); University of California at Los Angeles (Los Angeles); University of California at Riverside (Riverside); University of Redlands (Redlands); University of Santa Clara (Santa Clara); University of Southern California (Los Angeles); Whittier College (Whittier)

COLORADO

Adams State College (Alamosa); Colorado College (Colorado Springs); Colorado State College (Greeley); Colorado State University (Fort Collins); University of Colorado (Boulder); University of Denver (Denver); Western State College of Colorado (Gunnison)

CONNECTICUT

Central Connecticut State College (New Britain); St Joseph College (West Hartford); Southern Connecticut State College (New Haven); Trinity College (Hartford); University of Connecticut (Storrs); Wesleyan University (Middletown); Yale University (New Haven)

DELAWARE

University of Delaware (Newark)

DISTRICT OF COLUMBIA

American University (Washington, D C); Catholic University of America (Washington, D C); Georgetown University (Washington, D C); George Washington University (Washington, D C); Howard University (Washington, D C)

FLORIDA

Barry College (Miami); Florida State University (Tallahassee); Stetson
University (Deland); University of Florida (Gainesville); University of Miami
(Coral Gables)

GEORGIA

Atlanta University (Atlanta); Emory University (Atlanta); University of
Georgia (Athens)

HAWAII

University of Hawaii (Honolulu)

IDAHO

Idaho State University (Pocatello); University of Idaho (Moscow)

ILLINOIS

DePaul University (Chicago); Illinois State University (Normal); Northern
Illinois University (Dekalb); Northwestern University (Evanston); Southern
Illinois University at Carbondale (Carbondale); University of Chicago (Chicago
University of Illinois at Urbana (Urbana); Western Illinois University (Macomb

INDIANA

Butler University (Indianapolis); DePauw University (Greencastle); Indiana
University (Bloomington); Purdue University (Lafayette); University of
Notre Dame (Notre Dame)

IOWA

Drake University (Des Moines); State College of Iowa (Cedar Falls);
University of Iowa (Iowa City)

KANSAS

Fort Hays Kansas State College (Hays); Kansas State College at Pittsburg
(Pittsburg); Kansas State Teachers College (Emporia); Kansas State University
(Manhattan); University of Kansas (Lawrence); Wichita State University
(Wichita)

KENTUCKY

Eastern Kentucky University (Richmond); Morehead State University (Morehead);
University of Kentucky (Lexington); University of Louisville (Louisville)

LOUISIANA

Louisiana Polytechnic Institute (Ruston); Louisiana State University
(Baton Rouge); Loyola University (New Orleans); Northeast Louisiana State
College (Monroe); Northwestern Louisiana State College (Natchitoches);

Tulane University (New Orleans); University of Southwestern Louisiana (Lafayette); Xavier University of Louisiana (New Orleans)

MAINE

University of Maine (Orono)

MARYLAND

Johns Hopkins University (Baltimore); St Joseph College (Emmitsburg); University of Maryland (College Park)

MASSACHUSETTS

Amherst College (Amherst); Boston College (Boston); Boston University (Boston); Clark University (Worcester); Harvard University (Cambridge); Mount Holyoke College (South Hadley); Smith College (Northampton); State College at Fitchburg (Fitchburg); Tufts University (Medford); University of Massachusetts (Amherst); Wellesley College (Wellesley); Williams College (Williamstown)

MICHIGAN

Siena Heights College (Adrian); University of Detroit (Detroit); Wayne State University (Detroit)

MINNESOTA

Bemidji State College (Bemidji); Moorhead State College (Moorhead); St John's University (Collegeville); University of Minnesota (Minneapolis)

MISSOURI

Northeast Missouri State College (Kirksville); St Louis University (St Louis); University of Missouri (Columbia); Washington University of St Louis (St Louis)

MISSISSIPPI

Mississippi State University (State College); University of Mississippi (University); University of Southern Mississippi (Hattiesburg)

MONTANA

Montana State University (Bozeman); University of Montana (Missoula)

NEBRASKA

Kearney State College (Kearney); Municipal University of Omaha (Omaha); University of Nebraska (Lincoln); University of Omaha (Omaha); Wayne State College (Wayne)

NEVADA

University of Nevada (Reno)

NEW HAMPSHIRE

Rivier College (Nashua); University of New Hampshire (Durham)

NEW JERSEY

Fairleigh Dickinson University (Rutherford); Rutgers State University
(New Brunswick)

NEW MEXICO

Eastern New Mexico University (Portales); New Mexico Highlands University
(Las Vegas); University of New Mexico (Albuquerque)

NEW YORK

Brooklyn College of the City University of New York (Brooklyn); Canisius
College (Buffalo); City College of the City University of New York (New York);
Cornell University (Ithaca); Columbia University (New York); C W Post College
(Brookville, Long Island); Fordham University (New York); Hunter College of
the City University of New York (New York); Long Island University (Brooklyn);
New York State Teachers College (New York); Niagara University (Niagara);
St John's University (Jamaica); Sarah Lawrence College (Bronxville); Siena
College (Loudonville); State University of New York at Buffalo (Buffalo);
State University of New York College at Buffalo (Buffalo); Syracuse University
(Syracuse); Wagner College (Staten Island); Wells College (Aurora)

NORTH CAROLINA

Duke University (Durham); East Carolina University (Greenville); North
Carolina College (Durham); University of North Carolina at Chapel Hill
(Chapel Hill); University of North Carolina at Greensboro (Greensboro);
Wake Forest College (Winston-Salem); Western Carolina University (Cullowhee)

NORTH DAKOTA

University of North Dakota (Grand Forks)

OHIO

Bowling Green University (Bowling Green); Case-Western Reserve University
(Cleveland); John Carroll University (Cleveland); Kent State University (Kent);
Miami University (Oxford); Oberlin College (Oberlin); Ohio State University
(Columbus); Ohio University (Athens); University of Cincinnati (Cincinnati);
University of Toledo (Toledo); Wittenberg University (Springfield)

OKLAHOMA

Northwestern State College (Alva); Oklahoma East Central State College (Ada);
Oklahoma State University (Stillwater); University of Oklahoma (Norman);
University of Tulsa (Tulsa)

OREGON

Pacific University (Forest Grove); University of Oregon (Eugene)

PENNSYLVANIA

Bucknell University (Lewisburg); Carnegie-Mellon University (Pittsburgh); Duquesne University (Pittsburgh); Indiana University of Pennsylvania (Indiana); Lehigh University (Bethlehem); Pennsylvania State University (University Park); Shippensburg State College (Shippensburg); Swarthmore College (Swarthmore); Temple University (Philadelphia); University of Pittsburgh (Pittsburgh); Villanova University (Villanova); West Chester State College (West Chester)

RHODE ISLAND

Brown University (Providence); University of Rhode Island (Kingston)

SOUTH CAROLINA

University of South Carolina (Columbia); Wofford College (Spartanburg)

SOUTH DAKOTA

South Dakota State University (Brookings); University of South Dakota (Vermillion)

TENNESSEE

George Peabody College for Teachers (Nashville); Siena College (Memphis); University of Tennessee (Knoxville); Vanderbilt University (Nashville)

TEXAS

Austin College (Sherman); Baylor University (Waco); East Texas State University (Commerce); Hardin-Simmons University (Abilene); Howard Payne College (Brownwood); Midwestern University (Wichita Falls); North Texas State University (Denton) Rice University (Houston); St Mary's University (San Antonio); Southern Methodist University (Dallas); Southwest Texas State University (San Marcos); Southwestern University (Georgetown); Stephen F Austin State College (Nacogdoches); Sul Ross State College (Alpine); Texas Agricultural and Mechanical University (College Station); Texas Arts and Industries University (Kingsville); Texas Christian University (Fort Worth); Texas Technological University (Lubbock); University of Houston (Houston); University of Texas at Austin (Austin); University of Texas at El Paso (El Paso); West Texas State University (Canyon)

UTAH

Brigham Young University (Provo); University of Utah (Salt Lake City); Utah State University at Logan (Logan)

VERMONT

University of Vermont (Burlington)

VIRGINIA

University of Richmond (Richmond) University of Virginia (Charlottesville); William and Mary College (Williamsburg)

WASHINGTON

Central Washington State College at Ellensberg (Ellensburg); Gonzaga University (Spokane); University of Washington (Seattle); Washington State University at Pullman (Pullman)

WEST VIRGINIA

Marshall University (Huntington); West Virginia University (Morgantown)

WISCONSIN

Beloit College (Beloit); Marquette University (Milwaukee); University of Wisconsin (Madison)

WYOMING

University of Wyoming (Laramie)

FOREIGN COLLEGES AND UNIVERSITIES

Acadia University (Wolfville, Nova Scotia, Canada); Ca Foscari Institute (Venice, Italy); Cambridge University (Cambridge, England); Carleton University (Ottawa, Ontario, Canada); Dalhousie University (Halifax, Nova Scotia, Canada); Jagiellonian University (Cracow, Poland); Leeds University (Leeds, England); McGill University (Montreal, Quebec, Canada); McMaster University (Hamilton, Ontario, Canada); Memorial University of Newfoundland (St John's, Newfoundland, Canada); Mount Allison University (Sackville, New Brunswick, Canada); Mount Saint Vincent (Halifax, Nova Scotia, Canada); Oxford University (Oxford, England); Queen's University (Kingston, Ontario, Canada); Saint Mary's University (Halifax, Nova Scotia, Canada); Sheffield University (Sheffield, England); University College of Cork (Cork, Ireland); University of Adelaide (Australia); University of Alberta (Edmonton, Alberta, Canada); University of British Columbia (Vancouver, British Columbia, Canada); University of Caen (Caen, France); University of Canterbury (Canterbury, England); University of Gottingen (Gottingen, Germany); University of London (London, England); University of Manchester (Manchester, England); University of Montreal (Montreal, Quebec, Canada); University of New Brunswick (Fredericton, New Brunswick, Canada); University of Ottawa (Ottawa, Canada); University of Saskatchewan (Saskatoon, Saskatchewan, Canada); University of Toronto (Toronto, Ontario, Canada); University of Wales (Wales); University of Warsaw (Warsaw, Poland); University of Western Australia (Australia); University of Western Ontario (London, Ontario, Canada); University of Windsor (Windsor, Ontario, Canada)

TABLE OF CONTENTS

FOREWORD   vii
LIST OF INSTITUTIONS   ix
INDIVIDUAL AUTHORS
    Joseph Addison   1-29
    Aelfric   30-37
    Richard Aldington   38-40
    Matthew Arnold   41-168
    Roger Ascham   169-172
    Jane Austen   173-268
    Francis Bacon   269-298
    James Barrie   299-324
    Francis Beaumont   325-347
    Samuel Beckett   348-370
    Thomas Lovell Beddoes   371-375
    Max Beerbohm   376-380
    Brendan Behan   381-384
    Mrs Aphra Behn   385-417
    Arnold Bennett   418-419
    Richard Doddridge Blackmore   420-422
    William Blake   423-522
    James Boswell   523-542
    The Brontes   543-610
    Rupert Brooke   611-615
    Thomas Browne   616-635
    The Brownings   636-899
    Edward Bulwer-Lytton   900-911
    John Bunyan   912-942
    Edmund Burke   943-946
    Fanny Burney   947-966
    Robert Burns   967-999
    Robert Burton   1000-1010
    Samuel Butler   1011-1041
    George Gordon, Lord Byron   1042-1234
    Thomas Carlyle   1235-1315
    Lewis Carroll   1316-1318
    Joyce Cary   1319-1336
    George Cavendish   1337-1338
    William Caxton   1339-1340
    George Chapman   1341-1361
    Geoffrey Chaucer   1362-1733
    Lord Chesterfield   1734-1741
    Gilbert Keith Chesterton   1742-1768
    John Clare   1769-1773
    Arthur Hugh Clough   1774-1784
    Samuel Taylor Coleridge   1785-1904
    Wilkie Collins   1905-1910
    William Collins   1911-1916
    William Congreve   1917-1936
    Joseph Conrad   1937-2302
    Abraham Cowley   2303-2310
    William Cowper   2311-2331
    George Crabbe   2332-2345
    Richard Crashaw   2346-2364

Samuel Daniel	2365-2374
William D'Avenant	2375-2380
John Davies	2381-2382
Daniel Defoe	2383-2446
Thomas Dekker	2447-2480
Walter de la Mare	2481-2489
Thomas Deloney	2490-2500
Thomas DeQuincey	2501-2507
Charles Dickens	2508-2648
Benjamin Disraeli	2649-2664
John Donne	2665-2834
Michael Drayton	2835-2846
William Drummond	2837-2849
John Dryden	2850-2929
Lawrence Durrell	2930-2972
Maria Edgeworth	2973-2983
George Eliot	2984-3093
John Evelyn	3094-3097
Henry Fielding	3098-3193
Edward Fitzgerald	3194-3198
John Fletcher	3199-3212
Ford Madox Ford	3213-3234
John Ford	3235-3249
Edward Morgan Forster	3250-3279
Christopher Fry	3280-3299
John Galsworthy	3300-3376
David Garrick	3377-3384
George Gascoigne	3385-3389
Elizabeth Cleghorn Gaskell	3390-3407
John Gay	3408-3426
William Schwenck Gilbert	3427-3434
George Robert Gissing	3435-3451
William Godwin	3452-3463
William Golding	3464-3499
Oliver Goldsmith	3500-3550
John Gower	3551-3559
Robert Graves	3560-3568
Thomas Gray	3569-3585
Graham Greene	3586-3644
Robert Greene	3645-3673
Lady Augusta Gregory	3674-3678
Fulke Greville	3679-3686
Thomas Hardy	3687-3894
William Hazlitt	3895-3922
George Herbert	3923-3979
Robert Herrick	3980-4007
Thomas Heywood	4008-4020
Thomas Hobbes	4021-4024
Gerard Manley Hopkins	4025-4111
Alfred Edward Housman	4112-4134
William Henry Hudson	4135-4142
David Hume	4143-4146
Leigh Hunt	4147-4153
Aldous Huxley	4154-4187

Thomas Henry Huxley   4188-4194
Francis Jeffrey   4195-4199
Samuel Johnson   4200-4291
Ben Jonson   4292-4395
James Joyce   4396-4490
John Keats   4491-4629
Charles Kingsley   4630-4646
Rudyard Kipling   4647-4687
Charles Lamb   4688-4709
Walter Savage Landor   4710-4720
William Langland   4721-4741
D H Lawrence   4742-4844
T E Lawrence   4845-4849
Edward Lear   4850-4852
F R Leavis   4853-4855
Vernon Lee   4856-4857
Cecil Day Lewis   4858-4860
Clive Staples Lewis   4861-4876
John Locke   4877-4887
Richard Lovelace   4888-4890
Malcolm Lowry   4891-4902
John Lyly   4903-4931
Thomas Babington Macaulay   4932-4937
George MacDonald   4938-4941
Louis MacNeice   4942-4945
Thomas Malory   4946-4975
Katherine Mansfield   4976-5006
Christopher Marlowe   5007-5100
John Marston   5101-5109
Andrew Marvell   5110-5140
John Masefield   5141-5156
Philip Massinger   5157-5166
William Somerset Maugham   5167-5191
George Meredith   5192-5243
Thomas Middleton   5244-5261
John Stuart Mill   5262-5267
Alan Alexander Milne   5268-5271
John Milton   5272-5628
Lady Mary Wortley Montagu   5629-5631
George Moore   5632-5644
Thomas Moore   5645-5653
Thomas More   5654-5683
William Morris   5684-5709
Thomas Nashe   5710-5719
John Henry Newman   5720-5752
Sean O'Casey   5753-5774
Liam O'Flaherty   5775-5777
George Orwell   5778-5796
John Osborne   5797-5800
Wilfred Owen   5801-5806
Walter Pater   5807-5825
Coventry Patmore   5826-5834
Thomas Peacock   5835-5852
George Peele   5853-5863
Samuel Pepys   5864-5875

Arthur Pinero	5876-5877
Harold Pinter	5878-5885
Alexander Pope	5886-5960
John Cowper Powys	5961-5963
J B Priestley	5964-5966
Matthew Prior	5967-5970
Ann Radcliffe	5971-5979
Walter Raleigh	5980-5990
Charles Reade	5991-5996
Samuel Richardson	5997-6017
Richard Rolle	6018-6023
The Rossettis	6024-6066
John Ruskin	6067-6094
George William Russell	6095-6097
Siegfried Sassoon	6098-6100
Walter Scott	6101-6187
Thomas Shadwell	6188-6195
Shaftesbury	6196-6199
Shakespeare	6200-7246
George Bernard Shaw	7247-7380
Percy Bysshe Shelley	7381-7508
Richard Sheridan	7509-7523
James Shirley	7524-7531
Philip Sidney	7532-7568
The Sitwells	7569-7577
John Skelton	7578-7589
Christopher Smart	7590-7602
Tobias Smollett	7603-7620
C P Snow	7621-7627
Robert Southey	7628-7632
Robert Southwell	7633-7639
Muriel Spark	7640-7647
Herbert Spencer	7648-7650
Stephen Spender	7651-7654
Edmund Spenser	7655-7921
Richard Steele	7927-7937
James Stephens	7938-7941
Laurence Sterne	7942-7967
Robert L Stevenson	7969-8000
Lytton Strachey	8001-8003
John Suckling	8004-8007
Arthur Seymour Sullivan	8008-8010
Jonathan Swift	8011-8128
Algernon Charles Swinburne	8129-8155
John Millington Synge	8156-8196
Jeremy Taylor	8197-8201
William Temple	8202-8204
Alfred Tennyson	8205-8353
William Thackeray	8354-8388
Dylan Thomas	8389-8431
Francis Thompson	8432-8465
James Thomson	8466-8486
J R R Tolkien	8487-8502
Cyril Tourneur	8503-8512

Thomas Traherne	8513-8529
Anthony Trollope	8530-8565
Henry Vaughan	8566-8585
Horace Walpole	8586-8598
Hugh Walpole	8599-8603
Izaak Walton	8604-8606
Mrs Humphrey Ward	8607-8610
Isaac Watts	8611-8617
Evelyn Waugh	8618-1835
John Webster	8636-8675
H G Wells	8676-8689
John Wesley	8690-8694
William Hale White	8695-8698
Oscar Wilde	8699-8727
Charles Williams	8728-8737
John Wilmot	8738-8745
Mary Wollstonecraft	8746-8752
Virginia Woolf	8753-8813
William Wordsworth	8814-8938
William Butler Yeats	8939-9000
GENERAL INDEX	
THESIS AUTHOR INDEX	

JOSEPH ADDISON

1 ASTON Mabel B   The Critical Opinions of Joseph Addison as Reflected
   in His Writings   MA Univ of Oklahoma 1942
2 BLAIR Elizabeth H   Addisonian Tradition in the Familiar Essay of
   the Twentieth Century   MA Univ of Pittsburgh 1926
3 BUCK Doris T   Joseph Addison's Influence in the Social Reform of
   His Age   Texas Woman's Univ ·1936
4 CARLETTI Ilda   Joseph Addison's *Cato*   MA Ca Foscari (Italy) 1967
5 DOUGHTIE M E W   Joseph Addison's Literary Criticism as Found in
   The Spectator   MA North Texas St Univ 1950
6 EDELIN, Sophia M   American Reputation of Joseph Addison 1700-1850
   MA Howard Univ 1930   21 p
7 ELLENWOOD W R   The Fictitious Editor in the Periodicals of
   Steele and Addison   MA Alberta (Canada) 1963
8 GRAHAM Paul R   The Christianity of Joseph Addison as Shown in His
   Essays   MA Univ of Pittsburgh 1959
9 HALPERN Mark I   Joseph Addison's Essay on the *Pleasures of the
   Imagination:* A Theory of Its Significance and a Study of
   Some Scholarly Views of It   MA Columbia 1955   142 p
10 HERMAN Jane   Joseph Addison: The Advocate of Friendship and the
   Anomaly of His Quarrels   MA Columbia 1955   79 p
11 HUDNALL Alice A   His Own Springs or Another's: A Study of
   Joseph Addison's *Remarks on Italy*   MA San Diego St Coll 1962   87 p
12 HUGUELET Eugene W   Joseph Addison's *Pleasures of the Imagination*
   an Innovation in English Critical Theory   MA East Carolina Univ
   1963
13 JONQUET Eugene M   The Narratives in the Periodical Essays of
   Steele and Addison   MA Washington Univ at St Louis nd   110 p
14 LEACH Sr Dorothy   Joseph Addison's Influence in American
   Periodicals 1722-1805   MA St John's Univ 1942
15 LEWIS Virginia M   Theatrical Criticism of Addison and Steele
   MA Univ of Richmond 1955   117 p
16 McDONOUGH John M   Oriental Lore in the *Tatler, Spectator, Guardian*
   and *Freeholder* of Addison and Steele   MA Boston Univ 1948
17 McMILLAN K M   Addison Versus Pope   MA Univ of North Carolina at
   Chapel Hill 1934
18 MAHONEY John L   Mark Akenside: A Study in the Philosophic Influence
   of Addison and Shaftesbury on Eighteenth Century Poetry
   MA Boston Coll 1952
19 MATTHEWS Ruth E   The Classical Element in the Works of Joseph Addison
   MA Howard Univ 1932   44 p
20 MORGAN E C   The Politics of Joseph Addison   MA Univ of North Carolina
   at Chapel Hill 1951
21 MORRISSEY Albert J   Horace's and Addison's Theories of Satire:
   A Comparison   MA St Louis Univ 1932   58 p
22 PAIGE Muriel M   Joseph Addison's Reading   MA Columbia 1937
23 PETREE Colbert G   Joseph Addison's Tragedy: His Theory and Practice
   MA Univ of Tennessee nd
24 PLUMB Robert J Jr   Joseph Addison's *Cato*, the Traditional Stoic in
   English Drama   MA Univ of North Carolina at Chapel Hill 1950   94 p
25 POLICARDI Silvio   Joseph Addison's Influence on the English People
   of His Times   MA Ca Foscari (Italy) 1921
26 RUTH Mary V   The Literary Criticism of Joseph Addison
   MA Washington Univ at St Louis 1934   172 p
27 SINGER Abraham D   Joseph Addison in the 19th Century   MA Columbia 1936
28 SOUKUP Kenneth J   Joseph Addison's Theory of Satire and a Comparison
   of that Theory with those of His Predecessors and Contemporaries
   MA Univ of Tennessee 1930
29 UNDERWOOD Marilyn H   Joseph Addison's Comments on Physicatheology in

The Spectator   MA Texas Agricultural & Mechanical Univ 1969   78 p
See also 6995

AELFRIC

30 BUCHANAN Constance R Studies in the Syntax of Aelfric's Old English
    Translation of the Vulgate *Genesis* MA Univ of Texas at Austin 1922
31 HART Mary A A Study of Aelfric's *Homilies* MA Utah St Univ 1965
32 HAYNES L L Nomenclature of Grammatical Terms in Aelfric's
    Translation of the Latin Grammar MA Univ of North Carolina at
    Chapel Hill 1940
33 HENDERSON Robert An Etymological Examination of Aelfric's *Passion
    of Saint Sebastian, Martyr* MA North Texas St Univ 1963
34 HIGASHI Yasunori The Survival of the Words Used in Aelfric's
    Colloquy MA Univ of Texas at Austin 1953   77 p
35 HORLICK Bernard Aelfric's Anglo-Saxon Latin Grammar Translated,
    with Introduction, Notes and Appendices MA Columbia 1937
36 STANSELL Dorothy The Lost Words of Aelfric MA Univ of North
    Carolina at Chapel Hill nd
37 WILSON R B Aelfric, Abbot of Eynsham: A Translation of Aelfric's
    Homilies, with an Introductory Chapter on Aelfric's Relation
    to Old English Culture MA Univ of North Carolina at Chapel Hill 193

RICHARD ALDINGTON

38 BANFICHI Paola Richard Aldington: A Study Ma Ca Foscari (Italy) 1935
39 MALADORNO Emilio Richard Aldington, a Novelist of the New Generation
    MA Ca Foscari (Italy) 1935
40 PEASLEE Alice R Richard Aldington MA Boston Univ 1935

MATTHEW ARNOLD

41 AKRIGG George P V Matthew Arnold: The Early Years MA Univ of
    British Columbia (Canada) 1940
42 ANGHERA' Francesca The Poetry and the Literary Criticism of
    Mr Matthew Arnold (1822-1888) MA Ca Foscari (Italy) nd
43 BALDWIN Marguerete F Matthew Arnold as a Literary Critic
    MA Univ of Oklahoma 1940
44 BARBOUR James F Spinoza and Arnold MA Washington Univ at St Louis
    1960   110 p
45 BARBOUR Michael M An Examination of Some Attitudes Underlying
    Matthew Arnold's Preface to the Edition of 1853, and Their
    Influence Upon His Poetry BA Univ of British Columbia (Canada) 1967
46 BARRETT Martha J Matthew Arnold and Ernest Renan: A Comparison of
    Their Religion, Their Ideas and Principles of Criticism and Their
    Style MA Univ of Arkansas 1931
47 BARTON Jenny D Matthew Arnold's Critique of Poetry
    MA Auburn Univ 1952   143 p
48 BAXTER Julia E An Appraisal of Matthew Arnold's Poetry by
    Contemporary Nineteenth Century Literary Periodicals
    MA Columbia 1941
49 BECKER Laurence A Continuity Within Change: A Study of
    Matthew Arnold's Thought in His Poetry and Selected Literary
    Criticism MA Univ of Texas at Austin 1966   150 p
50 BEEDE Margaret A The Hebraic in Matthew Arnold MA Univ of
    North Dakota 1922   55 p
51 BENSON Carol F The Modernity of Matthew Arnold, A Study of His
    Religious, Social and Political Thought MA Univ of Texas at
    Austin 1938   128 p
52 BERMACK Ruth A Comparative Study of Henry Adams and Matthew Arnold

MA Columbia 1953   45 p
53 BINDER Raymond K Arnold and Senancour MA Columbia 1966   56 p
54 BOWER Susan J Matthew Arnold's Poetry and the Ethical Implications
      of "Disinterestedness" MA Univ of Oklahoma 1963
55 BRINTON Mary R Matthew Arnold MA Univ of Arizona 1933
56 BROOKS Heather The Literary Criticism of Matthew Arnold and
      T S Eliot MA Univ of British Columbia (Canada) 1959   173 p
57 BUNDENTHAL Theodore K Arnold's Road to Emmaus MA Washington Univ
      at St Louis 1960
58 BYARS John A A Comparison of the Social Criticism of Matthew Arnold
      and T S Eliot MA Univ of North Carolina at Chapel Hill 1956
59 CARR William Matthew Arnold and the Contemporary Journalism
      MA Cambridge (England) 1962
60 CARTER Bonnie J Matthew Arnold and His Contributions to Education
      MA Univ of Tulsa 1947
61 CHELABI Sajeda A Criticism of Arnold's Poetry Before 1889
      MA Univ of Maryland at College Park 1951   107 p
62 CHETKOW B H Matthew Arnold's "Hebraism": A Study of His Indebtedness
      to the Old Testament BA Univ of British Columbia (Canada) 1951
63 CLIPPER Lawrence J Matthew Arnold on Tour 1883-84 MA George Wash-
      ington Univ 1964   124 p
64 CONNORS James E The Theme of Matthew Arnold BA Amherst 1957
65 COOPER Alan The Place of Education in Matthew Arnold's Criticism
      MA Columbia 1954   126 p
66 COPLEY Patricia A Matthew Arnold's Discourses in America MA Univ of
      Texas at Austin 1954   93 p
67 CORNER M N The Literary Criticism of Matthew Arnold: Its
      Characteristics and Directions in Relation to the Contemporary
      Literary and Critical Background and that of the Earlier Nine-
      teenth Century MA Univ of London (England) 1965
68 COULLING Sidney M B III Matthew Arnold's Indebtedness to Ernest Renan
      MA Univ of North Carolina at Chapel Hill 1949   94 p
69 CRISTINA Louise Matthew Arnold and *The Poetry of Experience*
      MA Columbia 1963   131 p
70 CUFF Eileen P Survey of the Reception of Arnold's Religious Essays
      in Magazines MA Columbia 1941
71 DAILEY John F The Conflict of Faith and Doubt in Certain Lyrical
      Poems of Matthew Arnold MA St Louis Univ 1936   59 p
72 DALTON Mary E Suggestions of a Wordsworthian Influence in the
      Phrasing, Imagery and Ideas of the Poetry of Matthew Arnold
      MA Texas Technological Univ 1966   40 p
73 DAVIS Dale W The Naturalistic Humanism of Matthew Arnold: A Critical
      Reinterpretation of His Imaginative Vision MA Univ of Oklahoma 1968
74 DAVIS Jewel Matthew Arnold's Conception of Religion in the "Whole Man"
      MS Auburn Univ 1926   30 p
75 DAVIS Murray S Jr Matthew Arnold's Free Verse and Its Influence
      MA Columbia 1940
76 DeFILIPPI Beatrice Matthew Arnold and Italy MA Columbia 1940
77 DeLORME Edward F An Investigation of the Educational Principles
      of Matthew Arnold with Special Emphasis on *A French Eton and
      Schools and Universities on the Continent* MA Niagara Univ 1966
78 DOLTON Donald E A Re-interpretation of Matthew Arnold's "High
      Seriousness" MA Oklahoma St Univ 1957   62 p
79 DOYLE Gerald P Matthew Arnold and Foreign Languages MA Lamar Tech-
      nological Univ 1967   99 p
80 EDER Doris L "Sunday Morning" by Wallace Stevens and *Empedocles
      on Etna* by Matthew Arnold MA Hunter Coll 1965
81 EMSON Mary E A Re-examination of Matthew Arnold's Critical
      Principles MA Saskatchewan (Canada) 1965
82 FARRINGTON Lorna D *Empedocles on Etna* (A Jungian Perspective)

MA Carnegie-Mellon Univ 1970
83 FAUST Seymour Word Order and Matthew Arnold's Poems MA Columbia 1960
84 FRENCH William W The Concept of Nature in the Poetry of
       Matthew Arnold MA Univ of Pittsburgh 1960
85 FREUND Hans J Towards a Harmony of Opposites: A Study of Empedocles
       of Akragas and His Relations to the Poetry of Matthew Arnold
       and Friedrich Holderlin MA Columbia 1954 166 p
86 FURTWANGLER Albert J "Arnold's Missionary Muse" BA Amherst 1964
87 GALE Charles R Aspects of Matthew Arnold's Poetry: The Search
       for Harmony MA Columbia 1959 47 p
88 GILL Alice E Labor in *Piers Plowman*, Matthew Arnold's Wordsworth,
       and The Poe-Fay Exchange: A Critical Edition MA Pennsylvania
       St Univ 1965
89 GODDARD Elizabeth Matthew Arnold and Sainte-Beuve: A Comparison
       MA Univ of Arkansas 1933
90 GOEDEKER Sr M Lucina The Educational Theories of Arnold, Huxley
       and Newman MA St Louis Univ 1939 58 p
91 GOLDSMITH Desire Matthew Arnold's Visit to America MA Boston Univ
       1940
92 GOSS L C The Influence of Marcus Aurelius Upon Matthew Arnold
       MA Univ of North Carolina at Chapel Hill 1942
93 GREGG Paul L Matthew Arnold's Criticism of American Society Compared
       with that of Twentieth-Century American Novelists MA St Louis Univ
       1934 87 p
94 GROVES Anna K A Bibliography of Matthew Arnold's Writings and Ana
       from January 1, 1935 to January 1, 1940 MA Univ of Kentucky 1942
95 GROWALL Sally T S Eliot and Matthew Arnold, A Comparative Study of
       Their Critical Views MA Univ of Pittsburgh 1958
96 GULBRANDSON Helen R The Break in Friendship Between Matthew Arnold
       and Arthur Hugh Clough MA George Washington Univ 1952 136 p
97 HADSELL Sardis R Matthew Arnold: What is Poetry? BA Univ of Oklahoma
       1904
98 HAMM Mary L The Ethical Bias of Matthew Arnold's View of Literature
       and of Criticism MA Univ of Texas at Austin 1942 150 p
99 HAY Francis R Matthew Arnold's Concept of Nature MA Univ of
       Oregon 1939
100 HENNESSY W G Matthew Arnold as Poet-Philosopher MA Boston Univ 1924
101 HILLIARD Billie B British Authors in America from Paine to Arnold
       MA Southern Methodist Univ 1934
102 HOFMAN Dorothy E The Religion of Matthew Arnold MA Boston Univ 1932
103 HUTCHINS Pearl Matthew Arnold's Debt to Hellenism BA Univ of
       Oklahoma 1908
104 JONES Beatrice M Matthew Arnold's Interpretation of Nature as
       Revealed in His Poetry MA Univ of Tulsa 1949
105 JORDAN Marguerite The Influence of Matthew Arnold on Henry Arthur Jones
       MA Southern Methodist Univ 1937
106 KAUFFMAN Willa L Matthew Arnold: From Poet to Prophet M Ed Henderson
       St Coll nd
107 KEARNEY Maryadelle Arnold as an Educator MA Univ of Iowa 1934
108 KESTLER C B The Influence of Goethe upon Matthew Arnold MA Univ of
       North Carolina at Chapel Hill 1933
109 KILLAM G D The Literary Critical Principles of Matthew Arnold as
       Applied to the English Romantic Poets in the Light of Succeeding
       Criticism BA Univ of British Columbia (Canada) 1955
110 LASITER Helen Z Matthew Arnold's Literature and Dogma and Its
       Victorian Critics MA Univ of Texas at Austin 1952 115 p
111 LENOSKI Daniel S Pragmatic Elements in Matthew Arnold's Thought
       MA Manitoba (Canada) 1966
112 LYNCH James J Matthew Arnold's Attitude Toward History, with an
       Index to Passages Related to the Subject MA Columbia 1941

113 McCONNELL Anna L A Study of Matthew Arnold's *Merope* and *Empedocles on Etna* MA Univ of Oklahoma 1943
114 McFETRIDGE Katherine L An Evaluation of Matthew Arnold's Place as a Poet Based on the Criticisms of Eighty-Five Years MA Tulane Univ 1935
115 McGUIRE Dorothy S The Influence of Homer and Sophocles upon Arnold's Poetry MA Southern Methodist Univ 1933
116 McINNIS M A Matthew Arnold's Theory of Culture MA Boston Univ 1926
117 McKENZIE Allan I Arnold's Poetry in the Light of His Criticism MA Queen's (Canada) 1965
118 MACKEY J D The Hero in the Poetry of Matthew Arnold MA North Texas St Univ 1967
119 MATHEWS R D The Literary Critical Principles of Matthew Arnold, Examined and Traced Through His Social and Religious Criticism BA Univ of British Columbia (Canada) 1955
120 MATHEWSON D The Poetry of Matthew Arnold: A Study in Versification MA Brigham Young Univ 1965
121 MAXIE Doris L Mountain Imagery in the Poetry of Matthew Arnold MA Lamar Technological Coll 1968 94 p
122 MEGINNIS Frances S Matthew Arnold: Victorian Educator MA Univ of Maryland at College Park 1965 79 p
123 MERMEL Ann Matthew Arnold: Thinker and Reformer MA Univ of Houston 1965 98 p
124 MIHILLS Mildred Studies in the Poetry of Matthew Arnold MA Univ of Texas at Austin 1915
125 MILES Albert The Imagery of Religious Doubt in the Poetry of Matthew Arnold MA Lehigh Univ 1965
126 MILLER Robert H A Study of Matthew Arnold's Writings on the Irish Question and Their Relation to *Culture and Anarchy* MA Bowling Green Univ 1961
127 MILLER Scott E Current Views of Matthew Arnold's Criticism MA Univ of Pittsburgh 1956
128 MINTER Margaret E Sainte-Beuve's Influence on the Literary Criticism of Matthew Arnold MA Univ of North Carolina at Chapel Hill 1958
129 MITCHELL Patrick An Examination of Matthew Arnold's "Sohrab and Rustum" BA Univ of British Columbia (Canada) 1968
130 MOONEY James J The Influence of *The Bhagavad-Gita* on the Poetry of Matthew Arnold MA Niagara Univ 1966
131 MORGAN Jeanette P The Solitary Figure: Studies in Six Poems by Matthew Arnold MA Univ of Houston 1963 138 p
132 MORRIS Geraldine R The Poetry of Matthew Arnold as a Criticism of Life MA Oklahoma St Univ 1954 48 p
133 NAM Doon W Matthew Arnold's Social Criticism and His Critics MA Univ of Rhode Island 1963 97 p
134 NEVINS Laura The Philosophical Association of Matthew Arnold and Arthur Hugh Clough MA Univ of Maryland at College Park 1937 28 p
135 PENIL Mary J Arnold and Kierkegaard: A Stage in Life's Way MA Cornell Univ 1966
136 PURVIS Tomsye D Quietism in the Poetry of Matthew Arnold MA Univ of Tennessee 1970 117 p
137 READ Minnie Theories of Poetry of Arnold's Time, and Theories of the Present Time MA Univ of Oklahoma nd
138 REED Delores J Matthew Arnold's Approach to Mass Culture through Education MA Idaho St Univ 1966
139 REGAN Miriam E The Influence of the Writers of Classical Antiquity upon Matthew Arnold's Literary Work MA Boston Univ 1948
140 RIGHTOR Ella E Some Aspects of Matthew Arnold MA Tulane Univ 1902
141 ROBERTSON Marie H Matthew Arnold's Relationship with France MA Arkansas St Coll 1964

142 ROBBINS William Matthew Arnold as a Social and Religious Reformer,
     and His Influence as Reflected Mainly in Periodical Literature
     MA Univ of British Columbia (Canada) 1934
143 SAGERT Louis A Matthew Arnold's Early Verse as an Expression of
     Doubt MA Univ of Iowa 1931
144 ST CLAIR David W The Duality of Matthew Arnold BA Amherst 1956
145 SALE Richard B Criticism of Poets and Poetry in the Poems of
     Matthew Arnold MA Univ of Texas at Austin 1954 76 p
146 SAMPSON Helen X The "Higher Self" of Matthew Arnold and the "Higher
     Will" of Irving Babbitt MA Univ of Iowa 1940
147 SCOTT Emma A Matthew Arnold's Critical Opinions of His Contemporaries
     MA Univ of Oregon 1939
148 SCRUTCHINS James R The Major Critical Evaluations of the Religious
     Writings of Matthew Arnold 1888-1965 MA Baylor Univ 1968 116 p
149 SICILIANO E A Merope in French, Italian and English Literature
     MA Boston Coll 1939
150 SIGAL Laurie A Tale Retold: A Study of Matthew Arnold's *Tristram
     and Iseult* MA Columbia 1966 90 p
151 SMALLBONE Jean A St Paul and Protestantism: Its Place in the
     Development of Matthew Arnold's Thought MA Univ of London (England)
     1950
152 STEPHENS Edna B Matthew Arnold's Philosophy MA Univ of Arkansas 1933
153 STRICKER Margery Romantic Aspiration in the Poetry of Matthew Arnold
     MA Indiana Univ 1965
154 THANNIKARI Sr M G Matthew Arnold's Ideal of Preparation for Higher
     Education MA Boston Coll 1958
155 TIMOTHY Helen D P The Reputation of Arnold During His Life
     MA Toronto (Canada) 1963
156 TOLLERS Vincent L A Study of Matthew Arnold, With a Bibliography
     of Arnoldiana (1932-1964) MA Univ of Colorado 1965
157 TRUESDELL Lynn G Matthew Arnold as Literary Critic BA Amherst 1958
158 TULLY Margot J Arnold and Renan MA Univ of Florida 1965
159 VIGNEAULT John A Comparative Study of Arnold and Renan MA Toronto
     (Canada) 1965
160 VINING Ima J The Reception of Matthew Arnold's Early Critical Work,
     1861 to 1865 MA Univ of Texas at Austin nd
161 WAITE Richard S Matthew Arnold, His Critical Vocabulary MA Univ of
     Arizona pre 1933
162 WARNER Francis C Matthew Arnold: The Critic-Poet MA Texas Woman's
     Univ 1966
163 WATT F W The Critical Ideal in Matthew Arnold BA Univ of British
     Columbia (Canada) 1950
164 WAYMAN Virginia A Study of the Changing Concepts Held by
     Matthew Arnold as to Man's Place in the Universe MA Bowling
     Green Univ 1937
165 WEAR Richard T S Eliot on Matthew Arnold: A Study of Dissidence
     Florida St Univ 1963
166 WEINSTEIN Rita J Matthew Arnold's Invasion of America
     MA Columbia 1940
167 YEAGER Mabel L Matthew Arnold, as Revealed by His Letters, Poetry
     and Criticism MA Univ of Arizona 1936
168 YINGER Daniel W The Uses of Time Juxtaposition in the Poetry of
     Matthew Arnold MA Bowling Green Univ 1969
See also 1781, 2855, 4964, 5267

ROGER ASCHAM

169 ANDERSON Elizabeth K A Study of the Vocabulary of Roger Ascham
     MA Southern Methodist Univ 1935
170 HAFNER Mamie Morals and Ethics in the Works of Roger Ascham

MA Univ of North Carolina at Chapel Hill 1953   78 p
171 HALL Roger S   The Influence of Xenophon and Plato upon the Educational
    Principles of Roger Ascham, as shown in *Toxophilus* and
    The Scholemaster   MA Columbia 1940
172 PALUMBO Roberta M   Roger Ascham: His Contributions to English
    Literature as Prose Writer and Literary Critic   MA Coll of the
    Holy Names at Oakland 1968

JANE AUSTEN

173 ALLEN Stella M   Some Techniques of Jane Austen   MS Kansas St Coll at
    Pittsburg 1940
174 ALLISON Frances   Dramatic Elements in the Novels of Jane Austen
    MA Montreal (Canada) 1963
175 ANDERSON Judith   Jane Austen on the Nature of Passion, with Special
    Reference to *Sense and Sensibility*   BA Univ of British Columbia
    (Canada) 1964
176 ANDERSON Judith S   Concept and Presentation of Love in Jane Austen
    MA Univ of British Columbia (Canada) 1970
177 ANGELO Beatrice H   The Durable Jane Austen: A Critical Survey of
    the Jane Austen Criticism   MA Sul Ross St Coll 1966
178 ATHEY Frances E   A Study of the Moral Values Found in Four of
    Jane Austen's Novels: *Northanger Abbey, Mansfield Park, Emma*
    and *Persuasion*   MA Auburn Univ 1966
179 BAKER Judith E   A Study of Intelligence in the Novels of Jane Austen
    MA Bowling Green Univ 1960
180 BEAL George   Reflection of the Times of Jane Austen in Her Writings
    MA Boston Univ 1936
181 BENDER Barbara T   Jane Austen's Use of the Epistolary Method
    MA Univ of Richmond 1967   102 p
182 BILLER J   The Novel of Society as Written by Fanny Burney, Jane Austen
    and Susan Ferrier   BA Univ of British Columbia (Canada) 1937
183 BISSON Lillian M   The Value of His Preference: A Study of the
    Rejected Suitors in Jane Austen's Novels   MA Univ of Massachusetts
    1964
184 BLONG Beatrice A   Jane Austen: Hero as Fulcrum   MA Univ of Iowa 1965
185 BLYTH Marion D   The Ironic Observer: A Study of Jane Austen
    MA Fresno St Coll 1952   47 p
186 BOHANAN M   Jane Austen: The Unresolved Conflict Between Sensibility
    and Sense   MA San Diego St Coll 1966
187 BOWEN B A   Jane Austen and Her Critics 1940-1954   MA North Texas
    St Univ 1955
188 BRANDON Eugenie J   Jane Austen's Attitude Toward the Gothic Novel
    MA Univ of Arizona 1936
189 BRECK Catherine   Universality of Appeal in Jane Austen's Novels
    MA Univ of Pittsburgh 1925
190 BROOKS Laura J J   The Position of Women in the Early 19th Century
    as Shown in the Novels of Jane Austen   MA Univ of Oklahoma 1928
191 BROWN Elizabeth J   The Evolution of Jane Austen's Art   BA Univ of
    Delaware 1940   70 p
192 COOPER Thomas A   A Study of Jane Austen's Irony   MA Univ of Tulsa
    1960   88 p
193 COREY Victoria K   Jane Austen's Clergymen: Fact or Fiction?
    MA Univ of Omaha 1966
194 CURRY Lyverne B   Irony in Jane Austen's Major Novels   MA Florida St
    Univ 1953
195 de BRUYN J   The Treatment of the Human Emotions in the Works of
    Jane Austen and Charlotte Bronte: A Study in Contrast, Involving
    a Comparative Discussion of Their Lives and Times   BA Univ of
    British Columbia (Canada) 1949

AUSTEN Con't   8   196-224

196 DEFENSOR Ella B A Study in Jane Austen's Reaction to the Gothic Novel
      and the Novel of Sensibility MA Oklahoma St Univ 1955 66 p
197 DINGFELDER Dorothy R The Clerical and Naval Men of Jane Austen's
      Novels MA Univ of Hawaii 1961 71 p
198 DOWNES Claire V Jane Austen as a Satirist MA Florida St Univ 1953
      89 p
199 DUNN Catherine H Jane Austen: Her Family and Early Life and the
      Relationship Between Her Juvenilia and Mature Novels MA Boston
      Univ 1948
200 EGELSTON Martha Jane Austen: A Study of the Evidences of Romanticism
      in the Novels after 1812 and in the Fragments MA Oklahoma St Univ
      1940 99 p
201 FARIS Mildred T Anti-Romantic Attitudes in the Novels of Jane Austen
      MA Univ of New Mexico 1936
202 FIELDS Suzanne B Moral Judgment in Two Novels of Jane Austen: *Sense
      and Sensibility* and *Mansfield Park* MA George Washington Univ
      1965 110 p
203 FRANCKE Warren T Tipping the Tea Table: An Argument for Reforming
      an Image, from the Austere Miss Austen to Jolly Aunt Jane
      MA Univ of Omaha 1966
204 GILLEY Iris M Social Criticism in the Novels of Jane Austen
      MA Saskatchewan (Canada) 1967
205 GREEN Elmer A The Humor of Jane Austen MA Williams Coll 1905
206 HALL Thelma M The Use of Misunderstanding in the Novels of
      Jane Austen MA Auburn Univ 1963
207 HAYWARD Madlyn E Feminism as Exemplified by Mary Wollstonecraft
      and Jane Austen MA Washington Univ at St Louis 1936 214 p
208 HEDIN Constance L Jane Austen's Use of Social Amusements in Her
      Novels MA Univ of Maine 1944 116 p
209 HEFFRON Margery M The Condemned Chapters of *Persuasion*: A New
      Edition of the Manuscript with a Critical Introduction
      MA Columbia 1966 101 p
210 HENCH Katrina Misfortune as a Test of Character in Jane Austen
      MA Stetson Univ 1965
211 HIGGINS Catherine E The Reliability of the Biographical Writings
      about Jane Austen M Ed Temple Univ 1947 183 p
212 HINKEL Jolayne J Human Values and Meaning in Jane Austen MA Univ
      of Arizona 1966
213 HNATKO Eugene Courtship and Marriage in Austen's Novels MA Bowling
      Green Univ 1955
214 HONEY Glenys The Humour of Jane Austen as Exemplified in Her
      "Country House Comedies" MA Texas Technological Univ 1935
215 HOWARD Pierce J Rhetoric in *Northanger Abbey* MA East Carolina Univ
      1967
216 HYMAN Esther C Jane Austen and Eighteenth Century Provincial England
      MA Univ of Pittsburgh nd
217 JONES Vivian L Reflections of the Life and Customs of the English Upper
      Middle Class of the Late Eighteenth and Early Nineteenth Centuries
      in the Novels of Jane Austen MA Boston Univ 1945
218 KENYON Lorraine F Jane Austen's Novels: The Heroine in Her Society
      MA Univ of Maryland at College Park 1969 72 p
219 KINCAID William P Jr Some Aspects of Jane Austen's Theory and Practice
      MA Univ of Kentucky 1948 66 p
220 KIRSCHENBAUM Stephen I The Art of Jane Austen BA Amherst 1955
221 KROEBER Karl Jane Austen's Techniques MA Columbia 1951
222 LANDRAM William H A Study of the Parent-Child Relationships in
      the Novels of Jane Austen MA Univ of Oklahoma 1966
223 LaROCQUE Sr Francis M A Function of Irony and Point of View in
      Jane Austen's *Emma* MA Boston Coll 1962
224 LATHAM John A Propriety in Jane Austen's Novels BA Amherst 1966

225 LYON Patsy L Characteristics of Romanticism in the Major Novels
    of Jane Austen MA Univ of Tulsa 1967 76 p
226 McALEER John J The Rise of Jane Austen as a Satirist with an
    Evaluation of the Role Sensibility Takes in this Development
    MA Boston Coll 1949
227 McCRACKEN Kathryn A Marriage and Maturity in Jane Austen's Novels
    MA McGill (Canada) 1966
228 McKINNEY Irene M The Letters of Jane Austen: A Biographical and
    Critical Study MA Univ of Pittsburgh 1934
229 McLEOD Charlotte Jane Austen's Heroines MA Southern Illinois
    Univ at Carbondale 1951 166 p
230 MOORE D E Jane Austen's American Reputation MA Boston Univ 1939
231 MURPHY Elisabeth The Heroines in the Novels of Jane Austen
    MA Univ of North Carolina at Chapel Hill 1931
232 NICHOLSON Darrell H A Study of the Influence of the Gothic Romance
    on *Northanger Abbey* MA Univ of Louisville 1966 158 p
233 O'BRIEN Mary J Analysis of Some Figurative Techniques in Jane Austen's
    Mansfield Park MA Dominican Coll of San Rafael 1965
234 OEFELEIN Irma I The Malice of Jane Austen's Irony MA St Louis Univ
    1936 62 p
235 OLIVER Ruby M Jane Austen's Moral Insight in Her Portrayal of
    Character MA Southern Illinois Univ at Carbondale 1958 77 p
236 OLLIVIER Alfred P Jane Austen's Male Characters MA Boston Coll 1950
237 PAPENFUSS Elaine An Analysis of the Character of Darcy in *Pride and
    Prejudice* MA Brigham Young Univ 1966
238 PARKER Margaret A The Role of the Comic Heroine: A Study of the
    Relationship between Subject Matter and the Comic Form in the Novels
    of Jane Austen MA Univ of British Columbia (Canada) 1967 142 p
239 PERRAULT Lillian M The Value of His Preference: A Study of the
    Rejected Suitors as Seen Through the Eyes of Jane Austen's Heroines
    MA Univ of Massachusetts 1964
240 PIRETTI Annamaria Jane Austen MA Ca Foscari (Italy) 1953
241 POPE Zelma Jane Austen's World MA Univ of Texas at Austin 1940 117 p
242 PORTER Patricia A Jane Austen as a Johnsonian Moralist MA Univ of
    New Brunswick (Canada) 1965
243 POTEET Lewis J Religion and Moral Censure in Jane Austen MA Univ of
    Oklahoma 1962
244 POTHIER Guy Jane Austen: The Recognition of Irony in the Major
    Novels MA Dalhousie (Canada) 1966
245 QUATTLEBAUM Martha C Empirical Sources in Jane Austen's *Emma*
    MA George Washington Univ 1940 79 p
246 RANNE Virginia A Jane Austen's Commentary on Contemporary Female
    Education MA Toronto (Canada) 1967
247 REYNOLDS Thomas E Commitment and Marriage in the Fiction of
    Jane Austen MA Univ of Iowa 1964
248 RIEKER Richard A Comic Elements in Jane Austen's Fiction MA Univ of
    Pittsburgh 1960
249 ROSA Ermenegilda Jane Austen MA Ca Foscari (Italy) 1938
250 RUBIN Mary P A Study of the Characterization of Mothers in
    Jane Austen's Novels MA Univ of Tennessee 1964
251 RUBLE Shirlee B Types of Satire in Jane Austen's Novels
    MA Mankato St Coll 1961 51 p
252 SAMPEY Jane R Point of View in Jane Austen's *Northanger Abbey*,
    Pride and Prejudice and *Persuasion* MA Univ of North Carolina
    at Chapel Hill 1958 122 p
253 SANDEFER Mary L Structure and Characterization in the Novels of
    Jane Austen MA Univ of Texas at Austin 1918
254 SANDERS Helen M A Flaw in Jane Austen's *Mansfield Park*
    MA Syracuse Univ 1949 88 p
255 SCHMIDT Mary J Occupation and Characterization in the Novels of

Jane Austen   MA Univ of Pittsburgh 1934

256 SCHWAGER Mary L   Jane Austen's Detractors   MA Univ of Colorado 1965
257 SMITH Judith A   The Individual and Society in the Novels of
     Jane Austen   MA Univ of Iowa 1966
258 STRANGE Rebecca P   The Position of Jane Austen's Heroines
     MA Texas Agricultural & Mechanical Univ 1967   160 p
259 SULLIVAN M M   Characterization in *Pride and Prejudice, Emma* and
     Persuasian by Jane Austen   MA Boston Univ 1924
260 SUWANNABHA Sumitra   Reason and Passion in Jane Austen's Heroines
     MA Univ of Oklahoma 1966
261 THOMAS Carma A   The Personality and Art of Jane Austen   MA Univ of
     Texas at Austin 1932
262 THORNTON John   Amusements, Games and Sports Mentioned in Six Novels
     of Jane Austen   MA Boston Univ 1945
263 THORNTON K L   The Moral Judgments of Jane Austen   MA North Texas
     St Univ 1968
264 TURNER B C   The Polite Novel after Jane Austen   B Litt Oxford Univ
     (England) 1944
265 WAYLAND Audrey   A Critical Appraisal of Jane Austen's Rejection of
     Her Unpublished Work   MA Oklahoma St Univ 1957   78 p
266 WEBBER Elizabeth P M   Romanticism in Jane Austen's Novels   MA Univ of
     Delaware 1965   100 p
267 WHITE Frances C   Satire on Women in Jane Austen's Novels   MA Univ of
     Texas at Austin 1956   141 p
268 ZIMMERMAN Everett   Jane Austen and Sensibility: A Study of Tradition
     and Technique   MA Temple Univ 1966
See also 586, 588, 955, 963, 2414, 3091, 3114, 4450

FRANCIS BACON

269 BARNHILL Harry L   Sir Francis Bacon's Reputation and Influence as a
     Historian: A Study of Selected Criticism   MA Univ of North Carolina
     at Chapel Hill 1954   111 p
270 CANNON Donald E   Bacon and Machiavelli   MA Columbia 1950
271 CLUETT Robert IV   John Evelyn and His Debt to Francis Bacon
     MA Columbia 1961   155 p
272 DEMOS Peter G   Some Aspects of the Problem of the Immediate Historical
     Background of Francis Bacon   MA Univ of Pittsburgh 1927
273 GAHAGAN M K   Montaigne's Influence on Bacon's Essays   MA Boston
     Coll 1938
274 GARNER Collie   The Relation of More's *Utopia* and Bacon's *New Atlantis*
     to the Advancement of Learning in Their Times   MA Univ of North
     Carolina at Chapel Hill 1929
275 GEARIN J J   The Essays of Francis Bacon 1597-1625   MA Boston Coll 1954
276 GERCHOW William D   The Critical and Aesthetic Beliefs of Bacon,
     Descartes and Hobbes, and Their Effects upon the Status and
     Function of Seventeenth-Century English Poets   MA Columbia 1962 88 p
277 GLASS Florence   The Utopian Situation in More's *Utopia*, Campanella's
     City of the Sun and Bacon's *New Atlantis*   MA Hunter Coll 1963
278 GREEN Helen   Emerson's Indebtedness to Bacon   MA Univ of Texas at
     Austin 1929
279 GREEN Howard E   Sir Francis Bacon's Break with Mediaeval Tradition
     MA Washington Univ at St Louis 1929   129 p
280 HANNA Elsa B   The Life and Character of Francis Bacon as Reflected
     in His Essays   MA Univ of Arizona 1940
281 HARRIS Vivian M   Francis Bacon's Philosophy of Truth   M Ed Henderson
     St Coll nd
282 HOGAN Patrick G Jr   The Literary and Critical Opinions of
     Sir Francis Bacon   MA Univ of Mississippi 1948   112 p
283 HOLTON E A   An Introduction to Bacon's Essays   MA Boston Univ 1915

284 KELLY Thomas E A Study of the Nature and the Origin of the Idols of Francis Bacon MA St Louis Univ 1933 62 p
285 KIRK Rudolph A Literary Study of Bacon's Henry VII MA Univ of Iowa 1924
286 KRUPA Gene Polydore Vergil and Francis Bacon: Two Views of Henry VII and History MA Columbia 1966 108 p
287 LEVEY David K The Nature and Function of Imagery in Bacon's *Essays* MA Columbia 1960 109 p
288 MABUSTH Mary H The Basis of Bacon's Theory of Personal Conduct MA George Washington Univ 1941 77 p
289 MacCURDY Burnet Francis Bacon's Science of Success MA Univ of North Carolina at Chapel Hill 1946 97 p
290 MANNA Jehad K The Elements of the Courtesy Book in Elyot and Bacon MA George Washington Univ 1963 157 p
291 OLSEN W A Francis Bacon's Ideas on the Aim of Learning MA Univ of North Carolina at Chapel Hill 1927
292 PEATTIE Edward G Bacon to Boyle, A Method and Its Uses MA Temple Univ 1953
293 PILKINGTON J The Growth and Development in Francis Bacon's Essays MA Univ of London (England) 1962
294 RATTE E H A Comparison of the Essays of Montaigne and Bacon MA Boston Univ 1940
295 REAVES H M Origin of Francis Bacon's Theories of the Method and the Purpose of Science MA Univ of North Carolina at Chapel Hill 1924
296 STOUT W W Platonic Ideas in Bacon MA Univ of North Carolina at Chapel Hill 1922
297 WEIGEL Clyde L The Bible in Bacon's Essays MA Univ of Texas at Austin 1949 113 p
298 YODER LaVerne E Bacon's Employment of Allusion and Figures of Speech MA Univ of Iowa 1935
See also 2304, 4286, 6442

JAMES MATTHEW BARRIE

299 AMUNDSON James D Recurrent Character Types in the Works of James Matthew Barrie MA Rice 1963
300 BAROLINI Antonietta The Modern English Drama with Special Regard to Barrie MA Ca Foscari (Italy) 1938
301 BARRY M E James M Barrie's Treatment of Female Characters MA Boston Coll 1934
302 BROOKE Esther H A Critical Study of the Works of Sir James Barrie in Relation to His Life MS Ft Hays St Teachers Coll 1938 126 p
303 BUIKSTRA Eunice Reflections of Margaret Ogilvy in the Heroines of James M Barrie's Plays MA Oklahoma St Univ 1938 77 p
304 CERESOLA Clorinda Sir James M Barrie MA Ca Foscari (Italy) 1930
305 CROW Charles R Serious and Humorous Elements in the Fiction of J M Barrie MA Univ of Pittsburgh 1931
306 DROHAN W M Sir James M Barrie, Dramatist MA Boston Coll 1933
307 EWING M J Sir James M Barrie MA Boston Univ 1921
308 GLYNN Helen A The Humor in the Plays of Sir James M Barrie MA Boston Univ 1935
309 HOWARD Kathleen E The Use of Sentiment in James M Barrie MA Boston Univ 1934
310 JONES Mart W J M Barrie's Technique of Exposition MA Texas Technological Coll 1934 49 p
311 KREISCHER Marjorie The Victorian Woman as Presented by J M Barrie MA Bowling Green Univ 1941
312 LAHR Natalia E Child Life as Shown in Riley's *Child World* and Barrie's *Sentimental Tommy* MA Purdue Univ 1897

313 LAMARCA Jacqueline M Barrie: The Man and His Works MA Boston Univ
     1931
314 LAVIA John T Sir James M Barrie: His Works and Reputation
     BA Rutgers St Univ 1961 55 p
315 LORENZETTO Maria J M Barrie and His Plays MA Ca Foscari (Italy) 1949
316 LYNCH William J A Philosophy of Life as Evidenced in the Plays of
     Sir James Matthew Barrie MA Boston Coll 1958
317 O'FLAHERTY John G The Aim and Purpose of Make-Believe in the Plays
     of James M Barrie MA St Louis Univ 1935 69 p
318 PHILLIPS Elizabeth C Barrie and the Development of the Literary
     Stage Direction MA Univ of Tennessee 1949
319 ROBERTSON Pensive C The Relation of Sir James Matthew Barrie to the
     Development of English Sentimental Drama MA Texas Christian Univ
     1936 206 p
320 ROSE Virjama Autobiographical Material Used in the Plays of
     J M Barrie MA Univ of Oklahoma 1940
321 SMITH Sr Mary P Philosophical Basis of Sir James M Barrie's Plays
     MA Boston Coll 1942
322 TOOMBS Edith O The Nostalgia of the Characters of J M Barrie
     MA Univ of Texas at Austin 1940 95 p
323 VALLAS Beverley W The Women of Barrie's Plays MA Tulane Univ 1925
324 ZANON DAL BO Margherita The Plays of J M Barrie MA Ca Foscari (Italy)
     1935
See also 7370

                            FRANCIS BEAUMONT

325 ATTLEE George G Structure in the Tragicomedies of Beaumont and
     Fletcher MA Syracuse Univ 1950 122 p
326 BARRY Lucille Studies in the Collaboration of Beaumont and
     Fletcher MA Univ of Iowa 1932
327 BOCCATO Alberta Francis Beaumont: *The Woman Hater* MA Ca Foscari
     (Italy) 1960
328 BRONZINI Maddalena Beaumont and Fletcher: *The Knight of the
     Burning Pestle* MA Ca Foscari (Italy) 1960
329 BUCHANAN Alllye P Parallelism and Contrast in the Plays of
     Beaumont and Fletcher MA Indiana Univ 1940
330 BURLESON Joyce J *The Knight of the Burning Pestle*: A Showcase
     of Burlesque Techniques MA Texas Technological Univ 1968
331 CHAPMAN Kathleen W The Play, *The Knight of the Burning Pestle*
     MA New Mexico Highlands Univ 1965
332 GUNDERSON Ellen D The Heroes of Beaumont and Fletcher MA Univ of
     North Dakota 1932 95 p
333 HAMPTON Lelia Studies in Beaumont and Fletcher's Theories of
     Kingship MA Univ of North Carolina at Chapel Hill 1931
334 HERRING Gertrude M A Study of English Dramatic Burlesque from
     Beaumont to Sheridan MA Univ of Oregon 1932
335 LACY Roy C The Development of Tragi-Comedy as a Generic Dramatic
     Type from Its Earliest Examples through Beaumont and Fletcher;
     A Study in Comparative Literature MA Texas Christian Univ 1939
     200 p
336 LANDON Hazel M The Romance Element in Beaumont and Fletcher
     MA Univ of Oklahoma 1933
337 MARSHALL Mary E The Renaissance Theory of Honor and Its Use in
     the Plays of Beaumont and Fletcher MA Florida St Univ 1955
338 MATSON Cecil A Production and Prompt Book of Beaumont and Fletcher's
     Philaster or *Love Lies Bleeding* MA Univ of Iowa 1935
339 PEZZATO Giovanna A Joint Authorship: Francis Beaumont and
     John Fletcher MA Ca Foscari (Italy) 1948
340 PITSCH Marcella F A Study of the Stage Directions in the First Folio

of Beaumont and Fletcher   MA Univ of Iowa 1931
341 PLUMMER Freda S   A Critical Bibliography of the Beaumont and Fletcher
     Plays   MA Univ of Oklahoma 1932
342 SURVANT Joseph W   Atmosphere in *The Maid's Tragedy*   MA Univ of
     Delaware 1966   58 p
343 TERRY Mary H   A Study of the First Acts in Eight of Beaumont and
     Fletcher's Plays   MA Univ of Texas at Austin 1940   99 p
344 TESH Gardner L   Ideas of Kingship in the Plays of Beaumont and
     Fletcher   MA George Washington Univ 1946   70 p
345 TOMASINI Imelde   *The Maid's Tragedy* by Beaumont and Fletcher. Edited
     with Introduction and Notes   MA Ca Foscari 1958
346 VERMEERSCH Sr Mary J   Implied Production Notes in Four Beaumont-
     Fletcher Plays   MA St Louis Univ 1945   103 p
347 WENCK Robert W   *The Knight of the Burning Pestle*: Analysis of
     Production in a Public Theater and a Private Theater in Seventeenth
     Century London   MA Texas Agricultural & Mechanical Univ 1966   125 p
See also 3201, 3203, 3206, 3207, 3208, 3209, 3210, 4298, 6611, 6960

SAMUEL BECKETT

348 ALBERT Gordon E   Parallel Structures in the Dramatic Techniques
     of William Butler Yeats and Samuel Beckett   MA Mankato St Coll
     1969   70 p
349 BELL Richard A   Thematic Development in Four Beckett Plays   MA Univ
     of Richmond 1969   58 p
350 DAMASHEK Richard   Samuel Beckett's *Waiting for Godot*   MA Columbia
     1965   121 p
351 FLANDERS Wallace A   A Study of Samuel Beckett's Trilogy: *Molloy,
     Malone Dies* and *The Unnamable*   MA Columbia 1959   142 p
352 FOTHERGILL Robert A   The Retrospective Hypothesis: A Study of the
     Pursuit of Identity in Samuel Beckett's Trilogy   MA McMaster
     (Canada) 1964
353 FRASER Donald M   Samuel Beckett; The Prophet of the Absurd
     BA Acadia (Canada) 1966
354 GARZILLI Henry F   A Philosophical Evaluation of Three Novels by
     Samuel Beckett   MA Univ of Rhode Island 1966   80 p
355 GELB Harold   Time and Time Again: A Study of Beckett's *Waiting for
     Godot* and *Play*   MA Columbia 1965
356 GIBAU Barbara P   Samuel Beckett's Trilogy   MA Univ of Rhode Island
     1960
357 GINGLES John R   Samuel Beckett: The Power of the Irresolvable
     MA Univ of Arizona 1966
358 GLOTZER Marguerite   Laughter in Purgatory: Some Interpretations
     of Samuel Beckett   MA Columbia 1963   176 p
359 GRATTAN Robert III   The Method in Beckett's Madness: A Critical
     Study of Samuel Beckett's Drama   MA Univ of Richmond 1965   114 p
360 HARRISON Robert L   Theseus Threadbare: A Study of Samuel Beckett's
     Murphy   MA Univ of Texas at Austin 1960
361 HEIKEN Patricia M   Samuel Beckett and Harold Pinter, a Comparative
     Study   MA Northern Illinois Univ 1966
362 KOHEN Willard J   From Here to Absurdity: Where Then? A Study of
     the Works of Samuel Beckett   MA Long Island Univ 1961   89 p
363 LAWSON JoAnn D   Language Philosophy in the Novels of Samuel Beckett
     MA Mankato St Coll 1967   116 p
364 LOGOTHETI Fkaterini   The Clown Motif in Samuel Beckett's Play
     Waiting for Godot   MA Alberta (Canada) 1964
365 MENDOZA Joseph D   An Analysis and Production Book of Samuel Beckett's
     Waiting for Godot   MA East Texas St Univ 1964
366 MITCHELL Jenelle E   Man's Ineffectiveness; a Study of the Plays by
     Samuel Beckett, Eugene Ionesco and Harold Pinter   MA Pacific Univ

1967
367 ORNER Frederic H The Human Image as Fool in Samuel Beckett's *Waiting for Godot* MA Columbia 1965 100 p
368 PAROLA Gene J An Interpretation of the Thought in *Waiting for Godot* MA Indiana Univ 1962
369 SCHOTTER Richard D Structure and Image in Three Plays by Samuel Beckett MA Columbia 1966 68 p
370 WHITE Patricia Existential Men in Three Novels by Samuel Beckett MA Illinois St Univ 1966
See also 5884

THOMAS LOVELL BEDDOES

371 APPLEGATE E H Thomas Lovell Beddoes MA Univ of Kentucky 1926
372 HAMILTON Elizabeth Attitude of Thomas Lovell Beddoes toward the Elizabethan Tragic Dramatists MA Univ of Pittsburgh 1928
373 LEEPER Robert R Beddoes and the Elizabethan Dramatists MA George Washington Univ 1942 83 p
374 MAGNI Maria L Thomas Lovell Beddoes MA Ca Foscari (Italy) 1967
375 ZAMPAROTTI Agostino Thomas L Beddoes, a Monography MA Ca Foscari (Italy) 1950

MAX BEERBOHM

376 BAILEY Richard C The Essays of Max Beerbohm MA Univ of Texas at Austin 1932
377 FELS William C Max Beerbohm's Dramatic Criticism MA Columbia 1940
378 NORBY Beverly J Max Beerbohm as a Literary Critic MA Univ of British Columbia (Canada) 1968 171 p
379 REILLY Mary A Max Beerbohm, a Writer of Satire MA Univ of Pittsburgh 1936
380 STACK Conrad J Max Beerbohm: A Critic of His Time MA Univ of New Mexico 1956
See also 2221

BRENDAN BEHAN

381 BEDELL Jeanne F The New British Drama 1956-1966 a Critical Study of Four Dramatists: John Osborne, Brendan Behan, Arnold Wesker and John Arden MA Univ of Richmond 1967 128 p
382 BOYLE Mary T Characteristics of Comedy in Two Plays by Brendan Behan MA Univ of Nebraska 1966
383 McNARY Nancy A Brendan Behan: Clown MA Columbia 1965 85 p
384 MALLOY Ione M Notes on Brendan Behan's *The Hostage* with Introductory Chapters on Behan's Life and Works MA Boston Coll 1964

MRS APHRA BEHN

385 BELANGER Terry Mrs Aphra Behn: The Novelist as Historian MA Columbia 1964 63 p
386 BOWMAN Wayne The Comedies of Mrs Aphra Behn MA Univ of North Carolina at Chapel Hill 1940
387 CLARK Edith L The Negro in Fiction: A Historical and Critical Sketch MA Univ of Texas at Austin 1902
388 DAVIS Marguerite F Woman's Contribution to Drama MA Austin Coll 1932
389 GORDY Jessalyn L Aphra Behn's *Oroonoko* MA Syracuse Univ 1940 102 p
390 GROAK Stephen M Aphra Behn's *Oroonoko* in Dramatic Form, 1696-1788 MA Univ of Maryland at College Park 1968 62 p
391 HILL Carrie S A Study of the Use of Source Material in the Plays of Mrs Aphra Behn MA Univ of Oklahoma 1943

392 KEELER Donald S   Literary Patronage and Mrs Aphra Behn   MA Columbia
       1940
393 McREYNOLDS John A   Characters in the Novels of Mrs Aphra Behn
       MA Univ of Oklahoma 1950
394 PENCE Anna M   Methods of Characterization in the Novels of Aphra Behn
       MA Univ of Pittsburgh 1948
395 PIOVAN Angelo M   Aphra Behn   MA Ca Foscari (Italy) 1955
396 SCHULTZ Mrs Gene   Mlle De Scudery and the Novels of Aphra Behn
       MA Univ of Texas at Austin 1937   103 p
397 TINDER Nancy   The Characterization of Women in Aphra Behn's Comedies
       MA Univ of Kentucky 1961   101 p
398 WALDENMAIER Elizabeth A   The Literary Reputation of Aphra Behn
       MA Univ of North Carolina at Chapel Hill 1952   95 p
399 WAKEFIELD-RICHMOND M W   The Life and Works of Mrs. Aphra Behn,
       with a Special Study of *Oroonoko*   B Litt Oxford Univ (England) nd
400 WEAVER Kitty D   The Poetry of Aphra Behn   MA George Washington Univ
       1933   88 p
See also 2385, 6192

ARNOLD BENNETT

401 BOHON E   Arnold Bennett as a Novelist   MA Univ of Louisville 1923
402 CEOLATO Cecilia   Arnold Bennett e le Sue Migliori Opere   MA Ca Foscari
       (Italy) 1949
403 HANDS S   Proverbial Reference in the Novels of Arnold Bennett
       MA Leeds Univ (England) 1966
404 JEWELL Dorothy M   Time the Dispossessor: A Study of the Theme of Time
       in the Works of Arnold Bennett   MA Hunter Coll 1969
405 KELLER N Florence   The Novels of Arnold Bennett; a Critical Estimate
       MA Univ of Oklahoma 1919
406 KING Bettye R   Characterization in the Major Novels of Arnold Bennett
       MA Univ of Texas at Austin 1955   264 p
407 KLUTEY Anna M   The Short Stories of Arnold Bennett   MA Indiana Univ
       1940
408 KNECHT Christian   The Origin and Sources of Arnold Bennett's *The Old
       Wives' Tale*   MA Indiana Univ 1935
409 LANGEVIN G R   Formative Influences on Arnold Bennett as Revealed in
       Five Representative Novels   MA Boston Univ 1940
410 MARCONI Ernesta A   Bennett's Novels   MA Ca Foscari (Italy) 1935
411 MILFORD Russell T   The Social Consciousness of Arnold Bennett
       M Ed Temple Univ 1939   156 p
412 MOON Harold D   Realism in Arnold Bennett's Five Towns Novels
       MA Univ of Texas at Austin 1939   102 p
413 NEILL Robert L Jr   Limitation or Expansion? A Study of Four Realistic
       Novels of Arnold Bennett   BA Amherst 1960
414 NORTHCROFT David J   The Craft of Arnold Bennett. A Study of His
       Realism in Relation to the Late Nineteenth-Century French Novel
       and to Contemporary Criticism   M Litt Cambridge (England) 1969
415 REDEWILL Helena M   The Realistic Fiction of Arnold Bennett
       MA Univ of Arizona pre 1933
416 SHIRLEY Johnnie   The Human Interest of Arnold Bennett   MA Univ of
       Texas at Austin 1940   118 p
417 SOHNGEN Mary L   Arnold Bennett: Upward Social Mobility in His Novels
       MA Miami Univ 1965
418 SOLOMON Mignon J   The Provincialism of Arnold Bennett   MA Washington
       Univ at St Louis 1937   181 p
419 STOCKDALE John C   Themes of Family Tensions and Financial Ambitions
       in the Novels of Arnold Bennett   MA Univ of New Brunswick (Canada)
       1963
See also 2401, 5173

RICHARD DODDRIDGE BLACKMORE

420 DANZIGER Belle B   Concerning the Art of Richard Doddridge Blackmore
     MA Univ of Texas at Austin 1935
421 MADAMBA Adriano N   Rime and Rhythm in Blackmore's Prose,
     Lorna Doone MA Oklahoma St Univ 1933
422 SPEAK Gwendolene M   A Critical Estimate of Richard Doddridge
     Blackmore's Novels MA Leeds Univ (England) 1950
See also 2915

WILLIAM BLAKE

423 ABRAHAMS Cecil   An Annotated Index to *The Four Zoas* of William Blake
     MA Univ of New Brunswick (Canada) 1965
424 ANDERSON William D   A Study of Blake's *The Four Zoas* MA Univ of
     Texas at Austin 1962
425 BANDY Flossie M   Evil and the Fall in the Poetry of William Blake
     MA Univ of Idaho 1965
426 BLACK John S   Evidences of Neoplatonism in the Work of William Blake
     MA St Louis Univ 1936   73 p
427 BOOKER N B   William Blake's *Annotations to Sir Joshua Reynolds'
     Discourses* MA Univ of North Carolina at Chapel Hill 1940
428 BORCHERS Louise H   William Blake's Poetry and Engravings
     MA Boston Univ 1935
429 BORCK Jim S   The Theme of Sexual Repression in William Blake's
     The Book of Thel MA Univ of Florida 1965
430 BRIDGE Thomas J   William Blake's *Mental Traveller*: An Explication
     BA Univ of British Columbia (Canada) 1962
431 BRIDGES Mary E   William Blake as a Critic of *The Canterbury Tales*
     MA Univ of Oklahoma 1951
432 BRIGGS Fred A   Development and Criticism of William Blake MA Baylor
     Univ 1940   301 p
433 BROOKS Elmer L   Traits of the Poete Maudit in Blake, Coleridge and
     Wordsworth MA Univ of Oklahoma 1948
434 BUNN James H   The Blakean Eye MA Wake Forest Coll 1965
435 BURKE Fenton G   An Annotated Index to the Minor Prophetic Works
     of William Blake MA Univ of New Brunswick (Canada) 1964
436 CARNER Frank K   Blake's Use of Smiles and Frowns: A Study of
     Contrariety MA Temple Univ 1967   53 p
437 CHRISTENSEN Sylvia L   William Blake and Zohar: Parallels in Thought
     MA Temple Univ 1963   56 p
438 CIOCCO Loretta G   Metaphoric and Symbolic Use of Color in the Poetry
     and Engravings of William Blake MA Temple Univ 1965   54 p
439 CLARKE Jack C   William Blake's *Jerusalem*, the Cosmic Projection of
     the Inner Life of a Prophetic Mystic MA Bowling Green Univ 1959
440 CLOUGH Frances C   The Aphorisms of William Blake MA Univ of Oklahoma
     1951
441 DARDIS Margaret M   Cherub and Chariot; Ezekiel's Vision of God and
     Society in the Poetry of William Blake MA Temple Univ 1965   112 p
442 DIKE Donald A   Blake's Answer to His Age MA Columbia 1942
443 DOMKE Charlotte F   The Problem of Good and Evil in Blake MA Univ of
     Houston 1960   94 p
444 DOUGLAS J A   William Blake's Theory of Religion and Art MA Boston
     Coll 1941
445 DUCKER Bruce   William Blake's *Songs of Innocence* MA Columbia 1963 80 p
446 DUMBAUGH Winifred   William Blake's Vision of America MA Stetson Univ
     1964
447 EEKMAN John S   Blake's Marginalia on Reynolds' *Discourse on Painting
     and the Fine Arts* MA Univ of Tennessee 1954   83 p

448 ENGER Norman L Blake's *Prophetic Books* and Analytical Psychology
     MA Columbia 1959 117 p
449 FANELLI Roselee B Several Features of William Blake's Aesthetic
     Mode MA St Joseph Coll 1966
450 FENN Don F A Study of William Blake BA Amherst Coll 1956
451 FINNINGAN Michael J The Arc Symbol in William Blake's Works
     MA Central Washington St Coll 1964
452 FLATTO Elie William Blake: A Vindication of Man MA Columbia 1958
     140 p
453 FRIEDMAN David J A Reading of Blake's *The Grey Monk* MA Columbia
     1967 42 p
454 FRUEN Bernice P Interpretations of *Songs of Experience*: Summary
     and Commentary MA Columbia 1960 124 p
455 GASTON Karen C The Significance of William Blake's Poetry in
     Joyce Cary's *The Horse's Mouth* MA North Texas St Univ 1970
456 GOLDFARB Richard L William Blake's Concept of Vision MA Columbia
     1964 66 p
457 GRAFTON Brian Jungian Light on the Blakean Archetype BA Univ of
     British Columbia (Canada) 1964
458 GREENBERG John S Generalization of an Idiot; Blake's Prophetic
     Perspectives BA Amherst 1970
459 GROSS Robert V William Blake's Numerological Symbolism in *Milton*
     and *Jerusalem* MA George Washington Univ 1953 71 p
460 GUNTER Mary A The Influence of Mary Wollstonecraft's Life and
     Writings on William Blake's *Visions of the Daughters of Albion*
     MA Temple Univ 1966 70 p
461 HALL Madge Moral Philosophy of William Blake in Relation to His Time
     MA Univ of Oklahoma 1937
462 HALL William H The Aesthetics of Blake's Drawing and Engraving
     MA Univ of Houston 1966 59 p
463 HESTER Kathleen D William Blake's *Marriage of Heaven and Hell*:
     A Formal Analysis MA Univ of North Carolina at Greensboro 1969
464 HERBERT Jack William Blake and the Integration of Poetry and
     Painting M Litt Cambridge (England) 1959
465 HERSCHEL James A Blake's *Jerusalem*: Images for the Imageless Truth
     MS Syracuse Univ 1968 110 p
466 HIGGINS David M William Blake: The Myth of the Imagination
     MA Bowling Green Univ 1968
467 HILL Kathleen B The Role of Orc as Redeemer MA Columbia 1963 72 p
468 HILL Viola J Blake and the Bible MA Indiana Univ 1940
469 HODGES Norma L Gulley Jimson as William Blake MA Univ of Iowa 1965
470 JACOBY John B William Blake and the Religion of Art BA Amherst 1966
471 KOPER Peter T Finite and Infinite in *Vala; or the Four Zoas*
     MA Washington St Univ 1969 96 p
472 LeDOUX Larry V The Contraries: Blake's Reintegration
     MA Sacramento St Coll 1966
473 McCLOY Bonnie J William Blake as Seen by His Contemporaries
     MA Univ of North Carolina at Chapel Hill 1948 50 p
474 MATHER George V The Sex Factor in Blake's Cosmology MA Univ of
     New Mexico 1948
475 MIRANDA Irene The Punctuation in Blake's *Jerusalem* MA Univ of
     Massachusetts 1965
476 MITCHELL Jeffrey D Blake's *Last Judgments* MA Columbia 1966 74 p
477 MOODY Willa A Mysticism in the Poetry of William Blake
     MA Boston Univ 1934
478 MOTT Bernard E A Comparison of William Blake's Theology and Some
     Aspects of Modern Christian Doctrine MA Univ of Oregon 1932
479 MURPHY Susan Blake as a Satirist: A Study of *An Island in the
     Moon* and *The Marriage of Heaven and Hell* BA Univ of British
     Columbia (Canada) 1970

480 ORMOND Wilbur C William Blake's Use of the Bible MA East Carolina
     Univ 1965
481 ORTOLANI Corrado William Blake as a Lyric Poet MA Ca Foscari
     (Italy) 1937
482 OSBORN Winifred Vates Ludens: William Blake's *The Four Zoas,*
     Sub specie ludi MA Columbia 1965 89 p
483 PERLMUTTER Eila S Blake and Natural Religion: The Philosophical
     and Religious Controversy in *Jerusalem* MA Kent St Univ 1966
484 RABINOVITZ Rubin Old Testament Influences in William Blake's
     The Four Zoas MA Columbia 1961 89 p
485 ROSENGARD Robert S The Lamb and The Tiger: A Search for Power in
     the Minor Prophetic Works of William Blake BA Amherst 1961
486 SAMPSON Minnie Blake and 18th Century Taste MA Univ of Oklahoma 1950
487 SAMUELS Jayne N William Blake's Use of Color Symbolism in *The Four
     Zoas* MA Washington St Univ at Pullman 1939
488 SANFERRARE Joanna R Symbols of Vegetation in William Blake's *Songs
     of Innocence and of Experience* MA Columbia 1966 83 p
489 SCHWARTZ Howard E The Form of the Fall: A Study of Blake's
     The Mental Traveler MA Washington Univ at St Louis 1969 43 p
490 SCOTT Andrew A Comparison of William Blake's *Songs of Innocence
     and of Experience* and Allen Ginsberg's *Howl* BA Univ of British
     Columbia (Canada) 1969
491 SCOTT Merry D The Symbolism of William Blake's Poetry MA Kansas St
     Coll at Pittsburg 1940
492 SEVIER Marcus W A True Poet and of the Devil's Party: A Study of
     the Mythic Symbols in the Prophetic Books of Blake MA Univ of
     Houston 1967 91 p
493 SHANDLER Annette The Developing Cosmos of William Blake MA Temple
     Univ 1963 53 p
494 SHAPIRO Clara The Wise and Foolish Woman: A Study of the Debates
     between Vala and Jerusalem in the Prophetic Works of William Blake
     MA Columbia 1962 126 p
495 SHROYER Richard J An Examination of William Blake's *An Island in
     the Moon* MA Toronto (Canada) 1964
496 SIMMONS Robert E Blake's *Book of Urizen:* A Study of Text and Design
     M Phil Toronto (Canada) 1966
497 SKRETKOWICZ Florence E The Female in the Writings of William Blake
     MA Univ of New Brunswick (Canada) 1967
498 SKRETKOWICZ Victor Blake's Creation Myth with Reference to
     Jacob Boehme MA Univ of New Brunswick (Canada) 1967
499 SMITH Helen C Three Poets in Changing World: The Metamorphoses of
     Ovid, Milton and Blake MA Univ of Oklahoma 1950
500 SMITH Judith A Outline of Identity: A Study of William Blake's
     Emerging Public Image MA Colorado St Coll 1965
501 SOBELL Guy J A Critical Discussion of the *Songs of Innocence and
     of Experience* BA Univ of British Columbia (Canada) 1966
502 SPIVACK Joan William Blake and the Apocalypse of Art MA Hunter Coll
     1963
503 STEELE Marjorie A William Blake's Theme of Energy MA Columbia 1959
     76 p
504 STERLING Allan C William Blake's Poetical Sketches: The Span and
     Order of Their Composition MA Columbia 1964 93 p
505 STERN Herbert J Foundations of Blake Criticism: A Study of Blake
     Criticism and Commentary in the Nineteenth and Early Twentieth
     Centuries MA Columbia 1953 128 p
506 SVATIK Stephen The Influence of Jacob Bryant on William Blake
     MA Univ of Maryland at College Park 1969 69 p
507 TATE A Five Literary Influences on William Blake's *The Marriage of
     Heaven and Hell* MA Univ of Texas at Austin 1966 63 p
508 TAYLOR L John William Blake: Christian Critic of Christianity;

Prophecy and Poesy: An Imaginary Conversation between
William Wordsworth and Joseph; and Eugene O'Neill: A Man of
Thought and Feeling in an Era of Unbelief MA Brigham Young Univ
1960 72 p

509 THOMASON Jessie W William Blake: A Wild-Eyed Revolutionary Rebel
of the Eighteenth Century MA Arkansas St Coll 1964

510 TRACHTMAN Paul William Blake's *America*: A Study of the Prosody
MA Columbia 1961 89 p

511 UNDERWOOD Richard S William Blake as an 18th Century Figure
MA Univ of Pittsburgh 1928

512 VOSSLER Albert E William Blake as a Critic of Literature MA Syracuse
Univ 1947 75 p

513 WARSHAW Nancy R Jacob Bryant and William Blake MA Columbia 1962 105 p

514 WILLIAMS Harry S Some Characteristics of the Visionary Poet:
William Blake and Dylan Thomas MA Univ of Maryland at College Park
1969 87 p

515 WILSON David L William Blake: The Responsibility of Vision
BA Amherst 1960

516 WILSON Raymond R Blake's Imagery: *Songs of Innocence* MA West Texas
St Univ 1937 84 p

517 WITEK John C Pictorial Expression in the *Songs of Innocence and of
Experience* MA Hunter Coll 1968

518 WOLFF George A A Critical Analysis of Blake's *Visions of the
Daughters of Albion* MA Washington Univ at St Louis 1959 115 p

519 WOLSEY Sarah The Influence of the French Revolution on the Writings
of Blake, Wordsworth and Coleridge MA Brigham Young Univ 1963 143 p

520 YORK Ella M Imagery from the Technology of the Industrial Revolution
in the Poetry of William Blake MA Univ of Arizona 1960 58 p

521 YOUNG Beatrice Some Points of Likeness in the Philosophy of Blake
and Browning MA Univ of Pittsburgh 1923

522 ZWERLING L Steven Eternity in an Hour: A Critical Study of the
Ninth Night of William Blake's *The Four Zoas* MA Columbia 1961 71 p

See also 1835, 1890, 1999, 4524, 5305, 5331, 7354, 7507

JAMES BOSWELL

523 BARBOUR Roberta B Boswell's Tour to the Hebrides as a Basis for
the Life of Johnson MA Univ of Oklahoma 1939

524 BATAILLE Robert R A Literary Analysis of Boswell's *London Journal*
MA Univ of Kansas 1966

525 BRAWLEY Georgia W Fresh Impressions of Dr Johnson from the Newly
Published *Boswell Papers* MA Univ of Iowa 1935

526 DALTON Joyce V Z Histrionic Boswell: The Influence of Drama on
His Life MA Lamar Technological Coll 1965 103 p

527 DODD Diana L An Investigation of the James Boswell-William Johnson
Temple Friendship and Correspondence MA Southern Illinois Univ
at Carbondale 1954 128 p

528 EGGEMEYER Emeline An Account of Boswell's Reading MA Univ of
Kentucky 1941 190 p

529 HOWELL Elmo Boswell Versus Johnson MA Univ of Florida nd

530 JONES Harold E James Boswell as a Critic of English Life
MA Howard Univ 1939 42 p

531 LYNCH Rev John W The Classification of and Reason for the Changes
in James Boswell's "Printed Version" of the Tour of the Hebrides
with Samuel Johnson, LL D MA Boston Coll 1948

532 McGUFFIE Helen L The Personality of James Boswell MA Univ of
Pittsburgh 1937

533 McULWEE Sonia L Samuel Johnson and James Boswell: A Comparison of
Their Political Views MA Lamar Technological Coll 1966

534 MEIER Tom K Johnson and Boswell in Scotland MA Columbia 1963 118 p

535 MIDGETT Wallace R James Boswell and the Law MA Univ of Tennessee 1964
536 MOTSCH Charles P Boswell's Revision of His *Life of Samuel Johnson*
     MA Univ of Texas at Austin 1947 71 p
537 NEESON John F English Biography from Boswell to Stanley MA Univ of
     Pittsburgh 1933
538 PHENIX Ruby The Moral Philosophy of James Boswell MA North Texas
     St Univ 1948
539 SELLERS Pamela C Boswell's Melancholy MA Georgetown Univ 1968 55 p
540 STICKMAN Barbara B Influence of the Drama on James Boswell
     MA Marshall Univ 1965
541 SUMMERS Minosa F The Epistolary Style of James Boswell MA Texas Tech-
     nological Univ 1963 141 p
542 TERRILL Robert K Boswell's Melancholia: The Utrecht Period
     MA Univ of Texas at Austin 1955 63 p
See also 3534, 4264

                            THE BRONTES

543 ALLEN William R The Animal World of Emily Bronte MA Univ of Louisvill
     1966 105 p
544 ALLENDER Beulah L The Labor Movement in the Novels of Bronte, Eliot
     and Gaskell MA Univ of Oklahoma 1933
545 ALEXANDER Irene Imagery in Emily Bronte's *Wuthering Heights*
     MA Boston Coll 1954
546 ANDERSON H A Gothic Elements in the Novels of Charlotte, Emily and
     Anne Bronte MA Univ of North Carolina at Chapel Hill 1933
547 ANENDELL Beverly B The Brontes' Concept of the Independent Woman
     MA Texas Technological Univ 1968
548 BAILEY George H The Animals of *Wuthering Heights:* An Analysis in
     the Main Stream of Bronte Criticism MA Boston Coll 1966
549 BARRETTE Sr Mary E Color Symbolism: A Technique of the Plot in
     Jane Eyre MA Boston Coll 1961
550 BARTH Marian G The Indebtedness of May Sinclair to the Bronte Sisters
     MA Univ of Toledo 1931
551 BELTZ Dorothy S Charlotte Bronte in the Nineteenth Century Novel:
     Romantic, Victorian, Realist MA Southern Illinois Univ at
     Carbondale 1950 106 p
552 BOLAND Zuleika E Biographical Data Used by Charlotte Bronte as
     Material for Her Novels MA Univ of Oklahoma 1942
553 BRADFORD Ethel R Popularity of Charlotte Bronte as Evidenced by
     the Periodicals (1847-1900) MA Univ of Oklahoma 1948
554 BROWN Mitzi Heathcliff: The Alter-Ego of Emily Bronte MA Univ of
     Southern Mississippi 1966
555 BUTLER Barbara M The Gothic Element in the Bronte Novels
     MA Boston Univ 1946
556 BYERS John R Jr The Use of Models from Life and from Fiction in
     the Novels of Charlotte Bronte MA Univ of North Carolina at
     Chapel Hill 1954 121 p
557 CARR Dorothy D Autobiography in the Bronte Novels MA Univ of
     Kentucky 1932
558 CECCONI Lucina Symbolism in *Wuthering Heights* by Emily Bronte
     MA Ca Foscari (Italy) 1969
559 CERVETTI Maria A Emily Bronte MA Ca Foscari (Italy) 1939
560 COCHRAN Janet Charlotte Bronte's *Villette:* The Confessional
     Perspective MA Univ of North Carolina at Greensboro 1966
561 DALY Irene F Charlotte Bronte: An Appraisal of Certain Criticism
     of Her Novels, with Special Reference to the Manuscript
     Caroline Vernon MA Syracuse Univ 1942 162 p
562 DELANEY Martha A An Analysis and Evaluation of Technical Deficiencies
     in the Novels of Charlotte Bronte MA Oklahoma St Univ 1940 91 p

563 DRAKE Pauline E The Master-Pupil Relationship in the Novels of
     Charlotte Bronte MA Bowling Green Univ 1959
564 EDELMAN John R The Literary Reputation of Charlotte Bronte from the
     Time of the Publication of *Jane Eyre* to the End of the Nineteenth
     Century MA Villanova Univ 1964
565 FACEN Elda Women in Charlotte Bronte MA Ca Foscari (Italy) 1936
566 FADEM Richard Emily Bronte: A Dynasty of Loneliness MA Columbia
     1963   145 p
567 FERRITER Sr Mary L Imagery in Emily Bronte's Poetry MA Boston Coll
     1954
568 FREEDMAN Frances S Charlotte Bronte and Feminism MA Montreal
     (Canada) 1964
569 GOWEN Marianne S Creativity and the Search for Unity in the Work
     of Emily Bronte MA Stanford Univ 1940
570 HARDEN L June Some Aspects of the Life of Emily Bronte as Revealed
     by Her Imagery MA Howard Univ 1946   53 p
571 HART Sr St Agatha Charlotte Bronte as a Literary Critic
     MA Indiana Univ 1935
572 HENRY Neil O The Characterization Techniques of Charlotte Bronte
     MA Alberta (Canada) 1966
573 HICKEY G T Naive Genius of Emily Bronte MA Boston Coll 1940
574 HOEY Sr Mary A The Search for Identity: The Theme of
     Charlotte Bronte's Novels MA Boston Coll 1961
575 KEARNS Ruth A The Role of Children in the Novels of Charlotte,
     Emily and Anne Bronte MA St Louis Univ 1962   116 p
576 LAKE Fredric D Jr Alienation and the Victorian Narrator in
     Wuthering Heights and *Jane Eyre* BA Amherst 1964
577 LONG Maida The Worlds of Heaven and Hell: Apocalyptic and
     Demonic Imagery in *Wuthering Heights* with Some Reference to
     the Poetry of Emily Bronte BA Univ of British Columbia
     (Canada) 1966
578 LOOMIS Chauncey C Jr Charlotte Bronte and Her Sense of Lonliness
     MA Columbia 1955   83 p
579 McCABE James E The Gothic Tradition in the Brontes' Novels
     MA Mankato St Coll 1966   66 p
580 McCUE Eleanor L The Position of Woman in the Works of the Brontes
     MA Univ of Maine 1933   143 p
581 MacKAY Ruth M *Wuthering Heights:* A Mosaic, An Analytical Study
     of the German, Irish and English Influences on Emily Bronte's
     Novel MA Brigham Young Univ 1962   110 p
582 MANSFIELD Maureen H Emily Bronte Biography MA Univ of Montana
     1934   176 p
583 MILES Susan The Novels of Charlotte and Emily Bronte MA Univ of
     Texas at Austin 1929
584 NEVIN Carol A The Literary Reputation of *Jane Eyre* in the Nineteenth
     Century MA Univ of Maryland at College Park 1963   79 p
585 NOFTSKER Orpha Parallels in Characters and Situations in
     Charlotte Bronte's Novels MA Univ of Oregon 1935
586 NYLUND Laimi Finnish Translations of the Works of Jane Austen,
     Charlotte Bronte, Emily Bronte and George Eliot MA Columbia 1937
587 PASSEL Anne W Charlotte Bronte's Novels: The Artistry of Their
     Construction MA Pacific Univ 1967   248 p
588 PAWLYK John E Some Uses of Nature in the Delineation of Character:
     Alexander Pope, Henry Fielding, Jane Austen and Emily Bronte
     MA Syracuse Univ 1959   104 p
589 PRITCHARD William P A Study of the Fiction of Anne Bronte
     MA Univ of Pittsburgh 1950
590 PUBLICOVER Isabel F Victorian Attitudes Toward Education as Reflected
     in the Novels of Charlotte and Anne Bronte MA Saint Mary's
     (Canada) 1965

591 RAGSDALE Inez T The Elements of Mysticism in the Works of Emily Bronte
    MA Texas Christian Univ 1967 170 p
592 REIGSTAD Paul M The Critics of *Wuthering Heights* MA Univ of
    New Mexico 1956
593 SCHREINER Wilhelmina R The Criticism of Emily Bronte MA Univ of
    Pittsburgh 1937
594 SEARS Evelyn The Enigma of Emily Bronte MA Washington Univ at
    St Louis 1947 131 p
595 SHUNAMI Gideon The Structure of Emily Bronte's *Wuthering Heights*
    MA Columbia 1960 72 p
596 SPITZER Elizabeth Concepts of Heredity and Environment in
    Wuthering Heights MA Columbia 1963 79 p
597 STARRETT Agnes L The Mysticism of Emily Dickinson and Emily Bronte
    MA Univ of Pittsburgh 1925
598 STRETCHER Joyce S Charlotte Bronte and George Eliot: Their
    Reaction to the Victorian Heroine MA Auburn Univ 1968
599 TOWLES Sarah B *Wuthering Heights*: A Study MA Tulane 1906
600 TREVISANI Leonilla The Poetry of Emily Bronte MA Ca Foscari
    (Italy) 1958
601 TRUSSLER G A Comparative Examination of the Treatment of the Theme
    of Renunciation in the Novels of Charlotte Bronte and George Eliot
    M Phil Univ of London (England) 1967
602 VAN HORN Belle R A Study of Character Delineation in *Jane Eyre*
    MA Tulane 1910
603 VAZZOLER Anna M The Sources of Charlotte Bronte's Novels
    MA Ca Foscari (Italy) 1954
604 WAGNER Sr M Ildefonse The Philosophy of Life Reflected in the
    Poetry of Emily Jane Bronte and Christina Georgina Rossetti
    MS Ft Hays St Coll 1944 99 p
605 WAIDE Helen I The Reception of Mrs Gaskell's *Life of Charlotte Bronte*
    MA Columbia 1941
606 WARD Mary E Charlotte Bronte's Feminine Characters; A Revolt Against
    Some Victorian Ideals MA Univ of Pittsburgh 1931
607 WHITEHEAD Constance U The Bronte Country, the Bronte Hardships
    and Some Results in the Bronte Novels MA Boston Univ 1945
608 WILLS Jack C The Brontes: A Comparative Study of Temperament as
    Reflected in the Novels MA Univ of Delaware 1963 53 p
609 ZANCONATO A Maria Romantic Elements in Emily Bronte's Works
    MA Ca Foscari (Italy) 1949
610 ZANCONATO Giovanna Romantic Elements in Charlotte Bronte's Works
    MA Ca Foscari (Italy) 1949
See also 195, 963, 3404, 4634, 6016

RUPERT BROOKE

611 COLACO Margarida M The Sonnets of Rupert Brooke Edited with an
    Introduction and Notes MA Boston Coll 1964
612 DAVIS Lucile The Life and Works of Rupert Brooke MA Univ of Texas
    at Austin 1930
613 DeLAURENTIS Lydia Rupert Brooke and His Poems MA Ca Foscari (Italy)
    1936
614 GUIDI Vittorio The Poetry of Rupert Brooke MA Ca Foscari (Italy) 1967
615 SCAPIN Giovanni Rupert Brooke, An Essay on Psychological Analysis
    Through His Poems MA Ca Foscari (Italy) 1939

THOMAS BROWNE

616 ANGELL Richard C Sir Thomas Browne in the Nineteenth and Twentieth
    Centuries MA Univ of New Mexico 1962
617 BRENNAN Sr Alice The Influence of Sir Thomas Browne on

Emily Dickinson MA Boston Coll 1963
618 DEANS E V Jr Sir Thomas Browne's Botanical Learning as Illustrated
      in His Writings MA Univ of North Carolina at Chapel Hill 1939
619 EOYANG Eugene C Aspects of the Quincuncial Mind: A Study of
      Sir Thomas Browne MA Columbia 1960 106 p
620 FRAYNE John P Sir Thomas Browne: Antiquarian and Virtuoso
      MA Columbia 1961 100 p
621 FREELAND Stephen L The Influence of Travel Literature on
      Sir Thomas Browne MA Columbia 1935
622 FULLER Nelle I A Study of the Relation of Sir Thomas Browne to
      Two Special Phases of 17th Century Thought MA Smith Coll 1936
623 FUSON James R Sir Thomas Browne and the Neo-Platonic Theory of the
      Microcosm MA Univ of Oklahoma 1958
624 HURT Ellen L Sir Thomas Browne, Baroque Stylist MA Univ of
      Oklahoma 1958
625 KENNY Margaret A Sir Thomas Browne and the Microcosm MA Columbia
      1960 100 p
626 KOCH Albert W An Analysis of Sir Thomas Browne's Diction in His
      Religio Medici MA St Louis Univ 1940 66 p
627 LENNING Ann *Moby Dick* and the Works of Sir Thomas Browne: A Com-
      parison of Metaphysical Modes MA Marshall Univ 1966
628 McKNIGHT Winifred L Sir Thomas Browne of the *Religio Medici*, a
      Study of Attitudes MA Univ of Pittsburgh 1935
629 MAGID Joel From Gardens to God: A Study of Structure and Meaning
      in *The Gardens of Cyrus* by Sir Thomas Browne MA Columbia 1965
630 O'SULLIVAN Robert J Sir Thomas Browne on Death MA St Louis Univ
      1941 56 p
631 POLO Alessandro Sir Thomas Browne as a Demiurge MA Ca Foscari
      (Italy) nd
632 REED Laurie T Sir Thomas Browne: A Study of His Christianity and
      His Stoicism MA Univ of North Carolina at Chapel Hill 1955
633 SCHILLER David J A Study of Three Works by Sir Thomas Browne
      MA Columbia 1965 116 p
634 VICARI Eleanor P Myth and Imagination in Sir Thomas Browne
      MA Toronto (Canada) 1963
635 WISE James N Some Seventeenth Century Animadversions on
      Sir Thomas Browne's *Religio Medici* MA Univ of Florida 1964
See also 2822

                          THE BROWNINGS

636 ABBOTT Maude E The Dramatic Monologue in Browning and Tennyson
      MA Boston Univ 1906
637 ALDRICH Johnnie R An Annotated Robert Browning Bibliography,
      1951-1960, with an Analysis of Critical Trends MA Univ of
      Colorado 1966
638 ANDERSON B Browning as a Dramatist BA Univ of British Columbia
      (Canada) 1956
639 ANDERSON Sara E Browning's Intepretation of Euripides' *Alcestis* in
      Balaustion's Adventure MA Washington St Univ at Pullman 1916
640 ARCHULETA Br Anthony C Browning's Attitude Toward Miracles as
      Manifested in His Poems MA Saint Mary's at San Antonio 1939 63 p
641 ATCHLEY Donovan O Inconsistencies in Browning's *Doctrine of
      Imperfection* MA Univ of Tennessee 1964
642 AUSTIN Sylvia Robert Browning's *Pippa Passes*: A Study in Self-
      Delusion BA Univ of British Columbia (Canada) 1966
643 BATES Ada W The Influence of Swedenborg on the Brownings
      M Ed Temple Univ 1943 101 p
644 BATES Ann L Browning's Literary Theory MA Univ of North Carolina
      at Chapel Hill 1955 93 p

645 BEASLEY Elizabeth A Elements of Pessimism in the Poetry of
    Robert Browning MA Univ of Tennessee 1953 97 p
646 BEASLEY Ruth Nineteenth Century Criticism of *The Ring and the Book*
    MA Univ of Texas at Austin 1950 91 p
647 BEATTIE Hazel M Robert Browning's Dramas BA Univ of Oklahoma 1917
648 BECK Charlotte H An Examination of the Conclusions to Browning's
    Dramatic Monologues MA Univ of Tennessee 1966
649 BECKER Allen W Browning on Byron: A Record of Admiration and
    Protection MA Univ of Tennessee 1950
650 BELL Ellen B Browning's Use of Molinism in *The Ring and the Book*
    MA Univ of North Carolina at Chapel Hill 1951
651 BERMAN Lena The Artist in Browning MA Boston Univ 1932
652 BERRIGAN Agnes Browning's Philosophy BA Univ of Oklahoma 1913
653 BIBB Josephine Elizabeth Barrett Browning's Interest in Italian
    Affairs as Shown in Her Poetry with Explanatory Notes
    MA Univ of Arkansas 1931
654 BISHOP Selma L *The Ring and the Book:* A Study in Characters
    MA Univ of Texas at Austin 1933
655 BLACK Audrey D Elizabeth Barrett Browning and Social Reform
    MA Howard Univ 1939 104 p
656 BLACK Ruth Renaissance Themes and Figures in Browning's Poetry
    MA Texas Technological Univ 1937 50 p
657 BLAIR Carolyn L Browning as a Critic of Poetry MA Univ of Tennessee
    1948
658 BLAKNEY P S Browning's *The Ring and the Book* in Twentieth-Century
    Criticism MA North Texas St Univ 1955
659 BLODGETT Margaret E Love of Man and Woman in Robert Browning's
    Poetry MA St Louis Univ 1936 53 p
660 BOOTHBY Edith M The Influence of Personal and Social Environment
    upon the Poetry of Elizabeth Barrett Browning MA Boston Univ 1932
661 BOSWELL Genevieve M A Decade of Browning Criticism MA Univ of Texas
    at Austin 1948 132 p
662 BOTTENFIELD Eanid W The Love Poems of Browning MA Univ of Tulsa 1949
663 BOULWARE M Sketches of Robert Browning's Women MA Univ of Louisville
    1929
664 BOWERS Leroy Browning's Theory of Evil MA Univ of Kentucky 1917
665 BOX Grace An Essay Toward a Romantic Biography of Elizabeth Barrett
    Browning (1813-1845) MA Southwestern Univ 1928
666 BOYLE Sr Mary E Browning's Treatment of Catholicism MA Univ of
    Pittsburgh 1920
667 BRACK O M Jr The Philosopher's Stone: The Final Meaning of *Paracelsus*
    MA Baylor Univ 1961 85 p
668 BRADY Thomas Browning's Negative Definition of the Ideal in *The Ring
    and the Book* MA Midwestern Univ 1968 101 p
669 BREITHAUPT Thelma Browning's Theory of Poetry, Music and Painting
    MA Texas Christian Univ 1933 157 p
670 BRISCOE S Backgrounds of the Correspondence between Robert Browning
    and Elizabeth Barrett MA St Mary's at San Antonio 1949 75 p
671 BROWN Elizabeth Pound and Browning: Image and Persona MA Alberta
    (Canada) 1963
672 BROWN Nellee L An Examination of the Non-Dramatic Poems of Robert
    Browning's Third Period (1846-1869) MA Univ of Texas at Austin 1906
673 BROWN Sr Roberta M The Development of Robert Browning's Optimism
    MA Boston Coll 1963
674 BRYAN M Charlotte Twenty Men of Browning MS Kansas St Coll at
    Pittsburg 1932
675 BUHL Paulina E The Criticism on Robert Browning's *The Ring and the Book*
    1868-1908 MA Univ of North Carolina at Chapel Hill 1953 99 p
676 BURLISON Prudence B Man's Growing Concept of God as Seen in Selected
    Poems of Robert Browning MA Univ of Idaho 1966

677 BURTON Ruth H Life: A Continuous Growth; A Comparative Study of
     the Philosophies of Wordsworth and Browning MA Washington Univ
     at St Louis 1920
678 BUTLER Ella L Christianity in the Poetry of Robert Browning
     MA Univ of Texas at Austin 1906
679 BYRNES William A Browning's Knowledge of Painters and Sculptors and His
     Inferences about Art Values MA Indiana Univ of Pennsylvania 1967   58 p
680 CALDWELL Alma A A Critical Analysis of Browning's *The Inn Album*
     MA Texas Technological Univ 1933   69 p
681 CAMPBELL Katherine G Robert Browning and Religion MA Univ of Kentucky
     1940
682 CANDLER T T The Struggle for Italian Unity and Its Reflection in
     Mrs Browning's Poetry MA Univ of North Carolina at Chapel Hill 1897
683 CARACCIA Anthony L Browning's Treatment of the Law and the Lawyers
     in *The Ring and the Book* MA Univ of Rhode Island 1966   105 p
684 CARIGAN William E Jr Browning's View of the Role of the Poet: An
     Appraisal from Evidence in His Works MA George Washington Univ
     1964   120 p
685 CARR Sr Mary C Book X, *The Ring and the Book* MA Univ of Texas at
     Austin 1950   175 p
686 CARTER Gloria A Browning's Characterization of Women MA Univ of
     Texas at Austin 1948   171 p
687 CATANACH Rev The Roman Catholic Clergyman in the Works of Robert
     Browning MA St Mary's at San Antonio 1940   73 p
688 CARVER Mildred Gothic Traits in Robert Browning's Shorter Poems
     MA Univ of Texas at Austin 1942   161 p
689 CAWOOD Nancy M Some Nineteenth Century American Criticism of the Work
     of Elizabeth Barrett Browning MA Univ of Kentucky 1955   178 p
690 CHANDLER Carrie M A Study of Dramaturgical Elements in Three of
     Browning's Closet Dramas MA Oklahoma St Univ 1959   125 p
691 CHAPMAN Doris V The Changing Attitudes in Browning Criticism
     MA Univ of Maine 1960   70 p
692 CHOATE Mary J Franceschini: A Dramatization of *The Ring and the Book*
     MA Univ of Texas at Austin 1950   92 p
693 CLAPP Sarah L Robert Browning's Theory of Poetry MA Univ of Texas
     at Austin 1918
694 CLEE David The "Defense of the Indefensible": A Study of the
     Relationship between Aesthetic Sympathy and Moral Judgment in a
     Group of Browning's Poems BA Univ of British Columbia (Canada) 1963
695 CLEWELL Lynne A Robert and Elizabeth Barrett Browning: The Legend of
     the Perfect Marriage MA Univ of Maryland at College Park 1956   80 p
696 COLLEY Mary E The Technique of Character Setting and Point of View
     in Browning's Longer Poems MA Boston Univ 1936
697 COURTNEY Eleanor L Elizabeth Barrett Browning and Christina Georgina
     Rossetti: A Comparative Study of Popularity and Appeal MA Univ
     of Arizona 1957   58 p
698 CRAGG Edward C Browning's Art Poems BA Univ of British Columbia
     (Canada) 1968
699 CUNDIFF Paul A A Source Study of Robert Browning's *The Ring and the
     Book* MA Univ of Kentucky 1936
700 CURRY Mary L Who's Who Among Browning's Friends MA Baylor Univ 1938
701 CURTIS Tina M A Study in the Diction of Browning's *The Ring and the
     Book* MA Univ of Texas at Austin 1950   119 p
702 CURTIS Wynn J Christian Existentialism and Situation Ethics
     Illustrated by Robert Browning's Lovers MA Univ of Tennessee 1969
703 DEERING Dorothy J Browning and Modern Critical Trends MA Baylor Univ
     1960   167 p
704 DERRICK Margaret C Recent Interest in Robert Browning (1890-1933)
     MA Univ of Oklahoma 1934
705 DeWITT Paul B The Early History of Browning's Plays MA Univ of Iowa

1932
706 DICKISON Betty O The Complex Character of Browning's Bishop Blougram
       MA Univ of New Mexico 1962
707 DIEBELS Alice E The Relation of Knowledge and of Love to Life as
       Deduced from the Poems of Robert Browning MA Marquette Univ 1930
708 DOHERTY S M The Nature and Consistency of Browning's Optimism
       BA Univ of British Columbia (Canada) 1931
709 DOLAN William E The Development of Robert Browning from Dramatist
       to Dramatic Monologuist: A Study of His Plays MA Syracuse Univ
       1964   92 p
710 DOUGHTON L M Browning's Theory of Immortality MA Boston Univ 1927
711 DRISCOLL Elizabeth M Browning the Singer MA Boston Univ 1931
712 DROLL Naomi R Elizabeth Barrett Browning: Browning's Ideal of
       Womanhood MA St Louis Univ 1936   108 p
713 DROWN Helen O Robert Browning BA Univ of Oklahoma 1903
714 DUMLOP Margaret R Nature in Browning as Seen in Dramatic Lyrics,
       Dramatic Romances, Men and Women and Dramatic Personae MA Texas
       Technological Univ 1940   84 p
715 EAGAR Margaret M Imagery in Twenty-Five Poems of Browning MA Boston
       Univ 1948
716 EASON J L Browning's Interpretation of Leading Renaissance Ideas
       MA Univ of North Carolina at Chapel Hill 1915
717 ELDRIDGE Elizabeth F Browning's Personal and Literary Associations
       with France MA Univ of Kentucky 1917
718 ENGLISH Walter H Robert Browning and the New Testament Theology
       MA Howard Univ 1934   48 p
719 EVANS Carolyn J Gide and Browning: A Study of Influence MA Texas
       Christian Univ 1968   94 p
720 EYFORD Glen A Language and Communication in Browning MA Toronto
       (Canada) 1965
721 FAULKINBERRY John L Browning in the Popular Press, 1900-1950
       MA Baylor Univ 1966   149 p
722 FERGUSON Lois E The Relationship of Browning's Plays to His Dramatic
       Monologues MS Kansas St Coll at Pittsburg 1945
723 FINE Lita Hierarchical Patterns in Browning's Nature Imagery
       MA Columbia 1963 . 143 p
724 FLANAGAN Thomas J The Pre-Raphaelites and Browning's Art Poems
       MA Univ of Maryland at College Park 1965   50 p
725 FOX Bernice L Browning's Revision of *Paracelsus* MA Univ of
       Kentucky 1934
726 FOX Gladys Characterization in Browning's Dramas MA Univ of Texas
       at Austin 1933
727 FRAZER Jennie M Elizabeth Barrett Browning's Relations with Con-
       temporary Women Writers MA St Mary's at San Antonio 1938   80 p
728 GARDNER Bessie B Other Women in the Life of Robert Browning
       MA St Mary's at San Antonio 1949   97 p
729 GARLAND Betty B Animate Nature in the Poetry of Robert Browning
       MA Florida St Univ 1949
730 GARRIOTT Harold M Browning's Use of Metaphor in the Two Guido
       Monologues of *The Ring and the Book* MA Indiana Univ 1955
731 GILL Helen V R The Influence of Elizabeth Barrett Browning upon
       the Poetry of Robert Browning MA Univ of California at Berkeley
       1923
732 GILMORE Sr Julia Browning's Self-Revelations; His Unconscious
       Dramatization of His Most Poignant Experience MA St Louis Univ
       1942   93 p
733 GLEASON Katherine F The Dramatic Art of Robert Browning MA Univ of
       California at Berkeley 1897
734 GOLL Marguerite M The Influence of Music on the Poetry of
       Robert Browning MA Temple Univ 1935   81 p

735 GOLDSMITH Richard W Browning as Poet-Prophet: An Examination of
    Pauline, Paracelsus, Sordello and *The Ring and the Book*
    MA Univ of North Carolina at Chapel Hill 1951
736 GREEN Ruth S Animal Imagery in Browning's *The Ring and the Book*
    MA Univ of North Carolina at Chapel Hill 1951 101 p
737 GREGORY Lura N Is Browning Really Dramatic in the So-Called Dramatic
    Poems? MA Univ of Texas at Austin 1943 117 p
738 GRIFFIN Claudius W The Portrayal of Historical Character in
    Browning's Poetry MA Univ of Richmond 1960 129 p
739 HAGEMAN Elizabeth The Comic Vision of *The Ring and the Book*
    MA Columbia 1964 68 p
740 HAMILTON Harry W The Mind of Elizabeth Barrett Browning MA Univ of
    Texas at Austin 1909
741 HAND Carolyn E Browning's Theory of Success in Failure MA Univ of
    Florida nd
742 HARRELL J M Browning as a Religious Beacher MA Boston Univ 1925
743 HARROD Hazel L Mrs Browning's Poetry: An Evaluation MA Univ of
    Texas at Austin 1944 158 p
744 HARVEY Lois H Browning and Music MS Mankato St Coll 1968 64 p
745 HASKELL Margaret English Poetic Drama from Robert Browning to
    Stephen Phillips MA Univ of Maine 1939 197 p
746 HAWKES Mildred Browning's Attitude Toward Institutionalized
    Religion MA Univ of Texas at Austin 1941 174 p
747 HEFFERMAN Dorothy Browning as a Dramatic Creator MA St Louis Univ
    1934 84 p
748 HEIGEN Janice T Robert Browning and Henry James: A Study in
    Parallelism MA Univ of Tennessee 1964
749 HIGHLEY Mona P Elizabeth Barrett Browning and Christina G Rossetti:
    A Comparative Study MA Univ of Texas at Austin 1939 121 p
750 HIGHSMITH Mary Jo A Study in Browning's Artistic Uses of the Past
    MA Univ of Texas at Austin 1950 132 p
751 HILL Mary C The Early Poems of Robert Browning MA Univ of Texas
    at Austin 1916
752 HITNER John M A Study of Browning's Gothic Imagery MA Univ of
    Hawaii 1961
753 HOLT Albert E A Study in Biblical Allusion in Robert Browning's
    The Ring and the Book MA Ohio St Univ 1956
754 HOOD Lillian D Robert Browning's Philosophy of Life as Reflected
    in His Poetry MS Kansas St Coll at Pittsburg 1942
755 HOSTETTER Patricia A The Pope's Monologue in *The Ring and the Book*:
    Apex of Browning's Religious and Philosophical Thinking
    MA Univ of North Carolina at Chapel Hill 1956 102 p
756 HOWARD Elizabeth His Star: A Romantic Drama of Elizabeth Barrett
    Browning in Three Acts MA Southwestern Univ 1936
757 ISLE Pearle Browning as a Playwright MA Univ of Oklahoma nd
758 JACOBS Alberta F A Comparison of the Artistry of Edwin A Robinson
    and Robert Browning M Ed Temple Univ 1934 79 p
759 JACOBSEN Martha C Mrs Browning and *Aurora Leigh* MA Columbia
    1953 112 p
760 JAMISON Emma L Robert Browning, Interpreter of Paintings MA Univ
    of Arizona 1942
761 JEFFERS D L The Ethics of Browning MA Boston Univ 1911
762 JENKINS K A Browning's Criminals MA Univ of North Carolina at
    Chapel Hill 1929
763 JENNINGS Theresa J The Publication, Sources and Literary Analysis
    of Browning's Soul MA St Mary's at San Antonio 1946 46 p
764 JOHNSON Martha A Comparison of Browning's and Tennyson's Dramas
    MA Baylor Univ 1938
765 JOHNSON Wanda M Elizabeth Barrett Browning's Influence on
    Robert Browning MA Oklahoma St Univ 1932

766 JOHNSTON John W Browning on Protestantism MS Kansas St Coll at
     Pittsburg 1966
767 JOHNSTON R A Passion in the Poetry of Robert Browning MA Univ of
     London (England) 1953
768 JOINER Eunice C Browning and Whitman: A Comparative Study
     MA Southwestern Univ 1924
769 JONES S F The Women in Browning; Types of Feminine Personality
     in the Works of Robert Browning MA Boston Univ 1928
770 JOYNER Nancy C Violence in Browning MA Columbia 1959 84 p
771 KALLISON Fannie R The Criticism of the Prevailing Themes in
     Mrs Browning's Longer Poems MA St Mary's at San Antonio 1948
772 KENLEY Polk M The Influence of Elizabeth Barrett Browning on the
     Works of Robert Browning MA Univ of Texas at Austin 1928
773 KENNEDY Etta C Louis Napoleon in Browning's *Prince Hohenstiel-
     Schwangau:* A True Portrait of a Double Personality MA Univ of
     Tennessee 1949
774 KENNEDY Marian V The Teachability of Browning's Poems on Art
     MA Univ of Texas at Austin 1950 109 p
775 KERR John K *The Ring and the Book,* a Review of the Criticism
     MA Baylor Univ 1963 97 p
776 KINCAID Elizabeth An Analysis of Some of Browning's Major
     Characters MA North Texas St Univ 1936
777 KLEINKE Viola L Robert Browning: A Study of His Poetic Mind
     MA Univ of Hawaii 1926 57 p
778 KNETZGER Sr Mary C The Music Poems of Robert Browning MA St Louis
     Univ 1926 68 p
779 KRETSINGER Elwood An Interpretative Analysis of Browning's
     Andrea del Sarto MA Univ of Oklahoma 1941
780 LAMBERT Betty G A Study of Robert Browning's Use of Artists and
     Musicians as Characters in His Monologues MA Auburn Univ 1969
781 LANGFORD Virginia L A Selection from Browning's Characters on the
     Basis of Sensitivity MA West Texas St Univ 1968 114 p
782 LaPAZ Leota J Early and Modern Criticism of Browning's *Pauline,
     Paracelsus* and *Sordello* MA Univ of New Mexico 1958
783 LEE Mary V An Analysis of the Response of Browning's Contemporaries
     to *Fifine at the Fair* MA Univ of Oklahoma 1963
784 LEMAY Theatus J Browning's Interest in the Physical Aspects of His
     Character MA Hardin-Simmons Univ 1954
785 LEVY Margaret P The Art of Elizabeth Barrett Browning MA Univ of
     Texas at Austin 1912
786 LINDBERT Evlyn M A Study of the Head and Heart Symbolism in
     Robert Browning MA Texas Christian Univ 1952 149 p
787 LITZINGER Boyd A Robert Browning's Reputation as a Thinker, 1889-1955
     MA Univ of Tennessee 1956 343 p
788 LOBETTI BODONI Giuseppina Elizabeth Barrett Browning's Love Poetry
     MA Ca Foscari (Italy) nd
789 LOCKHART John H The History of the Dramas of Robert Browning
     MA Univ of Texas at Austin 1948 113 p
790 LONG Wilhema Critical Interpretations of the Form and Content of
     Browning's *Pippa Passes* MA St Mary's at San Antonio 1948 82 p
791 LOWERY Doris C Browning: The Poet of the Grotesque MA Univ of Tulsa
     1965 91 p
792 LYTTLETON Laurita A The Renaissance, as Portrayed in the Poems of
     Robert Browning from 1842-64 MA Univ of Texas at Austin 1929
793 McCANDLESS Lucy B The Modernity of Elizabeth Barrett Browning
     MA Univ of Pittsburgh 1930
794 McCARTHY Terence A The Function of Symbolism in *The Book of the
     Duchess* MA Boston Coll 1968
795 MacINTIRE Frances W Three Life Views: That of Ecclesiastes, of
     Omar Khayyam and of Robert Browning MA Boston Univ 1929

796 McINTIRE Norma E The Jewish Philosopher in *Rabbi Ben Ezra* and the
    Pope in *The Ring and the Book* MA St Mary's at San Antonio 1938 67 p
797 McLAURIN Nancy D Earthy Images in the Poetry of Robert Browning
    MA Univ of North Carolina at Chapel Hill 1946 179 p
798 MARSHALL Mary J Authors on Browning Since 1900 MA Baylor Univ 1936
    287 p
799 MASON Melvin R Narrative Form in *The Ring and the Book* MA Univ of
    Texas at Austin 1951 36 p
800 MATERA Elizabeth C Robert Browning and the Drama MA Temple Univ
    1967 53 p
801 MATZEN B Andrew A Thought-Subject Index of the Poetry of
    Robert Browning MA Univ of Maryland at College Park 1923 115 p
802 MAXWELL Sadie H Italian Renaissance Painters and Pictures in the
    Poems of Robert Browning MA St Mary's at San Antonio 1938 98 p
803 MAYALL Mary L The Literary Influence of Elizabeth Barrett Browning
    upon Robert Browning MA Univ of Oklahoma nd
804 MERONEY Howard The Treatment of Nature in the Poetry of
    Robert Browning MA Univ of Texas at Austin 1928
805 MEYERS Alicia C The Dramatic Monologue in Tennyson and Browning
    MA Tulane Univ 1929
806 MICHIE Sue Browning and Art MA Texas Technological Univ 1937 45 p
807 MILLER Anne U Critical Opinions of Some Nineteenth Century Poets
    on the Poetry of Robert Browning MA George Washington Univ 1965
808 MILLS Carla J Imagery of Characterization in Browning's Dramatic
    Monologues MA Temple Univ 1967 37 p
809 MITCHELL James E Browning's Bishop Blougram Considered as
    Cardinal Wiseman MA St Louis Univ 1931 61 p
810 MONAHAN Sr T M *The Book of the Duchess* MA Boston Coll 1950
811 MOORE George B Robert Browning and the Military Mind MA Columbia
    1951
812 MUKOYAMA Atsuko Paradox in Browning's Poetry MA Baylor Univ 1969
    265 p
813 MULLIN Dianna L Robert Browning's "Obscurity" in Modern Perspective
    MA Univ of Houston 1968 103 p
814 MULLINS James J Robert Browning and *A Blot in the 'Scutcheon:*
    Background and Analysis MA Univ of Colorado 1965
815 MURPHY Sr Marie C Guido: A Character Study of Browning's *The Ring
    and the Book* MA St Louis Univ 1932 57 p
816 NELSON Charles E Creative Consciousness in *The Ring and the Book*
    MA Univ of Oklahoma 1963
817 NEWSOM Francis W An Evaluation of the Formal and Emotional Effects
    of the Poetry of Robert Browning Considered from the Humanistic
    Viewpoint MA Boston Univ 1932
818 NORTHRUP Frederick W The Influence of Vasari upon the Art Poems
    of Robert Browning MA Univ of Arizona 1942
819 OLMSTEAD Jane H Browning's Correspondence to the Rev J D Williams,
    1874-1889 MA Univ of Texas at Austin 1966 108 p
820 PARCHMAN Mary E Browning's View of "Humanity in Action" in *Men and
    Women* MA Univ of Texas at Austin 1963 103 p
821 PARNELL Kenneth D Relativism in the Defense Lawyer's Pleadings in
    The Ring and the Book MA Texas Christian Univ 1969 141 p
822 PARROTT Helen L The Literary and Social Significance of
    Mrs Browning's *Aurora Lee* MA Univ of Iowa 1932
823 PASQUALATO Gabriella Robert Browning's *Pippa Passes, Men and Women*
    and *The Ring and the Book* MA Ca Foscari (Italy) 1941
824 PASTERNAK Walter P A Study of Browning's Use of Imagery in *The Ring
    and the Book* MA George Washington Univ 1948 93 p
825 PAXTON Mildred A Study of Browning's *Sordello* MA Univ of Texas at
    Austin 1918
826 PAYNE Barbara Browning and Drama MA East Carolina Univ 1965

827 PEARCE Theodore Browning's Knowledge and Criticism of Music
     MA Boston Univ 1948
828 PEIRCE E C Race in Browning's Poetry MA Boston Univ 1926
829 PERKINS Mary K Doubt in Religious Faith and the Function of Evil
     in Robert Browning's Poems MA Univ of Texas at Austin 1937
830 PERSON Amy L Versification of Browning MA Univ of Kentucky 1927
831 PHELPS Mary G Critical Opinions of Robert Browning as a Craftsman,
     1950-1965 MA Baylor Univ 1968 103 p
832 PHILLIPS Marie E Love in the Non-Dramatic Poems of Browning
     MA Univ of Texas at Austin 1920
833 PICKETT John R The Browning Criticism of Henry James and
     George Santayana MA Univ of Texas at Austin 1952 196 p
834 POTTS Isabel The Ultimate Failure of Mrs Browning's *Aurora Leigh*
     MA Univ of Tennessee 1951 126 p
835 PRIEST Lydia P Truth and Knowledge in Browning's *Sordello* and
     The Ring and the Book MA George Washington Univ 1967 192 p
836 PROUDFIT Isabel B Henry James' Last Duchess: A Study of the
     Influence of Robert Browning on Henry James MA Columbia 1958 80 p
837 PUCKETT Claire M The Confessional Motif in the Poetry of
     Robert Browning MA Texas Arts and Industries Univ 1952
838 PUCKETT Walter E The Nineteenth Century Foundations of the
     Robert Browning-Ezra Pound Bridge to Modernity in Poetry
     MA St Louis Univ 1961 303 p
839 PUNTNEY Albert T Robert Browning as a Dramatist MA Univ of
     Kentucky 1928
840 REICHARDT Sr Mary A Objective Religion in Browning MA St Louis
     Univ 1926 75 p
841 RICH Margaret R Art in the Poems of Browning MA Univ of Oklahoma
     1943
842 ROBBINS Wilma Elizabeth Barrett's Influence on the Poetry of
     Robert Browning MA Texas Technological Univ 1938 66 p
843 ROBERTS E W The Social Poetry of Elizabeth Barrett Browning
     MA Univ of North Carolina at Chapel Hill 1933
844 ROBINSON Elizabeth D A Study of the Philosophy of Robert Browning
     MA Univ of Tulsa 1953 75 p
845 RODGER J C Browning and the Italian Renaissance BA Univ of British
     Columbia (Canada) 1944
846 ROSENBERGER Leroy P An Inquiry into the Influence of Walter Savage
     Landor's *Imaginary Conversations* on the Dramatic Monologues of
     Robert Browning M Ed Temple Univ 1943 130 p
847 ROYSTER Beatrice H The Reputation of Browning's *Sordello*, 1863-1950
     MA Howard Univ 1954
848 RUTHERFORD Winifred J Philosophical Implications in Browning
     MA Boston Univ 1948
849 RYAN Anna C Dramatic Art of Wordsworth, Byron, Shelley, Tennyson,
     Browning and Swinburne MA Univ of Louisville 1918
850 SEARS O Henry The Rent Veil: Devine Revelation-Inspiration in the
     Poetry of Robert Browning MA Baylor Univ 1969 117 p
851 SCHERLE Phyllis J Browning's Humanism MA Southern Illinois Univ at
     Carbondale 1958 75 p
852 SCHULZE Mary M Imagery in Browning's *The Ring and the Book*
     MA Rice 1958
853 SCHWITALLA Sr Mary G The Problem of Evil in Browning and Hawthorne
     MA St Louis Univ 1931 81 p
854 SHAFFER Alma A A Critical Study of the Browning-Wedgewood Letters
     MA St Mary's at San Antonio 1938 62 p
855 SHELTON J A Browning's Literary Reputation: 1833-1870 MA North
     Texas St Univ 1961
856 SHOUSE Claude F Robert Browning's Personal and Literary Relationship
     with Germany MA Univ of Kentucky 1939

857 SIMMONS Mary L   A Study of Robert Browning's Conception of God
     MA Hardin-Simmons Univ 1947
858 SINCLAIR Jean   Parodies of the Poems of Robert Browning   MA Univ of
     Maryland at College Park 1948   145 p
859 SKINNER Mary L   Browning's Listeners   MA Univ of Tennessee 1965
860 SMITH Constance R   Browning's Role as Priest in His Early Works
     MA St Louis Univ 1967   108 p
861 SMITH Martha L   A Study of Browning's and Robinson's Doctrine of
     Success in Failure   MA Emory Univ 1935   98 p
862 SMITH Nathan J   The Ring and the Book and The Old Yellow Book
     MA Boston Univ 1936
863 SOLIMINE Joseph   Summary of the Literary Criticism of Robert Browning's
     The Ring and the Book   MA Univ of Rhode Island 1959
864 SONINO Bice   Elizabeth Barrett Browning   MA Ca Foscari (Italy) 1941
865 SORRELL Elizabeth N   Robert Browning in College Anthologies
     MA Univ of Texas at Austin 1948   113 p
866 SPENCER Virginia C   The Philosophy of the Imperfect in the Poetry
     of Robert Browning from 1833-1855   MA Univ of North Carolina at
     Chapel Hill 1952   134 p
867 STALLARD Sadye   A Study of The Ring and the Book   MS Purdue Univ 1900
868 STEVENS Lewwl R   Robert Browning as a Myth-Maker in The Ring and the
     Book   MA Univ of Oklahoma 1963
869 STRIMPLE Virgile   Browning's Half-Gods: A Study of the Development
     of Browning's Usage of Classical Mythology, 1833-1855   MA Baylor
     Univ 1966   137 p
870 SWAIN G Jacqueline   The Irony of Truth in The Ring and the Book
     MA George Washington Univ 1967   86 p
871 SWIM Lillian B   The Literary Opinions of the Brownings as Expressed
     in Their Letters   MA Univ of Maine 1942   113 p
872 TALBOT Jones H III   Robert Browning: Character and Monologue
     BA Amherst 1970
873 THOMAS Marjorie B   The Literary Reputation of Elizabeth Barrett
     Browning as Seen in the Periodicals of England and America from
     1840-1865   MA Columbia 1940
874 THOMASON Caroline W   Elizabeth Barrett Browning's Theory of Social
     Reform   MA Univ of California at Berkeley 1921
875 THOMPSON Beatrice S   Modernistic Elements in Robert Browning's
     Victorianism   MA Univ of Texas at Austin 1937   118 p
876 THWAITES M R   A Study of The Ring and the Book   B Litt Oxford Univ
     (England) 1947
877 TIETZE Paulita A   Reprints for American Readers of Contemporary
     British Criticism of Browning   MA St Mary's at San Antonio 1946
878 TODD Lucile   The Background and Leading Women of Robert Browning's
     First Three Dramas   MA St Mary's at San Antonio 1947   55 p
879 ULRICKSON Linda W   The Humanitarianism of Elizabeth Barrett Browning
     MA Univ of Texas at Austin 1938   154 p
880 VANN Bess W   Browning's Pompilia, Caponsacchi and Pope as Symbols
     MA St Mary's at San Antonio 1940   60 p
881 VINCENZI Maria T   Italy in Elizabeth Barrett Browning's Poems
     MA Ca Foscari (Italy) 1946
882 WALDAUER Joyce A   Authorial Presence in the Monologues of Three
     Characters of The Ring and the Book: Caponsacchi, Pompilio and
     Guido   MA Univ of Massachusetts 1965
883 WALDRIP Louise B   Browning's Turf and Towers   MA Baylor Univ 1961   162 p
884 WALL Patricia A   Browning and Theatrics   MA Texas Christian Univ
     1964   98 p
885 WATTERS E A   The Materials of The Ring and the Book   MA Univ of
     Arkansas 1929
886 WILCOX John H   Robert Browning's Debt to Classical Literature
     MA Univ of Kentucky 1910   41 p

887 WILEY Barbara U The Criticism of Browning's *Childe Roland*: A Study
     of Psychological Aspects MA Northern Arizona Univ 1968
888 WILKINS Ada C A Study of Robert Browning's Use of Nature in His
     Love Poems MA Hardin-Simmons Univ 1949
889 WILSON Eleanor S The Existential Choice: A Study of Four Browning
     Characters MA Texas Technological Univ 1965 104 p
890 WOMACK Dollins A Study in Browning's Shorter Verse MA Univ of
     Texas at Austin 1954 ·59 p
891 WOOD Bernice The Infinite Moment and the Themes of Art, Religion and
     Love in the Poetry of Robert Browning BA Univ of British Columbia
     (Canada) 1968
892 WOOD Jean H The Bible in Browning: Biblical Allusions in Browning's
     Poetry Exclusive of *The Ring and the Book* MA Univ of Texas at
     Austin 1939 161 p
893 WRAY Martha M Browning's Attitude Toward Catholicism MA Univ of
     Tennessee 1950 95 p
894 WRIGHT Mary Browning and the Pre-Raphaelites, Rossetti, Morris and
     Swinburne MA Univ of Maryland at College Park 1940 55 p
895 YATES Frances T Browning Interest in Texas MA Texas Christian Univ
     1941 88 p
896 YATES Mildred C Browning and Jeffers: A Comparative Study MA Lamar
     Technological Univ 1962
897 YOUNG Dorothy A The Methods of Argumentation in Five of Browning's
     Casuistic Poems MA Univ of North Carolina at Chapel Hill 1959 159 p
898 ZIMMER Diana Lee Who, What and Why: Three Aspects of Robert Browning's
     Theory of the Poet MA Auburn Univ 1969
899 ZYLSTRA Henry Goethe and Browning: A Comparative Study MA Univ of
     Iowa 1933
See also 521, 1090, 1999, 4634, 5218, 5571

EDWARD BULWER-LYTTON

900 BAATZ Wilmer H Bulwer-Lytton's Prose Fiction Theories and Their
     Applications in His Historical, Criminal, Fashionable and Home
     Life Novels MA Indiana Univ 1945
901 BOWMAN Virginia M Studies in the Plays of Edward Bulwer, Lord Lytton
     MA Univ of Texas at Austin 1938 139 p
902 CLEAR Patrick F Bulwer-Lytton's *Richelieu*: A True Portrait?
     MA St Louis Univ 1939 58 p
903 GIBSON Martha K Bulwer-Lytton's Place in the English Drama of the
     Middle Nineteenth Century MA Univ of Louisville 1941
904 HARRIS Frances B Bulwer-Lytton's Critical Theories MA Texas
     Christian Univ 1942 64 p
905 METZE Mabel W Science and Psuedo-Science in Representative Novels
     of Bulwer-Lytton MA Boston Univ 1932
906 MORRIS Verna A Characterization in the Historical Novels of
     Edward Bulwer-Lytton MA Univ of Texas at Austin 1935
907 ROSSIGNOL Lois J Bulwer-Lytton and the Theater MA Columbia 1941
908 SIEPI Adriana The English Novels by Edward Bulwer, First Baron
     Lytton of Knebworth MA Ca Foscari (Italy) 1939
909 VITALI Erminia The Historical Novels of Edward G Bulwer, Lord
     Lytton, 1803-1873 MA Ca Foscari (Italy) 1929
910 WADE Mary K Bulwer-Lytton as Dramatist MA Howard Univ 1933 27 p
911 WIGGIN David C The Sources of Bulwer-Lytton's *Richelieu* MA Univ
     of Maine 1967 107 p
See also 6154

JOHN BUNYAN

912 BARTLETT Helen C Benjamin Keach and the Bunyan Tradition
     MA Columbia 1936

913 BERRY Charles E John Bunyan's Dominant Characteristics as Reflected
     in His Works MS Kansas St Coll at Pittsburg 1944
914 BUNYAN Dorothy E A Study of John Bunyan's Place in the Ancestry of
     the English Novel MA Oklahoma St Univ 1938 49 p
915 CHRISTIAN Eleanor The Narrative Art of John Bunyan MA Univ of Texas
     at Austin 1934
916 COBAU William W John Bunyan and the Reading of Allegory
     BA Amherst 1955
917 COBAU William W John Bunyan's *Grace Abounding* and *Pilgrim's Progress*:
     Allegory as Metaphor and Extended Metaphor MA Columbia 1960 103 p
918 DOBSON Willis B Bunyan's Knowledge and Use of the Bible, as Seen in
     His Non-Allegorical Works MA Univ of Texas at Austin 1929
919 DUGDALE Clarence E John Bunyan, the Preacher MA Univ of Texas at
     Austin 1932
920 GAMBIGLIANI ZOCCOLI Cesarina A Study of the Sources of Bunyan's
     Allegory MA Ca Foscari (Italy) 1943
921 GOODYKOONTZ William F Some Aspects of John Bunyan's Influence on
     the Art of George Bernard Shaw MA Univ of North Carolina at
     Chapel Hill 1952 179 p
922 HORNER Richard W The Influence of the Authorized Version of the Bible
     (1611) on the Style and Literary Art of John Bunyan MA Univ of
     Rhode Island 1968 107 p
923 JEPPERSON Shirley D Vision and Quest: *Piers Plowman* and *The Pilgrim's
     Progress* Compared MA San Diego St Coll 1968 173 p
924 KERIG Laurence E The Old Testament Influence in John Bunyan's
     Pilgrim's Progress MA Boston Coll 1964
925 LEDFORD Florence M A Survey of Criticisms of Bunyan's *Pilgrim's
     Progress* MA Univ of Oklahoma 1936
926 LITTLE T A Bunyan's Indebtedness to His Times MA Univ of North
     Carolina at Chapel Hill 1924
927 LOVEJOY Robert B Bunyan's Debt to John Foxe MA Univ of Kentucky
     1960 76 p
928 MADDEN Estelle E The Bible in Bunyan's *Pilgrim's Progress* and
     Milton's *Paradise Lost* M Ed Temple Univ 1933 104 p
929 NAUGHTON Rev Edward V John Bunyan and Predestination: An Aspect
     of Restoration and Puritanism MA Boston Coll 1964
930 NEAL Lucy H The Social Doctrines of Gerrard Winstanley and
     John Bunyan MA Univ of Kentucky 1961 65 p
931 NURICK Evan Allegorical Isolation in *The Pilgrim's Progress*
     MA Columbia 1966 84 p
932 ONION Margaret K Modes of Characterization in the Fiction of
     John Bunyan MA Univ of Vermont 1969 108 p
933 PICKEL Laura C Bunyan and the Bible MA Washington Univ at
     St Louis 1930 108 p
934 PRIOR R R A Psychological Study of John Bunyan MA Ohio St Univ
     1932
935 PRYDE Marion J Bunyan's Use of Country Life MA Howard Univ 1968 110 p
936 RHINES H D The Diction of Realism as Illustrated in *Mandeville's
     Travels*, *Pilgrim's Progress* and *Robinson Crusoe* MA Boston Univ 1911
937 SHARROCK R I The Methods and Models of Bunyan's Allegories
     B Litt Oxford Univ (England) 1947
938 THOMPSON Richard F John Bunyan and the Critics of Two Centuries
     MA Univ of Maryland at College Park 1964 72 p
939 TUHEY John T Principles of Religious Allegory Reflected in
     John Bunyan and C S Lewis MA Univ of Rhode Island 1965 109 p
940 TURNER Henry A John Bunyan's Reading Exclusive of the Bible and the
     Allegories MA Univ of Texas at Austin 1930 182 p
941 VOS Sarah M Three Religious Moralists M Litt Cambridge (England) 1950
942 WALKER John D John Bunyan and the Metaphysical Style MA Columbia 1951

EDMUND BURKE

943 BECK Richard P Edmund Burke: Eighteenth-Century Politician and
     Writer MA Butler Univ 1967
944 GELDERS Max C Edmund Burke: Utilitarian or Natural Lawyer?
     MA Florida St Univ 1965
945 MERGLER Esther Religion in the Works of Edmund Burke MA Univ of
     Kansas 1933
946 NIGRO Virginia T Edmund Burke and the Anti-Jacobin MA Western St
     Coll of Colorado 1932 71 p
See also 1296, 3901

FANNY BURNEY

947 ALLEN Annie H The Place of Miss Burney in the Development of the
     Novel of Manners MA Univ of California at Berkeley 1903
948 ALVIS Lota S The Technique of Fanny Burney (Madame D'Arblay)
     MA Univ of Texas at Austin 1935
949 BAKER Julia M The Analysis of Fanny Burney's Camilla MA Rice 1960
950 BAXTER Susanna G Frances Burney: Diarist and Letter Writer
     MA Univ of Texas at Austin 1935
951 BOGARDUS Helen L Madame D'Arblay's Literary Friendships and
     Associations 1793-1840 MA Southern Methodist Univ 1926
952 CARLTON Sydell T The Early Novels of Fanny Burney: The Creation
     and Control of a Small World MA Indiana Univ 1960
953 CONRAD Pearl W Eighteenth Century Manners and Customs in Fanny Burney
     MA Univ of Oklahoma 1925
954 EAKER Julia M The Analysis of Fanny Burney's Camilla MA Rice 1960
955 FINN Julia M Jane Austen's Debt to Fanny Burney MA Univ of Oregon 194●
956 FORNARO Ugo Fanny Burney MA Ca Foscari (Italy) 1950
957 GROLLA Giovanni Fanny Burney: The Diary and the Novels MA Ca Foscari
     (Italy) 1966
958 LAL R R Women in the Novels of Fanny Burney, Charlotte Smith, Ann Rad-
     cliffe and Maria Edgeworth MA Univ of London (England) 1965
959 McNEESE Willie J Entertainment in the World of Fanny Burney
     MA East Tennessee St Univ 1960
960 NOGAMI Yasuko The Relation between Social Convention and Morality
     in the Novels of Fanny Burney MA Univ of Massachusetts 1964
961 RANSON Nell J A Study of Fanny Burney's Cecilia MA Rice 1946
962 SHAW Russell B Fanny Burney's Cecilia: A Critical and Historical Intr●
     duction for a New Shortened Edition MA Georgetown Univ 1960 206 p●
963 TAHMIZAN Z D The Evolution of the Heroine in the Novels of Fanny Burne●
     Jane Austen, the Brontes, George Eliot and Edith Wharton
     MA Boston Univ 1926
964 TINDALL Maxine Life in the Eighteenth Century as Depicted by
     Fanny Burney MA Rice 1934
965 VESPIGNANI Anna The Novels of Fanny Burney MA Ca Foscari (Italy) 1957
966 WARD Nora B The Diaries of Fanny Burney as Sources of Characters in
     Her Novels MA Univ of Texas at Austin 1940
See also 182

ROBERT BURNS

967 ANGELL Sue The Influence of Wine, Women and Song as Reflected in
     Selected Works of Robert Burns M Ed Henderson St Coll nd
968 BERNTSON Lloyd The Common Man in Wordsworth and Burns MA Washington
     St Univ at Pullman 1966
969 BROWN Eva L The Love Life of Robert Burns and Its Effects on His
     Writings M Ed Henderson St Coll nd
970 BURGESS Hugh F Robert Burns as a Satirist: A Study of Nine of Burns'
     Most Important Satires MA Univ of Massachusetts 1954

971 BYRD Neva B Robert Burns: Pegasus Harnessed to a Plow
      M Ed Henderson St Coll nd
972 CASELLI Rossana The Scottish Popular Ballad in W Scott and
      Robert Burns MA Ca Foscari (Italy) 1941
973 CASTOR Shirley K Sentimentalism in the Poems and Songs of Robert Burns
      MA Clemson Univ 1965
974 CHIARA Luciana Robert Burns MA Ca Foscari (Italy) 1930
975 CLELLAND Frank W Robert Burns and His Social Environment MA Boston
      Univ 1910
976 COTTINGHAM William T Cultural Influences in the Life and Works of
      Robert Burns MA Emory Univ 1938 81 p
977 DAVIS Vella W Poetic Qualities that Made Robert Burns Immortal
      M Ed Henderson St Coll nd
978 GLEASON William D The Literary Kinship of Catullus and Robert Burns
      MA Univ of Massachusetts 1968 93 p
979 HANFORD Josephine The Political Opinions of Robert Burns MA Boston
      Univ 1924
980 HORNE Ruth Robert Burns: The Man and the Poet M Ed Henderson St
      Coll nd
981 HOWARD Joyce S Burns' Fame in America During the Nineteenth Century
      MA Univ of North Carolina at Chapel Hill 1946
982 KENNEDY Jessie L Intimate Acquaintances in the Songs of Robert Burns
      MA Univ of Pittsburgh 1935
983 KENNEY Reginald A Robert Burns and the Old South MA William and
      Mary Coll 1935
984 LONG Ezra M Satire in the Poetry of Robert Burns MA Oklahoma St
      Univ 1943 85 p
985 McCLUNEY Miriam M Folklore in the Poetry of Robert Burns MA Texas
      Christian Univ 1961 142 p
986 MARZARI Francesco The Poetry of Robert Burns MA Ca Foscari (Italy)
      1941
987 MILLER Camille The Forces of Inspiration in the Literary Development
      of Robert Burns M Ed Henderson St Coll nd
988 MITCHELL J G Satire in Burns BA Univ of British Columbia (Canada)
      1945
989 MOONEYHAM Jacquelin A Study of the Popular Ballads upon Which
      Burns Based Twenty-Five of His Well-Known Poems MA Univ of Texas
      at Austin 1936
990 OLLEY Francis R Robert Burns and the Eighteenth Century Stream of
      Satire MA Temple Univ 1955
991 PAPPS Elizabeth M The Satires of Robert Burns MA Bowling Green Univ
      1950
992 PRESTON Thomas R Burns and the Critics: 1786-1832 MA Rice 1960
993 REES Janie H The Treatment of Burns in Fiction MA Univ of Kentucky
      1939
994 RICE Berkeley D The Peasant Poet: Robert Burns and the Eighteenth-
      Century Tradition of the Natural Poetic Genius MA Columbia 1962
995 SHULL Virginia I Peasant Life in the Poetry of Robert Burns
      MA Boston Univ 1942
996 SNIPES Wilson C Satire in Robert Burns' Poetry MA Florida St Univ
      1950
997 STORY J M Burns as a Revolutionary BA Univ of British Columbia
      (Canada) 1926
998 STUART Floyd C Sylvander and Clarinda: The Burns Correspondence
      with Agnes M'Lehose MA John Carroll Univ 1965
999 TUTTLE Helen I The Effect of Robert Burns' Politics on His Life
      and Poetry MS Kansas St Coll at Pittsburg 1955

ROBERT BURTON

1000 CALDON Barbara E Proverb Lore in *The Anatomy of Melancholy*
       MA Baylor Univ 1941 129 p
1001 CHIMSKY Matthew Robert Burton and Capitalism MA Columbia 1951
1002 GREET Anne H Robert Burton, a Study in Style MA Columbia 1954 47 p
1003 GROS LOUiS Kenneth R Robert Burton's "Love-Melancholy" MA Columbia
       1960 85 p
1004 HARPER Guy G The Place of Robert Burton's Ideal Commonwealth in the
       Tradition of Utopias MA St Louis Univ 1940 68 p
1005 HAUGEN Mary E Robert Burton's Treatment of Religious Melancholy
       MA Univ of Arizona pre-1933
1006 JACKSON Paul R A Revaluation of Robert Burton's Religious Position
       MA Columbia 1959 147 p
1007 LEVINE George R Robert Burton's Attitude toward War MA Columbia
       1952 83 p
1008 NOCHIMSON Richard L Burton's Sense of Self in *The Anatomy of
       Melancholy* MA Columbia 1962 67 p
1009 STEWART Gladys S Robert Wilton Burton: A Biographical Sketch
       Including a Selection of His Writings MA Auburn Univ 1932
1010 THOMAS Bernice L Robert Burton's Observations on Contemporary
       English Life MA Howard Univ 1960 104 p

SAMUEL BUTLER

1011 APPOLONI Sabri An Historical and Critical Review of Samuel Butler's
       Work of Fiction MA Ca Foscari (Italy) 1937
1012 BLACK Laurence N Samuel Butler (1835-1902) as a Literary Critic
       and Commentator MA Univ of Houston 1952 98 p
1013 BUELL L W The Satire of Samuel Butler as Seen in His *Erewhon,
       The Way of All Flesh, The Fair Haven, Erewhon Revisited*
       MA Boston Univ 1926
1014 BURNHAM David C The Development of Samuel Butler's Religion and
       Ethics MA Univ of Massachusetts 1962
1015 CANDIOLO Giovanni A Study of Samuel Butler, Author of *Hudibras*,
       with a View to Set off the Neglected Importance and Literary
       Value of His Minor Poetical Work and His Prose Writings
       MA Ca Foscari (Italy) nd
1016 CONN Edwin H Samuel Butler and *The Way of All Flesh* MA Columbia
       1941
1017 DANDRIDGE Rita B Satire in Samuel Butler's *Hudibras* MA Howard
       Univ 1963 102 p
1018 ELLIOTT J Samuel Butler and the Bondage of Ideas BA Univ of British
       Columbia (Canada) 1943
1019 ENGLER William H *The Way of All Flesh*: An Apprenticeship to Life
       MA Columbia 1965 108 p
1020 FIELDS Elinor C *Hudibras* and *Don Quijote* MA Univ of Florida 1953
1021 GRANT John D Samuel Butler and the Victorian Compromise MA Univ of
       British Columbia (Canada) 1941 45 p
1022 GILLHAM Mary M The Development of the Genealogical Novel in England
       and America from Samuel Butler's *Way of All Flesh* to
       John Galsworthy's *On Forsyte 'Change* MA Univ of Toledo 1931
1023 GRANT John D Samuel Butler and the Victorian Compromise MA Univ of
       British Columbia (Canada) nd
1024 GUILFORD M A Samuel Butler, Man of Letters MA Boston Univ 1928
1025 HIPPS Gary M Samuel Butler: Character Writer of the Restoration
       MA Univ of North Carolina at Chapel Hill 1959 60 p
1026 KEITH Mary L A Study of the Satire of Samuel Butler MA Southern
       Methodist Univ 1928
1027 McCONNELL Julian C The Problem of the Christian Ethic in Three

Modern Novels: *An American Tragedy* by Theodore Dreiser, *The Way
of All Flesh* by Samuel Butler and *A Portrait of the Artist as a
Young Man* by James Joyce MA Columbia 1959 71 p

1028 MACRORIE Kenneth Samuel Butler (1835-1902) on the Art of Writing
      MA Univ of North Carolina at Chapel Hill 1948 117 p
1029 MARA Gilda Samuel Butler, the Novelist MA Ca Foscari (Italy) 1951
1030 MARTENS Marcia L *The Way of All Flesh*: An Approach MA Columbia
      1964 86 p
1031 MILAN Dervio Samuel Butler: *Hudibras* MA Ca Foscari (Italy) 1958
1032 MOODY Ora M Samuel Butler, a Professional Heretic MA Washington
      St Univ at Pullman 1926
1033 MURPHY Lena B Samuel Butler's Satire in Fictional Form MA Univ
      of Texas at Austin 1932
1034 O'KELLY Dorothy The Humor of Samuel Butler MS Auburn Univ 1945 73 p
1035 REICHMAN Richard M Butler and Swift Versus the Puritans
      MA Washington Univ at St Louis 1950 78 p
1036 ROSENMAN John Evangelicalism in the Works and Thought of
      Samuel Butler MA Kent St Univ 1966
1037 SHORB Ellis Samuel Butler, a Critical Estimate MA Univ of New
      Hampshire 1950 60 p
1038 STRANG Marilee J The Targets of Samuel Butler's Satire MA Southern
      Illinois Univ at Carbondale 1952 149 p
1039 TABUNAR Elisa G *Erewhon* as a Synthesis of Samuel Butler's Ideas
      MA Columbia 1955 80 p
1040 YANTHA Priscilla M Comic Techniques in Butler's *Hudibras*
      MA Toronto (Canada) 1966
1041 YUREWICZ John R Satiric Techniques in Samuel Butler's *Hudibras*
      MA Boston Coll 1956
See also 7293, 7317, 7366

                    GEORGE GORDON, LORD BYRON

1042 ADAMS Elaine V Byron on Government and Freedom MA Univ of Texas
      at Austin 1945 123 p
1043 ALLARD Aline *Don Juan*: Theme and Variations BA Univ of British
      Columbia (Canada) 1966
1044 ALLEN Paul L Bowles-Byron Controversy on Pope MA St Louis Univ 1943
1045 ALLISON Herbert M Lord Byron in Contemporary American Critical Reviews
      MA Univ of Maryland at College Park 1940 92 p
1046 ANGELO Ansi N The Appeal of Byron in America MA Boston Univ 1946
1047 ARCHER Luta B Byron's Use of Levantine Materials in His Early Poetry
      MA Univ of Texas at Austin 1952 107 p
1048 AVISON Margaret K The Style of Byron's *Don Juan* in Relation to the
      Newspapers of His Day MA Univ of Toronto (Canada) 1964
1049 AYCOCK Roy E Lord Byron and Bayle's *Dictionary* MA Univ of North
      Carolina at Chapel Hill 1952 67 p
1050 BASS Mary B Influences of Environment and Temperament Upon the
      Writing of Lord Byron M Ed Henderson St Coll nd
1051 BAUSO Thomas M Some Approaches to Cock-Heroic: The Imaginative
      Worlds of Pope, Gay, Fielding and Byron BA Rutgers St Univ 1967 87 p
1052 BEAMISH Francoise T Byron and His Criticism of Continental Literature
      MS Purdue Univ 1961 106 p
1053 BENSON Jane A The Active Life: A Comparison of *Don Juan* and
      The Idylls of the King MA Midwestern Univ 1969 163 p
1054 BICLEY Nelwyn K Variations in Byron's Treatment of Geography in
      His Poems MA Northeast Louisiana St Coll 1966
1055 BLYTHE Wayman K The Narrative Element in Byron's Poetry
      MA Southern Methodist Univ 1926
1056 BOGOSTA William Byron's *Cain* and the Legend MA Syracuse Univ 1951
1057 BOOHER Marcia A Revaluation of Byron's *Cain* MA Columbia 1965 54 p

1058 BRAND Elizabeth K   A Study of the Relationship of Imagery to Satiric
         Themes in the First Five Cantos of Byron's *Don Juan* MA Bowling
         Green Univ 1956
1059 BRYAN Marie D   The Controversy between Robert Southey and Lord Byron
         MA Univ of Maryland at College Park 1945   125 p
1060 BURDETTE Frances R   The Freedom Theme in Byron's Verse Tales
         MA George Washington Univ 1969   88 p
1061 CAMPBELL Dorothy M   Byron as Portrayed through His Letters
         MA Howard Univ 1943   49 p
1062 CARLTON Willa G   The Byron Life Records, 1788-1816   MA Univ of Texas
         at Austin 1951   47 p
1063 CARPENTER James B   Byron's Attitude Toward History in *Childe Harold*
         and *Don Juan* MA Stetson Univ 1966
1064 CARROLL William M   The Sea in the Life and Poetry of Lord Byron
         MA Indiana Univ 1940
1065 CARVER J E   Byron and Shakespeare   MA Univ of North Carolina at
         Chapel Hill 1930
1066 CHILDS Ralph W   Social Criticism in *Don Juan*   MA Univ of Iowa 1933
1067 CHRISTOPHER Willie M   Pessimism in Byron   MA Univ of Texas at Austin
         1928
1068 CLUBBE John L   Byron and Greece: A Study in Romantic Hellenism
         MA Columbia 1960   95 p
1069 CONLEY Robert J   A Study of the Genesis Theme in Lord Byron's Plays
         MA Midwestern Univ 1968   118 p
1070 COOPER Ruth   Byron's Influence on the Poetry of Poe   MA Univ of
         Alabama 1937
1071 COSS David L   The Neo-Classic Influence in Byron's *Don Juan*
         MA Illinois St Univ 1966
1072 COULTER J L Jr   Byron's Ethical, Religious and Political Principles,
         as Revealed in His Judgment of Men   MA Univ of North Carolina at
         Chapel Hill 1936
1073 COYNE Rita L   The Byronic Hero in Four Turkish Tales by George Gordon,
         Lord Byron   MA John Carroll Univ 1966
1074 CRAWFORD Patricia   Comic Theory and *Don Juan:* An Attempt to Formulate
         Byron's Theory of Comedy   MA Washington St Univ at Pullman 1933
1075 CROWTHER Joan D   Byron's Mystery Plays   BA Univ of British Columbia
         (Canada) 1961
1076 CUSENZA Marianne S   The Byronic Hero in the American Television
         Western   MA San Diego St Coll 1966   130 p
1077 DAVIS Ann H   The Unbounded Spirit: A Study of Prometheanism in the
         Dramatic Works of Lord Byron   MA Univ of Houston 1969   127 p
1078 DAVIS Beatrice   The Development of the Byronic Hero   MA Tulane Univ
         1936
1079 DeSIMONE Paula A   A Study of the Heroes of Byron's Historical Dramas
         MA Columbia 1966   62 p
1080 DEVLIN Joseph F   The Development of the Hero-Type in Byron's Poems
         MA Boston Coll 1959
1081 DICKINSON Lucy E   Byron and Poe: A Comparison and a Study of Byron's
         Influence upon Poe   MA Auburn Univ 1941
1082 DICKSON H H   Byron on His Contemporaries   BA Univ of British Columbia
         (Canada) 1959
1083 DOYLE John R Jr   Poe's Debt to Byron, Coleridge, Moore and Shelley:
         A Study of Influences in the Development of a Poet's Art
         MA Univ of Virginia 1937
1084 DRAMIN Edward I   Byron and the Gothic Movement   BA Amherst 1963
1085 DUCHEMIN Henry P   Byron and Satiric Tradition   MA Toronto (Canada)
         1966
1086 DUNSON D G   The Juvenalian Influence on Byron's *Don Juan*
         MA North Texas St Univ 1967
1087 DYER Lilian L   Byron's Influence on Echeverria   MA Univ of Texas

at Austin 1937 121 p
1088 EDSON Thomas H The Friendship of Byron and Shelley: Virginia Woolf's
      Search for Reality MA Univ of Texas at Austin 1967
1089 EDWARDS Hazel Byron's Early Reading and Its Influence on His Early
      Works MA Univ of Texas at Austin 1923
1090 EGGLESTON Mary B Italy in the Poetry of Byron, Shelley and
      Browning MA Univ of Toledo 1932
1091 ELKINS Aubrey C Imagery in Byron's Don Juan MA Univ of Texas at
      Austin 1963 93 p
1092 ELLIOT Billye Byron's Use of Storms in His Poetry MA Hardin-Simmons
      Univ 1950
1093 ENGLAND H A Byron as Revealed in Childe Harold's Pilgrimage
      MA North Texas St Univ 1944
1094 FAULEY Franz E A Critical Analysis of Cantos II, III and IV of
      Lord Byron's Don Juan MA Bowling Green Univ 1964
1095 FINNEGAN John Purity, Platonism and Pathos: A Study of the Love
      Lyrics of Byron, Shelley and Keats MA Univ of Texas at El Paso
      1966 199 p
1096 FISHER James H Byron's Use of the Theme of Destruction and a Study
      of the Mythological Aspects of John Updike's The Centaur
      MA Univ of Texas at Austin 1968
1097 FORDYCE-CLARK Charles A Byron as a Satirist MA Univ of British
      Columbia (Canada) 1925 81 p
1098 FOX Charles F The Byronic Heroine of the Oriental Tales and Manfred
      MA Indiana Univ 1955
1099 FRISKEL Robert Analysis of Structure of Byron's Don Juan
      MS Kansas St Coll at Pittsburg 1959
1100 FOWLER Marian E The Social Context of Byron's Don Juan MA Toronto
      (Canada) 1965
1101 FUNG Kwok Y Byron and Shelley as Dramatists MA Univ of Pittsburgh
      1936
1102 GATZ Marlene H The Women in Byron's Don Juan MA Municipal Univ of
      Omaha 1964
1103 GERMACK Mariagrazia The Tragedy of Byron MA Ca Foscari (Italy) 1965
1104 GEYER Alice L Byron's Cain: Its Inception and Reception MA Univ of
      Maryland at College Park 1951 116 p
1105 GIBB Peter L Metaphysical Ideas in Byron's Cain BA Univ of British
      Columbia (Canada) 1965
1106 GOLDFARB William B The Bible in the Life and Works of Byron
      MA Columbia 1951
1107 GOLDSTEIN Stephen L Scenes of Destruction in Byron's Poetry
      MA Columbia 1966 80 p
1108 GOULET Claire Varieties of Irony in Byron's Don Juan, Cantos I-V
      MA Montreal (Canada) 1965
1109 GREGORY Hoosag K Lord Byron and Thomas Wolfe: A Comparison of Their
      Philosophical and Personal Problems MA Univ of Illinois 1940
1110 GROBE Camilla Byron's Idea of Liberty in the Poetry of the
      Childe Harold Period MA Rice 1953
1111 HANKS H S Don Juan in Hell MA North Texas St Univ 1961
1112 HART Anabel F The Character of Lord Byron as Shown in Eight English
      Novels MA Univ of Kentucky 1937
1113 HASSLER Donald M II Lord Byron's Marino Faliero: A Study and
      Interpretation MA Columbia 1960 115 p
1114 HATCH Roger W Lord Byron in Landscape: A Study of the Structure
      of the Poet's Nature Imagery in Childe Harold's Pilgrimage
      MA Univ of New Hampshire 1969 99 p
1115 HAYDEN John O The Humorous Techniques in Don Juan Analyzed with
      the Aid of Bergson's Theory of the Comic MA Columbia 1959 94 p
1116 HEADRICK Allan W Digressions in Don Juan: Their Structure and
      Purpose MA Queen's (Canada) 1965

1117 HERAKLY T G Francis Jeffrey as a Literary Critic with Special
      Reference to His Criticism of Byron and Keats MA Univ of London
      (England) 1963
1118 HICKS Catherine I Byron: His Religious Beliefs and Doubts and
      Their Implications MA Univ of Arkansas 1953
1119 HILL Griffitha M Byron and Italy; a Consideration of Italian
      Political, Social and Religious Influences on the Life and Work
      of George Noel Gordon, Sixth Lord Byron MA Columbia 1941
1120 HOWARD William J Growth Through Experience in Byron's *Don Juan*
      BA Univ of British Columbia (Canada) 1967
1121 INGLEBY P Byron's Poetic Theory: Its Development and Application
      M Phil Univ of London (England) 1967
1122 JENKINSON Irene E Byron's Religion and Philosophy MA Western St
      Coll of Colorado 1929 56 p
1123 JOHNSON Nancy S Byron's Criticism of His Contemporaries MA Texas
      Technological Univ 1941 183 p
1124 JONES Lindsay M A Critical Study of Byron's *Cain* MA Univ of British
      Columbia (Canada) 1968 90 p
1125 JONES Willie D Autobiography in Byron's Plays MA Louisiana St Univ
      1941
1126 KESSI Mary Byron and Tasso MA Univ of Oregon 1939
1127 KLEMM G P Lord Byron's Attitude toward Napoleon MA North Texas
      St Univ 1962
1128 KLIEGL Helen L Lord Byron and the Religious Quest MA Columbia 1959
1129 KNIGHT Patricia C The Byronic Hero in James Fenimore Cooper's
      Sea Novels MA Texas Technological Univ 1968 111 p
1130 KNUCKLES Thomas C Rousseau and Byron: A Comparison, with Special
      Reference to the Influence of Rousseau on Byron MA Univ of
      Maryland at College Park 1950 122 p
1131 KRUKOWSKI J D Lord Byron's Interest in British Politics MA North
      Texas St Univ 1963
1132 LALL Diyamir S Comic Devices in Byron's *Don Juan* MA Oklahoma St Univ
      1960
1133 LANE E S Byron and the Fine Arts: Music, Architecture, Painting
      and Sculpture MA Univ of North Carolina at Chapel Hill 1938
1134 LEONARD Venus R Determination in Byron's Dramas and *Childe Harold's
      Pilgrimage* MA Univ of Texas at Austin 1959 198 p
1135 LOCKRIDGE Ross F Jr Byron and Napoleon MA Indiana Univ 1940
1136 LYNN Harry B Byron and Scotland MA Univ of Texas at Austin 1957 124 p
1137 MACA Suanne A Complex of Religious Beliefs as Found in the Life and
      Works of Lord Byron MA North Texas St Univ 1967
1138 McASKIE Catriona Byron's Use of the Turkish Element in Four Verse
      Tales and *Don Juan* BA Univ of British Columbia (Canada) 1966
1139 McCAWLEY Katherine J The Nature of Byron's Satire MA St Louis Univ
      1936 43 p
1140 McFARLAND Mary A Byron's Reading and Its Influence on His Works
      from 1807 Through the First Canto of *Childe Harold* MA Univ of
      Texas at Austin 1925
1141 McGUIRE Cora H The Spirit of Democracy in Byron MA Univ of
      California at Berkeley 1914
1142 McKEMY Anna Lord Byron's Wit: A Freudian Study of *Don Juan*
      MA Columbia 1963 91 p
1143 MARKIDOU Ariadne N Lord Byron and the Dramas of the Greek Liberation
      MA Northeast Missouri St Coll 1958
1144 MARTIN Ellen B The Personalities and Literary Relationship of
      Byron and Shelley MA Tulane Univ 1932
1145 MASEY Crystal Reflections of Lord Byron's Life in His Writings
      M Ed Henderson St Coll nd
1146 MATHEWS Alice M The Significance of Animals in the Life and Writings
      of Lord Byron MA North Texas St Univ 1965

1147 MAZZOLENI Luciana George Gordon, Lord Byron and Criticism
       MA Ca Foscari (Italy) 1928
1148 MILLER Mary A Thematic Imagery in Lord Byron's *Don Juan* MA Rice 1964
1149 MONCRIEF Sallie B Byron in the Satiric Tradition MA Baylor Univ
       1942 115 p
1150 MORGAN Lucretia B Byron's Influence on Villiers de l'Isle-Adam
       MA Univ of Georgia 1965
1151 MORGAN Mary E A Study of *Manfred* MA Univ of Oklahoma 1918
1152 MUKHERJEA S K The Influence of Byron on Lermontov B Litt Oxford Univ
       (London) 1945
1153 MYERS James R The Clay Eagles: A Study of the Heroes of Byron's
       Oriental Tales MA Columbia 1966 72 p
1154 NEAD Marshall Byron Portrayed by the Reviews MA Columbia 1943
1155 NEWTON W R Polysyllabic Rime in *Don Juan* MA Lamar Technological
       Univ 1965
1156 NOBBE George Satire and Romanticism in Byron MA Washington Univ
       at St Louis 1920 54 p
1157 NORMAN Arthur M The Dramatic Effectiveness of Byron's Historical
       Tragedies MA Univ of Texas at Austin 1951 112 p
1158 O'BRIEN John J Attitude of Byron toward the Catholic Church
       MA Boston Coll 1942
1159 OPPERMAN Charlein Byron in the English and American Novel MA Univ
       of Oklahoma 1942
1160 OSTER Edward Byron, Leigh Hunt and *The Liberal* MA Rutgers St Univ
       1950 99 p
1161 OSTROWSKI Paul S Costume and the Poetry of Lord Byron MA Columbia
       1958 83 p
1162 PARKER John H A Chronology of the Travels and Experiences of
       Lord Byron: April 23, 1816 to October 5, 1816 MA Univ of
       Tennessee 1969 46 p
1163 PATIN Marjorie C Metaphorical Language in Byron's *Don Juan*
       MA St Coll of Iowa 1966
1164 PATTISON D A Variorum Edition of Byron's *English Bards and Scotch
       Reviewers* M Phil Univ of London (England) 1967
1165 PEREZ Carmen A Bibliography of Lord Byron's Writings and Ana
       from January 1, 1935 to December 31, 1940 MA Univ of Kentucky
       1944 100 p
1166 PERRY Dale J Lord Byron's Concern with the Theme of Death MA Univ
       of Oregon 1940
1167 PETERS Michael Byron's Attitude toward War MA Texas Technological
       Univ 1967 70 p
1168 PILKINTON Annie B A Study of English and American Criticism of
       Byron since 1924 MA Howard Univ 1939
1169 PISANCESCHI John P The Development of the Byronic Hero in
       Lord Byron's Major Works MA Villanova Univ 1964
1170 PITTMAN C L Byron and the Counter-Revolution MA Univ of North
       Carolina at Chapel Hill 1932
1171 POE Patty S The Byronic Hero in Some Novels and Plays of the
       Eighteenth Century MA Univ of Oklahoma 1934
1172 PRATT Lyda S The Evolution of the Don Juan Legend MA Western St
       Coll of Colorado 1933
1173 RAPPAPORT Linda M The Evolution of Byron's Attitude toward Solitude
       MA Columbia 1960 75 p
1174 REAGH Elizabeth M A Study of Byron's *Manfred* BA Univ of British
       Columbia (Canada) 1968
1175 REEVES Joyce A Study of Byron's *Manfred* MA Columbia 1963 100 p
1176 RODENCHUK E The Byronic Heroine BA Univ of British Columbia
       (Canada) 1948
1177 ROESLER A Study of Some Early Byron Criticism MA St Mary's at
       San Antonio 1947 63 p

1178 ROGERS Neva The Plays of Lord Byron BA Univ of Oklahoma 1918
1179 ROGERS Rutherford D Byron's Attitude toward the Oppressed
      MA Columbia 1937
1180 ROXBY Robert J L'Influence de Lord Byron sur les Premieres
      Poesies d'Alfred de Musset MA Georgetown Univ 1966
1181 RUYLE Benjamin J Don Juan MA Texas Christian Univ 1939 56 p
1182 SADOWSKI Charles F Lord Byron's Manfred: A Historical Survey of
      Criticism and Scholarship MA Georgetown Univ 1968 87 p
1183 SALVIDIO Frank A Satan, Manfred and Cain: A Study in Myth
      MA Univ of Connecticut 1963
1184 SCHAEFFER Joan Byron and Scotland MA Columbia 1966 128 p
1185 SCHAIDT Anna L Literary References to the Story of Cain and Abel
      MA Univ of Maryland at College Park 1932 65 p
1186 SCHOOLS Maxwell R The Travels of Lord Byron MA Univ of Richmond
      1949 126 p
1187 SCHROTH Joseph F A History of the Literary Criticism of Lord Byron's
      Lyrical Dramas MA Univ of Pittsburgh 1950
1188 SCOTT Albert E Sea and Water Imagery in Byron's Childe Harold's
      Pilgrimage and Don Juan MA Univ of New Mexico 1962
1189 SHIRAKAWA Samuel H The Unified Vision; a Study of the Search for
      Redemptive Truth in the Poetry of Lord Byron MA Temple Univ 1966
1190 SHORTER Mary D Faust and Byron: A Study of the Influence of Goethe's
      Faust on Certain Writings of Lord Byron MA Texas Technological
      Univ 1965 59 p
1191 SILBAUGH Hugh R Jr Lord Byron and the Indestructible Hero: A Study
      of the Narrative Poetry of George Gordon, Lord Byron BA Amherst
      1954
1192 SIMONIDES Howard A An Analysis of Lord Byron's Attitude toward
      Alexander Pope MA Univ of Texas at El Paso 1968 75 p
1193 SIRCY O C Jr A Study of Byron's Approaches to Reality in Don Juan
      MA North Texas St Univ 1968
1194 SKINNER Mildred L Lord Byron's Health: Its Effect upon His Work
      and Mind MA Univ of Maryland 1938 36 p
1195 SMITH Eta D Have Byron's Works Been Successful or Influential?
      MA Univ of Oklahoma 1925
1196 SMITH Ethel F Byron's Plagiarism as Judged by His Contemporaries
      MA Boston Univ 1937
1197 SMITH Judy F Lord Byron's Self-Portrayal in Don Juan MA North
      Texas St Univ 1964
1198 SMITH Lahoma Byron's Use of History in His Poetry MA Univ of
      Texas at Austin 1959 124 p
1199 SNYDER Richard C The Literary Attitudes of Lord Byron as Reflected
      in His Letters MA Univ of Pittsburgh 1942
1200 SORRELLS Suzanne K Byron and Chateaubriand: A Comparison
      MA East Texas St Univ 1966
1201 STEPHENSON William A The Influence of Byron's Don Juan on the
      Don Juan Tradition in Western Literature MA Texas Technological
      Univ 1965 89 p
1202 STONE Donald O An Examination of Lord Byron's Political Beliefs
      as Revealed Chiefly in His Prose to June 1821 MA Florida St Univ
      1962
1203 STOTT Jon C The Historical Dramas of Lord Byron BA Univ of British
      Columbia (Canada) 1961
1204 STRINGER David H Lord Byron's Imaginative Vision BA Amherst 1964
1205 SUHWEIL Eveline S The Moslem Near East and Lord Byron MA Columbia
      1960 117 p
1206 SUMMERS Jon L Lord Byron and Modern Existentialism MA Texas
      Technological Univ 1969 64 p
1207 SUNDAY Angeline M The Influence of the Old Testament on George Gordon,
      Lord Byron's Poetry MA Univ of Maryland at College Park 1944 133 p

1208 SUVAJIAN Garabed K The Near Eastern Color in Byron's Poetry
      MA Texas Christian Univ 1959 103 p
1209 SWANSON Martha A Some Byron Family Letters MA Univ of Texas at
      Austin 1941 120 p
1210 TALLMAN Marion A Byron, Revealer of the World of Idea MA Univ of
      Toledo 1932
1211 TAYLOR Wayne W Byron's Religious Views with Special Reference to
      the Hebrew Melodies MA Univ of Arizona 1942
1212 TAYLOR Welford D The Dramas of Byron: An Evaluation MA Univ of
      Richmond 1961 62 p
1213 TEACHOUT Peter R Plucking Various Fruit: A Study of Byron
      MA Amherst 1962
1214 TERRELL Theresa The Democracy of Lord Byron MA Univ of Texas at
      Austin 1929
1215 THOMAS Gordon K Social Commentary and Criticism in Four Versions
      of the Don Juan Theme MA Brigham Young Univ 1960 62 p
1216 THOMAS Robert L The Heroes of Byron: A Study of Their Origin,
      Development and Meaning in the Poetry of George Gordon, Lord Byron
      MA Pacific Univ 1956 134 p
1217 TONSMEIRE Sue G A Study of Byron's *English Bards and Scotch
      Reviewers* MA Tulane Univ 1933
1218 TRAHAN Emile R The Byronic Hero as a Wanderer MA Boston Coll 1965
1219 TRAMMELL Robert T Byron's Regular Dramas MA Univ of Florida 1964
1220 TURNER Susan J Byron's Knowledge of the Eighteenth Century
      MA Univ of Kentucky 1936
1221 UEBELE Ruth C Byron's Use of the Bible MA Indiana Univ 1942
1222 WADSWORTH M E The Literary Criticism of Lord Byron MA Boston Univ
      1942
1223 WALKER Ralph H Lord Byron's Acquaintance with Madame de Stael and
      other French Writers MA Univ of Texas at Austin 1949 118 p
1224 WARNER Josephine M Nature and Natural Man in Byron's Poetry
      MA Univ of Texas at Austin 1935
1225 WASSON Margaret Byron's Contacts with Men MA Southern Methodist
      Univ 1931
1226 WATSON Jack C Women in the Life of Lord Byron MA Univ of Texas at
      Austin 1935
1227 WEBER Harry F Byron as a Literary Critic MA George Washington Univ
      1939 68 p
1228 WHITEHEAD Diane E Byron and Neoclassicism MA Villanova Univ 1966
1229 WHITMORE Allen P Byron the Dramatist MA Univ of Maine 1959 79 p
1230 WHITWORTH Louis D Psychotic Elements in the Works of Lord Byron
      MA Northeast Louisiana St Coll 1966
1231 WILCOX Sidney W Lord Byron's Use of the Bible MA Univ of Oklahoma
      1939
1232 WILEY Louise M The Personal and Literary Relations of Byron and
      Shelley MA Univ of Tennessee 1917
1233 WILSON W L A Problem in Byron's Prosody: What Does Rime-Variation
      in Byron's Four-Stress Iambic Tales Show of His Artistic Power and
      Growth? MA Univ of North Carolina at Chapel Hill 1928
1234 ZIMMERMAN Paul D Byron, the Story of His Literary Career
      BA Amherst 1960
See also 649, 849, 1347, 1356, 1361, 2887, 3895, 4657, 7148

THOMAS CARLYLE

1235 BAILEY Lucretia The Sartor-World and the Sacred City: A Reading
      of Thomas Carlyle's *Sartor Resartus* MA Columbia 1967 51 p
1236 BARNES Samuel G The Newtonian Pattern in Thomas Carlyle's
      Sartor Resartus MA Univ of North Carolina at Chapel Hill 1946
1237 BRUCKNER Paul J Characteristics of the Epic Imagination as Found

in Carlyle's *Sartor Resartus* MA St Louis Univ 1933 69 p
1238 CALDWELL Rachel M A Comparison of the Thought of Thomas Carlyle
       and Walt Whitman MA Univ of Louisville 1958
1239 CALLENDER Jack T The Real Significance of Carlyle's 1830 Essay on
       Jean Paul Richter MA Univ of Kentucky 1951 108 p
1240 CAMPBELL Mable G The Influence of Christian Socialism upon Carlyle,
       Ruskin and Mrs Humphrey Ward as Reflected in Their Works
       MA Texas Woman's Univ 1935
1241 CHAMBERLAIN Benjamin D Carlyle as a Portrait Painter MA Univ of
       Pittsburgh 1927
1242 CHINN Harold B Carlyle's Attitude toward Social Reform
       MA Howard Univ 1933 106 p
1243 COLE Marion G Thomas Carlyle MA Williams Coll 1908
1244 COLLINS David M The Function of Style in *Sartor Resartus*
       MA St Louis Univ 1954 117 p
1245 CONNIHAN Sr M Columcille Thomas Carlyle and Eric Gill as Critics
       of the Capitalist-Industrialist System MA Marquette Univ 1950
1246 CONNOLLY Elizabeth J Thomas Carlyle's Letters to Varnhagen Von Ense,
       1837-1857 MA Columbia 1951
1247 CURTIN P T Medievalism in Carlyle's *Past and Present* MA Boston
       Coll 1942
1248 DEINES Mercedes The Literary Reception of Thomas Carlyle's *Past and
       Present* MA Univ of Rhode Island 1967 73 p
1249 DUPERTUIS Germaine Thomas Carlyle MA Washington St Univ at Pullman 19
1250 DUTTON Robert R Hebraism and Hellenism as Seen in *Sartor Resartus*
       and *Wilhelm Meister's Apprenticeship* MA Pacific Univ 1951 76 p
1251 FARQUHARSON Robert Carlyle's Idea of God and Man's Destiny
       MA Univ of British Columbia (Canada) 1956 161 p
1252 FAULSTICH Bernard G Carlyle in Catholic Criticism in English Before
       1886 MA St Louis Univ 1939 70 p
1253 FERGUSON Ruth M Carlyle and Emerson: A Comparative Study
       MA Southwestern Univ 1924
1254 FLESHER Lyla Macaulay and Carlyle: A Study in Victorian Contrasts
       MA North Texas St Univ 1940
1255 GRAVES Lila V The Disparate Visions of Carlyle and Emerson
       MA Auburn Univ 1968
1256 GROSS John J Carlyle and the Social Novelists MA Univ of Oregon 1942
1257 HANAWALT Murvle H Carlyle and the New Morality MA Univ of Iowa 1935
1258 HANCOCK Jimmye R Vitalism in Carlyle MA East Texas St Univ 1965
1259 HARKEY Bennie E Thomas Carlyle and German National Socialism: A Study
       of the Nazi Interpretation of Carlyle's Thought MA Univ of Oklahoma
       1950
1260 HARRIS Carolyn V A Comparison of the Froude and Wilson Biographies
       of Thomas Carlyle MA Auburn Univ 1941
1261 HORNER Charles W A Bibliography of Thomas Carlyle from January 1, 1934
       to December 31, 1938 MA Univ of Kentucky 1940
1262 HUNTER James S Carlyle's Hero MA Univ of Pittsburgh 1934
1263 JONES Iona E Analysis of Carlyle's *Sartor Resartus* and *Heroes and
       Hero Worship* from the Standpoint of Diction, Mechanics and Style
       MS Kansas St Coll at Pittsburg 1933
1264 KELLEY Gloria L Individualism in the Political Philosophies of
       Carlyle, Emerson and Thoreau MA Univ of Texas at Austin 1955 154 p
1265 KERCKHOFF Walbraut E A Bibliography of Thomas Carlyle's Writings
       and Ana from January 1, 1939 to January 1, 1950 MA Univ of
       Kentucky 1951 106 p
1266 KING M P The Influence of Carlyle's Biographical Criticism of Authors
       on British Periodicals of His Time MA Univ of London (England) 195?
1267 KOSTKA Elain V Nature and the City: A Study of Thomas Carlyle's
       Imagery MA Univ of Massachusetts 1969 82 p
1268 KRAL Edna M Carlyle's Interest in Biography MA Mankato St Coll

1960   87 p
1269 KRAUS Robert L   Carlyle's Attitude toward Catholicism   MA St Louis
Univ 1944   57 p
1270 KUSSY Bella   The Social Theories of Carlyle and Nietzsche
MA Columbia 1937
1271 LALLY F J   Periodical Opinions of Carlyle from 1827-1882   MA Boston
Univ 1939
1272 LAMB Robert J Jr   Carlyle's Contribution to the Concept of
Nationalism   MA Columbia 1954   72 p
1273 LAMBDIN Margaret   Thomas Carlyle's Theory of Government   MS Kansas
St Coll at Pittsburg 1938
1274 McCLOIN Joseph T   Carlyle's "Hero" and the Modern Dictator
MA St Louis Univ 1943   129 p
1275 MARK Eva H   A Comparison of Carlyle's Doctrine of the Hero with
the Nietzschean Theory of the Superman   MA Texas Woman's Univ 1931
1276 MARRS Edwin W   A Calendar of Carlyle Letters with an Introduction
MS Syracuse Univ 1961   178 p
1277 MARTIN V M   Carlyle as a Critic of Literature   MA Oklahoma St Univ 1917
1278 MASON Marjorie E   Thomas Carlyle as Historian of the French Revolution
MA Texas Technological Univ 1968   77 p
1279 MASSIRER Mary R   The Development of the Idea of Progress in the Early
Works of Thomas Carlyle   MA Baylor Univ 1962   137 p
1280 MEYER Florence J   The Vogue of Carlyle in England and America
MA Univ of Arizona 1936
1281 MILLER Alan C   Carlyle as Humanitarian   MA Indiana Univ 1940
1282 MOON Barbara A   Three Essays in English: English and Spanish Ballads;
Carlyle and Nabokov; T S Eliot's Nightingales   MA Pennsylvania
St Univ 1966
1283 MURDOCK Robert   Carlyle's Hero-Leadership and Democracy   MA Washington
Univ at St Louis 1959
1284 NEWCOMB Mildred E   A Study of the Puritanism and Romanticism in
Carlyle: A Comparison and Contrast   MA Indiana Univ 1942
1285 NYSTROM Leonard G   The Influence of Thomas Carlyle on Selma Lagerlof
MA Southern Methodist Univ 1936
1286 OWNSBY Jessie M   Carlyle's Relation to the Economic Thought of His
Time   MA Texas Woman's Univ 1931
1287 PACE Harold E   The Religious Views of Thomas Carlyle and
John Stuart Mill   MA Univ of Kentucky 1948   64 p
1288 PEARCE Haywood J   An Inquiry into the Style and Characteristics of
Thomas Carlyle   MA Emory Univ 1915   47 p
1289 POHL Oskar   Thought and Poetry in Carlyle's *Sartor Resartus*
MA Ca Foscari (Italy) 1950
1290 POWER Theresa E   Carlyle as a Biographer   MA Univ of Texas at Austin
1935
1291 REITH Helen W   Thomas Carlyle as a Social Reformer   MA Univ of
British Columbia (Canada) 1927
1292 RINGO Sr Margaret A   Orestes A Brownson: An Interpreter of Carlyle
MA Boston Coll 1960
1293 ROSENGARTEN Frank   Thomas Carlyle: A Prophet of the Hero
MA Columbia 1951
1294 RUFF Joseph R   Carlyle as Historian: The Example of the French
Revolution   MA Temple Univ 1963   56 p
1295 SCHNEIDER M Barry   Thomas Carlyle and the Eighteenth Century
BA Rutgers St Univ 1956   72 p
1296 SEIBERT Betty A   Burke, Carlyle and Dickens on the French Revolution
MS Kansas St Coll at Pittsburg 1942
1297 SEIGEL Jules P   Thomas Carlyle and the Periodical Press: A Study
in Attitudes   MA Univ of Maryland at College Park 1965
1298 SHUTTS Katherine   The Influence of Carlyle on Ruskin   MA Univ of
Oklahoma 1914

1299 SMITH Anne Educational Philosophy of Thomas Carlyle M Ed Temple
      Univ 1930
1300 SOKOLOFF Heloise C Thomas Carlyle: Poetry and Morality MA Columbia
      1965 117 p
1301 STODDARD Martha A Carlyle's Theory of the Hero and Its Importance in
      History MA Boston Univ 1943
1302 STOWEL Frank S Thomas Carlyle's Adaptation of the Jocelin Chronicle
      for the Second Book of His *Past and Present* MA Univ of Oregon 1932
1303 TAYLOR Eleanor K Origins of Carlyle's Biographical Attitudes
      MA Univ of Pittsburgh 1929
1304 TETREAULT Ronald Carlyle's Doctrine of Work: A History of His Idea
      BA Univ of British Columbia (Canada) 1969
1305 THOMAS Alan C Parallels and Influences in Some Selected Works of
      Carlyle and Dickens MA Toronto (Canada) 1964
1306 THOMPSON Doris C The Influence of Carlyle upon the Social Novel
      of the Victorian Period MA Texas Woman's Univ 1934
1307 THOMPSON M M Jr The Influence of Carlyle's *Life of Friedrich Schiller*
      on Later Schiller Biography in English MA Louisiana St Univ 1938
1308 TRAPNELL Jean B The Critical Reception Accorded Carlyle's Works
      in Contemporary American Periodicals MA Columbia 1937
1309 VIDA Elizabeth M The Influence of Fichte's *Die Bestimmung des Menchen*
      on Carlyle's *Sartor Resartus*: A Comparison MA Toronto (Canada) 1964
1310 WALKER Lee H Carlyle's Conception of History MA Univ of Iowa 1935
1311 WALKER Morton Thomas Carlyle on Poetry and the Poets MA Univ of
      Kentucky 1933
1312 WILKINS Charles T A Bibliography of Thomas Carlyle's Writings and
      Ana from September 13, 1928 to January 1, 1934 MA Univ of Kentucky
      1941
1313 WOLFSHOLL Clarence J The Language of Thomas Carlyle's *Sartor Resartus*:
      A Study of Source and Subject of Diction, Allusions and Figurative
      Language in I, iv; II, vii-ix; and III, iii MA Univ of Idaho 1966
1314 YOUNG Margaret L The Emerson-Carlyle Relationship MA Univ of Iowa 1947
1315 ZOLBROD Paul G Carlyle's *Sartor Resartus*: An Interpretation
      MA Univ of Pittsburgh 1962
See also 1821, 4265, 4644, 4729, 4933

LEWIS CARROLL

1316 LATHAM Jean C The Satire of Lewis Carroll MS Kansas St Coll at
      Pittsburg 1952
1317 PATERNI Alessandra M The Literature of Children and One of Its English
      Elements: Lewis Carroll MA Ca Foscari (Italy) nd
1318 ZINS Rose M Lewis Carroll Revisited: A Century of Criticism
      MA Mankato St Coll 1965 55 p
See also 2615

JOYCE CARY

1319 AICHINGER C P The Political Element in the Works of Joyce Cary
      MA Ottawa (Canada) 1963
1320 BARON Howard Joyce Cary: Ways of the Creative Individual MA Univ of
      Arizona 1965
1321 BATTS Bertha B The Novels of Joyce Cary MA Washington Univ at St Louis
      1953 73 p
1322 BUTLER Georgette R Patterns in Joyce Cary's First Trilogy MA Trinity
      Coll in Connecticut 1965
1323 DAVIES Marily J The One Proteus: A Study of the Novels of
      Joyce Cary MA Dalhousie (Canada) 1964
1324 DROMGOLD Pegi L Destructive Creativity: The Theme of Joyce Cary's
      First Trilogy MA Univ of Oklahoma 1962

1325 DUNN Mary T Joyce Cary: The Affirmation of Life MA Univ of
        Massachusetts 1967 37 p
1326 FERRELL Retta B Joyce Cary's Affirmation of the Creative Imagination
        in the First Trilogy MA Univ of Texas at Austin 1966 78 p
1327 GOLDEN Sanford M Joyce Cary: A Bibliography of Works and Criticism
        MA Wayne St Univ 1965
1328 HARRIS Paul A Hampered Pilgrimage: The World of Joyce Cary
        MA George Washington Univ 1953 68 p
1329 HEALEY Eleanor C Character Creation: Joyce Cary MA Columbia 1954
1330 McNEAL Frances S Religion in the Novels of Joyce Cary MA Univ of
        Delaware 1960 139 p
1331 MERCER Jack E Depiction of Character Through Style in Joyce Cary's
        Political Trilogy MA Univ of British Columbia (Canada) 1962 204 p
1332 PEARCE Scott C Freedom and Responsibility in Five of Joyce Cary's
        Novels MA Washington St Univ at Pullman 1965
1333 PRICE Maurice G Joyce Cary's Perspective of Human Behavior
        MA Univ of Texas at Austin 1953 68 p
1334 SHANKMAN Roy Man Is Creation in the Act: A Study of "Character"
        in Joyce Cary's First Trilogy MA Dalhousie (Canada) 1967
1335 THORP Almus M Jr Joyce Cary: The Self-Conscious Moralist; A Study
        of *Mister Johnson* and the First Trilogy BA Amherst 1963
1336 VANDERHOOF Peter R Joyce Cary and the Subjective Nature of Reality
        MA Washington St Univ at Pullman 1969
See also 455, 3642

GEORGE CAVENDISH

1337 GRAHAM Robert E Roper's *More* and Cavendish's *Wolsey:* A Study in
        Early English Biography MA Boston Coll 1951
1338 STONE Alan N The Structure of Cavendish's *Life of Wolsey* and the
        De Casibus Tradition MA Columbia 1966 109 p

WILLIAM CAXTON

1339 KOURDAY R William Caxton: England's First Editor MA C W Post Coll
        nd 96 p
1340 O'BRIEN James A William Caxton's Contribution to English Literature
        as a Critic, Translator, Editor, Writer and Printer MA Univ of
        Rhode Island 1961 99 p
See also 4970

GEORGE CHAPMAN

1341 AIROLDI Tilde George Chapman: *Charlemagne* MA Ca Foscari (Italy)
        1956
1342 BARBIERI Angela *The Widow's Tears* by George Chapman MA Ca Foscari
        (Italy) 1965
1343 CASINI Edoardo *All Fools* by George Chapman MA Ca Foscari (Italy)
        1963
1344 CUTBIRTH Nancy A Study of Structural and Dramatic Elements in *Ovid's
        Banquet of Sence* by George Chapman MA Univ of Texas at Austin 1966
1345 GADDIS Arthur G A Variorium Edition of George Chapman's *The Tragedy
        of Caesar and Pompey* MA Oklahoma St Univ 1951 115 p
1346 GALUPPO Maria E *The Revenge of Bussy D'Ambois* by George Chapman
        MA Ca Foscari (Italy) 1965
1347 GIBBONS Sr Marina Personal Responsibility in Chapman's *Bussy D'Ambois*
        and *The Conspiracy and Tragedy of Byron* MA Boston Coll 1960
1348 GOFF Virginia R Chapman's *The Blind Beggar of Alexandria:* The
        Renaissance Hero in Ludicrous Context MA Univ of Oklahoma 1964
1349 KASKE Robert E An Analysis of Chapman's Tragedies, Based on a

Consideration of Tragic Theory and the Fundamental Types of
Tragedy MA Univ of North Carolina at Chapel Hill 1946
1350 KESTER Dolores A The Psychology of George Chapman as Revealed in
His Comedy *All Fools* MA Univ of Oklahoma 1964
1351 LARSEN S Chapman's Ideal Man and His Tragic Heroes BA Univ of
British Columbia (Canada) 1960
1352 MADDOCKS L Jane The Early Tragedies of George Chapman and the
De Casibus Tradition MA Bowling Green Univ 1958
1353 MILLER Vida Terminology of Supernatural Beings in Chapman, Daniel,
Drayton, Marlowe and Spenser MA Univ of North Carolina at
Chapel Hill 1934
1354 PASTORELLO Agostino George Chapman: *Bussy D'Ambois* MA Ca Foscari
(Italy) 1961
1355 POLLACK Michael The Tragic Heroes of Marlowe and Chapman MA Columbia
1964 74 p
1356 REESE Jack E Chapman's Byron Plays and the Earl of Essex MA Univ of
Kentucky 1953 85 p
1357 RISLEY Helen M Classical Mythology Used by Chapman in His Tragedies
MA Rutgers St Univ 1950 42 p
1358 SCAFIDEL Jimmy R George Chapman and the Comedy of Humors MA Univ of
Mississippi 1966
1359 STOVALL Sidney T Chapman's and Pope's Translations of the First
Book of Homer's *Iliad:* An Analysis and Criticism with Comment
on Some Reflections of the Seventeenth and Eighteenth Centuries
MA Columbia 1952 142 p
1360 WASSER Frances R Studies in *Eastward Ho* MA George Washington Univ
1953 85 p
1361 XAUSA Giuseppe *The Conspiracy of Byron* by George Chapman MA Ca Foscari
(Italy) 1965
See also 1103, 2866, 4304, 5682, 6672, 6855, 8657

GEOFFREY CHAUCER

1362 ADAMS Agusta C Chaucer's Friar, Mallock's Religion, Thoreau's Heroes
MA Pennsylvania St Univ 1965
1363 ADAMS George R Chaucer's General Prologue: A Study in Tradition
and the Individual Talent MA Univ of Oklahoma 1961 152 p
1364 ADAMS John A Comparative Study of Chaucer's *Sir Thopas* and the
Popular Ballads MA Univ of Tennessee 1932
1365 ALGARIN Miguel An Edition of the Verse in Morton's *Compendium
Physicae*; Characterizations in *Where Angels Fear to Tread* and
in *A Room with a View,* and Chaucer's Fairy Tale: A Review of
the Criticism on the "Squire's Tale" MA Pennsylvania St Univ 1965
1366 ALLEN M T Destinal Forces in the Narrative Pattern of the
Canterbury Tales MA Univ of North Carolina at Chapel Hill 1939
1367 ALLEN Robert F Chaucer and the Chaucerians: A Study of the English
and Scottish Poets from Chaucer to Spenser MA Boston Univ 1909
100 p
1368 ANDERSON M Dale Chaucer's Franklin MS Ft Hays St Teachers Coll
1961 43 p
1369 ANDERSON Martha J Musical Instruments in Fourteenth Century England
as Found in Chaucer's Works MS Kansas St Coll at Pittsburg 1948
1370 ANDERSON Mary M Geoffrey Chaucer: Two Hundred Years of Translation
MA Univ of Hawaii 1957 176 p
1371 ANDERSON Norma J Physiognomy as a Literary Device in the *Canterbury
Tales* MA Texas Christian Univ 1960 116 p
1372 ANGUS Doublas R The Art of Satire in the Prologue to the *Canterbury
Tales* MA Univ of Maine 1935 118 p
1373 APPERSON Elder B A Study of Chaucer's Influence on English Literature
through Dryden MA Univ of Richmond 1954 127 p

1374 ARBOGAST Jules J A Study of Rhetorical Amplification in Chaucer's
     "Wife of Bath's Tale", "The Franklin's Tale" and "The Nun's
     Priest's Tale" MA St Louis Univ 1930 48 p
1375 ARCHIBALD Rosamond M The Influence of Boethius on Chaucer's
     Canterbury Tales MA Smith Coll 1908
1376 ARNDT Irene A Biblical Passages in the Canterbury Tales MA Washington
     Univ at St Louis 1937 99 p
1377 ATKIN Ralph The Use of Rhetoric in Chaucer and Henryson, with
     Special Reference to Troilus and Criseyde and The Testament of
     Cresseid MA Western (Canada) 1965
1378 BABINGTON Mima A Grammatical Survey of Chaucer's Works MA Louisiana
     St Univ 1942
1379 BAGLEY Carolyn Chaucer's Use of Dramatic Technique in Troilus and
     Criseyde MA Oklahoma St Univ 1932 36 p
1380 BAKER Elizabeth D A Study of Three Rhetorical Devices in the
     Canterbury Tales: The Exemplum, Exemplary Figure and Appeal
     to Authority MA Univ of Oklahoma 1957
1381 BALL David A Rhetorical Device in "The Merchant's Tale" MA Univ
     of Maryland at College Park 1966 60 p
1382 BANKS John P Biblical Quotations in the "Tale of Melibee", "The
     Wife of Bath's Prologue" and "The Summoner's Tale MA Boston Coll
     1955
1383 BARRETT Sr Ellen T The Debate on Sovereignty in Chaucer's
     Canterbury Tales MA Boston Coll 1958
1384 BAXTER Frances L A Comparison of the Use of the Troilus and Cressida
     Story by Chaucer and Shakespeare MS Kansas St Coll at Pittsburg
     1948
1385 BEARDEN Ruth R Some Word Innovations of Chaucer's MA Texas Tech-
     nological Univ 1937 80 p
1386 BEDNOWICZ Rev Joseph S A Study of the Sources of Chaucer's "Seconde
     Nonne's Tale" MA St Louis Univ 1933 183 p
1387 BELL Ellen S Three Critical Essays: Comparison of Chaucer and
     Henryson; T B Read's Sonnets; Evaluations of Colin MacInnes
     MA Pennsylvania St Univ 1966
1388 BIRNEY A E Chaucer's Irony BA Univ of British Columbia (Canada) 1926
1389 BISHOP Carolyn J The Narrators of Chaucer's Love Visions
     MA Southern Methodist Univ 1965
1390 BIVINS Sarah A Canterbury Tales: A Selection for Dramatic Use
     Adapted from Geoffrey Chaucer MA West Texas St Univ 1965 138 p
1391 BLAKEMAN Winifred M The Men Characters in Chaucer MA Boston Univ 1940
1392 BLASSINGAME Roy Classical Mythological Allusions in Chaucer's Major
     Works MA East Texas St Univ 1966
1393 BOGG Joan M A Study of "The Reeve's Tale" MA Washington Univ at
     St Louis 1963 75 p
1394 BOLTON Frances The Women of Chaucer's Day According to the Literature
     of the Period MA Smith Coll 1926
1395 BONNELL Judith E A Definition of "Gentilesse" in the Works of
     Geoffrey Chaucer MA Univ of Idaho 1965
1396 BOONE Lalia P Literary Criticism in the Works of Geoffrey Chaucer
     MA Univ of Oklahoma 1947
1397 BOURNE Lucy V The Dream Motif in Chaucer's Poetry MA Univ of
     Tennessee 1927
1398 BOYER Bruce Husbandly Virtues in "The Shipman's Tale" MA Lehigh
     Univ 1966
1399 BRACK Donald W Chaucer's Use of Abbreviation MA Boston Coll 1964
1400 BRADLEY Carol "Ther Was Also a Nonne, a Prioress" MA Univ of
     Rhode Island 1962 122 p
1401 BRADLEY Sr Ritamary Chaucer's Translation of the Bible MA St Louis
     Univ 1945 95 p
1402 BRISCOE Mary L The Prioress, the Merchant and the Miller

MA Bowling Green Univ 1961

1403 BRODY Saul N Geoffrey Chaucer and the Principle of Plentitude MA Columbia 1960 98 p

1404 BROWN Gerald L The Wife of Bath's Motives MA Indiana Univ of Pennsylvania 1966 40 p

1405 BROWN Ruth A Study of Chaucer's Attitude toward Life as Reflected in *Troilus and Criseyde* MA Univ of Oregon 1940

1406 BROWN Ruth A Chaucer's Knight and Criticisms of Knighthood in the Late Fourteenth Century MA Bowling Green Univ 1968

1407 BUCKNER Mary D Chaucer's Redaction of the Character of Cressida MA Texas Technological Univ 1929 58 p

1408 BUESCHER Jimmie L Chaucer and the Lancasters MA Univ of Texas at El Paso 1967 67 p

1409 BUNGE Eldo F Chaucer's Knight MA Univ of Iowa 1932

1410 BUNN Olena S Chaucer in English and American Belle-Lettres Since 1900 MA Univ of North Carolina at Chapel Hill 1947 129 p

1411 BURJORJEE Dinshaw M The Pilgrimage of Troilus' Sailing Heart in Chaucer's *Troilus and Criseyde* MA Georgetown Univ 1969 37 p

1412 BURNS Robert A Chaucer's Troilus in Perspective: A Study of Two Critical Traditions and a Review of Recent Scholarship and Criticism MA Univ of Maine 1969 147 p

1413 BUSSELL Archie An Analysis and Interpretation of the Structural Elements in Chaucer's *Canterbury Tales* MA Univ of New Mexico 1951

1414 BYERLY Margaret J A Comparison of Two Medieval Storytellers: Geoffrey Chaucer and John Gower MA Pacific Univ 1967 93 p

1415 CALL Reginald M Chaucer's "Cook's Tale" and Fourteenth Century Apprenticeship MA Columbia 1942

1416 CALLAHAN Mary P Chaucer as a Traditional Figure MA Univ of Iowa 1933

1417 CALLUNAN J A Elements of Narrative Technique in the *Canterbury Tales* and Chaucer's Approach to Short Story Writing MA Boston Univ 1916

1418 CAPPER Victor L Chaucer's Characterization of the Women in the *Canterbury Tales* MA Univ of Oklahoma nd

1419 CARDLE Margaret Chaucer's "Knight's Tale" MA Univ of Iowa 1934

1420 CARLOCK Mary S Dryden's Interpretation of Chaucer MA Univ of Texas at Austin 1935 135 p

1421 CARNAGHI Raymond An Interpretation of the Symbolic Significance of the Number Three in Geoffrey Chaucer's *Troilus and Criseyde* MS Ft Hays St Coll 1966

1422 CAVANAUGH Estella M Chaucer's Treatment of Nature in the *Canterbury Tales* MA St Louis Univ 1932 80 p

1423 CHADWICK William R Chaucer's Varying Uses of the Garden of Love Motif MA Toronto (Canada) 1963

1424 CHAMBERLIN Mallory Jr Sea Imagery in the Works of Geoffrey Chaucer MA Univ of Tennessee 1964

1425 CHAMBERS Kathleen R A Study of Imaginative Figures of Speech in the Works of Geoffrey Chaucer MA Univ of Maine 1941 188 p

1426 CHAMBERS Patricia Chaucer as a Lyric Poet MA Hunter Coll 1965

1427 CHEW Lucretia C An Investigation of Chaucer's Use of Dreams MA Univ of Texas at El Paso 1967 113 p

1428 CLARK Thomas L Chaucer's Persona and Narrator MA Univ of Utah 1966

1429 CLARKE Dolores D Eileen Power's Treatment of the Medieval Nun with Special Reference to Chaucer's Prioress MA Boston Coll 1955

1430 CLINE Dorothy M An Aesthetic Approach to Mutability in Selected Poems of Chaucer and Spenser MA Univ of Delaware 1965 66 p

1431 CLOUGHER Roberta E Chaucer's Religion MA Boston Univ 1937

1432 COFFEY Mary E Chaucer's Use of the Love Vision in *The Book of the Duchess* MA St Louis Univ 1945 52 p

1433 COHEN Gladys L Chaucer's Allusions to Music in the *Canterbury Tales* MA Columbia 1954 150 p

1434 COLEMAN Helen L Chaucer's Ecclesiastics in the *Canterbury Tales*
        MA Univ of Richmond 1968 83 p
1435 COLLMER Robert G Annotated Bibliography of Geoffrey Chaucer Based
        on Holdings of the Library of Hardin-Simmons Univ 1956
1436 CONNER Margaret Some Renaissance Aspects of Chaucer MA Univ of
        Iowa 1933
1437 CONNERS Lucy A Three Studies in English: Chaucer's *Troilus and
        Criseyde*; Shelley's Dramas; and Three Mencken Letters
        MA Pennsylvania St Univ 1966
1438 COOPER Ursula C Chaucer's Use of Ovid and Virgil MA Tulane Univ 1930
1439 COULTER Humphrey M Chaucer and the Medieval Temple MA Univ of
        Tennessee 1960 83 p
1440 CRAIG Cynthia A Three Critical Studies in Poetry: The Narrator in
        Chaucer's *Troilus and Criseyde*; Sappho in the Poetry of Swinburne;
        and Death in the Poetry of Emily Dickinson MA Pennsylvania St
        Univ 1966
1441 CULLY Esther L A Study of the Character of Criseyde MA Columbia
        1958 58 p
1442 CUMMINGS Mary L The Romance Element in Chaucer (in collaboration)
        MA Univ of Iowa 1934
1443 CUNDIFF V E The Contribution of Scholarship toward an Understanding
        and Appreciation of Chaucer MA North Texas St Univ 1954
1444 CUNNINGHAM Lorene The Genre of Chaucer's "Squire's Tale" MA Texas
        Christian Univ 1941 123 p
1445 CURRAN Thomas M Biblical Quotations in the "Man of Law's Tale",
        "The Pardoner's Tale" and "The Knight's Tale" MA Boston Coll 1956
1446 DAFFRON Phillip V Chaucer's Pandarus: A Character Study
        MA Univ of Richmond 1967 72 p
1447 DAGLEY Elizabeth M Medieval Manners and Customs as Reflected in
        the Works of Geoffrey Chaucer and in the *Romount of the Rose*
        MA Univ of Oklahoma 1937
1448 DAVIDSON Richard B The Prologue to Chaucer's *Legend of Good Women*
        BA Amherst 1963
1449 DAVIS Charlotte I Social Backgrounds of Chaucer's Treatment of
        Marriage MA Univ of Maine 1947 102 p
1450 DAVIS D Bruce An Analysis of Historical Attitudes toward Chaucer's
        Ribaldry, through an Examination of the Handling of "The Miller's
        Tale" by Modernizers MA Univ of Maryland at College Park 1969
        108 p
1451 DAWSON Janice F The Characterization of Theseus in Chaucer
        MA Univ of North Carolina at Greensboro 1964
1452 DeFIORE Sr M Consiglia The Art of Chaucer's Narrative Technique in
        the *Canterbury Tales* MA Villanova Univ 1965
1453 DE LA VEGA SAUCEDO Mary C Chaucer's Debt to Graunson MA Univ of
        Texas at El Paso 1968 54 p
1454 DENHAM William E Chaucer's Translation of Boethius' *De Consolatione
        Philosophiae* MA Tulane Univ 1927
1455 DENIOUS Robert W Narrative Technique in Chaucer's *The Book of the
        Duchess, House of Fame, Parliament of Fowls* and *Prologue* of the
        Legend of Good Women BA Amherst 1959
1456 DERBY Diana L The Seven Ages of the Church in "The Man of Law's
        Tale" MA Columbia 1966
1457 DEVLIN Joseph D A Re-Evaluation of Chaucer's Wife of Bath According
        to the Scotistic Principle of Individuation MA Boston Coll 1964
1458 DEWEESE Jo J Ovidian Motifs in Chaucer's *Troilus and Criseyde*
        MA Univ of North Carolina at Chapel Hill 1956 73 p
1459 DEXTER Phyllis F The Concept of Fame from Chaucer's Boccacio and
        Spenser's *Faerie Queene* MA Univ of Tennessee 1949
1460 DIAMOND Arlyn Chaucer and the Cliches of Courtly Love MA Columbia
        1962 57 p

1461 DOBBINS Austin C Pope's Employment of Chaucer: A Study in Literary
        Apprenticeship MA Univ of North Carolina at Chapel Hill 1946
        181 p
1462 DRENNAN Robert E Chaucer's Ironic Vision: A Study of the Canterbury
        Pilgrims MA Trinity Coll 1965
1463 DUFFEY W A A Study of Determinism in Chaucer in the Light of
        Medievalism MA Boston Coll 1941
1464 DUGAN Janice Female Portraits in Chaucer's *Canterbury Tales*
        MA Univ of Texas at El Paso 1966 163 p
1465 DUNBAR Leila L Chaucer's Use of Proverbs MA Indiana Univ 1935
1466 DUPUIS Mary M A Comparison of the Syntactic Devices in Chaucer's
        Poetry and Prose MA Purdue Univ 1963 95 p
1467 DUSENBURY Julia T Duke Theseus in Chaucer's "Knight's Tale"
        MA Univ of Florida 1964
1468 DYER Mildred The Romance Element in Chaucer (in collaboration)
        MA Univ of Iowa 1934
1469 EASTERLY Hettie C The Costumes of Chaucer's Pilgrims MS Ft Hays
        St Teachers Coll 1952 145 p
1470 ELMORE E B Traditionality of Chaucer Note-Making MA Univ of North
        Carolina at Chapel Hill 1929
1471 EVANS Deanna G Antifeminism in Chaucer's *Canterbury Tales*
        MA Univ of Texas at Austin 1966 167 p
1472 FAIREY Francis G The Art of Chaucer's "Wife of Bath's Tale" MA Univ
        of Maryland at College Park 1967 79 p
1473 FANG Edith K Chaucer's Use of Setting in *Troilus and Criseyde*
        MA Windsor (Canada) 1967
1474 FELTS M P Chaucer's Devices for Securing Verisimiltude in the
        Canterbury Tales MA North Texas St Univ 1952
1475 FENLEY V M Structural and Verbal Repetitions in Chaucer MA Univ of
        North Carolina at Chapel Hill 1927
1476 FERRARIS Enrico The Language of Chaucer and Langland MA Ca Foscari
        (Italy) 1921
1477 FINCKE Lillian O Chaucer as a Lyric Poet MA Tulane Univ 1933
1478 FLATTERY George W A New Assessment of the Influence of the *Roman
        de la Rose* on Chaucer MA Univ of Oklahoma 1964
1479 FLETCHER Edward W Woman in English Literature of the Age of Chaucer
        MA Williams Coll 1930
1480 FINAN Karen B Chaucer's "Nun's Priest's Tale", The Mariner and the
        Critics and Whitman's Adamic Songs MA Pennsylvania St Univ 1964
1481 FISHER Richard E Chaucer's Troilus: A Celebration of Fleshly Love
        MA Univ of New Hampshire 1959 57 p
1482 FOLEY Sr Vincent F The Syntax of the Sentence in the *Canterbury
        Tales* MA St Louis Univ 1932 44 p
1483 FORD Cora M Chaucer's Narrative Techniques in *Troilus and Criseyde*
        MA Univ of Pittsburgh 1947
1484 FOWLER Carl M Demonstrations of Chaucerian Influence on Southern
        Language MA West Texas St Univ 1966 166 p
1485 FRICKE Hans W Treatments of Cressida from Chaucer to Shakespeare
        MA C W Post Coll 1963 91 p
1486 FULLER Bruce K Chaucer in the Eighteenth Century, 1700-1775
        MA George Washington Univ 1941 75 p
1487 FUQUA Lois Prolegomenon to a Study of Chaucer's Theory of Poetry
        MA Univ of Oregon 1941
1488 GARCIA Edward C A Study of Poetic Justice in the Tales of Chaucer
        MA Univ of California at Berkeley 1916
1489 GARDNER E D "The Man of Law's Tale" and Its Analogues MA North Texas
        St Univ 1953
1490 GARLAND John F Jr The Nature and Impact of the Parson's Religion in
        Chaucer's *Canterbury Tales* MA Arkansas St Coll 1964
1491 GARLAND Mirian M The Development of Realism in Chaucer MA Univ of

California at Berkeley 1919
1492 GEIBEL Mary G Food and Drink in Chaucer MA Univ of Florida 1965
1493 GEORGE M Elizabeth The "Sedulous Ape" and Chaucer: A Study of
  Chaucer's Theory and Practice of Rhetoric MA Boston Univ 1932
1494 GEROW B K Critical and Scholarly Interest in Chaucer (1775-1850)
  MA Univ of North Carolina at Chapel Hill 1945
1495 GETTY Agnes K Chaucer's Changing Conception of the Humble "Lover"
  MA Univ of Montana 1931 17 p
1496 GILCHRIST Marie E A Study of Some of Chaucer's Similes MA Smith
  Coll 1921
1497 GLOTFELTER Manone Anglo-French Nouns in Chaucer's "Knight's Tale";
  Their Etymology and Semasiology MA Univ of Oklahoma 1924
1498 GOLDEN E J Elements of Satire in Chaucer's Treatment of the Pardoner
  and the Friar in the Canterbury Tales MA Boston Coll 1928
1499 GOLDRUP Lawrence P The Traditional Courtly-Love Evil and Its
  Application in Chaucer's Troilus MA Brigham Young Univ 1965
1500 GOODMAN Mamie M An Analysis of the Anglo-Saxon and Continental
  Influences on Chaucer BA Univ of Oklahoma 1906
1501 GOSNELL Donald K The Development of Twentieth Century Criticisms
  of the Canterbury Tales MA Pacific Univ 1967 117 p
1502 GOWAN Samuel C Chaucer, Naturalism and the Troilus and Criseyde
  MA Boston Coll 1966
1503 GRANGER Mary B The Interpolated Lyric in Chaucer's Longer Poems
  MA Univ of Tennessee 1930
1504 GRANT Clyde M A Study of Chaucer's Vocabulary MA Univ of Oklahoma
  1951
1505 GRATZ Eugene C 'Tis Pity: A Study of Chaucer's Use of Analogues
  in the "Wyf of Bathe's Prologue" MA Toronto (Canada) 1966
1506 GREER Allen W Chaucer's Troilus and Criseyde: The Tragicomic
  Dilemma MA Univ of Florida 1965
1507 GREGORY Cornelie H Sir Thopas and the Critics MA George Washington
  Univ 1956 133 p
1508 GRIFFITH Richard R An Interpretation of Chaucer's Pandarus
  MA Univ of Kentucky 1948 96 p
1509 GRIGGS Virginia Chaucer's Knowledge of Dreams MA Texas Christian
  Univ 1940 75 p
1510 HAAVISTO Anne H Evaluation of Chaucerian Conception of Criseyde from
  the Interpretations of Critics MA Boston Univ 1940
1511 HADLOCK Annie F The Boethian Cycle in Chaucer's "Knight's Tale"
  MA Univ of New Hampshire 1967 67 p
1512 HAMPTON Sr Mary P Did Chaucer Write An Holy Medytaction?
  MA St Louis Univ 1942 68 p
1513 HANLEY Marguerite G Chaucer's Use of Dreams and Visions MA Tulane
  Univ 1927
1514 HARMAN Roland N An Introduction to the "Knight's Tale" of Chaucer
  MA Georgetown Univ 1934
1515 HARMON James O The Use of "Shall" and "Will" in the Canterbury Tales
  MA Univ of Maryland at College Park 1949 41 p
1516 HARRIS Margaret E Troilus and Criseyde, a Study of Chaucer's
  Narrative Art MA Univ of California at Berkeley 1912
1517 HART Katherine A Poetic Imagery in Chaucer's Love-Visions
  MA Syracuse Univ 1949 95 p
1518 HARVEY William R A Bibliography of Chaucer, 1954-1957 MA Florida
  St Univ 1959
1519 HASELDEN Shirley R Chaucer's Use of Setting MA Univ of Florida 1954
1520 HAZELTON V F A Study of Chaucer's House of Fame MA Rice 1962
1521 HEAD James L Chaucer's Portrayals of the Friar and the Summoner
  MA Texas Christian Univ 1966 159 p
1522 HEBERLEIN Gertrude K Chaucer's Man: An Examination of Their Positions
  in Society, Their Characters, Their Interests and Activities, Their

Dress; and a Discussion of Chaucer's Method of Characterization
MA Indiana Univ 1942

1523 HENDRICKSON Melanie R *Troilus and Criseyde* and *La Celestina*, an
Analysis of the Two Works in Terms of Their Three Major Protagonists
MA Univ of Iowa 1966

1524 HERLIHY J B A Study of the Complete Personality of Chaucer's Host
MA Boston Coll 1940

1525 HERNDL George C Lyrical Elements in the Poetry of Chaucer
MA Univ of North Carolina at Chapel Hill 1955   135 p

1526 HEUSTON E F Unity in the *Parlement of Foules* MA Boston Coll 1958

1527 HIRSH John C Chaucer's Holy Women: Some Theological Implications
in the "Man of Law's Tale" and the "Second Nun's Tale"
MA Lehigh Univ 1966

1528 HOLLINGSHEAD Margaret P Proverbs in Chaucer's *Troilus* MA Baylor Univ
1948   160 p

1529 HOLMES Frederick W Procedures in Realism from Chaucer to 1900
MA Boston Univ 1931

1530 HOOKER Elisabeth Chaucer's Use of the *Roman d'Eneas* MA Smith Coll
1936

1531 HORNEY W J Poetic Interpretation of Nature: Chaucer and Wordsworth
Compared MA Univ of North Carolina at Chapel Hill 1899

1532 HUFF Lloyd D Place Names in Chaucer MA Indiana Univ 1950

1533 HUTCHINGS Dimple E The Women in Chaucer's *Canterbury Tales*
MA Univ of Texas at Austin 1954   148 p

1534 HUTMACHER William F A Comparison of Chaucer and Gower's Use of Six
Episodes from Ovid MA Univ of Houston 1954   57 p

1535 HYDE Louise A Collection of Criticisms to the Rank of Chaucer
Among Classics MA Smith College 1910

1536 INMAN Sarah E Chaucer in America MA Univ of North Carolina at
Chapel Hill 1940

1537 IRESON Corinne C The Four English Versions of the Troilus and
Cressida Story MA Univ of Texas at Austin 1934   143 p

1538 ISTED Sharon A The Wife of Bath in Criticism BA Univ of British
Columbia (Canada) 1965

1539 IVEY Elizabeth D *Troilus and Criseyde* Expanded: A Prologue and
an Epilogue to Chaucer's Poem MA Univ of Tulsa 1961   89 p

1540 JACKSON Jocelyn W Treachery and Betrayal in *Troilus and Criseyde*
MA Georgetown Univ 1966

1541 JAUNZEMS J "Murthe and Doctryne" in the "Nonne's Preeste's Tale"
MA McMaster (Canada) 1965

1542 JOHNSON Carole Chaucer and Spain MA Univ of Texas at El Paso 1966
125 p

1543 JOHNSON Lillian C Birds and Bird Lore in Chaucer MA Univ of
Maryland at College Park 1950   78 p

1544 JONES Judith A Fourteenth Century London as Revealed in the Works
of Geoffrey Chaucer MA Howard Univ 1968   211 p

1545 JOYNER William Beatrice and the Mass in Book III of Chaucer's
Troilus and Criseyde MA Univ of New Hampshire 1968   61 p

1546 KANNEL Gregory J The Artistic Unity of Chaucer's "Pardoner's Tale"
MA Kent St Univ 1966

1547 KELLOGG Orrie B A Background for Presenting Chaucer MS Kansas St
Coll 1936

1548 KENNEALLY Patricia A The Minor Characters in Chaucer's *Troilus and
Criseyde*: A Study in Technique MA Boston Coll 1960

1549 KIMBROUGH Ray A Geoffrey Chaucer: "The Franklin's Tale"
MA Brown Univ 1966

1550 KING William H The Wife of Bath as a Medieval Socialite
MA Shippensburg St Coll 1965

1551 KIRK Mary C "The Knight's Tale": Conflicting Critical Opinions,
1900-1963 MA Univ of Texas at Austin 1965   168 p

1552 KLEIN Karen W An Interpretation of Chaucer's *Troilus and Criseyde* and Malory's *Morte Darthur* as Medieval "Tragedies" MA Columbia 1959 118 p

1553 KMEN Audrey J A Study of the Oaths in Chaucer's Poems MA Florida St Univ 1951

1554 KNOCK Madeline Chaucer's Awareness of Costume as Shown in the *Canterbury Tales* MS Kansas St Coll at Pittsburg 1948

1555 KNOWLTON Thomas A The Role of the Internuntius in Chaucer's *Troilus and Criseyde* and Boccaccio's *Il Filostrato* MA Boston Coll 1952

1556 KOHL James A Chaucer and *The Romaunt of the Rose* MA Univ of Delaware 1964 73 p

1557 KREBS Margaret R Medieval Rhetorical Devices in Chaucer's *Canterbury Tales* as Exemplified by the "Knight's Tale" and the "Manciple's Tale" MA Washington Univ at St Louis 1951 401 p

1558 LAKAS Robert R Source Studies of Chaucer's Short Poems: A Critical Bibliography MA St Louis Univ 1945 79 p

1559 LAMKIN Billy D Chaucer and Publilius Syrus MA Baylor Univ 1955 55 p

1560 LAMMOGLIA Anna M *Troilus and Criseyde:* A Structure of Analogies MA Georgetown Univ 1965 62 p

1561 LANDRY Cecile J Chaucer's Allegorical Evaluation of Courtly Love: *The Book of the Duchess, The House of Fame* and *The Parliament of Fowls* MA Univ of Southwestern Louisiana 1967 117 p

1562 LANGLEY Louise K Medieval Medicine in the *Canterbury Tales* MA Texas Christian Univ 1942 96 p

1563 LARMOUR Victoria A The Character of Criseyde: A Comparison of the Character of Creseyde in Chaucer's *Troilus and Creseyde* with that of Griseida in Boccacio's *Il Filostrato*, Supplemented by a Comparison with Briseida in Benoit's *Roman de Troie* MA Smith Coll 1912

1564 LASH Muriel A An Analysis of Geoffrey Chaucer's Criseyde as the Culmination of a Literary Love Tradition MA Univ of Rhode Island 1963

1565 LEININGER Lorie J Chaucer's Use of Proverbs in the *Troilus and Criseyde* MA Univ of Arizona 1961 63 p

1566 LENZ Barbara J Musical Instruments in the Works of Geoffrey Chaucer MA Univ of Florida 1964

1567 LEVY Lynn T Glossary to Chaucer's *Troilus and Criseyde* MA Western St Coll of Colorado 1954 60 p

1568 LEWIS Elsie H The Astrology in the Works of Chaucer MA Boston Univ 1934

1569 LEWIS Jack S Chaucer and Modern Dream Psychology MA Alberta (Canada) 1966

1570 LIGHTFOOT Omarie W Chaucer's Portraits of the Regular Clergy MA Univ of Texas at Austin 1951 106 p

1571 LINN Eva L The Originality of the *Canterbury Tales* MS Purdue Univ 1898

1572 LISTON Paul F Chaucer's Parody of Matins in "The Miller's Tale" MA Georgetown Univ 1969 28 p

1573 LOCKE Margaret S Chaucer's Use of Women and Children as Characters in His Stories MA Boston Univ 1934

1574 LORD Florence M Chaucer and Satire in the *Canterbury Tales* MA Tulane Univ 1935

1575 LOSEE Vernon O A Comparative Study of Some Aspects of John Gower's *Confessio Amantes* and Geoffrey Chaucer's *Canterbury Tales* MA Univ of Connecticut 1961

1576 LYON Joan B A Study of Chaucer's Criseyde as a Courtly-Love Heroine MA Univ of Texas at Austin 1963 77 p

1577 McCABE Sr Mary C The Christian Ideal in Chaucer's Women MA Boston Coll 1944

1578 McCAIN L H Linguistic History and Semantic Values of Representative
        Words in the "Prologue" of the *Canterbury Tales* MA Univ of North
        Carolina at Chapel Hill 1935
1579 McCAUSLAND Elizabeth The Knight of Curtesy and the Fair Lady of
        Faguell: A Study of the Date and Dialect of the Poem and Its
        Folklore Origins MA Smith Coll 1922
1580 MACEDO Celestino D Probable Sources of the Prioress' Tales MA Boston
        Coll 1958
1581 McELLIGOTT Thomas J The Problem of the Two Prologues to Chaucer's
        Legend of Good Women: A History of Critical Opinion MA Boston
        Univ 1949
1582 McHALE Sr Mary J Chaucer's Use of Humor in the *Canterbury Tales*
        MA St Louis Univ 1933 68 p
1583 McMAHON Sr Catherine B "The Nun's Priest's Tale": Trends in
        Criticism 1960 through 1964 MA Boston Coll 1966
1584 McMURRY Margaret A Comparison of Chaucer's Verse Forms and Metrical
        Practices with those of His French Contemporaries: Machant,
        Deschamps and Froissart MA Texas Technological Univ 1932 61 p
1585 McNELLY Cleo A Structural Analysis of *Troilus and Criseyde*
        MA Columbia 1966 83 p
1586 MANSON Eleanor G In the Honour of Love: Readings of M S Fairfax 16
        and M S Gg 4.27 Cambridge, Two Versions of the Prologue to
        The Legend of Good Women MA Western (Canada) 1965
1587 MARCHALONIS Shirley L Chaucer's Wife of Bath MA Univ of New
        Hampshire 1968 90 p
1588 MARTIEN Norman Chaucer's *Troilus and Criseyde*: Contrast and Use
        of Tradition MA Univ of California at Riverside 1962
1589 MARTIN Genevieve E Color and Color Symbolism in Chaucer
        MA St Louis Univ 1944 128 p
1590 MARTIN Lawrence H Themes of Causation in the Constance Stories
        of Trivet, Gower and Chaucer MA Univ of Massachusetts 1966
1591 MASSEY Isaac L The Friar as Portrayed by Chaucer and Langland
        MA Univ of Texas at Austin 1902
1592 MASSEY Thomas W Chaucer's Italian and Spanish Journeys and Their
        Possible Resultant Literary Influences on His Works MA Univ of
        Texas at Austin 1963 126 p
1593 MAYER Yvonne S Characterization as the Vehicle of Boethian Philosophy
        in *Troilus and Criseyde* MA Claremont Graduate School 1965
1594 MEDEIROS Sr Lucille Sincerity in Criseyde MA Boston Coll 1968
1595 MILLER Austellena M Democratic Trends in the Age of Chaucer
        MS Kansas St Coll at Pittsburg 1944
1596 MILLER E Matilda Chaucer's Portrayal of the Common Man in the Light
        of Medieval English Tradition MA Univ of Arizona 1938
1597 MILLER James I *Parliament of Fowls*: An Interpretation MA Univ of
        Oklahoma 1953
1598 MILLS Howard J Chaucer's Comic Techniques: Precursors of the
        Modern MA Stanford Univ 1965
1599 MILLS M S Imagery in Chaucer and Dryden: A Comparative Study of
        the Images of Chaucer's "Knight's Tale", "Wife of Bath's Tale"
        and "Nun's Priest's Tale" and in Dryden's Versions of Those
        Stories MA Univ of North Carolina at Chapel Hill 1937
1600 MINTON Mary M The Relations of Early Spanish Literature from
        Chaucer to Shakespeare MA Univ of Tennessee 1927
1601 MOLLEMA Peter C The Garden in Chaucer MA Univ of New Hampshire 1964
        128 p
1602 MOLONY Alice J The Canterbury Rogues MA Tulane Univ 1924
1603 MONTAGUE Gene B The Chaucerian Adaptations of Thomas Godfrey
        MA Univ of Texas at Austin 1952 127 p
1604 MOOMAW Sarah L Chaucer's Imagery in Relation to His Personality
        MA Oklahoma St Univ 1941 138 p

1605 MOORE Dorothy A Study of Color Words Used by Geoffrey Chaucer
         MA Univ of New Mexico 1943
1606 MOO-YOUNG Kathleen T "The Nun's Priest's Tale" as Allegory, *Aeneid*
         in *Paradise Lost* and Classical References in Thoreau's *Walden*
         MA Univ of Tennessee 1964
1607 MORRIS Francis J The Role of the Narrator in Chaucer's *Book of the
         Duchess* MA Columbia 1960 60 p
1608 MORRIS Muriel "The Miller's Tale" and the Miracle Plays: A Confusion
         of Values BA Univ of British Columbia (Canada) 1970
1609 MOSS D B Some Aspects of Chaucer's Literary Reputation in England
         from 1400 to 1600 MA Univ of North Carolina at Chapel Hill 1940
1610 MOYER Mabel P Analysis and Criticism of Ten Versions of Chaucer's
         Canterbury Tales as Adapted for Children MA Univ of Florida 1957
1611 MOYLE Cyprian Fifty Years of Critical Opinion on Chaucer's Prioress
         and Her Tale MA Barry Coll 1966
1612 MURRAY John F Renaissance Criticism of Chaucer MA St Louis Univ
         1941 86 p
1613 MURRAY Sr Mary P Rhetorical Amplification in Chaucer's "Knight's
         Tale" MA St Louis Univ 1937 53 p
1614 MYLOTT M I Literary Criticism in the English Works of Geoffrey Chaucer,
         John Wyclif and John Gower MA Boston Univ 1939
1615 NELSON Clifford C Some Nautical Terms from Chaucer's Period
         MA Columbia 1942
1616 NELSON Judy Chaucer's Use of the Forest in the *Canterbury Tales*
         BA Univ of British Columbia 1968
1617 NUNAN Joseph C The Interpretation of Chaucer's *Parlement of Foules*
         MA Emory Univ 1932 74 p
1618 O'BRIEN Janet E The Relation of Chaucer's Wife of Bath, Her Prologue
         and Tale to Their Sources MA Toronto (Canada) 1964
1619 O'BRIEN Patricia F Chaucerian Prosody: Background and Origins
         MA Alberta (Canada) 1966
1620 O'CONNOR Jane H The Relationship of the "Man of Law's Tale" to Its
         Narrator MA Boston Coll 1968
1621 O'HARA Charles M Chaucer's Attitude toward Religion, with Special
         Reference to His Portrayal of the Pardoner MA St Louis Univ 1929
         80 p
1622 O'HARA Setsuko A Survey of the Interpretation of Chaucer's *Troilus
         and Criseyde*: 1956 through 1965 MA Duke Univ 1966
1623 OLMERT Kenneth M "The Canon's Yeoman's Tale": An Interpretation
         MA Georgetown Univ 1965 47 p
1624 OSBORNE Don Chaucer's Gentle Criticism: A Study of *Troilus and
         Criseyde* MA Stanford Univ 1966
1625 OVERHOLSER Renee V Chaucer's Venus MA Hunter Coll 1969
1626 PACKMAN Ronald E The Adaptation of French Words to Middle English
         by Chaucer and Gower, Containing a Bibliography of John Gower
         MA Univ of Denver 1964
1627 PAPPAS Angline J A Comparison of Chaucer's and Shakespeare's
         Treatment of Troilus and Cressida MA Boston Univ 1950
1628 PARKER Margaret A A Study of Selected Head-Links and End-Links
         in the *Canterbury Tales* MA Duquesne Univ 1965
1629 PARKINSON Francis C Chaucer's *Troilus and Criseyde*: A Dramatic
         Interpretation of the "Double Truth" Theory MA Univ of British
         Columbia (Canada) 1962 101 p
1630 PARNELL Estelle F Chaucer's Treatment of Friendship and Family
         Relationships MA Texas Christian Univ 1950 124 p
1631 PESCHEL Constance C Chaucer's Poetry from a Sound Perspective:
         A Selective Study MA Univ of Colorado 1965
1632 PHILLIPS Mary J Twenty Modern Critics and Geoffrey Chaucer's
         Troilus MA Columbia 1951
1633 PHIPPS Thomas M The Influence of French on Chaucer MA Univ of

Pittsburgh 1944

1634 PIERSON Elizabeth A Chaucer's Women MA Indiana Univ 1942

1635 PLATT Annette E Pope's Modernization of Chaucer MA Univ of Texas
      at Austin 1957 141 p

1636 POPE Dorothy V Chaucer's Methods of Portraying Character
      MA Tulane Univ 1927

1637 POPYACH Joan Chaucer's Art and Aim in "The Summoner's Tale"
      MA Lehigh Univ 1966

1638 POWERS Adda Words of Measure from Chaucer and *Piers Plowman*:
      A Study in the Ways of Words MA Univ of Oklahoma 1921

1639 POWERS Austin Geoffrey Chaucer and John Masefield: A Comparison
      of Two Great Beloved Storytellers MA St Louis Univ 1932 80 p

1640 POWERS Edward E Venus and Chaucer's *Troilus and Criseyde* MA Univ
      of New Hampshire 1962 95 p

1641 PREDOEHL Louise P Chaucer's Use of Occupation MA Univ of Maryland
      at College Park 1967 78 p

1642 PUCKETT Wayne W An Analysis of the Comic Content of Chaucer's
      Canterbury Tales MA Oklahoma St Univ 1939 113 p

1643 PURCELL Sr Margaret J Rhetorical Amplification in Chaucer's
      "Monk's Tale", "Man of Law's Tale" and "Clerk's Tale" MA St Louis
      Univ 1932 66 p

1644 QUINN Polly S Chaucer's Use of Contemporary Events in the *Canterbury
      Tales* MA Univ of North Carolina at Chapel Hill 1946

1645 RAGOW Faith T Chaucer's Marriage Group: Fact or Fiction?
      MA Univ of Miami 1966

1646 RAMIREZ Elayne Fortune and Chaucer's Characters MA Emory Univ 1965

1647 RAMSEY Oliver F Dryden's Theory and Practice as an Adapter of Chaucer
      MA Texas Technological Univ 1931 43 p

1648 RAMSEY Roy V Tradition and Chaucer's Unfaithful Woman MA Univ of
      Oklahoma 1964 448 p

1649 REINER Anita G An Analysis of the Cosmic Elements in Chaucer's
      "Miller's Tale" MA Rice 1960

1650 RILEY Sr Mary L The Prioress and the Wife of Bath: Two Feminine
      Extremes in Chaucer's *Canterbury Tales* MA St Louis Univ 1929 107 p

1651 RIPPY Thelma L The Influence of Chaucer on Masefield, with Particular
      Reference to the Prologue to the *Canterbury Tales* and Part I of
      Reynard the Fox MA Univ of Texas at Austin 1926

1652 ROACH Joyce G Animals in the *Canterbury Tales* MA Texas Christian
      Univ 1965 83 p

1653 ROLLICK Gloria E The Concept and Treatment of Death in Chaucer
      MA Toronto (Canada) 1963

1654 RUPP Henry R Courtly Love and Marriage in Selected *Canterbury Tales*
      MA Univ of North Carolina at Chapel Hill 1955

1655 RUSSELL N Cyclic Imagery and Fortune's Wheel in Chaucer MA Univ of
      London (England) 1968

1656 SAMPLE Veda M A Study of the Multi-Faceted Character of the Host
      in *Canterbury Tales* MA Arkansas St Coll 1966

1657 SARGENT Edwin H "The Miller's Tale": The Cuckold and the Critics
      MA Lehigh Univ 1966

1658 SAYLORS Rita D Epic Characteristics in Chaucer's *Troilus and
      Criseyde* MA Univ of Houston 1969 92 p

1659 SCANLAN Sr Mary B The French Influence on Chaucer's Portrait of
      the Squire and upon the "Squire's Tale" MA Boston Coll 1954

1660 SCHAEFER Elizabeth M Three Studies in Poetic Method: "Frost at
      Midnight"; The Ballad "Little Musgrave and Lady Barnard"; and
      Troilus and Criseyde MA Pennsylvania St Univ 1965

1661 SCHWEIKERT Judith J An Analysis of the Character of Criseyde
      MA Univ of Rhode Island 1966 109 p

1662 SCRUGGS Virginia L The Women of Chaucer MA Tulane Univ 1924

1663 SEEFF Adele F Theme and Technique in the "Nun's Priest's Tale":

An Essay in Interpretation   MA Univ of Maryland at College Park
   1968   62 p
1664   SEIDELL Mary M   Chaucer and Marriage   MA Central Connecticut St Coll
   nd
1665   SEWALL Marjorie   Chaucer's Literary Criticism   MA Texas Christian
   Univ 1939   167 p
1666   SEYMOUR Evan S   A Survey of One Hundred Representative *Troilus and
   Criseyde* Studies   MA Univ of Delaware 1966   73 p
1667   SHAKER David   Chaucer: "The Miller's Tale"; Wordsworth: "The World
   is too Much With Us"; and Melville: *Redburn*   MA Pennsylvania
   St Univ 1965
1668   SHAPIRO Michael E   The Durability of Chaucer's Laughter: A Theory
   and an Analysis   MA Long Island Univ 1968   97 p
1669   SHAW Harry B   Similarities between "The Clerk's Tale" and The Book
   of Job   MA Illinois St Univ 1965
1670   SHEA Virginia   Chaucer's Comic Vision   MA Temple Univ 1966   64 p
1671   SHIELDS Martha F   The Pardoner: No Final Verdict   MS Kansas St Univ
   1965
1672   SHIPLEY Harriet   *House of Fame*: Indications of Early Composition
   MA Washington Univ at St Louis 1912   179 p
1673   SILVIA Daniel S Jr   The Structure and Motifs of the Tales in Chaucer's
   Marriage Group   MA Univ of North Carolina at Chapel Hill 1958   91 p
1674   SKELLY Laurence   Biblical Quotations in "The Parson's Tale"   MA Boston
   Coll 1959
1675   SKELTON Jean W   The Humor of Chaucer   MA Univ of British Columbia
   (Canada) 1936
1676   SMITH Billie G   Characters and Conventions in "The Franklin's Tale"
   MA Oklahoma St Univ 1969   27 p
1677   SNYDER Orpha B   Chaucer as Revealed by His Imagery   MA Univ of Arizona
   1938
1678   SOMERVILLE Walter G Jr   The Genitive Case of Nouns in Chaucer
   MA Univ of North Carolina at Chapel Hill 1949
1679   SOMMERVILLE Marie   Predestination in Chaucer's Tales   MA Univ of
   New Mexico 1952
1680   SORNBORGER Nancy W   Nature in the Works of Chaucer   MA Boston Univ 1930
1681   SPRADO Evelyn L   A Bibliography of Chaucer, 1924-1934   MA Columbia 1935
1682   STATHAM Denis P   Chaucer and the "Ordre Destynal"   MA Univ of Oklahoma
   1946
1683   STEIN Dona L   The Argument of Love: *Troilus and Criseyde*   MA Clark
   Univ 1969
1684   STEIN Richard L   The Art of the Conventional in Chaucer's "Clerk's
   Tale"   BA Amherst 1965
1685   STEINBERG Clarence   The Classical Development of the Proserpina
   Myth and Its Use in Chaucer   MA Univ of Connecticut 1957
1686   STELLINI Saviour J   Chaucer's Structural and Thematic Use of Courtly
   Love   MA Alberta (Canada) 1965
1687   STIFLER Martha H   Astrology and Astronomy in Chaucer's "Franklin's
   Tale"   MA Columbia 1943
1688   STOBIE Harold R   Prolegomenon to the Study of Rhetoric in Chaucer
   MA Univ of Oregon 1942
1689   STOKES Thomas R   Chaucer's Use of Satire in the *Canterbury Tales*
   MA St Louis Univ 1932   99 p
1690   STOUT Jack H   Levels of Style in Chaucer's *Troilus and Criseyde*
   MA Univ of Oklahoma 1965
1691   STRASSER William C   Child Characters and Allusions to Children and
   Youth in Chaucer   MA Univ of Maryland at College Park 1959   111 p
1692   STRIPLING Edna H   The Treatment of Women in the Poetry of Chaucer
   MA Univ of Maryland at College Park 1960   100 p
1693   SULLIVAN John J   Chaucer's Method of Characterizing Narrator by
   Tale in "Wife of Bath's Tale", "The Pardoner's Tale" and "The Nun's

Priest's Tale"   MA Boston Coll 1949
1694   SULLIVAN R W   Geoffrey Chaucer, the Man and His Works   MA Boston
      Coll 1929
1695   SUTTON Carl   Chaucer's Color Usage   MA Texas Christian Univ 1940   83 p
1696   TAYLOR Letha E   A Study in Syntax Based on Chaucer's "Mannes Tale
      of Lawe"   MA Univ of Oklahoma 1933
1697   TAYLOR M E   A Comparison of Chaucer's and Shakespeare's Treatments
      of the Troilus-Cressida Story   MA North Texas St Univ 1951
1698   TOROSSIAN Agnes S   The *Canterbury Tales*: A Study of Endings
      MA Univ· of Maryland at College Park 1968   76 p
1699   TOWNSEND Guibor   Characterization in Chaucer's *Canterbury Tales*
      MA St Louis Univ 1942   282 p
1700   TOWNSEND Marion J   Experience and Authority in Selected *Canterbury
      Tales*   MA Univ of North Carolina at Chapel Hill 1959
1701   TUCKER Ann A   Chaucer's Use of Musical References in *Troilus and
      Criseyde*   MA Boston Coll 1962
1702   VANCE Nancy J   Chaucer's Musical Lore   MA Texas Christian Univ 1942
      69 p
1703   VANDERBURG Naoma   Religious People in Chaucer's *Canterbury Tales*
      MA Texas Arts and Industries Univ 1958
1704   VAN KLUYVE Robert A   Astrological Healing and Death in Chaucer
      MA Univ of Rhode Island 1958
1705   VAN LIERE Carma P   Chaucer's Clerks   MA Indiana Univ 1950
1706   VAUGHAN Sr Mary T   Chaucer's Knowledge of Alchemy as Shown in
      "The Chanouns Yemannes Tale"   MA Univ of California at Berkeley 1923
1707   VAUGHAN Sadie O   A Literary History of the Wife of Bath   MA Univ of
      Texas at Austin 1948   172 p
1708   VESTERMAN William R   Alisoun and Molly: The Earthy Female in Chaucer
      and Joyce   BA Amherst Coll 1964
1709   VON KREISLER Nicolai A   *Parlement of Foules*: A Survey of Scholarship
      and a Re-Evaluation   MA Univ of Texas at Austin 1966   219 p
1710   VUYANOVICK Lois J   Chaucer's Use of Classical Themes and Materials
      in the *Canterbury Tales*   MA Boston Univ 1950
1711   WADE Margaret W   The Aesthetic Problem of Distance in Chaucer's
      "Merchant's Tale"   MA Oklahoma St Univ 1969   25 p
1712   WARD Helen S   Stress of Romance Words in Chaucer's Prologue
      to the "Knight's Tale"   MA Univ of Louisville 1909
1713   WARNOCK John P   A Reading of Chaucer's *Troilus and Criseyde*
      BA Amherst 1963
1714   WATERHOUSE Ruth M   Chaucer and the New Spirit of the Fourteenth
      Century   MA Boston Univ 1932
1715   WEATHERBEE George B Jr   Contemporary Treatment of Fourteenth Century
      English Life: A Comparative Study of the Attitudes and Methods
      of Robert Mannyng, Langland and Chaucer   MA Univ of Maine 1938   118
1716   WEBB Lois J   Chaucer's References to His Own Times   MA Univ of Texas
      at El Paso 1967   78 p
1717   WEISS Alexander   The Kiss in Chaucer   MA Univ of Maryland at
      College Park 1967   111 p
1718   WEYER Irene I   Chaucer's Use of Color   MA Indiana Univ 1942
1719   WHEAT Mary A   The Influence of Boethius on Chaucer and the English
      Renaissance   MA Univ of Iowa 1933
1720   WHEELER Barclay M   Chaucer's Use of the Exemplum in the *Canterbury
      Tales*   MA Univ of Oklahoma 1953
1721   WHITE Maura C   Augustinian Thought in Chaucer's *Troilus and Criseyde*
      MA Boston Coll 1964
1722   WHITMORE Nyeulah   Medieval Preaching: *Canterbury Tales*   MA Univ of
      Iowa 1934
1723   WILEY E W   Realism and Satire in Chaucer's Miller Robbins of the "Gener
      Prologue"   MA Oklahoma St Univ 1917
1724   WILLARD Daniel D   A Metrical Comparison of the *Romaunt of the Rose*

with Some of Chaucer's Early Known Works MA Univ of Maryland at
        College Park 1940   52 p
1725 WILLGING Herbert M The Romance Element in Chaucer (in collaboration)
        MA Univ of Iowa 1934
1726 WILSON Julia Chaucer's Knowledge and Use of the Classical Story of
        Troy MA Emory Univ 1935   73 p
1727 WILSON M M The Women Characters in Chaucer's Works MA Boston Univ
        1940
1728 WILSON Marie S Dress in the Poetry of Geoffrey Chaucer MA Indiana
        Univ 1942
1729 WINSLOW Genevieve G Chaucer's Use of Metaphor in *Troilus and Criseyde*
        MA Univ of Pittsburgh 1952
1730 WISEMAN Etta W Chaucer's *Canterbury Tales* as a Reflection of the
        Metamorphosis of the Medieval Knight MA C W Post Coll nd 66 p
1731 WOOD June P The Tournament in the "Knight's Tale": A Contemporary
        Scene MA Univ of Houston 1958   61 p
1732 WORTLEY Marilyn P Deception and Delusion: A Study of Theme and
        Characterization in *Troilus and Criseyde* MA Manitoba (Canada) 1966
1733 WYATT George R A Comparison of the Uses of Astrology in the Works
        of John Gower and Geoffrey Chaucer MA Univ of Richmond 1952 90 p
See also 431, 2906, 4725, 5932, 6328, 6568, 6699, 6739, 6790, 6967

LORD CHESTERFIELD

1734 ASHFORD Guy W A Survey of the Educational Letters of Lord Chesterfield
        to His Son and Godson MA Univ of Texas at Austin 1943   164 p
1735 CLARK Grace Lord Chesterfield's Literary Criticism MA Univ of
        Oklahoma 1933
1736 MORRIS R J The Character of Lord Chesterfield as Drawn from His Letters
        MA Boston Coll 1941
1737 NOVAK Pauline A Lord Chesterfield's Later Letters, 1754-1772
        MA John Carroll Univ 1966
1738 SMITH Grace B Light Thrown upon Social and Political Conditions in
        England by Lord Chesterfield's Letters to His Son MA Univ of Iowa 1933
1739 SULLIVAN Maurice T Chesterfield: A Personality and Letter Writer of
        the Eighteenth Century MA Boston Univ 1943
1740 THOMPSON Lucille Z Lord Chesterfield and Women in the Eighteenth Century
        MA Univ of Kentucky 1945
1741 WOODTKE Frederick J The Changes in Lord Chesterfield's Ideas as Reflected
        by His Letters to His Son and to His Godson MA Boston Coll 1949

GILBERT KEITH CHESTERTON

1742 BAWCOM Burney E G K Chesterton's Philosophy as a Solution for the
        Problems of His Time MS Kansas St Coll at Pittsburg 1941
1743 BEHLEN Mother Winifred Chestertonian Temperance MA Boston Univ 1948
1744 BENARD C Gardner The Paradoxes of Gilbert Keith Chesterton
        MA Boston Coll 1945
1745 CAHALANE Charles W Gilbert Keith Chesterton: The Laughing Crusader
        MA Boston Coll 1948
1746 CALLAN Alice C Chesterton's Tendency towards Catholicism as Seen
        in His Poetry MA Boston Coll 1939
1747 CASEY Mary E G K Chesterton's Views on an Ideal Society MA Boston
        Univ 1945
1748 CASTELFRANCHI Sara G K Chesterton MA Ca Foscari (Italy) 1929
1749 COLLINS James A The Novel of Ideas: A Study of Gilbert K Chesterton's
        Prose Fiction Technique MA Columbia 1955
1750 COTTER D J Prose Works of G K Chesterton: His Philosophy MA Boston

Coll 1934
1751 DAKIN Sr M A Criticisms from the Works of G K Chesterton MA Boston
       Coll 1950
1752 DRUMMOND Edward J The Literary Element as a Measure of the Effective-
       ness of the Catholic Apologetic Essay as Seen from the Writings
       of England, Brownson and Chesterton MA St Louis Univ 1930 63 p
1753 FLANAGAN Sr Mary M An Anthology: Chesterton's Ideas on Education
       MA Boston Coll 1953
1754 FLETCHER Noreen M G K Chesterton: The Quality of Imagination and
       Imagery in Some of His Fiction BA Univ of British Columbia (Canada)
       1964
1755 HICKS Olan L Gilbert Keith Chesterton as an Essayist MA Univ of
       Texas at Austin 1935
1756 HOLLOWAY Jean M The Paradox of Chesterton MA Texas Christian Univ
       1948 83 p
1757 KILEY Sr Marguerite L Satiric Verse in G K Chesterton's Weekly
       MA Boston Coll 1949
1758 LEONARD Vivien R Gilbert Chesterton as a Literary Critic
       MA Columbia 1953 165 p
1759 LORDAN Sr Mary A G K Chesterton's Code in Journalism MA Boston
       Coll 1949
1760 McCARTHY Sr M Justina The Early Development of Chesterton's
       Religious Philosophy MS Kansas St Coll at Pittsburg 1945
1761 McCORD Bertha The Logical as Compared with the Conventional
       Grammatical Analysis of the Structure of the Sentence with
       Special Reference to the Language of Gilbert K Chesterton
       MA Univ of Iowa 1931
1762 McGUIRE Mother Dorothy The Wonderland of G K Chesterton
       MA Boston Coll 1950
1763 MENDELSON Ellen B G K Chesterton: Limited Wonder and Boundless
       Vision MA Columbia 1964 99 p
1764 MERCIER Sr Rose-Imelda The Marian Theme in Chesterton's Poems
       MA Rivier Coll 1959
1765 O'HALLORAN F M Chesterton and Medievalism MA Boston Coll 1935
1766 ROSS Margaret I The Thought of G K Chesterton MA Toronto (Canada)
       1964
1767 TAYLOR Irene O G K Chesterton as a Critic MA Univ of Arizona
       pre-1933
1768 VESSELS Br William G K Chesterton: Critic of Victorian Literature
       MA St Mary's at San Antonio 1942 71 p
See also 4655, 7380

JOHN CLARE

1769 COLTON Ruth M A Study of the Poetry of John Clare MA Columbia 1936
1770 ERRERA Lea John Clare the Northamptonshire Peasant Poet MA Ca Foscari
       (Italy) 1950
1771 HOWARD William J John Clare and the Poetic Process MA Univ of
       British Columbia (Canada) 1969 114 p
1772 STENGEL Joan M Childhood and Nature in the Poetry of John Clare
       MA Univ of Maryland at College Park 1969 74 p
1773 WARNER Paul S John Clare: Poet of Nature MA Syracuse Univ 1940 187

ARTHUR HUGH CLOUGH

1774 BOWERS Lucy The Satiric Poetry of Arthur Hugh Clough MA Duke Univ 196
1775 GAMBI Bianca M Arthur Clough MA Ca Foscari (Italy) 1949
1776 HOLCOMBE Jean L The Growth of Religious Thought in Arthur Hugh Clough
       MA Columbia 1936
1777 JOHARI G P The Intellectual Life of A H Clough, with Particular

Reference to His Poetry B Litt Oxford Univ (England) nd
1778 KELLEY Sr R Loretta Qualities of the Metaphysical in the Lyrics
      and Sonnets of Arthur Hugh Clough MA Boston Coll 1965
1779 McEWEN Mary J Arthur Hugh Clough: *Amours De Voyage* MA Texas Tech-
      nological Univ 1967 47 p
1780 MUSGRAVE Marianne E The Biographical Sources of Realism in the Poetry
      of Arthur H Clough MA Howard Univ 1946
1781 REID M R Arthur Hugh Clough and Matthew Arnold as Moral Idealists
      BA Univ of British Columbia (Canada) 1949
1782 RODGERS Lillian D Arthur Hugh Clough: Disciple of Action
      MA Univ of Maryland at College Park 1969 56 p
1783 SAMS Vera E Arthur Hugh Clough: A Study of His Thought MA Univ
      of Texas at Austin 1927
1784 WELLS Margo C The Dialectical Principle in the Poetry of
      Arthur Hugh Clough MA Univ of British Columbia (Canada) 1963
See also 96, 134

                        SAMUEL TAYLOR COLERIDGE

1785 ALDRICH James S Coleridge's "Wedding Guest" and "Fallen Optimism"
      MA Univ of New Hampshire 1957 80 p
1786 ALTHAUS Phoeba Coleridge in Emerson MA Univ of Louisville 1962
1787 AUDLIN David J Coleridge and the Gothic Tradition MA Syracuse Univ
      1952 78 p
1788 BAIRD Douglas G The Influence of German Romanticism on
      Samuel Taylor Coleridge MA C W Post Coll 1964 109 p
1789 BALDWIN Grace D Coleridge's Theory of Art: A Study of Its Sources
      and Effects MA Univ of Montana 1926 40 p
1790 BARBER Marion D The Projected Works of Samuel Taylor Coleridge
      MA Univ of Florida 1951
1791 BARNAUD E E The Supernatural in the Poetry of Samuel Taylor Coleridge
      MA Boston Univ 1942
1792 BARRY Gerald M Coleridge as Critic of Shakespearean Drama MA Boston
      Coll 1946
1793 BEAVER Doris D The Oral Interpretation of Coleridge's *Christabel*
      MA Univ of Oklahoma 1952
1794 BRANNAN Robert L The Political Development of Samuel Taylor Coleridge
      MA Univ of Texas at Austin 1952 148 p
1795 BRIM Patricia C Archetypes of Folklore and Superstition in
      Coleridge's Poetry MA American Univ 1964
1796 BROWN Ann W A Psychological Study of Samuel Taylor Coleridge
      MA Texas Technological Univ 1963 102 p
1797 BUTLER Agnes F A Defense of Coleridge MA Univ of Louisville 1962
1798 CARAGONNE Jean M Coleridge's "Kubla Khan": An Archetypal Interpre-
      tation MA Univ of Houston 1966 128 p
1799 CARMEAN Hillis The Methods of Poe and Coleridge in Attaining a
      Weird, Uncanny Effect MA Stetson Univ 1926
1800 CARR B C Coleridge and Kant: Significant Parallels and Contrasts
      in Ethical and Religious Ideas MA North Texas St Univ 1969
1801 CARTER Zelma T The Folk Element in the Poetry of Coleridge, Keats
      and Tennyson MA Univ of Tulsa 1939
1802 COLLOS Alana Coleridge and the Wandering Jew's Burden of Guilt
      MA Columbia 1966 79 p
1803 COWEN Margaret E The Influence of the Mediaeval Ballad upon
      Coleridge and Wordsworth MA Washington Univ at St Louis 1926 131 p
1804 CRAIN Warren B Jr The Influence of Coleridge's Theory of the
      Imagination on Selected Writings of Leigh Hunt MA Univ of
      Mississippi 1968
1805 CRUTCHER Mary L The Spiritual and Supernatural Elements in Selected
      Works of Samuel Taylor Coleridge M Ed Henderson St Coll nd

1806 CUBINE M V The Religious History of Samuel Taylor Coleridge to 1807
        MA Univ of North Carolina at Chapel Hill 1944
1807 DATER Walton F Coleridge and the Collective Unconscious MA Syracuse
        Univ 1963 103 p
1808 DAVIS S I The Doctrine of Necessity in the Early Philosophical
        Periods of Coleridge and Shelley MA Univ of North Carolina at
        Chapel Hill 1945
1809 DELAFIELD Mary L Twentieth Century Approaches to Coleridge's
        Rime of the Ancient Mariner MA Columbia 1955 65 p
1810 DRAMIN Edward I Horror in Coleridge's Poetry MA Columbia 1965 289 p
1811 EGE Rhea E Relationship of Lessing and Coleridge MA Univ of
        Pittsburgh 1920
1812 ENGLE John D Jr A Bibliography of the Writings and Ana of
        Samuel Taylor Coleridge from January 1, 1945 to January 1, 1950
        MA Univ of Kentucky 1953
1813 FALCON Olga J A Time to Sow and a Time to Weed: The Theme of
        Sympathy in Coleridge's Shakespearean Criticism MA Boston Coll
        1969
1814 FITZGERALD Louise Y Coleridge's Introduction into America
        MA Univ of North Carolina at Chapel Hill 1950 83 p
1815 FOWLER James C Coleridge: The Doctrine of Original Sin MA Univ of
        Oklahoma 1949
1816 FULMER Oliver B Criticism of *The Rime of the Ancient Mariner*,
        1927-1957 MA Univ of North Carolina at Chapel Hill 1958 152 p
1817 GARRATT William The Pathetic Fallacy in Coleridge and Ruskin
        MA Univ of Florida 1955
1818 GOOD James M The Huntington *Coleridge MS HM 8195* MA Western
        (Canada) 1965
1819 GORDON Lorenne M *The Rime of the Ancient Mariner:* A Modern
        Interpretation BA Univ of British Columbia (Canada) 1962
1820 GOTTSCHALK Karl D The Post-Enlightenment Pattern of Conversion:
        Its Manifestations in the Art and Life of Samuel Taylor Coleridge
        MA Univ of Mississippi 1965 142 p
1821 GRAEFFE Lotte B A Sample Comparison of Coleridge and Carlyle as
        Translators of Schiller's *Wallenstein* MA Univ of Florida 1956
1822 GRIFFIN Bonnie C Evidences of Coleridge's Influence upon the
        Development of Emerson's Religious Ideas and upon His Main Theories
        of Nature, Soul, Mind and Criticism MA Auburn Univ 1939
1823 HALDEMAN Linda W Modern Criticism on the Moral in *The Rime of the
        Ancient Mariner* MA Pennsylvania St Univ 1965
1824 HARDY Barbara G Coleridge's Theory of Communication MA Univ of
        London (England) 1949
1825 HARDY Gene B Jr Religious Musings: A Commentary MA Univ of
        Oklahoma 1949
1826 HARRIS John D The Method of Coleridge's Literary Criticism
        MA Univ of British Columbia (Canada) 1966 139 p
1827 HATSCHER Mary H The Poetic Theory of Samuel Taylor Coleridge
        MA Washington Univ at St Louis 1949
1828 HEALY Margaret L The Development of Coleridge's Philosophy and
        Its Expression in *Dejection: An Ode* MA Univ of North Carolina
        at Chapel Hill 1949 108 p
1829 HENNIGER Isabel Some Aspects of Coleridge's Poetic Theory MA McGill
        (Canada) 1965
1830 HIBBS Eleanore C The Level Stream: The Consistency of Coleridge's
        Criticism MA Univ of Pittsburgh 1960
1831 HICKS Phoebe M The Religion of Samuel Taylor Coleridge as Revealed
        in His Work MA Univ of Tulsa 1947
1832 HOODLEY Frank The Publication of Southey's *Wat Tyler* and Coleridge's
        Defense of Southey MA Univ of Maryland at College Park 1938 145 p
1833 HORN Robert L II Samuel Taylor Coleridge: Philosophic Principles

and Poetic Practice   MA Columbia 1964   78 p

1834   HOWES Raymond F   Coleridge the Talker   MA Univ of Pittsburgh 1926

1835   HUDSON G E   A Discussion of the Fines of Literature as Exemplified in Wordsworth, Coleridge and Blake   MA Boston Coll 1941

1836   HUDSON Lola T   Coleridge's Theory of the Imagination   MS Kansas St Coll at Pittsburg 1946

1837   HURST Shelly A   The Role of Emotion in Coleridge's Religious Thought   MA North Texas St Univ 1965

1838   ITALIA Paul G   The Bard and the Problem of Evil in Coleridge's Three Major Poems   MA Columbia 1965   114 p

1839   JACKSON Clydean   The Mysticism of Coleridge   M Ed Henderson St Coll nd

1840   JACOBS Ann   A Study of Coleridge's *Zapolya:* Its Meaning and Use of Symbolism   BA Univ of British Columbia (Canada) 1970

1841   JACOBS Elizabeth M   The Contemporary Criticism of Coleridge's Poetry 1796-1834   MA Univ of Pittsburgh 1935

1842   JANSON-LaPALME Sr Marie B   The Relevance of Coleridge's Poetic Theory to His Own Poetry   MA Boston Coll 1962

1843   JONES Ruth L   *Christabel* and the Critics: A Review of Interpretations   MA Univ of Maryland at College Park 1969   82 p

1844   KAHN Shalom J   Science in the Poetry of Samuel Taylor Coleridge   MA Columbia 1942

1845   KEEP Rosalind A   Coleridge's Contribution to Literary Criticism   MA Univ of California at Berkeley 1911

1846   KING John P   Samuel Taylor Coleridge's Pantisocracy Dream of an American Utopia   MA Univ of New Hampshire 1967   67 p

1847   KING R F   Coleridge's Theory of Poetry   BA Univ of British Columbia (Canada) 1948

1848   KISS Stephen H   The Criticism of Samuel Taylor Coleridge   BA Amherst 1964

1849   KNIGHT Vicki L   The Function of Folk Elements in Coleridge's *Christabel*   MA Texas Technological Univ 1969   78 p

1850   LEHMANN Ruth P   The Organic Theory in Coleridge's General and Shakespearean Criticism   MA Auburn Univ 1958

1851   LEMISH Grace J   Coleridge's Use of Visual Imagery in the Conversation Poems   MA Rice 1959

1852   LIVINGSTON Olive E   The Critical Principles of I A Richards that Stem from Samuel Taylor Coleridge   MA Bucknell Univ 1953

1853   McGAVRAN James H Jr   A Study of the Marginal Gloss of Coleridge's *Rime of the Ancient Mariner*   MA Columbia 1965   113 p

1854   McGHEE Richard D   The Function of the Journeying Imagination in Coleridge's Conversation Poems   MA Univ of Oklahoma 1964

1855   McLEAN Sr Mary S   "Swell and Glitter": Coleridge's Principles of Poetic Diction   MA Coll of the Holy Names at Oakland 1970

1856   MADEWELL V D   Symbolism in Coleridge's Minor Poetry   MA North Texas St Univ 1968

1857   MALNIG Romeo L   Samuel Taylor Coleridge and His Criticism of Italian Life and Literature   MA Columbia 1940

1858   MILES Robert W Jr   A Bibliography of the Writings and Ana of Samuel Taylor Coleridge from January 1, 1930 to December 31, 1934   MA Univ of Kentucky 1948   138 p

1859   MORLAND Margaret W   Coleridge's Relationship to Christianity   MA Univ of North Carolina at Chapel Hill 1951   160 p

1860   MOTTE Sr Mary   Coleridge as Existentialist: The Relation of Theme in *Christabel* and "Kubla Khan" to the Mystery of the Present Moment   MA Boston Coll 1964

1861   MURPHY Carolyn M   Terror in the Poetry of Coleridge   MA Eastern Kentucky Univ 1969   85 p

1862   NATH Barbara   "Strange Power of Speech": The Development of the Narrative Guise in the Poetry of Samuel Taylor Coleridge   MA Columbia 1967   142 p

1863 NEWBURN Barbara R Samuel Taylor Coleridge's Translation of
        Schiller's *Wallenstein* MA Univ of Massachusetts 1966
1864 NORTH John S Anticipations of "the Ancient Mariner" in the Early
        Poetry of S T Coleridge MA Univ of British Columbia (Canada) 1965
1865 O'BRIEN Frances M Imagery and the Pattern in *The Rime of the
        Ancient Mariner* MA Toronto (Canada) 1964
1866 O'BRIEN P E The Philosophy of S T Coleridge MA Boston Coll 1933
1867 OLDENBURG Grace M Coleridge and Poe MA Univ of Maryland at
        College Park 1933 71 p
1868 OLNEY Warren IV Fusion and Confusion: The Poetry and Poetics of
        Samuel Taylor Coleridge BA Amherst 1959
1869 OLSON Kristin L Coleridge on the Understanding MA Emory Univ 1966
1870 O'NEIL Nancy J "The Idea, with the Image": A Study of Nature
        in the Poetry of Coleridge MA Queen's (Canada) 1964
1871 OSTRO Lynne H A Critical Analysis of Coleridge's *Remorse*
        MA Columbia 1965 77 p
1872 PERRY Carole D A Study of Selected Imagery and Certain Figures
        of Speech in the Poetry of Samuel Taylor Coleridge MA Eastern
        Tennessee St Univ 1965
1873 PRATT Arline V T S Eliot and the Coleridgean Political Tradition
        MA Columbia 1941
1874 PRIESTLEY Celia S Organic Form in the Writings of Samuel Taylor
        Coleridge MA Leeds Univ (England) 1966
1875 REEVES Floyd Coleridge's Use of the Physical Function of the Eye
        in His Philosophy of Creativity MA Univ of Oklahoma 1962
1876 ROSENBAUM Jeanie W Kantian Aesthetics in the Prose and Poetry
        of Coleridge MA Midwestern Univ 1966 79 p
1877 ROUSH George C Coleridge's Poetry: The One Life BA Amherst 1968
1878 SANSON B A Coleridge's Concept of the Symbol BA Univ of British
        Columbia (Canada) 1959
1879 SATTERFIELD Ellen S Coleridge as Seen by His Contemporaries
        MA Tulane Univ 1931
1880 SCHLUETER H V *The Rime of the Ancient Mariner*: Critical Commentary,
        1798-1968 MA North Texas St Univ 1969
1881 SEIDEN Leo B Jr Coleridge's Readings in English Rational and Platonic
        Theology of the Seventeenth Century MA Univ of Florida 1951
1882 SHIELDS Ruth A Coleridge and the Supernatural MA Tulane Univ 1930
1883 SHOOK Barbara J Interpretations of *Christabel* MA Columbia 1952 66 p
1884 SINGER Siegfried W Coleridge's Translations of German Drama
        MA Univ of Maine 1966 106 p
1885 SPALTEHOLZ Hans G The Sacramental Vision of Samuel Taylor Coleridge
        in Three of His Minor Poems MA Columbia 1961 155 p
1886 SPURGEON Gertrude Samuel Taylor Coleridge's *Christabel*: The Psycho-
        dynamics of Its Antecedents and Analogues MA Beloit Coll 1965
1887 STAVROS George The Image and Idea of Hope in the Poetry of
        Coleridge MA Columbia 1964 79 p
1888 STEIN R Scientific Terminology and Analogy in Coleridge's Poetic
        Theory and Practice B Litt Oxford Univ (England) 1946
1889 SURETTE Philip L Wordsworth and Coleridge: Two Poetic Modes
        MA Toronto (Canada) 1963
1890 THOMAS Frankie E The Supernatural in Blake and in Coleridge
        MA Univ of Tennessee 1930
1891 TOMEI Margherita The Feeling of Nature in Wordsworth and Coleridge
        MA Ca Foscari (Italy) 1941
1892 TURNER Ruth G Damaged Archangel: A Study of the Character of
        Coleridge as Revealed in His Letters MA Howard Univ 1949
1893 UPDIKE Marie A A Study of Four Romantic Dramas: Wordsworth's
        Borderers, Coleridge's *Remorse*, Shelley's *The Cenci* and Keats'
        Otho the Great MA Washington Univ at St Louis 1919 48 p
1894 VALENTI Peter L A Survey of the Interpretive Criticism of

Coleridge's *Christabel*   MA East Carolina Univ 1969

1895 VAN HAITSMA Glenn A   Coleridge, the Christian Politician   MA Syracuse
      Univ 1950   89 p
1896 WALKER Kenneth E   Stevens' and Coleridge's Concern with the Imagination
      MA Wake Forest Coll 1965
1897 WHITE M E   Influence of Coleridge on Poe   MA New York St Coll for
      Teachers 1940
1898 WHITE Marion M   A Study of Coleridge's Drama *Remorse* in Relation to
      the Early Nineteenth Century English Theatre   MA Univ of Arizona
      pre-1933
1899 WHITE-HURST Bernard M   The Element of Experience in the
      Poetry of Samuel Taylor Coleridge   MA Univ of Richmond 1937   161 p
1900 WILDE Heidrun E   Coleridge's Criticism and Coleridge's Plays: Critical
      Principles and Playwriting   MA Columbia 1966   75 p
1901 WILSON Curtis W   *The Rime of the Ancient Mariner*   MA Texas Christian
      Univ 1966
1902 WRIGHT Mildred   Contemporary Evidence as to the Character of
      Samuel Taylor Coleridge   MA Univ of California at Berkeley 1921
1903 YANO Fumiko   Coleridge's Criticism of His Contemporaries   MA Northeast
      Missouri St Coll 1957
1904 YOUNG Caryl J   Samuel Taylor Coleridge's Quest for the Unification
      of the Real and the Unreal   M Ed Henderson St Coll nd
See also 433, 519, 1083, 1480, 1660, 4494, 5721, 6428, 6429, 6819

                          WILKIE COLLINS

1905 ADAMS Ruth M   Wilkie Collins: His Dramatic Work and the Dramatic
      Elements in His Novels   MA Columbia 1943
1906 BRUTTOMESSO Gabriella   *The Moonstone* by Wilkie Collins   MA Ca Foscari
      (Italy) 1968
1907 DAL MASCHIO Milena   William Wilkie Collins   MA Ca Foscari (Italy) 1955
1908 HOLT John A   The Melodramatic Expression of Adventure and Objective
      Morality in the Novels of Wilkie Collins   MA Boston Coll 1951
1909 KISER David H   The Novels of Wilkie Collins   MA Univ of Pittsburgh 1938
1910 MESEROLE Harrison T   Wilkie Collins' Medical Interests as Reflected
      in Novels   MA Univ of Maryland at College Park 1953   83 p

                          WILLIAM COLLINS

1911 AKINS Dee W   William Collins: A Study in Sensibility   MA Univ of
      Kansas 1966
1912 CUSHMAN Charles S   William Collins and the Sublime   MA Univ of
      Massachusetts 1965
1913 DAVIS W C   An Examination of the Eclogues of William Collins
      MA Columbia 1940
1914 MITCHELL Marion B   William Collins   MA George Washington Univ 1936
      64 p
1915 WEBB Eugene III   William Collins: A Study of His Poetry   MA Columbia
      1962   162 p
1916 WESLEY Isabel S   A Study of the Epithet as Used in the Poetry of
      William Collins   MA Columbia 1936

                          WILLIAM CONGREVE

1917 BALLENGER Judith W   The Disguise in the Works of William Congreve
      MA Univ of Oklahoma 1959
1918 BONFANTI Annamaria   Congreve's Comedies   MA Ca Foscari (Italy) 1957
1919 BURNS Patrick J   Sex and Marriage Witticism in the Restoration
      Comedies of Sir George Etherege, William Wycherley and
      William Congreve   MA Fairleigh Dickinson Univ 1966

1920 CHILLMAN Dawes Congreve's *The Way of the World*: A Critical
      Appreciation MA Univ of Texas at Austin 1960 77 p
1921 CLARKE Alan B William Congreve: A Critical Study MA Univ of
      Richmond 1924 117 p
1922 CRAVEN Linda G Rumours in William Congreve's Comedies MA Wake Forest
      Coll 1966
1923 DANIEL M J A Study of Seventeenth Century Spelling as Represented
      by the Comedies of William Congreve MA North Texas St Univ 1963
1924 DUNN Carol M Congreve's *The Double Standard*: An Examination of a
      Problem Comedy MA Syracuse Univ 1963 122 p
1925 FOX Allan B Artistic Development in the Comedies of William Congreve
      MA Temple Univ 1963 46 p
1926 McNEELY Samuel S Jr A Study of the Dramatic Career of William Congreve
      MA Louisiana St Univ 1936
1927 MARSTON Louise G Congreve's Theory and Practice of Comedy MA Univ
      of Tennessee 1936
1928 NASCIMBEN Alcide *The Double Dealer* by William Congreve MA Ca Foscari
      (Italy) 1968
1929 NICKSON Joseph R Congreve's Theory and Practice of Comedy MA Univ
      of North Carolina at Chapel Hill 1946 79 p
1930 RANIOLO Marianna Wit in the Comedies of Congreve MA Ca Foscari
      (Italy) 1950
1931 SHARPE, Alice V Satiric Types of Women in the Comedy of Dryden,
      Etherege, Wycherley, Vanbrugh and Farquhar MA Univ of Kentucky
      1946 142 p
1932 SMITH Herbert H *The Way of the World*: A Critical Re-Evaluation
      MA Syracuse Univ 1965 113 p
1933 TEER Barbara A Congreve's *Love for Love*: Valentine's Voices
      MA Texas Woman's Univ 1966
1934 WANG Hsi-Lan The Classical Learning of William Congreve MA Univ
      of Tennessee 1951 81 p
1935 WILLIAMS S R The Morality and Wit of Congreve and Sheridan in the
      Comedy of Manners MA North Texas St Univ 1958
1936 WOOD Starling J Congreve's *Old Batchelor* MA Univ of Tennessee 1941
See also 5236, 5922, 7518

                           JOSEPH CONRAD

1937 ADAMS Edwin H The Structure of Joseph Conrad's Novels MA Washington
      St Univ at Pullman 1931 102 p
1938 ADLAM Percy J The Lonely Man: A Study of Characterization in the Novel
      of Joseph Conrad BA Mount Allison Univ (Canada) 1959 112 p
1939 ALDEN Howel H The Malaysian Fiction of Joseph Conrad MA Univ of
      Kansas 1928
1940 ALLEN Robert T Alchemy and Experience: The Concept of Alter Ego in
      Heart of Darkness and *Moby Dick* MA Cornell Univ 1966
1941 ALLEN Thomas C Joseph Conrad: Point of View in the Early Marlow
      Fiction MA Rice 1963
1942 ALSOP Ethlyn M The Life of Joseph Conrad as Reflected in His Novels
      MA Kansas St Univ 1931
1943 ANDERSON Gerald Symbolism in Six Works of Joseph Conrad MA North
      Texas St Univ 1950 97 p
1944 ARNOLD Gale H Joseph Conrad: A Study in Irrationality MA George
      Washington Univ 1970 74 p
1945 ASKINS Donald H Isolation and Solidarity in Conrad's Works MA Univ
      of Virginia 1962 42 p
1946 ASTOR Stuart L Joseph Conrad's Drama MA Columbia 1959 65 p
1947 AVINGER Judith Conrad and Human Institutions MA Texas Technological
      Univ 1964 60 p
1948 BAKER Arthur K Life, Man and the Fixed Idea: A Study of Joseph Conrad
      MA Univ of Iowa 1965

CONRAD Con't 69 1949-1981

1949 BALKAN Sadik M Joseph Conrad: The Man Behind His Work MA Lehigh Univ
1937 89 p
1950 BARTHOLOME Mary Sources of the Latin Element in the Works of
Joseph Conrad MA Univ of Texas at Austin 1939 102 p
1951 BATTIN Joan A Study of the Treatment and Development of the Characters
in Conrad's Works MA Wells Coll 1955
1952 BECKER Robert J Recurring Themes in the Fiction of Joseph Conrad
MS Mankato St Coll 1962 44 p
1953 BIER Ruth S Reality of Characterization in the Novels of Joseph Conrad
MA Univ of Pittsburgh 1931 329 p
1954 BLAESS F J Handbook on Conrad MA Univ of Adelaide (Australia) 1943
1955 BOARD D H Joseph Conrad MA Sheffield Univ (England) 1958
1956 BOEBEL Charles E Irony and Belief in Joseph Conrad MA Univ of Iowa
1962 148 p
1957 BOERSCH Alfred H Ford Madox Ford: A Study of His Collaboration and Its
Effect upon His Novels with Joseph Conrad MA Univ of Minnesota 1950
1958 BOGER Ruth B Joseph Conrad's Treatment of Nature MA Univ of Texas at
Austin 1941 94 p
1959 BOWROU Gayle L The Conradian Hero MA Alberta (Canada) 1952 88 p
1960 BOYETT Annie L Joseph Conrad: Raconteur MA Columbia 1924 50 p
1961 BRACKENBURY Beverly J A Study of the Elizabethan Characteristics in
Some Works of Joseph Conrad MA Univ of Nevada 1964
1962 BRANDY Elsie G The Credibility of Joseph Conrad MA Boston Coll 1943
1963 BRASHEAR Minnie M The Angle of Narration in the Fiction of
Joseph Conrad MA Univ of Missouri 1922 147 p
1964 BRAUCH Lillian M The Hamartia in Conrad's Heroes MA Ohio St Univ
1925 25 p
1965 BRIGGS Austin E The Heights of Illusion in a World of Darkness
BA Harvard Univ 1954
1966 BROWN Beneva J Moral Responsibility in Conrad's Political Novels:
A Study of *Nostromo, The Secret Agent* and *Under Western Eyes*
MA Columbia 1966 83 p
1967 BROWN Emerson L Joseph Conrad's Last Novels: *The Shadow Line,
The Arrow of Gold* and *The Rover* MA Syracuse Univ 1958 62 p
1968 BROWN Leonard S The Expositional and Moralizing Substance in the
Novels of Joseph Conrad MA Univ of Nebraska 1925 59 p
1969 BRUECHER Werner The Concept of the "Double" in Joseph Conrad
MA Univ of Arizona 1962
1970 BUCK Jule R A Study of Some of the Important Characters of
Joseph Conrad BA Wells Coll 1949
1971 BUDZIAK Lydia M Joseph Conrad as a Novelist MA St Louis Univ
1930 51 p
1972 BUSZA A Conrad's Polish Literary Background and Some Illustrations
of the Influence of Polish Literature on His Work MA Univ of
London (England) 1964
1973 CANNING Peter C An Examination of *Nostromo* BA Harvard Univ 1959
1974 CAREY Robert Joseph Conrad: Self-Recognition MA Wesleyan Univ 1961
1975 CASH Joe L The Evolutionary Development of Women Characters in the
Works of Joseph Conrad MA Texas Technological Univ 1967 90 p
1976 CHARBONNEAU Louis H Jr The Nature and Significance of Joseph Conrad's
Morality MA Univ of Detroit 1949 75 p
1977 CHIPPINDALE Nigel K Tragedy and Technique in the Novels of
Joseph Conrad MA Univ of British Columbia (Canada) 1970
1978 CLARK Rupert E Racial and National Types in the Works of Joseph Conrad
MA Univ of Texas at Austin 1936
1979 CLARK Wesley L Christian Symbolism as Reflected in Selected Novels
by Joseph Conrad MA Oklahoma St Univ 1968 97 p
1980 CLARK Winnifred Conrad's Man Against the Universe MA Univ of Tulsa
1963
1981 CLARKE Kenneth W The Treatment of Race Prejudice in Joseph Conrad
MA Washington St Univ at Pullman 1949 83 p

1982 CLARKSON Max The Short Story in England in the Later Nineteenth
        Century MA Toronto (Canada) 1946 114 p
1983 CLEMENS Anne B Joseph Conrad's Theory of Fiction as Embodied in
        Lord Jim BA Univ of British Columbia (Canada) 1961
1984 CLOTHIER Selma V A Study of Joseph Conrad's Interpretation of
        Character MA Univ of Southern California 1935 62 p
1985 COCKE Leta M Joseph Conrad's Portrayal of Malay Characters MA Univ
        of Texas at Austin 1938
1986 COFFEY Ada O Joseph Conrad: A Dictionary of Characters MA Univ of
        Kansas 1939
1987 COLE John O Conrad's Typhoon: An Analysis Emphasizing the Logic
        of Its Creative Development MA Univ of Rhode Island 1967 124 p
1988 COLEMAN P Some Influences of the Sea Career of Joseph Conrad on His
        Novels BA Univ of British Columbia (Canada) 1960
1989 COLFER Brian J Myth and Symbol in Joseph Conrad's The Nigger of the
        Narcissus MA Boston Coll 1968
1990 COLSON J A "Positive" and "Negative" Characters in Joseph Conrad's
        Fiction MA North Texas St Univ 1951
1991 COMMAGER Henry S The Problem of Evil in Conrad's Heart of Darkness
        BA Harvard Univ 1952
1992 CONLON Rosalie M The Collaboration of Joseph Conrad and
        Ford Madox Ford MA Columbia 1945 51 p
1993 CONNELL Penelope L Elements of the Gothic in Melville and Conrad
        MA Univ of British Columbia (Canada) 1970
1994 COOK William J Jr A Study of the Light and Dark Imagery in the Early
        Works of Joseph Conrad: 1895-1900 MA Auburn Univ 1964
1995 COOK William W Joseph Conrad and His Critics, 1942-1955 MA Univ of
        Maine 1966
1996 COOKE Leta M Joseph Conrad's Portrayal of Malay Character MA Univ
        of Texas at Austin 1938 90 p
1997 CORGIATI LOYA Erina Joseph Conrad MA Ca Foscari (Italy) 1933
1998 COULTER Celeste M Marlow: Conrad's Prismatic Perspective
        MA Univ of Wyoming 1965
1999 COX Joseph C Andre Gide and His Interest in Blake, Conrad, Browning
        and Whitman MA Univ of Illinois 1952 49 p
2000 CRAMBLETT Mary L Idea and Theme in the Fiction of Joseph Conrad
        MA Univ of Iowa 1955 114 p
2001 CRAMER Frances I The Irony of Joseph Conrad MA Ohio St Univ 1931
        50 p
2002 CROZIER G L The Literary Values in the Novels of Joseph Conrad
        MA Univ of Nebraska 1922 52 p
2003 CZUBAKOWSKA H The Narrator in the Structure of Three Novels by
        Joseph Conrad: Heart of Darkness, Lord Jim and Chance
        MA Jagiellonian Univ (Poland) 1958
2004 DALUGA Richard B Suicide, Isolation and Joseph Conrad MA Univ of
        Massachusetts 1968 36 p
2005 DANNER Marguerite F The Interpretation of the Common Elements in
        the Fiction of Conrad and Dostoevski MA Ohio St Univ 1932 35 p
2006 DAULTON Patricia A The Contrast of Illusion and Reality in Three
        Novels by Joseph Conrad: Heart of Darkness, The Nigger of the
        Narcissus and Nostromo MA Univ of Cincinnati 1955 176 p
2007 D'AVANGO Mario L The Function of Marlow in Three Novels of
        Joseph Conrad MA Trinity Coll 1954
2008 DAVIDSON Donald The Inversive Method of Narration in the Novels and
        Short Stories of Joseph Conrad MA Vanderbilt Univ 1922
2009 DAVIS Stephen L Imagery in the Fiction of Joseph Conrad MA Univ
        of Maine 1966 121 p
2010 DAWSON Carl Joseph Conrad: A Vision in Light and Dark MA Columbia
        1960 83 p
2011 DAY Esther Joseph Conrad's Use of the Double MA Univ of Houston

1963   91 p

2012   DEARMAS Delia W   A Study of Joseph Conrad and *Heart of Darkness*
       MA Stetson Univ 1962

2013   DEES Mary C   Joseph Conrad's Dominant Tone of Sobriety as Revealed
       by an Analysis of His Works   MA Univ of Texas at Austin 1940   85 p

2014   DEWITT Robert H   Joseph Conrad's View of Life as Shown Principally
       by His Descriptions   MS Kansas St Coll at Pittsburg 1938   44 p

2015   DICKENSON Maude A   The Continuing Characters in the Stories of
       Joseph Conrad   MA Ohio St Univ 1925   51 p

2016   DICKSON Harry H   The Sympathetic Bond in the Works of Joseph Conrad
       MA Univ of British Columbia (Canada) 1964

2017   DIETIKER Don W   *The Rover:* A Study of the Change in Conrad's
       Narrative Technique   MA Columbia 1960   90 p

2018   DIGGS Della A   Literary Citation in the Works of Joseph Conrad
       MA Univ of Arizona 1938   20 p

2019   DILLARD Richard I   Irony: The Integrant in the Art and Philosophy
       of Thomas Hardy and Joseph Conrad   MA Univ of Montana 1931   169 p

2020   DISHMAN Benjamin E   The Theme of Responsibility and Command in Four
       Works by Joseph Conrad   MA Univ of Massachusetts 1969   49 p

2021   DOWD C R   The World of Conrad   MA Boston Univ 1924   41 p

2022   DUDLEY Edward J   Patterns of Imagery in Conrad's Early Fiction
       MA Univ of Minnesota 1951

2023   DUFFY William B Jr   Conrad: The Moral Adventure   BA Amherst Coll 1955

2024   DUGGAN Sr Mary R   The Function of Landscape Description in
       Joseph Conrad's *Nostromo*   MA Catholic Univ of America 1963   48 p

2025   DUNN Frederick D   The Dark Powers: A Study of Joseph Conrad
       MA Wesleyan Univ 1960

2026   EAGER Hannah   Joseph Conrad   MA Columbia 1918   20 p

2027   EAMES R P   The Depiction of National Characteristics in the Novels
       of Joseph Conrad   MA Wesleyan Univ 1938

2028   EBERHARD Florence L   A Study of Stage Settings in the Novels of
       Joseph Conrad   MA Ohio St Univ 1925   95 p

2029   EDDLEMAN Ruth E   The Function of Marlow in Joseph Conrad's Fiction
       MA Univ of Oklahoma 1962

2030   ELLIOTT Lorris   *Lord Jim*: A Study in Imagery   BA Univ of British
       Columbia (Canada) 1962

2031   ELLIS James N   The Short Stories of Joseph Conrad   MA Univ of Oklahoma
       1958

2032   ELLIS Sharon   The Limited Man: A Study of the Conradian Hero
       MA Florida St Coll 1969   70 p

2033   ENDERS Anthony F   Aspects of Structure in Conrad's *Victory* and
       Forster's *A Passage to India*   BA Harvard Univ 1959

2034   EPP Harold B   The Quest for Identity in Joseph Conrad's Fiction
       MA Univ of British Columbia (Canada) 1968   99 p

2035   ESLICK Thomas W   The Awkward Focus: A Study of Women and Love in
       the Fiction of Joseph Conrad   MA Univ of New Hampshire 1968   70 p

2036   ESPIE Stephen B   Reality and Its Foe: A Study of Five Novels of
       Joseph Conrad   BA Amherst Coll 1953

2037   FAY Janet A   Conrad the Moralist   MA Columbia 1962   90 p

2038   FEASTER Jacob H   The Position of the Adverb "Only" in the Works
       of Joseph Conrad   MA Louisiana St Univ 1930

2039   FERGUSON Bessie E   Joseph Conrad and His Critics   MA Univ of Kansas
       1926

2040   FERRELL William R   Some Aspects of Thematic Development in Five of
       Conrad's Novels: *Heart of Darkness, Lord Jim, Nostromo, Victory,*
       and *The Rover*   BA Swarthmore Coll 1954   96 p

2041   FICHTER Robert P   Joseph Conrad's Political Novels   BA Harvard Univ
       1961

2042   FLEMING Emily L   Mood Effects in Conrad and Galsworthy   MA Ohio St
       Univ 1924   39 p

2043   FLETCHER John W   A Criticism of Modern Urban Civilization and in
         the Writings of Joseph Conrad   MA Oklahoma St Univ nd
2044   FOLDA Olga   Joseph Conrad and Russia   MA Univ of Chicago 1930   77 p
2045   FRANCIS K W   A Study of Animism in the Writings of Joseph Conrad
         MA Univ of Iowa 1930   43 p
2046   FRANZONI Orfeo J   Conrad's Attitude Towards the Civilization of
         Spanish America   MA Siena Coll 1959   69 p
2047   FRIEDMAN Joseph H   Joseph Conrad: The Making of His Reputation
         MA Columbia 1947   219 p
2048   FRY Ruth J   A Study of the Collaboration of Joseph Conrad and
         Ford Madox Ford   MA Univ of Texas at Austin 1938   86 p
2049   FURPHY A A   The Development of the Technique of Conrad as an
         Ironical Novelist   MA Univ of Manchester (England) 1953
2050   GARD Robert R   A Study of Joseph Conrad's Humanitarianism
         MA Univ of Illinois 1950   73 p
2051   GARDNER Naomi   Joseph Conrad's Theory of Narrative Art   MA Univ of
         Colorado 1939   94 p
2052   GARRUTO John C   Conrad's Ideas on Illusion and Reality and Their
         Employment in *Nostromo*   MA Univ of Virginia 1952   82 p
2053   GARST Tom   Beyond Realism: Short Fiction of Kipling, Conrad and
         James in the 1890's   MA Washington Univ at St Louis 1969   247 p
2054   GEDDES Gary R   Conrad and the Creative Process   MA Toronto (Canada)
         1966
2055   GIACOBELLI Francesco   *Nostromo*: A Tale of the Seaboard   MA Ca Foscari
         (Italy) 1968
2056   GILE Elizabeth   The Technique of Authentication in the Novels of
         Joseph Conrad   MS Univ of Minnesota 1925
2057   GILLON Adam   Isolation in the Life and Works of Joseph Conrad
         MA Columbia 1954   221 p
2058   GILMORE Nora E   Characterization in Joseph Conrad's Novels   MA West
         Texas St Univ 1951   148 p
2059   GOLDBERG Ethel   Ships, Men and Joseph Conrad   MA Columbia 1924   43 p
2060   GOLSON Julian A   "Positive" and "Negative" Characters in Joseph Conrad
         MA North Texas St Univ 1951
2061   GORDON Velma V   The Major Symbolism in the Voyage Novels of
         Joseph Conrad   MA Whittier Coll nd
2062   GRABCZAK E   Oriental Vocabulary in Conrad and Orwell   MA Univ of Warsa
         (Poland) 1962
2063   GREEN Helen   Conrad's Concept of Evil   M Ed Henderson St Coll nd
2064   GREENBERG Elizabeth L   The Friendship and Literary Collaboration
         Between Joseph Conrad and Ford Madox Ford   MA Univ of Maryland at
         College Park 1949   95 p
2065   GRENZOW Daisy B   Narrative Method in Four Novels of Joseph Conrad
         MA Ohio St Univ 1931   75 p
2066   GRIFFIN Elsie A   The Role of Tragedy in the Major Novels of
         Joseph Conrad   MA North Carolina Coll 1965
2067   GRIFFISS John M   Joseph Conrad's Concept of the Tragic and Heroic
         Figure   BA Univ of North Carolina at Chapel Hill 1962   96 p
2068   GUETTI James L   The Rhetoric of Joseph Conrad   BA Amherst Coll 1959
         47 p
2069   GUIET Pierre   A Dream and a Fear: A Study of Joseph Conrad
         MA Columbia 1950   112 p
2070   GUTHRIE William B   The Technique of Chronology in Some Novels of
         Joseph Conrad   MA Univ of Virginia 1952   96 p
2071   HALE Thomas   The Element of Avarice in the Works of Joseph Conrad
         MA Univ of Texas at Austin 1943   186 p
2072   HAMILTON Eloise C   Selection and Use of Setting in the Novels of
         Joseph Conrad   MA Univ of California at Los Angeles 1929   70 p
2073   HANCOX P   The Treatment of the Theme of Betrayal in the Novels and
         Stories of Joseph Conrad   MA Univ of Minnesota 1938

2074 HARVEY David D The Collaboration of Ford Madox Ford and Joseph Conrad
      MA Columbia 1958
2075 HERNANDEZ Jose M The Philosophy of Joseph Conrad MA Univ of Notre
      Dame 1931
2076 HILL Minnie L Some Aspects of the Philosophy of Joseph Conrad
      MA Univ of Louisville 1917
2077 HILL Ordelle G Hero-Villain Relationships in Representative Novels
      of Conrad MA Auburn Univ 1959 119 p
2078 HOBLITZELLE Harrison Jr *Lord Jim*: A Study in Narrative Technique
      MA Columbia 1951
2079 HOFFMANN Stanton de V Joseph Conrad's Use of Burlesque Within the
      Framework of Moral Allegory MA Pennsylvania St Univ 1957 61 p
2080 HOLDER Robert C The Idea of Duty in Joseph Conrad's Novels
      MA Ohio St Univ 1947
2081 HOLLINGSWORTH Joseph K The Technique of Joseph Conrad, with
      Particular Reference to His Handling of the Point of View
      MA Univ of Chicago 1931 102 p
2082 HOLLOWAY Lowell H The Reading of Joseph Conrad MA Ohio St Univ
      1938 76 p
2083 HOOD Leslie I Conrad and the Orestes Myth MA Stanford Univ 1950
2084 HOOD Valerie L The Political Novels of Joseph Conrad: *Nostromo,
      The Secret Agent* and *Under Western Eyes* MA George Washington Univ
      1965 120 p
2085 HOWARD Hubert C The Development of Women Characters in Joseph Conrad's
      Novels MA Ohio St Univ 1928 100 p
2086 HOWLETT Theodor J Joseph Conrad's Technique MA Acadia Univ (Canada)
      1938 82 p
2087 HUNTER Robert A Conrad's Use of Marlow in Two Novels and Two Tales
      MA Columbia 1953 138 p
2088 INNISS Kenneth B Conrad's Human Geography, Two Explorations
      MA Indiana Univ 1955
2089 JAMISON Laura The Ships in the Stories of Joseph Conrad MA Ohio
      St Univ 1925 100 p
2090 JOHNSON Eunah Comparison of the Descriptive Powers of Conrad and
      Ruskin MA Stetson Univ 1926
2091 JOHNSON Frank W Studies of Joseph Conrad: Essays on Reality and
      the Imagination in the Early Fiction BA Rutgers St Univ 1968 114 p
2092 JOHNSON Gladys M Elements of Moral Conflict in Joseph Conrad MA Univ
      of Iowa 1960 94 p
2093 JOHNSTONE Douglas B The Three Phases of Joseph Conrad: An Examination
      of Changing Theme in the Novels MA Wesleyan Univ 1965
2094 JONES Harriette C Dona Rita Considered Between the Women of Conrad's
      Early and Late Novels MA Ohio St Univ 1930 53 p
2095 JONES Sarah R Does Joseph Conrad Present a Fixed Feminine Type?
      MA Columbia 1933 91 p
2096 KADET Sanford R Joseph Conrad: An Existentialist Approach
      MA Columbia 1953 91 p
2097 KAMIENNY J Joseph Conrad: The Painter of the Sea MA Univ of Warsaw
      (Poland) 1950
2098 KANE Robert J Some Novels of Mr Joseph Conrad MA Ohio St Univ 1922
      60 p
2099 KATZ Michael S The Moral Struggle in Conrad BA Amherst 1966
2100 KAUFMAN Christopher L Aspects of the Turn-of-the-Century Romance
      in James, Conrad and Lawrence BA Amherst 1967
2101 KAUFMAN Judith A Understanding and Judging Conrad's Use of Reflectors
      MA Tufts Univ 1966
2102 KAY Hubert A Joseph Conrad's Creation of Atmosphere MA Columbia 1929
      36 p
2103 KEEFEE Daniel J An Analysis of Joseph Conrad's Short Stories
      MA Vanderbilt Univ 1941

2104 KEITH Priscilla Conrad's Theme of Self-Discovery MA Wells Coll 1960
2105 KENNEDY Nellie A Abnormal Psychology in Joseph Conrad's Characters
      MA Univ of Texas at Austin 1940 73 p
2106 KILLINGSWORTH Robert B Jr Aspects of the Mode of Romance in Malory,
      Scott, Stevenson and Conrad BA Amherst 1965
2107 KING Laureen Religious Imagery in Joseph Conrad's The Nigger of the
      Narcissus BA Univ of British Columbia (Canada) 1970
2108 KIRSCHNER P A Study of Conrad's Use of the Principles of Dramatic
      Technique and Construction in His Fiction, with a Comment on His
      Three Plays MA Univ of London (England) 1956
2109 KOCH Ivan L Conrad's Microcosm MA Univ of Wyoming 1962 89 p
2110 KOLBERT Richard S Lord Jim and His Friends: A Study of Conrad's
      Novel MA Columbia 1962 69 p
2111 KOLODZIEJCZYK J The Role of the Description of Nature in the Narrative
      of Conrad's First Three Novels: Almayer's Folly, An Outcast of the
      Islands and The Nigger of the Narcissus MA Jagiellonian Univ
      (Poland) 1958
2112 KUCZYNSKI A Portraits of the Sailors in Joseph Conrad's Novels
      MA Univ of Warsaw (Poland) 1960
2113 KURETH Sr Julia The Fatalism of Joseph Conrad and Thomas Hardy
      MA Duquesne Univ 1935
2114 LaBEAUME Nora C Joseph Conrad's Application of His Artistic Theories
      MA Univ of Arkansas 1929
2115 LANE Sherri Narrative Modes in Conrad: A Selective Study MA Columbia
      1967 122 p
2116 LEAM Harold S Conrad and Villainy: A Study of the Villains in His
      Major Novels MA Lehigh Univ 1959 129 p
2117 LEAMON Dorothy Joseph Conrad and Pierre Loti as Interpreters of the
      Sea MA Ohio St Univ 1923 45 p
2118 LEE Maurice A The Structure of Fear and Horror in Benito Cereno,
      Heart of Darkness and The Turn of the Screw MA Oklahoma St Univ
      1967 120 p
2119 LEE Robert F Joseph Conrad and the White Man's Burden MA Vanderbilt
      Univ 1953
2120 LEESE M J Joseph Conrad as a Poetical Novelist MA Univ of Manchester
      (England) 1955
2121 LEVY Gain S The Remarkable Hero: Joseph Conrad's Moral Ideal
      MA Tufts Univ 1965
2122 LEVY Lora S Joseph Conrad's Artistic Treatment of Women: An Analysis
      MA Univ of Arizona nd 116 p
2123 LEWIS Jane E A Critical Exposition of Joseph Conrad's Heart of
      Darkness MA Univ of Mississippi 1969
2124 LEWIS Lawrence B Four Character Types in the Fiction of Joseph Conrad
      MA Univ of Missouri 1955 103 p
2125 LEWIS William H The Hero of Isolation in the Novels of Joseph Conrad
      BA Harvard Univ 1961
2126 LILLIARD Richard G Irony: The Integrant in the Art and Philosophy
      of Thomas Hardy and Joseph Conrad MA Montana St Univ 1931 169 p
2127 LIPSKA J Women Characters in Joseph Conrad's Works MA Univ of Warsaw
      (Poland) 1949
2128 LOHMAN Mary M A Critical and Historical Survey of the Stream of
      Consciousness Technique in Contemporary Fiction MA Columbia 1942
      82 p
2129 LONG Jerome A Conrad's Nostromo: Reception, Theme, Technique
      MA Loyola Univ 1961
2130 LOVE Evelyn S The Brutal Gentlemen in Joseph Conrad's Victory,
      George Meredith's The Egoist, Henry James' The Portrait of a Lady
      BA Wells Coll 1957
2131 LUDDY Thomas E Two Plays by Joseph Conrad : A Matter of Form
      MA Boston Coll 1965

2132 McCARTHY Donald C Joseph Conrad MA Trinity Coll 1918
2133 McCLELLAN David Freudian Ideas in Three Tales by Joseph Conrad
        MA East Tennessee St Univ 1956 48 p
2134 McCLURG Finas A Joseph Conrad, Mariner MA East Texas St Univ 1942
2135 McCONNELL Ruth The Theme of Isolation in the Work of Joseph Conrad
        MA Univ of British Columbia (Canada) 1958 162 p
2136 McCORKLE Julia N A Study of Stylistic Departures from the Con-
        ventional in Twenty Representative British and American Novelists
        of the Present Day (1920-1924) MA Univ of Southern California
        1926 237 p
2137 McCUNE Samuel A Comparison between the Style of Joseph Conrad and
        That of W Somerset Maugham MA Louisiana St Univ 1936
2138 McDONALD Dorothy R Narcissus: Identity and Suicide in *Moby Dick*
        and *Lord Jim* MA Univ of Hawaii 1963 229 p
2139 MacLENNAN Janet F The Philosophy of Joseph Conrad MA Oberlin Coll
        1928 48 p
2140 McPHERSON Clarence L The Narrative Method of Joseph Conrad
        MA Columbia 1925 21 p
2141 MANN Charles W Dominant Traits in Conrad's Characters MA Pennsylvania
        St Univ 1954 95 p
2142 MARK Maxine C The Tragic in Early Conrad MA Colorado St Coll 1966
2143 MARTIN Christopher W Conrad as a Delineator of Human Life
        MA Catholic Univ of America 1926
2144 MARTIN David M The Development of the Idea of Self-Knowledge in
        Conrad's Early Phase MA Univ of Rhode Island 1959
2145 MARTIN Harriette R Joseph Conrad and Studies in Fear MA Univ of
        Arizona pre-1933
2146 MASON Louie M Aspects of Joseph Conrad's Art MA Mills Coll 1935
2147 MAY Nell A Conrad, Malraux, Lowry: The Journey to the Interior
        MA Emory Univ 1962
2148 MEANS Ann An Analysis of Figurative Language in Joseph Conrad's
        The Nigger of the Narcissus and Related Works for Teaching
        Imaginative Literature M Ed Howard Payne Coll 1967 75 p
2149 MENDILOW Adam A Time and the Novel MA Univ of London (England)
        1952 245 p
2150 MERRIX Robert P Joseph Conrad's Portrait of Marlow MA Butler Univ
        1960
2151 MESSENGER William E Historical Background, Sources and Composition
        of Joseph Conrad's *The Secret Agent*, with a General Interpretation
        of the Novel and Its Meaning MA Cornell Univ 1959
2152 MEYER Elizabeth A Ideals as Deception: A Study of Disillusionment
        in Three Works by Joseph Conrad MA Univ of Massachusetts 1968
        29 p
2153 MILLER Raymond R Conrad's *The Secret Agent*: "A Simple Tale" of
        Irrationality MA Univ of Delaware 1969 67 p
2154 MILLS H B Conrad's Use of People He Knew as Illustrated by His
        Use of Dominic Cervoni MA Boston Univ 1941
2155 MITCHELL Sidney H Ideals and Illusions in Conrad's Short Stories
        MA Univ of Virginia 1952 78 p
2156 MONK D E A Study of Selected Novels by James and Conrad as Evidenced
        in Their Literary Theory and Exemplified in These Selected Novels
        by Each of Them MA Univ of Manchester (England) 1959
2157 MONRO Charles B Conrad's Use of Description MA Univ of Pittsburgh
        1926
2158 MOORE Carolyn *Heart of Darkness*: The Moral Affirmation MA Univ of
        Massachusetts 1968 29 p
2159 MOORE Patricia B A Study of the Theory and Practice of Fiction in
        Conrad-Ford Collaboration MA Rice 1955
2160 MORAN Berenice A The Tragedy in the Novels and Stories of
        Joseph Conrad MA Ohio St Univ 1932 125 p

2161 MOREINES Harvey A "New" Novel: Joseph Conrad's *Heart of Darkness*:
      A Study of Image and Structure MA Univ of Maryland at College Park
      1962 145 p

2162 MOREY Elizabeth K A Study of the Themes of Four English Novels
      MA Columbia 1923 145 p

2163 MOREY John H Joseph Conrad and the Milieu of Man MA Cornell Univ 1955

2164 MORGAN Joseph T The Philosophy of Joseph Conrad MA Ohio St Univ
      1931 59 p

2165 MORRIS Lena A Joseph Conrad: His Literary Inheritance MA Univ of
      Texas at Austin 1940 82 p

2166 MOSES Elizabeth P A Study of Character in the Novels of Joseph Conrad
      MA Washington St Univ at Pullman 1939 68 p

2167 MOSS Robert F Moral Relativism in Three Novels of Joseph Conrad
      MA Columbia 1965 107 p

2168 MOWAT Angus M A Critical Study of the Life, Philosophy and Art of
      Joseph Conrad MA Univ of Saskatchewan (Canada) 1935

2169 MUNTZ Herbert E Conrad's Use of Autobiographical Material in His
      Short Stories and Novels MA Ohio St Univ 1930 83 p

2170 MURPHY Daniel J Conrad the Novelist MA Univ Coll of Cork (Ireland)
      1949

2171 MURPHY Marian I The Theme of Isolation in the Novels of Joseph Conrad
      MA Atlanta Univ 1966

2172 MURRAY Phyllis M The English Novel of the Sea from Smollett to
      Conrad MA McGill (Canada) 1927

2173 MUSIO Gustavo Joseph Conrad MA Ca Foscari (Italy) nd

2174 NALESSO Marilena *The Secret Agent* and *Under Western Eyes* by
      Joseph Conrad MA Ca Foscari (Italy) 1969

2175 NAPIER Edna M Joseph Conrad's Women MA Univ of British Columbia
      (Canada) 1920 65 p

2176 NELSON Kenneth G Irony in Joseph Conrad's Early Novels
      MA Northern Illinois Univ 1961

2177 NEWLANDS P Joseph Conrad's Artistic Achievement in the Light of His
      Own Criticism BA Univ of British Columbia (Canada) 1931

2178 NIKETAS George The Eastern Spirit of Resignation Versus the Western
      Spirit of Action in Joseph Conrad's Fiction MA Univ of South
      Carolina 1961

2179 NOLAN John A A Critical Study of Selected Short Stories of
      Joseph Conrad with Reference to Themes Found in the Novels
      MA Canisius Coll 1957

2180 NOLEN JoAnn T The Individual and the Community in the World of
      Joseph Conrad MA Johns Hopkins Univ 1962

2181 NORTH Douglas M Joseph Conrad and the "Facts" MA Syracuse Univ 1965
      71 p

2182 OAKLANDER Lucille Political Symbolism in the Novels of Joseph Conrad
      MA Smith Coll 1950 98 p

2183 ODDEN Edmund S The Concept of the Frailty of Idealism in Conrad's
      Works MA Univ of Arizona 1962

2184 ODELL Maryann E The Theme of Betrayal in Joseph Conrad's *Nostromo*
      MA Dominican Coll of San Rafael 1958 61 p

2185 O'HANLON Sr Mary K The Theme of Discipline and Conflict in Conrad's
      Heart of Darkness MA Dominican Coll of San Rafael 1960 43 p

2186 OKAMURA Sonoho The Orientalism in Joseph Conrad MA Smith Coll 1942
      103 p

2187 OVERTON Cora M The Treatment of Duty in the Writings of Joseph Conrad
      MA Univ of Iowa 1928 160 p

2188 OWEN Lyman B The Polish-French Joseph Conrad MA New York St Coll
      for Teachers 1937

2189 PACKARD George V Jr *Heart of Darkness* by Joseph Conrad MA Columbia
      1960 92 p

2190 PALMER Anita R A Study of Some Memorable Women Characters in the

Novels of Joseph Conrad MA Univ of Texas at Austin 1937 110 p
2191 PARKER Robert W The Slavic Aspects of Joseph Conrad MA North Texas
      St Univ 1955
2192 PARKIS Patricia K Conrad's Narrator Marlowe: The Relationship between
      Fate and Will in Three Tales MA Univ of Massachusetts 1969 35 p
2193 PASQUALATO Roberto *The Nigger of the Narcissus* by Joseph Conrad
      MA Ca Foscari (Italy) 1969
2194 PEIRCE William P Africa as a Literary Symbol in *Heart of Darkness*
      and *Henderson the Rain King* MA Univ of Maryland at College Park
      1966 77 p
2195 PELFREY Charles J Conrad's Malaysians MA Univ of Kentucky 1950 89 p
2196 PENDERGAST Constance Joseph Conrad and the Remorse of Conscience
      BA Wells Coll 1945
2197 PERRY Gwendolyn G Joseph Conrad and Composition MA Univ of California
      at Berkeley 1923
2198 PETERS Agnes D The Art of Joseph Conrad: His Theory and Practice
      MA Stanford Univ 1928
2199 PETTIGREW Elizabeth Ford Madox Ford and Joseph Conrad MA Vanderbilt
      Univ 1942
2200 PEZET Maurice J A Psychological Study of Conrad's Main Characters
      MA Univ of Caen (France) 1958 109 p
2201 PHILLIPS Mary H Joseph Conrad: The Depth of Courage MA Columbia
      1954 86 p
2202 POLLEY Phillip J The Relationship of Joseph Conrad's Political
      Thought to His Literary Art MA Northern Illinois Univ 1966
2203 POSPISIL Robert Joseph Conrad: Illusion and Solidarity MA Queens
      (Canada) 1954 144 p
2204 POWIS M B The Individual and Society in Conrad's Novels MA Univ of
      London (England) 1957
2205 PRATT Mary The French Contacts of Joseph Conrad MA Univ of Indiana
      1928 188 p
2206 PROFITT Doris L The Novellas of Joseph Conrad: A Study in Crafts-
      manship MA Stanford Univ 1959
2207 PUZON Mother Mary B Joseph Conrad and His Reviewers MA Boston Coll
      1964
2208 PYSZHOWSKI Richard J Joseph Conrad Korzeniowski and His Polish
      Heritage MA Univ of Ottawa (Canada) 1952 103 p
2209 QUICK D E The Technique of Conrad in Relation to the Moral Conduct
      of His Characters MA Univ of Wales (Wales) 1953
2210 RABEY Hetty R Joseph Conrad MA Wittenberg Univ 1930
2211 READY Marie E Joseph Conrad's Women MA Univ of Wyoming 1955 131 p
2212 REES Florence H Recent Developments in Narrative Methods MA Ohio
      St Univ 1920 66 p
2213 REGAN Sr Rose E A Study of Man in Conflict in the Sea Stories of
      Joseph Conrad and in Herman Melville's *Moby Dick* MA Mount Saint
      Vincent (Canada) 1967
2214 REYNOLDS Anne Prose-Poetry in Joseph Conrad MA Univ of Texas at
      Austin 1938 145 p
2215 RIDD John C Conrad's Lingard Novels: An Index of Change MA Univ of
      Manitoba (Canada) 1955 145 p
2216 ROBERTS Iris S Nine Women in the Fiction of Joseph Conrad MA North
      Texas St Univ 1961
2217 ROBERTS Wilma A Joseph Conrad: The Effect of His Polish Birth and
      British Citizenship Upon His Writings MA Univ of Denver 1959
2218 RODES Roberta M The Eternal River: A Study in Conrad and Melville
      MA Occidental Coll 1958
2219 ROEHL Sr Barbara M Joseph Conrad: A Study of His Theory and Tech-
      niques MA St Louis Univ 1941 122 p
2220 ROONEY Lawrence F A Symbolic Pattern in Conrad's Early Fiction
      MA Montana St Univ 1950 83 p

2221 ROSELLI Br Alexander   The Parodies of Max Beerbohm on Joseph Conrad
      and Henry James   MA Univ of Notre Dame 1964
2222 ROSEME Diane   The Threefold Interpretation of the *Heart of Darkness*
      MA Sacramento St Coll 1958   104 p
2223 ROWLANDS Hobart E   Joseph Conrad and the Russian Novelists   MA Ohio
      St Univ 1923   63 p
2224 ROY Jaqueline C   Joseph Conrad and France   MA Univ of Cincinnati
      1952   116 p
2225 RUDD May   Conrad's Power of Developing Scene and Characterization
      MA Univ of South Dakota 1923   168 p
2226 SAYRE Ira C   Conrad's Treatment of the Short Story   MA Ohio St Univ
      1931   54 p
2227 SCHEER Roberta   Joseph Conrad's Views of Idealism   MA Hunter Coll 1968
2228 SCHUNK Karl   Der Zufall bei Joseph Conrad   MS Univ of Gottingen
      (Germany) 1941   140 p
2229 SCHWARTZ Edward   The Destructive Element   MA Columbia 1948   66 p
2230 SCHWERTMAN Mary P   Materialism and the Individual in Conrad's
      Nostromo   MA Columbia 1953   114 p
2231 SEAVER Lillian F   Some Patterns of Imagery in Joseph Conrad's
      Typhoon   MA Dominican Coll of San Rafael 1960   61 p
2232 SECOR Robert A   Conrad and Hawthorne   MA Brown Univ 1963   169 p
2233 SELDEN Nancy A   The Gallery of Women in Conrad's Political Novels
      MA Univ of Iowa 1964
2234 SHAPIRO Barbara   Modes of Being: Illusion and Actuality in
      Joseph Conrad   BA City Coll of New York 1963   52 p
2235 SHARON Adeline   Nationalism in the Works of Joseph Conrad   MA Univ
      of Iowa 1934   62 p
2236 SHAW William F   A Study of Self-Portraiture and Technique in the
      Marlow Group in Joseph Conrad's Fiction   MA Univ of Texas at Austin
      1936
2237 SHELTON Evie L   Joseph Conrad: A Study of His Creative Imagination
      at Work   MA Univ of Texas at Austin 1935
2238 SIKES James R   Style and Thought in Conrad's *Lord Jim*   BA Harvard
      Univ 1957
2239 SINGLETON Emma M   Joseph Conrad's Personal Philosophy of Life
      MA Univ of California at Los Angeles 1935   146 p
2240 SLATER Mary M   A Structural Study of Joseph Conrad   MA Univ of
      Toronto (Canada) 1934   96 p
2241 SLOAN Eugene H   Joseph Conrad and the Classical Ideal   MA Ohio St
      Univ 1926   85 p
2242 SMALL Ray   Joseph Conrad's Use of Superstition and Tradition in Nine
      of His Novels   MA Univ of Texas at Austin 1941   139 p
2243 SMIALKOWA A   Conrad's Passion for the Sea and Ships   MA Univ of
      Warsaw (Poland) 1950
2244 SMITH Annie E   Dominant Character Traits of Conrad's Men   MA George
      Peabody Coll for Teachers 1936   141 p
2245 SMITH John W   Character Relations in Some of Conrad's Fiction
      MA Toronto (Canada) 1965
2246 SMOCK George E   Joseph Conrad's Theory of the Art of Fiction   MA Univ
      of Chicago 1928
2247 SMOLLER Sanford J   The Fall and Abyss in Joseph Conrad's Fiction
      MA Columbia 1964   137 p
2248 SNELL Frank M   The Truth of Existence and Fidelity to Life
      MA Columbia 1950   63 p
2249 SNYDER H Evan   The Relationship between Theme and Narrative Technique
      in Three Joseph Conrad Novels   BA Amherst 1958
2250 SOLOMON Barbara   Conrad's Marlow as a Narrator and a Character.
      MA Univ of Kansas 1960
2251 SOLOMON Vera   Symbolism in Selected Works of Joseph Conrad
      M Ed Henderson St Coll nd

2252 SOMERMIER Cornelia E Idee Fixe as It Manifests Itself in Certain
     of Conrad's Characters MS Kansas St Teachers Coll of Emporia 1933
2253 SPALDING Branch Conrad's Evolved Descriptive Method MA Univ of
     Virginia 1931 63 p
2254 STASKO Sr Mary L A First Translation into English of the World of
     Conrad's Novels and Tales by Jozef Ujejski and a Consideration of
     Ujejski's Critique in the Light of Recent Conrad Criticism
     MA Canisius Coll 1954
2255 STAUFFER Ruth M Joseph Conrad: His Romantic Realism MA Univ of
     California at Berkeley 1919 139 p
2256 STEPP Nancy T The Ideal Woman in the Work of Joseph Conrad MA Univ
     of Virginia 1962 44 p
2257 STERNBERG Sima Two Aspects of the Voyage: A Critical Study of
     Moby Dick and *Heart of Darkness* BA City Coll of New York 1957 102 p
2258 STORY Mattison L Jr Joseph Conrad: Autobiographical Elements in His
     Works MA Univ of Texas at Austin 1938 95 p
2259 STRANDBERG Edith A Characterization in the Novels of Joseph Conrad
     MA DePaul Univ 1944
2260 STRONACH Eunice E Plot and Point of View in Conrad's *Nostromo*
     MA Univ of British Columbia (Canada) 1965
2261 STUCKERT Frances A Conrad and Melville: The Sea Aspects of Their
     Works MA Univ of Texas at Austin 1938 163 p
2262 TAEGE Allan L Human Relationships in the Major Novels of Joseph Conrad
     1900-1911: A Study of Four Novels; *Lord Jim* (1900), *Nostromo* (1904),
     The Secret Agent (1907), and *Under Western Eyes* (1911) MA Univ
     of Canterbury (England) 1961 196 p
2263 TAGGART Michael Joseph Conrad: His Vision of Existence MA Colorado
     Coll 1962 61 p
2264 TAYLOR Edith C Joseph Conrad MA Washington St Univ at Pullman 1923
2265 TAYLOR Gordon O Guilt and Self-Redemption in Conrad's *Under Western
     Eyes* and Dostoevsky's *Crime and Punishment* BA Harvard Univ 1960
2266 TAYLOR Harry H The Imagination of Disaster MA Columbia 1954 83 p
2267 TAYLOR Ouita W Social and Political Conservatism in Joseph Conrad's
     Fiction MA North Texas St Univ 1951
2268 TEARE Richard Joseph Conrad's *Dombey and Son* BA Harvard Univ 1958
2269 THOMERSON Charles B The Island World of Joseph Conrad's *Victory*
     MA San Diego St Coll 1967 133 p
2270 THOMPSON David S The Subjective Novel: Joseph Conrad and Andre Gide
     MA Columbia 1951 103 p
2271 TIPTON Margaret E Joseph Conrad's Artistic Use of Silence MA Ohio
     St Univ 1923 20 p
2272 TKACZECKI B Polish Themes in Conrad's Works MA Univ of Warsaw (Poland)
     1961
2273 TREANOR Marie T The Relation of Character to Theme in Joseph Conrad's
     Nostromo MA Univ of Hawaii 1960 58 p
2274 TURNBULL Isabel Joseph Conrad as a Novelist of Subjective Adventure
     MA Univ of Manitoba (Canada) 1919 160 p
2275 TURNER L H Conrad's Craftsmanship MA Univ of Western Australia
     (Australia) 1943
2276 UHL Bernard Conrad's Colour Imagery BA Univ of British Columbia
     (Canada) 1968
2277 UNWIN G H Structural Studies in Modern Fiction MA Univ of Toronto
     (Canada) 1928 85 p
2278 VERDONER Josefine A Study of Structure, Imagery and Symbolism in
     Conrad's *Victory* MA Univ of North Carolina at Chapel Hill 1958
     74 p
2279 WAGNER Jane S A Study of the Relationship of the Political and the
     Psychological Theme in *Heart of Darkness* MA Univ of Redlands 1966
2280 WALKER Helen *The Rover*: A Study of Joseph Conrad MA Birmingham-
     Southern Coll 1931

2281 WALKER Judith D Conrad's Women: A Study in Negation MA Brigham
      Young Univ 1966
2282 WARREN Helen F Human Solidarity as a Recurring Theme in the Eleven
      Novels and Longer Tales of Joseph Conrad MA Indiana Univ of
      Pennsylvania 1966 80 p
2283 WARREN Stanley Tragedy in Two Early Novels of Joseph Conrad
      MA Hunter Coll 1966
2284 WARSCHAUSKY Sidney The Ego and the Darkness: A Study of the Early
      Works of Joseph Conrad MA Columbia 1949 120 p
2285 WEBER George L The Problem of Self-Knowledge and Self-Identity
      in Four Works of Joseph Conrad MA Univ of Notre Dame 1956
2286 WEEKS N Wendell Christian Faith of the Characters in the Fiction
      by Joseph Conrad and Its Relation to the Author's Personal
      Philosophy MA New York St Coll for Teachers 1938
2287 WELS Alena The Nineteenth Century Background of Conrad's Revolution-
      aries MA Columbia 1961 113 p
2288 WESOLOWSKI Florence Illusion and Reality in the Theme and Structure
      of Conrad's *Chance* MA Univ of Detroit 1963 88 p
2289 WHELAN Robert Joseph Conrad and the Romantic Feeling of Reality
      MA Niagara Univ 1957 141 p
2290 WHITELEY Thomas S The Technique of Joseph Conrad's Fiction as Revealed
      in the Pantai Group of His Novels MA Univ of Texas at Austin 1940
      144 p
2291 WHITEMEN Roger T A Comparative Analysis of Joseph Conrad, Henry James
      and Ernest Hemingway MA Pacific Univ 1954
2292 WHITTIER Henry S Self-Sacrifice in Selected Works of Joseph Conrad
      MA Univ of New Hampshire 1955 180 p
2293 WILCOCK Edith Joseph Conrad, Theory and Practice BA Wells Coll nd
2294 WILHELM Frederick O The Place of Memory in Joseph Conrad's Novels
      MA Wesleyan Univ 1944
2295 WILLIAMS Eluned Joseph Conrad: A Study in the Spiritual Values of
      His Work MA Pennsylvania St Univ 1931 47 p
2296 WITT D V The Epic Strain in Joseph Conrad MA North Texas St Univ 1968
2297 WITTMEYER Herman F The Spirit of Man in the Writings of Joseph Conrad
      MA Univ of North Carolina at Chapel Hill 1939 85 p
2298 WOOD William P The Evolution of the Concept of Innocence in Four
      Short Stories of Joseph Conrad BA Harvard Univ 1954
2299 WRIGHT Edgar Joseph Conrad: His Expressed Views about Technique
      and the Principles Underlying Them, with a Study of Their Relevance
      to Certain Novels MA Univ of London (England) 1955
2300 WRIGHT Penny Technique and the Role of Time in Joseph Conrad's
      Nostromo: A Tale of the Seaboard BA Univ of British Columbia
      (Canada) 1968
2301 WRIGHT Walter O III The Concepts of Work and Action in Joseph Conrad
      MA Columbia 1962 103 p
2302 ZELLAR Leonard E Joseph Conrad, 1898-1904: A Study of His Philosophy
      and Technique MA Univ of Denver 1953
See also 3222

ABRAHAM COWLEY

2303 ABRAMS Mabel H Tradition and Originality in the Non-Dramatic Writings
      of Abraham Cowley BA Univ of British Columbia (Canada) 1958
2304 ASKEW Annette C Aspects of Seventeenth Century Education as Seen
      in the Works of Bacon, Milton, Cowley and Locke MA Duke Univ 1965
2305 HERRING Charles A A Comparison of Cowley's *Davideis* and *Paradise Lost*
      MA Univ of Iowa 1933
2306 IWANICKI Charles P Mid-Seventeenth Century Epic Theory as Illustrated
      by Davenant's *Gondibert* and Cowley's *Davideis* MA George Washington
      Univ 1936 73 p

2307 PEARCE Sheena M The Plays of Abraham Cowley, as Examples of Some
         Dramatic Fashions Current in His Time MA Columbia 1953 56 p
2308 PIGOT David C The Matter and Context of Cowley Criticism from
         1660 to 1800 MA Dalhousie (Canada) 1966
2309 SCHAEFER Earlene H An Analysis of Abraham Cowley's Love Poem
         "The Mistress" MA Oklahoma St Univ 1962 57 p
2310 SHEPHERD Dora Y An Analysis of Abraham Cowley's Prose Style
         MA George Washington Univ 1940 70 p
See also 5140

WILLIAM COWPER

2311 ADAMS Ruth J William Cowper's Personal Religion as Reflected in His
         Memoir, Poems and Letters MA Univ of Tennessee 1952 79 p
2312 ALSTON Mary E Cowper's Literary Reputation from 1782 to 1935
         MA Howard Univ 1947 89 p
2313 BARTLETT Lester W Cowper: His Place in the Eighteenth Century and
         His Treatment of Nature MA Univ of California at Berkeley 1910
2314 BLACK Jimmy Hymning a New Order MA Texas Christian Univ 1968
2315 BYRD Jimmie E Boadicea in English Poetry MA Louisiana St Univ 1944
2316 COUND Fern P William Cowper: Evangelical Poet of the Humanitarian
         Movement MA Univ of Texas at El Paso 1956 133 p
2317 COX Helen S Criticism in Cowper's *Task* MA Univ of North Dakota 1933
2318 EVANS Kathleen T A Study of the Sublime in William Cowper's Poetry
         MA Univ of Massachusetts 1966
2319 EVERSOLE Ruth L The Background of Cowper's *Tirocinium* MA Univ of
         Oregon 1940
2320 FOLEY H B Contribution of William Cowper to Eighteenth-Nineteenth
         Centuries MA Boston Coll 1934
2321 FRATTI Mario William Cowper, the Poet of Sorrow MA Ca Foscari
         (Italy) 1950
2322 GIBBS Mary L The Personae in Cowper's *Olney Hymns* MA Univ of
         Massachusetts 1968 45 p
2323 HAUGHT Evelyn H The Bible in William Cowper's *The Task* MA Northern
         Illinois Univ 1965
2324 HOWE W A William Cowper as a Poet of Methodism in the Eighteenth
         Century MA Ohio St Univ 1924
2325 LAWTON Edith William Cowper as a Representative of Eighteenth
         Century Criticism MA Boston Univ 1930
2326 MAGUIRE Myrtie M Animal Lore in the Poetry of Cowper MA Boston Univ
         1910
2327 MIRES Carol William Cowper's Literary Opinions MA Univ of Oklahoma
         1940
2328 REMMEL M R Newton and Cowper and the *Olney Hymns* MA Boston Univ 1926
2329 SIMPSON H Cowper's Contribution to English Nature Poetry in Relation
         to His Predecessors in the Eighteenth Century BA Univ of British
         Columbia (Canada) 1953
2330 STREHLE Sue A An Analysis of Humor in the Letters of William Cowper
         MA Sacramento St Coll 1965
2331 SUGG Redding S The Enthusiastic Gentleman: An Essay on
         William Cowper MA Univ of Texas at Austin 1948 120 p

GEORGE CRABBE

2332 BROWN D A Satire in the Works of George Crabbe before *The Borough*
         MA Univ of North Carolina at Chapel Hill 1932
2333 CHAMBERLAIN Robert L Love, Reason and the Spirit in George Crabbe's
         Tales of the Hall MA Syracuse Univ 1950 138 p
2334 FORSYTHE Sally Psychopathic Characters in the Poetry of George Crabbe
         MA Columbia 1951

2335 GARMON Gerald M Actuality and Realism in the Poetry of George Crabbe
      MA Univ of Richmond 1960 109 p
2336 GRAYBURN William F The Qualities of the Narrative Poetry of
      George Crabbe MA Univ of Pittsburgh 1950
2337 HARTMAN Ethel R Studies in the Poetry of George Crabbe MA Univ of
      Texas at Austin 1938 155 p
2338 McCLOSKEY Sr Marie Traditional Morality in Crabbe's Characters
      MA St Louis Univ 1943 68 p
2339 McDANIEL Gerald The Poetic Personae of George Crabbe MA Midwestern
      Univ 1968 196 p
2340 NEILAN Bernaece I A Study of the Early Nineteenth Century Criticism
      of the Poetry of George Crabbe MA Rice 1942
2341 PARKS Adela G Crabbe's Literary Reputation from 1780 to 1832
      MA Howard Univ 1937
2342 RASKOPF Nancy A Satire and Sympathy: The Paradox of George Crabbe's
      Mature Poetry MA Univ of Tennessee 1969 99 p
2343 SCHILEO Liliana George Crabbe and His Poetry MA Ca Foscari (Italy)
      1956
2344 WALKER Mary J George Crabbe and His Times MA Washington St Univ at
      Pullman 1931
2345 WINEHOUSE B I "Never by Passion Quite Possessed": A Study of the
      Expression of the Conflict Between "Passion" and "Reason" in the
      Poetry of George Crabbe M Phil Univ of London (England) 1967

                              RICHARD CRASHAW

2346 BENNIS Sr M Anna The Catholicity of Richard Crashaw MA Columbia
      1952 109 p
2347 BERRY Barbara J The Influence of St Teresa of Jesus on
      Richard Crashaw MA Columbia 1950
2348 BRADFORD Joseph E The Fount of Ecstasy: A Study of the Imagery of
      Crashaw's English Sacred Verse MA Univ of Oklahoma 1961
2349 CALLAHAN Sr Ann B Baroque Music in Richard Crashaw MA Boston Coll 196
2350 CAMMARATA Bernard C Richard Crashaw and Francis Thompson: Contrasts
      in Mystic Poetry MA Columbia 1951
2351 CRONIN Francis C Thematic Structure in the *Carmen Deo Nostro* Poetry
      of Richard Crashaw MA Univ of Pittsburgh 1959
2352 DeLAURA David J The Baroque in the Poetry of Richard Crashaw
      MA Boston Coll 1958
2353 DOYLE Sr Teresa A Catholicism in the Poetry of Richard Crashaw,
      Seventeenth Century Religious Poet MA Univ of Kansas 1938
2354 GALBREATH Kate Richard Crashaw as an Exponent of the Poetry of Wit
      MA Louisiana St Univ 1937
2355 GARVEY Marie M The Contemporary Reputation of Richard Crashaw
      MA Columbia 1953 56 p
2356 HALLEY Thomas A Crashaw's Religious Poetry: A Study in Petrarchan
      and Patristic Influences MA St Louis Univ 1943 97 p
2357 HOLT Barbara F Invisible Things Understood by Things that are
      Made: Crashaw and the Emblem Writers MA Columbia 1964 74 p
2358 LEBEDINSKY Marcia H The Religious Viewpoint in the Poetry of
      Richard Crashaw MA Univ of Pittsburgh 1953
2359 McDONALD John B Crashaw and Francis Thompson: A Comparative Study
      MA Univ of Iowa 1931
2360 McGILLEY Sr Mary J The Influence of Saint Teresa of Avila on the
      Poetry of Richard Crashaw MA Boston Coll 1951
2361 PETTOELLO Laura D The Poetry of Richard Crashaw M Litt Cambridge Univ
      (England) 1954
2362 RAMIREZ Adela O Crashaw's Imagery: A Study Based on the *Carmen Deo
      Nostro* MA Georgetown Univ 1957 78 p
2363 REILLY Robert T Francis Thompson's Debt to Richard Crashaw in

Poetical Thought and Content MA Boston Univ 1948
2364 WATERS Leonard A A Study of the Poetry of Richard Crashaw and His
      Relation to the Metaphysical School MA St Louis Univ 1935 93 p
See also 3943, 3969, 5464

SAMUEL DANIEL

2365 BISSELL Betty J Samuel Daniel: His Theory and Practice MA Univ of
      North Carolina at Chapel Hill 1958 109 p
2366 COBRIN Allen M Samuel Daniel: The First English Interpretative
      Historian MA Columbia 1959 65 p
2367 HIMELICK James R Samuel Daniel's Musophilus: Containing a General
      Defense of All Learning MA Indiana Univ 1950
2368 HORN Jefferson L Poetic Theory and Practice in the Work of
      Samuel Daniel MA Univ of Texas at Austin 1951 93 p
2369 MIATELLO M Paola The Tragedy of Cleopatra by Samuel Daniel
      MA Ca Foscari (Italy) 1968
2370 ROMAN James Samuel Daniel's Delia: An Appreciation MA Temple Univ
      1964 60 p
2371 ROSECRANCE Jackson Samuel Daniel MA Columbia 1941
2372 SESSUMS A C Studies in Samuel Daniel MA Univ of North Carolina at
      Chapel Hill 1925
2373 STAGNI Alessandra The Tragedy of Philetas by Samuel Daniel
      MA Ca Foscari (Italy) 1965
2374 WYANT Jerome L Samuel Daniel: A Senecan Tragedy MA John Carroll
      Univ 1965
See also 1353, 2838

WILLIAM D'AVENANT

2375 BERRY William G Sir William Davenant and the Seventeenth Century
      Theatre MA McGill (Canada) 1935
2376 JOHNSTON Albert S Jr The Wits and The Platonic Lovers by
      William D'Avenant MA Univ of Florida 1951
2377 MOSHER Mary T The Life of Sir William Davenant MA Columbia 1935
2378 MYERS James P The Pre-Commonwealth Tragicomedies of Sir William
      D'Avenant MA Univ of Arizona 1965
2379 THOMAS Wesley W A Study of Gondibert, a Heroic Poem by
      Sir William D'Avenant MA Columbia 1951
2380 WALKER William D Jr Madagascar with Other Poems by
      Sir William Davenant MA Columbia 1935
See also 2306

JOHN DAVIES

2381 COX Mary N Sir John Davies' Nosce Teipsum: Its Reputation in the
      Seventeenth and Eighteenth Centuries MA Univ of Kentucky 1959 80 p
2382 KRAMER Pauline The Light Fantastic: A Study of the Background and
      the Sources of Sir John Davies' Orchestra MA Columbia 1940

DANIEL DEFOE

2383 ANGELL C E Pragmatism as the Religion of Defoe MA North Texas St
      Univ 1957
2384 AYCOCK Lonnie W Defoe's Woman: Her Place in Life and Fiction
      MA Washington Univ at St Louis 1960 72 p
2385 BATHANIEL Gaylord Aphra Behn and Daniel Defoe: A Study of Comparative
      Verisimilitude MA North Carolina Coll 1959 52 p
2386 BOREN Elizabeth The Educational Views of Daniel Defoe MA Univ of
      Texas at Austin 1931 147 p

2387 BRAGG Juliama Defoe's Treatment of the English Upper Classes
      MA Howard Univ 1939   56 p
2388 BREWER Mattie S Defoe's *Moll Flanders*: Its Historical Background
      MA Univ of Texas at Austin 1935
2389 BROWN Grace A A Study of the Religious Aspects of Defoe's Major
      Works MA Howard Univ 1936
2390 BURGER Mary M The Critical History of a Classic: A Study of
      Robinson Crusoe MA Colorado St Coll 1961
2391 CANNIZZO Francesco Daniel Defoe MA Ca Foscari (Italy) 1930
2392 CHARLTON John E Defoe the Journalist MA Boston Univ 1908
2393 CURTIS Constance H The Natural Man in the Eighteenth Century as
      Shown in Defoe's *Robinson Crusoe* MA Columbia 1942
2394 DAVIS Margaret Defoe's Loyalties as Manifested in His *Review of the
      Affairs of France* MA George Washington Univ 1941   81 p
2395 DEHNICK Philip C Defoe's Criminal Characters M Ed Temple Univ 1955
      44 p
2396 DILLMAN Mildred M The Theme of Isolation in Four Novels of
      Daniel Defoe MA Pacific Univ 1967   146 p
2397 ELWOOD William A Aspects in Individualism in Defoe's Narratives
      MA Univ of Mississippi 1959   159 p
2398 ENDERBY M E Defoe's Attitude Toward the Position of Women in the
      Eighteenth Century MA North Texas St Univ 1967
2399 EVANS Nancy D Defoe's Use of the Supernatural MA Univ of Kentucky
      1954 121 p
2400 EWING R P Daniel Defoe: The Father of Modern Journalism
      MA Ohio St Univ 1927
2401 EYRE Dorothy J Certain Realistic Novels of Daniel Defoe and
      Arnold Bennett MA Boston Univ 1931
2402 FLORY Dan L *Die Landstortzerin Courasche, Moll Flanders, Das Leben
      der Schwedischen Grafin von G.....*: A Study in Development
      MA Univ of Tennessee 1966
2403 FONTAINE Phyllis D The Dissenting Theme in *Robinson Crusoe*
      MA East Tennessee St Univ 1969
2404 FRIEDMAN Murray N Daniel Defoe and His Economics MA Columbia 1936
2405 GIEBEL Norbert J The Military Motive in British Fiction from Defoe
      to Dickens MA Univ of Toledo 1931
2406 GOERGEN Nicholas J Evidence of Socio-Economic Classlessness in
      the Major Fiction of Daniel Defoe MA South Dakota St Univ 1965
2407 GOODWIN A M Defoe's Versatile Adoption of the Social, Political
      and Religious Movements of His Day to Literary Uses MA Boston
      Univ 1927
2408 GORE Daniel Plot and the Doctrine of Providence in *Robinson Crusoe*
      MA Univ of North Carolina at Chapel Hill 1956   118 p
2409 HALL Blanche E Comparison of Defoe's Picaresque Novels and the
      Spanish Picaresque Novel MA Univ of Texas at Austin 1934
2410 HATCH Ronald The Moral Universes of Defoe and Fielding BA Univ of
      British Columbia (Canada) 1963
2411 HENDLEY William C The Narrative Method of Daniel Defoe: Aspects
      of Reality and Use of Biography MA Univ of Texas at Austin 1966
2412 ILLINGWORTH E The Political Ideas of Daniel Defoe MA Leeds Univ
      (England) 1961
2413 INGALLS Iolani A Critical Index of Defoe's *Review* MA Univ of
      Oregon 1942
2414 ISE Hulda L A Study in the Criticism of Prose Fiction from Daniel Defo
      to Jane Austen MA Univ of Kansas 1912
2415 KADISH Doris Rousseau and the Defoe of *Robinson Crusoe*: A Study
      in Affinities and Divergencies MA Columbia 1964   104 p
2416 KAHN Edward P Secrecy as an Organizing Theme in Defoe, Fielding
      and Scott BA Amherst 1965
2417 KIRK Frankie J A Century of Defoe Criticism, 1731-1831 MA Rice 1952

2418 KORN Frederick B A Study of Diction in the Narratives of Daniel Defoe
       MA Washington St Univ at Pullman 1963
2419 LADNER Christine H Daniel Defoe: Advocate of Religious Toleration
       MA Univ of Houston 1965 101 p
2420 LENNON J K Defoe: The First Modern Novelist MA Boston Coll 1932
2421 LIND Carl B Daniel Defoe the Soldier: A Study of Defoe's Military
       Accounts in *Memoirs of a Cavalier* and *Colonel Jacque*
       MA Columbia 1963 135 p
2422 McDANIEL Sr Marion Defoe's *Review* and the Stage MA Univ of Texas
       at Austin 1959 89 p
2423 McKEE Jane The Literary Reputation of Daniel Defoe as a Novelist,
       1719-1935 MA Univ of North Carolina at Chapel Hill 1940
2424 MANSFIELD Joseph G Ironic Intention in Defoe's *Roxana* MA Boston
       Coll 1968
2425 MAYHALL Pearle R Daniel Defoe as the Forerunner of the English
       Novel MA Florida St Univ 1940
2426 MUIR Ross L Considerations of the Laboring Poor in the Writings
       of Mandeville and Defoe MA Columbia 1950
2427 MURRAY Norma D Defoe and the English Middle Classes MA Howard Univ
       1940 78 p
2428 NASH Charles C Daniel Defoe's *Moll Flanders*: Innovation and
       Tradition MA Hunter College 1967
2429 NEUHAUS C H Jr The Theme of Isolation in the Novels of Daniel Defoe
       MA North Texas St Univ 1960
2430 PITTS Carol M A Study of Defoe's *Captain Singleton, Colonel Jacque*
       and *Roxana* as Tradesmen MA Univ of North Carolina at Chapel Hill
       1957 106 p
2431 RICE Kenneth W The Origins of Defoe's Ideas as Set Forth in His
       Essay upon Projects MA Columbia 1950
2432 ROITER Howard The Growth of Religious Awareness in Isolation: The
       Dissenting Position in Defoe's *Robinson Crusoe* MA Columbia 1961
       95 p
2433 SANDERS Winifred E An Examination of the Factual Basis for the
       Newgate and Transportation Sections of *Moll Flanders* MA Columbia
       1952 171 p
2434 SANSING John W Fielding's Comic Sense: A Corrective to Deficiencies
       in the Works of Defoe, Richardson and Smollett BA Amherst 1965
2435 SCHULTZ John H The Castaway Story in Literature Before *Robinson Crusoe*
       MA Univ of Texas at Austin 1934
2436 SEN Srichandra Daniel Defoe: His Mind and Art M Litt Cambridge Univ
       (England) 1947
2437 SEYMOUR Thaddeus The Literature of the South Sea Bubble: With Some
       New Light on the Lives and Writings of Defoe, Pope, Swift and Gay
       MA Univ of North Carolina at Chapel Hill 1951 142 p
2438 SMALLEY Donald A Defoe's Purpose in Its Relation to His Novels
       MA Indiana Univ 1935
2439 SOGLIERO Albert A The Art and Mind of Defoe MA Boston Coll 1951
2440 TOWNS Robert M Defoe as a Guide and Counselor in the Home
       MA Indiana Univ 1950
2441 WALLIS Mary L An Investigation of the Historical Aspects of
       Daniel Defoe's Writings M Ed Henderson St Coll nd
2442 WATSON John E Charles Morton, Tutor to Daniel Defoe MA Univ of
       Maine 1947 62 p
2443 WHITE Ruth B Defoe's Methods of Establishing the Impartiality and
       Reliability of His *Review* in the Controversy Over Union of Scotland
       and England Ma Washington Univ at St Louis 1947 179 p
2444 WILLIAMSON Eunice C Defoe and Picaresque Fiction MA Tulane Univ 1932
2445 WORTMAN Walter R The Statement of Christian Fundamentals in
       Daniel Defoe's *Robinson Crusoe* MA Lamar Technological Univ 1966
       100 p

2446 WRIGHT T Techniques in the Presentation of Psychology in the Novels
          of Defoe, Richardson and Sterne M Phil Univ of London (England)
          1967
See also 936, 3525, 4917

THOMAS DEKKER

2447 ABBIATICI Erfa *The Virgin Martyr* by Philip Massinger and Thomas Dekker
          MA Ca Foscari (Italy) 1961
2448 BEAMAN Milburn F Democratic Ideas Reflected in Dekker's Dramatic
          Work MA Oklahoma St Univ 1939 45 p
2449 BEEDE Helen F The Elements Common to the Civic Pageants and the
          Plays of Thomas Dekker MA Smith Coll 1918
2450 BERGER Theodore S Thomas Dekker: The Years 1599-1610, an Elizabethan
          Faces the Jacobean World MA Columbia 1965
2451 BERNET Ruth E Popular Elizabethan Psychology in the Works of
          Thomas Dekker MA St Louis Univ 1940 109 p
2452 BRAGLIA Norberto Dekker's *Old Fortunatus* MA Ca Foscari (Italy) 1956
2453 BUCKMASTER Elizabeth M Evidences of Unity in Dekker's *The Honest
          Whore, Parts I and II* MA Univ of Delaware 1967 52 p
2454 CARLSON Norma Collaboration on *The Honest Whore, Part I* MA Rutgers
          St Univ 1958 92 p
2455 CERUTI Mariarosa Thomas Dekker: *Westward Hoe* MA Ca Foscari (Italy)
          1959
2456 CHRISMAN Pauline C A Study of Six Comedies of Dekker MA Univ of
          Texas at Austin 1937 155 p
2457 CORTELLI Paola A *If It Be Not Good, the Devil Is In It* by
          Thomas Dekker MA Ca Foscari (Italy) 1966
2458 CRISTINA Giuseppina *The Honest Whore* by Thomas Dekker MA Ca Foscari
          (Italy) 1959
2459 DUFFY Dorothy V The Artisan in the Plays of Thomas Dekker MA Fordham
          Univ 1956
2460 FULTON Joseph D Thomas Dekker's Composition of His Source Material
          in *The Shoemaker's Holiday* MA Univ of Texas at Austin 1934
2461 GALLO Maria L Thomas Dekker: *The Bellman of London* MA Ca Foscari
          (Italy) 1964
2462 GALLOWAY Phyllis H Religion and the Plague Pamphlets of Thomas Dekker
          MA Howard Univ 1966 45 p
2463 GARLANDA Franca Thomas Dekker: *The Shoemaker's Holiday* MA Ca Foscari
          (Italy) 1955
2464 GRATZ Charles The Plays of Thomas Dekker with Special Reference to
          Old Fortunatus, The Honest Whore and *The Shoemaker's Holiday*
          MA Univ of Pittsburgh 1951
2465 KING Mary E A Study of the Bourgeoise in Thomas Dekker's Plays
          and Prose Pamphlets MA Univ of North Carolina at Chapel Hill
          1949 72 p
2466 KIRBY M R Life of the Elizabethans as Reflected in Dekker MA Boston
          Univ 1926
2467 LUCHI Laura Thomas Dekker: *The Seven Deadly Sins of London*, News
          from Hell MA Ca Foscari (Italy) 1964
2468 MANCINI Anna R *The Witch of Edmonton* by Samuel Rowley, Thomas Dekker
          and John Ford MA Ca Foscari (Italy) 1961
2469 MERCER Tracy E Social Comment and Criticism in Selected Works of
          Thomas Dekker BA Univ of British Columbia (Canada) 1967
2470 MOORE Donald K The Plague in Dekker's Pamphlets and Stow's
          Annales MA Univ of Delaware 1969 89 p
2471 OWEN Guy Jr The Dramatical Satire of Thomas Dekker MA Univ of
          North Carolina at Chapel Hill 1949 138 p
2472 PAXTON George B Jr A Production Book for Thomas Dekker's *Shoemaker's
          Holiday* MA Univ of Tennessee 1951 116 p

2473 RACCA Ida Thomas Dekker: A Tragicomedy Called *Match Me in London*
        MA Ca Foscari (Italy) 1961
2474 SCARAMUZZA DE MARCO Anna M *Patient Grissil* by Thomas Dekker,
        William Houghton and Henry Chettle MA Ca Foscari (Italy) 1961
2475 SCHIFFHORST Joseph A Critical Edition of Thomas Dekker's *Old
        Fortunatus* MA St Louis Univ 1963 117 p
2476 SCHNAKENBERG Charlotte S The Citizen Comedies of Thomas Dekker
        and Thomas Heywood MA Columbia 1951
2477 STOUT Rev O Hugh Thomas Dekker's Treatment of the Middle Class
        MA Villanova Univ 1965
2478 TIENGO Luciana Thomas Middleton; Thomas Dekker: *The Roaring Girl
        or Moll Cutpurse* MA Ca Foscari (Italy) 1959 29 p
2479 WADDLE Amber Thomas Dekker's Pamphlets MA Univ of Kansas 1932
2480 WEIR Ruth D Parallelism and Contrast in the Plays of Dekker and
        Ford MA Indiana Univ 1940
See also 6877

                        WALTER DE LA MARE

2481 CHIARI Gilda Children in Contemporary English Literature:
        Walter de la Mare MA Ca Foscari (Italy) 1950
2482 FOX Martha C Walter de la Mare's Use of Fantasy in the *Memoirs of
        a Midget* MA Univ of Texas at Austin 1938 122 p
2483 GREHAN Eileen P Walter de la Mare and Dream Poetry MA Columbia 1951
2484 HARBIN Katherine Studies in the Poetry of Walter de la Mare
        MA Univ of North Carolina at Chapel Hill 1933
2485 OLSEN Dorothy A The Terrible Vision of Walter de la Mare MA Bowling
        Green Univ 1969
2486 PLANCHER Maria Walter de la Mare MA Ca Foscari (Italy) 1937
2487 STUMPF Edna C Walter de la Mare and the Supernatural: A Study of
        His Short Stories MA Pennsylvania St Univ 1966
2488 WESTON Joanna M Thresholds in the Prose Fiction of Walter de la Mare
        MA Univ of British Columbia (Canada) 1969 101 p
2489 WOOD C A A Critical Examination of the Poetry of Walter de la Mare,
        with Special Reference to the Poetry of 1902-1913 MA Univ of
        London (England) 1967
See also 4396

                        THOMAS DELONEY

2490 DAVEY L M A Study of the Realistic Elements in the Novels of
        Thomas Deloney MA Univ of North Carolina at Chapel Hill 1936
2491 FASSINA Giuliana *Thomas of Reading* by Thomas Deloney MA Ca Foscari
        (Italy) 1965
2492 HARD C F Studies in Deloney's Prose MA Univ of North Carolina at
        Chapel Hill 1924
2493 HAYDOCK James J Deloney's Proverb Lore MA Baylor Univ 1952 130 p
2494 HYSHAM Marjorie The Realism of Thomas Deloney's Novels MA Univ of
        Iowa 1932
2495 OFFUTT Edwyna A Characterization in the Novels of Thomas Deloney
        MA Indiana Univ 1942
2496 PERISSUTTI Maria Thomas Deloney: *The Pleasant History of
        John Winchcomb in His Younger Years Called Jack of Newberie*
        MA Ca Foscari (Italy) 1964
2497 SCOTT Mary E Thomas Deloney, Elizabethan Novelist MA George
        Washington Univ 1943 102 p
2498 VITALI Margherita *The Gentle Craft* by Thomas Deloney MA Ca Foscari
        (Italy) 1965
2499 WEAVER Robert B Technical Aspects of Thomas Deloney's Prose Fiction
        MA Univ of Texas at Austin 1957 132 p

2500 WOLSKI Helen W The Novels of Thomas Deloney MA Boston Coll 1959

THOMAS DeQUINCEY

2501 CORNELISON Fern J The Dream Literature of Thomas DeQuincey
      MA Washington Univ at St Louis 1943
2502 CRESCINI Anna Thomas DeQuincey: Some Aspects of His Work
      MA Ca Foscari (Italy) 1938
2503 FORBES Minnie M Thomas DeQuincey MA Univ of Oklahoma 1911
2504 FUTRELL John C Horror in DeQuincey MA St Louis Univ 1953 165 p
2505 HADEN Gladys   A Comparison of Thomas DeQuincey's 1882 and 1866
      Confessions of an English Opium Eater MA Eastern New Mexico Univ
      1961
2506 HOLLINGER Robert E The Wit and Humor of Thomas DeQuincey MA Univ of
      North Carolina at Chapel Hill 1947 99 p
2507 MERCER M M Imagery of Thomas DeQuincey MA Ohio St Univ nd

CHARLES DICKENS

2508 ADAMS Ruth R Dickens and Slavery MA Univ of Maryland at College Park
      nd 79 p
2509 ADAMSON Martha A "Most Ingenious Practitioners": A Study of Lawyers
      and Clerks in Six Novels by Charles Dickens MA Univ of Texas at
      Austin 1961 127 p
2510 ANGUS-SMITH Joanne The Quest for Identity in *Great Expectations* and
      Related Dickens Novels MA Alberta (Canada) 1966
2511 AUGBURN Gerald Dickens' Conversion in the *Pickwick Papers* MA Univ
      of Maryland at College Park 1962 66 p
2512 BANKS Paul F Charles Dickens' *Hard Times:* A Study of Character
      Portrayal MA Boston Coll 1955
2513 BARKER Mary *The Posthumous Papers of the Pickwick Club*: A Study
      in Amiable Humor MA Vanderbilt Univ 1965
2514 BARNES Gladys A The Influence of Charles Dickens on Education
      BA Univ of Oklahoma 1917
2515 BARRETT Barbara A Dickens' Theme of Childhood: The Child as Victim
      of the Victorian Age MA Central Connecticut St Coll 1966
2516 BEAMAN Evelyn A Dickens' Relationship to Tobias Smollett MS Univ of
      Massachusetts 1935
2517 BELL Mary E The Doctors in Dickens' Works MS Kansas St Coll at
      Pittsburg 1960
2518 BERGE Margaret C The Literary Treatment of the Criminal in
      Charles Dickens' *Great Expectations* and Victor Hugo's *Les Miserables*
      MA Syracuse Univ 1949 72 p
2519 BERNSTEIN Diane An Examination of Some of Dickens' Death Scenes
      MA Wayne St Univ 1965
2520 BLOUNT T J An Investigation of Materials and Method in Dickens'
      Bleak House MA Univ of London (England) 1962
2521 BONNER Nancy L Hearth and Home in *Bleak House* MA Emory Univ 1965
2522 BROADBENT Clairene R A Study of the Immediate American Response
      to Dickens' *American Notes* MA San Diego St Coll 1956 78 p
2523 BROCKINGTON Philipp L Jr *Bleak House*: The Problem of a Public
      Voice in the Victorian World BA Amherst 1962
2524 BROOKS Florence C Dickens' Religious Beliefs as Revealed in His
      Novels M Ed Temple Univ 1942 116 p
2525 BURGAMY Nona P Ralph Nickleby: The Development of a Villian in
      Nicholas Nickleby MA Texas Technological Univ 1966
2526 CALHOUN Ruth R Character and Illustration in Three Novels by Dickens:
      Oliver Twist, David Copperfield and *Great Expectations*
      MA Louisiana Polytechnic Institute 1966 194 p
2527 CARTER Reta N Quotable Quotations from the Novels of Charles Dickens

MA Univ of Kansas 1948

2528 CHARLTON Judith L Dickens' Fiction for the Young Reader MA Univ of Iowa 1965

2529 CHEEK Edwin R Dickens' Contribution to the Short Story MA Univ of North Carolina at Chapel Hill 1958 155 p

2530 CLARK Sr Eileen M The Ideal of Charity Portrayed in the Life and Works of Charles Dickens Is That of Humanitarianism MA Boston Coll 1942

2531 CLARK Harold F Jr The Energy that Thwarted Itself: A Biographical Criticism of Charles Dickens BA Amherst 1957

2532 CLINE Clarence L A Study of the Men in the Novels of Charles Dickens MA Univ of Texas at Austin 1931

2533 COLLIER D H The Presentation of Character in the Early Novels of Charles Dickens: The *Pickwick Papers* to *Martin Chuzzlewit* MA Leeds Univ (England) 1958

2534 COUGHLIN Matthew N Toward the Light: The Changing Outlook of Dickens Symbolized in His Novels from *Bleak House* to *Great Expectations* MA Villanova Univ 1966

2535 CRENSHAW Thaddeus H III The *Pickwick Papers*: Focal Point of Dickens' Career MA Auburn Univ 1942

2536 CROMWELL Alexandra F House, Family and Domesticity as Central Images in Dickens' Novels MA Univ of British Columbia (Canada) 1970

2537 CUTLER Edward J The Undisciplined Heart Theme in the Latter Novels of Charles Dickens MA Columbia 1963 58 p

2538 DEMAREST George S The Egoism of Charles Dickens as Revealed in His Life and Novels MA Rutgers St Univ 1938

2539 DE STEFANI Maria Children in Dickens' Novels MA Ca Foscari (Italy) 1933

2540 DICE Jess E Liquor in the Novels of Dickens MA Indiana Univ 1950

2541 DICK John A The Dramatic Interests of Charles Dickens MA Univ of North Carolina at Chapel Hill 1949 113 p

2542 DICKERMAN Ethel K Educational Reforms Advocated in Dickens Fiction MA Texas Christian Univ 1959 118 p

2543 DILLINGHAM Jennie R Structure in Charles Dickens' *Nicholas Nickleby* MA Texas Technological Univ 1966

2544 DOCKERY Ruth M Dickens' *Household Words* as Popular Literature MA St Louis Univ 1937 84 p

2545 DOERNENBURG Emil Der Einfluss Dickens auf Raabe MA Northwestern Univ 1908

2546 DOTSON Doris A Dickens' Comic Villains MS Kansas St Coll at Pittsburg 1968

2547 EATON Arthur D An Analytical Survey of the Critical Approaches to Dickens' Fiction MA Manitoba (Canada) 1965

2548 EATON Richard B Jr Detective Story Characteristics in *Bleak House* MA Univ of North Carolina at Chapel Hill 1954 78 p

2549 ENGLISH Helen E Nature in the Novels of Charles Dickens MA Indiana Univ 1940

2550 FABER Arthur The Ideological Pattern in Charles Dickens' *Hard Times* MA Bowling Green Univ 1960

2551 FARLEY Mary I The Portrayal of Humble Life by Charles Dickens MA Univ of Texas at Austin 1927

2552 FEENY Virginia L *Marianela* and *The Old Curiosity Shop*: A Comparative Study MA Univ of Texas at Austin 1960 89 p

2553 FERLAND Wilfrid Charles Dickens and the Child MA Montreal (Canada) 1964

2554 GANNON Sr Dorina Pictures of Poverty in the Works of Charles Dickens MA Univ of North Dakota 1932 77 p

2555 GARDNER Harvey C Fantastic Elements in *Bleak House* MA Columbia 1951

2556 GARRIGUS Charles Freedom and Confinement: Comic Character and Theme in *Little Dorrit* MA Fresno St Coll 1963 45 p

2557 GAYDON M A Autobiographical Elements in the Works of Charles Dickens
       MA North Texas St Univ 1950
2558 GIBSON E M The Autobiographical Element in the Novels of
       Charles Dickens BA Univ of British Columbia (Canada) 1938
2559 GISH Carol S Popular Attitude towards Dickens and Thackeray from
       1850 to 1925 MA Univ of Oklahoma 1929
2560 GOLAY Eleanor K The Criminals in Dickens' Novels MA Indiana Univ 1935
2561 GREEN Marjorie A The Uncultured Rich Man in Dickens' Late Novels:
       Hard Times, Little Dorrit and *Our Mutual Friend* MA Texas Agricul-
       tural and Mechanical Univ 1967 136 p
2562 GREGORY Charles T Progressive Pessimism in Dickens as Viewed in the
       Central Symbols of the Late Novels MA Columbia 1958 105 p
2563 GRINNELL Ray E The Background of Dickens' Satire MA Univ of North
       Dakota 1931 128 p
2564 GRUNLUND B E The Presentation of Children in Dickens' Novels as
       Social, Comic and Pathetic Characters BA Univ of British Columbia
       (Canada) 1948
2565 GUNSTEAD Alice Aspects of Reform in Certain Novels of Charles Dickens
       MA North Texas St Univ 1945
2566 HACKER Mary S Dickens and Steinbeck MA Univ of Iowa 1947
2567 HARRINGTON Richard C Dickens as Editor of Fiction in *All the Year
       Round* MA St Louis Univ 1944 116 p
2568 HARRIS Justine F The Delineation of Childhood in the Novels of
       Charles Dickens MA Univ of Texas at Austin 1927
2569 HARVEY Isobel Dickens and De Morgan MA Univ of British Columbia
       (Canada) 1919
2570 HERRIN Mary B Analysis and Evaluation of Some Recent Abridgments
       of Dickens' Classics MA East Tennessee St Univ 1951
2571 HIGHFIELD Esther L Types of Children in Dickens' Novels MA Univ of
       Louisville 1930
2572 HINDMAN Geraldine Painters of Nineteenth Century Metropolitan
       Masses: Dickens and Balzac MA Univ of Pittsburgh 1936
2573 HINDS Dorothy H A Study of Dickens' Unfinished Novel MA Univ of
       Arizona 1966
2574 HINES Jessie M Charles Dickens: A Study of His Treatment of Children
       in Certain of the Novels MA Oklahoma St Univ 1942 74 p
2575 HUGHES H H Character Description in Dickens MA Univ of North Carolina
       at Chapel Hill 1909
2576 HUGHES Jacqueline M Dramatic Techniques in Some Selected Novels of
       Charles Dickens MA Univ of Pittsburgh 1961
2577 HUNTRESS Elizabeth J Charles Dickens and George Cruikshank MA Univ
       of Maryland at College Park 1963 78 p
2578 HYNES Frances C A Study of the Widow Characters in the Novels of
       Charles Dickens MA St Mary's at San Antonio 1944 80 p
2579 JANES Sophie Charges of Sentimentality Against Dickens MA St Louis
       Univ 1944 90 p
2580 KAJII Jasuko Charles Dickens and American Slavery MA San Diego
       St Coll 1965 88 p
2581 KAPLAN Fred Dickens: A Modern Novelist. A Study of the Style of
       Bleak House, Little Dorrit and *Our Mutual Friend* MA Columbia 1961
       124 p
2582 KEER Karen L Teaching a Novel in High School: An Approach to
       Charles Dickens' *David Copperfield* MA Cornell Univ 1965
2583 KERR Bernice A Some Implications of Selected Writings of
       Charles Dickens for Contemporary Education MA Kent St Univ 1966
2584 KIRK Gerald A An Analysis of Charles Dickens' Criticism of
       Victorian Society through the Use of the Symbols of the Prison
       and the Criminal MA Univ of Houston 1955 69 p
2585 KNAUS Bertha M Prison Reform through Fiction MA Austin Coll 1937
2586 LESHAN David J Dickens and Love: A Study of Romantic Love Relation-

ships in Five Novels by Charles Dickens MA Columbia 1965   77 p
2587 LEVY Melania La Influencia de Dickens en Galdos MA Columbia 1937
2588 LEWIS Douglas J Dickens on Education as Seen in *Hard Times for These Times* MA Columbia 1965   125 p
2589 LIN Peggy Gothic Elements in Three of Charles Dickens' Novels BA Univ of British Columbia (Canada) 1969
2590 LITTELL Penelope P Charles Dickens: Aspects of Narrative Technique MA Columbia 1965   123 p
2591 LUNDGREN Bruce R The Function of Romance in *Martin Chuzzlewit, Dombey and Son* and *Hard Times* MA Western (Canada) 1966
2592 McCARTHY Carolle Dickens and the Theatre MA Univ of Pittsburgh 1962
2593 McMURCHIE Karen R The Women Characters in the Novels of Charles Dickens MA Univ of South Dakota 1965
2594 MALONE James F Dickens' Villains MA Univ of Texas at El Paso 1962   88 p
2595 MANEY Florence A Structure and Symbol in *Great Expectations* MA Univ of Hawaii 1951   95 p
2596 MARCUS Steven P Dickens' Novels as They Relate to His Culture M Litt Cambridge Univ (England) 1954
2597 MARKLEY Meredith S Dickens' Use of His Family Relationships in His Fiction MA Texas Christian Univ 1955   110 p
2598 MESCOLA Emma Dickens' Whimsical Characters MA Ca Foscari (Italy) 1941
2599 MILLER I S A Study of the Children in the Works of Charles Dickens BA Univ of British Columbia (Canada) 1922
2600 MILLER Pamela A From Comedy to Humor: A Study of Dickens' Minor Women Characters MA Pennsylvania St Univ 1965
2601 MOORE M A The Humour of Dickens BA Univ of British Columbia (Canada) 1933
2602 MURPHY Mary J Imagery of Theme and Character in *Bleak House* by Charles Dickens MA Univ of Louisville 1966
2603 MYERS V L Dickens and Melodrama: Themes and Techniques of the Theatre in the Early Novels M Phil Univ of London (England) 1968
2604 NELSON Barbara K Dombey, Dorrit and Dickens: A Study of Fathers MA Bowling Green Univ 1968
2605 NETTERVILLE Dora G Plot Structure in the Novels of Charles Dickens MA Univ of Texas at Austin 1922
2606 OEHMSON Meta "The Dandy-Gentleman" as Seen in Four of Dickens' Novels MA Columbia 1963   63 p
2607 PATTERSON Charles I The Predecessors of *Pickwick Papers* MA Emory Univ 1940   176 p
2608 PATTON Alva L The Social Criticism of Charles Dickens MA Univ of Tulsa 1956   132 p
2609 PIRSIG Ruth A Dickens' Darlings: A Study of the *Angel in the House* Female Characters in Dickens' Novels MA Bowling Green Univ 1969
2610 POTTS Helen M Dickens' Social Satire on the American People and Institutions MA Univ of Kentucky 1937
2611 PRIOUR Kate A George Cruikshank as Illustrator for Charles Dickens MA Univ of Texas at Austin 1939   104 p
2612 RIDDEL Caroline M A Study of the Benevolent Gentlemen in Dickens' Novels MA McGill (Canada) 1966
2613 RIEPE Olga Charles Dickens and Social Reform MA Univ of Iowa 1934
2614 ROBERTS Minnie Y The Portrayal of Woman in the Novels of Charles Dickens MA Univ of Texas at Austin 1927
2615 ROBERTSON Heather The Use of the Child as a Technique of Fiction by Three Victorians: Dickens, Kingsley and Carroll MA Columbia 1964   170 p
2616 ROBINSON Roselee Dickens' Creation and Use of Minor Characters MA Toronto (Canada) 1966
2617 RODDIE Carol B Romantic Elements in Dickens MA Univ of Texas at Austin 1962
2618 ROSEN L C The Portrayal of Women in the Novels of George Eliot between

1850 and 1860 as Contrasted with that of Charles Dickens in the
Same Period BA Univ of British Columbia (Canada) 1947

2619 ROTHWEIN Alma F A Study of Australia as Presented in *Household Words*
and *All the Year Round*, Under the Editorship of Charles Dickens
(1850-1870) MA Columbia 1942

2620 SAINT WILFRED Sr A Study of the Child in the Early Novels of Dickens
MA Western (Canada) 1965

2621 SAUNDERS John K The Use of Triangular Familial Relationship in
Dickens' *Great Expectations* MA Oklahoma St Univ 1968 78 p

2622 SAWYER R M Child Characters in the Dickens' Novels MA Boston Univ 194(

2623 SCHMIEDENDORF Isabel M A Comparison of the Treatment of the Lower
Classes of Society in the Novels of Charles Dickens and in Those
of Pio Baroja MA Univ of Arizona 1938

2624 SCHONER Alta A A Search for Truth: A Study of Non-Conscious States
in the Novels of Charles Dickens MA Texas Technological Univ 1966

2625 SHLEFFAR Jo E Household Deeds: A Consideration of the Relationship
between the Disintegrating Vision of Charles Dickens and the
Crucial Years of His Private Life, 1857-1858 MA Temple Univ 1966
50 p

2626 SINCLAIR Lela The Preparation of the Reading Public for the *Pickwick
Papers* MA Univ of Oklahoma 1930

2627 STEPHENS Ruby J Charles Dickens: Oral Reader MA Univ of Oklahoma 194?

2628 STERN Henry H Jr Towards Hearth and Home: Charles Dickens' Conception of Moral Change BA Amherst 1959

2629 STILLER June A Study of the Casual Characters in Dickens' Novels
MA Univ of Toledo 1951

2630 STOUT Wynona M The Gothic Motif in the Novels of Charles Dickens
MS Kansas St Coll at Pittsburg 1965

2631 STUBBS Grady G The Elements of Purpose in Dickens' Novels MA Indiana
Univ 1940

2632 TATHAM Campbell The Satirical Method of Charles Dickens BA Amherst 19

2633 THURLEY G J Dickens' Conception of the Moral Responsibility of the
Individual as Shown in the Treatment of Some of His Heroes MA Univ
of London (England) 1964

2634 TROUT Charles H The Comedy of Charles Dickens BA Amherst 1957

2635 TUDOR Jayne V Charles Dickens' Theory of Villainy in *Nicholas Nickleby*
Oliver Twist and *Old Curiosity Shop* MA Texas Technological Univ
1967 72 p

2636 VARMUS Harold E The Murder of Evil: A Study of Charles Dickens
BA Amherst 1962

2637 WALLACE Alva D Grotesque in the Novels of Charles Dickens MA Texas
Technological Univ 1929 77 p

2638 WHITTON Etta M Villains and Their Punishment in Dickens' Novels
MA Florida St Univ 1950

2639 WILL Sr Mary L The Clown and Comics in *Pickwick Papers* and *Our Mutual
Friend* MA Coll of the Holy Names at Oakland 1968

2640 WILLIAMS G L The Theory and Practice of Humour in Dickens MA Univ of
London (England) 1962

2641 WILLIAMS Sharon L The Heroes of Charles Dickens: A Study in Inward-
ness MA Univ of Tulsa 1966 62 p

2642 WOLL Barbara L Imagery in Dickens Later Novels MA Univ of Maryland
at College Park 1964 73 p

2643 WORDON John L Jr Dickens and Interpersonal Communications MA San
Diego St Coll 1965 132 p

2644 WRIGHT Susie T Education in the Writings of Dickens MA Southern
Methodist Univ 1923

2645 WYKES David Art and Autobiography in Dickens: *Oliver Twist,
David Copperfield* and *Great Expectations* MA Miami Univ 1964

2646 YOUNG Harriet M Dickens and Anglo-American Copyright, 1836-1870
MA Columbia 1937

2647 YOUNG Susan N From Hunted to Hunter: A Study of Four Murderers in
        Dickens MA Washington Univ at St Louis 1970 87 p
2648 ZANE E Virginia Widows of Dickens M Ed Temple Univ 1938   154 p
See also 1296, 1305, 2405, 3392, 4634, 5485, 6186, 7380

BENJAMIN DISRAELI

2649 BEACH Sr Mary A The Attitude of Benjamin Disraeli toward Catholicism
        and the Roman Catholic Church as Revealed by His Novels, 1826-1880
        MA Marquette Univ 1946 94 p
2650 BLOOM Paul B The End of the Season: The Novels of Benjamin Disraeli
        BA Amherst 1966
2651 CRESTANA Lamberta Disraeli MA Ca Foscari (Italy) 1947
2652 GETTMANN Laurene E The "Condition-of-England Question" as Dealt with
        in the Novels of Benjamin Disraeli MA Univ of Oregon 1934
2653 GOVE Leslie J The Political, Social and Religious Elements in
        Disraeli's Trilogy MA Boston Univ 1948
2654 LEGRIS Maurice Theme and Structure in the Autobiographical Novels
        of Benjamin Disraeli MA Univ of North Carolina at Chapel Hill
        1957 137 p
2655 MERRITT James D The Novels of Benjamin Disraeli: A Study MA Univ of
        Wisconsin 1964
2656 MOORE John T The Portraiture Question in the Political Novels of
        Benjamin Disraeli MA Boston Coll 1952
2657 NOLAN Robert F Benjamin Disraeli: A Study of His Religious Develop-
        ment and Racial Consciousness MA Univ of Maryland at College Park
        1951 119 p
2658 RAMSEY Goldie A Study of Disraeli's Novels MA Univ of Louisville
        1966 114 p
2659 SCHUPF Henri A The Political Philosophy of Benjamin Disraeli
        BA Amherst 1957
2660 SIMPSON Harriet U Social Problems in the Fiction of Benjamin Disraeli
        MA Univ of New Mexico 1943
2661 STEPHENS John C The Novels of Benjamin Disraeli, Earl of Beaconsfield
        MA Emory Univ 1938 135 p
2662 TRERE Sergio Benjamin Disraeli: Statesman and His Times MA Ca Foscari
        (Italy) 1941
2663 WALKER Floyd A Benjamin Disraeli's Young England Trilogy: The Minor
        Characters and Their Function MA Texas Christian Univ 1967 70 p
2664 WYLIE Pauline R Young England in Disraeli's Trilogy MA Univ of
        Kentucky 1940

JOHN DONNE

2665 ANDERSON Ruth A John Donne and Petrarchism: The Tradition and the
        Major Poems MA San Diego St Coll 1968 171 p
2666 ARMITAGE Christopher M Donne's Poems in Huntington Manuscript 198:
        A Textual Study MA Western (Canada) 1964
2667 AUSTIN Alexander J Reading Matter of John Donne MA Boston Coll 1939
2668 BAIRD Eleanor B Metaphysical Conceits Involving Death in the Writings
        of John Donne MA Pacific Univ 1963 78 p
2669 BAKER E M The Poetry of John Donne and the World of Plotinus
        MA Univ of London (England) 1953
2670 BALDWIN Helene L The Cult of John Donne in the Twentieth Century
        MA George Washington Univ 1959 82 p
2671 BALSEVICH Mary Leonard Cohen and John Donne: The Divine Sceptics
        BA Univ of British Columbia (Canada) 1969
2672 BARNES Henry D The Conversion of John Donne: A Study in the Renewal
        of Poetic Vision MA Univ of Rhode Island 1963 78 p

2673 BARTON Alice F Metaphysical Poetry: A Study of the *Songs and Sonnets*
      MA Columbia 1961 86 p
2674 BEARD Vada L The Evolution of Donne's Religious Thought MA Univ of
      Oklahoma 1949
2675 BEATON Archibald E Autobiographical Evidences in the Poetry of
      John Donne MA Boston Coll 1942
2676 BELL Kathelene John Donne's Divine Poems MA Univ of California at
      Riverside 1962
2677 BENSON Crayton R Jr The Dating of John Donne's Poems MA Univ of
      North Carolina at Chapel Hill 1949 78 p
2678 BESPALOFF Alexis J The Consummation and the Cost: A Study of Some
      of the Lyric Poems of John Donne BA Amherst 1955
2679 BILLINGSLEA Cenia B John Donne: The Evolution of His Theology and
      Philosophy MA Univ of Oklahoma 1960
2680 BROADWIN Vita H John Donne's Preoccupation with Death, Studied in
      Relation to the Whole of His Life and Thought MA Columbia 1943
2681 BROWN Josephine John Donne as a Poet of Love MA Univ of Texas at
      Austin 1938 107 p
2682 BRUCE George H Donne's Augustinian Theology MA Univ of New Hampshire
      1958 73 p
2683 BRYAN Robert A The Reputation of John Donne in England during the
      Years 1785-1832 MA Univ of Kentucky 1951 163 p
2684 BURKS William John Donne's Wit: An Analysis of the Figures of
      Contradiction and Contrariety in the Lincoln's Inn Sermons
      MA Univ of Tennessee 1956 73 p
2685 BUTCHER Martha A Comparative Study of the Concepts in John Donne's
      Secular Verse and Religious Prose MA East Tennessee St Univ 1965
2686 CAHILL Robert J The Contrasting Moods of John Donne's Poetry
      MA Boston Coll 1947
2687 CAMERON Allan B The Verse Letters of John Donne: A Study of the
      Rhetorical Traditions of the Verse Epistle MA Windsor (Canada) 1965
2688 CASEY John W Theme of Love in the Poetry of John Donne MA Boston Coll
      1939
2689 CASKIE Gladys L An Analysis of the Prose Style of John Donne
      MA Florida St Univ 1954
2690 CASTILLO Frances E Donne's Images in *Songs and Sonnets* MA Univ of
      Rhode Island 1962 145 p
2691 CATES William F John Donne: A Study in Scholastic Metaphysics
      MA Univ of North Carolina at Chapel Hill 1950 70 p
2692 CHANEY William O The Use of Place Names in John Donne's Poetry
      MA Bowling Green Univ 1965
2693 CHETKIN Robert D The Dynamic Affirmation: *Call It Sleep;* Libertine
      Naturalism: John Donne; *The Wheel and the Martyr* MA Univ of
      Iowa 1966
2694 CITRON Lowell S Existential Anxiety of John Donne: A Study of the
      Devotions upon Emergent Occasions, Anniversarie Poems, Holy Sonnets
      and *A Litanie* MA Columbia 1960 65 p
2695 CLARKE Barbara C John Donne, Paradox and Problem; The Significance
      of the "Decay of Nature" Theory in John Donne's Work MA Smith Coll
      1935
2696 COFFIN C M The Romanticism of John Donne MA Ohio St Univ 1925
2697 COLLMER Robert G John Donne's Interest in Death MA Baylor Univ 1949
      156 p
2698 COONEY Rev Adrian J The Concept of Grace in the Writings of John Donne
      MA Boston Coll 1960
2699 CORETH Joseph H Neoplatonism in Donne's *Songs and Sonnets* MA Cornell
      Univ 1966
2700 COSTA Prudence M A Seventeenth Century Poetic of Wit: John Donne
      and Don Luis de Gongora MA Columbia 1965 103 p
2701 COTTON Elanor G John Donne MA Univ of Texas at El Paso 1952 132 p

2702 COX Warren E The Northern Passage: Donne on Death MA Columbia 1951
2703 CROW Betty G John Donne and the Classical Elegy MA North Texas
      St Univ 1967
2704 DANKER Frederick E Anti-Courtly Elements in Donne and Cervantes
      MA Boston Coll 1965
2705 DIEB Ronald K Flesh and Spirit: A Study of Donne's Love Poetry
      MA Texas Christian Univ 1955 103 p
2706 DOGGETT Frank A Innovation in the Poetry of John Donne MA Emory Univ
      1933 69 p
2707 DUPONT Georges L John Donne and the Individual Soul MA Columbia
      1953 68 p
2708 DURRWACHTER Carol J John Donne and Gerard Manley Hopkins: A Comparison
      MA Pennsylvania St Univ 1966
2709 EIBNER Gerald A Study of John Donne's Use of the Metaphysical Conceit
      MA Mankato St Coll 1969 53 p
2710 EL-KNUDAIRI Nadira A Critical Consensus of John Donne's Character
      MA Howard Univ 1967
2711 FEINBERG Susan E John Donne's Religion of Love as Evidenced in the
      Songs and Sonnets MA Boston Coll 1968
2712 FERGUSON B L Jacobean Pulpit Oratory, with Special Reference to the
      Sermons of Lancelot Andrewes and John Donne BA Univ of British
      Columbia (Canada) 1939
2713 FINI Rev Gilbert G The Mariology of John Donne MA Boston Coll 1953
2714 FLANAGAN James M Early Years of John Donne MA Univ of Pittsburgh 1928
2715 FLYNN Dennis John Donne and the Middle Way MA Columbia 1962 60 p
2716 FRASER Glorene Donne and the New Critics MA Univ of Tulsa 1951
2717 FRIESEN Benno W "Thy Firmness Draws My Circle Just": A Study of
      Discipline in the Poems of John Donne MA Univ of Arizona 1966
2718 GAEBELEIN Isabel N Hall, Donne and the Roman Satirists MA Columbia
      1943
2719 GIAQUINTA Josephine M Verb Structure in the Religious Poetry of
      John Donne and of Several Contemporaries MA Georgetown Univ 1960
      119 p
2720 GOETZ Murrel L John Donne and the Petrarchan Tradition MA Univ of
      Oklahoma 1949
2721 GOLDBERG Jonathan S The Idealization of Women in Donne's Occasional
      Poetry MA Columbia 1965 84 p
2722 GOLDBERG Joseph P A Reconsideration of Current Concepts of the School
      of Donne MA Univ of Maryland at College Park 1959 140 p
2723 GRAFIOUS Louis V Philosophy of Love in the Poetry of John Donne in
      Relation to Renaissance Traditions MA Univ of Oregon 1935
2724 GREEN Myrtle I A Study of John Donne in Relation to Contemporary
      Comments and Criticism MA Louisiana St Univ 1936
2725 GUTIERREZ Larry John Donne and Some Spanish Poets of el Siglo de Oro
      and the Later Spanish Renaissance MA Wayne St Univ 1965
2726 HABENICHT Rudolph E John Donne's Concept of Homiletic Eloquence and
      Its Application to His Sermons MA Columbia 1951
2727 HAGGARD Frank E John Donne and the Concept of Self-Knowledge
      MA Univ of Kansas 1965
2728 HALL Dick H John Donne the Preacher MA Univ of Louisville 1925
2729 HAMILTON Carl H The Lincoln's Inn Sermons of John Donne MA Univ of
      Tulsa 1963 89 p
2730 HAYES Noreen L Death as a Theme in the Sermons of John Donne
      MA Univ of Louisville 1964
2731 HAYTER Sharon A The Influence of Courtly Love on the Elegies of
      John Donne MA Auburn Univ 1968
2732 HEANEY William H Devotional "Wit": An Approach to Selected Religious
      Poems of John Donne and George Herbert BA Amherst 1968
2733 HEIMAN Mary A A Re-Evaluation of Donne's Use of Classical Allusion
      and Mythology in His Poetry MA Univ of Florida 1964

2734 HEJKE Gene M A Definitive Analysis of the "Metaphysical" Style
     of John Donne MA Fairleigh Dickinson Univ 1966
2735 HENRY Marie L Dynamic Imagery in the *Songs and Sonnets* of John Donne
     MA Boston Coll 1953
2736 HERLIHY Thomas John Donne and His Poems MA Boston Univ 1938
2737 HIGHTOWER Dorothy G John Donne: English Master of Gongorism
     MA Pacific Univ 1969 152 p
2738 HILYARD Joseph R The Symbolism of Light in the Poetry of Donne,
     Herbert and Vaughan MA Univ of Massachusetts 1955
2739 HINTON Norman D Correspondences in the Poetry of John Donne and
     George Herbert MA Univ of Tulsa 1954 78 p
2740 HODGES Norfleet D Sensuous Imagery in the Poetry of John Donne
     MA East Carolina Univ 1964
2741 HOFFMAN Jill J The Use of the Negative: A Study of Donne's
     Nocturnall upon St Lucies Day MA Columbia 1960 135 p
2742 IRMSCHER William F The Conventional Aspects of John Donne as a Love
     Poet MA Indiana Univ 1950
2743 JANZEN Henry D The Satires of John Donne MA Windsor (Canada) 1964
2744 JONES Freda E Meaning and Metaphor in John Donne's *Elegies*
     MA Univ of Montana 1965
2745 JONES Mary C John Donne and the Circle of Love MA Long Island Univ
     1966 117 p
2746 KEATING John L Sermon Writings of John Donne MA Boston Coll 1947
2747 KELLER William L John Donne: Similarities between the Anniversary
     Poems and the *Devotions upon Emergent Occasions* MA Columbia 1951
2748 KNIGHT Dorothy R The Configuration of the Cross as a Mode of Tension
     in the Poetry of John Donne MA Boston Coll 1966
2749 KRIECKHAUS Robert The Temperament of John Donne in *The Sunne Rising*
     MA Columbia 1962 75 p
2750 KUHRE Walter W The Doctrine of the Natural Law and the Prose Works
     of John Donne MA Univ of Pittsburgh 1961
2751 KURTINITIS Sandra L The Greek Anthology and the Love Poetry of
     John Donne MS Univ of Maryland at College Park 1969 85 p
2752 LEARY Sr Mary M Corporate Unity in Donne's *Devotions upon Emergent
     Occasions* MA Boston Coll 1958
2753 LEFKOWITZ Judith J The Microcosm-Macrocosm Imagery of John Donne
     MA George Washington Univ 1964 73 p
2754 LEREW Donna M Paradoxes of the Renaissance in the *Songs and Sonnets*
     of John Donne MA George Washington Univ 1965 162 p
2755 LESEN Ruth A Reading of John Donne's *Anniversaries* MA Columbia
     1965 158 p
2756 LIBOWITZ Harvey M Image-Forms Available to the Poetry of the Coming
     Decades: Observations Based upon Similarities in Image-Forms in
     Donne and Shakespeare and the Contrast in Their Employment
     MA Univ of Pittsburgh 1958
2757 LINNEMAN Sr Rose A The Death Image in the Works of John Donne
     MA Xavier Univ of Louisiana 1964
2758 LOWTHER Leo M John Donne and Womankinde MA Idaho St Univ 1966
2759 McCARTHY Kathleen J Donne's "Air and Angels": A Question of Meaning;
     Allegorical Tendency in *Jude the Obsure*; and a Hawthorne Problem:
     The Psyche and the Butterfly MA Pennsylvania St Univ 1965
2760 McCONNOCHIE James Drama in John Donne's Poetry MA Long Island Univ
     1969 71 p
2761 McDANIELS Jack D John Donne's Revolt Against Courtly Love MA Baylor
     Univ 1955 135 p
2762 McGLAUN Rithia A John Donne's Two *Anniversaries* MA Univ of North
     Carolina at Greensboro 1964
2763 McKNIGHT George The Autobiographical Element in the *Songs and Sonnets*
     of John Donne MA McMaster (Canada) 1965
2764 MacLEAN Jessie L The "Impure Motive" in Dr Donne MA McGill (Canada)

1967

2765 MacLEOD Sr Mary C Rhythmic Structures in the Poetry of John Donne:
     A Study in Technique MA Mount Saint Vincent (Canada) 1967

2766 McMENAMIN Marie E The Friendship between John Donne and
     Magdalen Herbert MA Georgetown Univ 1959 91 p

2767 MacPHERSON Frances B The Significance of Reformation Thought for
     John Donne MA Columbia 1955 130 p

2768 McSORLEY Barbara T A Study of Donne's Use of Imagery in His Sermons
     MA Boston Coll 1951

2769 MALONEY Carol F Donne's Influence on the Elegies of John Dryden
     MA Boston Coll 1966

2770 MARAS Emil B The Medieval Element in John Donne MA Univ of Arizona
     1938

2771 MARK Lily L The Figure of Death: A Study of the Minds and Uses of
     Imagery in Selected Sermons of John Donne MA Mount Holyoke Coll
     1966

2772 MARTELLA Sandra L John Donne and George Garrard: The Study of a
     Friendship MA Georgetown Univ 1967 131 p

2773 MERS Sr M Bernardine Reputation of John Donne in the Nineteenth
     Century MA St Louis Univ 1942 128 p

2774 MIDDLETON J A Ideas on Transience and Permanence in the Poems of
     Donne MA Univ of London (England) 1962

2775 MILLMANN Robert H Donne and the Seventeenth Century Sonnet
     MA St Louis Univ 1938 96 p

2776 MOLLENKOTT Virginia R Revaluating John Donne: A Study of Donne
     Criticism since 1912 MA Temple Univ 1955

2777 MOORE Raymond L The Idea of Death in Donne's Poetry MA West Virginia
     Univ 1967 84 p

2778 MOSER Anita M John Donne: A Study of His Literary Reputation among
     His Contemporaries MA St Louis Univ 1938 56 p

2779 MULLIGAN Louise E John Donne's Ideas of Marriage as Shown in His
     Sermons MA Boston C 1968

2780 MURPHY Virginia M Imagery on the Secular Poetry of John Donne
     MA Boston Univ 1948

2781 NEILL Mary L The Language of the 1611 Bible and of Donne's Sermons:
     A Study in Late Elizabethan English MA Stanford Univ 1939

2782 NEILSON Frederic W The Thinking Heart: A Study of Donne's Use
     of Religious and Erotic Imagery MA Columbia 1960 98 p

2783 NOBLE Thomas A The Reputation of John Donne among His Contemporaries
     MA Univ of North Carolina at Chapel Hill 1952 108 p

2784 O'CONNOR M Joyce The Circle Image: Index to Donne's Mind
     MA Boston Coll 1962

2785 PAGE Lois M The Influence of the Counter-Reformation on John Donne's
     Songs and Sonnets MA West Virginia Univ 1963 101 p

2786 PECKOVER Sarah L A Study of John Donne through His Poetry MA Boston
     Univ 1920

2787 PERKINS Alice M The Pictorial in the Sermons of John Donne MA Univ
     of Arizona 1940

2788 PETTIS M L Medicine in the Poetry of John Donne MA Univ of North
     Carolina at Chapel Hill 1940

2789 PFATTEICHER Philip H Anguish Pietie: The Role of Self-Torment in
     the Poetical Works of John Donne BA Amherst 1957

2790 PICCO Ulises R The Poetic Vision of Death in Jorge Manrique and
     John Donne MA Columbia 1960 81 p

2791 PRINDLE Roderic M A Reading of the Songs and Sonnets and the Sermons
     of John Donne BA Amherst 1960

2792 RANDALL Helen W Donne's Position in Literary History MA Smith Coll
     1931

2793 RAY R An Investigation of the Denotative Value of Donne's Imagery
     MA Univ of London (England) 1965

98

2794 REESE Mary M Three Studies in Poetry: Donne's "Aire and Angels";
      Paradise Lost in *The Prelude*; and Ransom's "First Travels of Max"
      MA Pennsylvania St Univ 1965
2795 REEVES George B The Microcosm in the Works of John Donne MA Univ
      of Pittsburgh 1934
2796 REYNOLDS David S The Movement to Donne: A Study in Poetic Iconoclasm
      BA Amherst 1970
2797 RICHARDSON Stewart B Structural, Thematic and Other Parallelisms
      Between Certain Poems of John Donne and of T S Eliot MA Columbia
      1950
2798 RIMEL Robert D The Lyrics of Jonson and Donne: A Comparative Study
      MA Univ of Delaware 1964 84 p
2799 ROBERTS Mathalie R Puritanism and Hedonism in the Poetry of
      John Donne MA Oklahoma St Univ 1932
2800 ROBERTS Tim J The Poetic Experience in Donne: A Comparison of the
      Poetry of John Donne and Jean De Sponde BA Univ of British
      Columbia (Canada) 1966
2801 ROBINSON F W Robert Southwell, Giles Fletcher and John Donne: An
      Analysis and Comparison of Their Religious Poetry BA Univ of
      British Columbia (Canada) 1947
2802 ROGERS Mary T Selected Poems with a Comparison of the Religious
      Sonnets of Donne and Hopkins MA North Texas St Univ 1970
2803 ROODHOUSE Anne C An Analysis of *The Canonization* by John Donne
      MA Univ of Oklahoma 1961
2804 ROSEBAUGH Constance G Aspects of Renaissance Melancholy in the
      Works of Spenser, Raleigh and Donne MA Columbia 1943
2805 ROSS Loretta M The Influence of the Cabala on the Works of
      John Donne MA Boston Coll 1962
2806 ROXBURGH J W The Jacobean Lyric with Emphasis on John Donne
      BA Univ of British Columbia (Canada) 1936
2807 SARNO Ronald A John Donne: His Role as a Renaissance Poet and
      How It Was Changed by the New Astronomy MA Boston Coll 1966
2808 SENNHENN Carl B Within the Meditative Tradition: A Study of
      John Donne's *Devotions upon Emergent Occasions* MA Univ of
      Oklahoma 1960
2809 SHOLLEY Susan John Donne's "A Litany": The Poem of Re-Creation
      MA Columbia 1967 106 p
2810 SIBLEY Agnes M A Comparative Study of John Donne and T S Eliot
      MA Univ of Oklahoma 1936
2811 SMITH Paul E Donne's Use of Biblical Paradox in the *Divine Poems*
      BA Bowling Green Univ 1963
2812 SMITH Paul E Trends in Donne Criticism: 1912-1965 MA Miami Univ
      1966
2813 SMITH Scott R The Redemption Theme in Donne's "La Corona", "A Litany",
      "Holy Sonnets" and Hymns MA Auburn 1969
2814 SPRAGUE Richard S The Reputation of John Donne as Poet from His Own
      Time to the Present MA Univ of Maine 1949 90 p
2815 STAHR William E John Donne and the Law MA Univ of Maryland at
      College Park 1953 70 p
2816 STRINGER Gary A The Biblical Element in Donne's Poems of Sacred
      and Profane Love MA Univ of Oklahoma 1970
2817 SULLIVAN Elizabeth M John Donne's *Letters to Several Personages*:
      A Re-Evaluation MA Brown Univ 1966
2818 SUMMERS Richard M Love Imagery in the Poetry of John Donne and
      Sir Philip Sidney MA Bowling Green Univ 1964
2819 SUN Mary The Epithalamions of John Donne MA Georgetown Univ 1968
      71 p
2820 SUNDQUIST Erik L Latin Verse Satire and the *Satyres* of John Donne
      MA Columbia 1967 145 p
2821 SWAIN Victor C The Love-Elegies of John Donne MA Columbia 1951

2822 SWARTCHILD William G   The Treatment of Death in John Donne and
        Sir Thomas Browne   MA Columbia 1959   92 p
2823 THORNTON Grace J   Imagery in the Poetry of John Donne   MA Univ of
        Oklahoma 1940
2824 TULLER Stuart S Jr   John Donne: A Study in Literary Continuity
        BA Amherst 1957
2825 VAIL Benjamin A   The Idea of Love as Eros and Agape in the *Songs
        and Sonnets* and the *Divine Poems* of John Donne   MA George
        Washington Univ 1953   208 p
2826 VANDOVER Sr Mary L   Donne and the Maps: A Study in the Thematic
        Relation between Image and Idea   MA St Louis Univ 1967   123 p
2827 WADMAN John C   The Excitement in John Donne's Love Poetry
        BA Amherst 1957
2828 WALKER B B   Classical Mythology in the Secular Poetry of John Donne
        MA North Texas St Univ 1967
2829 WEISS Robert H   Renaissance Ideas in John Donne's *Anniversaries*
        MA Temple Univ nd   77 p
2830 WOLFE Jane E   Donne's "La Corona": A Telling Transition   MA Syracuse
        Univ 1963   70 p
2831 WOOD Lucie A   Death and Resurrection in John Donne's Easter-Day
        Sermons   MA Columbia 1950
2832 WOOD Virginia M   Theories Concerning the Relation of Body and Soul
        in Donne's Poetry   MA Univ of North Carolina at Chapel Hill 1946
2833 YATES Miles L   The Court Preaching of John Donne   MA Columbia 1943
2834 ZUNDER William L   The Relations between Donne's *Elegies* and Ovid's
        Amores   MA McMaster (Canada) 1964
See also 3969, 4056, 4062, 4312, 4326, 5117, 5460, 5903, 6731

                            MICHAEL DRAYTON

2835 DI FEO Maria F   Michael Drayton: *Idea*, Edited with Introduction and
        Notes   MA Ca Foscari (Italy) 1961
2836 HALSEY Joan E   The Sources of the Arthurian Material in
        Michael Drayton's *Poly-Olbion*   MA Claremont Graduate School 1966
2837 HOHMAN Mary J   "In Love and Armes Delighting": A Critical Study of
        Drayton's *Nimphidia*   MA Temple Univ 1962
2838 LeBLANC Roland   Some Aspects of Historical Imagination in Daniel and
        Drayton   MA Toronto (Canada) 1966
2839 LONG Edgar   Studies in the Fairy Lore of Michael Drayton   MA Univ of
        North Carolina at Chapel Hill 1916
2840 LOSS Archie K   Three Studies in Style and Taste: Drayton's Later
        Style; Cubism, Montage and *Ulysses*; and American Popular Theater
        (1938-1939)   MA Pennsylvania St Univ 1966
2841 MILANI Franca   *Edimion and Phoebe* and *The Man in the Moone* by
        Michael Drayton   MA Ca Foscari (Italy) 1961
2842 PALESTIN Seymour J   The Pastoral Poetry of Michael Drayton
        MA Columbia 1936
2843 PARISI Peter E   Drayton's Revisions of *Idea*   MA Columbia 1965   52 p
2844 PEFOZA Annamaria   *The Legend of Matilda* by Michael Drayton
        MA Ca Foscari (Italy) 1962
2845 REED James C   Drayton's Proverb Lore   MA Baylor Univ 1956   102 p
2846 WILSON Harry B   Michael Drayton and the Erotic Tradition   MA Univ
        of Tennessee 1956   74 p
See also 1353, 6537

                            WILLIAM DRUMMOND

2847 FURSTENBURG William L   Contemptus Mundi in William Drummond of
        Hawthornden   MA Columbia 1964   107 p

2848 HOWELL Constance M A Critical Consensus Concerning the Poet
      William Drummond of Hawthornden MA Howard Univ 1967 79 p
2849 MILAN Nancy M William Drummond of Hawthornden: Poet of Meditation
      MA Univ of North Carolina at Chapel Hill 1959 66 p

                        JOHN DRYDEN

2850 ALLEN Eileen D Normative Use of Nature in Dryden's Criticism
      MA George Washington Univ 1949 96 p
2851 BARBEAU Anne The Religious Thought of John Dryden MA Hunter Coll 1964
2852 BEARD Elmer Religious Affiliations and Concepts of John Dryden as
      Reflected in Selected Works M Ed Henderson St Coll nd
2853 BISCHOFBERGER George John Dryden's Defense and Final Rejection of
      the Rhyming Couplet MA St Louis Univ 1935 87 p
2854 BOCASKY Carole C John Dryden: "Reason" in *Religio Laici*
      MA Boston Coll 1963
2855 BONNELL James F The Social Criticism of Dryden, Arnold and Eliot
      MA Boston Coll 1968
2856 BOURQUE Darrell The Social Offenders in Dryden's Comedies and
      Tragicomedies MA Univ of Southwestern Louisiana 1968 74 p
2857 BROWN Elizabeth J The Dramatic Use of Music in the Comedies of
      John Dryden MA Univ of Maryland at College Park 1961
2858 BYBRAND Glenna L A Comparison of Dryden's *Absalom and Achitopel*
      and Its Biblical Source M Ed Henderson St Coll nd
2859 CAROTHERS Mary T The Influence of Lucretius on Dryden MA Rice 1930
2860 CARROLL Mildred V Does the Literary Practice of John Dryden Correspond
      with His Critical Theory? MA Boston Univ 1933
2861 CHANDLER John W *Absalom and Achitopel:* A Collation MA Texas
      Christian Univ 1969 116 p
2862 COCHARN Judith C Dryden's *MacFlecknoe* and Pope's *Peri Bathous*
      as Satires on Augustan and Eighteenth Century Literary Mediocrity
      MA Colorado St Coll 1968 100 p
2863 COOPER Juliette C A Study of Dryden's Dramatic Criticism in
      Relationship to the Critical Theories of Corneille MA Oklahoma
      St Univ 1951
2864 COSTA Gian B Dryden's Fables and Their Sources MA Ca Foscari (Italy)
      1948
2865 CUTTS Richard A Study of the Rimed Heroic Tragedy and Its Culmination
      in the English Opera as Revealed in the Works of John Dryden
      MA Univ of Maine 1949 107 p
2866 DAMON Howard C Theories of English Translators from George Chapman
      to John Dryden MA Univ of Maine 1948 131 p
2867 DELTOUR Rev Sylvere A Reassessment of Dryden's Intellectual
      Background MA Villanova Univ 1965
2868 EBBS John D The Characterization of the Lovers in John Dryden's
      Comedies MA Univ of North Carolina at Chapel Hill 1949 145 p
2869 EIDMANS Kathleen M Dryden's *The Medal:* A Text and a Study MA Univ
      of London (England) 1950
2870 ELLIOT Emory B An Examination of Dryden's Adaptations of Shakespeare
      with Emphasis upon the Characters of Miranda, Cleopatra and
      Cressida MA Bowling Green St Univ 1966
2871 ERNST Manfrid P Dryden's Debt to Other Seventeenth Century Critics
      MA Washington Univ at St Louis 1932
2872 EVANS Betty D Dryden's Imagery in His Nondramatic Poetry MA Univ
      of Oklahoma 1957 368 p
2873 FALSEY Elizabeth A "And His Occasion Having Brought You Here":
      Classical Rhetoric in John Dryden's *Prologues* and *Epilogues*
      MA Columbia 1966 162 p
2874 FINGER Rev Joseph Attacks on Dryden's Catholicism MA Marquette Univ
      1935 107 p

2875 FITTABILE Leo F A Comparison of the Satirical Methods of John Dryden
      and Alexander Pope MA Boston Coll 1940
2876 FORD Zarepha The Literary Versatility of John Dryden with Emphasis
      on *Absalom and Achitophel* M Ed Henderson St Coll nd
2877 FORDE Henrietta E The Character of Cressida from Benoit to Dryden
      MA Univ of Maine 1940 110 p
2878 FOWLER Gertrude L The Dramatic Criticism of John Dryden MA Texas
      Christian Univ 1941 99 p
2879 GANGEWERE Robert J Dryden's Abortive Opera MA Univ of Connecticut
      1961
2880 GOOCH Bryan N Poetry and Music in England, 1660-1760: A Comparison
      Based on the Works of Dryden, Purcell, Pope and Handel MA Univ
      of British Columbia (Canada) 1962 196 p
2881 HALL Elmo M Dryden's Happy Adaptations in *Absalom and Achitophel*
      MA Texas Christian Univ 1965 78 p
2882 HANTHORNE Cleo M John Dryden in the Eighteenth Century MA Univ of
      Oklahoma 1936
2883 HARTSELL Robert C A Study of Dryden's *Religio Laici* as a Defense
      of Traditional Christianity MA Wake Forest Coll 1965
2884 JONES Betty M Certain Rhetorical Effects in Dryden's *Prologues* and
      Epilogues MA Vanderbilt Univ 1965
2885 JONES Helen G The Religious Development of John Dryden MA George
      Washington Univ 1935 54 p
2886 KAHN Arthur D A Comparative Study of Milton's *Paradise Lost* and
      Dryden's *State of Innocence* MA Rutgers St Univ 1942 85 p
2887 KENNELLY L B Significant Parallels in the Heroes of John Dryden and
      Lord Byron MA North Texas St Univ 1969
2888 KLEIN Don T Poetic Diction in Dryden's Original Nondramatic Poetry
      MA St Louis Univ 1940 96 p
2889 LESCHETSKO Helen John Dryden's Dramatic Criticism MA Columbia 1953
      67 p
2890 LYONS Rev Robert J Reason and Emotion in the Tragic Theory of
      John Dryden MA Niagara Univ 1965
2891 McKEON Michael The Uses of History in Poetry: Dryden's Verse and
      Historical Tradition MA Columbia 1966 105 p
2892 MARY THERESA Sr Discovery Scenes in Dryden's Serious Plays
      MA Univ of Oregon 1939
2893 MALONE Carol Ann Swift's Relationship with Dryden MA Texas
      Technological Univ 1970
2894 MEREDITH Johanna R Dryden and Shakespeare in Critical Perspective
      MA Univ of Oklahoma 1953
2895 MORGAN Henry D Some Influences of Political Philosophy and
      Government in the Works of John Dryden MA Southwest Texas St
      Univ 1938
2896 MORGAN Hubert John Dryden's Characteristic Temper of Mind BA Univ
      of British Columbia (Canada) 1963
2897 MUNSON Eva K A Detailed Study of Dryden's Translation of Virgil's
      Aeneid MA Louisiana St Univ 1937
2898 NEWCOMB Rebecca Dryden in the Light of Aristotle MA Washington
      Univ at St Louis 1929 171 p
2899 O'GORMAN Ignatius G St Augustine and John Dryden: Some Parallels
      MA Boston Coll 1960
2900 O'LEARY Frank L The Reputation of John Dryden as a Dramatist,
      1700-1779 MA Temple Univ nd 82 p
2901 PADBERG Mary J The Tragic Theodicy in Dryden MA St Louis Univ
      1935 108 p
2902 PALMER Ellen N Verb Forms from Selected Plays of John Dryden
      MA Oklahoma St Univ 1961 59 p
2903 PALMER J J Literary Patronage in the Time of Dryden B Litt Oxford
      Univ (England) 1940

2904 PATTEN Alta M The Influence of the French Critics on John Dryden's
      Criticism MA Washington Univ at St Louis 1935
2905 PICKARD Linda H John Dryden's *All for Love*: A Study of the Themes
      MA Texas Woman's Univ 1965
2906 POMERLEAU Mary F John Dryden's Theory of Poetry as Exemplified in
      His Translation of Chaucer's "The Knight's Tale" MA Carnegie-
      Mellon Univ 1966
2907 PRINCE Helen M The Critical Attitude Toward the Epic from Aristotle
      to Dryden MA Univ of New Hampshire 1964 76 p
2908 RANKIN H A Jr Scientific References in Dryden's Works MA Univ of
      North Carolina at Chapel Hill 1927
2909 REINHOLTZ Helen G John Dryden's Criticism of Ben Jonson as a Comic
      Dramatist Compared with Later Views MA Univ of Rhode Island 1968
      69 p
2910 RICHMOND G A John Dryden's Shakespearean Criticism MA Boston Univ
      1938
2911 ROBBINS Ora M The Foreign Influences in the Critical Writings of
      Dryden MA Texas Technological Univ 1935 47 p
2912 ROWLEY Grace K Dryden's Attitude Toward Shakespeare MA Smith Coll
      1930
2913 RUSS John R The Historical Development of the Beast Fable and the
      Debate from Their Origins to John Dryden MA Univ of New Hampshire
      1964 76 p
2914 SCHADE Florence A John Dryden as a Critic and Adapter of Shakespeare
      MA Washington Univ at St Louis 1927
2915 SHIRLEY Irma R The Quarrels of John Dryden and Sir Richard Blackmore
      MA Univ of Texas at Austin 1937 116 p
2916 SMITH Walter H Disguises, Music and Letters in Dryden's Comedies:
      A Study of Dramatic Method MA Univ of Tennessee 1964
2917 STIGA Paul F The Literary Relationships of John Dryden's *Religio
      Laici* MA Columbia 1960 59 p
2918 STINSON Massie C Jr Dryden's Adaptation of Shakespeare MA Univ of
      Richmond 1966 115 p
2919 STOKES William H The Reputation of John Dryden as a Dramatist
      MA Univ of Pittsburgh 1947
2920 THORSEN Lenora S *Oedipus Rex* by Seneca and Its Influence upon Dryden,
      Voltaire and Cocteau MA Univ of Oklahoma 1964
2921 TRAIN Lilla An Analysis of John Dryden's Literary Criticism
      MA Smith Coll 1934
2922 TUSKAN Regina C Religious Literature, 1638-1682: A Study of the Genes
      of Dryden's *Religio Laici* MA Ohio St Univ 1966 92 p
2923 TWEDDLE Mary C A Study and Evaluation of the Comic Techniques in
      the Satiric Poetry of Dryden, Swift and Pope MA Univ of Delaware
      1968 82 p
2924 URAGANI Reiko N A Comparative Study of John Dryden's Heroic Theory
      and Practice MA DePauw Univ 1957 101 p
2925 WHALEN John F Dryden's Dramatic Expression of Emotion MA Boston
      Coll 1954
2926 WHITTINGTON Pauline K The Epistolary Poems of John Dryden
      MA Univ of Oklahoma 1957
2927 WILLIAMS Sandra L John Dryden: A Study of His Principles and
      Descriptions Concerning the Poet MA Texas Woman's Univ 1964
2928 WIRTH John G The Heroic Drama of John Dryden MA Univ of Delaware
      1966 56 p
2929 WOHLSCHLAEGER Richard John Dryden: An Analysis of *The Medal*
      MA Columbia 1964 87 p
See also 1373, 1420, 1599, 1647, 1931, 2769, 4022, 4351, 5117, 5297, 5457,
      5492, 5534, 5895, 5906, 5932, 5956, 6204, 6309, 6534, 6568, 6675,
      6783, 7027, 7113, 7206, 7227

LAWRENCE DURRELL

2930 BARKATT Ariela Lawrence Durrell: *The Alexandria Quartet* MA Columbia
      1961 88 p
2931 BATTEN Mary Place as an Archetype in the Works of Lawrence Durrell
      MA Columbia 1962 96 p
2932 BOHRER Jennie The Theme of Exile in the Prose of Lawrence Durrell
      MA Columbia 1964 92 p
2933 BRIGHAM James A Prospero's Cell: Lawrence Durrell and the Quest
      for Artistic Consciousness MA Univ of British Columbia (Canada) 1965
2934 BRISCOE Donald C The Play-Element in Lawrence Durrell MA Columbia
      1965 81 p
2935 CLOVER Carol A *The Alexandria Quartet*: An Analysis of Modern Love
      MA Texas Technological Univ 1969 78 p
2936 COWAN Sandra E "The Heraldic Aspect of Reality": A Consideration
      of Certain Images and Symbols in *The Alexandria Quartet*
      MA McMaster (Canada) 1965
2937 CROOKS Alan F The Heraldic Universe of Lawrence Durrell: An Intro-
      ductory Analysis of His Thoughts and Poetry MA Utah St Univ 1965
2938 DASCH Robert A The Role of the Artist in the Modern World: A Study
      of Lawrence Durrell's *Alexandria Quartet* MA Sacramento St Coll 1966
2939 DAVIS Robert B Character Presentation in Lawrence Durrell's
      The Black Book and *The Alexandria Quartet* MA Long Island Univ 1968
      92 p
2940 FIFFICK Alicia L Theoretical and Symbolic Bases of Lawrence Durrell's
      Alexandria Quartet MA Villanova Univ 1965
2941 FOSTER Dorothy L Lawrence Durrell and British Diplomatic and Military
      Tradition MA Univ of Delaware 1967 93 p
2942 FRY P L The Artist in Durrell's *Alexandria Quartet* MA North Texas
      St Univ 1964
2943 HESTER Ernest C Jr Relativity and the Theme of Love in
      Lawrence Durrell's *Alexandria Quartet* MA Univ of North Carolina
      at Greensboro 1967
2944 HUNT Winifred M Lawrence Durrell: Towards the Heraldic Universe;.
      A Study of *The Sonnet of Hamlet* MA Columbia 1950
2945 HUOKONEN Ritva T Lawrence Durrell's Conception of Literary Art in
      Our Time MA Indiana Univ 1963
2946 HURST Darrell W The Critical Reception of Lawrence Durrell's
      Alexandria Quartet MA East Carolina Univ 1967
2947 KAPLAN Morton N Projections of an Artist: A Study of Character
      Structure in Lawrence Durrell's *The Alexandria Quartet* MA Columbia
      1962 167 p
2948 KRAUSE Leslie A The Role of Modern Love in *The Alexandria Quartet*
      MA North Texas St Univ 1965
2949 KROLL Alex Lawrence Durrell's Holy City: An Investigation into the
      Pattern and Unifying Elements of *The Alexandria Quartet* BA Rutgers
      St Univ 1962 118 p
2950 KRUPPA Joseph E Metaphor and Cosmology: The Structure of
      Lawrence Durrell's *Alexandria Quartet* MA Columbia 1961 99 p
2951 LOUTON Arlene S *The Alexandria Quartet* MA Ohio St Univ 1969
2952 MAGEE Marilyn *The Alexandria Quartet*: Studies in Syncretism
      MA Syracuse Univ 1966 81 p
2953 MATTESON Judith I An Analysis of Artistic Development in the Prose
      and Poetry of Lawrence Durrell MA Univ of Rhode Island 1965 81 p
2954 MILLS Judith H Lawrence Durrell's *Alexandria Quartet*: A Study of
      Characterization MA Queen's (Canada) 1965
2955 O'SHEA John V The Role of Unreality in the Characterization of
      The Alexandria Quartet MA Colorado St Coll 1966
2956 OTIS Paul J Durrell's Comic Satire MA San Diego St Coll 1965 129 p
2957 OUTTEN Judith E The Aesthetic of Fiction of Lawrence Durrell MA Univ

of Massachusetts 1965
2958 POST Kirby M Appearance Versus Reality in *The Alexandria Quartet*
      MA Texas Christian Univ 1965 147 p
2959 QUILLEVERE Hanne G Characters and the City in *The Alexandria Quartet*
      MA Univ of British Columbia (Canada) 1965
2960 REEVE Phyllis M The Mythopoesis of Lawrence Durrell MA Univ of
      British Columbia (Canada) 1965
2961 ROEBUCK William G The Implications of Time in *The Alexandria Quartet*
      MA McMaster (Canada) 1966
2962 SCHWETMEN John W Lawrence Durrell's *Alexandria Quartet*: A Metaphor
      for Relativity MA Baylor Univ 1965 108 p
2963 SHEINER Naomi F Masks and Masquerades: A Study of Lawrence Durrell's
      Alexandria Quartet MA Columbia 1961 71 p
2964 SKLAR Judith S The Artist and Reality: Darley's Relation to
      Alexandria in Lawrence Durrell's *Alexandria Quartet* MA Columbia
      1964 84 p
2965 SPAGNUOLO Geraldine D The Conception of Alexandria in
      Lawrence Durrell's *Alexandria Quartet* MA Univ of Massachusetts
      1967 38 p
2966 STARR Jacqueline M Labyrinth of the Soul: *The Alexandria Quartet*
      MA Boston Coll 1967
2967 STOUCK David H A Study of the Literary Influences of T S Eliot on
      Lawrence Durrell MA Toronto (Canada) 1964
2968 TABER Gisela An Examination of Modern Love in Lawrence Durrell's
      The Alexandria Quartet MA Washington St Univ at Pullman 1966
2969 TOMSHANY Robert A Relativity and Dramatic Irony: A Study of
      Lawrence Durrell's *Alexandria Quartet* MA Univ of Tulsa 1968 77 p
2970 WHEELOCK Webster The Wounded Inhabitants of Lawrence Durrell's
      Alexandria MA Columbia 1963 78 p
2971 WRIGHT Gene M Chronological Discrepancies in *The Alexandria Quartet*
      MA Texas Christian Univ 1968 76 p
2972 ZARIN Eve The Quest Motif in *The Alexandria Quartet* MA Columbia
      1961 140 p

                              MARIA EDGEWORTH

2973 ADAMS Dorinda A English Society in Novels of Maria Edgeworth
      MA Univ of Maine 1933 151 p
2974 ANDREOLI Maria F The Irish Novels of Maria Edgeworth MA Ca Foscari
      (Italy) 1959
2975 CIVAN Judith The Evil Jew in the Fiction of Maria Edgeworth
      MA Columbia 1963 111 p
2976 EGLESTON Helen F Maria Edgeworth: Novel Writer MA Univ of
      Pittsburgh 1927
2977 FARR C J Maria Edgeworth as a Precursor of Realism MA North Texas
      St Univ 1958
2978 HEARD Lutie Maria Edgeworth's Stories for Children MA Austin Coll 19
2979 MAY Willena The Novels of Maria Edgeworth MA Univ of Texas at Austin
      1930
2980 PADOVAN Carolina Maria Edgeworth MA Ca Foscari (Italy) 1937
2981 PENN Wanda Maria Edgeworth: Fiction in the Service of Education
      MA Texas Woman's Univ 1934
2982 RAMEY Shirley R The Novels of Maria Edgeworth MA Lamar Technological
      Univ 1966 103 p
2983 SMITH Estelle F The Literary Reputation of Maria Edgeworth
      MA Columbia 1940
See also 958
                              GEORGE ELIOT

2984 ALLEN Della C ¨Autobiographical Elements in the Writings of

George Eliot MA Florida St Univ 1941
2985 AMARASINGHAM Gwendoline M A Comparison of the Attitudes of
Mrs Gaskell and George Eliot, as Revealed in Their Novels, to
the Class System of Nineteenth Century England MA Boston Coll 1958
2986 ANTICO Peter J Inheritance and Commitment in *Daniel Deronda*
MA Columbia 1965 89 p
2987 ARMSTRONG Tila M Empiricism, the Basis of George Eliot's Moral
Philosophy MA Texas Woman's Univ 1935
2988 ASP Waldo B Through Pain and Suffering to Sympathy and Finally Love:
The Humanistic-Religious Theme in George Eliot's Early Novels
MA Mankato St Coll 1967 110 p
2989 BAILEY Mildred F The Philosophy and Art of George Eliot MA Boston
Univ 1943
2990 BAROSSO Fernanda Pensiero e Sentimento in George Eliot MA Ca Foscari
(Italy) 1942
2991 BELSON Abby A Similarities in the Treatment of the Theme of Marriage
and the Superior Woman by Henry James and George Eliot
MA Columbia 1959 58 p
2992 BLACKMON Billie A Character Development in Selected Novels of
George Eliot MA Northwestern St Coll 1966
2993 BLOCK Leon F The Psychological Dynamics in the Characters of
George Eliot MA Univ of Pittsburgh 1949
2994 BOTSFORD H V The Maturing Emotion of George Eliot MA North Texas
St Univ 1943
2995 BROWN Carolin C The Social Position of George Eliot's Heroines
MA Univ of Oregon 1934
2996 BROWN Helen L Literature Read in Rural England between 1790 and
1835 as Seen in the Provincial Novels of George Eliot MA Columbia
1942
2997 BRUBAKER Nora E Religious Motifs in George Eliot's *Adam Bede* and
Middlemarch MA Univ of Texas at Austin 1953 78 p
2998 CAMPBELL Charles F A Study of George Eliot's *Middlemarch* MA Bowling
Green Univ 1963
2999 CAMPBELL Patrick *Middlemarch* and Reality: A Study of the Development
of George Eliot's Ethical Creed MA Univ of British Columbia
(Canada) 1959 130 p
3000 CHONG Swan-Peng Moral Themes in the Shorter Fiction of George Eliot
MA Univ of New Brunswick (Canada) 1966
3001 CHRYSTOWSKI Madeline The Treatment of Provincialism in *Madame Bovary*
by Flaubert and in *Middlemarch* by George Eliot MA Univ of New
Hampshire 1960 89 p
3002 CLAUS Audrey E Three Bray-Hennell Thought Patterns in the Novels of
George Eliot MA Washington Univ at St Louis 1952
3003 COMBS John R The Clerical Characters in George Eliot's Novels
MA Texas Agricultural and Mechanical Univ 1964 208 p
3004 COYLE William The Omniscient Point of View as Used by George Eliot
MA Univ of Pittsburgh 1941
3005 CRAWFORD Linda R George Eliot's Treatment of Love and Marriage
MA Dalhousie (Canada) 1964
3006 CUNNINGHAM Ethel B The Tragic Error: A Study of Disastrous
Commitment in the Novels of George Eliot MA Columbia 1966 135 p
3007 DAIKER Victoria A Vision and the Quality of Choice: A Study of
George Eliot's *Romola, Felix Holt, Middlemarch* and *Daniel Deronda*
MA Indiana Univ 1964
3008 DALES Duane D George Eliot and Henry James MA Columbia 1955 71 p
3009 DANCER Murtel The Intrusive Author as Revealed in the Novels of
George Eliot MA Univ of New Mexico 1936
3010 DARRELL Nelda P Villains in George Eliot's Novels MA Hardin-Simmons
Univ 1969
3011 DAVIS Barbara J A Critical Study of George Eliot's *Romola*

MA Univ of Florida 1965
3012 DAVIS Estelle B The Scientific Content of George Eliot's Novels
     MA Oklahoma St Univ 1933
3013 DENT Carrie L George Eliot's Heroes MA West Virginia Univ 1900 32 p
3014 EDENS Agnes The Place of Religion in George Eliot's Novels MA Univ of
     Texas at Austin 1931
3015 EMERSON Ona M Provincial Life in the Novels of George Eliot MA Univ
     of Oklahoma 1925
3016 FISK Viva Religion and Tradition in the Novels of George Eliot
     MA Univ of New Mexico 1958
3017 FULTON A A Theory to Explain the Difference between the Earlier and
     Later Novels of George Eliot (Based on Her Psychological Pre-
     occupation) BA Univ of British Columbia (Canada) 1933
3018 GETMAN Oneita L Unity in *Middlemarch* through Time, Interrelation-
     ship of Plots and Tempo MA Univ of Louisville 1967 126 p
3019 GILMORE Mary George Eliot: A Critical Examination of Her Art as
     a Novelist MA Tulane Univ 1896
3020 GOODY Ila The Idea of the Self in the Novels of George Eliot and
     Henry James MA Toronto (Canada) 1966
3021 GROZIER Mary M The Theme of Isolation in *The Mill on the Floss*
     MA Columbia 1960 110 p
3022 HART Charles W *Adam Bede*: A Critical Revaluation MA Columbia 1962
     101 p
3023 HESS Virginia F George Eliot: Feminism and Women's Vocations
     MA Rice 1969
3024 HODGES Thomas K A Survey of the Criticism of George Eliot's Novels
     MA Univ of Pittsburgh 1941
3025 HOOYBOER John J Certain Aspects of the Conflict between Reason and
     Emotion in George Eliot MA Univ of Oregon 1938
3026 HORTON Bertha A George Eliot's Portrayal of Women MA Univ of Texas
     at Austin 1924
3027 HUMPHREY Danisa M The Portrayal of Female Characters in George Eliot's
     Novels: *Adam Bede, The Mill on the Floss* and *Middlemarch* MA Univ
     of Oklahoma 1959
3028 HUNSICKER Carol Social Disorientation in the Novels of George Eliot
     MA Columbia 1963 57 p
3029 JAMES David L Isolation in George Eliot's Novels MA Univ of British
     Columbia (Canada) 1966
3030 JELLISON Pauline W The Young Women Characters in George Eliot's
     Novels MA Univ of Maine 1940 102 p
3031 JONES Jesse C George Eliot and the Evangelical Mind MA North Texas
     St Univ 1966
3032 JONES Verna George Eliot's Portrayal of Men MA Univ of Texas at
     Austin 1925
3033 KELLEHER D J Humanitarianism of George Eliot MA Boston Coll 1933
3034 KELLEY Marguerite S George Eliot's Religion of Sympathy MA Univ
     of Maryland at College Park 1965 112 p
3035 KLAEGER Irene S The Subjective Element in the Novels of George Eliot
     MA Texas Christian Univ 1961 102 p
3036 LAROCHE James N George Eliot and Her Contemporary Critics
     MA Univ of Texas at Austin 1950 127 p
3037 LEE Mary M Mrs Gaskell and George Eliot as Ethical Interpreters of
     Their Age: A Comparative Study MA Univ of Texas at Austin 1932
3038 McCORMICK Sr M Eustochia The Realism of George Eliot MA Univ of
     Pittsburgh 1931
3039 McCULLOCH R W Relation of George Eliot to Mrs Gaskell MA Univ of
     North Carolina at Chapel Hill 1911
3040 McDONALD Sylvia V George Eliot's Doctrine of Responsibility and
     Retribution MA Central Connecticut St Coll 1965
3041 McDOWELL Curtus F George Eliot's Treatment and Development of the

Feminine Character in Her Novels MA Boston Univ 1943
3042 MANCINI Gino Scenes of Clerical Life and Religious Problems in
George Eliot MA Ca Foscari (Italy) 1934
3043 MANCUSO Sr Mary H Complexity, Consistency and Confinement in
George Eliot's Characterization MA Villanova Univ 1964
3044 MARCHETTI Giuseppina George Eliot and Italy MA Ca Foscari (Italy)
1929
3045 MASTERSON Mariana Sources of Ambiguity in the Portrayal of
Dorothea Brooke in *Middlemarch* MA Cornell Univ 1966
3046 MEGEE Willie E Plot Structure in the Novels of George Eliot
MA Univ of Texas at Austin 1916
3047 MILLER Daniel J Didactic Strategy in the Novels of George Eliot
MA Univ of Massachusetts 1965
3048 MILLER Lillie George Eliot: A Study of Her Philosophy of Life as
Shown in Her Works BA Univ of Oklahoma 1904
3049 MONEY Darlene E Social Setting in the Novels of George Eliot
MA Toronto (Canada) 1965
3050 MOREHEAD E W George Eliot's Life and Philosophy as Reflected in
Certain Characters of Her Four Early Novels MA North Texas St
Univ 1944
3051 NAGY Dolores M The Uses of Water and Water Episodes in the Novels
of George Eliot MA Univ of Pittsburgh 1955
3052 NAKAMURA Caroline C The Notion of Work in George Eliot's *Middlemarch*
MA Univ of Hawaii 1964 81 p
3053 NECOMB Mary J Christianity in the Works of George Eliot MA Kansas
St Univ 1965
3054 NICHOLS Elliff A Imagery as Characterization: The Main Plot of
Middlemarch MA Univ of Texas at Austin 1963 122 p
3055 OLDFIELD D E The Prose Style of *Middlemarch* MA Univ of London
(England) 1964
3056 PACK Isabelle M George Eliot's Ethical Sensibility: A Study of Five
Heroines MA Columbia 1955 121 p
3057 PARKER Beryl M The Role of the Mentor in George Eliot's Novels
MA McGill (Canada) 1965
3058 PATERSON Gary H The Aesthetic of George Eliot MA Toronto (Canada)
1964
3059 PFAFF Winnifred L A Study of the Chorus in the Novels of George Eliot
with Special Reference to Those of the Early Group MA Univ of
Texas at Austin 1936
3060 PHILLIPS Thelma H The Victorian Age as Revealed in the Novels of
George Eliot MA Indiana Univ 1940
3061 PRICE Ruth The Principles of Retribution in the Novels of George Eliot
MA Indiana Univ 1940
3062 PROVENCE Christine Biographical Data as Revealed in George Eliot's
Novels MA Univ of Oklahoma 1939
3063 PUCCI Raffaella George Eliot's Moral Realism MA Ca Foscari (Italy)
1948
3064 QUEEN Larry T Confrontation Scenes in *Middlemarch* MA Univ of North
Carolina at Greensboro 1970
3065 RAFF Walter S Patterns of Temptation in George Eliot's Novels
MA Univ of British Columbia (Canada) 1969 204 p
3066 RANDALL Bryce Moral Interest in the Novels of George Eliot
MA Temple Univ 1964 106 p
3067 RARIG Frank M Biblical Diction and Religious Belief in the Novels
of George Eliot MA Northwestern Univ 1905
3068 REGOSA Rebecca T The Realism of George Eliot MA Boston Univ 1935
3069 ROGERS Winslow S The Truth of Feeling: George Eliot's Doctrine
of Sympathy BA Amherst 1966
3070 ROSENBERG Rose S George Eliot: A Study in Conflicts MA Univ of
Pittsburgh 1932

3071 RUST James D George Eliot as a Literary Critic MA Indiana Univ 1940
3072 SANTANGELO Gennaro A The Clerical Characters in the Novels of
      George Eliot MA Univ of North Carolina at Chapel Hill 1953
3073 SCHLUETER Martin A The Intellectual Powers of George Eliot as
      Revealed in Her Fiction MA Southern Illinois Univ at Carbondale
      1964 98 p
3074 SCHNEIDER Alvin The Problem of Unity in *Daniel Deronda* MA Washington
      Univ at St Louis 1964 100 p
3075 SPAIN Leona G The Influence of Greek Drama on the Novels of
      George Eliot MA Univ of Arizona 1960 84 p
3076 STONE Albert Jr Technique and Idea in George Eliot's *Felix Holt*
      MA Univ of Houston 1956 65 p
3077 STONEMAN P M A Study of the Development of George Eliot's Methods
      of Presenting Character from *Scenes of Clerical Life* to *Romola*,
      with Special Reference to Linguistic Aspects of Her Technique
      MA Univ of London (England) 1964
3078 STRINGFELLOW William M The Influence of Biblical Higher Criticism
      upon the Life and Works of George Eliot MA Univ of New Mexico 1948
3079 SUKENICK Lynn The Two Worlds of Daniel Deronda MA Hunter Coll 1968
3080 SULLIVAN F E Social Consciousness in George Eliot's Novels
      MA Boston Univ 1914
3081 SWANEY M Imogene The Teachings of George Eliot MS Kansas St Coll
      at Pittsburg 1937
3082 TAFT Robert W Henry James and George Eliot: Inclusiveness and
      Selectivity in the Narrative Voice BA Amherst 1959
3083 TARBOX William G George Eliot's Art of the Novel MA Univ of Oklahoma
      1949
3084 TAYLOR Geneva R The Clergyman in George Eliot's Novels MA Univ of
      North Dakota 1932 59 p
3085 THORNTON Miriam A Bibliography of George Eliot's Writings and
      Selected Ana from January 1, 1930 to January 1, 1940 MA Univ of
      Kentucky 1944 137 p
3086 UNDERWOOD Gary N The Treatment of Love in Four George Eliot Novels:
      Adam Bede, The Mill on the Floss, Middlemarch and *Daniel Deronda*
      MA Texas Agricultural and Mechanical Univ 1964 199 p
3087 VIZZARDELLI Vittoria George Eliot's *Romola* MA Ca Foscari (Italy) 195
3088 WALKER Hallie D The Interpretation of Humble Life in the Novels of
      George Eliot MA Univ of Texas at Austin 1914
3089 WILLIAMS Abbie F The Influence of Scientific Studies on the Diction
      of George Eliot MS Northwestern Univ 1902
3090 WILLIAMSON Lillian A A Critical Study of Character Analysis in the
      Novels of George Eliot MA Univ of British Columbia (Canada) 1926
3091 WILPISZEWSKI Marianne *Emma* and *Middlemarch*: A Study in Parallel
      Thought MA Univ of Maryland at College Park 1967 58 p
3092 YARKER Roberta M A Study of the Development of Distorted Vision
      in the Major Characters of *Middlemarch* MA Columbia 1960 93 p
3093 YOST Agnes B A Study of the Influence of French Philosopher
      Auguste Comte on George Eliot MA Univ of Houston 1955 104 p
See also 544, 586, 598, 601, 963, 2618, 3114, 3787, 8553

JOHN EVELYN

3094 DENNY Margaret John Evelyn: Fellow of the Royal Society MA Smith
      Coll 1929
3095 HALE Margaret N The Friendship of John Evelyn and Samuel Pepys
      MA Univ of Arizona 1934
3096 ORTON Helen M A Study of the Literary Interests of Evelyn
      MA Univ of Iowa 1932
3097 WEBSTER R G John Evelyn's *Sylva*: Its Place in the Science of
      Forestry and in English Literature MA Univ of New Hampshire 1930

26 p
See also 271, 5869, 5875

HENRY FIELDING

3098 ADAMS Naomi E The Influence of the Latin Classics on the Work of
       Henry Fielding MA Univ of North Dakota 1930 154 p
3099 AHARONI A A Fielding's *Tom Jones* M Phil Univ of London (England) 1967
3100 AMORY Hugh Lex Loquens: A Study of the Formal Meaning of the Law
       in *Tom Jones* MA Columbia 1961 236 p
3101 ANDREW Jean E Fielding's Narrative Technique MA Univ of British
       Columbia (Canada) 1933
3102 ASHMORE Charles D Henry Fielding, Literary Critic: A Study of an
       Eighteenth Century Critical Mind MA George Washington Univ 1949
       115 p
3103 BARNARD Caroline K Structure and Change in Fielding's Novels or the
       Diminished Levity MA Brown Univ 1966
3104 BAUMAN Charles P Henry Fielding's *Amelia*: The Novel and Social
       Criticism MA Columbia 1960 63 p
3105 BELL Phyllis B Henry Fielding's Theory of the Novel and Its Applica-
       tion to *Joseph Andrews, Tom Jones* and *Amelia* MA Univ of Kentucky
       1948 77 p
3106 BEYER Betty M Humility, Charity and Poverty in Fielding's
       The Champion: A Key to His Clergymen MA Texas Agricultural and
       Mechanical Univ 1968 97 p
3107 BLAKE Lillie B A Consideration of the Problems of Good and Evil in
       the Works of Henry Fielding MA Rice 1931
3108 BROWN Alling C The Voice of Henry Feilding BA Amherst 1955
3109 BYNELL Harlan B The Forty-Five and *Tom Jones* MA Columbia 1965 67 p
3110 CARR William The Interpolated Tale in *Joseph Andrews* and
       Roderick Random MA Brooklyn Coll 1966
3111 CATLETT LaRue S The Function of Innocence: *Joseph Andrews, A Tale
       of a Tub* and *The Beggar's Opera* MA Univ of Texas at Austin 1962
       154 p
3112 CLARKE Linda The Theme of Marriage in *Tom Jones* BA Univ of British
       Columbia (Canada) 1966
3113 COHEN M A The Plays of Henry Fielding MA Leeds Univ (England) 1958
3114 COOPER Elaine P The Father-Daughter Theme in *Clarissa, Tom Jones*
       and *Emma* MA Columbia 1962 113 p
3115 CRAIG Ruth N Anticipations of Socio-Psychological Education in the
       Development of *Tom Jones* MA Bowling Green Univ 1949
3116 CUKERBAUM Bernard L Henry Fielding as an Essayist MA Univ of
       Pittsburgh 1930
3117 CULLINAN Mary E The Treatment of Marriage in Selected Works of
       Henry Fielding MA Univ of Iowa 1965
3118 D'AMICO Paris T The Appearance of Fielding's Fictional Characters
       in His Miscellaneous Prose Works MA Columbia 1936
3119 DAVIES E O A Critical Edition of *Pasquin* and *The Historical Register*
       by Henry Fielding B Litt Oxford Univ (England) nd
3120 DeKORTE Richard W An Approach to the Novels of Henry Fielding
       BA Amherst 1957
3121 EDWARDS Phillis J Henry Fielding's Interest in Law and Its Influence
       upon His Novels MA Boston Univ 1943
3122 EGG Norma The Use of the Chorus in the Novels of Fielding MA Univ
       of Texas at Austin 1928
3123 EUBANKS Katharine L Fielding's Political Plays: A Study in Back-
       grounds and Allusions MA Univ of Texas at Austin 1937 207 p
3124 FASKEN Joseph S Fielding the Essayist as Discovered in His Novels
       MA Texas Christian Univ 1925 129 p
3125 FEHR James K *Tom Jones* and the Picaresque Tradition MA Mankato St

Coll 1966   60 p
3126 GENTILE Jimmie K   The Basis of Morality in Henry Fielding's Novels
      MA Univ of Houston 1966   83 p
3127 GIFFEN Lynette L   Modes of Development and Meaning in *Tom Jones*
      MA Syracuse Univ 1956   90 p
3128 GRINDLE Rufus M   Irony in the Novels of Fielding   MA Univ of Maine
      1934   236 p
3129 HAASE-DUBOSC Danielle H   Some French Precursors of Henry Fielding:
      A Comparative Study   MA Columbia 1960   99 p
3130 HAILES Roger P   Moral Basis in Fielding's Irony   MA Univ of Richmond
      1969   56 p
3131 HAND Sally T   Fielding's Use of Horace in His Novels   MA Florida St
      Univ 1957   63 p
3132 HARRINGTON Alberta   Criticism in Henry Fielding's *Tom Jones*:   Classical
      Influences   MA Louisiana St Univ 1938
3133 HAYS May   The Philosophy of Henry Fielding as Expressed in His Novel
      Tom Jones   MA North Texas St Univ 1941
3134 HENRY Rolanne   The Significance of "An Enquiry into the Causes of
      The Late Increase of Robbers" to Henry Fielding, the Reformer
      MA Columbia 1966   136 p
3135 HIGBIE Robert G   Fielding's Nature: An Examination of Henry Fielding's
      Literary Character as Seen in *Tom Jones*   BA Amherst 1960
3136 HINNANT Charles H   Henry Fielding's *The Author's Farce* and *Pasquin*:
      A Study in Dramatic Satire   MA Columbia 1960   92 p
3137 HOWE Jean M   Studies in the Plays of Henry Fielding   MA Univ of Texas
      at Austin 1938   151 p
3138 HUDSON Susie M   A Comparative Study of the Growth in Artistic
      Purpose: Miguel Cervantes, Henry Fielding and Mark Twain
      MA West Texas St Univ 1963   102 p
3139 HUVANE James J   The Influence of the Drama on Henry Fielding's Novel
      Joseph Andrews   MA Columbia 1959   84 p
3140 JERIC Marta   Fielding's Novels: A Study in Technique   MA Ca Foscari
      (Italy) 1959
3141 JOHNSON Christine E   The Literary Essay in Fielding's *The Covent-
      Garden Journal*   MA Univ of Delaware 1967   69 p
3142 KALPAKGIAN Mitchell A   Prudence and Luck in *Joseph Andrews*   MA Univ
      of Kansas 1966
3143 KORN Barbara C   A Study of the Narrator of *Tom Jones* and *Joseph Andrews*
      MA Univ of Idaho 1966
3144 LEOPOLD Robert E   Henry Fielding's Dramatic Use of the Country Inn
      in *Joseph Andrews* and *Tom Jones*   MA Temple Univ 1955   87 p
3145 LePAGE Peter V   Fielding's Equivocal Ladies: Varium et Mutabile Semper
      Faemina   MA Bowling Green Univ 1961
3146 LESSARD Sr M of St Rose-Frances   La Bruyere and Fielding: Character
      Painters of Their Times   MA Boston Coll 1966
3147 LINDSAY Louis A   Henry Fielding's Treatment of Crime and the Criminal
      Type in His Novels and Political Pamphlets   MA Temple Univ 1958   72
3148 MacKENZIE Elizabeth D   Love and License in Fielding's Comedies:
      The Conscience of a Humorist   MA Columbia 1965   128 p
3149 McMILLAN Connie B   A Comparative Study of Henry Fielding's
      Joseph Andrews (1742) and Sarah Fielding's *David Simple* (1744)
      MA Texas Technological Univ 1967   65 p
3150 McWILLIAMS David J   The Technique of Henry Fielding   MA Univ of Texas
      at Austin 1933
3151 MARSHALL Geoffrey   Fielding and the Perception of True Merit
      MA Rice 1961
3152 MATTHEWS Joan V   Translatable Names: The Effect of the Descriptive
      Name in *Tom Jones* and *Joseph Andrews*   MA Columbia 1967   69 p
3153 MEAGHER Keith J   Henry Fielding's Use of Satire   MA Univ of British
      Columbia (Canada) 1966

3154 MONAHAN Josephine W The Nature of Fielding's Standard of Values
      and the Impact of the Standard Since the Time of Fielding
      MA Boston Univ 1935
3155 MORRISSETTE Rene R The Families in Fielding MA Univ of Massachusetts
      1965
3156 MOSELEY Jean Henry Fielding: Critic of the Drama MA American Univ
      1966
3157 MYERS Sidney R A List of Occurrences in Fielding's Major Prose
      Fiction of the Concepts of Fortune and Providence with an Intro-
      ductory Essay and an Annotated Bibliography of Criticism Treating
      His Use of Those Concepts MA Univ of Louisville 1969   49 p
3158 NELSON Paul J A Study of Henry Fielding's Attitude toward the
      Doctrines of Methodism and Deism MA Florida St Univ 1960
3159 PAPADOPOULOU Katina E The Comedies of Henry Fielding as a Possible
      Source of Tom Jones MA Smith Coll 1931
3160 PERKINS James A Ironic Narration in Tom Jones: Fielding's Second
      Self as Intruder MA Miami Univ 1965
3161 POLK Anna C The Importance of the Burlesque Aspects of Joseph Andrews,
      a Novel by Henry Fielding MA Oklahoma St Univ 1969   96 p
3162 QUINN Joseph A Henry Fielding's Conception of Benevolence as
      Revealed through a Study of Tom Jones MA Boston Coll 1958
3163 RAECHICK Ruth E Fielding's Criticism in Tom Jones MA Univ of North
      Dakota 1932   43 p
3164 RAYNAL Margaret A Study of the Structure and Doctrine of
      Henry Fielding's Amelia MA Univ of North Carolina at Chapel Hill
      1955   68 p
3165 READ Kather An Eighteenth Century French Translation of Joseph Andrews
      MA Rice 1951
3166 RECKLEY Ralph Comedy Versus Satire in Fielding's Novels MA Howard
      Univ 1966   154 p
3167 REGAN Daniel Generous Deception: A Study of the Narrator's Relation-
      ship with the Reader in Tom Jones BA Amherst 1966
3168 RICHETTI John J The Christian Ethical Critique of Fieldings'
      Tom Jones MA Columbia 1961   108 p
3169 ROBERGE Phyllis I Henry Fielding's Use of the Persona MA Colorado
      St Coll 1968
3170 ROBERTS Edna G Sentimental Elements in the Writings of.
      Henry Fielding MA Univ of New Mexico 1941
3171 ROSENBALM John O Political and Social Significance in Selected Dramas
      of Henry Fielding MA North Texas St Univ 1966
3172 ROSENBLOOD Bryan N Fielding's Amelia: An Interpretive and Compara-
      tive Study MA McMaster (Canada) 1965
3173 SANBORN Barbara I The Concept of Good Works in the Prose Fiction of
      Henry Fielding MS Purdue Univ 1959   95 p
3174 SELLS Larry F Three Studies in English: Van der Moot and Spenser;
      Religion in Fielding's Novels; and Thomas Morton's Poetry: An
      Edition MA Pennsylvania St Univ 1966
3175 SHAVER R J A Comparative Study of Samuel Richardson and Henry Fielding
      MA North Texas St Univ 1941
3176 SHEA Eleanor A Fielding's Interpolated Tales: Handglass of Maturing
      Genius MA Hunter Coll 1964
3177 SHEEHAN Leonie M Henry Fielding and the Comic MA Boston Coll 1952
3178 SPIRES Gertrude F The Women in Fielding's Novels MA Univ of Maine
      1953   157 p
3179 STACK K E The Role of the Comic Spirit in the Novels of Henry Fielding
      and George Meredith MA Boston Univ 1938
3180 THOMAS D S Fielding's Amelia: A Critical Study of Its Themes and
      Their General Treatment by Fielding, with an Account of the Novel's
      Publication, Reception and Revision MA Univ of London (England)
      1962

3181 THOMAS M B The Humanitarian Interests of Henry Fielding as Mani-
     fested in His Writings MA Univ of North Carolina at Chapel Hill
     1932
3182 TRUSSLER S J A Generic Analysis of the Plays of Henry Fielding
     with Special Reference to the Forms of Regular Comedy and Dramatic
     Satire MA Univ of London (England) 1966
3183 TURNER William H Henry Fielding's Art of Fiction MA Toronto
     (Canada) 1963
3184 VAN LOON Nelles Characterization in *Tom Jones* MA Toronto (Canada)
     1963
3185 VASBINDER Samuel M The Persistence of the Quixotic Figure in Three
     Eighteenth Century Novels: *Joseph Andrews, Tristram Shandy* and
     Humphry Clinker MA Kent St Univ 1965
3186 WALKER Lynnette A Influence of the *Tatler* and the *Spectator* on
     Henry Fielding MA Univ of Maine 1926
3187 WEAVER John D The Political Writings of Henry Fielding MA George
     Washington Univ 1933 272 p
3188 WEEKS Janice F Henry Fielding and Essential Differences: A Study
     of the Plays *Joseph Andrews* and *Tom Jones* MA Columbia 1959 98 p
3189 WEINHOLD Marjorie W *Tom Jones*: The Masquerade MA Carnegie-Mellon
     Univ 1966
3190 WEISS Joan H The Common Lot of Folly: A Study of Henry Fielding's
     Method in the Drama MA Univ of Delaware 1965 86 p
3191 WHITE Sarah A Fielding's Early Prose Style: His Essays in
     The Champion MA Univ of Texas at Austin 1967 86 p
3192 WHITTY Emily E A Study of Fielding's *Parson Adams* and Sterne's
     Uncle Toby MA Columbia 1951
3193 WIETLISHPACH Ronald J The Method and Uses of Fielding's Epic
     Structure MA Univ of Iowa 1966
See also 588, 1051, 2410, 2416, 2434, 3413, 5211, 6009, 6014, 6015, 6017, 761

EDWARD FITZGERALD

3194 COLEMAN H E Edward Fitzgerald's Translations and Their Influence
     upon His Philosophy MA Univ of North Carolina at Chapel Hill 1933
3195 DAVIS Lisa E Edward Fitzgerald as a Translator of Calderon
     MA Univ of Georgia 1965
3196 DINKLE Ransy P The Personal and Literary Relationships of
     Edward Fitzgerald and His Contemporary English Men-of-Letters
     MA Univ of Kentucky 1933
3197 KALBERER Edward H The Letters of Edward Fitzgerald: An Expression
     of Personality MA Univ of Pittsburgh 1935
3198 SCOTT Norphlett Edward Fitzgerald: A Neglected Personality
     MA Univ of Texas at Austin 1939 83 p
See also 3844
JOHN FLETCHER

3199 BAKER Wilma E The Influence of John Fletcher upon James Shirley
     MA Univ of Oklahoma 1938
3200 BORLAND Wilson S The Poetry and the Music of the Songs of
     John Fletcher's Plays MA Univ of Pittsburgh 1931
3201 BROGAN Bessie E The Authorship of *The Knight of the Burning Pestle*
     MA Univ of Oklahoma 1930
3202 BROOKE Florence R Fletcher's Use of His Source Material in *The Two
     Noble Kinsmen* MA Univ of Texas at Austin 1930
3203 BROWN Helen Influence of Cervantes and Lope de Vega on the Plays
     of the Beaumont and Fletcher Folio of 1679 MA Univ of Pittsburgh
     1929
3204 COOK M S An Edition of the Brogyntyn Manuscript of John Fletcher's
     Demetrius and Enanthe with an Examination of Its Relationship to

the Text as Printed in the First Folio of 1647 B Litt Oxford Univ
(England) 1950
3205 HAUER Louis F The Figurative Language of John Fletcher MA Univ of
Iowa 1933
3206 MOLLOY Patricia A A Production Book for *The Knight of the Burning
Pestle* MA Boston Coll 1950
3207 MOODY Ila A Fletcher's *The Pilgrim* as Adapted by Vanbrugh
MA Boston Univ 1930
3208 NORMAN Colin J The Provenance of the First and Second Quartos of
Beaumont and Fletcher's *Philaster* MA Queen's (Canada) 1965
3209 PARKER W J The Concept of Tragedy and Tragi-Comedy as Revealed
in the Plays of Beaumont and Fletcher MA North Texas St Univ 1940
3210 RICHARDSON Mabel C *The Maid's Tragedy* on the London Stage Since 1710
MA George Washington Univ 1948 107 p
3211 TALOTTI Mariella *The Two Noble Kinsmen* by John Fletcher and
Philip Massinger MA Ca Foscari (Italy) 1961
3212 WEBB J B Decadent Elements of the Jacobean Drama with Special
Reference to Fletcher and His Collaborators M Phil Univ of London
(England) 1968
See also 325, 326, 328, 329, 330, 331, 332, 333, 335, 336, 337, 338, 339, 340,
341, 342, 343, 344, 345, 346, 347, 4298, 6611, 6960, 7239

                          FORD MADOX FORD

3213 AVERY Karl E Ford Madox Ford's *Parade's End*: A Study in Decline
MA Univ of Rhode Island 1962 100 p
3214 BARTELS Susan T Narrative Techniques of Ford Madox Ford MA Arizona
St Univ 1966
3215 BAUMWOLL Dennis The Fiction of Ford Madox Ford: Theory and Practice
MA Univ of Oklahoma 1964 320 p
3216 BRICKER David C F M Ford's *Parade's End*: Functions of Irony in the
Rendering of an Affair BA Amherst 1961
3217 BROOMFIELD Olga R A Critical Analysis of the Novels of Ford Madox Ford
MA Memorial (Canada) 1964
3218 BURNS Carolyn P Catholicism as Seen in the Major Novels of
Ford Madox Ford MA Bowling Green Univ 1963
3219 BUTLER Thorpe Ford Madox Ford: The Form of Comprehension
MA Claremont Graduate School 1965
3220 EVANS Oliver W Ford Madox Ford and the *English Review* MA Univ of
Tennessee 1941
3221 GIBSON Kenneth A Inside the Nightmare: An Examination of Ford Madox
Ford's *The Good Soldier* and *Parade's End* MA Queen's (Canada) 1964
3222 HARROD Lee V The Last Tories: The Ideal of the "Gentlemen" in
the Works of Ford Madox Ford and Joseph Conrad MA Pennsylvania
St Univ 1965
3223 HENNEY Frederic A An Investigation of the Structure of Ford Madox
Ford's *Parade's End* MA Univ of North Carolina at Chapel Hill 1958
79 p
3224 HILL Joan A The Last Surviving Tory: A Study of Ford Madox Ford's
Parade's End MA Univ of Toledo 1963
3225 KAULA David C The Achievement of Ford Madox Ford: A Critical Study
of His Novels MA Univ of Connecticut 1952
3226 KENNEDY Alan E *Parade's End* as a Comic Novel MA Univ of British
Columbia (Canada) 1966
3227 METZ Gerald M The Portrait of War in Ford Madox Ford's Tetralogy
Parade's End MA Univ of Rhode Island 1967 117 p
3228 NAUSE John D The Influence of D H Lawrence upon Ford Madox Ford as
Author of *The Good Soldier* MA Ottawa (Canada) 1967
3229 RICHTER Susan *Parade's End*: A World in Transition BA Univ of
British Columbia (Canada) 1968

3230 RUBIN Donald S Ford Madox Ford and the Theme of English Catholicism
        MA Toronto (Canada) 1966
3231 SHAW Peter Ford Madox Ford MA Columbia 1961 106 p
3232 TAYLOR Elinor D *Parade's End*: A Dramatic Adaptation of a Novel
        by Ford Madox Ford MA Marshall Univ 1966
3233 WEISS Leonard S Ford Madox Ford's Theory of the Novel MA Univ of
        Maryland at College Park 1964 69 p
3234 ZINGMAN Barbara G Ford Madox Ford's Attitude toward Life and Art:
        Parade's End and *The Good Soldier* MA Univ of Louisville 1962
See also 1957, 1992, 2048, 2064, 2074, 2159, 2199

JOHN FORD

3235 DEL BEL BELLUZ Teresa John Ford MA Ca Foscari (Italy) 1950
3236 DI NATALE Maria L John Ford: *Love's Sacrifice* MA Ca Foscari (Italy)
        1962
3237 ESSERY Elbert H John Ford's Characterization of Women in Five of
        His Dramas MA Univ of Texas at Austin 1940 102 p
3238 GARLING Kirsten The Gentleman Concept of Ford BA Univ of British
        Columbia (Canada) 1967
3239 GIBSON Richard J *'Tis Pity She's a Whore*: Three Centuries of
        Varying Attitudes Concerning John Ford's Tragedy MA Univ of Kansas
        1966
3240 HOWARD Robert G Stylistic Traits in the Dramatic Poetry of John Ford
        MA Syracuse Univ 1952 140 p
3241 JUBB Douglas E Mannerism in John Ford's *The Broken Heart* BA Univ
        of British Columbia (Canada) 1965
3242 KERSNAR William S Gravity in Merriment: John Ford's Use of Comedy
        MA Stanford Univ 1965
3243 MELONCINI Clara John Ford: *'Tis Pity She's a Whore* MA Ca Foscari
        (Italy) 1956
3244 MOSCOTTO Giovanna John Ford: *The Chronicle History of Perkin Warbeck*
        MA Ca Foscari (Italy) 1958
3245 PROVENCE Jean The Historical and Romantic Elements in John Ford's
        Perkin Warbeck MA Univ of Arizona pre-1933
3246 ROBERTS Moss An Interpretation of *'Tis Pity She's a Whore* Modified
        by Certain Seventeenth Century Platonic Love Doctrines MA Columbia
        1960 40 p
3247 SCHMITZ Elsie W A Critical Edition of John Ford's *'Tis Pity She's
        a Whore* M Litt Cambridge (England) 1962
3248 SLIGHTS William W The Love Motif in Three Tragedies of John Ford:
        The Broken Heart, *'Tis Pity She's a Whore* and *Love's Sacrifice*
        BA Amherst 1961
3249 STRUNK Sheila J A History of the Criticism of John Ford, 1628-1951
        MA Univ of Kentucky 1953 137 p
See also 2468, 2480, 5163, 5599

EDWARD MORGAN FORSTER

3250 ADLER Thomas P E M Forster's Cosmic Comedy: *A Passage to India*
        MA Boston Coll 1966
3251 BATCHELOR John B E M Forster and Cambridge MA Univ of New Brunswick
        (Canada) 1965
3252 BEHM Carl Theme and Personality in E M Forster's Edwardian Novels
        MA Univ of Maryland at College Park 1968 109 p
3253 BLODGETT John E Moral Fantasy: An Examination of the Tales of
        E M Forster MA Washington St Univ at Pullman 1966
3254 BLOOM Hugh A The Beliefs of E M Forster MA Univ of Pittsburgh 1955
3255 BROWN Carell The Personal Religion of E M Forster as Reflected in
        A Passage to India BA Univ of British Columbia (Canada) 1966

3256 CLARK Phyllis A A Study of E M Forster's Central Theme, the Undeveloped Heart, as Presented in His Novels MA Univ of Rhode Island 1963
3257 GRAHAM Calvin O E M Forster: A Technical Analysis of the Novels MA Oklahoma St Univ 1967 77 p
3258 GUARAGNO Grace C The Use of Music in the Major Works of E M Forster MA Columbia 1960 92 p
3259 HOAK Barbara A The Symbolic Moment in the Fiction of E M Forster MA Rice 1965
3260 HYDE Margaret A The Theme of Balance in Forster's Poems MA San Diego St Coll 1968 94 p
3261 KBERA Sunit B E M Forster and India, with Special Reference to *A Passage to India* MA Univ of New Brunswick (Canada) 1966
3262 KEIR W A E M Forster: A Critical and Historical Estimate B Litt Oxford Univ (England) 1949
3263 KERNS Joan M E M Forster's Short Stories MA Central Washington St Coll at Ellensburg 1968 86 p
3264 KIMURA Thomas S Primitivism in E M Forster's *The Longest Journey* MA Univ of Hawaii 1961 77 p
3265 LATHAM Jack P A Structural Analysis of the Novels of E M Forster MA Univ of Arizona 1966
3266 LESTER June A Expansive Structure in *A Passage to India* MA San Diego St Coll 1967 155 p
3267 LeSUEUR Joseph M An Analysis and Evaluation of the E M Forster-Eric Crozier Libretto for *Billy Budd* MA Columbia 1953 65 p
3268 LOW Virginia B E M Forster's and Virginia Woolf's Views of Their Changing Times MA Univ of Massachusetts 1968 22 p
3269 McGEE Helen C Aspects of Love in the Novels of E M Forster MA Univ of Tulsa 1966 78 p
3270 MONTGOMERY Austin P Jr The Elder E M Forster and the Very Young MA Columbia 1954 57 p
3271 PRADL Gordon M The Artistic Integrity of E M Forster BA Amherst 1965
3272 SAHNI Chaman L A Study of E M Forster's *A Passage to India* in Relation to Indian Thought MA Univ of Rhode Island 1968 114 p
3273 SINGH Rajendra E M Forster's *A Passage to India*: Theme, Symbol, Language and Structure MA Univ of Rhode Island 1967 108 p
3274 SUZUKI Kazuko Problems of Communication in E M Forster's *A Passage to India* MA Whittier Coll nd
3275 THOM Charles M E M Forster's *Howard's End*: The Qualified Achievement of Margaret Schlegel MA Columbia 1966 62 p
3276 VANTURE Paul S Some Women of Insight Who Inhabit the Novels of E M Forster and Virginia Woolf MA Columbia 1959 97 p
3277 WECHSLER Lorraine E M Forster in India, with Emphasis on How He Related Hinduism to His Philosophy MA Columbia 1952 93 p
3278 WOODWORTH Donald The Idea of Salvation in the Novels of E M Forster MA Univ of New Hampshire 1950 57 p
3279 WRONA June B The Dominant Theme in the Fiction of E M Forster MA Univ of Maryland at College Park 1962 93 p
See also 2033

CHRISTOPHER FRY

3280 BATTAGLIA Marcia J Dramatic Virtuosity in the Comedy of Jean Anouilh and Christopher Fry MA George Washington Univ 1960 78 p
3281 BLEDSOE Bennie G A Critical Analysis of *The Lady's Not for Burning* M Ed Henderson St Coll nd
3282 BRIGG Peter A Christopher Fry's Developing Views of Man's Situation MA Toronto (Canada) 1966
3283 DIPPOLD Diane The Becket Theme in Modern Drama: Eliot, Anouilh and Fry MA Univ of Maryland at College Park 1964 126 p

3284 FUSILLO Robert J A Record of a Centrally Staged Production of
        A Phoenix Too Frequent MS Ft Hays St Teachers Coll 1952 158 p
3285 GLEASON Judith The Function of Preciosity as Seen in the Works of
        Christopher Fry and Jean Giraudoux MA Columbia 1954 138 p
3286 HAHN Marian S The Elements of Quakerism in the Plays of
        Christopher Fry MA Univ of Pittsburgh 1960
3287 HARDWICK Diana L A Study of the Plays of Christopher Fry and
        T S Eliot with Relation to the Background of Recent Verse Drama
        MA Univ of Maine 1955 55 p
3288 KELLY Eileen P The Sources of the Plays of Christopher Fry MA Univ
        of North Carolina at Chapel Hill 1954 64 p
3289 KIRKALDY-WILLIS Iain D Quaker Elements in Christopher Fry's Dramas
        MA Univ of British Columbia (Canada) 1966 102 p
3290 McDONALD Robert F Christopher Fry: A Study BA Univ of British
        Columbia (Canada) 1964
3291 MELE Jean S Spiritual Crisis in the Plays of Christopher Fry
        MA Univ of Pittsburgh 1955
3292 MORAN Leonard W Christopher Fry's Idea of Verse Drama MA Columbia
        1954 65 p
3293 O'ROAK Nancy V The Plays of Christopher Fry: Theme, Language and
        Genre MA Queen's (Canada) 1964
3294 PELL Joan Structure and Poetry in the Tragedies of Christopher Fry
        MA Temple Univ 1964 82 p
3295 PETTY Donald Novelty and Ideas in T S Eliot's *The Family Reunion*
        and Christopher Fry's *A Sleep of Prisoners* MA Columbia 1966 74 p
3296 PICKENS Marjorie M The Development of Expression of Theme in the
        Poetic Drama of Christopher Fry MA Syracuse Univ 1955 88 p
3297 RYAN George E The Comedies of Christopher Fry MA Boston Coll 1953
3298 TAPLIN Claire A The Comedies of Christopher Fry MA Columbia 1961
        83 p
3299 THAMAN Joanne M A Critical Study of the Plays of Christopher Fry
        MA Univ of Texas at Austin 1955 123 p

JOHN GALSWORTHY

3300 ACTON Ellen R The Family in Galsworthy's Novels MA Univ of Texas at
        Austin 1946 134 p
3301 AHERN Eckoe M A Comparison of the Syntax of Fitzgerald and
        Galsworthy MA San Diego St Coll 1968 131 p
3302 AHRENS Rosalind K John Galsworthy's Criticism of the Aristocracy
        MS Kansas St Coll at Pittsburg 1937
3303 ALEXANDER Glendolyn M A Study of the Biographical Content in the
        Novels of John Galsworthy MA East Texas St Univ 1938
3304 BAKER Nannie R The Temper of Galsworthy MA Univ of Texas at Austin
        1950 128 p
3305 BARNES Grace John Galsworthy and the Dominance of "Property" in
        Present Day Thinking and Social Attitudes MA Univ of Maryland
        at College Park nd 57 p
3306 BECKER Barbara E Galsworthy's "Spire of Meaning" MA Univ of
        Arizona 1934
3307 BERGEN John R John Galsworthy: A Study in Development MA Columbia
        1953 95 p
3308 BINGHAM Fern C Galsworthy and the Theme of the Unhappy Marriage
        MA Univ of Arizona 1938
3309 BITTICK Edsell F John Galsworthy: Dramatist MA Univ of Texas at
        Austin 1951 142 p
3310 BLACKBURN Monce C An Evaluation of John Galsworthy as a Short
        Story Writer MA Oklahoma St Univ 1951 47 p
3311 BLAIR Thomas M John Galsworthy's Principles of Art MA Univ of
        Pittsburgh 1925

3312 BRADLEY Emmett Galsworthy's Dramatic Theory and Practice MA Univ of Kentucky 1926
3313 BRASTED Helene E Individualism in the Dramas of John Galsworthy MA Univ of Texas at Austin 1928
3314 BROWN Evelyn A The First Marriage of Ada Cooper Galsworthy as a Theme in John Galsworthy's Novels M Ed Temple Univ 1940 76 p
3315 BROWN Marjorie A John Galsworthy's Portrayal of Feminine Character in His Novels MA Boston Univ 1950
3316 CAFFERY Birtha Naturalism in the Galsworthy Theatre MA Marquette Univ 1926 43 p
3317 CAMPBELL Jack D An Examination of the Literary Relationship of John Galsworthy and Ivan Turgenev MA Oklahoma St Univ 1950 50 p
3318 CARBONNEAU Louis U The Short Stories of John Galsworthy MA Montreal (Canada) 1964
3319 CHATFIELD Harriet S Middle-Class England as Shown in John Galsworthy's The Forsyte Saga MA Univ of Kentucky 1940
3320 CONWAY Mary G The Plays of John Galsworthy: Dramatic Technique and Social Significance MA Boston Univ 1931
3321 DAVIS Betty J Social Criticism in the Plays of John Galsworthy MA Texas Christian Univ 1948 104 p
3322 De LANO Denise A Symbolism in John Galsworthy's The Forsyte Saga MA Marquette Univ 1950
3323 DENTI Renzo The Plays of John Galsworthy: A Critical Study MA Ca Foscari (Italy) 1937
3324 DIAMOND Dora A A Critical Study of the Drama of John Galsworthy MA Univ of Pittsburgh 1940
3325 DONELIN Kathleen The Short Stories of John Galsworthy MA Columbia 1954 148 p
3326 ECKMAN Mary L The Gentleman in Galsworthy's Novels MA Univ of Texas at Austin 1946 90 p
3327 FISCHER G John Galsworthy: His Concept of Beauty BA Univ of British Columbia (Canada) 1956
3328 FORBES Jean W The Realism of John Galsworthy, Especially English Society as Portrayed in His Novels MA Univ of Oklahoma 1925
3329 GOLD Lynn L Soames Forsyte: A Study in Characterization MA McGill (Canada) 1964
3330 GROSSMANN Robert M Pre-Marital Association with Ada Cooper Galsworthy as a Theme in John Galsworthy's Plays M Ed Temple Univ 1946 61 p
3331 HASSLER George J Galsworthy's Philosophy of Life as Found in His Dramas M Ed Temple Univ 1934 141 p
3332 HOUSER Helen B The Stream of Consciousness in Galsworthy MA Univ of Iowa 1935
3333 JAB Luisa The Forsyte Saga by John Galsworthy MA Ca Foscari (Italy) 1941
3334 JARDINI Anna M The Character of the English People in John Galsworthy's Forsyte Saga MA Ca Foscari (Italy) 1942
3335 JOINER Rebecca Galsworthy's Use of Symbolism MA Univ of Texas at Austin 1935
3336 KELTY Jane H John Galsworthy's Indebtedness to the Bible M Ed Temple Univ 1934 155 p
3337 KIMBALL F M Galsworthy's Presentation of Irene in The Forsyte Saga and Her Importance MA Boston Univ 1940
3338 KNAPP Elsie H Galsworthy's View of the Art of Fiction MA Univ of Iowa 1934
3339 LAKELAND Albert A Jr John Galsworthy: The Man and the Writer MA Columbia 1955 72 p
3340 LANDERS Madge V A Quarter of a Century of Social Criticism in the Plays and Novels of John Galsworthy MA Hunter Coll 1946
3341 LAY Dorothy C Forsyteism in the Works of John Galsworthy MA Univ of Texas at Austin 1948 92 p

3342 LES THIBAULT Roger M *The Forsyte Saga* by John Galsworthy MA Univ of
       Oklahoma 1941
3343 LINDEN John H John Galsworthy: Champion of the Individual
       MA Columbia 1953 88 p
3344 LINDGREN Charlotte H Galsworthy's Concept of Forsyteism MA Boston
       Univ 1947
3345 McLAUGHLIN E R The Ethical Ideals of John Galsworthy as Reflected
       in His Plays MA Univ of New Hampshire 1939 65 p
3346 MANER Adelaide S The Influence of John Galsworthy's Life on His
       Drama MA Univ of North Carolina at Chapel Hill 1950
3347 MORRIS Delyte W A Study of Literary Style in Galsworthy's Novels
       MA Univ of Maine 1934 99 p
3348 MOSS Erle L Craftsmanship in Galsworthy's Novels MA Univ of Texas
       at Austin 1930
3349 PAFFORD Jessie John Galsworthy: The Artist and Social Reformer
       MA Univ of Texas at Austin 1939 93 p
3350 PIPERNO Alba John Galsworthy as a Dramatist MA Ca Foscari (Italy)
       1934
3351 PRITCHARD V Geraldine The Characters of Galsworthy's Dramas
       MA Univ of Maryland at College Park 1941 48 p
3352 RASKIN Sherman John Galsworthy: A Study in Dramatic Technique
       MA Columbia 1961 67 p
3353 REEDY Lawrence D Turgenev and Galsworthy: A Comparative Study
       MA Univ of Oklahoma 1936
3354 REUTINGER Otto W Devices of Exposition in the Plays of
       John Galsworthy MA Univ of New Mexico 1934
3355 RICE Enid E Changing Attitudes toward Social Criticism in the
       Plays of Robertson, Pinero, Galsworthy and Maugham MA Univ of
       Maine 1941 76 p
3356 ROBINSON Elizabeth E Class Consciousness in Galsworthy's Novels,
       Plays and Essays MA Indiana Univ 1940
3357 ROBINSON William A Galsworthy the Dramatist: Expositor of Tolerance
       MA Univ of New Hampshire 1949 60 p
3358 ROGERS Richard E The Consistency of Soames Forsyte MA San Diego
       St Coll 1961 136 p
3359 RUNDELL Walter Social Studies in the Dramas of John Galsworthy
       MA Univ of Texas at Austin 1930
3360 RUSSELL Elsa The Individual Versus Fate-Through-Society in
       John Galsworthy MA Boston Univ 1933
3361 SCOTT Charlie Characterization in the Novels of John Galsworthy
       MA Univ of New Mexico 1936
3362 SELBY David L A Study of the Social Themes in *The Silver Box*,
       Strife and *Justice* to Show the Social Concern of John Galsworthy
       as a Dramatist MA West Virginia Univ 1964 59 p
3363 SELMAN Ida P Feminine Characters in the Novels of John Galsworthy
       MA Univ of Texas at Austin 1951 105 p
3364 SKINNER Virginia K Classification and Criticism of John Galsworthy's
       Essays and Short Stories MA Univ of Texas at Austin 1935
3365 SMITH Carl G A Study of the Sense of Property as a Theme in
       The Forsyte Saga MA Bowling Green Univ 1953
3366 STEAKLEY Pauline M The Women of the Forsyte Cycles MA Univ of
       Texas at Austin 1933
3367 STINCHCOMB LaFaye John Galsworthy's Sense of Justice MA Southern
       Methodist Univ 1936
3368 TOSARELLO Jole John Galsworthy as a Novelist MA Ca Foscari (Italy)
       1930
3369 TURCO Alma The Theatre of John Galsworthy MA Ca Foscari (Italy)
       1954
3370 TURKINGTON E E The Judicial Temper of John Galsworthy MA Boston
       Univ 1938

3371 WATSON Elizabeth W The English and American Estimates of Galsworthy
     as a Novelist MA Univ of Arizona 1938
3372 WEST Marion D A Study of John Galsworthy's Dramas and Novels
     MA Univ of Texas at Austin 1916
3373 WHITACRE William J John Galsworthy: The Man and His Drama
     BA Rutgers St Univ 1958 63 p
3374 WHITEHOUSE Alice G John Galsworthy and the Middle-Class Englishman
     MA Univ of Texas at Austin 1936
3375 WORKMAN C M Philosophy in The Forsyte Saga MA North Texas St Univ
     1942
3376 ZABORSZKY Dorothy E The Individual and Society: A Study of
     John Galsworthy's The Forsyte Saga MA Toronto (Canada) 1966
See also 1022, 2042

DAVID GARRICK

3377 BEATTIE Suzanne M David Garrick and the French Anglo-Maniacs:
     A Study in Anglo-French Criticism in the Eighteenth Century
     MA Univ of Oregon 1938
3378 CLUTTER Fairy H The Influence of David Garrick in the Theatre
     MA Univ of Pittsburgh 1942
3379 DOWNS O U The "Original" Dramatic Works of David Garrick MA Univ
     of North Carolina at Chapel Hill 1933
3380 JEWELL Kathyrn J Some Aspects of David Garrick's Prologues and
     Epilogues MA Univ of Delaware 1964 97 p
3381 McDANIEL Stella The Stage of David Garrick MA Univ of Texas at
     Austin 1928
3382 MILLER Joseph S David Garrick as Dramatist MA Long Island Univ
     1966 130 p
3383 RUSSELL Marshall Farce in David Garrick's Plays MA Louisiana St
     Univ 1938
3384 SOLDANI Sr M Virginia Eighteenth Century Acting Techniques as
     a Reflection of Literary Theory with Especial Reference to
     David Garrick MA Boston Coll 1959
See also 6989

GEORGE GASCOIGNE

3385 BYERS Jack W The Medieval and the Classical Elements in the Writings
     of George Gascoigne MA Univ of Texas at Austin 1943 107 p
3386 CAVAZZANA Mirka George Gascoigne: The Glass of Government
     MA Ca Foscari (Italy) 1962
3387 ROHR Maria R The Adventures of Master F J by George Gascoigne
     MA Ca Foscari (Italy) 1961
3388 STONE Elizabeth A Gascoigne's Poetic Theory and Practice MA Univ
     of North Carolina at Chapel Hill 1954 83 p
3389 WHITE W D Gascoigne's Proverb Lore MA Baylor Univ 1949 180 p

ELIZABETH CLEGHORN GASKELL

3390 BEDOGNI Elda Elizabeth C Gaskell: Her Life and Works MA Ca Foscari
     (Italy) 1939
3391 BOWER Miriam E Social Concerns of Mrs Gaskell MA Columbia 1954 90 p
3392 CARLIN C J Mrs Gaskell: Her Humanitarian Kinship to Dickens
     MA Boston Coll 1936
3393 CEROW Marjorie F Mrs Gaskell: Her Conscience and Her Art MA Columbia
     1966 117 p
3394 COK Primavera Elizabeth Cleghorn Gaskell MA Ca Foscari (Italy) 1962
3395 GALLAGHER Eugene F Mrs Gaskell's Social and Industrial Criticism
     MA St Louis Univ 1942 70 p

3396 GELLETICH Annie Mrs Gaskell MA Ca Foscari (Italy) nd
3397 KARMINSKI Anne S Writers in Manchester, 1831-1854 M Litt Cambridge
        (England) 1955
3398 LAKIN Carrie Mrs Gaskell's Social Attitudes in Relation to Her Times
        MA Univ of New Mexico 1954
3399 McLAUGHLIN Florence C Mrs Gaskell's Accomplishment as a Novelist in
        Her First Three Novels MA Univ of Pittsburgh 1932
3400 MIRZA Z The Theme of Mrs Gaskell's *Ruth* and the Reception of the
        Novel M Phil Univ of London (England) 1967
3401 OLIVER William E Mrs Gaskell's Short Fiction MA Columbia 1965 94 p
3402 PISANA Rosina Mrs Gaskell MA Ca Foscari (Italy) 1930
3403 REYDER Helen A Mrs Gaskell's Novels: A Study MA Univ of Texas at
        Austin 1934
3404 SHELSTON A J Elizabeth Gaskell: A Study of Four Major Works
        A Discussion of Her Development as a Writer with Detailed Reference
        to *Mary Barton, North and South, The Life of Charlotte Bronte* and
        Wives and Daughters MA Univ of London (England) 1968
3405 SIMPSON William J North or South: The Novels of Mrs Gaskell as They
        Relate to the Victorian Social Scene BA Amherst 1967
3406 TAYLOR Edna Elizabeth Gaskell and Constance Holme: An Appraisal
        and a Comparison MA Ohio St Univ 1939
3407 TYRE Nedra The Works of Mrs Gaskell MA Emory Univ 1938 157 p
See also 544, 605, 2985, 3037, 3039

JOHN GAY

3408 BALSHAM Joel John Gay's Intentions in *The Shepherd's Work* MA Temple
        Univ 1964 44 p
3409 BEST Evelyn G John Gay and the Fable Tradition MA Univ of
        Massachusetts 1966
3410 BULLOCK Melba R The Background of John Gay's *Beggar's Opera* MA Univ
        of Texas at Austin 1936
3411 CASKEY John H A Study in the *Beggar's Opera*, Including a Sketch of
        Opera in England from Its Beginning MA Baylor Univ 1915 64 p
3412 DALY Lawrence T The Poetry of John Cleveland, Gay's Pastorals and
        and Appraisal of John Cheever MA Pennsylvania St Univ 1965
3413 DRUMWRIGHT Charles M The Dramatic Burlesques of John Gay and
        Henry Fielding MA Univ of Texas at Austin 1955 181 p
3414 FIKE Duane J The Virgilian Influence in the Poetry of John Gay
        MA Univ of Colorado 1965
3415 FLAMMANG Emma M Social Criticism in John Gay's *Trivia* MA Univ of
        North Dakota 1933 39 p
3416 HANN Bruce F John Gay's Comic View of Society MA Univ of New Mexico
        1967
3417 KINGSLAND Janet M John Gay's Modification of the Comedy of Manners:
        A Search for Form MA Univ of Delaware 1969 57 p
3418 McGINNISS Caroline L The Dramatic Works of John Gay MA Columbia 1943
3419 NEUMAN Susan K The *Beggar's Opera* as a Play-Within-a-Play MA Columbia
        1960 111 p
3420 POMERLEAU Cynthia S The Parodic Structure of the *Beggar's Opera*
        MA Columbia 1966 93 p
3421 POSMANTUR Myrtle K An Edition of John Gay's *Mr Pope's Welcome from
        Greece*, with a Critical Introduction MA St Univ of New York at
        Buffalo 1965
3422 ROUSSEAU Jeanne G John Gay's *Trivia*: Craftsmanship in a Burlesque
        Georgic MA Texas Woman's Univ 1965
3423 SARETTI Fernanda John Gay's *Beggar's Opera* MA Ca Foscari (Italy) 1946
3424 SCHLEGEL Jeanne E The *Beggar's Opera* in Interpretation and Pro-
        duction since 1920 MA Columbia 1961 258 p
3425 SCHMIDT Dorothy J Literary, Religious and Social Satire in the

Works of John Gay MA Washington Univ at St Louis 1943
3426 THORNTON A G The *Beggar's Opera* and Its Perennial Popularity
      BA Univ of British Columbia (Canada) 1964
See also 1051, 2437, 3111, 5922, 5950

WILLIAM SCHWENCK GILBERT

3427 ALLEY J M Topical Allusions in the Savoy Operas MA Univ of North
      Carolina at Chapel Hill 1938
3428 BARTH Mabel D A Study of the Dialogue in the Plays of W S Gilbert
      and Its Influence on Drama MA Univ of Iowa 1924
3429 DAVIS Madge C The Relationship of the Bab Ballads to the
      Gilbert and Sullivan Librettos MA Louisiana St Univ 1936
3430 FLUDAS John Theatrical and Operatic Burlesque in the Savoy's
      Operas MA Columbia 1963 59 p
3431 HOERR Willmer A The Victorianism of Sir William Schwenck Gilbert's
      Savoy Libretti MA Univ of Pittsburgh 1932
3432 STACKHOUSE William J Social Criticism in Gilbert's Plays MA St Louis
      Univ 1944 100 p
3433 THALINGER Thelma W The Savoy: A Symbol of the Eighteen Nineties
      MA Washington Univ at St Louis 1934 245 p
3434 WALLACE Patricia E Seen and Heard at the Savoy MA Univ of Texas
      at Austin 1967 151 p
See also 8009, 8010

GEORGE ROBERT GISSING

3435 BAILEY J M An Introduction to George Gissing MA Boston Univ 1925
3436 CHOUTEAU Jennieve A Critical Analysis of Gissing's Revisions in
      Workers in the Dawn MA Oklahoma St Univ 1940 54 p
3437 FELEX Robert L Self-Identification in Four Novels of George Gissing
      MA Univ of British Columbia (Canada) 1962 97 p
3438 FIOCK Margaret L George Gissing: His Life and Work MA Univ of
      Arizona pre-1933
3439 GUERIN Margaret F George Gissing: A Pioneer in English Realism
      MA Boston Univ 1945
3440 HART John E George Gissing: A Study in Conflict MA Syracuse Univ
      1940 106 p
3441 KATZ John S George Gissing: A Portrait of the Artist as Shown in
      New Grub Street and *The Private Papers of Henry Ryecroft*
      MA Columbia 1961 67 p
3442 KERSHAW H Nancy Gissing's Literary Treatment of Poverty MA Columbia
      1937
3443 PERRY John O "Art, Veracity and Moral Purpose": George Gissing's
      Theory and Criticism of the Novel MA Univ of Florida 1952
3444 POSSENTI Anita George Robert Gissing MA Ca Foscari (Italy) 1950
3445 PROSSER Dorothy A From Altruism to Egoism in the Writings of
      George Gissing MA Univ of Oregon 1939
3446 RUTLAND R B The Realism of George Gissing: A Study of Five Novels
      MA Univ of London (England) 1961
3447 SELLERS William E George Gissing: Transitional Realist MA Boston
      Univ 1947
3448 SMITH J M An Examination of the Theme of Emancipation in Six
      Novels of George Gissing M Phil Univ of London (England) 1969
3449 STORK Gladys B Elements of Autobiography in George Gissing's
      Fiction MA Boston Univ 1934
3450 VAWTER Margaret S George Gissing: His Critical Standards and
      Appraisals MA Washington St Univ at Pullman 1954
3451 WRIGHT John E George Gissing as a Transitional Figure in the
      English Novel MA Univ of Pittsburgh 1925

See also 1982, 3866

WILLIAM GODWIN

3452 BEARD James F Psychology and Eclecticism in Godwin's Novels
        MA Columbia 1942
3453 BOVETTE Purvis E William Godwin as a Writer of Tragedy: A Study
        of His Plays and Novels MA Univ of Kansas 1962
3454 CHRISTIN Robert E The Novels of William Godwin MA Ohio St Univ 1949
3455 CROCKETT David A Study of the Causes of William Godwin's Literary
        Obscurity MA Oklahoma St Univ 1932   59 p
3456 JOHNSTON Thomas M William Godwin as Seen by His Contemporaries
        MA Tulane Univ 1931
3457 MEANS Beth Propaganda in the Novels of William Godwin MA Univ of
        Texas at Austin 1935
3458 NICHOLAS Ellwood R The Influence of William Godwin in the Works of
        Charles B Brown MA Univ of Maryland at College Park 1929   55 p
3459 PORTER Lahoma C The Influence of William Godwin's *Caleb Williams*
        on Charles Brockden Brown MA Univ of Oklahoma 1926
3460 SANDSTROM Glenn A Perfect Sincerity in the Novels of Godwin
        MA Washington St Univ at Pullman 1950
3461 SMITH Donald M William Godwin's *Caleb Williams* Against the Background
        of the Eighteenth Century Novel in England MA Columbia 1966   117 p
3462 SMITH J G Social Reform in William Godwin's Novels MA North Texas
        St Univ 1967
3463 STEWART Donald C An Evaluation of the Influence of William Godwin
        upon Shelley's *Queen Mab* MA Univ of Kansas 1952

See also 6005, 7389, 7396, 7496, 7498

WILLIAM GOLDING

3464 ARTHUR Richard L An Overview of Point of View in the Novels of
        William Golding MA Bowling Green St Univ 1965
3465 BELL Loren C Sources of Influence in William Golding's *Lord of the
        Flies* MA Adams St Coll 1966
3466 BOYLE Patricia M Human Freedom in the Novels of William Golding
        MA Toronto (Canada) 1967
3467 BRANAN Mary E William Golding's Existentialist Heroes MA Univ of
        Texas at Austin 1963
3468 BRIGGS Jane A Children in Contemporary Novels: Studies in
        Richard Hughes, J D Salinger and William Golding MA Florida
        St Univ 1964   101 p
3469 CLARKE Reginald D William Golding's View of Man: Variations on
        the Fall MA Brigham Young Univ 1968   90 p
3470 COLTER Larry W William Golding's Mystical Existentialism
        MA Colorado St Coll 1963
3471 DUFFY Carole J The Euripidean Vicious Circle in the Novels of
        William Golding MA San Diego St Coll 1967   177 p
3472 FEINSTEIN Michael D The Innocent, the Wicked and the Guilty in the
        Novels of William Golding MA Miami Univ 1965
3473 FOX Stephen D William Golding: The Experiment in the Contemporary
        Novel MA Emory Univ 1966
3474 GOLDSBERRY James R The Fusion of Traditions in William Golding's
        Lord of the Flies MA San Diego St Coll 1967   80 p
3475 GREEN David J A Study of Techniques and Thought in the Novels of
        William Golding MA Toronto (Canada) 1964
3476 HAGANS Marilyn T Evil, Negation and Affirmation in the Novels of
        William Golding MA Ohio St Univ 1962   46 p
3477 HARRIS Shelagh Golding and Camus: A Critical Comparison
        MA McMaster (Canada) 1965

3478 HICKS Gladys Existential Aspects in the Structure of William Golding's
      Free Fall MA Barry Coll 1966
3479 HYMAN Roger L William Golding and the Fall from Innocence
      MA Toronto (Canada) 1967
3480 KASTEL Eva M Egotism and Alienation in William Golding's Ambiguous
      World MA Coll of the Holy Names at Oakland 1968
3481 KOLUPKE Joseph A The Nature of Perception in the Novels of
      William Golding MA Univ of Iowa 1965
3482 LaCHANCE Paul R The Philosophy of Man in the Novels of
      William Golding MA Univ of Rhode Island 1964
3483 LACOSTE Br Andre The Use of Thematic Symbols in the Novels of
      William Golding MA St Mary's Univ at San Antonio 1965
3484 LEWIS Richard Symbols, Themes and Innocence: A Study of
      William Golding's *Lord of the Flies* MA Columbia 1963 87 p
3485 MacKINNON Alexander A The Novels of William Golding: A Dominance
      of Theme MA Windsor (Canada) 1964
3486 MARZULLO Marie T Some Patterns of Imagery in the Novels of
      William Golding MA St John's Univ 1965
3487 MERRILL Frederick H Four Golding Novels and Contemporary Literature
      MA Univ of Vermont 1967 176 p
3488 MILLER Gary E The Novels of William Golding MA McMaster (Canada) 1963
3409 MILLER Jeanne C Some Features of Style in the Novels of
      William Golding MA St Louis Univ 1964 86 p
3490 OSBURN Norma J The Idea of Order as a Basis for Comparison of
      Golding's *Lord of the Flies* and Hughes' *A High Wind in Jamaica*
      MA Univ of Oklahoma 1965
3491 PECK Barbara C William Golding: From Fabulist to Novelist
      MA Univ of Maryland at College Park 1966 99 p
3492 POTTER Robert J Communal Murder in the Novels of William Golding
      MA Bowling Green Univ 1969
3493 PRUITT Phillip R Sacrifice in *Lord of the Flies* MS Kansas St Coll
      at Pittsburg 1967
3494 ROGERS Leo J William Golding's *Lord of the Flies*: An Exposition
      of Man's Tragic Condition MA Temple Univ 1964 43 p
3495 SCHUMACHER Wayne A *Lord of the Flies*: A Modern Gulliver's Fourth
      Voyage MS Ft Hays Kansas St Coll 1966
3496 SIMMONS Marilyn M Three Studies in English: "Western Wind";
      Golding's Class Consciousness; *The New England Primer*
      MA Pennsylvania St Univ 1966
3497 SOLOMON Elizabeth F Theme and Imagery in Two Novels of
      William Golding MA Columbia 1963 93 p
3498 WHITE DeAnna M The Broken Chain of Being: A Study of
      William Golding's *Lord of the Flies* MA East Tennessee St Univ 1969
3499 ZALASKI Barbara Ego and Society in Four Allegorical Novels by
      William Golding MA Central Connecticut St Coll 1966
See also 5542

OLIVER GOLDSMITH

3500 ACHESON David Goldsmith and Humanitarianism MA Columbia 1940
3501 ANGLIN Jean C Social Criticism in the Minor Writings of
      Oliver Goldsmith MA Howard Univ 1943 66 p
3502 ARTHUR L R A Study of the *Vicar of Wakefield* MA North Texas St Univ
      1960
3503 BARDELLA Maria L Oliver Goldsmith: Considered as an Essay Writer
      MA Ca Foscari (Italy) 1954
3504 BILSLAND J W Oliver Goldsmith and the Social Problems of His Day
      BA Univ of British Columbia (Canada) 1949
3505 BYERLY Elizabeth C A Critical Study of the *Vicar of Wakefield*
      MA Columbia 1959 70 p

3506 CLARKE Kathleen O Oliver Goldsmith as a Literary Critic MA Univ of
     London (England) 1950
3507 CULVER Mary C Sentimentality in Goldsmith's *The Citizen of the World*
     MA Univ of Pittsburgh 1950
3508 EDELSON Mary E French Influence on the Theatre of Oliver Goldsmith
     MA Lamar Technological Univ 1965 103 p
3509 ERICKSON Elmer C Oliver Goldsmith as a Literary Critic MA Univ of
     North Dakota 1932 56 p
3510 FREEMAN Phyllis J The Critical Reception of the *Vicar of Wakefield*
     (1766-1866) MA Columbia 1953 373 p
3511 GARRETT Robert S Goldsmith's Prose Style MA Univ of Pittsburgh 1949
3512 GASKINS Pauline A The Vogue of Goldsmith and Sheridan in the
     New York Stage, 1773-1870 MA Howard Univ 1933 65 p
3513 GASS Mary E The Mind of Oliver Goldsmith MA Ohio St Univ 1945
3514 GEMMETT Robert J *The Deserted Village*: Goldsmith's Social Protest
     MA Univ of Massachusetts 1962
3515 GOLDMAN Irvin Goldsmith's Criticism of Contemporary Life and Thought
     in *The Citizen of the World* MA Indiana Univ 1935
3516 HALLER Robert S "And Even His Failings Leaned on Virtue's Side":
     Wit and the Good-Natured Fool in Oliver Goldsmith BA Amherst 1955
3517 HARRIMAN Robert E An Analysis of the Philosophic and Economic
     Principles of Happiness and Luxury in the Works of Oliver Goldsmith
     MA Univ of Maine 1966 177 p
3518 HAYDON Frances M Oliver Goldsmith as a Biographer MA Univ of
     Pittsburgh 1935
3519 HINES Samuel P Jr Goldsmith's Use of Borrowed Material in His
     Periodical Essays, 1759-1766 MA Univ of North Carolina at Chapel
     Hill 1958 103 p
3520 HOBSON Stanley P Oliver Goldsmith: A Critical Analysis of the Plot
     of *She Stoops to Conquer* M Ed Henderson St Coll nd
3521 HORRIGAN Sr Mary A Goldsmith's Treatment of the Peasant
     MA Boston Coll 1951
3522 HUDSON M A Comparative Study of Ideas in Montesquieu's *Lettres
     Persanes* and Goldsmith's *Citizens of the World* MA Ohio St Univ 1931
3523 INGLIS Gay Oliver Goldsmith: A Social Philosopher of the Eighteenth
     Century as Seen in *The Deserted Village* BA Univ of British
     Columbia (Canada) 1965
3524 JOSEPH Jean L Lower Class Women in Eighteenth Century Fiction,
     Richardson to Goldsmith MA Columbia 1943
3525 KABEL Martha R The Principal Women Characters in English Fiction
     from Defoe to Goldsmith MA Indiana Univ 1935
3526 KIRBY Sr Lonita M Goldsmith and the Neoclassical Opposition to
     Enthusiasm MA Univ of Oregon 1935
3527 LO Woo-Lih D Goldsmith's Chinese Letters through Chinese Eyes
     MA Boston Univ 1950
3528 LURANC Edward Satire in Goldsmith's *Citizen of the World*
     MA San Diego St Coll 1965 114 p
3529 McEWEN Fred B Critical Commentary on the *Vicar of Wakefield* from
     1766 to the Present MA Univ of Pittsburgh 1955
3530 MANAN Abdul The Social Views of Oliver Goldsmith MA Univ of North
     Carolina at Chapel Hill 1966
3531 MARTELL Sr Mary A The Literary Theories of Oliver Goldsmith
     MA Boston Coll 1958
3532 MELANSON George A Goldsmith, the Marivaux of English Literature?
     MA Boston Coll 1947
3533 MIRABELLI Luciana Oliver Goldsmith as a Dramatist MA Ca Foscari
     (Italy) 1955
3534 MORGAN Ira L Boswell's Portrait of Goldsmith MA Univ of Tennessee
     1950 90 p
3535 NASH Olive Goldsmith as a Critic MA Univ of Oklahoma 1929

3536 NECKERS Jeannette H   A Profile of Oliver Goldsmith   MA Southern
      Illinois Univ at Carbondale 1950 99 p
3537 O'CONNELL Sr Saint Cecilia Humanitarianism in Goldsmith
      MA Indiana Univ 1935
3538 O'CONNOR Dorothy Oliver Goldsmith as a Critic   MA Univ of Pittsburgh
      1938
3539 PATTERSON N S Oliver Goldsmith's Treatment of "Simplicity" and
      "Luxury" MA Univ of Texas at Austin 1935
3540 PATTERSON Sylvia W The Comic Style of Oliver Goldsmith MA Univ of
      Southwestern Louisiana 1965 72 p
3541 PELLET Magdelaine Commentary on Goldsmith's *Citizen of the World*
      in Connection with Other Works of the Same Kind, Particularly
      with Montesquieu's *Lettres Persanes* MA Smith Coll 1923
3542 PITMAN Norman H The Prose Style of Goldsmith MA Univ of Tennessee
      1897
3543 ROGERS James E Benevolence in Selected Works of Oliver Goldsmith
      MA Boston Coll 1965
3544 SAWYERS Charlotte Oliver Goldsmith: Romantic Neo-Classicist;
      a Study of the Classical and Romantic Elements in His life and
      Writing MA Fresno St Coll 1955 178 p
3545 SCOTT Robert L Oliver Goldsmith and His Relations with the Club
      MA Columbia 1041
3546 SMITH Beatrice E The Humor of Oliver Goldsmith MA Boston Univ 1936
3547 TYE Carol A The Economic Background to Oliver Goldsmith's
      The Deserted Village MA Boston Coll 1965
3548 VADNAIS Henry A Religion in Goldsmith's Works MA Boston Coll 1953
3549 WISSLER Helen L Goldsmith as a Literary Critic MA Univ of Iowa
      1935
3550 WYNKOOP William M The Two Oliver Goldsmiths MA Columbia 1950
See also 4048

                              JOHN GOWER

3551 ARNOLD Grace The Dream Motif in Gower and His Contemporaries
      MA Univ of Tennessee 1932
3552 BALDWIN Mary E The Latin Meters of John Gower's *Confessio Amantis*
      MA Toronto (Canada) 1966
3553 BRADLEY Carol D The Sober Observer: A Study of John Gower as a
      Critic of His Time as Represented by His Poem *Confessio Amantis*
      MA Columbia 1959 63 p
3554 BURLESON Allan W A Verbal Concordance to the Second Book of
      John Gower's *Confessio Amantis* MA Columbia 1937
3555 ELDREDGE Laurence M John Gower and the Medieval Ovid MA Columbia
      1959 129 p
3556 HOLLY Patricia M *Confessio Amantis* and *Metamorphoses*: Gower's
      Treatment of Tales from Ovid MA John Carroll Univ 1964
3557 MEAD John F The Syntax of the Infinitive in Gower's *Confessio Amantis*
      MA Univ of Texas at Austin 1930
3558 NEVILLE Marie E Gower's Use of the Bible in the *Confessio Amantis*
      MA St Louis Univ 1944 100 p
3559 TOWNSEND Eleanor M A Concordance of the Prologue and First Book
      of the *Confessio Amantis* of John Gower MA Columbia 1935
See also 1414, 1534, 1575, 1590, 1614, 1626, 1733

                            ROBERT GRAVES

3560 BOWERS Willard G Mind and Myth in the Poetry of Robert Graves:
      An Essay to Discover the Change in Graves' Poetic Technique Effected
      by His Study of the Muse of Poetry in *The White Goddess* MA Temple
      Univ 1963 65 p
3561 CAVANAUGH William C A Study of the Poetic Theory and Practice of

Robert Graves MA Univ of Pittsburgh 1959
3562 HAYLETT B C A Critical Study of the Poetry of Robert Graves
      MA Univ of London (England) 1963
3563 KIRKHAM M C The Development of the Concept of the White Goddess
      in the Poetry of Robert Graves M Phil Univ of London (England)
      1968
3564 OLMSTED Mary Humor in the Early Poetry of Robert Graves MA Columbia
      1964 78 p
3565 PALMER Max H Robert Graves and *The White Goddess*: A Study in
      Contemporary Paganism MA Columbia 1954 61 p
3566 WALSH T J The Poetry of Robert Graves MA Leeds Univ (England) 1962
3567 WILTGEN David Mythical Imagery in the Poetry of Robert Graves
      MA Mankato St Coll 1966 33 p
3568 WITMER Marian G The Case of Robert Graves Against the Apollonians
      MA Univ of Colorado 1965

                           THOMAS GRAY

3569 COBB Robert H Thomas Gray's Attitude toward Nature MA Tulane Univ
      1926
3570 COMER David B III Thomas Gray as a Critic MA Tulane Univ 1933
3571 GAZZINI Brunalba Moods and Themes of Melancholy from Gray to Keats
      MA Ca Foscari (Italy) 1942
3572 GRAYSTON D Words that Burn: A Stylistic Critique of the Poems
      of Thomas Gray BA Univ of British Columbia (Canada) 1960
3573 HARTMANN Marie M Thomas Gray's Letters as a Revelation of the
      Interests of an Eighteenth Century Scholar MA Univ of Iowa 1931
3574 LAMBERT Francis X Thomas Gray: Critic MA Boston Univ 1940
3575 LEATHWOOD William H Thomas Gray: Cause of His Scant Productions
      MA Univ of Oklahoma 1924
3576 MANCINI Glauco Romantic Themes and Modes in Gray's Works
      MA Ca Foscari (Italy) 1947
3577 MAYER Olive H Thomas Gray's Scholarship Manifested in His Poetry
      MA Boston Univ 1934
3578 MELLINGER Gladys L An Evaluation of Three Decades of Gray Criticism,
      1770-1800 M Ed Temple Univ 1954
3579 SARICK Hyman Reflections of Gray's Literary Personality in His
      Letters MA Toronto (Canada) 1966
3580 SCIGLIANO Anne R Thomas Gray and Richard Bentley MA Boston Coll 1966
3581 SWENSON Justine G The Composite Nature of Thomas Gray MA Florida
      St Univ 1949
3582 SWOR C E The Influence of Latin on the Poetry of Thomas Gray
      MA Univ of North Carolina at Chapel Hill 1934
3583 WHITE Lida I Thomas Gray as a Literary Critic MA Univ of Oklahoma
      1929
3584 WILLIAMS Leda N Classical and Romantic Elements in the Poetry of
      Thomas Gray MA Univ of Texas at Austin 1932
3585 WOOD R W Gray's Pride: A Reconsideration Based on a Study of His
      Correspondence MA Leeds Univ (England) 1967
See also 4273

                          GRAHAM GREENE

3586 BARRATT Harold Existentialism in Graham Greene's *The Name of Action*,
      The Heart of the Matter, *A Burnt-Out Case*: The Theme of Betrayal
      MA Windsor (Canada) 1964
3587 BELL Martha F Graham Greene and the Idea of Childhood MA North
      Texas St Univ 1966
3588 BOWEN Valerie F Graham Greene and the Roman Liturgy MA Univ of
      Hawaii 1962 178 p

GREENE Con't   127   3589-3615

3589 BOWES Sr Saint Martin of Lima   Graham Greene: Religious Dramatist
      MA Villanova Univ 1964
3590 BROOKS Sammy K Graham Greene and Mexico: A Critical Study of
      The Power and the Glory and Another Mexico   MA Univ of Texas at
      Austin 1966
3591 CARDINALE Vincent G Graham Greene's Conception of Evil   MA Boston
      Coll 1950
3592 CAWTHON Daniel D   The Themes of Alienation in the Major Novels of
      Graham Greene   MS Univ of Tulsa 1966   88 p
3593 CLINES Patrick   The Child and Being: Key to the Novels of
      Georges Bernanos and Graham Greene   MA Fresno St Coll 1966   119 p
3594 CONROY Esther A   American Critics on Four Novels of Graham Greene
      MA Rivier Coll 1961
3595 CRULL Mary E   "Down the Labyrinthine Ways": A Study of
      Graham Greene's Novels   MA Colorado St Coll 1959
3596 DAVIDSON Arnold C Graham Greene: A Writer of the Cross Rather
      than the Resurrection   MS Kansas St Teachers Coll 1966
3597 ELSON John T   The Concept of Order in the Novels and Entertainments
      of Graham Greene   MA Columbia 1954   124 p
3598 FITZGERALD Ellen F Difficulty Squared: Is Graham Greene a Great
      Catholic Novelist?   MA Columbia 1959   124 p
3599 FLAKE Elaine M Graham Greene's Obsession with the Lost Childhood
      Theme in His Novels, Short Stories and Essays   MA Brigham Young
      Univ 1968   85 p
3600 FLYNN Sr M Robert of Citeaux   The Utility of Suffering in the Novels
      of Graham Greene   MA Boston Coll 1965
3601 GALEN Ruth E   Graham Greene: A Study of Absolute and Relative
      Concepts of Morality   MA Univ of New Mexico 1953
3602 GINN Regis C   The Imaginary World Created by Graham Greene   MA Univ
      of Arizona 1961   189 p
3603 GROVEN John O   The Influence of Religion on the Works of
      Graham Greene   MA Univ of Colorado 1966
3604 GUEST Lawrence A   Christian Tragedy and the Works of Graham Greene:
      A Redefinition as Applied to Brighton Rock, The End of the Affair
      A Burnt-Out Case and The Power and the Glory   MA Fresno St Coll
      1969   74 p
3605 HOODECHECK Donald J   The Theme of Purgation in Graham Greene's
      The Power and the Glory   MA Mankato St Coll 1965   67 p
3606 HOPPER Walter D   The Peguy Motif in the "Catholic" Novels of
      Graham Greene   MA Univ of Rhode Island 1966   82 p
3607 HORNE Sandra G   Imagery as Exposition: A Study of Selected Novels
      by Graham Greene   MA Univ of Rhode Island nd
3608 JEAN-DE-LA-CHARITY Sr   Structure and Theme in Graham Greene's
      The Potting Shed   MA Rivier Coll 1959
3609 KAMBEITZ Clemens G   The Pessimistic Realism of Graham Greene
      MA Toronto (Canada) 1965
3610 KOBAN Charles   Theme, Character and Style in the Work of Graham Greene
      MA Columbia 1960   115 p
3611 LACHANCE Louis   Types of Fantasy in the Fiction of Graham Greene
      MA Montreal (Canada) 1966
3612 LEDEBOER Leroy D   The Despair that Leads to Faith: A Study of the
      Major Religious Novels of Graham Greene   MA Moorhead St Coll 1965
3613 LONGREE Georgia A   The Concepts of Belief and Non-Belief in the
      Writings of Graham Greene   MA Texas Christian Univ 1968   136 p
3614 LOVE Frances A   Graham Greene's Use of the Christian Concept of
      Descent   MA Texas Agricultural and Mechanical Univ 1969
3615 LYNES Charles M   The Whiskey Priest, an Atypical Martyr: An
      Examination of the Whiskey Priest of The Power and the Glory as
      a Reworking of the Standard Martyr Story   MA Fresno St Coll 1967
      53 p

3616 McCARTHY David R The Priest in Graham Greene: His Use and Failure
     MA Columbia 1961 163 p
3617 McCLENDON Margaret A God in a Godless World: A Study of
     Graham Greene, 1929-1951 MA Univ of Texas at Austin 1961 139 p
3618 McDONALD Marjorie M Sacred and Profane Love as Depicted in the
     Writings of Graham Greene MA Saint Mary's (Canada) 1965
3619 McLEOD Sr Madeleine S An Indexed Synthesis of the Critical Thought
     of Graham Greene and Patrick Braybrooke MA Siena Hts Coll 1958
     59 p
3620 MARLOWE Jeanne A A Comparison of Religious Themes in the Fiction
     of Graham Greene and Flannery O'Connor MA Bowling Green Univ 1969
3621 MILLER Helen M The Eschatology of Graham Greene MA Stetson Univ 1965
3622 MILLS Joseph L Plutchik's Emotive Theory as Applied to Eschatology
     Elements in Key Works of Graham Greene MA Morehead St Univ 1967
     117 p
3623 NEE James M Graham Greene's The Power and the Glory: A Source of
     Study MA Boston Coll 1964
3624 OMIBIYI A A The Treatment of Pain and Death in Five Novels of
     Graham Greene: The Man Within, It's a Battlefield, Brighton Rock,
     The Power and the Glory and The Heart of the Matter M Phil Univ of
     London (England) 1967
3625 PEPIN Sr Lucienne The Function of Imagery in Graham Greene's Fiction
     MA Rivier Coll 1957
3626 QUIRK Frank B Graham Greene and the Human Conditon MA Univ of
     Massachusetts 1965
3627 READ Donald R Pattern and Meaning in the Novels of Graham Greene
     MA Trinity Coll 1965
3628 ROTTINO Joseph F Despair in the Novels of Graham Greene MA Long
     Island Univ nd 39 p
3629 ROZSNAFSZKY Jane S The Search for Meaning of the Characters of
     Graham Greene: The Necessity of Suffering MA Drake Univ 1965
3630 RUSYN Br August S Ambiguity as a Literary Technique in Selected
     Novels of Graham Greene MA Univ of Rhode Island 1969 89 p
3631 SABINE Francisco J Graham Greene's Heroes: Regeneration through
     Experience MA Univ of British Columbia (Canada) 1969 175 p
3632 SANDERS Marvin C The Use of Ambiguity and Paradox in the Catholic
     Novels of Graham Greene MA Univ of Idaho 1962
3633 SHEEHAN Thomas M Graham Greene and the Problem of Good and Evil
     MA Univ of Louisville 1956
3634 SIFERD Nancy K Graham Greene's Attitudes toward Love and Marriage
     MA Bowling Green Univ 1964
3635 STAHL Norma M The Novels of Graham Greene: A Discussion of the
     Themes of Love and Pity and the Novelist's Technique MA Columbia
     1953 84 p
3636 STOWE Mary L The Significance of Interpersonal Relationships in
     the Novels of Graham Greene MA Washington St Univ at Pullman 1965
3637 SUAREZ Ralph P The Application of Catholic Criteria to the Works
     of Graham Greene MA C W Post College 1963 52 p
3638 SULLIVAN Virginia M The Heart of Darkness in Graham Greene: Some
     Critical Considerations of Greene's Vision of the World as It
     Relates to His Preoccupation with Death in His Novels and Enter-
     tainments, with Particular Emphasis on It's a Battlefield
     MA Columbia 1966 57 p
3639 TOLBERT Evelyn O The Greene Priest MA Univ of Houston 1965 98 p
3640 VILLANUEVA Rev Rodolfo E The Ethic of Graham Greene's Novels
     MA Mankato St Coll 1967 85 p
3641 WAGNER Nora E The Foundations of Graham Greene's Thought, with
     Particular Emphasis on the Concepts of Evil and Redemption as
     Presented in His Early Work MA George Washington Univ 1964 135 p
3642 WALTERS Dorothy J The Theme of Destructive Innocence in the Modern.

Novel: Greene, James, Cary and Porter   MA Univ of Oklahoma 1960   217 p
3643 WHIDDEN Sr Mary B   The Prophetic Artistry of Graham Greene   MA Univ
      of New Hampshire 1968   88 p
3644 ZERMAN Malvyn B   The Writer as Technician: A Study of the Literary
      Methods of Graham Greene   MA Columbia 1953   116 p

ROBERT GREENE

3645 BECKER David W   Sir Elgamour, a Source for Greene's *Menaphon*
      MA Rutgers St Univ 1949   48 p
3646 CLACK Alberta G   The Mother-Child Relationship in the Prose and Poetry
      of Robert Greene   MA Univ of Texas at Austin 1929
3647 COTHAM Margaret M   Greene and Lodge's *A Looking Glass for London and
      England*   MA Univ of Texas at Austin 1928
3648 DEANE Robert H   The Sick Soul of Robert Greene: A Study in Sixteenth
      Century Alienation   MA Univ of New Hampshire 1962   117 p
3649 DUNCAN Laura F   Portrayal of Feminine Character in Greene's Drama
      MA Hardin-Simmons Univ 1941
3650 ERGUN Dorothy K   Women in Robert Greene's Romances   MA Univ of
      Pittsburgh 1951
3651 FARRAR Charles B   Policy in the Plays of Robert Greene   MA Univ of
      North Carolina at Chapel Hill 1957   111 p
3652 FRAMARIN Silvia   Robert Greene: *The Comical History of Alphonsus,
      King of Aragon*   MA Ca Foscari (Italy) 1962
3653 GOREE Roselle G   The Narrative Art of Robert Greene as Shown in His
      Dramas and Romances   MA Univ of Texas at Austin 1922
3654 GUASTELLA Teresa   Robert Greene: *Pandosto*   MA Ca Foscari (Italy) 1965
3655 HOLLENBACH John W   A Study of the Anachronisms in the Plays of Lyly,
      Peele and Greene   MA Columbia 1935
3656 HOWELL James   The Rogue in Non-Dramatic English Literature to
      Robert Greene, Preliminary to a Study of the Rogue in Elizabethan
      Comedy   MA Univ of North Carolina at Chapel Hill 1931
3657 KELIUS Judith S   The Structure of Robert Greene's "Coney-Catching"
      Pamphlets   MA Univ of Delaware 1967   86 p
3658 LEONI Federica   Robert Greene: *Menaphon*   MA Ca Foscari (Italy) 1965
3659 MORAN Leila P   Imagery in the Plays of Robert Greene   MA George Wash-
      ington Univ 1951   151 p
3660 MORRIS Blanche F   The Dramatic Structure of the Plays of Robert Greene
      MA Univ of Texas at Austin 1923
3661 MURREDO Maria   *George A Greene* by Robert Greene   MA Ca Foscari (Italy)
      1960
3662 PERIL William   Earliest Elements of the English Novel in
      Robert Greene's Pamphlets   MA Univ of Pittsburgh 1929
3663 POLACCO Paola   *Orlando Furioso* by Robert Greene   MA Ca Foscari (Italy)
      1965
3664 ROCHE Kevin J   The Anti-Hero in Robert Greene   MA Boston Coll 1962
3665 ROCK Barbara   Sources of Greene's *Friar Bacon* and *James IV*
      MA Univ of Texas at Austin 1932
3666 THORNTON Ruby D   Characterization in the Plays of Robert Greene
      MA North Texas St Univ 1938
3667 TREADWELL Ara   Greene's *Alphonsus of Aragon*: An Analytical Study
      MA Univ of Texas at Austin 1938
3668 TUCHINSKY Joseph   Robert Greene's "Coney-Catching" Pamphlets and
      the Development of English Rogue Literature   MA Columbia 1965   91 p
3669 UTTERBACK Ethel I   Characteristics of the Novel as Exemplified in
      Robert Greene's Pamphlets   MA Univ of Oklahoma 1936
3670 VENDRAMIN Emma   Robert Greene: *A Notable Discovery of Cozenage,
      The Second Part of Coney-Catching* and *The Third and Last Part
      of Coney-Catching*   MA Ca Foscari (Italy) 1964
3671 WARD Elizabeth J   A Study of Setting in Robert Greene's Chief Plays

MA Univ of Pittsburgh 1931
3672 WATERFIELD Clement B Importance of Robert Greene's Work to Elizabethan
      Drama MA Univ of Oklahoma 1930
3673 WILSON Ollie J A Critical Bibliography of Robert Greene's Works
      MA Univ of Oklahoma 1935
See also 4913, 4922, 4931, 5072, 5260, 6801

LADY AUGUSTA GREGORY

3674 DEWAIDE Lucile The Concept of the Irishman in the Plays of
      Lady Gregory MA Univ of New Mexico 1952
3675 DILLON Sr Mary F Portrayal of the Irish People in Lady Gregory's
      Plays MA Boston Coll 1952
3676 FRAHER Sr Mary D The Conflict of Cultures in the Life and Works of
      Lady Gregory MA Boston Coll 1949
3677 GIBSON Katherine R A New View of Lady Gregory MA Wagner Coll 1966
3678 HENDERSON Linda L An Analysis of Lady Gregory's *Kiltartan Moliere*
      MA Univ of Texas at Austin 1967 96 p

FULKE GREVILLE

3679 BERNAT Paula L Of State and Nature: A Study of the Impact of
      Calvinism upon Political Theory in the Works of Fulke Greville
      MA Columbia 1962 103 p
3680 FROST William Fulke Greville's *Caelica*: An Evaluation MA Columbia
      1942
3681 GREENSTEIN David M The Human Condition in Fulke Greville's *Caelica*
      MA Columbia 1961 92 p
3682 O'CONNELL Carol A Greville and Humane Learning MA Columbia 1961 69 p
3683 ODARENKO Dora M Convention as Structure: An Examination of
      Fulke Greville's *Caelica* MA Columbia 1963 226 p
3684 PRYOR William D A Study of Fulke Greville's *Life of the Renowned
      Sir Philip Sidney* MA Florida St Univ 1950
3685 ROGERS Phillip W Illusion and Reality in Fulke Greville's *Caelica*
      MA Univ of Texas at Austin 1962 118 p
3686 WINSER Leigh The Religious Background of Greville's Poetry: A Study
      in Public Expediency and Private Meditation MA Columbia 1962 77 p

THOMAS HARDY

3687 ABRAHAM Fairfax Thomas Hardy: Existential Beginnings M Ed Henderson
      St Coll nd
3688 ADAIR John M Biblical References in Thomas Hardy's Six Major Novels
      MA Univ of Delaware 1967 163 p
3689 AGNEW Sr Patricia M An Analysis of the Functions of Animal Imagery,
      Fertility Symbols and Folk Legend in Hardy's *Tess* MA St Louis Univ
      1963 84 p
3690 ALLEN Bess The Influences of Greek Drama on the Wessex Novels of
      Thomas Hardy MA Oklahoma St Univ 1938 45 p
3691 ALLEN Mary Melodrama in Thomas Hardy's Novels MA Brigham Young Univ
      1963 117 p
3692 ANTHONY Henry Romantic Element in the Novels of Thomas Hardy
      MA Univ of Pittsburgh 1927
3693 BERGBUSCH Martin L Thomas Hardy's Use of Regionalism in His Novels
      MA Univ of British Columbia (Canada) 1964
3694 BHATIA Chandra Irony of Nature in the Novels of Thomas Hardy
      MA Boston Coll 1963
3695 BOGDONOWITZ Jacob A Study of Accident in Thomas Hardy's Novels
      MA Univ of Iowa 1933
3696 BONHAM Eupha The Use of Coincidence in the Novels of Thomas Hardy

MA Univ of Maine 1936
3697 BOTTALLA Ugo Thomas Hardy's Poems MA Ca Foscari (Italy) nd
3698 BRADDY Kenlock O Autobiographical Elements in the Works of
     Thomas Hardy MA Univ of Texas at Austin 1935
3699 BREARLEY Katherine W Some Manifestations of the Ironic Sense in the
     Works of Thomas Hardy MA Univ of British Columbia (Canada) 1939
3700 BRENNAN Helen C Hardy and Social Class MA Columbia 1941
3701 BREYER Bernard Values in the Poetry of Thomas Hardy MA Louisiana
     St Univ 1940
3702 BRINTON Patricia A Thomas Hardy's Theory of Tragedy MA Dalhousie
     (Canada) 1964
3703 BRYARLY Elizabeth Hardy's Use of Atmosphere MA Univ of Texas at
     Austin 1941 139 p
3704 BURLESON L M A Critical Survey of Thomas Hardy's The Return of the
     Native MA Texas Technological Univ 1942
3705 BUTLER A D The Bible in Thomas Hardy MA Univ of North Carolina at
     Chapel Hill 1929
3706 BYRD Forrest M The Evolution of the Male Character in the Novels
     of Thomas Hardy MA Texas Technological Univ 1960 45 p
3707 CADE Grace A Background in the Novels of Thomas Hardy MA Texas
     Technological Univ 1937
3708 CAMPBELL Dowling G The Wandering Character in Six of Hardy's Major
     Works MA Univ of Tennessee 1965
3709 CARROLL John M The Victorian Reception of Jude the Obscure, "A Full
     Look at the Worst" MA Colorado St Coll 1962
3710 CASS Martha C Hardy's Art and Ideas in His Prose and Poetry
     MA Univ of Texas at Austin 1930
3711 CHO Soong K A Korean Translation of Thomas Hardy's The Three
     Strangers and The Three Wayfarers MA DePauw Univ 1967 66 p
3712 CLARK Robert N Hardy and the Rustic Feeling: A Study of Folk-Ways
     in the Novels of Thomas Hardy MA Florida St Univ 1963
3713 CLARKE Robert W Thomas Hardy: The Madding Crowd MA Southern
     Illinois Univ at Carbondale 1957 88 p
3714 CLAY Roberta L Childhood as Portrayed by Thomas Hardy MA Columbia
     1942
3715 CLAYPOOL Ethel P Tragic Elements in the Novels of Thomas Hardy
     MA Fresno St Coll 1950 103 p
3716 CLONINGER Morris S Social and Economic Aspects of Wessex Life as
     Revealed in the Major Novels of Thomas Hardy MA Univ of Texas
     at Austin 1939 123 p
3717 COCHRAN Grace E Ghosts, Witches and Omens in the Poetry of
     Thomas Hardy MA Univ of Colorado 1965
3718 CONLEY Winfred B Between Two Worlds: The Tension between Ideas
     and Poetic Vision in Hardy's Novels MA Univ of Maryland at
     College Park 1969 108 p
3719 CONLIN Ruth E Elements of Folklore Found in the Novels of
     Thomas Hardy and the Creative Use Made of Them MA Syracuse Univ
     1946 78 p
3720 COOPE G A Short Study of Irony in the Works of Thomas Hardy
     BA Univ of British Columbia (Canada) 1922
3721 CORBISHLEY Johana S A Comparative Analysis of the Witchcraft Theme
     in The Return of the Native and Doctor Zhivago MA Indiana Univ 1956
3722 CORRIGAN Helen F The Influence of Schopenhauer on the Poetry and
     Prose of Thomas Hardy MA Marquette Univ 1930 73 p
3723 CRANE John K The Comic Motifs in the Novels of Thomas Hardy
     MA St Louis Univ 1964 174 p
3724 CRING Charles C Introduction and Notes to Thomas Hardy's Jude the
     Obscure MA Columbia 1935
3725 CULLEN Lee F A Night of Questionings; Thomas Hardy: Poet in an
     Age of Doubt MA Columbia 1962 150 p

3726   CUMMINGS James B   Thomas Hardy's World   MA Univ of Pittsburgh 1940
3727   DAVIS W Eugene   An Investigation into the Influence of Public Opinion
       on Thomas Hardy's Shift from Prose to Poetry   MA Bowling Green Univ
       1958
3728   DAY Charles G   A Study of *The Dynasts*   MA Columbia 1942
3729   DEAN Clara T   Contemporary Criticisms of Thomas Hardy in American
       Periodicals   MA Columbia 1950
3730   DEARDORFF Audrey J   Thomas Hardy's Use of the Bible   MA Univ of Idaho
       1966
3731   DEISS Joseph J   The Poetic Qualities of Hardy's Prose   MA Univ of
       Texas at Austin 1934
3732   DENVIR R F   The Sentimental Provincialism of Thomas Hardy   MA Boston
       Univ 1926
3733   DORAN Leonard G   Form in the Novels of Thomas Hardy   MA George Wash-
       ington Univ 1949   60 p
3734   DOTY Elisabeth   Chance in Relation to Thomas Hardy's Narrative
       Method   MA Univ of Pittsburgh 1948
3735   DUEHLMEIER Raymond A   Biblical References in the Major Novels of
       Thomas Hardy   MA Mankato St Coll 1966   60 p
3736   DURGAN Jerry P   Thomas Hardy's Architectural Training and Its
       Influence on His Prose   MA Sul Ross St Coll 1965
3737   FRASER Ross P   Patterns of Conflict in Hardy's Major Fiction
       MA Univ of British Columbia (Canada) 1967   101 p
3738   FRISCH Judith J   Thomas Hardy and D H Lawrence: Philosophy and
       Form in the Victorian and Modern Novel   MA Columbia 1962   154 p
3739   FULLER B S   The Element of Irony in the Work of Thomas Hardy
       BA Univ of British Columbia (Canada) 1926
3740   FURNISS John N   The Ideological Patterns in the Poetry of Thomas Hardy
       MA Univ of Alabama 1966
3741   GATES Mae C   Folklore in the Works of Thomas Hardy   MA Univ of
       Houston 1950   89 p
3742   GILMER Anna B   *The Dynasts* of Hardy and the *Oresteia* of Aeschylus
       MA Univ of Texas at Austin 1946   112 p
3743   GOINS Lovene P   The Narrative Development of the Dramatic Monologues
       of Thomas Hardy   MA Rice 1960
3744   GORDON Joseph W   Moods and Meters: Reading Thomas Hardy's Poetry
       BA Amherst 1970
3745   GRAVES Betty   The Development of Wessex in Thomas Hardy's Novels
       MA American Univ 1966
3746   GRIMES Martha   Shelleyan Platonics in Thomas Hardy's *The Well-Beloved*
       MA Univ of Maryland at College Park 1955   75 p
3747   GUY William C   Melodramatic Elements in the Novels of Thomas Hardy
       MA Univ of North Carolina at Chapel Hill 1946   92 p
3748   HACK Edward M   *Far from the Madding Crowd*;   Theme and Form: The Art
       of Renunciation and the Deeper Symmetry   MA Columbia 1966
3749   HALL James P   The Mysterious Stranger in the Fiction of Thomas Hardy
       MA Bowling Green Univ 1967
3750   HALSEY Courtland V   Thomas Hardy and Naturalism   MA Univ of Rhode
       Island 1952
3751   HALSTEAD Diane   The Nature of Tragedy in the Novels of Thomas Hardy
       MA Univ of Wyoming 1964
3752   HARRER Elizabeth V   A Study of Thomas Hardy's *A Pair of Blue Eyes*
       MA Univ of North Carolina at Chapel Hill 1949   146 p
3753   HARRIS J M   Thomas Hardy's Evolutionary Meliorism   BA Univ of British
       Columbia (Canada) 1948
3754   HARTMANN Ruth L   Thomas Hardy: Naturalist;   A Study of the Influence
       of Charles Darwin and Emma Hardy on His Novels   MA Univ of Texas
       at El Paso 1968   137 p
3755   HAWTHORNE Willie M   Hardy's Use of Dramatic Contrast in *Jude the
       Obscure*   MA Texas Technological Univ 1931

3756 HAYS Wanda M The Basis of Tragedy in the Characters of Hardy's
      Novels of Character and Environment MA Univ of Oklahoma 1937
3757 HERMANN Nancy E Thomas Hardy's Theory of the Novel MA Univ of
      Texas at El Paso 1969 100 p
3758 HEUNG Cecilia W Lawrence on Hardy: A Study in Interpretation and
      Influence MA McMaster (Canada) 1965
3759 HILL Clifford A Passivity: The Ethic of Irony in Thomas Hardy's
      Universe of Fate MA Columbia 1963 91 p
3760 HOBROCK Phyllis M Evidence of Thomas Hardy's Deepening Pessimism
      in the Marriage Theme of His Novels MA Utah St Univ at Logan 1967
3761 HOLLMIG Madie Thomas Hardy's Use of the Bible in His Prose
      MA Univ of Texas at Austin 1930
3762 HOORNEMAN Evan R An Understanding of Thomas Hardy BA Amherst 1960
3763 HOSTETTLER Ernst Tess as the Archetype of the Earth Goddess in
      Hardy's *Tess of the D'Urbervilles* MA Univ of North Carolina at
      Chapel Hill 1967
3764 HOUDAILLE Jacques A Nature in Thomas Hardy's Lyrical Poems
      MA Boston Coll 1948
3765 HUBBART Marilyn A Thomas Hardy's Meliorism MA Colorado St Coll 1963
3766 HUDSON Ruth The Relation of Thomas Hardy to Shakespeare with
      Particular Reference to Hardy's Eight Major Novels MA Univ of
      Texas at Austin 1926
3767 HUNTLEY Betty Woman in Thomas Hardy's Universe MA Montreal (Canada)
      1964
3768 HURLEY Charles L Thomas Hardy's Dominant Tone of Sobriety as
      Revealed by an Analysis of His Work MA Univ of Texas at Austin
      1941 85 p
3769 HUTTON Exa F Thomas Hardy: A Landscape Artist MA West Texas St
      Univ 1948 100 p
3770 HYNDS Ray Methods in the Craftsmanship of Thomas Hardy MA Texas
      Technological Univ 1940 82 p
3771 IRWIN H Elaine Animal Symbolism and Imagery in the Novels of
      Thomas Hardy MA Indiana Univ of Pennsylvania 1965 79 p
3772 IRWIN Mary E Thomas Hardy's Philosophy as Reflected in His Novels
      MS Kansas St Coll at Pittsburg 1940
3773 ISLAM-SOELDNER Anneros U The Alienation Theme in the Novels of
      Thomas Hardy MA Toronto (Canada) 1967
3774 JACKEL David A The Developing Structure in the Novels of Thomas Hardy
      MA Toronto (Canada) 1965
3775 JAMES Alan E Coincidences in the Novels of Thomas Hardy MA Rutgers
      St Univ 1931 74 p
3776 JENNINGS Bruce The Use of Chance in the Fiction of Thomas Hardy
      MA Univ of Oregon 1932
3777 JOHN David R A Critical Re-Assessment of the Tragic Achievement
      in Hardy's Novel MA McMaster (Canada) 1964
3778 JOHNSON Lillian G Social Conventions as Treated in Thomas Hardy's
      Novels MA Univ of Texas at Austin 1938 153 p
3779 JOHNSON Mina N Fancy, Eustacia and Tess: A Study of Hardy's Changing
      View of Women Characters MA Hardin-Simmons Univ 1962
3780 JONES Anita K Nature and Human Nature in Five of Thomas Hardy's
      Wessex Novels MA Univ of Texas at Austin 1966 111 p
3781 JUDD Anita P Usages of the Bible in Thomas Hardy's Novels MA Hardin-
      Simmons Univ 1969
3782 KARR Mary L Thomas Hardy's Use of the Forces of Nature in Character
      and Action in Three Representative Novels: *Far from the Madding
      Crowd, The Return of the Native* and *Tess of the D'Urbervilles*
      MA Univ of Idaho 1965
3783 KASS Miriam Themes in Thomas Hardy's Short Stories MA Rice 1960
3784 KATSUMURA Eiko Irony in the Poetry of Thomas Hardy MA Univ of Texas
      at El Paso 1964 93 p

3785 KAUR Surrinder   Ironic Fate in the Poetry of Thomas Hardy   MA Univ of
      Rhode Island 1963
3786 KEELER Phoebe F   Thomas Hardy's *Tess of the D'Urbervilles*: Inter-
      pretations, Evaluations and Analyses since 1891   MA Boston Univ 1943
3787 KENNEY T J   *Romola* and *Tess of the D'Urbervilles*   MA Boston Coll 1935
3788 KEYS J W   Thomas Hardy and Arthur Schopenhauer: A Comparative Study
      MA North Texas St Univ 1969
3789 KIMBLE Ralph J Jr   Thomas Hardy: Cosmos, Society and Reader
      BA Amherst 1967
3790 KUENSTLER Helen R   Thomas Hardy's *A Pair of Blue Eyes*: A Textual
      and Critical Study   MA Washington Univ at St Louis nd
3791 LANCE Donald M   A Comparison of *Dona Perfecta* and *The Return of the
      Native*   MA Univ of Texas at Austin 1962   87 p
3792 LANDON Robert D II   The Ballad and Thomas Hardy: An Approach to
      His Novels and Poems   BA Amherst 1962
3793 LAWLOR Mary B   The Influence of Thomas Hardy on the Poetry of
      W H Auden   MA John Carroll Univ 1965
3794 LAWSON Richard A   Hardy as a Satirist   MA Bowling Green Univ 1959
3795 LINCH Mary A   A Comparison of Tragic Characteristics in the Novels
      of Thomas Hardy and of William Somerset Maugham   MA Florida St
      Univ 1939
3796 LINKOUS Garland K Jr   Henrik Ibsen and Thomas Hardy: A Sociological
      Comparison   MA Univ of Richmond 1965   78 p
3797 LONG Kay P   The Rhetorical Use of Archetypes: Studies in Hardy,
      Rimbaud and Hemingway   MA Univ of Tulsa 1968   55 p
3798 LYNCKER Hilde   The Influence of the Tragedies of Sophocles on the
      Novels of Thomas Hardy   MA Smith Coll 1931
3799 LYNDS Richard J   The Dionysian in Thomas Hardy's *Far from the Madding
      Crowd* and *The Return of the Native*   MA Boston Coll 1965
3800 McCULLOUGH Norman V   Probability in the Novels of Thomas Hardy
      MA Ohio St Univ 1950
3801 McDAVID Grace E   The Structural Use of Comic Relief in the First Three
      of Hardy's Major Novels   MA Univ of Texas at Austin 1941   126 p
3802 McGUIRE John F   The Use of Mythology in Thomas Hardy's *Tess of the
      D'Urbervilles*   MA Pacific Univ 1967   87 p
3803 McGUIRE Paul M   Imagery in the Early Novels of Thomas Hardy   MA Texas
      Technological Univ 1941   78 p
3804 McKELLER John G   A Study of the Gradually Darkening Mood in
      Thomas Hardy's Novels   MA Brigham Young Univ 1962   110 p
3805 MACKERY Mamie L   The Influence of Environment upon the Characters
      in the Novels of Thomas Hardy   MA Florida St Univ 1940
3806 McMILLAN J B   Thomas Hardy's Views on Sex   MA Univ of North Carolina
      at Chapel Hill 1930
3807 MAHAFFEY Lois K   Beauty in Ugliness: A Study of Thomas Hardy's
      Concept and Practice of Poetry   MA Univ of Oklahoma 1944
3808 MALCOM Jeanne   Thomas Hardy's Poetry   MS Kansas St Coll at Pittsburg
      1943
3809 MANE Shobba   The Impact of the English Bible on the Thought and Art
      of Thomas Hardy   MA Toronto (Canada) 1963
3810 MANGOLD Charlotte W   Hardy's Fiction in Germany   MA Univ of Maryland
      at College Park 1954   73 p
3811 MARCUS Raymond   The Napoleonic Image in Hardy and Tolstoy   MA Columbia
      1951
3812 MARK Jerome   The Philosophy of Thomas Hardy   MA Univ of Tennessee 1926
3813 MARSDEN K   A Critical Study of the Shorter Poems of Thomas Hardy
      M Phil Univ of London (England) 1967
3814 MELTON Jeanne M   A Critical Analysis of Thomas Hardy's Prose Style
      MA Stanford Univ 1939
3815 MILLER Billie J   Thomas Hardy's Presentation of Women Characters
      M Ed Henderson St Coll nd

3816 MILLER Margaret P Thomas Hardy, Literary Artist and Deterministic
      Philosopher MA Univ of Arizona pre-1933
3817 MOORE Helen J Thomas Hardy's Views of His Fictional Methods
      MA Univ of Pittsburgh 1941
3818 MOORE Thomas I Evidences of a Religiously Based Morality in
      Thomas Hardy's Novels MA Univ of Wyoming 1965
3819 MURPHY Peter Patterns of Myth in *The Return of the Native* BA Univ
      of British Columbia (Canada) 1968
3820 NEIL Alice C Style in the Poetry of Thomas Hardy MA Univ of British
      Columbia (Canada) 1932 123 p
3821 NIELSON Elizabeth E The Influence of Thomas Hardy's Philosophical
      Preconceptions on Character Delineation MA Boston Univ 1932
3822 NOONAN John F The Poetry of Thomas Hardy and A E Housman: Charac-
      teristics of Their "Dark Views" MA Bowling Green Univ 1965
3823 NORVELL Charles A The Mind of Hardy's Earthbound Folk MA Univ of
      Texas at Austin 1938 88 p
3824 NUTT Constance R Thomas Hardy's Use of Physical Nature MA Univ of
      Montana 1934 48 p
3825 O'NEAL Eldon Thomas Hardy's Four Great Tragedies: A Study of His
      Philosophy, 1875-1895 MA Texas Christian Univ 1960 117 p
3826 ORR Rutha F Hardy and Schopenhauer MA Texas Christian Univ 1930 111 p
3827 OVERPECK Shirley A Thomas Hardy: A Study of Ambition in His Short
      Stories MA Southern Illinois Univ at Carbondale 1963 81 p
3828 PALMER Peter F Chance in Thomas Hardy MA Univ of British Columbia
      (Canada) 1926
3829 PARSONS Vesta M A Study of the Influence of the Wessex Setting on
      the Novels of Thomas Hardy with Particular Reference to the Main
      Characters MA Boston Univ 1929
3830 PENCE Eugenia C Animal Life in the Novels of Thomas Hardy Studied
      as an Aesthetic, Scientific and Philosophical Contribution to His
      Art MA Boston Coll nd
3831 PERRY Thomas P Critical Study of the Use of Coincidence in
      Thomas Hardy's Novels of His Major Period MA Northeastern Missouri
      St Coll 1959
3832 PITCUITHLY Mary S Nature in Thomas Hardy's *Far from the Madding Crowd,*
      The Return of the Native and *Tess of the D'Urbervilles* MA Texas
      Technological Univ 1969 99 p
3833 POLLARD D A A Comparison of the Poetry of William Barnes and
      Thomas Hardy MA Univ of London (England) 1966
3834 POPP Carole L Thomas Hardy's Attitude toward Women MA West Virginia
      Univ 1964 91 p
3835 POUND Sandra J A Comparison of *The Pit* and *The Mayor of Casterbridge*
      MA Bowling Green Univ 1963
3836 PRATT Dorothy J Thomas Hardy's Idea of the "Immanent Will" as
      Evidenced in His Works MA Baylor Univ 1968 129 p
3837 PRICE David Thomas Hardy: Twenty-Four Poems BA Amherst 1967
3838 PRICE Elizabeth J Thomas Hardy: Poet and Romanticism MA Univ of
      Oklahoma 1966
3839 RENO Raymond H Thomas Hardy's *The Dynasts* as a Tragedy MA George
      Washington Univ 1951 138 p
3840 RICH Howard The Short Stories of Thomas Hardy MA Columbia 1961 63 p
3841 RICHARDS Emily J The Reflection of Art in Thomas Hardy's Novels·
      MA Lamar Technological Univ 1963
3842 RISTY Mary J Observations in Thomas Hardy's *The Woodlanders*
      MA Auburn Univ 1966
3843 RIVERA Carmen L A Study of the Interrelation of Character and Fate
      in Thomas Hardy MA Florida St Univ 1947
3844 ROBERTSON Glen E A Study of Religious Pessimism in the Poetry of
      Hardy, Fitzgerald, Housman and Thompson MA Brigham Young Univ 1959
      72 p

3845   ROBINSON Lynn   A Comparison of Two Deterministic Philosophies:
       Thomas Hardy's Philosophy of Immanent Will and Leo Tolstoy's
       Theory of History   MA Midwestern Univ 1967   163 p
3846   ROBINSON Virginia L   The Classical Influence in Thomas Hardy's
       Novels from 1871 to 1880   MA Univ of Kentucky 1931
3847   RUSSELL R   The Minor Rustics in the Novels of Thomas Hardy
       BA Univ of British Columbia (Canada) 1943
3848   RYAN Marjorie J   A Comparative Study of Virgil and Hardy   MA Univ
       of Montana 1930   45 p
3849   SAKAI Helen C   The Relation between Imagery and Theme in *Tess of the
       D'Urbervilles*   MA Univ of Hawaii 1962   94 p
3850   SALKOFF Gladys B   Hardy and the Women of His Wessex Novels   MA Univ
       of Miami 1966
3851   SALTMAN Eva   "Divine Gloria Ruris": A Suggestion of the Influence
       of Virgil's *Georgics* upon Thomas Hardy's *Far from the Madding
       Crowd*   MA Smith Coll 1934
3852   SCHWARTZ Martha H   The Philosophy of Thomas Hardy's Fiction   MA Univ
       of Pittsburgh 1938
3853   SEARS Florence I   A Study of the Works of Thomas Hardy as an
       Expression of Humor   MA Univ of Texas at Austin 1939   133 p
3854   SHAW Will R   Tragic Figures in Thomas Hardy's Major Novels   MA Univ
       of Texas at Austin 1928
3855   SHELDON Georgia   A Study of the Irony in the Works of Thomas Hardy
       MA Univ of Oklahoma 1925
3856   SHERMAN George W   A Study of *The Dynasts*   MA Syracuse Univ 1946   187 p
3857   SIMPLER Maxine P   The Impact of Napoleon on the Minds of Three
       Nineteenth Century Men of Letters with Incidental Remarks on Their
       Philosophies of Life   MA Univ of Delaware 1949   112 p
3858   SMITH Clara M   Hardy's Use of Proverbs   MA Baylor Univ 1935   114 p
3859   SMITH Geneva M   Dramatic Irony: Some Views of Its Uses in the
       Novels of Thomas Hardy   MA Oklahoma St Univ 1938   118 p
3860   SMITH Katherine E   Thomas Hardy as a Short Story Writer   MA Univ
       of Texas at Austin 1939   111 p
3861   SOLETI Isabella   Thomas Hardy   MA Ca Foscari (Italy) 1936
3862   SPANN M W   The Treatment of Nature in Thomas Hardy's Six Major Novels
       MA North Texas St Univ 1959
3863   SPRING A J   Novels of Thomas Hardy and His Pessimism   MA Boston Coll
       1933
3864   SPRUCE Carol   A Classification of the Shorter Poems of Thomas Hardy
       MA Univ of Texas at Austin 1932
3865   STEELE Albert L   Thomas Hardy's Use of Technical Literary Devices
       in His Prose Works   MA Univ of Texas at Austin 1936
3866   STEVENS Roy T   Contemporary Criticism of Hardy, Gissing and
       "Mark Rutherford" as Novelists, 1870-1900   M Litt Cambridge Univ
       (England) 1954
3867   STOKES Dorothy E   Stylistic Effects in Thomas Hardy's Novels
       MA Univ of Texas at Austin 1938   96 p
3868   STONE Ruth R   The Influence of the Bible on the Major Novels of
       Thomas Hardy   MA Smith Coll 1931
3869   STROBEL Reaves E Jr   Robinson, Hardy and Williams: A Look at
       Estrangement   BA Amherst 1961
3870   SWETSKY Judith   Mythological Element in the Novels of Thomas Hardy
       MA Brooklyn Coll 1965
3871   SYERS Beatrice B   Folklore in Thomas Hardy's Major Wessex Novels
       MA Univ of Texas at Austin 1933
3872   TANDY Margaret   The Use of the Bible in Thomas Hardy's Novels
       MA Univ of Kentucky 1929
3873   TATE Marie T   The Short Stories of Thomas Hardy: An Analysis of
       Tone   MA Purdue Univ 1965   75 p
3874   TAYLOR Archie   Thomas Hardy's Philosophy   MA Texas Christian Univ 192

3875 TAYLOR C Ralph The Philosophy of Thomas Hardy as Revealed in His
      Novels MA Boston Univ 1931
3876 TERRY Anna H A Study of French Criticism of Thomas Hardy in the
      University of Texas Library MA Univ of Texas at Austin 1941 141 p
3877 TOPPING Donald M Social Criticism in the Novels of Thomas Hardy
      MA Univ of Kentucky 1956 86 p
3878 TREADWELL L W Hardy's Dark Ladies MA Univ of Arizona 1966
3879 VAN HAMMERSVELD Elizabeth W An Interpretation of the Spirits in
      The Dynasts MA Texas Christian Univ 1968 69 p
3880 VANNELL Nancy L Tragedy in the Novels of Thomas Hardy MA Texas
      Technological Univ 1967 65 p
3881 VINER Alexander E Thomas Hardy's Attitude toward Christianity
      MA Univ of North Carolina at Chapel Hill 1957 84 p
3882 WAGGONER Eleanore H Tree Imagery and Symbolism in Thomas Hardy's
      Far from the Madding Crowd, The Woodlanders, The Mayor of
      Casterbridge and Tess of the D'Urbervilles MA Texas Technological
      Univ 1963 78 p
3883 WALKER Harold S Jr The Bare Majority: A Moral Study of the Charac-
      ters in Thomas Hardy's Novels MA Columbia 1953 104 p
3884 WHEELER Jesse H The Critical Principles of Thomas Hardy the
      Novelist MA Auburn Univ 1940
3885 WICKENS Glen The Pattern of Sacrificial Images in Tess of the
      D'Urbervilles BA Univ of British Columbia (Canada) 1969
3886 WIESE Glen J Causality in the Novels of Thomas Hardy MA Brigham
      Young Univ 1959 111 p
3887 WILLIAMS Hazel M The Role of Nature in Selected Novels of
      Thomas Hardy MA Atlanta Univ 1965
3888 WILLIAMSON Adeline N Evidences of Evolutionary Meliorism in Lyrical
      Poems of Thomas Hardy MA Oklahoma St Univ 1942 56 p
3889 WINNE Eva A Study of Thomas Hardy's The Dynasts MA Univ of Texas
      at Austin 1932
3890 WINTER Carol A Hardy's Use of Setting in the Novels MA Toronto
      (Canada) 1966
3891 WOODFIELD James The Magic Touch: An Examination of Hardy's Use
      of Folklore and the Preternatural BA Univ of British Columbia
      (Canada) 1965
3892 WYND Catherine Fate and Hardy's Women MA Boston Univ 1929
3893 YEAGER Fannie A Psychological Analysis of the Characters in Hardy's
      Novels MA Univ of Oklahoma 1932
3894 ZINGER Anna Courtship and Marriage in the Novels of Thomas Hardy
      MA McGill (Canada) 1965
See also 1982, 2019, 2113, 2126, 2759, 5223, 6663

                          WILLIAM HAZLITT

3895 BEACH E K Hazlitt on Byron MA Univ of North Carolina at Chapel Hill
      1944
3896 BECKER Marion G The Religion and Social Ethics of William Hazlitt
      MA Washington Univ at St Louis 1948 113 p
3897 CAROTHERS Francis B Jr The Aesthetic Approach to Literature in the
      Criticism of William Hazlitt, Charles Lamb and John Keats
      MA Univ of Oregon 1941
3898 CURDA Paul M The Critical Reputation of William Hazlitt: A Survey
      and Synthesis MA Villanova Univ 1965
3899 DAVIS Russell E William Hazlitt's Political and Social Philosophy
      as Expressed in the Malthusian Controversy MA Columbia 1953 65 p
3900 DUNLAP Samuel R Hazlitt's Criticism of the Fine Arts MA Rice 1932
3901 DUSTIN Dorothy D Hazlitt on Burke: A Study of William Hazlitt's
      Conflicting Comments on, and the Frequency and Manner in Which
      He Quoted, Edmund Burke MA Univ of Omaha 1964

3902 EGGERS John P William Hazlitt as a Critic of Romanticism
      MA Columbia 1964 87 p
3903 EIKENBERRY Franklin J The Influence of William Hazlitt upon National
      American Literature with Special Reference to Poe MA Univ of Iowa
      1929
3904 ELLIS Anne P The Theories of Comedy in the Criticism of William Hazlit
      MA George Washington Univ 1944 126 p
3905 GARDNER Gerald M The Influence of Hazlitt on the Evolution of Keats'
      Aesthetic Theory MA Boston Coll 1969
3906 GEAR Sr Marion C The Formative Influence of William Hazlitt on the
      Prose Style of Louise Imogen Guiney MA Boston Coll 1949
3907 GLASS Martin Hazlitt's Maxims MA Columbia 1960 122 p
3908 GRIFFIN Warren B The Cockney School and Its Critics MA Howard Univ
      1938 61 p
3909 HANKINS Everett M A Study of Hazlitt's Style MA Univ of Iowa 1932
3910 HENDERSON Archibald Jr The Influence of William Hazlitt on
      John Keats MA Univ of North Carolina at Chapel Hill 1941
3911 HUGHES Samuel J The Spirit of the Age 1825-1850: A Chronological
      Study of the Social Criticism of Hazlitt, Mill, R H Horne and
      E P Hood MA Columbia 1954 126 p
3912 McBRIDE Emma B Hazlitt: Critic of His Own Times MA Univ of Tulsa
      1938
3913 McCARTHY Jane P Hazlitt on the Drama: The Theory and Practice of
      His Criticism MA Columbia 1963 93 p
3914 McCUTCHEON Helen H The Literary Reputation of William Hazlitt to
      1840 MA Tulane Univ 1927
3915 MASTROGIACOMO Ida *The Spirit of the Age or Contemporary Portraits*
      by William Hazlitt MA Ca Foscari (Italy) 1969
3916 OZOLINS Aija "Character" as Principle and Method in William Hazlitt's
      Criticism MA Univ of Maryland at College Park 1966 80 p
3917 PAISLEY Elizabeth The Reading of William Hazlitt MA Univ of
      Arkansas 1930
3918 QUINN Rosemary K William Hazlitt: His Criterion of Feeling
      MA Boston Coll 1963
3919 SHAW Joseph A Critical Study of Hazlitt's *Characters of Shakespeare's
      Plays* MA Univ of Tennessee 1941
3920 SMITH Hugh R A Comparison of the Literary Criticism of
      Walter Bagehot and William Hazlitt MA Univ of Montana 1933 86 p
3921 THOMPSON Richard H Jr Hazlitt's Use of Character MA Univ of Oklahoma
      1950
3922 WHEELER Frances L William Hazlitt's Literary Criteria as Interpreted
      by His Critics MA Univ of Iowa 1932
See also 4491, 6358

GEORGE HERBERT

3923 BAILEY Stephen George Herbert's Search for Simplicity in *The Temple:*
      Art and Life in the Image of God BA Univ of British Columbia
      (Canada) 1970
3924 BALLEW Joseph F George Herbert's Chief Prose Work *A Priest to the
      Temple or The Country Parson* as Courtesy Literature MA Univ of
      Tennessee 1955 129 p
3925 BAXTER Clyde E *The Temple*: The Revelation of George Herbert's
      Spiritual History MA Univ of Oklahoma 1956
3926 BENNETT Edith R George Herbert and the Humanist Tradition MA Columbi
      1960 80 p
3927 BERRA E J George Herbert: Poet of Anglicanism MA Boston Coll 1941
3928 BINDER Barrett Sin and Irony in George Herbert's *The Temple*
      MA Columbia 1961 89 p
3929 BINNETTE Mother Mary C An Annotated Bibliography of George Herbert

MA Boston Coll 1963
3930 BLAU Rivkah   George Herbert and the Psalm Tradition   MA Columbia
      1963   104 p
3931 BOX Florence A A Study of the Diction and Style of George Herbert's
      The Temple   MA Univ of Texas at Austin 1938   176 p
3932 BURNETT Ronald O A Study of the Poetry of George Herbert in Relation
      to the Fine Arts of His Period   MA Bowling Green Univ 1956
3933 BURNS Martha I   The Dragon and Saint George: A Study of
      George Herbert's Religious Problems   MA Columbia 1950
3934 CANAAN Howard L   Christian Allegory in the Poetry of George Herbert
      MA Columbia 1966   122 p
3935 CARICATO Frank S   George Herbert: A Study in Religious Sensibility
      MA Columbia 1960   89 p
3936 COHN Paula J   Order in the Poetry of George Herbert   MA Hunter Coll
      1966
3937 COLIN Carol   George Herbert: A Structural Study   MA Columbia 1961
      94 p
3938 COMPTON Elizabeth W   New Testament Allusions in the Poetry of
      George Herbert   MA Univ of Pittsburgh 1959
3939 CONNOLLY Brian W A Study of the Devotional Elements in the Poetry
      of George Herbert   MA Univ of Pittsburgh 1958
3940 DONOHUE Sr Rite   George Herbert, Renaissance Poet, Originator of
      the Religious Love-Lyric   MA Coll of the Holy Names at Oakland 1967
3941 DUCHARME Mother Saint Vincent F   George Herbert's Philosophy of Love
      MA Boston Coll 1947
3942 DYKES Sayre E   Music and Poetry of George Herbert   MA Rice 1966
3943 EDWARDS Marjorie B   The Attitude of the Metaphysical Poets toward
      Women   MA Howard Univ 1958   107 p
3944 EVETTS J   A Study of Some Features of George Herbert's Vocabulary
      and Syntax and Their Relation to His Poetic Form   M Phil Univ of
      London (England) 1967
3945 FELLIN Rev Joseph H   The Attributes of God in The Temple of
      George Herbert   MA Boston Coll 1951
3946 FREI Joan H   The Influence of George Herbert on the Poetry of
      Henry Vaughan   MA Univ of Tennessee 1955   139 p
3947 GOODSON Eleanor H   The Figures of Speech in the Poetry of George Herbert
      and Henry Vaughan   MA George Washington Univ 1935   37 p
3948 GREENE Edward P   Herbert's "Affliction" Poems: A Study in Continuity
      and Doctrine   MA Columbia 1966   105 p
3949 HALSTEAD Christina H   Herbert's Household Imagery   MA Univ of Richmond
      1967   80 p
3950 HARPER Sr Mary C   The Epithets and Images in George Herbert's English
      Poems   MA Marquette Univ 1939   70 p
3951 HAYDEN Evelyn E   George Herbert and Henry Vaughan: A Comparison of
      Their Mysticism   MA Columbia 1953   64 p
3952 HOOPES Robert G   The Formative Crises in the Life and Work of
      George Herbert   MA Boston Univ 1942
3953 JACOBSON Phyllis A   A Study of the Vocabulary of George Herbert
      MA Univ of Iowa 1931
3954 KAWANISHI Susumu   George Herbert: A Study of Religious Poetry
      BA Amherst 1956
3955 KELLY Gertrude R   The Patterns of Order: A Study of George Herbert's
      Imagery in Relation to His Major Themes   MA Columbia 1963   223 p
3956 KIRK Stephen S   The Curious Girdle: George Herbert's Poetry in
      Relation to His Age   MA Univ of Oklahoma 1949
3957 KLUTZ Sara   The Reputation of George Herbert in the Seventeenth
      Century   MA Univ of North Carolina at Chapel Hill 1952   100 p
3958 LAVERS Norman L   The Religion of George Herbert   MA Boston Univ 1943
3959 LEWIS Ruth H   The Conflicting Forces in the Life and Poetry of
      George Herbert   MS Kansas St Coll at Pittsburg 1935

3960 LUCIER Sr Mary D Music in the Poetry of George Herbert MA Boston
     Coll 1960
3961 McARRAVY Gwyneth The Poetic Style of George Herbert BA Univ of
     British Columbia (Canada) 1958
3962 McDONOUGH Donald P The Latin Poetry of George Herbert MA Columbia
     1966 90 p
3963 MARTIN David W The Humanism of George Herbert MA Temple Univ 1966
     45 p
3964 O'CONNOR Vivian George Herbert and Sir Philip Sidney: A Comparison
     MA Columbia 1960 125 p
3965 OSTERCAMP Janet F Edward Taylor's Homely Imagery Characterized
     through Comparison with George Herbert MA Pennsylvania St Univ 1965
3966 PARSONS Leslie C George Herbert's Use of Christian Paradox
     MA West Virginia Univ 1968 48 p
3967 PETERS Gail F Ambiguity in the Poetry of George Herbert MA Univ of
     Hawaii 1964 70 p
3968 RAMSEY Paul Jr Symbolism in the English Poems of George Herbert
     MA Univ of North Carolina at Chapel Hill 1948 176 p
3969 RANKIN John S Religious Themes from the Metaphysical Poets MA Texas
     Technological Univ 1934 67 p
3970 REED Richard A George Herbert's Poems about Poetry MA Emory Univ 1965
3971 REYNOLDS C E The Bible in the Life and English Works of
     George Herbert MA Univ of North Carolina at Chapel Hill 1931
3972 RICHARDSON N The Mysticism of George Herbert and Henry Vaughan
     MA Univ of British Columbia (Canada) 1952 135 p
3973 ROBERTS Ona P "The Collar": A Study of the Pull of the Worldly
     Versus the Pull of the Spiritual in the Life and Poems of
     George Herbert MA Texas Christian Univ 1949 98 p
3974 ROBIDA Sr Lucilla St Francois de Sales Possible Influence on the
     Poetry of George Herbert MA Boston Coll 1968
3975 ROBINSON Suzanne Irony and Paradox and George Herbert's "The
     Sacrifice" MA Columbia 1958 110 p
3976 STAMBLER Elizabeth George Herbert and the Courtly Lyric Tradition
     MA Columbia 1959 241 p
3977 TRIPPET Mary M The Precision of George Herbert's Poetry MA Texas
     Christian Univ 1957 109 p
3978 WIGGINS Mary C The Literary Reputation of George Herbert MA Univ
     of Florida nd
3979 WILLARD Frederic R Studies in the Lives, Works and Times of
     George Herbert and Henry Vaughan MA Boston Univ 1908
See also 2732, 2738, 2739, 4099, 5117

ROBERT HERRICK

3980 BARKER Edna L Robert Herrick's Poetry as a Poetry of Wit
     MA Louisiana St Univ 1937
3981 BARNES Frank D Pierre De Ronsard and Robert Herrick: Twin Peaks
     of the Lyric Renaissance MA Univ of Texas at Austin 1935
3982 BECK Paula G Robert Herrick's Descriptions of His Mistresses:
     The Key to an Imaginative Escape from the Transcience of
     Pleasure MA Columbia 1962 58 p
3983 BROWN Martha Robert Herrick: Pagan and Divine MA Univ of Texas
     at Austin 1938 106 p
3984 CINQUEMANI Anthony M Kinds of Love in the Poetry of Robert Herrick
     MA Columbia 1960 152 p
3985 COZART Dorothy T Some Aspects of the Use of Superstitions in
     Robert Herrick's Poems of *The Hesperides* MA Oklahoma St Univ
     1965 52 p
3986 CRAWLEY Thomas E Robert Herrick: A Study of His Poetic Reputation
     with a Critical Bibliography of the Poet and His Work MA Univ

of North Carolina at Chapel Hill 1953   106 p
3987 DROLETTE Wesley B   Robert Herrick: A Lyricist of the Seventeenth
      Century MA Boston Univ 1943
3988 DWYER Jon A Paradoxes in Robert Herrick's *Hesperides* MA West Texas
      St Univ 1965   137 p
3989 FREIS Willa H Herrick's Debt to Jonson MA Univ of Arizona 1936
3990 HENNESSEY Sr Julie P Robert Herrick's Topical Lyricism MA Boston
      Coll 1959
3991 HICKS Marion   Country Life and Lore in the Poetry of Robert Herrick
      MA Univ of Texas at Austin 1938   205 p
3992 LUCK Lawrence J Robert Herrick: Conflict of Idealist and Realist
      MA Bowling Green Univ 1967
3993 McKEON Martha W Robert Herrick: A Study in the Union of Music and
      Poetry MA Univ of Tulsa 1941
3994 MAYS Robert G A Detailed Study of the Poetry of Robert Herrick
      MA Univ of Oklahoma 1957
3995 MINARD Rosemary S Robert Herrick's Uses of the Petrarchan Conceits
      MA Univ of Houston 1969   76 p
3996 NEAGLE Rita T Parallels in the Poetry of Robert Herrick and Latin
      Authors MA Boston Univ 1934
3997 PONZIO Harold J Robert Herrick and the Theme of Success
      MA Long Island Univ 1967   72 p
3998 RAMSEY John S Folklore and the Poetry of Robert Herrick: Sources
      and Implications MA Univ of Maryland at College Park 1965   115 p
3999 ROBERTS Eunice E The Influence of Horace, Catullus and Martial on
      the Lyrics of Jonson and Herrick MA Univ of Texas at Austin 1934
4000 ROBINSON William R Epicurus and Robert Herrick on Pleasure
      MA Ohio St Univ 1956
4001 RODERICK W J A Critical Estimation of the Works of Robert Herrick
      MA Boston Univ 1938
4002 RUSHMORE Helen Country Customs and Folk Beliefs in the Poetry of
      Robert Herrick MA Univ of Tulsa 1938
4003 SHARP Maywood H Robert Herrick: Biblical Allusions in His *Noble
      Numbers* or His *Pious Pieces* MA Univ of New Mexico 1935
4004 SMITH Lorn H Society Verse in English Literature MA Univ of Texas
      at Austin 1913
4005 WESTON Priscilla R A Study of Nature in the Poetry of Robert Herrick
      MA Texas Christian Univ 1958   67 p
4006 WIEGAND Richard Naturalistic Tendencies in the Works of
      Robert Herrick MA Univ of North Carolina at Chapel Hill 1950   104 p
4007 WILLARD E P Jr Study in the Influence of Horace on Herrick's
      Hesperides MA Univ of North Carolina at Chapel Hill 1924

                              THOMAS HEYWOOD

4008 BADIALI Guido *Six Pageants* by Thomas Heywood MA Ca Foscari (Italy)
      1966
4009 CECOTTI Liliana Thomas Heywood: *The Four Prentices of London*
      MA Ca Foscari (Italy) 1965
4010 CONCOLATO Maria G Thomas Heywood: *A Woman Killed with Kindness*
      MA Ca Foscari (Italy) 1959
4011 EDWARDS Martha E Parallelism and Contrast in Certain Dramas of
      Philip Massinger and Thomas Heywood MA Indiana Univ 1940
4012 HANSEN Kathryn R The Settings of the Plays of Thomas Heywood
      MA Univ of Arizona pre-1933
4013 HATCH Mary C *If You Know Not Me, You Know Nobody* by Thomas Heywood,
      Edited with an Introduction and Notes MA Columbia 1941
4014 McCORD Hazel T A Study of Contemporary English Life in the Dramas
      of Thomas Heywood MA Univ of Texas at Austin 1941   119 p

4015 MANZUK Jean K Thomas Heywood: Domestic Dramatist MA Univ of
       Pittsburgh 1950
4016 MIONI Paola *The Fair Maid of the West Past* by Thomas Heywood
       MA Ca Foscari (Italy) 1968
4017 NEU Lucile M Characterization in the Plays of Thomas Heywood
       MA Univ of Texas at Austin 1933
4018 PATTERSON Thomas M Heywood's Use of His Sources in *A Woman Killed
       with Kindness* MA Univ of Texas at Austin 1936
4019 SMITH Alethia T The Popularity of Thomas Heywood as a Dramatist,
       1600-1670 MA Howard Univ 1934   33 p
4020 STOREY Paul S *The Wise Woman of Hogsdon* by Thomas Heywood; an Edition
       with an Introduction and Notes MA Univ of Pittsburgh 1955
See also 2476, 6672

                              THOMAS HOBBES

4021 DE SAULNIERS Lawrence B Machiavelli and Hobbes: A Criticism of
       Methods MA Boston Coll 1950
4022 KILLORIN Joseph I The Role of Heroic Virtue in Hobbes and Dryden
       MA Columbia 1958   87 p
4023 KLINEBERG Beatrice A A Discussion of the Problem of Relativity in
       Morals MA McGill (Canada) 1936
4024 NATIONS Caroline G The Influence of Thomas Hobbes upon the Resto-
       ration Wits MA Washington Univ at St Louis 1931   126 p
See also 276, 2761, 4880

                         GERARD MANLEY HOPKINS

4025 ABBOTT William H The Image of Time in the Poetry of
       Gerard Manley Hopkins MA Louisiana St Univ 1966
4026 AGNEW Janet K Gerard Manley Hopkins: A Victorian Critic and Poet
       MA Queen's (Canada) 1965
4027 ALGER Robert C Gerard Manley Hopkins: Contributions toward a Theory
       of Poetry MA Auburn Univ 1960
4028 BARRY Helen V Gerard Manley Hopkins: Sacramentalist and Incarna-
       tionist MA Butler Univ 1948
4029 BINGLE Beverly A A Critical Analysis on Linguistic Principles of
       Two Hopkins Sonnets MA Bowling Green Univ 1968
4030 BLOOM Lionel The Mystic Pattern in the Poetry of Gerard Manley Hopkins
       MA Columbia 1963   76 p
4031 BLUM Sr Magdalen L The Imagery in the Poetry of Gerard Manley Hopkins
       MA Univ of New Mexico 1950
4032 BOTTALLA Paola *The Wreck of the Deutschland* by Gerard Manley Hopkins
       MA Ca Foscari (Italy) 1968
4033 BRINLEE Robert W The Religion and Poetic Theory of
       Gerard Manley Hopkins MA Univ of Tulsa 1958   100 p
4034 BROWN Marie P The Sensuous Concept of Nature in Gerard Manley Hopkins'
       Poetic Images MA Georgetown Univ 1964   90 p
4035 BURR Carol Compound Epithets in the Poetry of Gerard Manley Hopkins
       MA Columbia 1967   100 p
4036 BURTON James R The Metrical Theory of Gerard Manley Hopkins
       MA Univ of Texas at Austin 1939   216 p
4037 BYRNE Virginia C Inscape in the Aesthetic Theory and Poetic Practice
       of Gerard Manley Hopkins MA Coll of the Holy Names at Oakland 1960
4038 CADY Joseph L Jr Gerard Manley Hopkins: Instress Stressed; The
       Liberation from Personal Experinece BA Amherst 1960
4039 CAFFERATA Florence Gerard Manley Hopkins' Use of Nature in His
       Poetry MA Univ of British Columbia (Canada) 1962   128 p
4040 CALIRI Sr Mary E The Poetic Theory of Gerard Manley Hopkins in the
       Light of the "New Criticism" MA Boston Coll 1952

4041 CARROLL Basilian A Study of the Conflict in the Sonnets of Desolation
     of Gerard Manley Hopkins MA Univ of Rhode Island 1966 66 p
4042 CHALAND Ann Paradox in the Poetry of Gerard Manley Hopkins
     MA Univ of British Columbia (Canada) 1969 101 p
4043 COLAVECCHIO Barbara M The Dominant Symbols in Gerard Manley Hopkins'
     The Wreck of the Deutschland MA Univ of Rhode Island 1963
4044 COLSON Ted D An Analysis of Selected Poems of Gerard Manley Hopkins
     for Oral Interpretation and a Study of His Poetic Theories
     MA Univ of Oklahoma 1963 243 p
4045 CONLIN Michael J A Bibliography of the Writings and Ana of
     Gerard Manley Hopkins from January 1, 1947 to January 1, 1958
     MA Univ of Kentucky 1961 108 p
4046 COX Dorothy S The Mind of Gerard Manley Hopkins MA Univ of Texas
     at Austin 1940 96 p
4047 DeGAFF Robert M Scotism in the Poetry of Gerard Manley Hopkins:
     A Study in Analogical Relationships MA Miami Univ 1966
4048 DELAHUNTY Kenneth R Guilt and the Grail; Hopkins, Poet in the Active
     Voice; and Wakefield, Mon Frere MA Pennsylvania St Univ 1965
4049 DELANEY Sr Anne C The Christocentricity of Gerard Manley Hopkins
     MA Boston Coll 1945
4050 DE SOUZA Frederick J Gerard Manley Hopkins: A Closer Look at the
     Terrible Sonnets MA Columbia 1963 45 p
4051 DORAIS Fabiola M The Poetry of Gerard Manley Hopkins: A Study of
     Light and Dark Symbolic Imagery MA Univ of Hawaii 1960 105 p
4052 EVARTS Prescott Jr Inscape and Symbol in the Poetry of
     Gerard Manley Hopkins MA Columbia 1962 80 p
4053 GIBBONS Mark L Metaphor and the Imagination in the Poems of
     Gerard Manley Hopkins BA Amherst 1964
4054 GILMAN William H Gerard Manley Hopkins: The Man MA George Wash-
     ington Univ 1943 57 p
4055 GLEESON William F Jr Gerard Manley Hopkins and the Society of Jesus
     MA Columbia 1952 70 p
4056 GREENBLATT Daniel L John Donne and Gerard Manley Hopkins: Two
     Religious Sensibilities BA Amherst 1970
4057 HACHE Mother Irene M The Place of the Incarnation in the Poetry
     of Gerard Manley Hopkins MA Boston Coll 1949
4058 HAMILTON Seymour C The Unified World Vision of Gerard Manley Hopkins
     MA Toronto (Canada) 1963
4059 HANNENKRAT Frank T Archetypal Patterns of Death and Rebirth in the
     Mature Poetry of Gerard Manley Hopkins MA Univ of Richmond 1968
     55 p
4060 HART Lucia C The Poetry of Gerard Manley Hopkins MA Univ of Texas
     at Austin 1965
4061 HERRING Mary L Gerard Manley Hopkins as a Critic of Poetry
     MA Univ of Tennessee 1964
4062 HOLMES Richard A Mannerist Approach to the Religious Sonnets of
     Donne and Hopkins BA Univ of British Columbia (Canada) 1970
4063 JOHNSON Ronald W Gerard Manley Hopkins: His Approach to Literary
     Criticism MA Colorado St Coll 1965
4064 KAMINSKY Marc The Victorian Hopkins MA Columbia 1967 234 p
4065 LAUDNER Mary L The Sermons of Gerard Manley Hopkins MA San Diego
     St Coll 1961 101 p
4066 LAWLER Donald L Gerard Manley Hopkins: Three Patterns of His
     Poetry MA Columbia 1960 49 p
4067 LIRETTE Sr Mary L Pitch; the Principle of Individuation in the
     Writings of Gerard Manley Hopkins MA Coll of the Holy Names at
     Oakland 1961
4068 LOMBA Marjorie L Hopkins the Beholder MA Coll of the Holy Names
     at Oakland 1968
4069 McDONOUGH Mary L An Investigation to Determine the Extent of the

Liturgical Echoes in the English Poems of Gerard Manley Hopkins
MA Bowling Green Univ 1949
4070 McGOWAN Madelon The Concept of Nature in the Poetry of
Gerard Manley Hopkins MA Univ of Southern California 1965
4071 McLAUGHLIN Rev John J The Influence of St Paul on Gerard Manley Hopkins
MA Boston Coll 1961
4072 MANN John S A Study in the Relation of Structure to Thought in the
Poetry of Gerard Manley Hopkins MA Columbia 1959 96 p
4073 MANUEL Hanora Mariology in the Poetry of Gerard Manley Hopkins
MA Univ of Texas at El Paso 1962 96 p
4074 MARKEN Ronald N Light and Dark Imagery in Hopkins' Major Verse
MA Alberta (Canada) 1965
4075 MASTRO Sr Mary L Hopkins' "Terrible Sonnets": A Fugue in Two
Voices MA Boston Coll 1968
4076 MELCHNER SR Mary R Hopkins and the Common Man MA Boston Coll 1942
4077 MEUTH Georgeanna S Gerard Manley Hopkins: Creator and Created
MA Columbia 1952 112 p
4078 MILLARD Janice "To What Serves Mortal Beauty": A Study in the
Aesthetics of Gerard Manley Hopkins BA Univ of British Columbia
(Canada) 1967
4079 MILLARD Mary J Hopkins' Inscape as Illuminated by a Consideration
of the Cinquecento Artistic Tradition and the Work of Michangelo
MA Univ of British Columbia (Canada) 1968 130 p
4080 MOAKLER Kenneth The Dark Night of Self: The Unifying Vision in
Gerard Hopkins MA Western Illinois Univ 1966
4081 MOON Nelson F Gerard Manley Hopkins' Use of Imagery MA Univ of
Oklahoma 1948
4082 MORRILL L M Blessings Not Unmixed: The Poetry of Gerard Hopkins
MA Boston Univ 1940
4083 MURPHY Sr Miriam J Gerard Manley Hopkins: Critic of His Contemporaries in the Nineteenth Century MA Univ of Pittsburgh 1943
4084 MURRAY Neil A The Prosodic Theory and Practice of Patmore, Hopkins
and Bridges MA Memorial (Canada) 1964
4085 NOONAN J J Evidences of the Supernatural in the Poetry of
Gerard Manley Hopkins MA Boston Coll 1937
4086 NORTHUP Eileen B Hopkins as a Student of Pater MA Univ of Rhode
Island 1958
4087 O'BRIEN Robert D Critical Mind of Gerard Manley Hopkins MA Boston
Coll 1942
4088 O'SHEA James H Hopkins and Bridges: A Study of the Critical
Relationship between Gerard Manley Hopkins and Robert Bridges
Insofar as It Concerned Itself with Hopkins' Poetry MA Univ of
Toledo 1959
4089 POCS John A Nationalism in the Poetry of Gerard Manley Hopkins
MA Bowling Green Univ 1960
4090 POUNCEY Lorene Gerard Manley Hopkins' Sextet of "Terrible" Sonnets:
An Analytical Study MA Univ of Houston 1963 110 p
4091 PROFFITT Edward L The Mastery and the Mercy: An Explication of
G M Hopkins' *The Wreck of the Deutschland* MA Columbia 1962 175 p
4092 RICKER Elizabeth A The Relation of Hopkins' Theories of Poetry to
His Applied Criticisms MA Boston Coll 1949
4093 ROBINSON Brian L Nature in the Poetry of Gerard Manley Hopkins
MA Columbia 1951
4094 SAVANT John Rhetorical Discipline in Hopkins' "The Blessed Virgin"
Compared to "The Air We Breathe" MA Dominican Coll of San Rafael
1966
4095 SHKOLNICK Sylvia Gerard Manley Hopkins: A Study in the Poetry of
Meditation MA Columbia 1959 93 p
4096 SHRAKE Joyce R The Poetic of Gerard Manley Hopkins: A Study of the
Relationship between the Philosophy of Duns Scotus and the Poetic

of Gerard Manley Hopkins MA Texas Christian Univ 1957 164 p
4097 SNAVELY Robert C Gerard Manley Hopkins: Mystic or Metaphysical
MA Univ of Omaha 1966
4098 SONSTROEM David A Gerard Manley Hopkins: The Winning Innocent
BA Amherst 1958
4099 STARK Sandra E The Importance of the Christian Frame of Reference
to the Poetry of George Herbert and Gerard Manley Hopkins
MA Univ of Texas at Austin 1967 86 p
4100 STEIN Karen F Hopkins' *The Wreck of the Deutschland*: An Aesthetic
Analysis MA Pennsylvania St Univ 1966
4101 STORM Melvin G Gerard Manley Hopkins: The Poet as Critic
MA Univ of Wyoming 1966
4102 SYLVESTER Howard E A Study of Gerard Manley Hopkins MA Univ of
New Mexico 1941
4103 TAMPLIN John G The Forsaken Forged Feature: A Study of
Gerard Manley Hopkins' Sonnet "Henry Purcell" MA Kent St Univ 1966
4104 TRUDEAU Sr Paul A A Commentary on the "Terrible" Sonnets of
Gerard Manley Hopkins MA Univ of New Mexico 1964
4105 VANCOS Mary J Gerard Manley Hopkins and Sacramentalism MA Boston
Coll 1951
4106 WALKER Alan J The Influence of Welsh Poetry on Gerard Manley Hopkins
MA Toronto (Canada) 1966
4107 WATSON Alice The Theme of Action in the Poetry of Gerard Manley Hopkins
MA Columbia 1962 86 p
4108 WEISS Theodore R Gerard Manley Hopkins MA Columbia 1940
4109 WHITE N E G M Hopkins: An Edition of the Last Poems (1884-1889)
with an Introduction and Notes M Phil Univ of London (England) 1968
4110 YETZER Bernard E The Victorianism of G M Hopkins MA Univ of Oklahoma
1965
4111 YOUNGBLOOD M A Elements of Old English Prosody in the Poetry of
Gerard Manley Hopkins MA North Texas St Univ 1969
See also 2708, 2802, 4516, 4595, 4622, 6026, 6052

ALFRED EDWARD HOUSMAN

4112 BLIDSTEIN Gerald J A E Housman: Poet of the Self-Conscious
MA Columbia 1961 90 p
4113 CAREY John L The Imagery and Poetic Theory of A E Housman MA Boston
Coll 1952
4114 CELLA Nicoletta A E Housman MA Ca Foscari (Italy) 1951
4115 CHANDLER Nada G The Narrow Measure: Variations, Themes of
A E Housman's *A Shropshire Lad* MA Columbia 1965 61 p
4116 COLANERI Marie E A E Housman's "Inverted Arcadia" MA Univ of Rhode
Island 1963
4117 CORRIGAN John C Jr And Deep Calls to Deep: Archetypal Patterns
in the Poetry of A E Housman MA Boston Coll 1960
4118 FAHY William L Pessimism in A E Housman MA San Diego St Coll 1968
152 p
4119 FLOX Richard E The Influence of the Bible on the Poetry of A E Housman
MA Indiana Univ 1950
4120 FORTNEY Alice E Classicism in the Poetry of A E Housman MA Univ of
Texas at Austin 1940 114 p
4121 GOLEMAN Barbara A A E Housman: Proud Rebel MA Florida St Univ 1954
4122 HARSCHEID Frank E Irony in the Poetry of A E Housman MA Univ of
Florida 1965
4123 LEGGETT Bobby J Theme and Structure in Housman's *A Shropshire Lad*
MA Univ of Florida 1965
4124 LEONE David F Irony and Empyreal Imagery in A E Housman's Poetry
BA Rutgers St Univ 1963 104 p
4125 LONG Bob Nature and Futility in A E Housman's Poetry MA West Texas

St Univ 1966 94 p
4126 NEWELL Alex A E Housman: A Biographical Study MA Univ of Pittsburgh
1953
4127 ORRICK Allan H A Study of the Imagery in the Poetry of A E Housman
MA Univ of Tulsa 1952
4128 PATRICK Michael D Recurrent Themes of A E Housman MA Southern
Illinois Univ at Carbondale 1957 73 p
4129 ROTA Elena The Poetry of A E Housman MA Ca Foscari (Italy) 1967
4130 SMITH M M Alfred Edward Housman (1859-1936): The Man and His Work
MA North Texas St Univ 1962
4131 SPARRON Wendell K A Comparison of the Poetry of A E Housman and
His Lecture "The Name and Nature of Poetry" MA East Carolina Univ
1965
4132 VALLIANT Ouida M The Art of A E Housman MA Univ of Texas at Austin
1931
4133 WALKER Norma J A Critical Study of the Basis of A E Housman's
Refusal to Include More Poems in His Published Works MA Oklahoma
St Univ 1954 40 p
4134 WHITE Marjorie Uniformity in the Poetry of A E Housman: A Study
of the Thought Content MA Univ of Florida 1934
See also 3822, 3844

WILLIAM HENRY HUDSON

4135 ALBERTSON Larrabee W H Hudson's Attitudes toward Nature MA Univ
of Hawaii 1937 71 p
4136 FOLEY Sr Alice J A Study of William Henry Hudson with Special
Reference to *Green Mansions*: Romance MA Mount Saint Vincent
(Canada) 1967
4137 LANDRY Rudolph J W H Hudson and the Vision of a Twin-Utopia
MA Boston Coll 1956
4138 McCUTCHEON David W H Hudson: An Estimate MA Univ of Pittsburgh
1939
4139 MASON M A The Prose Literature of Natural History, 1878-1927.
A Critical Study of the Chief Popular Writers on Natural History
with Special Reference to Richard Jefferies, William Henry Hudson
and Henry Williamson MA Univ of London (England) 1952
4140 OWEN Lula B The Language of the Folios Compared with Hudson's
Modernized Editions MA West Texas St Univ 1939 79 p
4141 SHIPP Ruby L The Autobiographical Elements in W H Hudson's
Romantic Prose MA Univ of Texas at Austin 1940 104 p
4142 YONKER Donald Y William Henry Hudson: The Naturalist in English
Literature M Ed Temple Univ 1935 119 p

DAVID HUME

4143 DORSI Evelyn G David Hume: Empirical Historian MA Syracuse Univ
1948 86 p
4144 KREINHEDER Albert G David Hume the Scotsman: A Study in Literary
Patronage MA Syracuse Univ 1940 112 p
4145 PRICE John V The Dialogues of Hume and Cicero on Natural Religion
MA Univ of Texas at Austin 1960 106 p
4146 SETSECK Michael A A Comparative Study of Hume's Criticism of English
Literature MA Univ of Texas at Austin 1961 170 p
See also 4881

LEIGH HUNT

4147 ALTAFFER Clara B Leigh Hunt as a Literary Critic MA Univ of
Oklahoma 1943

4148 GAHAGAN Nita Leigh Hunt: Liberal Editor MA Tulane Univ 1933
4149 HAMMER Jennings Criticism of the English Non-Dramatic Poets in
      the Essays of James Henry Leigh Hunt MA Univ of Pittsburgh nd
4150 KENDALL Kenneth E Leigh Hunt's *Reflector* MA Univ of Florida 1965
4151 KIRSCH Dorothy The Critical Opinions of Leigh Hunt MA George Wash-
      ington Univ 1939 75 p
4152 OLDFIELD Edward L Samuel Johnson and Leigh Hunt: Two Views of
      the Theatre MA Univ of British Columbia (Canada) 1961
4153 PARIGI Silvano Leigh Hunt as an Essayist MA Ca Foscari (Italy) 1955
See also 1160, 1804, 3908, 4505, 4520, 4550

                            ALDOUS HUXLEY

4154 BARBER Sherburne J John Whiting's *The Devils* and Aldous Huxley's
      The Devils of Loudun: A Study of a Playwright's Handling of a
      Source MA Univ of Tennessee 1965
4155 BASS Walter A From Limbo to the World of Light: An Examination
      of the Novels of Aldous Huxley MA Univ of Richmond 1950 76 p
4156 BELFIORE Anthony R What Aldous Huxley Owes to Italy MA Columbia 1937
4157 BENTLEY Burton A Metaphysics in Fiction: An Analysis of
      Aldous Huxley's *Those Barren Leaves* M Phil Toronto (Canada) 1966
4158 BENTLEY Joseph G Satirical Types in the Novels of Aldous Huxley
      MA Florida St Univ 1958
4159 BOWERING P E Development of the Moral Theme in the Major Novels
      of Aldous Huxley MA Univ of London (England) 1968
4160 BOWIE E The Literary Criticism of Aldous Huxley M Phil Univ of
      London (England) 1969
4161 BROUGHTON Levin A Survey of the Early Work of Aldous Huxley
      MA Columbia 1953 89 p
4162 BRUDEVOLD Bennett Aldous Huxley's Use of Music in *Point Counter
      Point* MA Univ of Montana 1940 75 p
4163 CALHOUN Robert D Jr Marcel Proust and Aldous Huxley: A Comparative
      Study MA Louisiana St Univ 1938
4164 CHARETTE Lee Q Aldous Huxley: A Study in a Changing Philosophy
      MA Pacific Univ 1940 117 p
4165 COPELAND Phyllis F Satire in the Novels of Aldous Huxley
      MS Auburn Univ 1941 109 p
4166 CRAWFORD Ruth R A Study of Progress as Related to Happiness in a
      Scientific Age in the Major Novels and Essays of Aldous Huxley
      MA Texas Arts and Industries Univ 1950
4167 FULTON Ethel Aldous Huxley: The Progressive Interest in Mysticism
      Shown in His Prose Works MA Univ of British Columbia (Canada)
      1960 180 p
4168 HAWVER Carl F Aldous Huxley's Theory of Education MA Bowling Green
      Univ 1939
4169 JABLKOWSKA Rose Aldous Huxley: A Critical Study of His Personality
      and Thought MA George Washington Univ 1948 104 p
4170 JOHNSTON Arthur R The Short Stories of Aldous Huxley MA Columbia 1951
4171 LAINO Barbara A Barnfield's *Lady Pecunis*: A Critical Edition;
      Huxley's Novel of Ideas and Disillusionment Writing; and
      Joyous Humility in Edward Taylor's *Meditations* MA Univ of
      Tennessee 1964
4172 LEFF Leonard J An Analysis of Four Satiric Devices Used in
      Aldous Huxley's *Brave New World* and George Orwell's *Nineteen
      Eighty-Four* MA Univ of Houston 1965 111 p
4173 LINCOLN John E Aldous Huxley as a Satirist MA Columbia 1950
4174 McCULLOUGH Peggy W Aldous Huxley and Technology: 1928-1938
      MA Midwestern Univ 1968 107 p
4175 MATHESON Gwen M A Commentary on Aldous Huxley's Last Novel, *Island*
      M Phil Toronto (Canada) 1966

4176 MATSON Virgie L A Study of Aldous Huxley's Literary Theories as
      Found in the Notebook of Philip Quarles and as Applied to
      Point Counter Point MA Univ of North Carolina at Chapel Hill
      1950 69 p
4177 MATTER William W Mechanization and the Isolated Man: Two Elements
      of Existentialism in Huxley's New World MA Texas Technological
      Univ 1968 47 p
4178 MESZBAN Mary P Objects of Satire in the Early Novels of Aldous Huxley:
      Four Major Universal Types MA Duquesne Univ 1966
4179 PETERSON Levi S An Evaluation of the Contribution of Burlesque to
      Aldous Huxley's *Brave New World*; Portent and Presentiment in
      Melville's *Pierre*; "Burial" MA Brigham Young Univ 1960 99 p
4180 READ James E *Point Counter Point* and *Eyeless in Gaza*: Experiments in
      Counterpoint BA Univ of British Columbia (Canada) 1963
4181 TURNER B R Maladjustment of the Chief Characters of the Novels of
      Aldous Huxley MA Boston Univ 1939
4182 UPTON Paul S The Role of the Intellectual Nonhero in the Novels
      of Aldous Huxley MA Alberta (Canada) 1966
4183 VIGLIA Luisa Aldous Leonard Huxley MA Ca Foscari (Italy) 1932
4184 WALSH J E The Narrative Technique of Aldous Huxley MA Boston Univ
      1940
4185 WARNER Deane M Aldous Huxley: From Cynic to Mystic MA Fresno
      St Coll 1958 132 p
4186 WATSON Thomas L Aldous Huxley: A Study in Values MA Univ of Texas
      at Austin 1949 141 p
4187 WATT Donald J The Human Fugue-Themes and Satirical Techniques in
      Four Novels of Aldous Huxley MA Boston Coll 1961

                        THOMAS HENRY HUXLEY

4188 ARSHAM Alice H The Spencer-Huxley Relationship: Its Influence on
      the Post-Darwinian Scientific Movement in England MA Columbia 1961
      142 p
4189 DAVIES Ora M Thomas Henry Huxley as an Educator M Ed Temple Univ
      1932
4190 HARVEY Mary J T H Huxley's Defense of Charles Darwin's *Origin of
      Species* MA Univ of Arizona 1960 67 p
4191 KUTCH Jane N T H Huxley and the Art of Controversy MA Lamar
      Technological Univ 1969
4192 SOLLER Mary The Influence of Thomas Henry Huxley's Essays on
      Scientific Thought of the Nineteenth Century MA Univ of Arizona
      1934
4193 SPEVACK Marjorie L Thomas Huxley's Warfare with Orthodoxy MA Univ
      of Houston 1962 92 p
4194 WOOTEN Lelia L A Comparative Study: Huxley and Darwin as Emotional
      Confreres of the Victorian Poets MA Mississippi St Univ 1964
See also 90
                        FRANCIS JEFFREY

4195 BOLAND Joseph E Jeffrey's Critical Principles and His Application
      of Them to the Poetry of Wordsworth MA St Louis Univ 1933 63 p
4196 LE PELLETIER Jerome A A Re-Assessment of the Critical Principles
      of Francis Jeffrey MA Univ of New Hampshire 1962 53 p
4197 MATTHEWS Virginia V Francis Jeffrey and His Contemporaries
      MA Southern Methodist Univ 1933
4198 SCHLABACH Barbara Francis Jeffrey and the *Edinburgh Review*
      MA Univ of Oklahoma 1917
4199 VINCE Ronald W Francis Jeffrey and the Lake School of Poetry
      MA Rice 1962
See also 1117

SAMUEL JOHNSON

4200 ACKERMAN Anna M   The Evaluation of Dr Samuel Johnson as a Literary
     Critic   MA Univ of North Dakota 1933   38 p
4201 ALLEN Adrienne   Samuel Johnson and the *Gentleman's Magazine*
     BA Univ of British Columbia (Canada) 1965
4202 ANDREWS Michael C   Samuel Johnson's Prejudice Against Scotland
     MA West Texas St Univ 1968
4203 ARKIN Stephen E   Aspects of Authority: A Study of Dr Johnson
     BA Amherst 1963
4204 BACOT Gladys R   The Dramatic Criticism of Samuel Johnson   MA Louisiana
     St Univ 1942
4205 BAND Margaret W   Characteristic Traits in the Prose Style of
     Samuel Johnson   MA Univ of Pittsburgh 1958
4206 BEAGAN Rosemary T   Johnson and Education   MA Boston Coll 1963
4207 BELFIGLIO Mary E   Samuel Johnson: A Study in Melancholy   MA Univ
     of Pittsburgh 1951
4208 BETTI Ines   Samuel Johnson as a Literary Critic   MA Ca Foscari
     (Italy) 1942
4209 BUCKLEY Patricia F   Samuel Johnson's Attitudes toward Catholicism
     MA Boston Coll 1951
4210 BURKE Sr Mary A   Samuel Johnson and the Pastoral   MA Boston Coll 1965
4211 CARIGG Mary E   The Religious Bias of Dr Johnson Recorded in the
     Dictionary   MA Boston Coll 1965
4212 CAVANAUGH Ellen R   An Evaluation of Johnson's Contributions to the
     Rambler and *Adventurer*   MA Univ of Iowa 1931
4213 CHERNIAVSKY Felix B   Dr Johnson on Genius   MA McGill (Canada) 1965
4214 COOGAN Margaret   The Conception of Service in the Writings and
     Conversation of Samuel Johnson   MA Smith Coll 1923
4215 CORBETT Ione T   Dr Samuel Johnson: A Study in the Art of Living
     MS Kansas St Coll at Pittsburg 1942
4216 COTTON Nancy C   The Art of Living: A Preliminary Investigation
     of Dr Johnson's Attitude toward Learning, Involving Primarily
     the *Rambler*, the *Idler* and the *Adventurer*   MA Univ of New Mexico
     1967
4217 CURRAN Paul   Attitudes toward Primitivism in the Works of
     Samuel Johnson and Benjamin Franklin   MA Bowling Green Univ 1962
4218 DAILY Mary M   Critical Analysis of Samuel Johnson's Poetry
     MA Boston Coll 1952
4219 DODDS Walter E   The Influence of the *Book of Common Prayer* on the
     Prose Style of Samuel Johnson's Prayers   MA Pacific Univ 1941   83 p
4220 DREYER Edward P   Dr Samuel Johnson as a Traveler   MA Tulane Univ 1931
4221 EIDSVIK Charles V   The Social Thought of Samuel Johnson   MA Univ of
     South Dakota 1966
4222 EMERY John K   Samuel Johnson and the Booksellers   MA Colorado St Coll
     1963
4223 FINK Andrew K   Johnson's Latin Poems   MA John Carroll Univ 1965
4224 FLEMMING Roberta M   Samuel Johnson's Scotch Prejudice and His Tour
     of the Western Islands of Scotland   MA Columbia 1936
4225 FOELBER Elmer E   The Moral Philosophy of Samuel Johnson   MA Indiana
     Univ 1935
4226 GAGNON Pierre A   To Teach and to Please: Theory and Practice in
     Samuel Johnson's Literary Criticism   MA Boston Coll 1966
4227 GEORGE Dorothy I   Aristotelian Elements in Samuel Johnson's Literary
     Criticism   MA Louisiana St Univ 1937
4228 GROHSKOPF Bernice A   Dr Johnson and Mr Strachey: A Comparison between
     Samuel Johnson's Theories of Biography and Lytton Strachey's
     Biographical Technique   MA Columbia 1954   56 p
4229 HARDING Louis A   The Critical Range of the English Preface in the
     Age of Johnson   MA Indiana Univ 1935

4230 HARWOOD Paul A Dr Johnson: Critic MA Univ of Nevada 1929
4231 HENDERSON Sara C A Study of Dr Johnson's Use of Spenser Quotations
       in the *Dictionary* MA Univ of North Carolina at Chapel Hill 1947
       68 p
4232 HESKETH-Williams P K The Earlier Literary Criticism of Samuel Johnson
       B Litt Oxford Univ (England) 1940
4233 HIGGINS David S A Survey of the Critical Response to Samuel Johnson's
       Rasselas MA Columbia nd
4234 HOOFMAN Jewel D Dr Johnson: Aspects of His Moral Character
       MA Florida St Univ 1951
4235 HOPPER Ruth The Religion of Dr Samuel Johnson MA North Texas St
       Univ 1949
4236 HORGAN G M The Influence of Johnson's Prose Style MA Boston Coll 1935
4237 HOWE John M The Relationship of Samuel Johnson's *Rasselas* to the
       Great Chain of Being and the Theme of Positive Action MA Boston
       Coll 1968
4238 HUGGINS Janie S The Social and Economic Views of Dr Samuel Johnson
       MA Univ of Tennessee 1938
4239 JOHNSON Margaret E Dr Samuel Johnson as Viewed through the Eyes
       of Contemporaries MA Univ of Delaware 1943 215 p
4240 KANTZ Katherine S Samuel Johnson's Editorship of the *Gentleman's
       Magazine*, 1738-1747 MA Texas Arts and Industries Univ 1955
4241 KILEY Paul J The Imitative Character of Samuel Johnson's Verse
       and Prose Satire MA Boston Coll 1948
4242 KIMBALL Anne G Johnson's *Rasselas* and the Hero of General Nature
       MA Univ of Vermont 1960 107 p
4243 KINT Erma L Minor Women Novelists of the Age of Johnson
       MA Indiana Univ 1935
4244 LAWERY Robert S Dr Johnson's Attitude towards the Established
       Institutions of His Day MA Indiana Univ 1935
4245 LE MASTERS Margaret H Dr Samuel Johnson's Attitude toward Science
       and Discovery MA Indiana Univ 1940
4246 LOVE C E The Moral Philosophy of Samuel Johnson MA North Texas
       St Univ 1949
4247 LUXTON David W Samuel Johnson and the *Book of Common Prayer*
       MA McMaster (Canada) 1965
4248 LYONS John F Dr Johnson's Attitude towards the Romantic Movement
       MA St Louis Univ 1935 145 p
4249 MADDEN Florence Dr Samuel Johnson as a Biographer: His Theory
       and Practice MA Indiana Univ 1935
4250 MADEK Gerald A Dr Johnson on Marriage and the Family MA Boston
       Coll 1969
4251 MAHER J A The Philosophy of Samuel Johnson MA Boston Univ 1941
4252 MAST Daniel D Samuel Johnson the Speculatist and Natural Philosophy
       MA Texas Agricultural and Mechanical Univ 1966 65 p
4253 MAYS Morley J Samuel Johnson: An Eighteenth Century Moralist
       MA Univ of Pittsburgh 1936
4254 METZ Gladys K Women and Samuel Johnson MA Florida St Univ 1952
4255 MILLER Lewis H Jr Samuel Johnson: In Quest of Certainty
       BA Amherst 1960
4256 MURPHY John L The Religious Practices of Samuel Johnson MA Univ
       of Florida 1951
4257 NELSON Sandra L Samuel Johnson: The Paradoxical Tory MA DePauw
       Univ 1964 138 p
4258 O'BRIEN M E Samuel Johnson as a Reviewer B Litt Oxford Univ
       (England) 1946
4259 OLIVER Robert T An Examination of Dr Samuel Johnson's Criticism
       of the Metaphysical Poets MA Univ of Oregon 1933
4260 O'SHEA Michael J An Exploration of the Key Terms of Dr Johnson's
       Literary Criticism MA Boston Coll 1965

4261 PATHMANN Rose B   Dr Samuel Johnson and His Relation to the Romantic
      Movement   MA Univ of North Dakota 1925   54 p
4262 PHILLIPS Jewell K   The Relationship of English Literary Criticism
      to the Art of Landscape Gardening from the Age of Pope through
      the Age of Johnson   MA Washington St Univ at Pullman 1943
4263 PONCE Abraham   The Benevolent Tyrant: Samuel Johnson   MA Univ of
      Texas at Austin 1967   99 p
4264 REWA Michael P   The Artful Biographer   MA Univ of Delaware 1961   63 p
4265 ROBINSON Jesse R   A Comparative Study of the Biographical Treatment
      of Samuel Johnson by Thomas Carlyle and Thomas Babington Macaulay
      MA North Carolina Coll 1964
4266 ROBLYER Pamela W   Johnson and Juvenal: A Comparison of *London* and
      The Vanity of Human Wishes with *Satires III* and *X*   MA Univ of
      Maryland at College Park 1969   65 p
4267 RUHE Edward L   Sources of Dr Johnson's *Life of Milton*   MA Columbia
      1951
4268 RUMBLE Exa W   The Poets of Dr Johnson's *Lives*: Their Contemporary
      and Late Reputations   MA Emory Univ 1933   80 p
4269 RUSSELL Brenda L   Johnson's Antiswiftianism   MA Univ of Utah 1966
4270 RYAN Charles J   The Relationship between *Rasselas* and Johnson's
      Attitude toward Fiction   MA Univ of Massachusetts 1968   41 p
4271 SCHUMACHER Cynthia J   The Religion of Dr Samuel Johnson   MA Florida
      St Univ 1951
4272 SEUBERT Eugene E   Dr Johnson's Opposition to the Romantic Movement
      MA Washington Univ at St Louis 1933   139 p
4273 SIEBERT Donald T   Samuel Johnson's Criticism of Thomas Gray
      MA Univ of Oklahoma 1964
4274 SILBERNAGEL Robert J   Samuel Johnson: An Evaluation of His Verse
      Satire   MA Boston Coll 1966
4275 SILCOX David P   Samuel Johnson's Concept of the Poet   MA Toronto
      (Canada) 1966
4276 SMITH Cecil H Jr   "Sublime" as a Critical Term in Samuel Johnson's
      Lives of the English Poets   MA Boston Coll 1951
4277 STACEY Iris   Samuel Johnson's Views on Women; from His Works
      MA Univ of British Columbia (Canada) 1963
4278 SUCH Peter D   An Interpretation of *Troilus and Cressida* with
      Reference to Johnson's Dramatic Techniques   MA Toronto (Canada)
      1966
4279 SULLIVAN Gerald J   Politics and Literature of Samuel Johnson
      MA Univ of Oklahoma 1964
4280 TAPP Theola L   Dr Samuel Johnson as a Critic   MA Texas Southern Univ
      1965
4281 TAYLOR Mary   The English Sermon as Literature (with Special Reference
      to Samuel Johnson's Contribution)   MA Howard Univ 1945
4282 THOMPSON William R   *Rasselas* as the Definitive Expression of
      Samuel Johnson's Critical Thought   MA Texas Christian Univ 1950
      151 p
4283 TIERNEY R J   Criticism of Samuel Johnson's *Lives of the English Poets*
      MA Boston Coll 1933
4284 TRAUBITZ Nancy L   The Inescapable Legacy: Samuel Johnson and the
      English Romantics   MA Univ of Maryland at College Park 1967   53 p
4285 TRAUGOTT William H   A Layman's Theology: Samuel Johnson   MA Univ of
      Houston 1964   164 p
4286 TUCKER L F   The Diction of the Prose Essay from Bacon to Johnson
      MA Boston Univ 1913
4287 WADE Joseph D   Johnson's Literary Club and Its Influence   MA St Louis
      Univ 1928   47 p
4288 WERTHEIMER Stephen   The Theory of Impersonal Poetry in the Literary
      Criticism of Samuel Johnson and T S Eliot: A Study of a Tradition
      BA Rutgers St Univ 1957   87 p

4289 WHITE Mary B Dr Samuel Johnson and the Stage MA Louisiana St Univ
      1942
4290 WOLFE James Samuel Johnson as Journalist MA Univ of California at
      Riverside 1957
4291 ZUCKER David H Samuel Johnson on the Marvelous MA Syracuse Univ
      1964 77 p
See also 242, 523, 525, 529, 531, 533, 534, 536, 4152, 4934, 5889, 6358,
      6718, 6995

                            BEN JONSON

4292 ABRAHAM Bernice B The Influence of the Classical Theories of Drama
      on Ben Jonson MA Columbia 1950
4293 AMIEL Joseph J How Rare Ben Jonson?: A Study of Jonson's Mature
      Comic BA Amherst 1959
4294 AYALA A L Ben Jonson: Literary Critic MA Univ of Texas at El Paso
      1953 196 p
4295 AZZI Costanza Epicoene or the Silent Woman by Ben Jonson
      MA Ca Foscari (Italy) 1964
4296 BARBOUR Douglas F Ben Jonson and the Morality Tradition MA Dalhousie
      (Canada) 1964
4297 BERGEN George T The Critical Opinions of Ben Jonson MA St Louis Univ
      1941 152 p
4298 BIVENS W P Use of the Negative in Ben Jonson and Beaumont and
      Fletcher MA Univ of North Carolina at Chapel Hill 1911
4299 BORDWELL Constance Ben Jonson's References to Classical Mythology
      and Their Sources MA Washington St Univ at Pullman 1932
4300 BORROR David P The Morality of Ben Jonson's Epigrammes, Book I
      MA Coll of the Holy Names at Oakland 1965
4301 BROCK D Heyward Poetic Principles Implicit in the Masques of
      Ben Jonson MA Univ of Kansas 1965
4302 BROWN Bonnie M Sejanus and Catiline: Ben Jonson's Satiric Tragedy
      MA Univ of Kentucky 1969 65 p
4303 BURSK John H Jonson, Brome and the Antiacquisitive Tradition
      MA Columbia 1964 91 p
4304 BUTMAN Robert H Richard Martin and the Jonson-Chapman Circle
      MA Univ of North Carolina at Chapel Hill 1949 94 p
4305 CAMPBELL Mary T Some Phases of English Life as Revealed in Jonson's
      Early Comedies MA North Texas St Univ 1937
4306 CANTONO Annamaria Bartholomew Fair by Ben Jonson MA Ca Foscari
      (Italy) 1965
4307 CASEY Sr Loretta Social Satire in the Comedies of Ben Jonson
      MA Villanova Univ 1964
4308 CENTER Edna P Parallelism and Contrast as Used by Ben Jonson in His
      Plays MA Indiana Univ 1940
4309 CERATO MORASSUTTI Fanny Ben Jonson and Italy MA Ca Foscari (Italy)
      1952
4310 COEN Paola The Alchemist by Ben Jonson MA Ca Foscari (Italy) 1965
4311 COGAN Stephen The Renaissance Concept of the Whole Man: A Study
      of Ben Jonson MA Columbia 1961 103 p
4312 COOK Clark The Artistic Integrity in the Poetry of John Donne and
      Ben Jonson BA Univ of British Columbia (Canada) 1963
4313 COOK Elizabeth The Tribe of Ben M Litt Cambridge Univ (England) 1951
4314 COOK Emmett W Dramatic Functions of Costuming in Plays by Ben Jonson
      MA Texas Technological Univ 1969
4315 CRABTREE John H Jr The Jonsonian Anti-Masque MA Univ of North
      Carolina at Chapel Hill 1951 151 p
4316 CRISSEY Carolotta Deception in Volpone MA Tufts Univ 1966
4317 DALE Leona F The Influence of Ben Jonson upon Ben Jonson
      MA Texas Technological Univ 1964 87 p

4318 DAMES Antoinette F The Influence of Ben Jonson on the Poetry of
       the Cavalier Poets MA Washington Univ at St Louis 1929 232 p
4319 ELLIOTT R C Character Writing and Its Influence on the Drama of
       Ben Jonson MA Univ of North Carolina at Chapel Hill 1935
4320 FEINBERG Harriet Ben Jonson's Masques MA Columbia 1961 87 p
4321 FELDMAN Rivkah *The Case is Altered*: An Anticipation of Jonson's
       Approach to Comedy MA Columbia 1960 46 p
4322 FLETCHER David R Poet and King in Ben Jonson's Masques MA McMaster
       (Canada) 1966
4323 FOLEY Louise The Doctrine of Humors in the Comedies of Ben Jonson
       MA Boston Univ 1949
4324 FREDEMAN Patsy D The Way of Ben Jonson's Dramatic World MA Univ
       of British Columbia (Canada) 1964
4325 FREEMAN R The Theme of Parenthood in Some Elizabethan and Jacobean
       Plays with Particular Reference to Kyd, Marston, Shakespeare
       and Jonson M Phil Univ of London (England) 1967
4326 FRIEDBERG Barton C The Influence of John Donne and Ben Jonson on
       the Poetry of Thomas Carew MA Columbia 1959 59 p
4327 GARO Marie T Abnormality in the Characterization of Jonson's Plays
       MA Univ of New Mexico 1933
4328 GOTTSCHALK Barbara O On Lucian's *Dialogues of the Dead*, *V-IX*, as
       the Source of the Plot of Ben Jonson's Play *Volpone* MA Univ of
       Arizona pre-1933
4329 GRAHAM H Richard Classicism and Didacticism in the Tragedies of
       Ben Jonson BA Temple Univ 1963 73 p
4330 GRAHAM Hugh R Ben Jonson's Didactic Tragedies *Sejanus* and *Catiline*
       MA Temple Univ 1966
4331 GREELEY Martin J Ben Jonson's Scholarship as Illustrated in
       Selected Works MA Boston Univ 1949
4332 GREEN Laura Jonson and the Dramatic Unities MA Texas Technological
       Univ 1936 56 p
4333 GUARDIA Charles E Richard Brome as a Follower of Ben Jonson
       MA Louisiana St Univ 1937
4334 HACKETT Mary The Sources of Ben Jonson's *Catiline* MA Univ of
       Oklahoma 1933
4335 HAILEY Jack D The Significance of the Language: The Masques of
       Ben Jonson BA Amherst 1967
4336 HALLETT Charles A The Unity of Jonson's *Volpone* MA Columbia 1963
       95 p
4337 HILL Alma G Ben Jonson as a Lyric Poet and His Influence on the
       Lyrics of the Seventeenth Century MA Boston Univ 1935
4338 HILL Bradford M Ben Jonson's Theory and Use of Satire in Comedy
       MA Boston Univ 1933
4339 HODNETT Josephine A A New Study of Ben Jonson as a Critic of
       Comedy MA Univ of Oklahoma 1929
4340 HUGGETT Milton A Proverb Lore in Jonson's Non-Dramatic Works
       MA Baylor Univ 1952 312 p
4341 HUNSAKER O Ben Jonson's Utilization of Three Elizabethan Dramatic
       Conventions: The Soliloquy, the Aside and the Disguise
       MA Brigham Young Univ 1964 102 p
4342 JONES Carol A Theory and Practice in Ben Jonson's Major Comedies
       MA Howard Univ 1966 315 p
4343 JONES Millard T Ben Jonson's Comic Theory and Practice
       MA Texas Christian Univ 1966 115 p
4344 KELLY Charles A The Artistic Value of Ben Jonson's Non-Dramatic
       Poetry BA Amherst 1953
4345 KISTLER Suzanne F The Development of Jonsonian Comedy MA Long Island
       Univ nd 65 p
4346 KOPP Marjorie A Stoicism in the Plays of Ben Jonson MA Univ of
       Maryland at College Park 1968 43 p

4347 KRAHENBUHL   The Influence of Inigo Jones on Ben Jonson's Masques
        MA Univ of North Carolina at Chapel Hill 1936
4348 KWASS Walter   The Main Argument: A Study of Ben Jonson BA Amherst 1963
4349 LAHIVE Anne   Tragic Satire in the Roman Tragedies of Ben Jonson
        MA Boston Coll 1956
4350 LEE Mary C The Masques of Ben Jonson MA Boston Coll 1965
4351 LEWIS Lora A A Comparison of the Dramatic Criticism of Ben Jonson
        and John Dryden MA Florida St Univ 1956
4352 LINDSAY Barbara N Terror of Decorum: Ben Jonson as a Tragic
        Dramatist MA Univ of Utah 1966
4353 LOGAN Dorothy M The Unifying Theme of Ben Jonson's Works as Shown
        in *Sejanus* and *Volpone* MA Univ of New Mexico 1966
4354 McCLAIN Vivian   The Historical Background of Ben Jonson's *Sejanus*
        MA Univ of Oklahoma 1929
4355 McGINNIS Paul J Jonson's *Discoveries*: A Study of Sources
        MA Univ of Oklahoma 1955
4356 McKENNON William C Critical Theory and Poetic Practice in Jonson
        MA Univ of Oregon 1937
4357 McMURTY Larry J Ben Jonson's Feud with the Poetasters, 1599-1601
        MA Rice 1960
4358 MARTIN Jeanne E Humanistic Doctrine in the Masques of Ben Jonson
        MA Univ of Southwestern Louisiana 1965 98 p
4359 MILLER Annie L Proverb Lore in Ben Jonson's Dramatic Works
        MA Baylor Univ 1951 358 p
4360 MILLER Dollie W Ben Jonson's Role in the Tradition of the English
        Epigram MA Univ of Texas at Austin 1964 85 p
4361 MILLIKEN Robert A Analysis of the Masques of Inigo Jones and
        Ben Jonson MA Univ of Maine 1965 141 p
4362 MILUNAS Joseph G The Problem of Free Will in Ben Jonson's Comedies
        MA St Louis Univ 1945 109 p
4363 MYERS Elsie B Literary Theory and the Concept of the Artist in
        Ben Jonson's Early Comedies MA Univ of Oklahoma 1959
4364 NORED Gary Counterpoint: Its Use in Ben Jonson's *The Alchemist*
        MA Texas Technological Univ 1970
4365 O'GRADY Gerald L Aristotleian Elements in the Criticism and Comedy
        of Ben Jonson MA Boston Coll 1955
4366 PIESCHEL June A *The Sower Sort of Shepherds*: Ben Jonson's Puritans
        MA Univ of Mississippi 1967
4367 PRESCOTT Ann L Abuse of Language in the Comedies of Ben Jonson
        MA Columbia 1961 127 p
4368 PROEBSTEL Lester The Progress in the Comedies of Ben Jonson from
        Pure Classicism to Pure Realism MA Univ of Oregon 1941
4369 READ James W *Sejanus, His Fall* and *Cataline, His Conspiracy*:
        Studies in Contrast to Ben Jonson's Ethical Code MA Southern
        Illinois Univ at Carbondale 1960 58 p
4370 RIGHETTI Angelo *Sejanus, His Fall* by Ben Jonson MA Ca Foscari
        (Italy) 1964
4371 RIOTTE Joseph H A Study of Sir George Etherege's Comedies as
        Innovations, or His Comedies as Imitations of Jonson and Moliere
        MA Southern Connecticut St Coll 1966
4372 RIVERS Isabel Jonson and the Idea of an Aristocracy MA Columbia
        1966 112 p
4373 ROBINSON Horace W A Production and Prompt Book of Ben Jonson's
        Epicoene, or the Silent Woman MA Univ of Iowa 1932
4374 ROUCE Helen D The Quality of Ben Jonson's Realism as Shown in
        Four Comedies MS Kansas St Coll at Pittsburg 1938
4375 SALING Virgie Self-Portrayal in the Plays of Ben Jonson MA North
        Texas St Univ 1938
4376 SCHAMBERG Ralph S The Critic in Ben Jonson's Plays MA Univ of
        Pittsburgh 1931

4377 SCHERESCHEWSKY E F Morale and Manners in Ben Jonson's Comedies
      MA Boston Univ 1938
4378 SCRITTORI Annarosa *Volpone, or the Fox* by Ben Jonson MA Ca Foscari
      (Italy) 1965
4379 SEWELL S W The Relation of *The Merry Wives of Windsor* to Jonson's
      Every Man in His Humour MA Univ of North Carolina at Chapel Hill
      1939
4380 SHY Zella M Ben Jonson: A Critical Study of His Women Characters
      MA Univ of New Mexico 1932
4381 SILBAUGH Morgan C A Study of the Comedies of Ben Jonson BA Amherst
      1957
4382 SPENCER H Allen Jonson's *Bartholomew Fair*: A Study MA Williams
      Coll 1967
4383 SPIRES Mary A Love Poetry of Ben Jonson MA Univ of California at
      Riverside 1958
4384 STODDARD Floyd G Imagery in Ben Jonson's *Sejanus* MA Univ of Texas
      at Austin 1958 90 p
4385 TOLIVER Hazel M Influence of Classical Comedy on Characterization
      in the Plays of Ben Jonson MA Univ of Arkansas 1933
4386 TRAVER Alice A An Analysis of Ben Jonson's Theories of Poetic
      Creation MA Univ of Oklahoma 1929
4387 TUCKER Virginia A Ben Jonson's Use of English Folk Ritual in the
      Court Masques MA Univ of North Carolina at Greensboro 1964
4388 UNRUE Darlene H Ben Jonson's *The Sad Shepherd* MA Marshall Univ 1964
4389 VALOIS Ellin E An Analysis and Reconstruction of the Performances
      of Ben Jonson's *The Masque of Queens* on the Night of
      February 2, 1609 MA Bowling Green Univ 1954
4390 VANDIVER E P Jr The Parasite in English Drama from Its Beginnings
      Up to and Including Ben Jonson MA Univ of North Carolina at
      Chapel Hill 1927
4391 VIZZINI Eleonora N The Influence of Machiavelli's *Il Principe*
      upon Shakespeare's *Richard III* and Ben Jonson's *Volpone*
      MA Hunter Coll 1967
4392 WALSH John J The Medieval Bases of Jonsonian Satire MA St Louis
      Univ 1940 76 p
4393 WATSON Charles N An Analysis of Ben Jonson's Inneract Material
      MA Univ of North Carolina at Chapel Hill 1951 79 p
4394 WILLIAMS Janet M The Affected Lady as a Humorous Character Type
      in the Comedies of Ben Jonson MA Wake Forest Coll 1965
4395 WILLIS Frank B Ben Jonson's Satire Against the Puritans: Six Plays
      MA Univ of Kentucky 1939
See also 2798, 2909, 3989, 6559, 6672, 6687, 6769, 6794, 7160

JAMES JOYCE

4396 ARNSPIGER Pearle Literary Ideals of Style MA Austin Coll 1934
4397 BARNETT Alan W *A Portrait of the Artist* in Imagery, Allusion and
      Myth MA Columbia 1951
4398 BENNETT Leon James Joyce's *Ulysses*: A Glossary of the First
      Three Episodes MA Southern Illinois Univ at Carbondale 1959 101 p
4399 BEECHHOLD Henry F James Joyce's *Ulysses*: Three Decades of British
      and American Criticism MA Oklahoma St Univ 1952 71 p
4400 BERNARD Cora M Irony in Joyce's *Portrait of the Artist* MA Univ of
      Florida 1965
4401 BOLLIN Gail K A Freudian Undercurrent in James Joyce's *A Portrait
      of the Artist as a Young Man* and Marcel Proust's *Du Cote de Chez
      Swann* MA Purdue Univ 1969 75 p
4402 BRESLIN James E The Interior Monologue as a Method of Characterization
      in James Joyce's *Ulysses* MA Univ of North Carolina at Chapel Hill
      1959 64 p

4403 BRICKWOOD John D The Influence of Mallarme and Rimbaud on James Joyce
     BA Cambridge Univ (England) 1958
4404 BUNTAG Eleanor B Sense Imagery in Relation to Theme in Joyce's
     A Portrait of the Artist as a Young Man MA Univ of Pittsburgh 1959
4405 CALLAHAN Edward F Jr Liturgical Motifs in James Joyce's *Ulysses*
     MA Boston Coll 1952
4406 CALLAHAN Jacqueline R An Examination of the Complementary Aspects
     of the Paralysis Motif of James Joyce's *Dubliners* and the Flight
     Motif of *A Portrait of the Artist as a Young Man* MA Univ of New
     Hampshire 1968 84 p
4407 CAMMAROTA Richard S Fabulous Artificer: The Emergence of James Joyce
     as a Prose Symbolist MA Columbia 1964 116 p
4408 CLEE David G The Theme of Class in James Joyce's *Dubliners* MA Univ
     of British Columbia (Canada) 1965 83 p
4409 COHEN Arthur J Elements of Satire in Joyce and Swift BA Rutgers
     St Univ 1967 46 p
4410 COLLINS B L Vico and James Joyce: An Application of the Theory of
     Cyclic History to *Dubliners, A Portrait of the Artist as a Young
     Man, Ulysses* and *Finnegan's Wake* MA Univ of Connecticut 1951
4411 COLVILLE Eleanor J New Settings for Joyce's *Chamber Music*
     MA Columbia 1953 41 p
4412 COOK Kelly F Irish History in James Joyce's *Dubliners, A Portrait of
     the Artist as a Young Man* and *Ulysses* With an Appendix of
     Historical Allusions MA Univ of North Carolina at Chapel Hill 1959
     54 p
4413 CRAWFORD John F Point of View as Thematic Definition: A Reading of
     James Joyce's *Stephen Hero* Disallowing Joyce's Aesthetic Theory
     MA Columbia 1963 122 p
4414 CUDDY Lois A The Concept of Self in the Ithaca Episode of
     James Joyce's *Ulysses* MA Univ of Rhode Island 1969 64 p
4415 D'AMBROSIO Vinnie-Marie "Ad Ballum Jocabimus": Bird and Orb in
     A Portrait of the Artist as a Young Man MA Brooklyn Coll 1965
4416 DAVENPORT G M James Joyce's Use of Symbolism B Litt Oxford Univ
     (England) 1950
4417 DeGIUSTI Lenore A Mulier Cantat: The Singing Woman in the Poetry
     and Prose of James Joyce MA Purdue Univ 1963 86 p
4418 DeMURO Paul W The Dramatic Theory of James Joyce MA Villanova Univ
     1965
4419 DEWITT David A The Joyce Menagerie: Animal Imagery in the First
     Three Novels MA Univ of Richmond 1967 88 p
4420 DiCESARE Mario A Jesuistical Joyce and Stephen Messiah: A Study
     of the Hero of James Joyce's *A Portrait of the Artist as a Young
     Man* MA Columbia 1954 134 p
4421 DUNCAN June A The Theme of the Artist's Isolation in Works by
     Three Modern British Novelists MA Univ of Oklahoma 1965
4422 EDELSTEIN Arnold The Plausible Mummer: A Study of the Function of
     Buck Mulligan in James Joyce's *Ulysses* MA Columbia 1962 108 p
4423 FELDMAN Burton E Language as Experience in *Finnegan's Wake*
     MA Columbia 1954 55 p
4424 FESHBACH Sidney The Green Rose: A Study of the Theme of Metamor-
     phosis in James Joyce's *A Portrait of the Artist as a Young Man*
     MA Columbia 1960 138 p
4425 FITZGERALD Joseph M The Short Story Sequence in Modern English
     Literature: James Joyce and William Faulkner MA San Francisco
     Coll for Women 1966
4426 FOLK Barbara N The Joycean Theory of Epiphany in Relation to
     Critical Interpretations of "The Dead" MA St Louis Univ 1962 66 p
4427 FORMAN Gail James Joyce's *Ulysses* and the Literary Critics
     MA Univ of Maryland at College Park 1964 88 p
4428 FRAMPTON Maralee L Dubliner's Dictionary: A Study of Characters

and Allusions in Joyce's Short Stories   MA Univ of Tulsa 1966
       261 p
4429   FRIEND Eleanor   Weaver of the Wind: A Study of the Clothing Imagery
       in James Joyce's *Ulysses*   MA Columbia 1954   87 p
4430   FURBERG Jon   Tragedy in James Joyce's *Dubliners*   BA Univ of British
       Columbia (Canada) 1967
4431   GATTUSO Josephine   The Double Stutter: An Essay on the Imagery of
       James Joyce's *Dubliners*   MA Columbia 1965   115 p
4432   GRAHAM Marie H   The "Anna Livia Plurabelle" Episode in James Joyce's
       Finnegan's Wake: An Interpretation   MA Univ of Idaho 1966
4433   HANCOCK Leslie F   The Macromorphology of a Novel: Notes to a Word-
       Index of James Joyce's *A Portrait of the Artist as a Young Man*
       MA Univ of Miami 1966
4434   HASKINS Lynda   The Awakening Soul: A Study of *A Portrait of the
       Artist as a Young Man*   BA Univ of British Columbia (Canada) 1963
4435   HAWK Robert E   James Joyce: Medieval and Modern: A Study of the
       Roman Catholic Influences on Three of James Joyce's Works
       MA Stetson Univ 1966
4436   HELGESON James E   A Critical Study of James Joyce's *A Portrait of
       the Artist as a Young Man*   MA Univ of Iowa 1964
4437   HERSHBERG Sarah   Women in the Works of James Joyce   MA Columbia 1955
       88 p
4438   HEUSEL Barbara S   Joyce's *Portrait of the Artist as a Young Man*:
       Some Doubts Regarding Ironic Interpretations   MA Univ of Louisville
       1967   160 p
4439   HOLDEN Carol J   The Development and Use of Comedy in the Writings
       of James Joyce   MA Univ of Pittsburgh 1956
4440   HOOKER Barbara E   Shem and Shaun in *Finnegan's Wake*   MA Univ of
       Kansas 1966
4441   HOUGHAM George   Bloom and Stephen: The Father-Son Relationship
       BA Univ of British Columbia (Canada) 1968
4442   HYDE Kathleen   The Mythological Approach to Life in James Joyce's
       A Portrait of the Artist as a Young Man and *Ulysses*   BA Univ of
       British Columbia (Canada) 1968
4443   JONES Paul   A Study of the Romantic and Ironic Pathos: Interpre-
       tations of James Joyce's *Ulysses*   BA Univ of British Columbia
       (Canada) 1970
4444   JOSEPH Margaret A   A Grammar of the "Anna Livia Plurabelle" Section
       of *Finnegan's Wake*   MA Univ of Kansas 1966
4445   KIELY Robert J   Dream and Myth in *Finnegan's Wake*   BA Amherst 1953
4446   KLINE Thomas J   Stream of Consciousness in the Novels of Joyce and
       Robbe-Grillet: *Ulysses* and *Les Gommes*   MA Columbia 1966   122 p
4447   LAREAU Eugene A   The Prism of Language: Aspects of Style in
       A Portrait of the Artist as a Young Man   MA Columbia 1966   63 p
4448   LEE John T   Stream of Consciousness Techniques in James Joyce's
       Ulysses   MA San Diego St Coll 1965
4449   LEVY Phyllis J   The Image of the Jew in James Joyce's *Ulysses*
       MA Univ of Richmond 1968   62 p
4450   McCRORY Thomas E   A Comparison and Contrast of the Art and Craft of
       the Descriptive Styles of Jane Austen and James Joyce Based on
       "Ergocentric" Analyses of Two Passages from *Mansfield Park* and
       The Portrait of the Artist as a Young Man   MA Columbia 1953   106 p
4451   McGOWAN Patricia M   The Streams of Life: Water and Related Imagery
       in James Joyce's *Ulysses*   MA Univ of Texas at Austin 1966   104 p
4452   McMANUS Anne   A Study of "Anna Livia Plurabelle" in James Joyce's
       Finnegan's Wake   MA Temple Univ 1960   74 p
4453   McNIECE Mildred   The Role of Confession in the Works of James Joyce
       MA Wayne St Univ 1965
4454   MAHER Raphael A   The Messianic and Trinity Motifs in *Dubliners*
       MA Western (Canada) 1965

4455 MALKOFF Karl The Search for the Father in the Early Fiction of
Dostoevsky and Joyce MA Columbia 1963 134 p
4456 MEYERSON Mark E The Uses of Myth in *Ulysses* BA Amherst 1963
4457 MEZEY Frederick C A Survey of the Criticism of James Joyce's
Ulysses BA Rutgers St Univ 1955 128 p
4458 MILLER Kenneth A The Wandering Rocks in Joyce's *Ulysses*: An Artist
in an Alien Society MA Cornell Univ 1965
4459 MILLER Mary A James Joyce's *Ulysses*: A Survey MA Univ of Texas at
Austin 1940 171 p
4460 MOZDZIERZ Carl A Molly Bloom's Monlogue: An Analysis of Molly's
Problems with Regard to Sex, Love and Marriage MA Univ of
Massachusetts 1967
4461 MUSGRAVE Reuben L Jr Characterization of Stephen Dedalus in
James Joyce's *Stephen Hero* and *A Portrait of the Artist as a
Young Man* MA Univ of Richmond 1967 93 p
4462 NEVILLE Margherita Stephen's Myth: The Use of Mythical Allusion
in Joyce's *Portrait* MA Univ of Tulsa 1964 159 p
4463 O'CONNELL Daniel Musemathematics: The Theme of Science in
James Joyce's *Ulysses* MA Columbia 1966 97 p
4464 POTVIN Janet H Portraits of the Artist: A Study of the Dynamics
of Character Interaction in James Joyce's *Ulysses* MA Texas
Christian Univ 1968 107 p
4465 PRITCHARD Roberta K James Joyce's Use of Epiphany in *Dubliners*
MA Texas Christian Univ 1968 106 p
4466 QUICK Jonathan R The Epic Dimensions of *Finnegan's Wake* BA Rutgers
St Univ 1963 76 p
4467 RENDLE Judith A A Reassessment of James Joyce's Poetry MA Alberta
(Canada) 1966
4468 RHODES James F Joyce's "Farced Epistol to the Hibruws" MA Univ of
Rhode Island 1965 74 p
4469 ROBERTSON Andrew An Interpretation of the "Circe" Episode in
James Joyce's *Ulysses* BA Univ of British Columbia (Canada) 1969
4470 RODARO Lea M The Literary Experiment of James Joyce as Seen Through
His Conception of Art MA Ca Foscari (Italy) 1941
4471 ROGERS Francis The Water Motif in James Joyce's *Ulysses* MA Columbia
1963 109 p
4472 ROGERS William F The Communion Motif in James Joyce's *Dubliners*
MA Univ of Hawaii 1965 134 p
4473 ROSENFELD Ruth The Wandering Rocks Episode: A Study of the Tenth
Chapter of James Joyce's *Ulysses* MA Columbia 1951
4474 ROSS Margaret I Ovid and James Joyce as Poets in the Metamorphic
Tradition M Phil Toronto (Canada) 1966
4475 SAMUELSON Ralph E Leopold Bloom: A Study of His Characterization
MA Columbia 1951
4476 SCARRY John M Shem and Shaun: John McCormack in the Works of
James Joyce MA Univ of Maryland at College Park 1965 84 p
4477 SCHMIDT Eleanor James Joyce's "The Dead" and Robert Musil's *Grigia*
MA Columbia 1963 74 p
4478 SMITH Jacqueline Mallarme and Joyce: A Question of Literary
Influence in *Ulysses* MA Temple Univ nd 107 p
4479 STEINHAUER Roger K The Search for Identity in James Joyce's *Ulysses*
BA Amherst 1956
4480 STEWART Colin E Character and Narrator in Four Early Chapters of
Ulysses BA Amherst 1970
4481 THORPE Dwayne L The Language of *Ulysses* MA Columbia 1962 238 p
4482 TISCHLER Christiana P Full Word Nominal Compounds in Joyce's
Ulysses MA Columbia 1965 49 p
4483 WARD David F Joyce in the School of Old Ibsen: A Critical Study
of Joyce's *Exiles* MA Univ of Tulsa 1966 60 p
4484 WARFIELD Marguerite R "I Paid My Way": A Theme of James Joyce's

Ulysses MA Columbia 1952 56 p
4485 WEIHE Edwin H Beloved Enemy: Love Themes in the Early Writings
      of James Joyce MA Univ of Iowa 1965
4486 WELSH James M *Stephen Hero* Examined: A Study of Joyce's Ur-
      Portrait MA Univ of Kansas 1965
4487 WETTER Judith A Humour in *Ulysses* MA Alberta (Canada) 1966
4488 WHITE Patrick T Didacticism in *Ulysses* MA George Washington Univ
      1955 91 p
4489 WILLIS John H Hats and Sticks: Their Symbolic Function in Joyce's
      Ulysses MA Columbia nd
4490 ZAHN Laura James Joyce and Italy MA Ca Foscari (Italy) 1950
See also 1027, 1708, 2840

                          JOHN KEATS

4491 AHREND Evelyn R Keats' Position in English Aesthetics, with Special
      Reference to the Influence of Hazlitt MA Columbia 1935
4492 ALSUP Velma D A Study of Keats' Poetic Development MS Kansas St
      Coll at Pittsburg 1935
4493 ANDERSON Mary R Intellectual Element in the Writings of John Keats
      MA Univ of Pittsburgh 1927
4494 ANGEVINE Margaret J Samuel Taylor Coleridge's Apparent Influence
      on John Keats' Great Odes MA Wichita St Univ 1966
4495 BALDI Ida John Keats: His Times, His Life and His Works
      MA Ca Foscari (Italy) nd
4496 BARRETT Ann E Sense Perception in Keats' Poetry MA Univ of Texas
      at Austin 1931
4497 BATES Madison C The Greek Element in the Life and Poetry of Keats
      MA Williams Coll 1905
4498 BEATTY Kenneth W Religious Values of John Keats' Poetry and Letters
      MA Boston Univ 1941
4499 BENNETT Marianne A Study of Time in Keats' "Ode to Autumn"
      MA Columbia 1965 65 p
4500 BRADFORD Melvin E Hellenism in the Poetry of John Keats MA Univ
      of Oklahoma 1956
4501 BRASWELL Margaret The Dramatic Element in the Mind and Works of Keats
      MA Univ of Texas at Austin 1925
4502 BROWN Donald N Melancholy: A Creative Force in the Poetry of Keats
      MA Indiana Univ 1942
4503 BROWN Standley D John Keats' "Beauty is Truth" as Interpreted since
      1957 by the Critics of the "Ode on a Grecian Urn" MS Ft Hays
      Kansas St Coll 1964
4504 BROWN Treva M Dominant Themes in the Poetry of John Keats MS Ft Hays
      Kansas St Coll at Pittsburg 1944
4505 BURCKHART Rose E Hunt's Influence upon the Early Poetry of Keats
      MA Univ of Iowa 1932
4506 BUTLER Gibbon Keats as Myth-Maker MA Washington Univ at St Louis
      1932
4507 CALLAN Larua F Fanny Brawne, an Influence on the Poetry of
      John Keats MA Baylor Univ 1939 140 p
4508 CAMPBELL Jean K Keats: A Study in Humanitarian Idealism MA Smith
      Coll 1937
4509 CAREY Robert G The Major Odes of John Keats; Recent Critical Inter-
      pretations MA Univ of Pittsburgh 1954
4510 CHALIFF Cynthia John Keats and Fanny Brawne: A Study of Their
      Relationship MA Columbia 1961 102 p
4511 CONNELLY Sr Agnes P Keats' Theory of Literary Criticism MA Boston
      Coll 1961
4512 COOPER Eula M Sense Perceptions in Keats' Poetry MA Baylor Univ
      1937 100 p

4513 COPPING Ann E Scotland and Her Visitors: John Keats and
     William Wordsworth MA Columbia 1960 52 p
4514 CROWE F C Keats' Interest in Things Italian and Its Influence on
     His Poems and Letters MA Univ of North Carolina at Chapel Hill
     1940
4515 CURTIS Ann F The Sonnets of John Keats MA Boston Coll 1958
4516 DILLIGAN Robert J The Influence of John Keats on Gerard Manley Hopkins
     MA Columbia 1964 57 p
4517 DUNLAP Patricia A "Independently and with Judgment Hereafter":
     A Study of the Revisions in John Keats' Endymion MA Univ of
     Texas at Austin 1964
4518 ESTERMAN Mark J The Dream Vision in Keats' Poetry BA Amherst 1965
4519 FELKER Karen R The Mansion of Life: John Keats' Philosophy of
     Poetry MA Brigham Young Univ 1963 94 p
4520 GADDIS Roger G Leigh Hunt's Political Influence on John Keats
     MA Univ of Tennessee 1969 105 p
4521 GRIFFIN Genevieve R Sensory Appeals in the Poems of Keats and
     Shelley MA Univ of North Dakota 1936 91 p
4522 HADLEY Olive R John Keats' Thinking of Religion as Revealed in His
     Personal Correspondence MA Indiana Univ of Pennsylvania 1967 121 p
4523 HANKE Amala M A Romantic Bruderschaft: A Comparative Study of
     Keats and Novalis MA Univ of Texas at Austin 1968 89 p
4524 HARDER Bernahard D Narcissus Englished: A Study of the Book of Thel,
     Alastor and Endymion MA Univ of British Columbia (Canada) 1966
4525 HARTMANN Barbara H Sensuous Vividness, Meaning and Brilliance:
     Nature in the Poetry of Vaughan, Marvell, Keats and Wordsworth
     MA George Washington Univ 1958 95 p
4526 HATCH Helen N John Keats: Bard of Beauty M Ed Henderson St Coll nd
4527 HAYES Elaine Some Medieval Influences on Certain Poems of John Keats
     MA North Carolina Coll 1964
4528 HENINGER Wylene C The Paradox Motif in the Poetry of Keats' 1820
     Lamia Volume: An Examination of His Letters MA Kansas St
     Teachers Coll 1966
4529 HENISEY Sarah L The Effect of Gothic Elements in the Medievalistic
     Poetry of John Keats MA Univ of Maryland at College Park 1969
     72 p
4530 HERRON Mary L A Study and Evaluation of the New Critics' Approach
     to the "Keats of the Odes" MA Miami Univ 1965
4531 HILL Elliott M A Bibliography of the Writings and Ana of John Keats
     from January 1, 1951 to January 1, 1956 MA Univ of Kentucky 1961
     184 p
4532 HILLMAN Dennis W The Poetic Arbour: A Study of the Vegetation and
     Water Imagery in Keats' Poetry BA Univ of British Columbia
     (Canada) 1966
4533 HITCHCOCK Mary L Medievalism in Keats' Poetry MA Indiana Univ 1950
4534 HOFF Mary J The Five Great Odes of John Keats MA Univ of Tulsa
     1961 63 p
4535 HOFFMAN Clementine The Function of Imagery in Four of Keats' Odes
     MA St Louis Univ 1940 57 p
4536 HOLT Dennis The Influence of Contemporary Romantic Writers on
     Keats M Ed Henderson St Coll nd
4537 HOLT Helen D Keats' Domestic Relations and Their Influence upon His
     Writings MA Univ of North Carolina at Chapel Hill 1946 107 p
4538 HUMPHREYS Margaret John Keats, the Brother MA Baylor Univ 1950
     103 p
4539 HUNTER William H Keats and the New Critics MA Univ of Tennessee
     1950 90 p
4540 HURD Carol E John Keats and the Cockney School of Poetry
     MA Georgetown Univ 1960 205 p
4541 JARRETT Dorothy L Keats in the English Magazines 1817-1848

MA Univ of Maryland at College Park 1933   120 p
4542 JONES Dana L   Critical Estimates and Interpretations of Keats'
      Endymion, The Eve of St Agnes and *Hyperion*   MS Univ of Oklahoma 1940
4543 JOUZEH Christina S   The Poetic Theory of John Keats, 1817-1819
      MA Bowling Green Univ 1958
4544 KANNAPELL Louise   Etude Comparative Sur L'hellenisme D'Andre
      Chenier et Celui Jean Keats   MA St Louis Univ 1932   67 p
4545 KENDALL Gayle J   A Study of the "Ode to the Nightingale"
      MA Univ of Colorado 1966
4546 KERN Cleveland C   The Reaction of John Keats to Literary Criticism
      MA Univ of Richmond 1936   110 p
4547 KESTNER Joseph A   Keats and Horace: A Comparative Study   MA Columbia
      1966   85 p
4548 KING V A   The Sensuous Element in Keats' Poetry   MA Boston Coll 1939
4549 KIVANC Nes'e   Myths in the Poetry of John Keats   MA Northeastern
      Missouri St Coll 1960
4550 LAKEMAN-SHAW Jeanne F   Hunt, Keats and Rossetti: A Study in Influence
      and Comparison   MA Univ of British Columbia (Canada) 1937   97 p
4551 LAPEYRE Julie A   Dreams, Barren and Fruitful: A Study of the Function
      of Dreams in Some Poems by Keats   BA Univ of British Columbia
      (Canada) 1963
4552 LEE Margaret G   A Consideration of the Aesthetic Thought of John Keats
      MA Northeast Louisiana St Coll 1965
4553 LEMFERT Wilma   The Letters of John Keats   MA Ca Foscari (Italy) 1952
4554 LEOFF Eve   From Ballad to Narrative: A Study of *La Belle Dame Sans
      Merci* and *Lamia*   MA Columbia 1963   88 p
4555 LEVY Allen R   The Classical Tradition in Four Poems of Keats
      MA Univ of Iowa 1966
4556 LOCKE Julius D   Keats and the Nature of Reality   MA Univ of Florida
      1955
4557 LOGAN Amelia J   A Study of the Narrative Artistry in John Keats'
      Endymion   MA Auburn Univ 1965
4558 LONG Amy   Literary Criticism in the Letters of Keats   MA Univ of
      Pittsburgh 1934
4559 LOWRY Lucie   An Analysis and Interpretation of Keats' *Endymion*
      MA Univ of Louisville 1940
4560 LURKIS Irene B   Keats' Attitude toward Women   MA Columbia 1965
4561 McBRIDE Helen M   John Keats as a Literary Critic   MA Univ of
      Oklahoma 1934
4562 McCARTY Minnie E   A Study of Keats' Theory of Beauty   MA Univ of
      Texas at Austin 1925
4563 McKELVIN Dennis J   Development of the Poetic Experience in the
      Odes of John Keats   MA Univ of Vermont 1963   81 p
4564 MacKENZIE Donald   The Significance of Keats' "Ode to Psyche"
      BA Univ of British Columbia (Canada) 1962
4565 McLANAHAN Fay H   Early Criticism of Keats: The History of a Legend
      MA St Mary's at San Antonio 1943   70 p
4566 McMINDES Monica F   A Review of Scholarship Concerning Two Versions
      of Keats' *Hyperion*   MA Georgetown Univ 1960   111 p
4567 MAGAW Edna L   A Study of the Work of John Hamilton Reynolds with
      Special Reference to His Influence on Keats   MA Louisiana St
      Univ 1946
4568 MARLEY Arthur E   John Keats and Greek Statuary: A Study of the
      Poet's Understanding of the Ancient Greek Statues   MA Univ of
      Rhode Island 1966   56 p
4569 MAYES Mildred J   John Keats' Debt to Science   MA Texas Woman's Univ
      1937
4570 MAYSE Shirley I   Nineteenth Century Criticism of John Keats
      MA Univ of British Columbia (Canada) 1935
4571 MEAGHER Mary H   A Study of Sense Impressions in Keats' Narrative

Poems   MA Smith Coll 1927
4572 MINTER Brian   Keats' Use of Lies in *La Belle Dame Sans Merci* and
      Lamia   BA Univ of British Columbia (Canada) nd
4573 MOONEY Sr Bernardine M   The Literary Reputation of Keats: A Study
      in the Tides of Literary Tastes   MA Columbia 1952   76 p
4574 MOORE Donna J   The Revealing Letters of John Keats   MA West Texas
      St Univ 1968   109 p
4575 MYERS Bernard J   Some Aspects of Keats' Language   MA Univ of Florida nd
4576 NAURAGIO Sr Mary A   Keats' Concept of Nature   MA Boston Coll 1964
4577 NEESON Sr Mary F   The Principle of Stationing in the Poetry of
      John Keats   MA Coll of the Holy Names at Oakland 1964
4578 NEWBOLD Heather   Keats' Treatment of Female Characteristics in
      Some of His Poems   BA Univ of British Columbia (Canada) 1969
4579 NOLEN Judith R   John Keats' Two *Hyperions*:   A Study   MA Baylor Univ
      1969   129 p
4580 NORRIS Helen A   Keats' Position in the Romantic Movement   BA Univ
      of Oklahoma 1910
4581 NOVOTNY James   John Keats and Isabella Jones: A Critical Review of
      Research   MA Univ of Illinois at Chicago Circle 1969
4582 O'BRIEN Patrick W   Keats and His English Contemporary Critics,
      1818-1820   MA St Louis Univ 1938   61 p
4583 OGATA Takeshi   Keats in Japan   MA Univ of Hawaii 1966   138 p
4584 PARKS Ruth A   A Study of the Similes and Metaphors in Keats' Poetry
      MA Univ of Oklahoma 1947
4585 PASSMORE Billie S   The Personality of John Keats as Revealed in His
      Letters   MA North Texas St Univ 1970
4586 PELTONEN Doris F   A Textual Analysis of John Keats' "Ode on a Grecian
      Urn"   MA Univ of Massachusetts 1968   74 p
4587 PHILIPS Jane   John Keats: A Study of a Developing Vision   MA Columbia
      1963   107 p
4588 PIERCE Marjorie L   A Study of Contemporary Reviews of John Keats'
      Poetry and of Reactions to and Effects of Those Reviews   MS Kansas
      St Coll at Pittsburg 1952
4589 POUND Ruth E   John Keats' Mastery of Color as an Element of Poetic
      Expression   MA Univ of Tulsa 1943
4590 POWELL Judith A   Philosophy and Imagination: A Study of Keats
      MA Indiana Univ 1956
4591 PRITCHARD Maude   Keats' Treatment of Medieval Subjects   MA Univ of
      North Carolina at Chapel Hill 1911
4592 RAMOS Leticia V   The Attitude of John Keats towards Evil   MA Columbia
      1954   71 p
4593 REISEN Diana   Quest for the Ideal: A Comparative Study of John Keats
      and Charles Baudelaire   MA Hunter Coll 1966
4594 RIFKIN Mona   Journeys Past the Scanty Bar: The Exotic in Keats'
      Endymion   MA Hunter Coll 1969
4595 RILEY Sr Maria A   A Comparative Study Showing the Influence of
      John Keats on Gerard Manley Hopkins   MA Florida St Univ 1963
4596 ROBERTS Lynne T   The Poet of the Vale: A Comparative Study of
      John Keats' *Hyperion* and *The Fall of Hyperion*   MA Columbia 1965
      79 p
4597 ROSENFELD J Peter   The Importance of Keats' Moods   MA Columbia 1961
      106 p
4598 ROSENFELT Deborah S   John Keats' *Lamia*:   An Analysis of Theme and
      Technique   MA Columbia 1965   145 p
4599 ROSENTHAL Nancy W   The Escape Theme in Keats' Poetry and Poetic
      Theory   MA Auburn Univ 1954
4600 ROVATTI Elleda   Keats' Medievalism   MA Ca Foscari (Italy) 1948
4601 RYAN Robert M   A Recourse Somewhat Human: The Place of Religion in
      the Life of John Keats   MA Columbia 1966 74 p
4602 SANDERS Sara E   The Harvest of Grand Materials: Keats' Concept of

the Working of the Poetic Imagination MA Univ of Texas at Austin
1969 70 p
4603 SANFORD Celeste A Study of John Keats' Poetry MA Univ of Tennessee
1923
4604 SCHIFF Mortimer Keats and Nerval: Isolation in Two Romantic Letter
Writers MA Columbia 1964 189 p
4605 SCOTT Sidney E *Lamia*: A Critical Edition MA Baylor Univ 1944 187 p
4606 SENN Howard B A Century of Keats' Criticism MA Univ of North Dakota
1936 183 p
4607 SHARKEY K F The Classic and Medieval Influence in Keats MA Boston
Univ 1942
4608 SHEPHERD Edith The Influence of Keats upon Rossetti, Morris and
Swinburne BA Univ of Oklahoma 1908
4609 SHINE W H The Influence of Keats on Rossetti MA Univ of North
Carolina at Chapel Hill 1925
4610 SILBERT Elizabeth W Keats: A Divided Poet MA Hunter Coll 1957
4611 SILLIMAN W W Jr Keats' Use of Tropes Based upon Classical Mythology
MA Univ of North Carolina at Chapel Hill 1933
4612 SMITH William J John Keats: A Biographical Record; An Annotated
Bibliography for the Years 1955-1964 MA Tufts Univ 1965
4613 STARKE Mary R Mythology in John Keats' *Hyperion* MA Auburn Univ 1968
4614 STOREY William The Pure Serene: The Classical in the Work of
John Keats BA Univ of British Columbia (Canada) 1969
4615 STOVALL Velma Keats as Seen through His Letters MA Baylor Univ 1946
120 p
4616 STRATMAN Sr Mary M A Study of Keats' Poetic Development MA St Louis
Univ 1936 66 p
4617 STROTHER Hattie B Revelations of Keats and His Poetry as Found in
His Letters MA Baylor Univ 1930 75 p
4618 TAYLOR Rolleen K John Keats: A Study in Conflicts MA Univ of
Tulsa 1950
4619 TEAGUE M B The Influence of John Keats on English Poets MA Boston
Univ 1926 33 p
4620 TEICH Nathanial "Beauty is Truth, Truth Beauty": Need We Know More?
Criticism and Keats' "Grecian Urn" MA Columbia 1962 134 p
4621 THORPE J E Jr John Keats as a Literary Critic MA Univ of North
Carolina at Chapel Hill 1937
4622 WALSH Maria J The Influence of Keats on Hopkins MA St Louis Univ
1966 75 p
4623 WATSON Barbara H The Critical Spectrum: Major Interpretations of
Keats' Beauty-Truth Relationship in the "Ode on a Grecian Urn"
MA Municipal Univ of Omaha 1965
4624 WINTON Flora E Keats and His Circle MA Baylor Univ 1933 171 p
4625 WOMACK Joseph L John Keats' "Ode on a Grecian Urn": A Study of
the Critical Opinions and Textual Material MA Baylor Univ 1967
202 p
4626 WOOD Glena D Some Aspects of John Keats' Critical Philosophy
MA Univ of Kentucky 1949 100 p
4627 WRIGHT Lillian B Keats and the Victorians MA Indiana Univ 1950
4628 YONG Grace H John Keats: Viewed through Japanese Criticism
MA Boston Coll 1968
4629 ZIMMERMAN Ruth M A Reappraisal of Keats' Religious Views MA Univ
of Florida 1956
See also 1095, 1117, 1801, 1893, 3571, 3897, 3905, 3910, 6528, 7387, 7466

CHARLES KINGSLEY

4630 CHARTER Harold R The Social Philosophy of Charles Kingsley: Its
Sources and Expression MA Univ of British Columbia (Canada) 1942
4631 CORONA Domenico Charles Kingsley and His Historical Novel

MA Ca Foscari (Italy) 1936
4632 FLOWERS Ruby H Charles Kingsley as a Romanticist MA Univ of
      Oklahoma 1927
4633 GOLD Ellen R Charles Kingsley on Sanitary Reform MA Univ of Kansas
      1966
4634 HENDREN Pearl L Literature and Educational Reform in Victorian
      England: A Study of Charles Kingsley, Charles Dickens,
      Elizabeth Barrett Browning and Charlotte Bronte in Relation to
      Educational Reform MA Univ of Tennessee 1950 128 p
4635 HOLTON Oscar D The Reflection of the Victorian Dilemma in the
      Novels of Charles Kingsley MA Texas Technological Univ 1965 56 p
4636 ISBELL Bernetta L The Religious Attitudes Revealed in Three Novels
      of the Nineteenth Century MA Texas Technological Univ 1941 146 p
4637 JONAITIS Thomas P Charles Kingsley and Sciences MA Columbia 1937
4638 LEIGHMAN Charles R Charels Kingsley's Yeast: A Portrait of England
      in Crisis MA Texas Agricultural and Mechanical Univ 1968 85 p
4639 MARMO Macario The Social Novel of Charles Kingsley MA Ca Foscari
      (Italy) 1933
4640 MARTIN R B An Edition of the Correspondence and Private Papers of
      Charles Kingsley, 1819-1856 B Litt Oxford (England) 1950
4641 MATLOCK Miriam The Novels of Charles Kingsley MA Univ of Texas at
      Austin 1932
4642 MENN William L Aspects of the Prejudice Against Spain and Catholicism
      in Kingsley's Westward Ho MA St Mary's at San Antonio 1940 70 p
4643 PREDA Adriana The Influence of the Social and Political Movement
      of His Time in the Works of Charles Kingsley MA Ca Foscari (Italy)
      1949
4644 SCHWARZ Milton D Kingsley's Debt to Carlyle MA Columbia 1953 102 p
4645 WARD Clara F Charles Kingsley and the Christian Socialist Movement
      MA Univ of Maryland at College Park 1934 93 p
4646 WINFREY David C The Historical Novels of Charles Kingsley MA Univ of
      Maryland at College Park 1957 110 p
See also 2615

RUDYARD KIPLING

4647 BAXTER B W The Poetry in Kipling's Verse MA Leeds Univ (England) 1956
4648 BELK Louise Implications of Imperialism as Shown in Selected Works
      of Rudyard Kipling M Ed Henderson St Coll nd
4649 BLAGG Mary E India in English and American Prose Fiction Since
      Kipling MA Texas Woman's Univ 1943
4650 BUGBEE L E The Contribution of Rudyard Kipling to the Short Story
      MA Boston Univ 1925
4651 CAIRNS Fred I The Use of the Bible in Kipling's Poetry MA Univ of
      Texas at Austin 1938
4652 CAMPBELL Mary I The Technique of Kipling's Verse MA Univ of Texas
      at Austin 1932
4653 CAZZATO Maria The Poetry of Rudyard Kipling MA Ca Foscari (Italy)
      1928
4654 CORNWELL Charles H The People of Rudyard Kipling's Fiction
      MA Univ of Texas at Austin 1931
4655 DALEY Sr Justina St J Nationalism in Kipling and Chesterton
      MA Boston Coll 1950
4656 DAVIS Helen C Clemens-Kipling: A Comparative Study of Social Concept
      MA Florida St Univ 1949
4657 DOHSE Milton Four Characteristics of the "Byronic Hero" in Kipling's
      The Light that Failed M Ed Henderson St Coll nd
4658 DVORKIN Etta La Vie Animale Dans les Fables de la Fontaine, les
      Jungle Books de Kipling et Dans Quelques Oeuvres de Joel Chandler H
      MA Hunter Coll 1930 or after

4659 GORDON Elizabeth G An Approach to the Study of Rudyard Kipling's
      Children's Books MA Univ of Houston 1954 78 p
4660 HORN Hester K A Study of the Anti-Intellectualism of
      Rudyard Kipling MA Univ of Oklahoma 1942
4661 HULME Francis P Kipling's Reading: A Preliminary Survey MA Emory Univ
      1937
4662 ISMA'IL Munir J Rudyard Kipling, India and the British Empire
      MA Kearney St Coll 1968 119 p
4663 JACKSON Nettie P Excursions of the Imagination into Animal Life:
      A Study of Rudyard Kipling's *Jungle Books* M Ed Henderson St Coll nd
4664 KEISER Merle W Some "Read-To" Books: A Study of Kipling's Juvenile
      Literature MA Lamar Technological Univ 1964 115 p
4665 LARKIN John J Study of Rudyard Kipling as the Literary Champion
      of Victorian Imperialism MA Boston Coll 1939
4666 LEA Grace Rudyard Kipling's Debt to Mark Twain and Bret Harte
      MA Tulane Univ 1913
4667 LIVERANI Pia Rudyard Kipling's World MA Ca Foscari (Italy) 1947
4668 LOHMAN Williams J The Influence of the Military Ethic on the
      Writings of Rudyard Kipling MA Duke Univ 1966
4669 McGOVERN A F The Poetry of Rudyard Kipling MA Boston Univ 1924
4670 MacKENZIE Norman Rudyard Kipling, Imperialist: A Reassessment
      MA Dalhousie (Canada) 1964
4671 MILLIKIN Ethel M The Bible in the Poetry of Rudyard Kipling
      M Ed Temple Univ 1932 111 p
4672 NOVI Teresa Rudyard Kipling MA Ca Foscari (Italy) nd 44 p
4673 OLPHERT William J Duty and Action in "The Law" of Rudyard Kipling
      and Their Presentation in His Poetry MA Niagara Univ 1965
4674 PARKER G B The Verse of Rudyard Kipling BA Univ of Oklahoma 1908
4675 PASS Maizie C The Rise and Progress of the Kipling Vogue in America
      MA Texas Woman's Univ 1938
4676 PITTOLA Umberto The Spirit of Roman Civilization in the Work of
      Rudyard Kipling MA Ca Foscari (Italy) 1949
4677 POLAND Emma Imperialism in Kipling's Poetry MA Boston Univ 1942
4678 POWERS Sr Mary P Kipling's Imperialism: A Revision MA St Louis
      Univ 1944 136 p
4679 ROBBERECHT Paul A Kipling et la France MA Dalhousie (Canada) 1963
4680 RYCZEK Martha H The Growth of Kipling's Imperialistic Ideas as
      Reflected in His Poetry MS Kansas St Coll at Pittsburg 1937
4681 SHOVREK Marion V Kipling and the Irish MA Univ of Pittsburgh 1960
4682 STOOKE D W Rudyard Kipling's English Themes in Verse and Prose from
      1896 M Phil Univ of London (England) 1968
4683 TEW Arnold G Kipling's "Recessional" MA Columbia 1961 74 p
4684 VAN PELT Louis J A Partial Linguistic Analysis of the Dialectal
      Poetry of Rudyard Kipling: A Study of Barrack-Room Ballads
      MA Texas Agricultural and Mechanical Univ 1968 131 p
4685 WARNER Lewis W Woman's Place in Kipling's Writing, 1885-1895
      MA Univ of Florida 1953
4686 WILLIAMS Nickol Rudyard Kipling: Poet of the Common Man
      M Ed Henderson St Coll nd
4687 YEATS Alvice W Kipling's Poetic Themes MA Univ of Texas at Austin
      1940 173 p
See also 1982, 2053, 4179

                            CHARLES LAMB

4688 CHADWICK Ellenletia M Historical Devices in Lamb's *Essays of Elia*
      MA Indiana Univ 1942
4689 CLEMENTS Rex S Jr Lamb's Literary Creation: *Elia* BA Amherst 1960
4690 COMFORT Hugh N Charles Lamb and Religious Conformity MA Univ of
      Oklahoma 1935

4691 DIGGS Ellabeth Personal Element in Lamb's Essays and Letters
MS Kansas St Coll at Pittsburg 1940
4692 FITZGERALD Peter H Charles Lamb: The Image and the Man MA Univ
of Maine 1965 124 p
4693 GALLOTTI Luisa Charles Lamb: An Appreciation MA Ca Foscari (Italy)
1937
4694 GIBBONS Catherine B A Famous "Fallacy" in Lamb MA St Louis Univ
1942 107 p
4695 GREEN Margaret E Charles Lamb and the Theatre MA Columbia 1950
4696 MacBRAYNE Daisy B Characterization of Charles Lamb MA Boston Univ
1936
4697 MANDELL Joan D The Essays of Charles Lamb: The Relation of Diction,
Organization and Theme MA Columbia 1960 87 p
4698 MARTIN Elizabeth C Charles Lamb's Essay on the Tragedies of Shakespeare MA Univ of Maryland at College Park 1951 60 p
4699 MAY Joyce Charles Lamb: Romantic on Education MA Univ of
Tennessee 1965
4700 MESSINI Moria Charles Lamb MA Ca Foscari (Italy) 1934
4701 NICKLIN David L The Shallow Fontlet of Charles Lamb MA Univ of
Omaha 1965
4702 NIELSON Lois E Charles Lamb's Treatment of the Past MA Boston Univ
1945
4703 OVERTON Laura H A Handbook of the Mythological and Biblical Allusions
in Lamb's *Essays of Elia* MA East Carolina Univ 1935
4704 POLATO Leonello *The Essays of Elia* by Charles Lamb MA Ca Foscari
(Italy) 1950
4705 POLIZZI Aida Charles Lamb: His Life and Writings with a Short
Introduction to the Significance of *The Essays of Elia* in the
Evolution of the English Essay MA Ca Foscari (Italy) 1933
4706 ROLFS Alvain R Charles Lamb, the Friend MA Tulane Univ 1934
4707 RUSHING P B Lamb's Self-Revelation as "Elia" MA North Texas St Univ
1968
4708 SMITH K B Charles Lamb's Criticism of His Contemporaries MA Univ
of North Carolina at Chapel Hill 1933
4709 WILCOX Robert H The Seventeenth Century Patina of the *Essays of Elia*
MA Univ of Pittsburgh 1951
See also 3897

WALTER SAVAGE LANDOR

4710 ARNEY Lewis J Rose Aylmer and Walter Savage Landor MA Univ of Iowa
1932
4711 CASEY Sr Ellen P Landor's Contemporaries in the *Imaginary Conversations* MA St Louis Univ 1945 107 p
4712 DE BONIS Corinna Walter Savage Landor MA Ca Foscari (Italy) 1951
4713 FERRARINI Maria P Life and Works of Walter Savage Landor
MA Ca Foscari (Italy) 1941
4714 FORD Aubrey M The Political Views of Walter Savage Landor Expressed
in His Classical *Imaginary Conversations* MA Univ of Tennessee
1969 79 p
4715 LOVE Marjorie J The Indebtedness of Walter Savage Landor to Catullus
MA Univ of North Carolina at Chapel Hill 1946 124 p
4716 McGALLIARD J C Classical and Romantic Elements in Walter Savage Landor
MA Univ of North Carolina at Chapel Hill 1925
4717 MAYES Bertha S Landor and His Critics MA Hunter Coll 1940
4718 PRATT A Walter Savage Landor: Interpreted and Criticized Primarily
as an Epicurean BA Univ of British Columbia (Canada) 1955
4719 RAWLINGS Louie M Landor the Classicist MA Univ of Tulsa 1939
4720 ZANETTO Marcello Walter Savage Landor MA Ca Foscari (Italy) nd
See also 846, 4003, 6120, 6176

WILLIAM LANGLAND

4721 BLOOMFIELD Morton W *Piers Plowman* Annotated, Together with an
     Introductory Essay MA McGill (Canada) 1935
4722 BRENNER Anthony J Manly's Imagery Test for *Piers Plowman* MA St Louis
     Univ 1945 216 p
4723 BYERS Vivian G Plowman Literature of the Fourteenth Century
     MA Univ of Oregon 1941
4724 CADOGAN Robert E A Critical Study of *Wynnere* and *Wastoure* and the
     A-Text of *Piers Plowman* MA Columbia 1966 89 p
4725 CLARK Audrey P The Seven Deadly Sins, a Medieval Literary Concept
     Utilized by Langland, Chaucer and Spenser MA Texas Arts and
     Industries Univ 1967
4726 DOTY Douglas M An Analysis of "Kynde" in *Piers Plowman* MA Columbia
     1965 86 p
4727 GLOBE Alexander V The Revelation of St John in *Piers Plowman* and
     The Faerie Queene MA Toronto (Canada) 1966
4728 HEMMERT Mother Mary Our Lady in *Piers Plowman* MA Boston Coll 1933
4729 HENNESSY Bernard C A Comparison of the Social Ideals in Langland's
     Piers Plowman (B-Text) and Carlyle's *Past and Present* MA Syracuse
     Univ 1949 76 p
4730 HUSSEY S S Eighty Years of *Piers Plowman* Scholarship: A Study of
     Critical Methods MA Univ of London (England) 1952
4731 KELLER Joseph R *Piers Plowman* and Medieval Philosophy: The Functions
     of Will, Reason and Conscience Related to Grace MA Syracuse Univ
     1948 93 p
4732 KOONCE Benjamin G The Use of Representatives of the Church in
     Piers Plowman: Materials for an Interpretive Study MA Univ of
     North Carolina at Chapel Hill 1948 181 p
4733 LANDIETH Virginia D Sources and Influences on the Harrowing-of-Hell
     Theme through *Piers Plowman* MA Miami Univ 1965
4734 LATTIN Linda L Medieval Number Symbolism in Langland's *Piers Plowman*
     MA Kansas St Teachers Coll 1965
4735 LEAVITT B D Temporal Structures in *Piers Plowman* MA Rice 1965
4736 O'BRIEN T F Langland: Teacher in *Piers Plowman* MA Boston Coll 1936
4737 SCHAUB Orise H A Comparison of the Uses of the Yoh in *Sir Gawain*
     and The Green Knight and *Piers Plowman* MA Northern Illinois Univ 1966
4738 SNOREK Gail M A Study of the Dialect of *Piers Plowman* Based on the
     Edition of the A-Text by George Kane MA Toronto (Canada) 1963
4739 SOLON John J Langland and Lollardy: The Orthodoxy of *Piers Plowman*
     MA Boston Coll 1947
4740 TORMEY G *Piers Plowman*: Comparison with the Spiritual Exercises
     of St Ignatius MA Boston Coll 1934
4741 ZAJCHOWSKI Richard A The Eternal in the Human: A Study of Medieval
     Drama and *Piers Plowman* BA Amherst 1961
See also 88, 923, 1476, 1591, 1638, 1715

D H LAWRENCE

4742 AKER Meredith E A Study of D H Lawrence MA Univ of Tulsa 1963 84 p
4743 ATKINS Judy "Living Relatedness" in *The Rainbow* BA Univ of British
     Columbia (Canada) 1968
4744 AZAR Diana L Critical Disagreement: A Study of Some Diverse Critical
     Interpretations of D H Lawrence's *St Mawr* and *Lady Chatterley's*
     Lover MA Columbia 1962 120 p
4745 BALL Miriam E The Role of Christian Elements in *The Rainbow*
     MA Cornell Univ 1965
4746 BALLIN Michael G The Functions of Imagery and Symbolism in
     D H Lawrence's *The Rainbow* and *Sons and Lovers* MA McMaster
     (Canada) 1964

4747 BLAZIC Theresa M The Development of Individuality and Polarity through
     Selected Women in the Early Novels of D H Lawrence MA Univ of
     Delaware 1967 105 p
4748 BLINCO, Ethelwynne M The Will-to-Power Relationship in D H Lawrence's
     Women in Love MA Florida St Univ 1963
4749 BOWMER William S The Resolution of Conflict in the Fiction of
     D H Lawrence MA Univ of Louisville 1941
4750 BROWN Homer O D H Lawrence and the Modern Novel: The Problem of
     Point of View MA Univ of Oklahoma 1962
4751 BROWN Jean E A Study of Symbolic Development in the Major Fiction
     of D H Lawrence MA Pacific Univ 1968
4752 BRUCE Harold R The White Goddess in the Early Novels of D H Lawrence
     MA Univ of Delaware 1967 79 p
4753 CALDIERO Julia D H Lawrence: Eros and the Religious Dimension in
     His Works MA Columbia 1961 72 p
4754 CHLOUBER Carla S Natural Symbolism in the Short Stories of
     D H Lawrence MA Oklahoma St Univ 1966 157 p
4755 CLARK L D D H Lawrence and the Apocalyptic Imagination MA Columbia
     1954 70 p
4756 COHEN Richard The Rananim of D H Lawrence: His Pursuit of the
     Utopia in the New World MA Univ of Texas at Austin at El Paso
     1955 111 p
4757 CONDIT John H D H Lawrence: Three Novels BA Amherst 1958
4758 CONOLLY Leonard W The Individual and Society in the Leadership Novels
     of D H Lawrence MA McMaster (Canada) 1964
4759 CORNISH Michael The Position of D H Lawrence in Relation to
     Christianity: An Examination of His Short Novels and Short Stories
     . MA Univ of Kansas 1960
4760 CUDLIPP Alice V A Study of Man and Religion in the Novels of
     D H Lawrence MA Univ of Richmond 1968 108 p
4761 DAL CER Franco D H Lawrence as a Story Teller: His Works and His
     Personality MA Ca Foscari (Italy) 1936
4762 DAVIDSON Eleanor I D H Lawrence and Mental Consciousness
     MS Ft Hays Kansas St Coll 1965
4763 DIX Ruth C D H Lawrence in His Novels MA Univ of Montana 1933 94 p
4764 DUNN Joan P A Study of Creative Force as Destructive Force in Four
     Major O'Neill Tragedies, D H Lawrence's Use of Nature Description
     in Sons and Lovers and "A Doll's House": An Original Short Story
     MA Brigham Young Univ 1959 75 p
4765 DURK Francis L Jr Reality Behind Reality: The Vision of D H Lawrence
     MA Columbia 1951
4766 EDGE Charles E Technique in Selected Short Stories of D H Lawrence
     MA Univ of North Carolina at Chapel Hill 1946 157 p
4767 ESPOSITO Paul J Transient Singularity and the Permanent Condition:
     Remarks on D H Lawrence's Women in Love and Jonathan Swift's
     Gulliver's Travels BA Amherst 1969
4768 ESSEX Ruth The Primitive Elements in the Work of D H Lawrence
     MA Brooklyn Coll 1965
4769 FELDMAN Leonard B D H Lawrence's Studies in Classic American Literat
     MA Columbia 1951
4770 FIDDES T M Strife, Balance and Allegiance: The Schemata of Will
     in Five Novels of D H Lawrence MA North Texas St Univ 1968
4771 FITZPATRICK William P The Love-Hate Phenomenon in the Major Novels
     of D H Lawrence MA Univ of Maryland at College Park 1969 96 p
4772 FRASER Keith W Quest for Wholeness: D H Lawrence's Shorter Fiction
     MA Univ of British Columbia (Canada) 1969 124 p
4773 FUCHS Cara S The Pursuit of the Primitive in D H Lawrence
     MA Columbia 1962 85 p
4774 GARD Rose A The Phoenix and the Stallion: A Study of Themes in the
     Works of D H Lawrence MA Univ of Kansas 1966

4775 GARY Barbara L The Ideal of Marriage in D H Lawrence's Short Stories
      MA Univ of Southwestern Louisiana 1969 96 p
4776 GLOVER Randal Y The Final Vision of D H Lawrence BA Univ of British
      Columbia (Canada) 1967
4777 GOLDBERG James F Women in Love and the English Novel BA Amherst 1961
4778 GRAYSON Nancy J D H Lawrence as a Short Story Writer MA Univ of
      Texas at Austin 1958 132 p
4779 GREENE Elizabeth S Lawrence's Voice in Look! We Have Come Through
      MA Univ of Rhode Island 1964 88 p
4780 GREY Spencer Y Symbolism in the Novels of D H Lawrence MA Columbia
      1960 116 p
4781 GURTOFF Stanley A An Introduction to the Plays of D H Lawrence
      MA Columbia 1958 179 p
4782 HANCOCK F B The Development of Symbols in D H Lawrence's The Rainbow
      and Women in Love MA Univ of London (England) 1962
4783 HARTMAN Nancy A D H Lawrence's Theory of Love in His Major Fiction
      MA Univ of Texas at Austin 1967 108 p
4784 HECHT Harvey L Amid the Whirlwinds: A Study of the Works of
      D H Lawrence BA Amherst 1958
4785 HELPHINSTINE Frances L Language Structures Carrying Tones of Power
      and Authority in the Short Stories of D H Lawrence MA Morehead
      St Univ 1968 90 p
4786 HEVENTHAL Charles R Jr D H Lawrence's Rupert Birkin: An Objective
      Consideration of His Language; an Existential Re-Thinking of His
      Problem MA Columbia 1955 77 p
4787 HOFFMAN D A The Monomythic Pattern in Three Novels of D H Lawrence
      MA North Texas St Univ 1968
4788 HUDSON Norma W Form and Symbol: Unity in D H Lawrence's The Plumed
      Serpent MA Univ of Tulsa 1969 60 p
4789 IRONS Doris E The Major Criticism, 1955-1965, of D H Lawrence's
      Sons and Lovers, The Rainbow and Women in Love MA Univ of Miami
      1966
4790 JACOBSON Steven M The Disintegrating World of D H Lawrence
      BA Amherst 1953
4791 JOFFE Philip H D H Lawrence as a Critic of Bloomsbury MA Univ of
      British Columbia (Canada) 1968 162 p
4792 JOHNS Robert E Design and Imagery in the Poetry of D H Lawrence
      MA Toronto (Canada) 1967
4793 JOHNSON Robert G D H Lawrence's Theory of Art: Its Development from
      and Application to His Prose Fiction MA Purdue Univ 1963 86 p
4794 KANE Richard C A Consideration of the Theme of Positive Destruction
      in the Shorter Fiction of D H Lawrence MA Temple Univ 1967 75 p
4795 KIRBY-SMITH Selden D H Lawrence in the United States of America
      MA Columbia 1951
4796 KNOTT Barbara J A Study of D H Lawrence's Concept of Quickness
      MA East Carolina Univ 1970
4797 KROUSE Agate N A Study of D H Lawrence's The Man Who Died
      MA Indiana Univ 1963
4798 LaMATTERY Jerry J D H Lawrence's The Rainbow: Art as Revelation
      MA San Diego St Coll 1966
4799 LEE Rose A The Boy in the Bush: A Study of the Collaboration of
      D H Lawrence and M L Skinner MA Univ of Texas at Austin 1967
4800 LEFF Arthur A Sex and Society in the Novels of D H Lawrence
      BA Amherst 1956
4801 LEVITAS Martin D H Lawrence: The Dilemma of Leadership MA Columbia
      1963 60 p
4802 LOVELL James H Hr D H Lawrence: The Taos Period MA Texas Christian
      Univ 1953 144 p
4803 MAGEE Douglas C Prophecy in Three Novels by D H Lawrence: The Rainbow,
      Lady Chatterley's Lover and Women in Love BA Amherst 1969

4804 MAMAS Helen D H Lawrence: Man and Artist MA Boston Univ 1946
4805 MARINELL James P The Development of "Lad-and-Girl Love" in *Sons and Lovers* and *Women in Love* BA Amherst 1968
4806 MASCIA Mario D H Lawrence: Sardinia Book and Italy MA Ca Foscari (Italy) 1951
4807 MELVIN Mary L D H Lawrence's Mexico MA Univ of Massachusetts 1965
4808 MEYER Virginia B The Effect of the Southwest upon D H Lawrence and His Writing MA Eastern New Mexico Univ 1969
4809 MILLS Marueen W Primitive Myth and Ritual in *The Rainbow* by D H Lawrence: An Interpretive Study MA Bowling Green Univ 1958
4810 MOODY Dianne The Feminine Prototypes in D H Lawrence's Early Novels MA Univ of Texas at El Paso 1966 126 p
4811 MOORE J A Dark Imagery in *Women in Love* MA North Texas St Univ 1967
4812 MORRISON Bryce Floral Vitalism in the Short Stories of D H Lawrence MA Dalhousie (Canada) 1965
4813 MOSKOWITZ Hilda S A Nest for the Phoenix: A Study of D H Lawrence's Mother Figures MA Univ of Maryland at College Park 1967 103 p
4814 NADEL Ira B Social Class in the Major Novels of D H Lawrence BA Rutgers St Univ 1965 63 p
4815 NEWBY Richard L The Treatment of Sex in D H Lawrence's Novels MA Southern Illinois Univ at Carbondale 1953 68 p
4816 NIEUWENHUIS Marjory D H Lawrence and the Novel: His *Women in Love* as an Expression of Yearning for Innocence Lost MA Columbia 1962 93 p
4817 OLDHAM Perry D D H Lawrence: Symbolism in the Early Novels MA Univ of Maryland at College Park 1966 80 p
4818 PALMER Paul R D H Lawrence and the Mediterranean World MA Columbia 1955 136 p
4819 PARSONS Robert D H Lawrence's Use of Symbolism in *The Rainbow* and *Women in Love* MA Univ of Colorado 1965
4820 PERZANOWSKI Dennis J Ideas and Technique in D H Lawrence's *The Rainbc* MA Temple Univ 1967 62 p
4821 PESSOLANO Frank J Jr A Critical History of the Novels of D H Lawrence MA Univ of Pittsburgh 1950
4822 RACKIN Phyllis F Imagery and Theme in Three of D H Lawrence's Novels MA Auburn Univ 1957
4823 ROBERTS Jane P Potential for Living: Themes in the Poems of D H Lawrence MA Texas Christian Univ 1969 87 p
4824 ROBINSON Richard J D H Lawrence's *Studies in Classic American Literature*: A Textual Study MA Univ of Iowa 1965
4825 ROSENBERG Judith The "Voice" of D H Lawrence MA Univ of Illinois at Chicago Circle 1969
4826 SCHWALBE Doris J D H Lawrence and Existentialism MA Univ of Toledo 1952
4827 SCHWARTZ Steven M Blood-Knowledge and *The Plumed Serpent* MA Univ of Richmond 1969 53 p
4828 SNYDER Nancy F The Metaphysical Goal of D H Lawrence as Dramatized in *The Man Who Died* MA Bowling Green Univ 1966
4829 SPILKA Mark The Love Ethic of D H Lawrence MA Indiana Univ 1955
4830 STALLMAN Robert L Symbolic Texture in a Selection of the Short Fictions of D H Lawrence MA Univ of New Mexico 1961
4831 STEELE Gilbert R The "Flight" Motif in the Fiction of D H Lawrence MA Columbia 1953 107 p
4832 SYNNOTT Burton J Spirit of Place in D H Lawrence: Its Development and Attainment BA Amherst 1963
4833 TEDLOW Roberta J Theory and Practice: D H Lawrence on Man, Woman and Society MA Georgetown Univ 1969 58 p
4834 THORNE Sylvia P Blutbruderschaft in the Major Novels of D H Lawrence MA Duke Univ 1965
4835 TSUCHIDA Bruce T The World of *The Rainbow* BA Amherst 1965

4836 TUDOR Kathleen Sexuality and Nature Imagery in the Major Novels of
       D H Lawrence MA Montreal (Canada) 1965
4837 TURNER Syd D H Lawrence's Use of American-Indian Symbolism in *The Plumed
       Serpent* MA Hardin-Simmons Univ 1951
4838 TYERYAR Gary L D H Lawrence's Political Philosophy as Expressed
       in His Novels MA Rice 1963
4839 VON KOHL Marilyn The Lawrentian Hero as a Study in Self-Definition
       MA Texas Christian Univ 1965 113 p
4840 WEBB John D H Lawrence's Criticism of the United States MS Auburn
       Univ 1950 192 p
4841 WEISS Daniel A The Evolution of *Lady Chatterley's Lover* MA Columbia
       1950
4842 WILLBERN David P D H Lawrence: Poet BA Amherst 1966
4843 WILLIAMS Hubertien H An Interpretation of *Women in Love* in Terms of
       the Lawrentian Metapsychology MA Bowling Green Univ 1963
4844 WOOD David V D H Lawrence and the Bloomsbury Novelists: A Com-
       parison BA Amherst 1960
See also 2100, 3228, 3738, 3758, 4421, 8553

                          T E LAWRENCE

4845 ABDOU Elias M Impulse into Nitria: T E Lawrence's Fictional
       Technique in *The Mint* MA Univ of Pittsburgh 1961
4846 BREITLING Wolfgang Thomas Edward Lawrence as Writer and Artist
       MA Ca Foscari (Italy) 1948
4847 HULLEY Sue E Lawrence of Arabia: Hero of a Troubled Generation
       MA Univ of Minnesota 1965
4848 KURTOVICH Robert Between Two Worlds: A Study of the Romantic
       and the Absurd in the Writing of T E Lawrence MA Fresno St Coll
       1970 53 p
4849 NOTOPOULOS Philip J Down on Paper: T E Lawrence and Literature
       BA Amherst 1967
See also 7286

                          EDWARD LEAR

4850 FOGLE Richard H Edward Lear: His Life and Nonsense Poetry
       MA Columbia 1937
4851 KENNY Thomas J The Clown's Mirror: Edward Lear as Seen in His
       Nonsense Verse MA Columbia 1964 115 p
4852 SCHWAB Robert P Edward Lear and Nonsense Literature MA Univ of
       North Carolina at Chapel Hill 1957 107 p
See also 5269

                          F R LEAVIS

4853 NORTH Charles L F R Leavis and the Problems of Evaluation
       MA Columbia 1964 171 p
4854 OLNEY James L A Study of the Criticism of F R Leavis MA Columbia
       1958 118 p
4855 SYNNOTT Burton J F R Leavis: Critic of Three Traditions MA Columbia
       1965 102 p

                          VERNON LEE

4856 BETTINI Liliana Vernon Lee and Her Literary Criticism on the
       Italian Eighteenth Century and Renaissance MA Ca Foscari (Italy)
       1947
4857 OLMINI Anita Vernon Lee and Italy MA Ca Foscari (Italy) 1937

CECIL DAY LEWIS

4858 BARTLETT Donald R The Fury and the Grace: A Study of the Poetry
      and the Poetic Development of C Day Lewis MA Memorial (Canada) 1965
4859 BARTON Edgar C The Poetry of Cecil Day Lewis MA Univ of British
      Columbia (Canada) 1948
4860 BENSON Paul F The Critical Theories of C Day Lewis MA Colorado St
      Coll 1969

CLIVE STAPLES LEWIS

4861 BOND Brian C The Mythical Element in C S Lewis' Trilogy MA Bowling
      Green Univ 1969
4862 BURLESON Lyman E An Analysis of Major Christian Doctrines in
      C S Lewis' Space Trilogy MA East Tennessee St Univ 1967
4863 CHIDDIE George A The Haunted World of C S Lewis: A Study of His
      Space Trilogy MA Univ of North Carolina at Greensboro 1968
4864 CHRISTOPHER Joe R The Romances of Clive Staples Lewis MA Univ of
      Oklahoma 1970
4865 FROESE R J C S Lewis' Concept of Myth and His Trilogy of "Science
      Fiction" BA Univ of British Columbia (Canada) 1967
4866 GARLAND Ruth E Image of the Tower of Babel in the Interplanetary
      Trilogy of C S Lewis MA Columbia 1951
4867 GREGORY Eloise C C S Lewis: Fantasy as an Illumination of Reality
      MA Pacific Univ 1967 94 p
4868 HONEY Diane C S Lewis' Treatment of Traditional and Created Mythology
      in the Science Fiction Trilogy MA Texas Technological Univ 1964
      81 p
4869 KUEKER Ted C S Lewis: Literary Critic MA Mankato St Coll 1965
4870 LINDAMAN Robert E The Literary Criticism of C S Lewis MA Mankato
      St Coll 1965 75 p
4871 MARTELL Clare L C S Lewis: Teacher as Apologist MA Boston Coll 1949
4872 MILLER R H Myth in the Fiction of C S Lewis MA North Texas St Univ
      1966
4873 RUTLEDGE Robert C The Literary Criticism of C S Lewis MA George
      Washington Univ 1957 96 p
4874 SOLT Marilyn J Christian Implications in C S Lewis' Chronicles of
      Narnia MA Bowling Green Univ 1966
4875 STUBBS David C C S Lewis' Theology and Its Reflection in His Fiction
      MA Florida St Univ 1957
4876 THOMAS Mary B The Fairy Stories of C S Lewis MA Univ of Oklahoma 1966
See also 939, 5008

JOHN LOCKE

4877 ARM Sigmund S The Influence of Locke and Montesquieu in the Early
      State Constitutions MA Columbia 1935
4878 CAREY Mother Barbara L John Locke's Theory of Natural Law MA Boston
      Coll 1959
4879 FISCHER G R John Locke as Semanticist MA North Texas St Univ 1950
4880 HAHN Fred E "Nature" in the Political Philosophies of Thomas Hobbes
      and John Locke MA Columbia 1953 82 p
4881 HALLIE P P Locke, Berkeley and Hume and the Perception of Exteriority
      B Litt Oxford Univ (England) 1951
4882 KOWALYSHYN Russell John Locke and the American Revolution
      MA Columbia 1943
4883 McGRAW Leslie E Matthew Prior's Response to Locke's "Essay Concern-
      ing the Human Understanding" MA Western (Canada) 1966
4884 MUMBULO Rachel E The Aesthetic Theory of John Locke MA Syracuse
      Univ 1942 69 p

4885 O'HARA John B John Locke's Philosophy of Discourse MA Univ of
      Oklahoma 1963
4886 O'KELLEY Thomas A An Examination of the Evidence Concerning the
      Influence of the *Regulae ad Directionem Ingenii* of Descartes upon
      John Locke's "Essay Concerning Human Understanding" MA Florida
      St Univ 1964
4887 SIEVERS Allen M An Investigation into the Nature and Scope of
      Economics Based on Certain Writings of John Locke MA Columbia 1941
See also 2304

RICHARD LOVELACE

4888 KENNEY William P Traditional and Individual Elements in
      Richard Lovelace's Poetry MA Boston Coll 1956
4889 QUIVEY James R A Critical Study of the Theme of Constancy in the
      Poems of Richard Lovelace MA Bowling Green Univ 1962
4890 SHERRY Walter L The Courtier and the Gallant: An Evaluation of
      Richard Lovelace and Sir John Suckling MA Syracuse Univ 1946 89 p

MALCOLM LOWRY

4891 ATKINS Shirley E Aspects of the Absurd in Modern Fiction, with
      Special Reference to *Under the Volcano* and *Catch 22* MA Univ of
      British Columbia (Canada) 1969 160 p
4892 BANHAM David S A Liverpool of Self: A Study of Lowry's Fiction
      Other than *Under the Volcano* MA Univ of British Columbia (Canada)
      1969 98 p
4893 CULLIS Tara A Structural Analysis of the Wheel Symbolism in
      Malcolm Lowry's *Under the Volcano* BA Univ of British Columbia
      (Canada) 1970
4894 CUNNINGTON Linda The Archetypal Pattern and Symbolism of Rebirth
      in Malcolm Lowry's *Under the Volcano* BA Univ of British Columbia
      (Canada) 1970
4895 EASTON Richard Collected Poetry of Malcolm Lowry BA Univ of
      British Columbia (Canada) 1969
4896 HOOGERS Evert R Thanatopsis: An Exploration of Death in the Works
      of Camus, Dostoyevsky and Malcolm Lowry BA Univ of British
      Columbia (Canada) 1968
4897 JOHNSON Carell The Making of *Under the Volcano*: An Examination of
      Lyrical Structure, with Reference to Textual Revisions MA Univ
      of British Columbia (Canada) 1969
4898 ROBERTSON Anthony Aspects of the Quest in the Minor Fiction of
      Malcolm Lowry MA Univ of British Columbia (Canada) 1966
4899 RUBBEN Juliette Discussion of Malcolm Lowry's *Hear Us O Lord from
      Heaven Thy Dwelling Place* BA Univ of British Columbia (Canada)
      1969
4900 SANDWELL Sherry The Use of Archetypal Landscape in Malcolm Lowry's
      Under the Volcano BA Univ of British Columbia (Canada) 1968
4901 THOMAS Hilda L Malcolm Lowry's *Under the Volcano*: An Interpretation
      MA Univ of British Columbia (Canada) 1965
4902 THOMPSON Sheryl A An Application of Albert Camus' Existential
      Principle to *Swamp Angel*: Ethel Wilson; *Beautiful Losers*:
      Leonard Cohen; *Under the Volcano*: Malcolm Lowry BA Univ of
      British Columbia (Canada) 1970
See also 2147

JOHN LYLY

4903 ABERNETHY C E Courtesy-Book Subjects and Ideas in the Comedies
      of John Lyly MA Univ of North Carolina at Chapel Hill 1935

4904 ADAM Giovanna John Lyly: *The Woman in the Moon* MA Ca Foscari
        (Italy) 1960
4905 BERTAPELLE Giancarlo *Gallathea* by John Lyly MA Ca Foscari (Italy)
        1961
4906 BUTLER Gary M Lyly's Proverb Lore MA Baylor Univ 1966 228 p
4907 CALORI Ethel V The Influence of Lyly on Elizabethan Drama MA Univ
        of Oklahoma 1933
4908 CANTON Roberto John Lyly: *Euphues, the Anatomy of Wit*
        MA Ca Foscari (Italy) 1964
4909 COSTA Sr Mary E Neoplatonism in John Lyly's Plays MA Boston Coll
        1957
4910 DE GRAFFENRIED Garland John Lyly's Use of Character Groups in the
        Structure of His Plays MA Univ of Texas at Austin 1950 152 p
4911 DI MARTINO Maria A *Midas* by John Lyly MA Ca Foscari (Italy) 1963
4912 DOCHERTY Helen A A Study of Euphuism in John Lyly's *Sapho and
        Phao* and *Midas* MA Boston Coll 1957
4913 FUSSEL Mildred A Study of the Treatment of the Time in the Plays
        of Lyly, Marlowe, Greene and Peele MA North Texas St Univ 1941
4914 GIORI Maria L The Plays of John Lyly with Particular Reference
        to Their Chronology, Sources and Satirical Elements MA Ca Foscari
        (Italy) 1954
4915 HARDIN LaRue A Study of the Plot-Structure of Lyly's Plays MA Univ
        of Texas at Austin 1936
4916 HENNELL Diana J A Study of Lyly's *Endimion* as Court Drama BA Univ
        of British Columbia (Canada) 1968
4917 KAYLOR Edward J The Development of Character Portrayal in the
        English Novel from Lyly through Defoe MA Boston Univ 1950
4918 LITTLEJOHN Joseph E John Lyly's *Endimion* as an Allegory of
        Elizabethan Court Intrigue MA Texas Christian Univ 1959 124 p
4919 LORENZONI Maria *Love's Metamorphosis* by John Lyly MA Ca Foscari
        (Italy) 1965
4920 MARTINI Mario *Alexander and Campaspe* by John Lyly MA Ca Foscari
        (Italy) 1963
4921 MIZELL L G The Women in Lyly's Plays with Reference to Selected
        Aspects of Contemporary Relationships and to High Comedy MA Univ
        of North Carolina at Chapel Hill 1943
4922 O'MEARA Katherine C Prologues and Epilogues of Elizabethan Plays,
        with Special Reference to Those of Lyly, Greene, Marlowe and Kyd
        MA Tulane Univ 1918
4923 OMMASSINI Giuseppina *Sapho and Phao* by John Lyly MA Ca Foscari
        (Italy) 1962
4924 PIAGGI M Wanda John Lyly and the Italian Renaissance MA Ca Foscari
        (Italy) 1946
4925 RAILSTON Annette G Lyly Prefers "s" in Poetry and "th" in Prose:
        His Use of the "s" and the "th" Endings in the Third Person
        Singular of the Present Tense MA Baylor Univ 1965 64 p
4926 RIVERS D E John Lyly's Prose and the Influence of His Style
        BA Univ of British Columbia 1942
4927 SLICER D H The Heritage of the Soliloquy of Classical and of Native
        English Comedy in the Plays of John Lyly MA Univ of North Carolina
        at Chapel Hill 1941
4928 STOLFA Breda John Lyly: *Mother Bombie* MA Ca Foscari (Italy) 1962
4929 TOOLE John K Lyly's Treatment of Women: The Beginnings of "Higher"
        Comedy in England MA Columbia 1959 51 p
4930 WALL Charles A An Interpretation of the Personal Allegory in the
        Dramas of John Lyly MA Emory Univ 1932 71 p
4931 WILSON L R Works of Lyly and Greene and the Pastoral Comedy of
        Shakespeare MA Univ of North Carolina at Chapel Hill 1902
See also 3655, 6325, 6373, 6594

THOMAS BABINGTON MACAULAY

4932 DIRKS Betty J A Study of the Contemporary Criticism of Macaulay's
     History of England (1840-1865) MA Kansas St Teachers Coll 1965
4933 HOLT Howard J Carlyle and Macaulay BA Univ of Oklahoma 1914
4934 HOLT Howard J Macaulay's Estimate of Johnson and Some Contemporaries
     MA Univ of Oklahoma 1929
4935 O'DONNELL Sr M Mildred Macaulay and the Biographical Essay MA Univ
     of Pittsburgh 1929
4936 OTTEN Terry R Macaulay's Critical Theory of Imagination and Reason
     and Its Background in European Thought MA Univ of Kentucky 1961
     101 p
4937 STAHL Emory W Oratorical Elements in the Writings of Macaulay
     MA Boston Univ 1928
See also 1254, 4265, 5428

GEORGE MACDONALD

4938 CARNELL Corbin S George MacDonald and "The Higher Faith" MA Columbia
     1953 120 p
4939 CHAMBERS Diana The Fairy Tales of George MacDonald MA Columbia 1953
     82 p
4940 DUFFY Lucy D An Analysis of George MacDonald and His Fantasy Tales
     for Children MA Southern Connecticut St Coll 1966
4941 LAURENT Martha H George MacDonald's Scottish Novels MA Auburn Univ
     1955
See also 6098

LOUIS MACNEICE

4942 HAWTHORNE Richard G The Early Poetry of Louis MacNeice: Biography
     of Mind and Style BA Amherst 1968
4943 ROSEN Bruce J The Poetry of Louis MacNeice MA Columbia 1954 70 p
4944 SAGER Nelson C Elements of Satire in the Works of Louis MacNeice
     MA Texas Technological Univ 1966 61 p
4945 STONE Julee A A Study of Louis MacNeice MA Columbia 1960 231 p

THOMAS MALORY

4946 BELYEA Barbara J The Influence of Malory's Tale of the Sangreal
     upon Spenser's *Faerie Queene*, Book One BA Univ of British Columbia
     (Canada) 1965
4947 BROWN Lila T A Comparison of Character Traits in Malory's *Le Morte
     d'Arthur* and Tennyson's *Idylls of the King* MA Eastern New Mexico
     Univ 1952 94 p
4948 CAMERON John R The Arthurian Adultery in English Literature with
     Special Emphasis on Malory, Tennyson, E A Robinson and T H White
     MA Univ of British Columbia (Canada) 1960 126 p
4949 CARTER Lois R The Knight as Clown: A Study of the Comic Element
     in the Chivalric Literature of Malory, Spenser and Shakespeare
     MA Oklahoma St Univ 1937 61 p
4950 CREEL Barbara H A Romance of Gaheriet: An Analogue of Malory's
     "Tale of Sir Gareth" MA Texas Christian Univ 1964 74 p
4951 CURRY Thomas W Sir Percival's Character in *Morte d'Arthur*
     MA St Louis Univ 1943 82 p
4952 DAGG Melvin H The Beasts beneath the Round Table: The Role of
     Animals in Malory's *Morte d'Arthur* MA Univ of British Columbia
     (Canada) 1969 161 p
4953 DeMOSS Marian S An Analytical Study of the Influence of Malory's
     Style in *Le Morte d'Arthur* on Dr Sebastian Evans' Style in

High History of the Holy Grael or *Perlesvaus* MA Oklahoma St Univ
1933 25 p
4954 DRYER Lloyd L A Comparison of Athletic Sports in Homer and Malory
MA Oklahoma St Univ 1935 37 p
4955 ELLIS Harold M Tennyson's Use of Malory's *Morte d'Arthur* and *The
Mabinogion* in the *Idylls of the King* MA Univ of Maine 1908 44 p
4956 HANA Nelly K Heroic and Christian Values in the Alliterative
Morte d'Arthur MA Univ of Utah 1966
4957 HULL Edith H A Comparison of the Treatment of the Arthurian Legends
by Malory, Tennyson, Morris and Swinburne MS Purdue Univ 1897
4958 KALBFLEISCH William J Gawain and His Family in Malory's *Le Morte
d'Arthur* MA Western (Canada) 1966
4959 LEHR Sr Angelica A Comparative Study of the Tristram Motif as
Developed by Sir Thomas Malory MA Boston Coll 1942
4960 LUTER David W Tragedy in Malory: Effects of Symbolic and Figural
Characterization MA Columbia 1966 54 p
4961 MacDONALD Martha B Dreams in Malory's Arthurian Tales MA Univ of
Maryland at College Park 1968 72 p
4962 MILLER Helena F The Infinitives in Sir Thomas Malory's *Morte d'Arthur*
MA Smith Coll 1912
4963 MOORE Amelia S Queens and Damsels in Distress: Medieval Tragedy
in Malory MA Auburn Univ 1967
4964 MORRIS Sr Mary M A Comparative Study of the Tristram Motif as
Developed by Malory, Wagner, Arnold and Tennyson MA Boston Coll
1949
4965 OLEFSKY Ellyn R Unity in the Writings of Sir Thomas Malory: Plot,
Characterization and Theme MA Univ of Maryland at College Park
1967 117 p
4966 PEPLOW Michael W Malory's Originality in "The Healing of Sir Urry"
MA Texas Christian Univ 1964 107 p
4967 SHANNON Carrie A The Influence of Malory on the Later English Poets
MA Texas Technological Univ 1934 116 p
4968 SHIRLEY Marjory The Evolution of the Character of Gawain from
Celtic Myth through Malory MA Bowling Green Univ 1967
4969 SHULTZ William C A Comparative Study of Malory's *Morte d'Arthur* and
Tennyson's *Idylls of the King* MA Univ of Kentucky 1914
4970 SIMKO J Word-Order in the Winchester Manuscript and in
William Caxton's Edition of Thomas Malory's *Morte d'Arthur* (1485):
A Comparison M Phil Univ of London (England) 1967
4971 STRICKLAND Arney L A Study of the Language of Sir Thomas Malory
MA Lamar Technological Univ 1965
4972 TINGLE Gladys E The Prose Style of Sir Thomas Malory's *Morte d'Arthur*,
Book I MA Oklahoma St Univ 1943 55 p
4973 TURCOT Sr Anne E Characterization in Lancelot: A Comparative Study
of the Methods Employed by Thomas Malory and E A Robinson
MA Boston Coll 1945
4974 WARD Catherine B Malory's Arthur MA Duke Univ 1965
4975 WHITEHEAD Graham G The Theme of Courtly Love in Sir Thomas Malory's
Le Morte d'Arthur MA Univ of New Brunswick (Canada) 1965
See also 1552, 2106, 6249, 8336

KATHERINE MANSFIELD

4976 BALDINI Leda Katherine Mansfield as a Short Story Writer MA Ca Foscari
(Italy) 1950
4977 BLUMENTHAL Estelle H Some Recent Tendencies in the Short Story
(1914-1934) MA McGill (Canada) 1935
4978 BROWN Nathanial H The Art of Katherine Mansfield MA Syracuse Univ
1955 183 p
4979 BURKE V M The Evolution of Katherine Mansfield's Art MA Boston

Univ 1942
4980 CARBONI Nella Women in the Novels of Three Modern Women Writers:
     Margaret Kennedy, Katherine Mansfield and Rosamond Lehman
     MA Ca Foscari (Italy) 1939
4981 CHAPMAN Catherine The Critical Tenets of Katherine Mansfield MA Texas
     Technological Univ nd   67 p
4982 COOKE Patricia J Themes from Her Childhood in the Short Stories of
     Katherine Mansfield MA Univ of Houston 1967   120 p
4983 DARLING Wanda Katherine Mansfield: Her Writing, Development and
     Literary Effect MA Columbia 1941
4984 EPP Anne M Katherine Mansfield's Treatment of Death BA Univ of
     British Columbia (Canada) 1970
4985 FAIRBAIRN Evelyn B Three Essays in Criticism: Jewett's *White
     Heron;* Mansfield and the Novel *Demeuble;* and Dante's Mythological
     Figures MA Brigham Young Univ nd
4986 FOLEY Sr Mary M Katherine Mansfield MA Boston Coll 1954
4987 GIBBONS Eileen Tone: Its Sources and Implications in Willa Cather's
     Death Comes for the Archbiship; Technique toward Dramatic Intensity
     in Katherine Mansfield's "The Daughters of the Late Colonel";
     "The Children", "Salt Water Sunday", and "When Phil Jones Died":
     Three Original Short Stories MA Brigham Young Univ 1960   119 p
4988 GREENWOOD Lillian B The Technique of Katherine Mansfield MA Univ
     of British Columbia (Canada) 1965
4989 HARDWICK Elizabeth B The Short Stories of Katherine Mansfield: A
     Critical Study MA Univ of Kentucky 1939
4990 HORTON M The Influence of Tchekov on Katherine Mansfield BA Univ
     of British Columbia 1952
4991 KATZ Estelle L The Writings of Katherine Mansfield and the Influence
     of Other Writers on Her Work MA Boston Univ 1934
4992 KEHR Grace H Katherine Mansfield and Her Art MA Indiana Univ 1940
4993 LESOK Kathryne P Similarity of Theme and Method in Anton Chekhov
     and Katherine Mansfield MA Texas Christian Univ 1947   62 p
4994 MELEEDY Sr Mary R A Study of the Short Stories of Katherine Mansfield
     MA Boston Coll 1938
4995 MIDDLETON B L Alienation in the Life and Works of Katherine Mansfield
     MA Rice 1966
4996 MITCHELL Charles H The Short Stories of Katherine Mansfield MA Univ
     of Pittsburgh 1931
4997 MORRISON Gail The Imagery of Katherine Mansfield BA Univ of
     British Columbia (Canada) 1961
4998 PATRICOLO Maria T Katherine Mansfield and Her Stories MA Ca Foscari
     (Italy) 1966
4999 PIAGGIO Alessandra Katherine Mansfield: A Brief Critical Study
     MA Ca Foscari (Italy) 1948
5000 PIRANI Lucia Katherine Mansfield MA Ca Foscari (Italy) 1933
5001 PROFETA Dorotea Katherine Mansfield's Art through Her Life and Work
     MA Ca Foscari (Italy) 1936
5002 ROWLAND J N The Differences in Katherine Mansfield and Anton Chekhov
     as Short Story Writers MA North Texas St Univ 1961
5003 STIGLER Elsie V Tonal Qualities of Katherine Mansfield's Short
     Stories MA Univ of Texas at Austin 1938   263 p
5004 STODDARD Hilda Transparence and Transcendence: Aspects of
     Katherine Mansfield's Fiction MA Univ of Louisville 1968   101 p
5005 TATE Gary L The Influence of Anton Chekhov on Katherine Mansfield
     MA Univ of New Mexico 1956
5006 TAUSS Beatrice Katherine Mansfield and the Snail Beneath the Leaf
     MA Columbia 1959   63 p

CHRISTOPHER MARLOWE

5007 AKERS Dorothy A Project in Stage Design for *The Jew of Malta*
MA Univ of Iowa 1933
5008 ANDERSON Carla L The Changing Face of Evil: A Study of Nine Devils
MA Univ of Delaware 1964 100 p
5009 BECK Florence E The Faust Legend in Elizabethan Drama MA St Louis
Univ 1927 47 p
5010 BECK Norman A The Changing Nature of the Protagonist in the Plays
of Christopher Marlowe MA Univ of Rhode Island 1964 87 p
5011 BELL Patricia J Some Aspects of Christopher Marlowe's English Usage
MA Univ of Oklahoma 1958
5012 BERGER Jonathan Tragedy in the Plays of Christopher Marlowe
BA Rutgers St Univ 1962 78 p
5013 BEST Larry G Christopher Marlowe: Imagery and the Tragic Hero
MA Brigham Young Univ 1966
5014 BETTO Saverio A Psychologic Aesthetical Analysis of
Christopher Marlowe's Works MA Ca Foscari (Italy) 1928
5015 BONTE Andries S The Villain before Marlowe in Eight Representative
Plays BA Univ of British Columbia (Canada) 1968
5016 BOWMAN Ruth E The Aspiring Mind: Marlowe's Concept of the Tragic
Hero MA Colorado St Coll 1966
5017 BRADLEY Peter G "Atheist" Marlowe's Affirmation of Christian
Idealism in His Drama MA Univ of Rhode Island 1966 93 p
5018 BROWN R M Hero and Leander: The Problem of Decorative Imagery
MA Univ of Connecticut 1951
5019 BRUNELLO Laura Christopher Marlowe: The Second Part of *Tamburlaine
the Great* MA Ca Foscari (Italy) 1961
5020 BURNS Cathleen The Man of the Renaissance: Christopher Marlowe
MA Boston Univ 1941
5021 CALDWELL William H Marlowe's Cosmology MA Univ of Richmond 1967 89 p
5022 CAMPBELL Lucien Q Characterization in the Dramatic Works of Marlowe
MA Univ of Texas at Austin 1924
5023 CARSON John F Tamerlane, A Literary Legend MA Univ of Texas at
El Paso 1962 94 p
5024 CARTER Norma F The Faust Legend in Marlowe, Goethe, Wolfe and Mann
MA East Tennessee St Univ 1968
5025 COOKE B M The Tragic Hero of Christopher Marlowe BA Univ of British
Columbia (Canada) 1934
5026 COWAN Jim M Objective Irony in *The Jew of Malta* MA Texas Technological Univ 1966 77 p
5027 DE MATTEIS Maria Christopher Marlowe MA Ca Foscari (Italy) 1926
5028 DIEHL Marie E Christopher Marlowe's Treatment of His Women Characters
MA Univ of Pittsburgh 1950
5029 DIMINI Lucia Some Aspects of Marlowe's *Dr Faustus* MA Ca Foscari
(Italy) 1950
5030 DOLAN Elizabeth M Imagery in the Plays of Christopher Marlowe
MA Boston Coll 1949
5031 DOWNN Jim M Objective Irony in *The Jew of Malta* MA Texas Technological
Univ 1966
5032 EMERY Emogene The Fame of Christopher Marlowe MA Univ of Oklahoma
1938
5033 ENGLISH J P *Tamburlaine the Great*: Triumph of the Will MA Rice 1967
5034 EWTON Gene S *Doctor Faustus* and Elizabethan Popular Theology
MA Rice 1961
5035 FORD H L A Comparison of Christopher Marlowe's *Edward II* and
William Shakespeare's *Richard II* MA North Texas St Univ 1960
5036 FRANCIS William A Plot-Structure in Marlowe's Plays MA Univ of Texas
at Austin 1922 178 p
5037 GIANNAKOPOULOS Judith Tamberlane: A Study of Marlowe's Gods

MA Toronto (Canada) 1967
5038 GLYNN F T A Comparative Study of Renaissance and Modern Thought as
      Expressed in Marlowe's *Faustus* and Goethe's *Faust* MA Boston Coll
      1939
5039 GRANT M Marlowe's Conception of Tragedy BA Univ of British Columbia
      (Canada) 1929
5040 HALPERT Juliette Ambition in Marlowe's Characters: A Reflection
      of the Elizabethan Spirit MA Univ of Arizona 1934
5041 HALSEY Joan "Ah, Mephistophles": A Study of Christopher Marlowe
      and the Faustian Spirit MA Univ of California at Riverside 1963
5042 HAMILTON Aleen C A Critical Edition of Marlowe's *Doctor Faustus*
      MA Southern Methodist Univ 1917
5043 HARDISON Osborne B Jr Marlowe's Treatment of Death in *Tamburlaine*
      and *Edward II* MA Univ of North Carolina at Chapel Hill 1950 131 p
5044 HARRIS Margie The Nature of Man in Marlowe's *Tamburlaine* MA Temple
      Univ 1966 84 p
5045 HARTMAN Mary E Marlowe Prefers "s": His Use of the "th" and the
      "s" Endings of the Third Person Singular of the Present Tense
      MA Baylor Univ 1961 24 p
5046 HAWLEY Mary B A Study of the Influence of Christopher Marlowe's
      Dramatic Works upon Those of William Shakespeare MA Syracuse Univ
      1950 179 p
5047 HAYNES Mary J A Study of the Structural Quality of Marlowe's
      Edward II MA Univ of North Carolina at Chapel Hill 1949 103 p
5048 HECHT Francis T The Damnation of Dr Faustus MA St Louis Univ 1943
      140 p
5049 HEINY Lloyd Figures of Repetition in Marlowe's Work MA Western St
      Coll of Colorado 1937 157 p
5050 HELLAL Farida Ambition in Marlowe's Drama MA Univ of Houston 1968
      151 p
5051 HERMANN Robert J Love of Pleasure as Cause of Faustus' Pain of Loss
      MA St Louis Univ 1966 107 p
5052 HEWITT Anna M The Pathos in Marlowe's *Edward II* MA Univ of Idaho 1966
5053 HILL John D An Investigation of the Contradition between Marlowe's
      Life and Marlowe's Work MA West Texas St Univ 1960 55 p
5054 HILMO Maidie The Tragic Elements in *Doctor Faustus* BA Univ of
      British Columbia (Canada) 1965
5055 HINKLEY Agnes T Myth in Marlowe's Dramas MA Univ of New Mexico 1958
5056 HOAR Linda M The Irony of Love: Christopher Marlowe's *Hero and
      Leander* MA Pacific Univ 1968
5057 HORN Frederick D *The Tragical History of Doctor Faustus* and the
      Morality Convention MA Univ of Delaware 1964 75 p
5058 HOSKINS H W Jr Christopher Marlowe's "High Astounding Tearmes":
      A Study of His Skepticism MA Columbia 1950
5059 JONES Richard P Acedia: The Major Sin of Doctor Faustus MA Univ
      of Massachusetts 1969 37 p
5060 KAMMER Michael P Marlowe's *Faustus*: A Script for Production
      MA St Louis Univ 1942 236 p
5061 KEIGHTLEY David N The Conjurer Laureate: The Artistic Significance
      of Marlowe's Renaissance Position BA Amherst 1953
5062 KENNEDY Yvonne E Studies in Marlowe MA Baylor Univ 1948 99 p
5063 LAMBERT Sallie C Christopher Marlowe: Dramatic Innovator M Ed Hen-
      derson St Coll nd
5064 LEVINE Robert Death and the Plays of Christopher Marlowe MA Columbia
      1958 79 p
5065 LINNEY Donabel C Christopher Marlowe's Uses of History in *The Jew of
      Malta* MA Univ of Oklahoma 1962
5066 MASINTON Charles G Apollo's Laurel Bough: Essays on the Theme of
      Damnation in Christopher Marlowe MA Univ of Oklahoma 1966 249 p
5067 MAWDSLEY Mary D The Influence of Marlowe on Shakespeare MA Univ of

British Columbia (Canada) nd
5068 MERDLER Tessa B Conflict and Coexistence: A Study of Marlowe's Use
     of Rhetoric at Points of Emotional Tension MA Toronto (Canada) 1964
5069 MONTGOMERY Robert M A Study of Setting in Christopher Marlowe's
     Plays MA Univ of Pittsburgh 1931
5070 MOORE Minnie L The Development of Blank Verse from Surrey to Marlowe
     MA Univ of Oklahoma 1933
5071 NOVAK Robert L Levels of Meaning in Marlowe's Plays MA Univ of
     Oklahoma 1958
5072 ONAFEKO Cynthia O A Comparative Study of Christopher Marlowe's
     Doctor Faustus and Robert Greene's *Friar Bacon* and *Friar Bungay*
     MA Howard Univ 1968 88 p
5073 O'RILEY Margaret Interests of the Renaissance Reflected in the
     Character Doctor Faustus MA Oklahoma St Univ 1937 43 p
5074 OWENS David C Women in Christopher Marlowe's Tamburlaine Plays
     MA North Texas St Univ 1965
5075 PECK Esther M Individualism as Reflected in Marlowe's Life and
     Works MA Oklahoma St Univ 1939 35 p
5076 PETERSON Edith H Cleopolis and Persepolis: A Comparison of Marlowe
     and Spenser MA Univ of New Mexico 1952
5077 PEZZINI Carla Christopher Marlowe: *The Tragedy of the Rich Jew of
     Malta* MA Ca Foscari (Italy) 1959
5078 POLONI Maria Christopher Marlowe: *The Tragedy of Dido Queen of
     Carthage* MA Ca Foscari (Italy) 1959
5079 REED Marian V The Humoral Psychology of Christopher Marlowe's
     Characters MA West Virginia Univ 1964 115 p
5080 RICKS Bob An Interpretation of the Mythological References in
     Marlowe's *Doctor Faustus* MA West Texas St Univ 1962 83 p
5081 ROBNETT Arlington R Marlowe's *Faustus* and Its Sources MA Univ of
     Oregon 1939
5082 RUNDLE Urvin Innovations in the Vocabulary of Christopher Marlowe:
     A Dictionary of New Words, Word Meanings, Forms and Functions
     MA Univ of New Mexico 1938
5083 SAMSEY Patricia C The Theme of the Evil in Man's Nature in the Plays
     of Christopher Marlowe MA Oklahoma St Univ 1967 123 p
5084 SARTIN Edith L Seneca's Influence upon Marlowe's *Jew of Malta*
     MA Univ of Arizona 1940
5085 SCHRAMM Harold B Marlowe's Artistry in *Dido, Queen of Carthage*
     MA Univ of Delaware 1967 92 p
5086 SCHRATZ Brice W A Comparison of the Stage Techniques in Parts I and
     II of *Tamburlaine* MA St Louis Univ 1947 141 p
5087 SCULLY Vincent A Jr Marlowe's Dramatic Poetry, *Tamburlaine* and
     Faustus MA Univ of Pittsburgh 1957
5088 SHAPIRO Michael Marlowe's Use of Sixteenth Century Literary and
     Dramatic Conventions in *Edward II* MA Columbia 1960 88 p
5089 SLOAN Timothy J The Comic Vision of the Dramatic Canon of
     Christopher Marlowe MA Univ of Massachusetts 1967
5090 SMITH Gertrude Y Marlowe's Use of Holinshed in *Edward II* MA Univ
     of Texas at Austin 1931
5091 SORENSON Anita F The Development of Christopher Marlowe's Dramatic
     Power MA Univ of Oregon 1942
5092 STEELE Oliver L The Moral Character of the Plays of Christopher
     Marlowe MS Auburn Univ 1951 149 p
5093 STORTI Amedeo Religion and Atheism in Marlowe MA Ca Foscari
     (Italy) 1947
5094 TALCOTT James H A Study of Christopher Marlowe's Four Dramas
     BA Amherst 1956
5095 TERRY William M Christopher Marlowe's *Tragical History of
     Doctor Faustus* BA Univ of Delaware 1942 36 p
5096 TUNG Mason The Theme of Marlowe's Tragedies: Thirst for Power

MA Baylor Univ 1957   144 p
5097 URBAN William H Machiavelli: The Machiavellian Legend and Marlowe
      MA Southern Illinois Univ at Carbondale 1959   112 p
5098 WELLWARTH George E The Development of Marlowe's Stagecraft; with
      Special Reference to *Dr Faustus* MA Columbia 1954   122 p
5099 WILLIAMS A L Christopher Marlowe and the Raleigh Circle MA Univ
      of North Carolina at Chapel Hill 1930
5100 WRIGHT Norman E Marlowe's Invitation to Death MA Colorado St Coll
      1966
See also 1353, 1355, 4913, 4922, 5713, 6383, 6492, 6537, 6731, 6855, 7114

JOHN MARSTON

5101 BERLAND Ellen D The Function of Irony in Three Plays by John Marston:
      Antonio and Mellida, Antonio's Revenge and *The Malcontent*
      MA Columbia 1962   69 p
5102 HERRON Helen An Examination of the Relation between Jaques of
      Shakespeare and Malevole of Marston MA Tulane Univ 1913
5103 JACOBS Alfred V "The Trembling Ground": An Examination of Malcon-
      tent Elements in the Dramatic Works of John Marston MA Columbia
      1959   82 p
5104 KAPLAN Joel H The Satyre's Dilemma: Role and Identity in the
      Comedies of John Marston MA Toronto (Canada) 1965
5105 MIDDLETON Ronald N The Satire of John Marston as Critical Literature
      BA Amherst 1960
5106 MOORE Josephine K Low Humor in Selected Comedies of John Marston
      MA Univ of Southwestern Louisiana 1966   67 p
5107 PEGG Barry M Identity, Disguise and Satire in Three Comedies of
      John Marston MA Univ of British Columbia (Canada) 1969   150 p
5108 RAVAGGI Maria T John Marston: *The Malcontent* MA Ca Foscari (Italy)
      1960
5109 SNYDER Merrill S The Drama of John Marston: A Study in Polarity
      MA Stanford Univ 1965
See also 4325, 8657

ANDREW MARVELL

5110 BERRY George M Jr The Pastoral Poetry of Andrew Marvell MA Univ
      of Maryland at College Park 1963   65 p
5111 BUCKER Henrietta H A Study of Religious Imagery in Andrew Marvell's
      Poetry MA Oklahoma St Univ 1963   79 p
5112 COLEMAN Peter E Public Man, Private Poet: The Poetry of
      Andrew Marvell MA Univ of British Columbia (Canada) 1964
5113 CUNDARI Vincentine E Andrew Marvell's Definition of Love MA Columbia
      1951
5114 ELLIS Wayne P Structure in *On Appleton House*: Marvell and the
      Critics MA Columbia 1966   118 p
5115 FULLMER Paul P Andrew Marvell and Four Modern Poets: A Comparative
      Study MA Univ of Pittsburgh 1954
5116 GRIECO Kay Marvell's Pastorals: A Pastoral Approach MA Fresno
      St Coll 1970   48 p
5117 HARRISON John L The Influence of Rhetoric in Shorter English Poems
      of the First Half of the Seventeenth Century M Litt Cambridge
      Univ (England) 1955
5118 HODGE Melanie A Andrew Marvell and His Critics MA Univ of Wyoming
      1965
5119 HOLLAND Richard D Andrew Marvell: His Critical Reputation as a
      Lyric Poet, 1681 to the Present MA Columbia 1959   55 p
5120 JENKINS Joan H The Place of Andrew Marvell in Seventeenth Century
      Poetry MA Texas Christian Univ 1956   127 p

5121 KENT Carolyn C Nature as Image and Idea in the Lyric Poetry of
       Vaughan and Marvell MA Columbia 1962 189 p
5122 KUNZ Don R Andrew Marvell's *Upon Appleton House, to My Lord Fairfax*
       MA Univ of Texas at Austin 1965 129 p
5123 LIMA Joseph Imagery in the Lyric Poetry of Andrew Marvell MA George
       Washington Univ 1951 110 p
5124 MITCHELL Barbara H Poetry of Judgment: The Devotional Poetry of
       Andrew Marvell MA Hunter Coll 1967
5125 NEUTHALER Paul D Andrew Marvell's Cromwell Poems MA Columbia 1965
       66 p
5126 NORFORD Don P The Ideal of Humility in the Poems of Andrew Marvell
       MA Columbia 1962 102 p
5127 PAULSON Allan R The Forward Youth that Would Appear: A Study of
       Andrew Marvell BA Amherst 1962
5128 PIAZZA Maria L Andrew Marvell MA Ca Foscari (Italy) 1950
5129 PIEPHO Edward L The Principle of Concordia Discors and Andrew Marvell'
       "The First Anniversary of the Government Under Oliver Cromwell"
       MA Columbia 1966 74 p
5130 POLE Elizabeth H Rhetorical Patterns in the Poetry of Andrew Marvell
       MA Univ of Richmond 1966 62 p
5131 PONSFORD Marion E "Various Lights" in the Lyrics of Andrew Marvell
       MA Columbia 1955 121 p
5132 RICE M The Sincerity of Andrew Marvell BA Univ of British Columbia
       (Canada) 1938
5133 ROWE Wallace H III The Interior Argumentation in the Poetry of
       Andrew Marvell MA Trinity Coll 1965
5134 SESSIONS William A Themes of Contemplation and Action in Six Poems
       of Andrew Marvell MA Columbia 1953 123 p
5135 SHIELDS Virginia M A Study of the Garden and Landscape Imagery of
       Andrew Marvell MA St John's Univ 1965
5136 SIEGEL June W A Reading of Andrew Marvell's *Upon Appleton House*
       MA Columbia 1963 79 p
5137 TAYLER Edward W The Garden of the Mind: A Study of Some of
       Andrew Marvell's Poems BA Amherst 1954
5138 WARD Phillip A The Poetic Technique of Andrew Marvell MA Univ of
       Oklahoma 1957
5139 WEIMAN Evelyn A Marvell's *Garlands of Repose* MA Columbia 1963 114 p
5140 ZASADA Arthur S Primitivism: A Criticism of Society in the Works
       of Marvell and Cowley MA Columbia 1951
See also 3943, 3969, 4525, 5443, 5562, 5572, 6731

                            JOHN MASEFIELD

5141 CONDON Marguerite A Study of the Treatment of the Sea in Masefield's
       Poetry MA Boston Univ 1932
5142 DRIMMER Frederick The Poems of John Masefield, 1902-1912 MA Columbia
       1941
5143 GORDON Isabel John Masefield: Poet and Dramatist MA Univ of
       Tennessee 1920
5144 HEINDEL Linda H Beauty's Minstrel: A Study of the Poetry of
       John Masefield MA Univ of Delaware 1963 118 p
5145 HILL Hilda A Convention and Revolt in the Poetry of John Masefield
       MA Howard Univ 1937 28 p
5146 MARTINE Leona H The More Distinctive Sea Poetry of John Masefield
       MA St Mary's at San Antonio 1943 81 p
5147 MOSELEY Virginia D The Aesthetics of John Masefield MA Univ of
       Oklahoma 1948
5148 PECKHAM Dorothy R Masefield as a Dramatist with Special Emphasis
       on the Shakespearean Influence MA Univ of Texas at Austin 1933
5149 RISPOLI Trusy The Sea in the Poetry of John Masefield MA Ca Foscari

(Italy) 1950
5150 ROSSINI Margherita   John Masefield   MA Ca Foscari (Italy) 1933
5151 SAMPLE Everett J   John Masefield's Adherence to His Poetic Creed
      MS Kansas St Coll at Pittsburg 1936
5152 SHELDRICK Helen M   The Narrative Technique of John Masefield's
      Longer Poems   MA Boston Univ 1930
5153 SMITH Edis A   The Art of John Masefield's Poetry   MA Univ of Texas
      at Austin 1933
5154 STINE Lula   The Art of Contemporary Narrative Poetry as Illustrated
      by Masefield's Dauber, Noyes' Drake and Robinson's Tristram
      MA Texas Technological Univ 1935   99 p
5155 SULLIVAN J J   The Realism of the Poetry of John Masefield   MA Boston
      Univ 1926
5156 WARREN Louise E   A Study of John Masefield as a Critic of Shakespeare's
      Plays   MA Univ of Texas at Austin 1937
See also 1639, 1651, 4967

                          PHILIP MASSINGER

5157 BADIELLO Loredana   Philip Massinger: *A New Way to Pay Old Debts*,
      Edited with Introduction and Notes   MA Ca Foscari (Italy) 1959
5158 EDEY Olivia B   Classical Mythology in Massinger   MA Rutgers St Univ
      1942   150 p
5159 KEBER Frida   Philip Massinger: *The Great Duke of Florence*
      MA Ca Foscari (Italy) 1957
5160 KRIENKE Marion D   The Moral Content in the Dramas of Philip Massinger
      MA Texas Agricultural and Mechanical Univ 1965   92 p
5161 MANNI Lauro   Philip Massinger: *The Fatal Dowry*   MA Ca Foscari (Italy)
      1965
5162 QUINLAN Genevieve A   Decadent Elements in the Romantic Comedies of
      Philip Massinger   MA Columbia 1933   128 p
5163 SANDERS Paul S   Middleton, Massinger and Ford: Their Relation to
      the Decline of Stuart Drama   MA Univ of Massachusetts 1965
5164 TUNNICLIFFE S   William Gifford, 1756-1826:   His Early Life, Literary
      Friendships and Editing of Massinger and other Jacobean Dramatists
      MA Univ of London (England) 1964
5165 WILSON Rodney E   Political Allusions in the Plays of Philip Massinger
      MA North Texas St Univ 1970
5166 WINTERGALEN Edward H   The Surprised Element Featured in Three
      Tragedies of Massinger   MA St Louis Univ 1932   114 p
See also 2447, 3202, 3211, 4011, 6848

                      WILLIAM SOMERSET MAUGHAM

5167 AVNER Shirley   W Somerset Maugham's Philosophy of Life as Found in
      His Plays   MA Marquette Univ 1949   46 p
5168 BAILEY Corinnea   Maugham the Misogynist   MA Univ of Texas at El Paso
      1966   115 p
5169 BAUDIN Maurice C   The South Sea Stories of W Somerset Maugham
      MA Columbia 1941
5170 BROWN Walter F   William Somerset Maugham: Novelist   MA Indiana Univ
      1940
5171 CAPRINI A M   William Somerset Maugham as a Novelist   MA Ca Foscari
      (Italy) 1942
5172 COMBS Martha L   The Language of the Cultural Chasm in Somerset Maugham's
      Of Human Bondage   MA Morehead St Univ 1968   115 p
5173 FLING John B   Three Recent Theories of the Novel: Maugham, Bennett
      and Wells   MA Columbia 1942
5174 GAFFNEY M J   The Narrative Technique of W S Maugham as Displayed in
      His Novels   MA Boston Univ 1939

5175 GIORDANO Liana William Somerset Maugham MA Ca Foscari (Italy) 1933
5176 GOLLADAY Maurice L Realism in W Somerset Maugham's Short Stories
       MA Univ of Pittsburgh 1959
5177 GREGORY Clara F The Enduring Qualities of the Short Stories of
       W Somerset Maugham MA Univ of Texas at Austin 1951 178 p
5178 HALE Ruthell William Somerset Maugham: An Analysis of *The Constant
       Wife* M Ed Henderson St Coll nd
5179 HAYWARD Alice L Characterization in the Chief Works of
       Somerset Maugham MA Washington Univ at St Louis 1946 152 p
5180 HELSEL Marjorie G William Somerset Maugham, Dramatist MA Indiana
       Univ 1945
5181 HENSON Betty J Arrogant Characters in the Short Stories of
       W Somerset Maugham MA Texas Agricultural and Mechanical Univ 1967
       60 p
5182 JAMES Albert W Jr Indirection in the Short Stories of W Somerset
       Maugham MA Univ of North Carolina at Chapel Hill 1958 68 p
5183 MURPHREE John D W Somerset Maugham as Writer and Critic of the Short
       Story MA Stetson Univ 1964
5184 POPOWSKI David J A Study of Naturalism and Existentialism in
       W Somerset Maugham's *Of Human Bondage*: Philip Carey's Journey
       to Freedom MA Mankato St Coll 1965 57 p
5185 PULLIAM Carole V A Critical Analysis of the Development of
       Philip Carey in *Of Human Bondage* MA Arkansas St Coll 1966
5186 SIMKIN Sarah William Somerset Maugham: Naturalist M Ed Temple
       Univ 1938 155 p
5187 SINGLETON Katherine L Restoration Comedy to Wilde and Maugham as
       and Introduction to the Study of Noel Coward's *Comedy of Manners*
       MA Univ of North Carolina at Chapel Hill 1957 75 p
5188 SPENCE Robert W S Maugham's *Of Human Bondage*: The Making of a
       Masterpiece MA Univ of Maryland at College Park 1948 45 p
5189 TINDALL Blossom M Satire in the Comedies of Hankin, Coward and
       Maugham MA Univ of North Carolina at Chapel Hill 1948 98 p
5190 VAN SCYOC Leo L An Evaluation and Interpretation of the Principal
       Characters in the Novels of W Somerset Maugham MS Ft Hays St Coll
       1950 118 p
5191 WILSON William A W Somerset Maugham's Re-Creation of Paul Gauguin
       as Charles Strickland MA Brigham Young Univ 1962 83 p
See also 2137, 3355, 3795

GEORGE MEREDITH

5192 ALLEN Stephen F George Meredith's *Modern Love* MA Wayne St Univ 1965
5193 BAILEY Dorothy D George Meredith and the Modern Temper MA Univ of
       Texas at Austin 1936
5194 BAKER Alice W A Critical Analysis of the Poetry of George Meredith
       MA Smith Coll 1913
5195 BAZZANA Angela Heroines and Female Characters in George Meredith's
       Novels MA Ca Foscari (Italy) 1936
5196 BECKLER Helen Woman in the Novels of George Meredith MA Univ of
       Texas at Austin 1916
5197 BRERETON Jane Meredith's Comic Practice in Three of His Novels
       MA Washington Univ at St Louis 1949
5198 COX Ruth C The Use of Aphorisms in Meredith's Novels MA Boston Univ
       1934
5199 DOWNING Bertha F George Meredith's Attitude toward Feminism
       MA Univ of Oklahoma 1929
5200 DUNCAN Mary E George Meredith's Ideas of Religion MA Univ of
       Louisville 1921
5201 FAY Lucy E The Chorus in the Novels of George Meredith MA Univ of
       Texas at Austin 1901

5202 FLOWER Juliet The Portrait of a Barbarian: George Meredith's
     Egoist MA Cornell Univ 1965
5203 FOORD Phillip E The Critical Reactions to the Comedy of Wit from
     Jeremy Collier to George Meredith: A Study in Taste MA Univ of
     Oregon 1935
5204 FOREMAN Frances B Meredith's "Love in the Valley" and *The Ordeal of
     Richard Feverel*: A Comparison MA Univ of Florida 1964
5205 FREUDENREICH Carol J Some Twentieth Century Concepts in
     George Meredith's Works MA Univ of Texas at Austin 1946 249 p
5206 GEIBEL James W George Meredith's *Modern Love*: A Critical Study
     MA West Virginia Univ 1963 99 p
5207 GODFREY Garland A George Meredith's Comic Spirit Directed Against
     Sentimentality as Illustrated in *Sandra Belloni* and Other of
     His Novels MA Oklahoma St Univ 1936
5208 GOLDBERG Amy R Meredith as Castigator of Folly: An Inquiry into
     the Development of His Moral Philosophy MA Syracuse Univ 1952
     124 p
5209 GOLDBERG Doris R The Struggle of the Sexes in George Meredith's
     Novels MA Univ of Toledo 1957
5210 HALL S G Meredith's Idea of Comedy and the Uses of the Comic
     Spirit MA Boston Univ 1924
5211 HEALD Effic C George Meredith's Debt to Henry Fielding MA Smith
     Coll 1932
5212 HERSETH Esther N Prototypes of Meredithian Characters MA Pacific
     Univ 1938 79 p
5213 HITCH Lawrence J Meredith's Concept of Natural Harmony
     MA Colorado St Univ 1966
5214 HODGES Thomas K A Survey of the Criticism of George Meredith's
     Novels MA Univ of Pittsburgh 1941
5215 HUTTANUS William D Philosophical Naturalism in the Poetry of
     Meredith and Swinburne MA Villanova Univ 1965
5216 INGRAHAM Elijah B The Poetry of George Meredith MA Univ of Texas
     at Austin 1912
5217 JOHNSTON Walter D Imagery in George Meredith's *The Egoist* MA Columbia
     1963 82 p
5218 KELLY Julia I Meredith: A Prose Browning MA St Louis Univ 1937 115 p
5219 KEYSER Elizabeth George Meredith's Egoists: The Search for a
     Larger Self MA Claremont Graduate School 1965
5220 KLEINMAN Peter D Nature and Society in Two Novels of George Meredith
     BA Amherst 1964
5221 LOMAX John A The Novels of George Meredith MA Univ of Texas at
     Austin 1906
5222 LONQUEST James L Modes of the Intellect and the Imagination in the
     Poetry of George Meredith MA Univ of Oklahoma 1961
5223 McGUIRE Stella V The Treatment of Nature in the Works of
     George Meredith and Thomas Hardy MA Univ of British Columbia
     (Canada) 1920
5224 MacKAY Katherine A Critical Study of the Women of George Meredith
     MA Univ of British Columbia (Canada) 1923
5225 McKAY Kenneth M The Relationship of Man and Nature: A Developing
     Theme in George Meredith's Poetry MA Manitoba (Canada) 1964
5226 McNEAL Frances S George Meredith: Of Marriage and Its Meaning
     BA Univ of Delaware 1956 182 p
5227 McNELLY Ruth J The Prototypes of George Meredith's Tragic Comedians
     MA Univ of Maryland at College Park 1956 89 p
5228 MATTHEWS Gladys S Studies in George Meredith's Longer Narrative
     Poems MA Univ of Texas at Austin 1929
5229 MAYER Frederick P Unity of Attitude in Meredith's Prose MA Univ
     of Pittsburgh 1924
5230 MONTALBERTI Gina Modern Thought in Meredith's Poems MA Ca Foscari

(Italy) 1947

5231 NELLIGAN Frances A Form and Content in the Poetry of George Meredith
     MA Univ of New Mexico 1935

5232 O'CONNOR P F Scientific Optimism of George Meredith MA Boston Coll
     1933

5233 OEMBER Marie S *The Egoist* and *The Portrait of a Lady* MA Univ of
     Delaware 1964 72 p

5234 PLUMMER T S Meredith's Exposition of Egoism BA Univ of British
     Columbia 1935

5235 REEVES Vistula E Tendencies toward Realism in Meredith's Novels
     MA Oklahoma St Univ 1945 54 p

5236 REYNOLDS Imogene E George Meredith's Women: The Comic Spirit in
     Their Creation with Comparisons from Congreve and Moliere
     MA Oklahoma St Univ 1935 104 p

5237 SCOTT Joyce S *Evan Harrington*: George Meredith's Use of Comedy as
     a Corrective to Sentimentality MA Univ of Richmond 1969 65 p

5238 SHIELDS John C George Meredith's Use of Zoroastrianism in Selected
     Novels and Poems MA Univ of Tennessee 1969 98 p

5239 STETSON Gladys Realism and Idealism in the Heroines of
     George Meredith MA Boston Univ 1927

5240 STEWART Gwendolyn O George Meredith's Time Continuum in *One of Our
     Conquerors* MA Columbia 1959 59 p

5241 STONE James S The Concept of Nature in the Poetry of Alfred Tennyson
     and George Meredith MA Univ of British Columbia (Canada) 1950

5242 WALKER Jacqueline L Metaphor and Method in Meredith's "Concentrated
     Presentment": A Study of Two Aspects of Metaphoric Structure in
     George Meredith's Novels MA Univ of Louisville 1964

5243 WILDER Emma C Four English Men of Letters in Meredith's Fiction
     MA Univ of Kentucky 1937

See also 2130, 3179, 7649

THOMAS MIDDLETON

5244 CANTOR Harold Thomas Middleton's Use of Irony in His Comedies of
     London Life MA Columbia 1951

5245 GABELNICK Faith The Tragicomedies of Thomas Middleton: An Identity
     of Opposites MA Univ of Massachusetts 1969 59 p

5246 GRISMAN Arnold E The Dramatic Development of Thomas Middleton
     MA Columbia 1942

5247 HOLMES David M The Structure and Theme of Thomas Middleton's
     A Fair Quarrel MA Windsor (Canada) 1964

5248 KENEL Helen M *Blurt Master Constable* or *The Spaniard's Night Walk*
     by Thomas Middleton, Edited with Notes MA George Washington Univ
     1940 113 p

5249 KLEIN Leonard S An Approach to Thomas Middleton through the Structure
     of His Plays MA Columbia 1966 87 p

5250 KIRKPATRICK Judith E The Moral Order of Thomas Middleton: Calvin-
     istic Influence in *Hengist, King of Kent, The Changeling* and
     Women Beware Women MA Univ of Delaware 1968 101 p

5251 LISTER Rotraud Calvinistic Elements in the Drama of Thomas Middleton
     MA Toronto (Canada) 1964

5252 MAGOWAN Claire C The Tragedies of Thomas Middleton MA Columbia 1965
     133 p

5253 MAY Zona E London Low Life as Seen in Middleton's Comedies MA Texas
     Technological Univ 1934 91 p

5254 MENEGAZZI Carla London Life in the Plays of Thomas Middleton
     MA Ca Foscari (Italy) 1950

5255 MILLER William An Edition of Thomas Middleton's *Widow* MA Rutgers
     St Univ 1939 191 p

5256 MOORE Catherine E Thomas Middleton's Prose Style in the Comedies

MA Univ of North Carolina at Chapel Hill 1954   182 p
5257 SHANKER Sidney Thomas Middleton: His Critics and His Problems
       MA Univ of North Carolina at Chapel Hill 1948   86 p
5258 STEFANCICH Giovanna *The Changeling* by Thomas Middleton and
       William Rowley MA Ca Foscari 1960
5259 TENER Robert Convention and Device in the Plays of Thomas Middleton
       MA Univ of British Columbia (Canada) 1956
5260 TIVNAN Joseph R Contrasting Conceptions of Womanhood in the Comedies
       of Thomas Middleton and Robert Greene MA Boston Univ 1935
5261 ZANON Maria G Thomas Middleton, the Writer MA Ca Foscari (Italy)
       1955
See also 2478, 5163

JOHN STUART MILL

5262 BIGGS Martha H Backgrounds of John Stuart Mill's Concepts of
       Liberty and Equality MA Baylor Univ 1968   150 p
5263 COOLEY Franklin D Saint Simon and John Stuart Mill MA Univ of
       Maryland at College Park 1933   457 p
5264 DRAPER Arthur G The Place of the Emotions in the Thought of
       John Stuart Mill MA Washington Univ at St Louis 1964   102 p
5265 JESSUP Bertram E The Transformation of Utilitarianism in
       John Stuart Mill Considered as an Expression of the Inner
       Victorian Spirit MA Univ of Oregon 1935
5266 LAZENBY Arthur L John Stuart Mill and the Subjection of Women
       MA Univ of British Columbia (Canada) 1968   212 p
5267 RIPPEL Susan J A Comparison: Arnold's *Culture and Anarchy* and
       Mill's *On Liberty* MA Columbia 1951
See also 1287, 3911, 4023, 5742, 5752, 7343

ALAN ALEXANDER MILNE

5268 BIRDWELL Lloyd W A Study of Six Plays by A A Milne MA Univ of
       Texas at Austin 1966   86 p
5269 COY Stephen C Children Versus Authority: A Study of the Children's
       Poems and Stories of Edward Lear and A A Milne BA Amherst 1953
5270 STARK Alfred Idealism in the Plays of A A Milne M Ed Temple Univ
       1932   121 p
5271 WILBERG Mary M A A Milne: An Apology MA Illinois St Univ 1964

JOHN MILTON

5272 ABBOTT Jody F Milton's Proverb Lore MA Baylor Univ 1953   128 p
5273 ACKERT Martha J Images of Christ in Milton's *Lycidas* MA Texas
       Christian Univ 1964   123 p
5274 ADAMS Albert C Milton's Justification of the Ways to God to Men in
       Paradise Lost MA Baylor Univ 1957   81 p
5275 ADAMS Dorris E Suggestions for the Teaching of Milton's Poems in
       High School MS Kansas St Coll at Pittsburg 1935
5276 ADAMS Elizabeth E The Study of Milton, 1730-1740 MA Univ of Texas
       at Austin 1925
5277 ADKINS Jane M Milton's Doctrine of Music: Its Origins and Influence
       on His Early Poems MA Univ of North Carolina at Chapel Hill 1958
       92 p
5278 AIKEN Marianne S Milton's Attitude toward Women MA Univ of North
       Carolina at Greensboro 1965
5279 ALLINGHAM Philip Heroic Elements in *Paradise Lost* as Reflections
       of Classical Epic Precedents with Emphasis upon the Role of Satan
       BA Univ of British Columbia (Canada) 1968
5280 AMIS George T Milton's Eclectic Muse: Structure and the Control

of Incongruity in *Lycidas* BA Amherst 1959
5281 ANAND Shahla The Liturgical Element in Three Religious Plays:
     Everyman, Samson Agonistes and *Murder in the Cathedral* MA Columbia
     1959 99 p
5282 ANONBY John A Milton's View of Human Destiny MA Univ of British
     Columbia (Canada) 1965
5283 ARGENT Russell H The Development of Milton's Concept of Religious
     Liberty Related to the Background of the Times MA George Wash-
     ington Univ 1959 76 p
5284 BAILEY Jean M The Battle Strategy of Milton's *Paradise Lost*
     MA Marshall Univ 1965
5285 BAKER John R A Study of Satan and the Politics of Hell in *Paradise
     Lost* MA Rice 1954
5286 BAKER Ruth O Milton's Indebtedness to Vergil in *Paradise Lost*
     MA Tulane Univ 1927
5287 BARNETT Frank W The Language of Milton's *Comus* MA Texas Agricultural
     and Mechanical Univ 1965 120 p
5288 BARTHOLOMEW Judith H A Comparison of Milton's *Paradise Lost* and
     Regained with Dante's *Divine Comedy* MA Boston Univ 1931
5289 BASEHEART Katherine A A Comparative Study of the *Paradise Lost* of
     Milton and that of Alcimus Ecdicius Avitus MA St Louis Univ 1933
     82 p
5290 BELL I F The Effect of the Christian Ideal on the Epic Elements of
     Paradise Lost BA Univ of British Columbia (Canada) 1951
5291 BENTLEY Burton A A Study of Milton's Satan MA Toronto (Canada) 1964
5292 BESSE LaVon Milton's *Paradise Lost* as a Compendium of the Learning
     of Its Time MS Kansas St Coll at Pittsburg 1946
5293 BESSENT Benjamin R The Development of Milton's Conception of the
     Godhead MA Hardin-Simmons Univ 1958
5294 BIRGE Verba L Milton's Attitude of Supremacy as Revealed in His Works
     M Ed Henderson St Coll nd
5295 BISHOP Nita N Studies in *Samson Agonistes*: A Synthesis MA Univ of
     Louisville 1959
5296 BITTING M E Contempt of the World in the Poetry of John Milton:
     A Study in Milton's Changing Personal and Artistic Emphases
     MA Univ of North Carolina at Chapel Hill 1937
5297 BLYTHE David E A Comparative Study of *The State of Innocence* and
     Paradise Lost MA Univ of Richmond 1966 84 p
5298 BOHANNON June A Christ and the Knowledge of Evil: An Analysis of
     Milton's *Paradise Regained* MA Columbia 1960 51 p
5299 BORDELON Roma B The Use of Verbal Repetition as a Structural Device
     in the Poetry of Milton MA Louisiana St Univ 1939
5300 BORLAND D Bruce The Principal Supernatural Characters of *Paradise
     Lost* and Their Antecedents in Classical Epics BA Univ of
     British Columbia (Canada) 1968
5301 BOWDEN William W A Comparative Study of Hamartiology in Milton's
     Paradise Lost and in the Old Testament: A Focus on the Origin
     and Early Disposition of Sin MA Univ of Tulsa 1965 51 p
5302 BOYD Helen H Early Formative Influences on the Development of
     Milton's Thought MA Univ of Texas at Austin 1938 134 p
5303 BRADEN Robert C The Idea of Fare and Dramatic Structure in Milton's
     Paradise Lost and *Samson Agonistes* MA Texas Technological Univ
     1967 60 p
5304 BRENNER Otto L Art and Religion in Milton's Critical Theory
     MA Univ of Richmond 1952 136 p
5305 BROWN Allan The Prosody of Blake's *Milton* BA Univ of British
     Columbia (Canada) 1969
5306 BROWN Mildred G Folklore in Milton's Poetry, with Special Reference
     to the Pre-Civil War Poems MA Saskatchewan (Canada) 1964
5307 BROWN Stanley D Studies in the Criticism of Milton Since 1823:

Milton and the Evangelical Tradition MA Univ of Maryland at
College Park 1935 138 p
5308 BUEHRER Bernardine Milton's Conception of Man MA Univ of Maine 1943
106 p
5309 BURNS J S Milton Criticism and the Biography MA Rice 1953
5310 BURSON Luree The Influence of Milton on Wordsworth's Poetry
MA North Texas St Univ 1950
5311 BUTTERFIELD Stephen Milton: Cathartic Elements in *Paradise Lost*
MA Tufts Univ 1965
5312 CAMPBELL Maurine P The Qualities of Ancient Greek Tragedy as Reflected
in Milton's *Samson Agonistes* M Ed Henderson St Coll nd
5313 CANNON Sadie C Milton's Knowledge of Music as Reflected in His Works
MA Southern Methodist Univ 1930
5314 CASWELL Wynema B Synod of Gods: The Infernal Council in Book II
of Milton's *Paradise Lost* MA Univ of Oklahoma 1959
5315 CHURCHMAN Anthony C *Paradise Lost, The Rape of the Lock* and *The
Dunciad*: A Study of Pope's Use of Miltonic Allusion MA Western
(Canada) 1965
5316 COHEN Steven L John Milton's Blindness: A Psychological Theory
MA Bowling Green Univ 1970
5317 COHEN William H Romantic Criticism of Milton MA Univ of Florida 1954
5318 COLEMAN Ann Milton's Concept of Freedom in *Paradise Lost* BA Univ of
British Columbia (Canada) 1958
5319 COLEMAN C A The Political Life and Prose Writings of John Milton
MA Boston Univ 1924
5320 COLLINS Dan S The Influence of Formal Rhetoric on the Treatment of
Nature in the Early English Poems of John Milton MA Univ of
North Carolina at Chapel Hill 1951 107 p
5321 COLLINS Joseph J Milton and Socinianism MA Univ of Richmond 1961
91 p
5322 COLLMER Linnie M Folklore in *Paradise Lost* MA Baylor Univ 1951 137 p
5323 COOK Sr Mary J The *Comus* Controversy MA Boston Coll 1957
5324 COOPER Miriam Rebellious Notes in Milton MA Baylor Univ 1947 138 p
5325 CORLEY Francis J A Study of Three Phases of the Personality of
John Milton with Special Reference to the Poetical Works
MA St Louis Univ 1938 105 p
5326 COX Paul H The Rhetoric of Recovery: Moral Didacticism in Milton's
Major Poetry MA Univ of Oklahoma 1970
5327 CROCKETT Edward P An Evaluation of the Autobiographical Interpretation of *Samson Agonistes* MA Univ of Richmond 1966 91 p
5328 CROSMAN Robert T "No Single Sense": A Study of *Paradise Regained*
MA Columbia 1965 81 p
5329 CROW Floyd G The Women in Milton's Life and Their Influence upon
His Delineation of Eve and Delila in *Paradise Lost* and in *Samson
Agonistes* MA Univ of Arizona pre-1933
5330 CUNNINGHAM Mary L The Combination of Pagan and Christian Doctrines
in the Poetry of John Milton MA Baylor Univ 1931 31 p
5331 CURRAN Catherine B Blake's Illustrations of Milton's Works
MA Boston Coll 1965
5332 DANIEL Berthe A The Dramatic Scheme of *Paradise Lost* MA Washington
Univ at St Louis 1924 109 p
5333 DARGEL Gerhard W *Samson Agonistes*: A New Critical Approach MA Univ
of Louisville 1967 117 p
5334 DAWSON Flora M Milton and Chateaubriand MA Tulane Univ 1918
5335 DEARBORN Bernice W A Study of Milton's Vocabulary MA Smith Coll 1907
5336 DeLONG C D A Comparison of the Influence of Virgil on Milton and
Spenser MA Univ of North Carolina at Chapel Hill 1936
5337 DENNER Karl A Translation of Milton's *Samson Agonistes* by
Dr C E Kreipe, with an Introduction and Notes MA Univ of Kentucky
1949 115 p

5338 DENT Robert W Higher and Lower Wisdom in Milton's Program of
      Education MA Univ of Oregon 1942
5339 DEVITT Barbara M *Samson Agonistes*: The Tragedy Without the Theology
      MA Colorado St Coll 1969
5340 DONOVAN James The Dogmatic Theology of John Milton MS Kansas St
      Coll at Pittsburg 1957
5341 DORAN Rev William J The Meaning of the "Plane and Open" Sense of
      Scripture in Milton's Polemical Prose MA Boston Coll 1965
5342 DOUGLAS Amelia J Structure and Idea in *Paradise Lost* and *Paradise
      Regained* MA Texas Christian Univ 1953 84 p
5343 DuBOSE Francis M The Relationship of Milton's Expansion of Scrip-
      ture to the Moral Significance of Christ's Temptation in *Paradise
      Regained* MA Univ of Houston 1957 63 p
5344 DUMARESQ William W The Epic and Tragedy of *Paradise Lost* MA Univ
      of British Columbia (Canada) 1961 164 p
5345 DUNDAS J The Sublime in *Paradise Lost* BA Univ of British Columbia
      (Canada) 1948
5346 DUNHAM Joe D Dramatic Conventions and Techniques in *Paradise Lost*
      MA Texas Arts and Industries Univ 1951
5347 DUNKLEBERG Ruth E Reason and Passion in *Paradise Lost* MA Baylor
      Univ 1953 107 p
5348 DUNN Robert The Hallow'd Fire: Mythical Consciousness in *Paradise
      Lost* MA Univ of British Columbia (Canada) 1967 118 p
5349 DURAYNI Mohamed R Milton's Knowledge of the Middle East MA Univ
      of Kentucky 1960 104 p
5350 DYSON Emily M The Scholarship on Milton as a Statesman MA Howard
      Univ 1938 64 p
5351 EDMUNDS Peter A Influences of Independency in Milton's Early Life
      MA Univ of Richmond 1964 103 p
5352 ELGIN Ruth S John Milton's Political Activities MA George Wash-
      ington Univ 1933 56 p
5353 ELLEGOOD Donald R *Samson Agonistes*: A Critical Interpretation
      MA Univ of Oklahoma 1950
5354 ELLEN Dorothy H Samson as a Classical Tragic Hero MA East Carolina
      Univ 1969
5355 ETHERTON Linda L Tragedy and the Sense of Balance in *Samson Agonistes*
      MA Univ of Colorado 1965
5356 EVANS Robert O A Study of Milton's Theory and Practice of Elision
      MA Univ of Florida nd
5357 FAGG Robert J Jr Milton and the Doctrine of the Synod of Dort
      Arminianism in Christian Doctrine and *Paradise Lost* MA Univ of
      Richmond 1964 65 p
5358 FALLON Robert T Captain or Colonel or Knight in Arms: Milton's
      Military Imagery; Its Growth and Function in His Art MA Columbia
      1962 83 p
5359 FARMER Janet R The Theme of Temperance in Selected Writings of
      John Milton MA Texas Technological Univ 1967 48 p
5360 FAY Mother Marieteresita R *Paradise Lost* and *The City of God*
      MA Hunter Coll 1964
5361 FEDORUK Rosalie B The Temptation and *Paradise Regained*: A Typo-
      logical Interpretation of Milton's Epic Poem MA Columbia 1967 127 p
5362 FELLOWES Frederick G The Development of Milton's Love for Liberty
      MA Univ of Arizona 1940
5363 FERRY Annie M Milton's Thought on Divorce MA Univ of Louisville 1941
5364 FIAWOO Gershon B *Lycidas*: The Turning Point of the Philosophical
      Mind of Milton MA North Carolina Coll 1965
5365 FINDLEY Margaret K Women in Milton's Writings and His Life MA Univ
      of Pittsburgh 1931
5366 FORD Jane F Satan as the Exemplar of Evil in *Paradise Lost* MA Univ
      of Pittsburgh 1934

5367 FOS Br John L Milton and Knowledge: A Survey of the Problem
      MA Univ of Texas at Austin 1955
5368 FOY Alice C Human Nature in Milton's *Paradise Lost* MA Univ of
      Pittsburgh 1939
5369 FLINKER Norman Milton's Use of the Psalms in *Paradise Lost*
      MA Columbia 1966   81 p
5370 FREEMAN A T Milton's Educational Theory MA Boston Univ 1923
5371 GERARD Bernice M Milton's Orthodoxy and Its Relation to the Form
      of *Paradise Lost* MA Univ of British Columbia (Canada) 1967
5372 GETTYS Pauline R A Study of Milton's Religious Views MA West Texas
      St Univ 1953   98 p
5373 GIBSON Sharan S Three Baroque Figures of Speech in Milton's Poetry
      MA Univ of Houston 1968   72 p
5374 GILLIS Lizzie M The Idea of Redemption in Milton's Poetry MA Texas
      Technological Univ 1954
5375 GIUGNI Guido Milton's Prose MA Ca Foscari (Italy) 1946
5376 GLASGOW Harvey B Patterns and Problems in *Paradise Lost* MA Texas
      Christian Univ 1968   104 p
5377 GLAUBERMAN Lois M Milton's *Samson Agonistes* and the Book of Job:
      A Study in Influence MA Columbia 1958   155 p
5378 GLYNN May G Was Milton a Misogynist? MA Tulane Univ 1924
5379 GOOLRICK William K Jr Milton and the Sharp and Double Edge of
      Liberty MA Columbia 1950
5380 GOSSMAN Ann M Man Plac't in a Paradise: A Comparative Study of
      Milton, St Ambrose and Hugh of St Victor MA Rice 1954
5381 GRAY Adina L The Mythological Background of Milton's *Lycidas*
      MA Columbia 1952   56 p
5382 GRAY James A The Role of Eve in *Paradise Lost* MA Rice 1962
5383 GREGSON John W *Samson Agonistes* Prefigures the Christ MA Stephen
      F Austin St Coll 1965
5384 GRIFFIN George R The Influence of Milton's Classical Elegies with
      a Translation of *Epitaphium Damonis* MA Marquette Univ 1928
5385 GRIFFIN Leah B Satan the Adversary of *Paradise Lost* MA Univ of
      Oregon 1941
5386 GUAZZO Dominic B The Theology of John Milton in *Paradise Lost*
      MA Boston Univ 1947
5387 GUTCHEON Jeffrey D *Samson Agonistes*: A Personal Essay BA Amherst
      1962
5388 HAMROCK Teresa A *Paradise Regained* and the Christian Imagination
      MA Boston Coll 1965
5389 HANNA Ralph III "Moral Recovery" in the Poetry of John Milton
      BA Amherst 1963
5390 HARBESON Geraldine M Nature in the Poetry of Milton and Spenser
      MA Florida St Univ 1944
5391 HARRELL Karl P The Nature of the Grotesque in Milton's *Comus*
      MA Univ of North Carolina at Chapel Hill 1950   153 p
5392 HARTSHORNE Doris R Epic Interests in Milton's Poetry and Prose
      before 1645 MA Univ of Oregon 1940
5393 HAWKINS Miriam A The Biblical, Classical and Personal Elements in
      Samson Agonistes MA Boston Univ 1935
5394 HELVEY James The Ways of God in *Paradise Lost* MA Univ of North
      Carolina at Greensboro 1966
5395 HEMBY James B Jr Milton's Satan: Idea and Image MA Texas Christian
      Univ 1964   118 p
5396 HENRY Jeanne H Milton's Concept of Woman MA Alberta (Canada) 1966
5397 HENRY N H Milton's Latin Secretaryship MA Univ of North Carolina
      at Chapel Hill 1933
5398 HERRING Jonnie J Sources of Sin and Death in *Paradise Lost* MA Univ
      of Houston 1965   87 p
5399 HESS Gertrude E The Technique of Milton's Poems and Early Latin

Poems M Ed Temple Univ 1935 111 p
5400 HESSELBERG Arthur K Milton and Catholicism MA Univ of New Hampshire
      1947 86 p
5401 HILL Laura N The Theme of Self-Knowledge in John Milton's *Paradise
      Lost* MA Wichita St Univ 1966
5402 HILL Melvin A Study of the Writings of John Phillips (1631-1706)
      Which Pertain to His Relationship with John Milton; with a Dis-
      cussion of Phillips' Early Years with Milton MA Columbia 1951
5403 HINES M M Literary and Philosophical Aspects of the Theme of Good
      and Evil in Milton's Poetry MA Univ of North Carolina at Chapel
      Hill 1941
5404 HO Margaret Y Milton's Imagery in *Paradise Lost* MA Univ of Hawaii
      1937 82 p
5405 HOGAN Mary M John Milton and the Commonplace Tradition MA St Louis
      Univ 1959 110 p
5406 HOLDEN Mary E John Milton's Theories of Education MA Univ of Texas
      at Austin 1934
5407 HOLMAN Ruth *Paradise Lost* as a Poem of Consolation MA Texas Tech-
      nological Univ 1957 93 p
5408 HOWARD Donald R Obscurantism in Milton MA Rutgers St Univ 1952 138 p
5409 HOWARD W F Interpretations of *Paradise Lost* MA Univ of Texas at
      Austin 1937 172 p
5410 HURT James R *Lycidas*: Toward a Variorum Edition MA Univ of Kentucky
      1957
5411 ICE Billy E Milton's Revisions to *Lycidas* and *Comus* in the Manuscripts
      and the Editions MA Oklahoma St Univ 1952
5412 IRRGANG Kenneth E The Relation of Samson in John Milton's *Samson
      Agonistes* to the Concept of the Tragic Hero of Aristotle's *Poetics*
      MA Mankato St Coll 1960 98 p
5413 JENNE Edward A Problem in Milton (1914-1934) MA Marquette Univ 1934
5414 JENSEN Ada Milton's Use of Classic Material MA Univ of North Dakota
      1918 54 p
5415 JOHNSON Katherine John Milton: A Study of the Relation between His
      Life and His Poetry MA Washington Univ at St Louis 1928 113 p
5416 JOHNSTON Evelyn M Order and the Individual in *Samson Agonistes*
      BA Univ of British Columbia (Canada) 1965
5417 JOHNSTON Joyce W The Great Dilemma: Milton as Moralist or as Artist
      MA Pacific Univ 1969
5418 JOHNSTON Nettie Sense Perceptions in Milton's *Paradise Lost*
      MA Baylor Univ 1934 82 p
5419 JONES M D The Record of Milton's Disillusionment as Found in His
      Writings MA Univ of North Carolina at Chapel Hill 1935
5420 JONES Maebelle L A Critical Study of John Milton's *Comus* MA Univ
      of Oklahoma 1960
5421 JOSEPH Ruth E The Poet in *Paradise Lost*: An "Instance of Example"
      MA Hunter Coll 1968
5422 JUSTICE Stephen Milton's Concept of God MA North Texas St Univ 1962
5423 JUSTMAN Shulamith Milton's Promethean Serpent MA Brooklyn Coll 1965
5424 KAPLAN Myron M The Emblem in *Paradise Lost* MA Columbia 1965 261 p
5425 KENDALL Lyle H Milton and Drama MA Univ of Texas at Austin 1948 267 p
5426 KETCHAM Lucia Milton's Treatment of Nature in His Poetry MA Indiana
      Univ 1935
5427 KILLIAN Viola Milton on Divorce MA Baylor Univ 1954 161 p
5428 KITTREDGE Paul M Macaulay's Essay on Milton: A Literary, Historical
      and Political Evaluation MA Univ of Florida 1951
5429 KNOWLTON Marianne On Reading Milton: Virtue and the Fall of Man
      MA Tufts Univ 1965
5430 KOON George W John Milton's "Nativity Ode": An Analysis of Imagery
      and Tradition MA Auburn Univ 1966
5431 KUHLMANN Hermann J Milton's Indebtedness to the Bible in *Paradise*

Lost MA Univ of Toledo 1927
5432 KURZ Myrtis T Milton and Shelley: A Study on Similarities and
      Parallels MA Florida St Univ 1940
5433 KUTNY Ronald Four Aspects of Milton's *Samson Agonistes*: Imagery,
      Comedy, Autobiography and Tragedy MA Univ of New Mexico 1959
5434 LANDER William A Milton's Imagination: Auditory or Visual?
      MA Alberta (Canada) 1966
5435 LANGTON Lary B "Love Both the Way and Guide": A Study of the Two
      Loves in *Paradise Lost* MA Wichita St Univ 1966
5436 LANHAM Louise Hymnic Elements in Milton's Poetry MA Univ of North
      Carolina at Chapel Hill 1927
5437 LASKOWSKY Henry J On the Style of *Paradise Regained* MA Syracuse
      Univ 1962 59 p
5438 LEA Dorothy Studies in the Diction of Milton's *Paradise Regained*
      MA Univ of Texas at Austin 1941 107 p
5439 LEAKE Mavis M Studies in the Diction of Milton's English Dramatic
      Poems MA Univ of Texas at Austin 1936
5440 LeBLANC Sr Marie P The Mediation of the Son of God in Milton's
      Paradise Lost MA Boston Coll 1965
5441 Le COMTE Edward S The "Haemony" Passage in Milton's *Comus* (lines
      629-641): An Inquiry into Its Origins, Background and Meaning
      MA Columbia 1940
5442 LEE Herbert G The Justification Theme in Milton's Work with Special
      References to *Paradise Lost* MA Univ of North Carolina at Chapel
      Hill 1946 67 p
5443 LIPPINCOTT Henry R Milton and Marvell and Samuel Parker MA Univ
      of New Mexico 1965
5444 LOVICK Laurence D Magnanimity: Milton's Concept of Heroic Man
      MA Univ of British Columbia (Canada) 1944
5445 LYONS Kathryn M Milton's *Moscovia*: A Study of Its Background and
      Sources MA Columbia 1940
5446 McCALL L J Periodic Interpretations of Milton's *Paradise Lost*
      MA North Texas St Univ 1944
5447 McCAWLEY Dwight L *Samson Agonistes*: Critical Interpretations,
      1930-1955 MA Univ of Tennessee 1957 70 p
5448 McCONNELL R B Structure, Pattern and Resonance in *Paradise Lost*
      BA Univ of British Columbia (Canada) 1964
5449 McCURRY Ruth Milton's Ideas of Liberty MS Kansas St Coll at Pitts-
      burg 1941
5450 McDILL J M A Study of Milton's Synonyms for the Major Characters
      in *Paradise Lost*, with Special References to Sylvester's *Du Bartas'
      Divine Weeks*, Caedmon's *Genesis* and the Bible MA Univ of North
      Carolina at Chapel Hill 1934
5451 McGRATH Marie L Milton's Reputation in America up to 1800
      MA Columbia 1935
5452 McKIE G M Review of Milton's Satan MA Univ of North Carolina at
      Chapel Hill 1907
5453 McLEOD Frances R Milton's View of Women as Shown by His Life and
      His Writings MA Auburn Univ 1945
5454 McNEW Louis D Milton, Conti and Classical Mythology MA Washington
      St Univ at Pullman 1948
5455 McQUILKIN Dwight E A Study of Milton's *Comus* MA West Virginia Univ
      1906 148 p
5456 MAGEALSON Viola A A Study of the Syntax of Milton's *Areopagitica*
      MA Univ of Pittsburgh 1934
5457 MANHEIM L Michael *The State of Innocence and Fall of Man* and *Paradise
      Lost*: An Analysis of the Relationship of Dryden's Work to that
      of Milton MA Columbia 1951
5458 MANN Clara C The Book of Job and Milton's *Paradise Regained* and
      Samson Agonistes MA Columbia 1953 112 p

5459 MANN David D John Milton's Use of the Bible in His English Sonnets
        MA Oklahoma St Univ 1963 68 p
5460 MAROTTA Joseph The Conflict of Body and Soul: A Study of John Donne
        and John Milton MA Brooklyn Coll 1965
5461 MARTIN P T Milton's Theodicy in *Paradise Lost* BA Univ of British
        Columbia (Canada) 1963
5462 MAULDIN Lois L The Domestic Life of John Milton as Presented in
        Anne Manning's Fiction MA Univ of Maryland at College Park 1959
        150 p
5463 MAULDIN Thelma H The Use of the Bible in Milton's Major Poems
        MA Univ of Texas at Austin 1949 195 p
5464 MEGARGEL Donald The Sensuous Element of the Baroque as Revealed in
        the Poetry of John Milton and Richard Crashaw BA Rutgers St Univ
        1962 44 p
5465 MENDELSOHN Judith John Milton's Doctrine and Discipline of Divorce
        MA Long Island Univ 1968 93 p
5466 MERKLE Crete M The Imagery of *Paradise Lost* MA Univ of Arizona 1938
5467 MESCALL Francis P Jr Milton, Emerson and the Way of Unity
        MA Brooklyn Coll 1965
5468 MILLER Milton G Milton's Religious Attitude in *Samson Agonistes*
        MA Univ of Louisville 1948
5469 MILLER Patrick L *Paradise Regained* in the Eighteenth Century
        MA Univ of Kansas 1965
5470 MOBERG George *Paradise Lost*: Lost and Regained; an Examination of
        Recent Criticism of *Paradise Lost* MA Colorado St Coll 1959
5471 MOORE F Dean Some Reconsiderations of the Prosody of *Samson Agonistes*
        MA Univ of Oregon 1942
5472 MOORE Helen L Parallelism between Milton and Virgil MA Boston Univ
        1933
5473 MORO T Russell Milton's Fall BA Amherst 1953
5474 MORRIS Clara M Poets of Patriotism: Virgil, Milton and Lowell
        MA Boston Univ 1902
5475 MORRIS William E The Immediate Results of Milton's Divorce Pamphlets
        MA Univ of Delaware 1953 170 p
5476 MORTON Jerry D An Examination of the Musical References in the
        English Poetry of John Milton MA Univ of Tennessee 1965
5477 MOSER Willard C A Study of the Development of John Milton's Concept
        of Church-State Relationships MA Univ of Houston 1962 150 p
5478 MOXLEY Cornelius F John Milton and Roman Catholic Critics in England
        MA Univ of Maryland at College Park 1950 52 p
5479 MURPHY Cornelius P Milton's Models and the Problem of Structure
        in Book XI and XIII of *Paradise Lost* MA Boston Coll 1969
5480 MURPHY Rita A The Nature of Man in Milton's *Paradise Lost*
        MA Columbia 1951
5481 MYERS William J Baroque Elements in John Milton's *Paradise Lost*
        MA Rutgers St Univ 1939 105 p
5482 MYRICK Edwin M The Idea of Freedom and Dramatic Structure in
        Paradise Lost MA Texas Technological Univ 1966 77 p
5483 NELSON Margaret Unity in *Paradise Lost* BA Univ of British Columbia
        (Canada) 1963
5484 NELSON Margaret V The Resolution of Dualities in Milton's English
        Poetry MA Univ of British Columbia (Canada) 1966
5485 NESTOR Sarah R Critical Studies of Milton, The Ossianic Contro-
        versy and Dickens MA Univ of Utah 1966
5486 NEUFELDT V A Sin and Evil as Conceived by Milton and Wordsworth
        BA Univ of British Columbia (Canada) 1957
5487 NEWELL Samuel W *Paradise Regained*: A Historical and Critical Study
        MA Emory Univ 1942 124 p
5488 ORDWAY Julia K The Influence of Virgil upon the Minor Poems of
        Milton MA Boston Univ 1912

5489 O'REGAN Jane D The Influence of Music upon the Sounding Quality of
      Milton's Verse MA Boston Coll 1948
5490 O'ROURKE Thomas E Historical Significance of Milton's *Eikonoklastes*
      MA Univ of Iowa 1935
5491 PANTUSO Giovanna The Trinity in the "De Doctrina Christiana" of
      John Milton MA St Mary's at San Antonio 1948 132 p
5492 PATTERSON Charles W Milton, Dryden and the Epic MA Columbia 1960
      86 p
5493 PATTERSON Daniel A Critical Study of John Milton's "On the Morning
      of Christ's Nativity" MA Univ of New Mexico 1961
5494 PATTON Dora D Flowers in Milton's Poetry MA Univ of Texas at Austin
      1952 81 p
5495 PATTON Ella S Milton and Twentieth Century Criticism M Ed Temple
      Univ 1955 47 p
5496 PEDEMONTI Alessandra Milton as a Dramatic Poet MA Ca Foscari (Italy)
      1941
5497 PELLETIER Robert R Shelley and Milton MA Boston Coll 1957
5498 PENDERGAST John E Milton's Treatment of Nature MA Boston Coll 1951
5499 PEYTON Hall A Study in the Development of Milton's Theology
      MA Baylor Univ 1953 161 p
5500 PITTS Ella J Milton's Views on the Qualifications for Leadership
      MA Howard Univ 1944 56 p
5501 PLUMMER Ruby B A Theory: Milton's Explanation of God's Ways to
      Men MA Arkansas St Coll 1965
5502 POHL Mary E Mediatorship in Milton MA Siena Coll 1965
5503 PRINCE L McDonald Milton's Synthesis of Material in *Paradise Lost*
      MA Univ of North Carolina at Chapel Hill 1926
5504 PRINS Alice S The Temptation Theme in *Paradise Lost, Paradise
      Regained* and *Samson Agonistes* MA Fairleigh Dickinson Univ 1966
5505 PRITCHARD H C A Study of Repetition as an Architechtonic Device
      in *Paradise Lost* MA Univ of North Carolina at Chapel Hill 1942
5506 PRITCHETT Early P III John Milton and the New Critics MA West Texas
      St Univ 1966 73 p
5507 PURNELL Rosentene B John Milton and the Doctrine of Sympathy:
      Deontology and Ambiance MA Univ of Oklahoma 1967 280 p
5508 PUTZEL Rosamond A Re-Examination of the Place of the Holy Spirit
      in *Paradise Lost* MA Univ of North Carolina at Chapel Hill 1951
5509 QUIGLEY Edward A Milton's Concept of Hell MA Kansas St Univ 1965
5510 RAINWATER Vera B Renaissance Background of Milton's *Of Education*
      MA Indiana Univ 1945
5511 RAMOS Maximo D Milton's Use of Folklore in His English Poems
      MA Indiana Univ 1950
5512 RASEY Mary B Milton's Concept of Woman MA Bowling Green Univ 1969
5513 RAWLINGS Mary L Truth, Theme and Structure in Milton's *Paradise
      Lost* MA Texas Technological Univ 1965 81 p
5514 REITZEL Frank X *Comus* in the Light of Modern Interpretations
      MA Toronto (Canada) 1966
5515 REWIS Helen S The Conflict between Humanism and Puritanism:
      Milton and His Predecessors MA Emory Univ 1937 121 p
5516 REYNOLDS J S The Similes in Book I of *Paradise Lost* Compared with
      Those in Book I of the *Faerie Queene* MA Univ of North Carolina
      at Chapel Hill 1940
5517 RICKS Beatrice The Literary History of *Lycidas*: An Essay and a
      Critical Bibliography MA Univ of Oklahoma 1950
5518 RINER Roy S Jr Milton and Cambridge: A New Look at an Old Attitude
      MA Univ of Richmond 1968 88 p
5519 RIPPERDA Jean M *Paradise Lost* in *The Waste Land* MA Texas Christian
      Univ 1968 114 p
5520 ROBERTSON Charles H The Use of the Bible in Milton's *Paradise Lost*
      MA Texas Christian Univ 1919

5521 ROBERTSON Grace E The Critical Influence of Bridges' *Milton's Prosody* MA Univ of North Carolina at Chapel Hill 1959 67 p
5522 ROBINS Harry F The Cosmology of *Paradise Lost*: A Reconsideration MA Indiana Univ 1950
5523 ROCKETT Helen M Milton's Use of the Biblical Samson MA Univ of Oklahoma 1964
5524 ROSE Sr M Carmeline Dissociation of Sensibility in Milton MA Boston Coll 1969
5525 ROSE N V Milton's Nature Images: A Study of Their Sources, Their Uses and Their Characteristic Qualities MA Univ of North Carolina at Chapel Hill 1937
5526 ROSE Patricia A Essentials of Epic Poetry: A Comparative Study of the *Iliad*, the *Chanson de Roland* and *Paradise Lost* MA Florida St Univ 1955
5527 ROSENBLATT Jason P A Revaluation of Milton's Indebtedness to Judaica in Book VII of *Paradise Lost* MA Brown Univ 1966
5528 ROSS John P John Milton, *Comus*, and the Christian Fusion: An Iconographic Study of *A Mask Presented at Ludlow Castle* MA Long Island Univ 1967 100 p
5529 ROTH Herbert J John Milton's Concept of Power MA Univ of Maryland at College Park 1965 103 p
5530 ROUSE Roscoe The Literary History of *Areopagitica*: An Essay and a Critical Bibliography MA Univ of Oklahoma 1952
5531 RUSCH Frederic E Milton's Muse in *Paradise Lost* MA Univ of Iowa 1966
5532 SANDERS Franklin D *Samson Agonistes* and the Critics MA Univ of North Carolina at Chapel Hill 1958 133 p
5533 SANDISON James Milton and the Non-Orthodox Reader: Chiefly a Study of the Human Elements in Eden MA Univ of British Columbia (Canada) 1953 101 p
5534 SAUCIER Evelyn N *Paradise Lost* and *The State of Innocence*: A Comparison of Plot, Characterization, Genre and Theme MA Univ of New Mexico 1968
5535 SAUNDERS Jeanne The Problem of Satan in Milton's *Paradise Lost* MA Univ of Richmond 1966 99 p
5536 SAYLES Nathaniel L Lowell's Criticism of Milton MA Indiana Univ 1950
5537 SCHLOSS Myrna The Concept of Will in Milton's *Paradise Lost* BA·Univ of British Columbia (Canada) 1962
5538 SCHRIER Virginia B Milton and Wordsworth: Some Parallels MA Columbia 1937
5539 SCOTT Allen H John Milton: Religious Independent MA Univ of Richmond 1957 110 p
5540 SCOTT Martha S The Stagings of Milton's *A Maske Presented at Ludlow Castle* MA Texas Christian Univ 1966 113 p
5541 SCOUTEN Lois M Milton's Second Adam in *Paradise Regained* MA Queen's (Canada) 1965
5542 SEARLES Joan C Three Studies on the Fall of Man: Structure in *Paradise Lost*, William Golding's *Free Fall* and Melville's "Bartleby" MA Pennsylvania St Univ 1965
5543 SELF Jacqueline Milton on Kingship MA Claremont Graduate School 1965
5544 SELIG Dorit M The Image Sequence in Milton's *Paradise Lost* MA Columbia 1953 115 p
5545 SEPIANU F C Milton's Reputation in France in the Seventeenth Century B Litt Oxford Univ (England) 1941
5546 SHANNON Pearl H Figures of Speech in Milton's English Poetical Works MA Univ of New Mexico 1931
5547 SHEEHAN Penelope M The Christianity of the Major Early Poems, Latin and English, of Milton MA Boston Coll 1968
5548 SHIRLEY Hunter B Characterization in *Paradise Lost* and *Samson Agoniste* MA Baylor Univ 1953 130 p
5549 SIEMERS Katie Milton's Satan: A Study of His Origin and Significance

MA Univ of British Columbia (Canada) 1953   173 p
5550 SMALL Charles Y   The Choral Odes of Milton's *Samson Agonistes*
      MA Fairleigh Dickinson Univ 1966
5551 SMITH James P   John Milton: A Study in Critical Views and Methods
      (1936-1958)   MA Univ of North Carolina at Chapel Hill 1959   97 p
5552 SNODDY C E   Milton and the English University in the Seventeenth
      Century   MA Univ of North Carolina at Chapel Hill 1926
5553 SODOWSKY Roland E   Numerical Symbolism in John Milton's "Nativity Ode"
      MA Oklahoma St Univ 1969   21 p
5554 SPELFOGEL Beverly K   The Renaissance Myths of Hercules and Circe
      in the Poetry of John Milton   MA Columbia 1959   85 p
5555 SQUIRES Ruamie C   Milton's Conception of Providence in *Comus* and
      Paradise Lost: A Study in Development   MA Univ of North Carolina
      at Chapel Hill 1958   85 p
5556 STAFFORD Florence P   Milton in the First Fifty Years of *The Quarterly
      Review*   MA St Mary's at San Antonio 1947   85 p
5557 STAHL Quentin S   Milton, History and Christian Truth   MA Univ of
      Houston 1956   85 p
5558 STEADMAN John M   "One Greater Man": A Consideration of Milton's
      Conception of the Second Person of the Trinity   MA Emory Univ 1941
      98 p
5559 STEVENS Irma N   Milton's Satan and Dante's Lucifer: A Comparison
      of the Symbols of Evil   MA Texas Christian Univ 1967   86 p
5560 STOLLMAN Samuel S   Milton and Judaism   MA Wayne St Univ 1964
5561 SULLIVAN Maureen T   Milton and the New Music, with Particular
      Reference to the Sonnets   MA Columbia 1958   87 p
5562 SUMIDA Stephen H   The Inward Light and the Visual Beam: Studies in
      John Milton and Andrew Marvell   BA Amherst 1968
5563 SUMMERHAYS Diana   Burn the Lyre and Sing: Milton's Choruses in
      Samson Agonistes   MA Columbia 1966   180 p
5564 SUNDELL Roger H   Internal Commentary in the Major Poems of
      John Milton   MA Washington Univ at St Louis 1965   180 p
5565 SUTHERLAND Jewell D   The Reputation of Milton in the Age of
      Queen Anne   MA Indiana Univ 1940
5566 SUTHERLAND William O Jr   Addison's *Paradise Lost* Criticisms in
      The Spectator   MA Univ of North Carolina at Chapel Hill 1946   100 p
5567 SUTTON C McK   Milton's Attitude toward Educational Theories of the
      Seventeenth Century   MA Univ of North Carolina at Chapel Hill 1924
5568 SVENDSEN J K   Milton's Use of Personal Epithet   MA Univ of North
      Carolina at Chapel Hill 1935
5569 SWANSON Anne L   Milton's Satan: A Study in Historical Criticism
      MA Howard Univ 1937   39 p
5570 SWARTLEY Stanley S   A Study of the *Areopagitica* of John Milton
      MA Boston Univ 1909
5571 SWARTZ David L Jr   Three Studies in English: Milton's "Sonnet XIX";
      Unreliable Narration: James and Browning; and E C Stedman's
      "Valentine"   MA Pennsylvania St Univ 1966
5572 SYMES M W   The Theme of the Garden and Its Relation to Man in the
      Poetry of Spenser, Milton and Marvell, with Consideration of
      Some Other Poetry of the Time   M Phil Univ of London (England) 1968
5573 TAGLIAVINI Pietro   Milton's Spiritual Testament: An Interpretation
      of *Samson Agonistes*   MA Ca Foscari (Italy) 1958
5574 TAGUE Harrell N   The Influence of Milton's Blindness on *Paradise Lost*
      MA Univ of Louisville 1932
5575 TARPLEY Ben   The Metaphorical Element of *Paradise Lost*   MA Univ of
      Texas at Austin 1946   96 p
5576 TATRO Clifton L   *Murder in the Cathedral* and *Samson Agonistes*: A
      Comparison   MA Univ of New Hampshire 1951   60 p
5577 TAYLOR Sarah V   A Study of the Influence of Italy and Her Culture
      upon the Life and Works of John Milton   MA Univ of Texas at Austin

1944   351 p
5578 TEAGUE Pelton   John Milton Is Samson Agonistes   M Ed Henderson St
      Coll nd
5579 TEMPLE Evan R   Milton's Views on Government and Their Bearing on His
      Defense of the Regicides   MA Univ of Arkansas 1967
5580 TERVO Esther F   Milton's Conception of Liberty   MA Univ of British
      Columbia (Canada) 1943   69 p
5581 TETHER Silvia   Christian Liberty in *Samson Agonistes*   MA Butler Univ
      1965
5582 THAMES Nena   A Study of *Samson Agonistes*: The Preface and the Poem
      MA Hunter Coll 1962
5583 THOMPSON Eric   Contemporary Criticism of Milton   MA George Washington
      Univ 1940   121 p
5584 THORPE Marjorie R   The Person of Eve in *Paradise Lost*   MA McGill
      (Canada) 1965
5585 TOBIN Patrick H   The Influence of Women on the Life and Thought of
      John Milton   MA Univ of Texas at Austin 1941   162 p
5586 TOLBERT James M   Milton's Use of Folklore   MA Emory Univ 1937   130 p
5587 TOUSLEY Marion   Milton as Myth-Maker   MA Louisiana St Univ 1939
5588 TOWNSEND Joyce B   "The Verse" and Milton's Practice and Rime
      MA Columbia 1962   60 p
5589 TREADWELL Mattie E   Studies in the Diction of Milton's English
      Lyrical Poems   MA Univ of Texas at Austin 1935
5590 TURNER Loyd I   *Comus* and the Seventeenth Century Masque   MA Baylor
      Univ 1940   100 p
5591 ULBRICH Edith V   The Satan of *Paradise Lost, Job* and *A Masque of
      Reason*   MA Texas Arts and Industries Univ 1956
5592 URBAN Otto H   John Milton's Concept of the Holy Trinity   MA West
      Texas St Univ 1966   106 p
5593 USSERY Annie W   Milton on Marriage and the Character of Woman
      MA Emory Univ 1943   226 p
5594 VERNON James K   The Position of the Speaking Voice in Milton's Poetry
      with Regard to Literature and Society   BA Amherst 1957
5595 VON DER MEHDEN Anne   The Consequences of Theme and Form in *Paradise
      Lost*   MA San Diego St Coll 1963   100 p
5596 VON ENDE Frederick A   The Role of the Sun in *Paradise Lost*   MA Texas
      Christian Univ 1966   116 p
5597 WADLINGER Maura C   Milton's Use of the Idea of Plenitude in *Paradise
      Lost*   MA Univ of Delaware 1968   56 p
5598 WAGNER Ralph A   *Paradise Lost*: A Fabric of Paradox   MA Texas
      Christian Univ 1967   103 p
5599 WALLACE Elizabeth T   Fit Conversation: A Study of Marriage and
      Divorce in Ford and Milton   MA Univ of Delaware 1968   48 p
5600 WALLINS Roger P   Reflections of *The History of Britain* in Milton's
      Poetry   MA Ohio St Univ 1964   95 p
5601 WEBER Rosalie F   Milton's Antipathy to Irregular Lines and Shapes
      MA Oklahoma St Univ 1969   105 p
5602 WEN Florence T   Analogues of Satan in *Paradise Lost*   MA St Louis
      Univ 1951   105 p
5603 WERLEIN Halsey E   Milton's *Tractate of Education* Considered as a
      Reflection of His Own Experience as a Student   MA Columbia 1962
      93 p
5604 WERMAN Golda   Conflicts between Christianity and Humanism Reflected
      in *Paradise Lost*   MA Butler Univ 1964
5605 WHEELER Dan W   Voltaire's English Essay on Milton Edited and with
      an Introduction   MA Univ of Oklahoma 1959
5606 WHITE Fay L   Some Antecedents of *Samson Agonistes*   MA Lamar
      Technological Univ 1966   132 p
5607 WHITE Rita S   A Study of Three Devices of Sound in Passages of
      Paradise Lost   MA East Tennessee St Univ 1966

5608 WHITEFIELD Tommie L Milton and Five Illustrators of *Paradise Lost*
      MA Texas Arts and Industries Univ 1963
5609 WILLIAMS Agnes D Some Religious, Political and Social Beliefs of
      Milton MA Univ of Arizona pre-1933
5610 WILLIAMS Garner L The Heavenly Muse of *Paradise Lost* MA Arkansas
      St Coll 1966
5611 WILLIAMS Herbert L A Rhetorical Analysis of the Language of
      Paradise Lost MA Univ of Mississippi 1941 148 p
5612 WILLIAMS Margaret P Humanistic Trends in Milton's Private Studies
      MA Baylor Univ 1935 203 p
5613 WILSON Augusta E The Theory of the Temptation in *Comus* as an
      Adumbration of the Theory of the Temptation in *Paradise Lost*
      MA Univ of Mississippi 1963 130 p
5614 WILSON Roger S John Milton's Theory of Religious Toleration
      MA Univ of Richmond 1963 101 p
5615 WINTER Keith J Milton's *Lycidas*: An Evaluation of Eight Approaches
      and the Proposal of a Ninth Approach MA Univ of British Columbia
      (Canada) 1965
5616 WITTREICH Joseph A Jr *Paradise Lost*: A Mirror of Renaissance Man
      MA Univ of Louisville 1962
5617 WOMACK Lucille L A General Commentary of *Samson Agonistes*
      MA Emory Univ 1944 195 p
5618 WOODRUFF Sara G *Samson Agonistes* and Its Biblical Source MA Univ
      of Rhode Island 1961 81 p
5619 WOOTEN Chesley E John Milton and the Question of Separation of
      Church and State MA Univ of Maryland at College Park 1959 135 p
5620 WRIGHT Robert G Milton's Christ: As Seen by the Critics of
      Paradise Lost and *Paradise Regained* Since 1900 MS Ft Hays St
      Teachers Coll 1962
5621 WYNN Valree F Milton's Sense of Vocation: MA Oklahoma St Univ 1951
      51 p
5622 YATES Lawrence Milton's Pronunciation of "e", "ee" and "ea"
      MA Univ of Kentucky 1926
5623 YOSHIMURA Rinko Geographical Allusions in Milton's *Paradise Lost*
      MA Boston Coll 1958
5624 YOUNG Helen F Theories Concerning the Personality of John Milton
      MA Univ of Arkansas 1931
5625 YU Hung-Chih Transformations in Milton's *Comus* MA Texas Agricul-
      tural and Mechanical Univ 1969 69 p
5626 ZAITZ Anthony W Imagery in *Paradise Lost* MA Boston Univ 1947
5627 ZIMMERMAN J E John Milton as Seen by the Critics MA Baylor Univ
      1930 134 p
5628 ZWICKY Laurie B Milton's Use of Time: Image and Principle MA Univ
      of Oklahoma 1959 122 p
See also 459, 499, 928, 1606, 2304, 2305, 2794, 2886, 3969, 4267, 5008, 5117,
      6393, 7467, 7815, 7909

LADY MARY WORTLEY MONTAGU

5629 CRILLY B L Lady Mary Wortley Montagu and Her Times MA Ohio St Univ
      1931
5630 KROFT Elmere P Lady Mary Wortley Montagu's Opinions on Literature
      and Education MA Washington Univ at St Louis 1947
5631 SLOAN Jean B The Literary Tastes of Lady Mary Wortley Montagu
      MA Univ of North Carolina at Chapel Hill 1952 100 p

GEORGE MOORE

5632 EDELSON Alfred M A Dialogue on George Moore's *Hail and Farewell*
      MA Columbia 1951

5633 EINHORN Merrie Is the Moore Pagan? An Inquiry into the Paganism
      of George Moore MA Columbia 1960 119 p
5634 GERMAN Sharon K The Influence of George E Moore's Philosophy of
      the Fiction of Virginia Woolf MS Purdue Univ 1961 153 p
5635 HOLLOW John W Circular Structure in the Novels of George Moore
      MA Rice 1962
5636 KENEIPP Lydia M The Transitions of George Moore MA Southern
      Illinois Univ at Carbondale 1953 56 p
5637 LICK Maxine V George Moore on Art and Artists MA Washington Univ
      at St Louis 1933
5638 NOZICK Martin The Influence of French Symbolism on George Moore
      MA Columbia 1942
5639 PRETO-RODAS Richard A The Nature of Good in the Philosophy of
      George E Moore MA Boston Coll 1960
5640 SAMMARELLI Miranda George Moore MA Ca Foscari (Italy) 1934
5641 SANDINI Angelo George Moore: A Study MA Ca Foscari (Italy) 1950
5642 STANFORD Edward B A Study of George Moore with Reference to His
      Celtic Temperamental Heritage MA Williams Coll 1939
5643 WILCOX James C Religion and Nature in the Novels of George Moore
      MA Univ of Rhode Island 1964 82 p
5644 WYATT Larry C The Quest for the Aesthetic Novel: A Study of
      George Moore MA Columbia 1961 112 p

                            THOMAS MOORE

5645 BUNNER Elizabeth J Thomas Moore's Place in Romanticism MA Univ of
      Pittsburgh 1938
5646 CARBONI Bianca Thomas Moore as a Biographer: A Critical Study
      MA Ca Foscari (Italy) 1956
5647 CASE Ivy P Thomas Moore and His Friends MA Tulane Univ 1937
5648 FINESSO Ermenegilda Thomas Moore MA Ca Foscari (Italy) 1936
5649 FLADLIEN Janet E A Critical Study of the Lyrical Qualities of
      Thomas Moore's Irish Melodies MA Bowling Green Univ 1959
5650 LUCCHESI Cesare Thomas Moore as a Poet and a Prosewriter
      MA Ca Foscari (Italy) 1935
5651 MARTIN Madelyn G Thomas Moore and the Irish Question MA Rice 1960
5652 PAFFORD Ward A Study of Thomas Moore: A Critical Analysis of the
      Reasons for the Rise and Fall of Moore's Literary Reputation
      MA Emory Univ 1933 50 p
5653 PRICE Cyril Greek Influence on the Life and in the Poetry of
      Thomas Sturge Moore, Contemporary English Poet, Critic and Wood-
      Engraver MA Howard Univ 1929 39 p
See also 1083

                            THOMAS MORE

5654 BARRY Sr Marie of the Trinity A Bibliography of the Works of or
      Relating to Sir Thomas More MA Boston Coll 1943
5655 BASS Robert W A Consideration of Sir Thomas More's Utopia as a Satire
      on Millennial Heresies MA Auburn Univ 1969
5656 BREUNIG Jerome E An Edition of Thomas More's Epigrams MA St Louis
      Univ 1942 86 p
5657 CAMPBELL John A The Background of More's Utopia MA Ohio St Univ 1937
5658 CAUDLE James E The Literary Reputation of Sir Thomas More in the
      Sixteenth Century MA Univ of North Carolina at Chapel Hill 1951
      83 p
5659 CHAPMAN Audre Sir Thomas More as a Social Reformer MA Oklahoma St
      Univ 1938 43 p
5660 CHRISTOFOLI Luther B Hythloday and More's Intent: An Investigation
      of Tone and Character in Utopia MA Auburn Univ 1965

5661 DICKEY Frank G Sir Thomas More's *Utopia* and Its English Background
     MA Univ of Kentucky 1942
5662 FALLAHAY Nolan M Traditional Rhetoric in Thomas More's *A Dialogue
     of Comfort Against Tribulation* MA St Louis Univ 1949 182 p
5663 FERGUSON Richard B More's *Utopia* and the Golden Age MA Texas
     Technological Univ 1970 46 p
5664 FINLAY Sr Mary G St Thomas More's Defense of the Blessed Sacrament
     MA Columbia 1940
5665 GAINEY Sr Mary S The Platonic Virtues in Thomas More's *Utopia, Book I*
     MA St Louis Univ 1952 202 p
5666 GRADY Sr Mary P Analogues in St Augustine and St Thomas More with
     Special Reference to the *Dialogue Concerning Tyndale* MA St Louis
     Univ 1943 149 p
5667 HALLORAN Ann More's Defense of Humanism: A Study of the Form and
     Content of Three of Thomas More's Letters MA Toronto (Canada) 1964
5668 HILLHOUSE Virginia C A Study of the Alliteration in St Thomas More's
     A Dialogue of Comfort Against Tribulation MA Auburn Univ 1967
5669 KRASS Alfred C The Changing Image of Thomas More BA Amherst 1958
5670 LATOUR Mother R C E The Exempla in More's *Dialogue of Comfort*
     MA Boston Coll 1956
5671 LeCLAIR Sr M Rose Poetic Elements in St Thomas More's *Dialogue of
     Comfort* MA Rivier Coll 1959
5672 McBRYAN Paul J Thomas More's *History of Richard III* a Medieval
     Exemplum MA St Louis Univ 1952 144 p
5673 McGINNIS Charles F The Literary Position of Thomas More MA Boston
     Coll 1949
5674 MAHONEY Louise Shakespearean Imagery and *The Book of Sir Thomas More*
     MA Boston Coll 1956
5675 OYEWALE John O Reflections of Sir Thomas More's *Utopia* on the
     Society of Sixteenth Century England MA Howard Univ 1966 133 p
5676 PERRY Charles H The Utopian and Post-Historical English Novel from
     Thomas More to George Orwell MA Univ of Maine 1950 118 p
5677 PHILBIN Richard G Salient Aspects of More's *Utopia* MA Boston Coll
     1951
5678 SCHENKEL Thelma The Dynamics of Utopia and War in the Land of
     Nowhere: Thomas More and Francois Rabelais MA Columbia 1964 75 p
5679 SEIDEL Michael C The Conscious Direction of the English Renaissance
     by Erasmus, Colet and More MA Southern Methodist Univ 1936
5680 TURNER Robert R Religion and the Church in More's *Utopia* MA Univ of
     Tennessee 1955 113 p
5681 TWOMEY Louis J The Element of Hope in the Writings of Thomas More
     MA St Louis Univ 1933 78 p
5682 WALSH Sr Mary St M *The Book of Sir Thomas More* and the *Tragedy of
     Chabot, Admiral of France* as Tragedies of Conscience MA Boston
     Coll 1959
5683 WRIGHT Thomas E Religion, Politics and Humanism in Sir Thomas More's
     Latin Epigrams MA Washington Univ at St Louis 1958 105 p
See also 274, 277

                              WILLIAM MORRIS

5684 BARTON Willette E The Place of William Morris in the Mediaeval Move-
     ment MA Univ of Texas at Austin 1933
5685 BLAKEY Dorothy A Critical Study of the Romances of William Morris
     MA Univ of British Columbia (Canada) 1922
5686 BUCKLIN G A William Morris' Conception of the Relation of Art in
     Society BA Univ of Oklahoma 1903
5687 BYRON Kenneth H A Study of the Color and Imagery of the Poetry of
     William Morris MA Univ of Richmond 1957 111 p
5688 CARPENTER Ruth L The Early Poems of William Morris MA Syracuse Univ

        1943   113 p
5689 CONCI Francesca   William Morris and His Poetry   MA Ca Foscari (Italy)
        1939
5690 DAVIS Anne E   The Curved Sword: A Study of William Morris' First
        Volume of Poetry, *The Defense of Guenevere and Other Poems*
        MA Columbia 1966   129 p
5691 DEWSNAP Terence F   The Development of the Gothic Symbol: Its Relation
        to William Morris   MA Boston Coll 1957
5692 DUTLI Margaret C   The Medievalism of William Morris: His Treatment
        of the Middle Ages in His Early Poetry and Later Prose
        MA Saskatchewan (Canada) 1966
5693 ERDMAN Edgar F   A Reconstruction of the Utopia of William Morris
        from His Later Romances   MA Univ of Richmond 1957   185 p
5694 GARDNER William L   Some of the Characteristics of William Morris'
        Early Romantic Poetry   MA Howard Univ 1950   110 p
5695 GEORGE John M   William Morris and Social Justice   MA DePauw Univ 1933
        131 p
5696 HOARE Agnes D   The Works of William Morris in Relation to the Norse
        Sagas   M Litt Cambridge Univ (England) 1927
5697 McDONALD Joseph E   Medievalism of William Morris as It Is Expressed
        in His Work *Dream of John Ball*   MA Boston Coll 1942
5698 MERCANI Edgardo   A Dreamer: William Morris   MA Ca Foscari (Italy) 1929
5699 MORRISON William N   William Morris and the Ideal Society   MA Carleton
        (Canada) 1965
5700 NEWCUM Mother Miriam   The Influence of Medieval Writings on the Poetry
        of William Morris   MA St Louis Univ 1944   113 p
5701 NIELSEN Margaret E   A Study of the Relationship between the Ethical
        Idealism and the "Medievalism" of William Morris   MA Syracuse Univ
        1965   77 p
5702 PAIGE Marjorie   Nineteenth Century Periodical Criticism of the Early
        Works of William Morris   MA Columbia 1935
5703 ROODY Sarah I   *Work-Pleasure*, an Edition of Certain Selections from
        the Works of William Morris for Twelfth Grade Students   MA Columbia
        1935
5704 SIMZIG Eugenia A   William Morris and Icelandic Literature
        MA Ca Foscari (Italy) 1954
5705 STEINGASS David H   The Narrative Backgrounds of William Morris'
        The Earthly Paradise   MA Univ of Maine 1964   227 p
5706 WALLACE Ruth F   A Study of the Women in the Prose of William Morris
        MA Univ of Pittsburgh 1937
5707 WALTHALL Nancy   William Morris: Modern Medievalist   MS Kansas St
        Coll at Pittsburg 1946
5708 WHITMAN Sr Mary E   The Sources of *The Earthly Paradise*:   A Study
        of William Morris' Literary Principles of Narration   MA St Louis
        Univ 1946   118 p
5709 WILLIAMS Mary J   The Organic Theory of Order in William Morris'
        Later Prose Romances   MA Univ of Rhode Island 1960
See also 894, 4608, 4957, 6038, 6123

                           THOMAS NASHE

5710 AMES Russell A   The Rhetoric of Thomas Nashe   MA Columbia 1936
5711 AUDETTE Richard A   The Influence of Rabelais on Thomas Nashe Recon-
        sidered   MA Boston Coll 1955
5712 HECHT Diane F   Thomas Nashe and the Supernatural   MA Columbia 1966
        100 p
5713 HOEFER Jacqueline S   A Refutation of Paul H Kocher's Claim that
        Thomas Nashe Wrote the Prose Scenes in Christopher Marlowe's
        Faustus   MA Washington Univ at St Louis 1955
5714 JOHNSON William J   Comedy in the Works of Thomas Nashe   MA Univ of

Texas at Austin 1963   89 p
5715 MILLER John K   The Prose Satire of Thomas Nashe   MA Columbia 1942
5716 NECARELLI Silvia   *The Unfortunate Traveller* by Thomas Nashe
      MA Ca Foscari (Italy) 1962
5717 PATTEN Maudie M   Nashe's Proverb Lore: A Study of His Diffused
      Humanism   MA Baylor Univ 1946   217 p
5718 RIEHEMANN Marguerite M   Thomas Nashe as a Defender of Learning
      MA St Louis Univ 1939   84 p
5719 ZINK Gerald   Thomas Nashe's Use of "Shall" and "Will"   MA Univ of
      North Dakota 1965

                        JOHN HENRY NEWMAN

5720 ALEXANDER Elizabeth S   A History of Modern Criticism Concerning
      Newman's *Idea of a University:*   1925-1962   MA Univ of Louisville
      1963
5721 ANDERSON Mary T   Newman and Coleridge on the Grounds of Belief
      MA Univ of Arkansas 1933
5722 BARSAGLIA Danilo   John Henry Newman   MA Ca Foscari (Italy) 1949
5723 BELLI Sr Antonina   John Henry Newman   MA Columbia 1943
5724 BENNETT Sr Miriam J   The Influence of Cicero in the Prose of
      John Henry Newman   MA Coll of the Holy Names at Oakland 1966
5725 BUCKLEY Sr M Ancille   Elements of Style in Newman's *Apologia Pro
      Vita Sua*   MA Siena Coll 1965
5726 BURGIS N F   An Edition of Newman's *Tamworth Reading Room*, with Intro-
      duction and Textual and Expository Apparatus   MA Univ of London
      (England) 1964
5727 BURT Forrest D   The Portrayal of the Victorian Dilemma in Newman's
      Apologia Pro Vita Sua   MA Texas Technological Univ 1965
5728 CAINE James P   A Study of Newman's Theory of Higher Education
      MA St Louis Univ 1932   59 p
5729 CRIPE George R   An Analysis of the Elements of Style in the
      University Sermons of John Henry Newman   MA Pacific Univ 1970
      68 p
5730 D'AGOSTINE R C   The Rhetoric and Styles of John Henry Newman's
      Parochial and Plain Sermons   MA Hunter Coll 1969
5731 FORREY Louis J   Rhetorical Parallelism as an Element of Style in
      the Sermons of John Henry Cardinal Newman   MA St Louis Univ 1931
      60 p
5732 FURST Kenneth W   Newman's Idea of Development Vis-a-Vis the Theory
      of Evolution   MA Columbia 1959   90 p
5733 HARVEY Sr Gertrude M   John Henry Newman's Idea of the Development
      of Christian Doctrine: An Evaluation   MA Villanova Univ 1965
5734 HAUKE Kathleen A   The Immanence of the Spiritual World in the
      Thought of John Henry Newman   MA Univ of Rhode Island 1963
5735 HIGGINS Sr Mary S   The Rhetorical Practice of John Henry Newman
      MA Boston Coll 1957
5736 HOERR Cecil E   The Human Sympathy of Cardinal Newman   MA St Louis
      Univ 1936   100 p
5737 KELLEY R G   John Henry Cardinal Newman: Poetic Genius   MA Boston
      Coll 1933
5738 LAHEY G   A Critical Study of Newman's *Apologia Pro Vita Sua*
      B Litt Oxford Univ (England) 1949
5739 MAHONEY Bernard J   The Empirical Tradition and the Place of the
      Conscience in John Henry Newman   MA Baylor Univ 1965   179 p
5740 MEHOK William J   The Historical and Philosophical Basis of Newman's
      Idea of a University in the Light of Catholic Tradition
      MA St Louis Univ 1936   89 p
5741 MESSIMER Madaline I   A Study of the Novels of John Henry Cardinal

Newman MA St Mary's at San Antonio 1942 87 p
5742 MICBALSKI Richard E Nineteenth Century Education: A Study in the
      Thought of John Stuart Mill and John Henry Newman MA Cornell Univ
      1965
5743 MURPHY Sr M Newman's Poetry MA Univ of Oklahoma 1933
5744 NEWTON Margaret M Educational Ideas Expressed by Thomas Arnold and
      Cardinal Newman MA Boston Univ 1938
5745 PACK John T Newman's Poetic Style and Intuition in the *Apologia*
      MA Boston Coll 1966
5746 RIEL A P Newman, the Rhetorician MA Boston Univ 1941
5747 RONAN Clifford J The Personal Use of Language: Remarks on
      John Henry Newman's *Idea of a University* BA Amherst 1957
5748 RYAN James C Newman's Psychological Insight as Revealed in His
      Catholic Sermons MA St Louis Univ 1932 75 p
5749 SILVER Sr Marilla A Study of the Sermons of John Henry Cardinal
      Newman; with Special Reference to His Use of Rhetoric
      MA Mount Saint Vincent (Canada) 1967
5750 SULLIVAN M E Important Influences of Newman's Faith MA North Texas
      St Univ 1951
5751 TERINO Edward O John Henry Newman's *Apologia Pro Vita Sua* BA Amherst
      1958
5752 WINTER Sr Mary V A Critical Comparative Study of the *Apologia Pro
      Vita Sua* of John Henry Cardinal Newman and the *Autobiography of
      John Stuart Mill* MA Oklahoma St Univ 1953 110 p
See also 90

SEAN O'CASEY

5753 ABRAHAM David H Realism and Non-Realism in the First Five Major
      Plays of Sean O'Casey MA Univ of Massachusetts 1968
5754 AIELLO Anthony Irony in O'Casey MA Columbia 1966 59 p
5755 ASHTON Angela D Himself in the Doorway: A Portrait of Sean O'Casey
      MA Miami Univ 1965
5756 CIPRIANI Bruna Sean O'Casey and the Abbey Theatre MA Ca Foscari
      (Italy) 1950
5757 COCHRAN Carolyn The Expressionism of Sean O'Casey's Plays
      MA Univ of Texas at Austin 1960 191 p
5758 DE BAUN Vincent C Sean O'Casey: His Artistic Development as a
      Dramatist MA Rutgers St Univ 1950 93 p
5759 DONOHUE Joseph W The Dramatic Theories of Sean O'Casey MA George-
      town Univ 1962 166 p
5760 ELLZEY Diana L The Opposition between Joie de Vivre and Convention-
      ality in the Plays of Sean O'Casey MA Univ of Texas at Austin
      1966 99 p
5761 GERSTEIN David The State of "Chassis": The Destructive Element
      in the Later Plays of Sean O'Casey MA Columbia 1959 52 p
5762 GRIMES V M Element of Futility in the Plays of Sean O'Casey
      MA Boston Coll 1936
5763 HARDIN Nicholas J The Plays of Sean O'Casey BA Amherst 1965
5764 JANOSEK Julius J The Protest of Sean O'Casey MA Long Island Univ
      nd 69 p
5765 LEYDEN William H Sean O'Casey: Early Triumph and Later Decline
      MA San Diego St Coll 1966
5766 MALONE M G The Plays of Sean O'Casey in Relation to Their Political
      and Social Background MA Univ of London (England) 1965
5767 MARKS William The Importance of Religion in the Works of
      Sean O'Casey BA Rutgers St Univ 1955 65 p
5768 MORAN Robert E The State of Ireland, 1916-1922, as Seen Through
      Three Plays of Sean O'Casey: *Juno and the Paycock, The Plough
      and the Stars* and *The Shadow of a Gunman* MA Indiana Univ 1962

5769 POGGEMILLER Marion Sean O'Casey's Last Plays: A Celebration of
     Life MA Univ of British Columbia (Canada) 1968 113 p
5770 SIMPSON Lewis P Sean O'Casey and His Plays MA Univ of Texas at
     Austin 1939 287 p
5771 SMITH Bobby L Satire in the Drama of Sean O'Casey MA Univ of
     Oklahoma 1965 215 p
5772 SNOWDEN J A Tradition and Experiment in the Plays of Sean O'Casey
     M Phil Univ of London (England) 1969
5773 TAYLOR Kathryn C A Comparative Study of the Women in Sean O'Casey's
     Autobiography and Plays MA Univ of North Carolina at Chapel Hill
     1950 92 p
5774 WEEKS Jeston R Naturalism and Expressionism in the Works of
     Sean O'Casey MA Univ of Houston 1950 105 p

                          LIAM O'FLAHERTY

5775 BOZZO Silvana Liam O'Flaherty as a Novelist and Story Teller
     MA Ca Foscari (Italy) nd
5776 MITCHELL Jean L Liam O'Flaherty: His Life and Works MA Columbia 1941
5777 WADE J A Irish Fiction and Its Background after 1922, with Special
     Reference to the Work of Liam O'Flaherty, Sean O'Faolain,
     Frank O'Connor and Flann O'Brien MA Univ of London (England) 1964

                          GEORGE ORWELL

5778 ALSMEYER Henry Political Thought in the Creative Writings of
     George Orwell MA Texas Arts and Industries Univ 1958
5779 BEHAR Jack George Orwell: Literature and Politics MA Columbia 1954
     134 p
5780 CALDER J R Imagination and Politics: A Study of George Orwell and
     Arthur Koestler MA Univ of London (England) 1966
5781 CHASE Joseph E The Entwined Philosophies of George Orwell MA Univ
     of Omaha 1965
5782 CORCORAN David A Sort of Pamphleteer: Politics, Art and Decency
     in the Novels of George Orwell BA Amherst 1969
5783 FIDERER Gerald L A Psycholoanalytic Study of the Novels of
     George Orwell MA Univ of Oklahoma 1967
5784 FONAROFF Benjamin S A Study of the Writings of George Orwell
     MA Univ of Louisville 1956
5785 GOLDINGER Leonard The Literary Criticism of George Orwell MA Univ
     of Maryland at College Park 1965 74 p
5786 GREENFIELD Robert The Ethical Views of George Orwell MA Columbia
     1961 91 p
5787 MAZER Charles D Orwell's *1984*, Zamyatin's *We* and the Sociology of
     Knowledge MA Texas Technological Univ 1968 59 p
5788 NUWAYSER Ruth A Orwell's Warnings: A Study of George Orwell's
     Purpose in Writing MA Univ of Richmond 1962 81 p
5789 PENDERGAST Herbert C Jr George Orwell's Analysis of the Totalitarian
     System MA Univ of Idaho 1955
5790 PICK Aline The Quest for the Absolute: Eschatology in the Works
     of Arthur Koestler, Andre Malraux and George Orwell MA Columbia
     1962 381 p
5791 REDDING Sr Mary A The Tradition of the Beast-Fable and George Orwell's
     Animal Farm MA Coll of the Holy Names at Oakland 1965
5792 SEXTON Jim George Orwell and "The Ersatz World" BA Univ of British
     Columbia (Canada) 1969
5793 SMITH Beth George Orwell: The Problem of Human Freedom MA Eastern
     New Mexico Univ 1965
5794 SMITH Marcus A Jr George Orwell's Insufficient Heroes MA Boston
     Coll 1961

5795 SPARK D The Class Theme in the Works of George Orwell BA Univ of
        British Columbia (Canada) 1960
5796 WELSH Howard The Genesis of Orwell's Political Philosophy MA Auburn
        Univ 1966
See also 2062, 4172, 4421, 5676

                              JOHN OSBORNE

5797 CULP Paul M Four Plays by John Osborne MA Univ of Texas at Austin
        1961 181 p
5798 JOHNSON Annette John Osborne's Vision of "The Entrapped Man"
        MA Univ of Massachusetts 1968 47 p
5799 MEDJUCK Joseph A John Osborne: A Playwright for England MA Toronto
        (Canada) 1966
5800 WALDRON Frances H The Substance and Development of John Osborne,
        Dramatist MA Univ of Maryland at College Park 1969 55 p
See also 381, 5883

                              WILFRED OWEN

5801 MARX Roy J Wilfred Owen: A Study of His War Poetry MA Kent St Univ
        1966
5802 MATTHEWS D J Blood-Images in the Poems of Wilfred Owen BA Univ of
        British Columbia (Canada) 1968
5803 METZGAR Judith M Images of Sensation in the War Poems of Wilfred Owen
        MA Indiana Univ of Pennsylvania 1967 77 p
5804 MOAN Margaret A Wilfred Owen and the Georgians MA Temple Univ 1967
        43 p
5805 NEWELL Everett E Wilfred Owen MS Kansas St Coll at Pittsburg 1951
5806 TERNER Sandra W Religious Thought in Wilfred Owen's Poetry
        MA St Univ of New York at Buffalo 1966

                              WALTER PATER

5807 ALLEN Richard E The Renaissance of Walter Pater: A Study of Pater's
        Early Aesthetic Theories as Revealed in *The Renaissance* MA Wash-
        ington Univ at St Louis 1949
5808 BLAKENEY Edward K Walter Pater as a Literary Critic MA Boston Univ
        1946
5809 BRAKE L R Walter Pater of *The Renaissance* M Phil Univ of London
        (England) 1969
5810 BROOKS Victor L Walter Pater: A Study in Critical Values MA Univ
        of Texas at Austin 1932
5811 BURKS Ray O Jr The Literary Criticism of Walter Pater MA Univ of
        Arkansas 1937
5812 COX C A The Ethical Aspects of Walter Pater's Aesthetics MA Univ
        of London (England) 1963
5813 DAVENPORT Marguerite R Contemporary Criticism of Walter Pater
        MA Tulane Univ 1933
5814 DE BLASE Samuel T Walter Pater: An Aesthetic Theory in Practice
        MA John Carroll Univ 1965
5815 GIGLI Gigliola The Influence of Walter Pater on Oscar Wilde
        MA Ca Foscari (Italy) 1957
5816 LANGFORD Thomas A Aestheticism, Ethics and Religion in the Writings
        of Walter Pater MA Texas Technological Univ 1963 88 p
5817 LOMBARDI Richard W Walter Pater and Ethical Relativism: Notes
        toward a Reappraisal of Paternian Thought MA Univ of Maryland
        at College Park 1969 61 p
5818 LYNCH Murl Walter Pater's Critical Philosophy MA St Louis Univ 1932
        74 p

5819 PEARCE Thomas M Critical Method of Walter Pater MA Univ of Pitts-
      burgh 1925
5820 PORTER Martha A A Study of the Aesthetic Backgrounds of Walter Pater's
      Criticism MA Univ of Iowa 1924
5821 REES Bethana A The Philosophy of Walter Pater MA Boston Univ 1937
5822 ROWE Donald W The Liturgy in *Marius the Epicurean* and *Gaston de Latour*
      by Walter Pater MA Columbia 1964 131 p
5823 VITTOZZI Aurelia A Study of Walter H Pater MA Ca Foscari (Italy) 1934
5824 WARD Hayden W Walter Pater and the Spirit of Art MA Columbia 1962
      227 p
5825 WEST Paul N Walter Pater and the Voices of Silence: A Study of a
      Narrowing Humanism MA Columbia 1953 84 p
See also 4086

                          COVENTRY PATMORE

5826 ADAM Sr M Deotila Patmore's Political Ideals MA Boston Coll 1936
5827 CAMPBELL G A Study of the Works of Coventry Patmore, with Special
      Reference to His Religious and Political Ideas MA Leeds Univ
      (England) 1957
5828 CULLINS Robert A The Philosophy of Love: A Study of Coventry Pat-
      more's Poetry MA Univ of Texas at Austin 1960 214 p
5829 EATON Vincent T The Works of Coventry Patmore MA Columbia 1942
5830 KIRCHMEYER W G Coventry Patmore's Nuptial Love MA Boston Coll 1936
5831 LEMIEUX Sr Gloria Patmore's Use of Symbols in *The Unknown Eros*
      MA Rivier Coll 1960
5832 McKENNA Mary Metaphysical Verse of Coventry Patmore MA Univ of
      Pittsburgh 1931
5833 McSWINEY M C Incarnation Was the Inspiration of Patmore's Poetry
      MA Boston Coll 1934
5834 STOREY Sr M D Patmore's Development of Divine Love MA Boston Coll
      1935
See also 4084, 6123

                          THOMAS PEACOCK

5835 BONARO Grace The Novels of Thomas Love Peacock MA Univ of Pittsburgh
      1945
5836 BRANNEN Dorothy V Literary Satire in the Novels of Thomas Love Peacock
      MA Univ of North Carolina at Chapel Hill 1951 87 p
5837 BROOKES Gerry H Green Tea and Ale: An Essay on the Novels of
      Thomas Love Peacock BA Amherst 1963
5838 BURROUGHS Patricia A Transitional Spirit of Thomas Love Peacock
      MA Temple Univ 1964 65 p
5839 CHAMBERS Susan R Peacock's World: The Satirical Novels of
      Thomas Love Peacock MA Washington Univ at St Louis 1950 123 p
5840 COX D Mitchell A Critical Examination of the Novels of Thomas Love
      Peacock MA Emory Univ 1936 164 p
5841 DeCAMP David Thomas Love Peacock and the Literary Criticism in His
      Novels with Extensive Bibliographies of Peacock MA Univ of New
      Mexico 1949
5842 DERSTINE Virginia Dialogue as a Major Element in the Narrative
      Art of Thomas Love Peacock MA Univ of Hawaii 1951 217 p
5843 DILWORTH Ernest N Peacock and the Romantic Dogma MA Univ of
      Pittsburgh 1937
5844 DuMOULIN Philip Three Aspects of Peacock's Satiric Novels
      MA Univ of Rhode Island 1963 137 p
5845 FERGUSON Byron L Satire in the Novels of Thomas Love Peacock
      MA Univ of British Columbia (Canada) 1950 99 p
5846 FOLEY Timothy F The Comic Art of Thomas Love Peacock MA St Louis

Univ 1964   103 p
5847 HENDERSON M E   Thomas Love Peacock's Criticism of His Literary
      Contemporaries   MA Univ of British Columbia (Canada) 1943
5848 HUMBLE James E   The Satire of Thomas Love Peacock   MS Kansas St
      Coll at Pittsburg 1950
5849 KILLOREN John J   Caricature in Thomas Love Peacock's Novels
      MA St Louis Univ 1940   69 p
5850 McCAULEY Lynne C   Thomas Love Peacock's Attitudes towards Romantic
      Convention as Evidenced in His Novels   MA St John's Univ 1965
5851 MALABY Iola H   The Development of Characterization Techniques in
      Thomas Love Peacock's Novels   MA Oklahoma St Univ 1961
5852 ROGERS Juanita   The Women Characters in Thomas Love Peacock's Novels
      MA Texas Christian Univ 1951   77 p

GEORGE PEELE

5853 BONATI Bruna   George Peele and the *Legend of Troy*   MA Ca Foscari
      (Italy) 1953
5854 COSSIO Maria G   George Peele: *David and Bethsabe*, with Introduction
      and Notes   MA Ca Foscari (Italy) 1958
5855 GORDON Mary F   Evolution of Dramatic Structure in Three Plays of
      George Peele   MA Columbia 1967   93 p
5856 GWYN Mary M   Characterization in the Plays of George Peele   MA Univ
      of Texas at Austin 1938
5857 HORTON L Diane   The Blank Verse of George Peele   MA Columbia 1960
      69 p
5858 LOZANO Ann M   Lyrics and Songs in Four Plays by George Peele
      MA St Mary's Univ 1966
5859 MANNING John J   George Peele and the English History Play   MA Boston
      Coll 1963
5860 PICCINI Cecilia   George Peele: *Edward I*, Edited with Introduction
      and Notes   MA Ca Foscari (Italy) 1958
5861 RAGAZZINI Maria G   *The Arraignment of Paris* by George Peele
      MA Ca Foscari (Italy) 1959
5862 SAMPLEY Arthur M   Plot Structure in Peele's Plays   MA Univ of Texas
      at Austin 1925
5863 WILKERSON Charles J   A Vocabulary Study of George Peele   MA Univ of
      Iowa 1931
See also 3655, 4913

SAMUEL PEPYS

5864 BALDWIN R G   Samuel Pepys as a Drama Critic of the Seventeenth
      Century   BA Univ of British Columbia (Canada) 1948
5865 BLACK Elizabeth R   Samuel Pepys and the Restoration Drama   MA Wash-
      ington Univ at St Louis 1958   127 p
5866 BRETT S M   Mr Samuel Pepys, Esquire: His Reading as Revealed in
      the *Diary*   MA Univ of North Carolina at Chapel Hill 1936
5867 CLEVER W Glenn   The Change in Samuel Pepys during the Period under
      Restoration Influence as Shown in the *Diary*   MA Ottawa (Canada)
      1966
5868 FIRSCH Robert Jr   Pepys' *Diary:* The Man Revealed   MA Hardin-Simmons
      Univ 1967
5869 GRANT Jeanette R   Literary and Other Connections between
      Samuel Pepys and John Evelyn, Diarists   MA Howard Univ 1962   84 p
5870 McAFFEE Helen F   Pepys on the Restoration Stage   MA Smith Coll 1914
5871 McQUEENEY Katherine R   A Consideration of the Domestic Aspects of
      the Life of Samuel Pepys as Revealed in the *Diary* and as Reflective
      of Life in the Seventeenth Century   MA Boston Coll 1948
5872 PAOLO Rev Francis E   The Influence of Latitude on Pepysian Morality

MA Boston Coll 1965
5873 PETERSON Margaret L Samuel Pepys and the Religious Controversies
     in His Time MA Univ of Pittsburgh 1951
5874 SILVESTRI Silvia Samuel Pepys as a Diarist MA Ca Foscari (Italy) 1950
5875 WEBBER Bernard G Samuel Pepys and John Evelyn as Restoration Virtuosi
     MA Univ of British Columbia (Canada) 1962   225 p
See also 3095

                          ARTHUR PINERO

5876 BAILEY D B Sir Arthur Wing Pinero's Treatment of Women in Four Social
     Plays MA North Texas St Univ 1967
5877 BARNES Margaret C The Technique of Sir Arthur Wing Pinero in
     Character Delineation MA Univ of Iowa 1934
See also 3355

                          HAROLD PINTER

5878 BORDNER Kenneth E Animal Imagery in the Plays of Harold Pinter
     MA Univ of Massachusetts 1965
5879 COLE Robert W Jr Comedy of Menace and Its Exemplification in
     Selected Plays of Harold Pinter MA DePauw Univ 1968   72 p
5880 COLUCCI Donald M The Art of Harold Pinter MA Univ of Nebraska 1966
5881 EDGAR Patricia The Essence of Pinter Drama BA Univ of British
     Columbia (Canada) 1967
5882 GIANNETTI Justine A The Neurotic Personality in the Plays of
     Harold Pinter MA Univ of Iowa 1965
5883 MASSOON Louis J Osborne, Delaney, Shaffer and Pinter: British
     Dramatists of the Fifties and Sixties MA Syracuse Univ 1967   172 p
5884 MAYHEW Anne L The Use of Ritual in the Theatre of the Absurd: A
     Study of Beckett, Pinter and Genet MA Univ of British Columbia
     (Canada) 1964
5885 SIMS Richard L Theme and Symbol in the Plays of Harold Pinter
     MA Univ of Delaware 1969   61 p
See also 361, 366

                          ALEXANDER POPE

5886 ARCARI Roberta Pope: The English Horace MA Ca Foscari (Italy) 1941
5887 BAKER Edwin Pope's Art in *The Rape of the Lock* MA Oklahoma St Univ
     1937   34 p
5888 BAKER Vernie M The Dominant Religious Ideas of the Age of Pope
     MA Washington Univ at St Louis 1933   168 p
5889 BECKER Roman W The Theory of the Pastoral from Pope to Johnson
     MA Washington Univ at St Louis 1930   198 p
5890 BIRD Jackson Alexander Pope as a Satirist M Ed Henderson St Coll nd
5891 BRANCH Billie C A Study of English Deism as Reflected in Pope's
     Essay on Man MA Baylor Univ 1963   122 p
5892 BROOKS I P The Philosophical Background of Pope's *Essay on Man*
     MA Univ of North Carolina at Chapel Hill 1932
5893 BRUNSWICK Gene A The Sensitivity of Alexander Pope: A Poet's
     Correspondence, 1719-1728 MA John Carroll Univ 1965
5894 BUCHANAN Margaret E Voltaire's Critique of Pope's Optimism
     MA Univ of Texas at Austin 1938   148 p
5895 BUSHNELL Nelson S The Poetic Art of Dryden and Pope MA Williams
     Coll 1926
5896 CAMPBELL Ramah N The Enduring Friendship of Alexander Pope: A
     Study of Scriblerian Correspondence MA Baylor Univ 1966   77 p
5897 CHANDLER William K A Variorum Text of Alexander Pope's *The Dunciad*
     MA Univ of Texas at Austin 1929

5898 CHILDS Kenneth W Poetic Identity in Alexander Pope's Horation
      Imitations MA Univ of Utah 1966
5899 CONWAY William D An Analysis of John Dennis' Role in the Famous
      Controversy with Alexander Pope MA Brigham Young Univ 1963 97 p
5900 COOK Stanley J An Examination of Three Features of Poetic Syntax
      in the Poetry of Pope MA Univ of Utah 1966
5901 COX Mary The Underlying Influences of Alexander Pope's Writings
      M Ed Henderson St Coll nd
5902 DAUGHETY Nancy M Youth and Old Age in Medieval Arthurian Literature:
      Pope's *Essay on Man* and Danforth's "Elegy on Madam Hannah Sewall"
      MA Pennsylvania St Univ 1965
5903 DAVEY F W Donne in the Age of Reason: A Study of Pope's Imitations
      of Donne's Satires BA Univ of British Columbia (Canada) 1961
5904 DIEBERT Rubie Satiric "Characters" of Women in Pope and Young
      MA Univ of Kentucky 1932
5905 DONNELLY D S Philosophy of Pope as Found in the *Essay on Man* is
      Contrary to Scholastic Philosophy MA Boston Coll 1933
5906 DOUGLAS Loyd The Mock-Epic in English Literature MA Texas Christian
      Univ 1933 189 p
5907 DREXLER Robert D Pope, Wordsworth and Yeats: A Study in Poetic
      Tradition BA Amherst 1963
5908 EDMONDSON Robbie W Pope as a Literary Critic MA Univ of Texas at
      Austin 1924
5909 EMERY Clark M The Philosophy of Alexander Pope MA Washington Univ
      at St Louis 1933 162 p
5910 FELPS Jettie I Pope's Common Sense MA Univ of Texas at Austin 1931
5911 FELPS Selety C A Study of Alexander Pope and His *Essay on Criticism*
      MA Univ of Texas at Austin 1940 150 p
5912 FISHER Joseph A Thomistic Aspects of Alexander Pope's *Essay on Man*
      MA Texas Christian Univ 1957 79 p
5913 FLEISCHAUER Warren L Leonard Welsted: The Career of One of Pope's
      Dunces MA Columbia 1940
5914 FOY Vesta H The Social Background of *The Rape of the Lock* MA Oklahoma
      St Univ 1938 27 p
5915 GARLAND Robert The Horatian Imitations of Pope and Swift MA Univ
      of New Mexico 1961
5916 GARNER Lafayette R Alexander Pope and the Comic Spirit MA Univ of
      Hawaii 1947 125 p
5917 GARRISON Marjorie B Nineteenth Century French and English Criticism
      of Alexander Pope MA Univ of Pittsburgh 1948
5918 GRUNDMANN Elvira M Theories of the Nature of Man in the Age of
      Pope MA Washington Univ at St Louis 1936 158 p
5919 HAHN Henry G Pope's New Vision: From Animus to Reformation MA Univ
      of Maryland at College Park 1966 108 p
5920 HARBISON Robert D Balance in the Poetry of Pope BA Amherst 1962
5921 HORAN T J Influence of Boileau on Pope MA Boston Coll 1934
5922 HUBBARD Murray P The Scriblerus Club: Its Genesis, Its Purposes
      and Its Major Literary Manifestations MA Univ of Wyoming 1965
5923 JOWSEY W H Pope's Version of the *Iliad* Considered as Illustrating
      His Theory of Translation and His Conception of the Heroic Style
      B Litt Oxford Univ (England) nd
5924 KELLEY William F The Relationship between Alexander Pope and
      William Warburton MA St Louis Univ 1939 59 p
5925 KIRKHAM John W The Pope-Cibber Controversy (1715-1744) MA Univ of
      Texas at Austin 1929
5926 LEVY Diane The Topsy-Turvy World of Alexander Pope's *Dunciad*
      MA Georgetown Univ 1967
5927 LOPEZ Cecilia L Alexander Pope: An Annotated Bibliography,
      1945-1962 MA Florida St Univ 1967 143 p
5928 McREYNOLDS Gwendolyn Essay on the Word "Nature" as It Was Employed

by Alexander Pope MA Florida St Univ 1940
5929 MANN Erica The Theme of Women in the Poetry of Pope: A Study of
      Conventional Sexual Language and Imagery in "Eloisa to Abelard"
      MA Columbia 1965 154 p
5930 MARTIN Elsie F Critical Attitudes toward Pope during the Eighteenth
      Century MA St Louis Univ 1938 57 p
5931 MEANS J A Pope's *Essay on Criticism*: A Study of the Technique
      M Phil Univ of London (England) 1968
5932 MIDGLEY E G Pope's Knowledge of English Literature from Chaucer to
      Dryden B Litt Oxford Univ (England) 1950
5933 MILLER Richard F Pope's Projected Blank Verse Epic MA Columbia 1937
5934 MOYNIHAN Paul V The Place of Thomas Cooke as a Literary Man in the
      First Half of the Eighteenth Century, with Special Emphasis on
      His Relationship with Alexander Pope MA Boston Coll 1959
5935 O'CONNELL Daniel H An Energy of Voice, The Satire of Alexander Pope
      BA Amherst 1966
5936 O'GRADY Walter A Pope's *Essay on Criticism*: A Study in Structure,
      Sound and Imagery MA Toronto (Canada) 1966
5937 PATON Wayne C Pope, Patriot Poet: The Latter Phase MA Columbia
      1960 101 p
5938 PERKINS Karen S Rhetoric and Style in Pope's *An Essay on Man*
      MA Texas Christian Univ 1965 64 p
5839 PETERSON Richard G The Moral Basis of Alexander Pope's *Epistles
      to Several Persons* MA Univ of Utah 1966
5940 POWER John E Pope's Horatian Imitators MA Toronto (Canada) 1963
5941 PRESTON John J III Alexander Pope's Aesthetics of Dramatic Emotion
      MA Temple Univ 1965 59 p
5942 REIDY Jo K Elements of Romanticism in the Poetry of Alexander Pope
      MA Southern Methodist Univ 1930
5943 RIMMER Juanita L Satire and Its Use in *The Rape of the Lock*
      MS Kansas St Coll at Pittsburg 1954
5944 RYAN Anna M Similarities Between the Memoirs of Martinus Scriblerus
      and Pope's Other Writings MA Boston Coll 1951
5945 SAVAGE David B Pope's Indignation MA Univ of British Columbia
      (Canada) 1969 115 p
5946 SEWARD William W The Quarrels of Alexander Pope MA Univ of
      Richmond 1935 148 p
5947 SIDWELL Sylvia J Wit and Judgment: An Analysis of Pope's Manu-
      script Revisions MA Univ of Maryland at College Park 1966 110 p
5948 SIGNORELLI Salvatore Alexander Pope and His Critics MA Ca Foscari
      (Italy) 1936
5949 SMITH Harry E Romantic Elements in the Life and Poetry of
      Alexander Pope MA Univ of Oklahoma 1927
5950 SMITH Shirley J The Relationship of Alexander Pope, John Gay and
      Ambrose Philips in the Pastoral War MA Univ of Tulsa 1967 63 p
5951 SULLIVAN Richard J Alexander Pope: The Poetry of Social Reference
      BA Amherst 1968
5952 TAYLOR Kent H Functional Morality in Alexander Pope's *Essay on
      Criticism* MA Univ of Georgia 1965
5953 TORLINE Sr Mary E Periphrases in Pope's Major Poems MA St Louis
      Univ 1946 123 p
5954 TUTHILL Hilda G A Measure of Horace in Pope's Imitations
      MA Temple Univ 1965 73 p
5955 ULEN Frederick E An Enquiry into the Changes in the Literary
      Reputation of Alexander Pope MA Univ of New Hampshire 1950 115 p
5956 WARD Robert S A Differentiation between the Satires of Dryden and
      Those of Pope MA Boston Univ 1933
5957 WHITE Sharon B A Study of Eighteenth Century Pronunciation Based
      on Analysis of Pope's Rhymes MA Oklahoma St Univ 1967 58 p
5958 WHITLEY Ray Satire, Pessimism and *The Dunciad* BA Univ of British

Columbia (Canada) 1969
5959 WILLIAMS G G A Study of Joseph Wharton's Essay on Pope MA Rice 1925
5960 WIRE Hermine P Alexander Pope as Satirist MA Univ of Maryland at
      College Park 1966 83 p
See also 17, 588, 1044, 1051, 1192, 1359, 1461, 1635, 2437, 2862, 2875,
      2880, 2923, 3421, 4262, 5315, 6486, 6731, 6995, 7149, 8083

                         JOHN COWPER POWYS

5961 CARIONI Anna M J C Powys and the Importance of the Countryside in
      English Contemporary Fiction MA Ca Foscari (Italy) 1946
5962 FOGEL Stanley H Theme as Structure in Three Novels of John Powys
      MA Univ of British Columbia (Columbia) 1970
5963 FOX Josef W A Study of the Novels of John Cowper Powys MA Louisiana
      St Univ 1938

                          J B PRIESTLEY

5964 CARRILLO Thomas Time and Brotherhood Themes in the Plays of
      J B Priestley MA Univ of Tennessee 1969 80 p
5965 LENAZ Gemma J B Priestley MA Ca Foscari (Italy) 1935
5966 OCCARI Dagmar J B Priestley MA Ca Foscari (Italy) 1941

                         MATTHEW PRIOR

5967 BARON William R Science in the Poetry of Matthew Prior MA Columbia
      1951
5968 CARTER Barbara S Man and Reason Versus God and Nature in the Poetry
      of Matthew Prior MA George Washington Univ 1967 86 p
5969 GUARIENTO Sante Matthew Prior: A Poet by Accident MA Ca Foscari 1960
5970 HARVEY Richard G Some Aspects of Satire in the Work of Matthew Prior
      MA Toronto (Canada) 1964
See also 4003, 4883

                         ANN RADCLIFFE

5971 CHAMNESS Martha The Novels of Mrs Ann Radcliffe MA Univ of Texas
      at Austin 1930
5972 GOVETT B M Presentation of Character in the Gothic Novel with
      Special Reference to *The Champion of Virtue* by Clara Reeve,
      The Mysteries of Udolpho by Ann Radcliffe, *Montalbert* by
      Charlotte Smith, *The Italian* by Ann Radcliffe, *Clermont* by
      Regina Roche, *The Benevolent Monk* by Melville and *The Forest of
      Montalbano* by Cuthbertson M Phil Univ of London (England) 1968
5973 KESSLER Betty C Realism in the Novels of Ann Radcliffe MA Temple
      Univ 1964 54 p
5974 MATHEWS Willa F A Comparison of Walpole's *The Castle of Otranto* and
      Mrs Radcliffe's *The Mysteries of Udolpho* MA Univ of Arizona 1942
5975 OWEN Irene B The Influence of Mrs Ann Radcliffe upon English Fiction
      MA Univ of Toledo 1913
5976 PRITCHARD Ernestine Ambivalent Attitudes toward Emotion in *The
      Mysteries of Udolpho* BA Univ of British Columbia (Canada) 1969
5977 ROSS J K Gothic Romances with a Special Comparison of Horace Walpole
      and Mrs Radcliffe MA Univ of North Carolina at Chapel Hill 1903
5978 SLOAN Elaine L The Servant as Comic Relief: A Key to Suspense in
      the Novels of Ann Radcliffe MA Texas Agricultural and Mechanical
      Univ 1969 68 p
5979 ULLERY Elizabeth S Mrs Ann Radcliffe as a Pioneer in the Use of
      Description in Fiction MA Smith Coll 1933
See also 958

WALTER RALEIGH

5980 BARRINGTON Sybil Edmund Spenser's Letter to Sir Walter Raleigh:
A Letter Prefixed to the *Faerie Queene*, Edited with Introduction
and Notes MA Univ of North Carolina at Chapel Hill 1923
5981 BRUNETTA Maria L Sir Walter Raleigh: The Poems MA Ca Foscari
(Italy) 1966
5982 CHEW Audrey Raleigh's Treatment of Pagan Mythology in His *History
of the World* MA George Washington Univ 1943 88 p
5983 FITZGERALD D J Sir Walter Raleigh MA Boston Coll 1933
5984 HARBER Billie D Sir Walter Raleigh and the Great Chain of Being
MA Univ of Kentucky 1960 96 p
5985 HEPLER Dianne K The Poetry of Sir Walter Raleigh: Its Relationship
to the Elizabethan and Metaphysical Traditions MA East Carolina
Univ 1968
5986 KERRIGAN William W Sir Walter Raleigh and the Lyric Poetry of the
Sixteenth Century MA Columbia 1966 152 p
5987 PAYLORE Patricia P Sir Walter Raleigh: Man of Letters MA Univ of
Arizona pre-1933
5988 PHIPPS Paul F Sir Walter Raleigh's Patronage of Poets and Scholars
MA Univ of North Carolina at Chapel Hill 1950 105 p
5989 STROUP T B Conventional Elements in Raleigh's *Discoverie of Guiana*
MA Univ of North Carolina at Chapel Hill 1927
5990 VICKERS Martha H Experience as Reflected in the Poetry of
Sir Walter Raleigh MA Univ of Arizona 1940
See also 2804, 5099, 7544

CHARLES READE

5991 DE FILIPPI Beatrice Charles Reade as a Novelist MA Ca Foscari
(Italy) 1936
5992 FAVERO Valentino The Social Novel in Charles Reade's Works
MA Ca Foscari (Italy) nd
5993 HARRISON Anne A The Humanitarian Novels of Charles Reade MA Univ
of Texas at Austin 1934
5994 KAIMANN Maryann E Charles Reade: Purpose Novelist MA Washington
Univ at St Louis 1947 111 p
5995 KOVNICK Edith E Social Problems in the Novels of Charles Reade
MA Univ of North Dakota 1932 54 p
5996 McGECHAEN John Charles Reade: A Study of a Literary Reputation
MA Univ of British Columbia (Canada) 1947 105 p
See also 2585,

SAMUEL RICHARDSON

5997 ANDERSON Irene P A Comparison of the Sentimentalism of Samuel
Richardson and Laurence Sterne MA Univ of North Dakota 1939 72 p
5998 BALLARDINI V V Richardson's Sentimental Design: A Critical Study
of the Relation between Sentimental and Moral Ideas as They Appear
in the Work of Samuel Richardson; with Reference to the Treatment
of Sentiment and Morality in the French Novel of the Late Seventeenth and Eighteenth Centuries MA Univ of London (England) 1963
5999 BARNES Nelle N Role and Characterization in Richardson's *Pamela*
MA Univ of Hawaii 1965 105 p
6000 CARDON Stanley P A Study of the Villains in the Novels of
Samuel Richardson MA Univ of Arizona 1944
6001 CLANCEY Richard W The Augustan Fair-Sex Debate and the Novels of
Samuel Richardson MA Univ of Maryland at College Park 1966
6002 ERVIN Ruth A Samuel Richardson's Use of Traditional Plot Themes
MA Florida St Univ 1948

6003 ESKRIDGE Mary L Literary Relations between England and France in
      the Eighteenth Century: Influence of Richardson upon Rousseau
      MA Univ of Tennessee 1915
6004 FITZGERALD Leon C Influence of Richardson on Seven Early American
      Novels MA Univ of Montana 1932 62 p
6005 FITZHUGH Mary H Political Analogy in *Clarissa, La Nouvelle Heloise,
      Les Liaisons Dangereuses* and *Caleb Williams* MA Columbia 1966 178 p
6006 HESTER Waverly E Poetical Justice in the Novels of Samuel Richardson
      MA Univ of North Carolina at Chapel Hill 1953 90 p
6007 HIGHTOWER Mary L Characterization in the Novels of Samuel Richardson
      MA Univ of Texas at Austin 1931
6008 IHLE Sandra N The Ritual Pattern in Tragedy: A Study of the
      Oresteian Myth as Adapted by Aeschylus, Euripides, O'Neill,
      Giraudoux, Sartre and Richardson MA Fresno St Coll 1968 74 p
6009 JONES Grenville C A Study of Sentimentalism in the Literature of
      the Eighteenth Century, Especially in the Novels of Samuel Richard-
      son and Henry Fielding MA Univ of Oregon 1933
6010 KUEBLER Anne Samuel Richardson's Scheme for the Formal Education
      of Clarissa MA Bowling Green Univ 1962
6011 McISSAC Paul W Richardson's *Clarissa*: A Tragedy of Sensibility
      MA Dalhousie (Canada) 1964
6012 NOBLE Fay Richardson's Moral Code and Its Influence MA Austin Coll
      1931
6013 O'CONNOR C I The Women in the Novels of Samuel Richardson MA Boston
      Univ 1939
6014 RAMSEY Herman E Moral Purpose and Practice in the Novels of
      Samuel Richardson and Henry Fielding MA Indiana Univ 1940
6015 ROBSON Mary S Politics and Government in the Novels of Richardson,
      Fielding, Smollett and Sterne MA Louisiana St Univ 1937
6016 SPATT Brenda *Pamela* and *Jane Eyre*: The Historical Sources of Their
      Differences MA Columbia 1962 89 p
6017 WATSON Melvin R Religion and the Church in the Novels of Richardson,
      Fielding, Smollett and Sterne MA Louisiana St Univ 1938
See also 2434, 2446, 3114, 3175, 3524, 7606

RICHARD ROLLE

6018 DALY John P The Prose Style of Richard Rolle: Euphuistic Elements
      MA St Louis Univ 1951 132 p
6019 DOBIE Bertha M The Influence of the Latin upon Richard Rolle of
      Hampole's *Prose Psalter* MA Univ of Texas at Austin 1918
6020 FARMER Marjorie The Mysticism of Richard Rolle MA Temple Univ 1954
      43 p
6021 GESNER Carol E Mysticism and Style in the Works of Richard Rolle,
      the Hermit of Hampole MA Univ of New Hampshire 1949 68 p
6022 NESBIT Frances E Richard Rolle's *Canor*: The Relation of Song to
      Form and Content in Rolle's English Prose MA Columbia 1966 75 p
6023 SHORES Doris Richard Rolle: Purpose and Language MA Columbia 1961
      63 p

THE ROSSETTIS

6024 ANDERSON A M The Religious Element in the Poems of Dante Gabriel
      and Christina Rossetti BA Univ of British Columbia (Canada) 1923
6025 ANTTONEN E J A Contrast of Christina Rossetti and Emily Dickinson
      to Which is Added a Critical Bibliography of Antecedent Writings
      about Them MA Boston Univ 1939
6026 AVISON Anne The Religious Spirit of Gerard Manley Hopkins and
      Christini Rossetti BA Univ of British Columbia (Canada) 1957
6027 AYRE Regina S Christina Rossetti's Poetry during the Collinson

Period MA Columbia 1965 212 p
6028 BARBOUR Betty A Study of Colour in the Poems of Dante Gabriel Rossetti
      MA Florida St Univ 1947
6029 BARTON E C Medievalism in Dante Gabriel Rossetti BA Univ of British
      Columbia (Canada) 1940
6030 BRILLHART Florence C Concreteness as Portrayed through the Poetry
      of Dante Gabriel Rossetti MA Oklahoma St Univ 1933 73 p
6031 BUBBA Lydia A Rossetti and the Occult MA Toronto (Canada) 1967
6032 BULLINGTON Charles S Dante Gabriel Rossetti and the Romantic Ideal
      MA Univ of Richmond 1969 93 p
6033 BUSH Sarah M A Comparison of the Lives and Poetry of Emily Dickinson
      and Christina Rossetti with Emphasis upon Similarity of Mystic
      Approach to Death and Immortality Themes MA Washington Univ at
      St Louis 1954
6034 CANN Heather E Christina Rossetti: The Two Ways; a Study in
      Religious Poetry MA Manitoba (Canada) 1967
6035 CORTLAND Peter A Method of Appreciating Christina Rossetti's Poetry
      MA Columbia 1960 95 p
6036 CUMMINGS Denise L Dante Gabriel Rossetti's *The House of Life* and
      the Biographical Imperative MA Univ of British Columbia (Canada)
      1963 124 p
6037 DARCO Michael A Dante Gabriel Rossetti's *The House of Life* MA Univ
      of Pittsburgh 1948
6038 DOLAN Mary E The Influence of Popular Poetry on the Literary Art
      of Dante Gabriel Rossetti and of William Morris MA Washington Univ
      at St Louis 1932
6039 DUBAY Martha Christina Rossetti MA Boston Coll 1940
6040 FALCOMER C M Christina Georgina Rossetti MA Ca Foscari (Italy) 1922
6041 GILL Donald A A Study of Rossetti Criticism, with a Bibliography
      of Rossettiana MA Univ of Colorado 1966
6042 GOODRIDGE Dorothy J Dante Gabriel Rossetti: A Literary Criticism
      MA Boston Univ 1935
6043 GRAZIOSI Maria L Christina Rossetti's Poems MA Ca Foscari (Italy) 1948
6044 HAFEN Marie K Christina Rossetti: Love, Death and Enigmas MA Brigham
      Young Univ 1966
6045 HENSLEY Charles S Studies in the Diction of Dante Gabriel Rossetti
      MA Washington Univ at St Louis 1943 92 p
6046 HILEMAN Evelyn A A Study of Rossetti for the High School Student
      MA Cornell Univ 1965
6047 HOUSTON Charles G A Critical Examination of Selected Devotional
      Works of Christina G Rossetti MA Univ of Pittsburgh 1948
6048 HOWELL Ruby Poe's Influence on Rossetti MA Louisiana St Univ 1929
6049 KENNEDY Joy P A Study of Dante Gabriel Rossetti in Relation to
      Nineteenth Century Romanticism: The Effect of Imagination upon
      Character in Shakespeare's Plays MA Smith Coll 1927
6050 LENNINGER Gertrude Literary Influences in the Poetry of
      Dante Gabriel Rossetti MA Ca Foscari (Italy) 1954
6051 McCLUSKEY Mary L Christina Rossetti: The Development of Her
      Character and Its Effect on Her Poetry MA Univ of Pittsburgh 1941
6052 McCROSSAN Sr Virginia E A Study of Two Poets of Faith in the
      Nineteenth Century: Christina Rossetti and Gerard M Hopkins
      MA Univ of Hawaii 1966 46 p
6053 MAHONEY A L The Interrelations of Painting and Poetry in the Verse
      of Dante Gabriel Rossetti MA Boston Univ 1927
6054 MANNUCCI Elisa The Rossettis MA Ca Foscari (Italy) 1935
6055 MILLMAN Sharon L Love and Death in the Works of Dante Gabriel Rossetti
      MA Columbia 1965 93 p
6056 MONOSON Anna Medieval Beliefs and Superstitions in the Poetry of
      Dante Gabriel Rossetti MA Columbia 1937
6057 PELAGATI Enrica The Latinity of Dante G Rossetti MA Ca Foscari

(Italy) 1950
6058 PRECIOUS M V Christina Rossetti: An Interpretation of Her Devotional
      Life and Religious Views MA Boston Univ 1939
6059 ROBERTS Harriett Main Currents in the Criticism of Christina Rossetti's
      Poetry MA Univ of Pittsburgh 1948
6060 ROWE Alice C The Medievalism of Dante Gabriel Rossetti MA Univ of
      British Columbia (Canada) 1935
6061 SANITA Luciana Christiana Rossetti as a Poetess MA Ca Foscari (Italy)
      1955
6062 SHELTON Winifred H Periodical Comment upon the Literary Work of
      Dante Gabriel Rossetti during His Lifetime and through the Year
      of His Death MA Columbia 1937
6063 SUGIMURA Kazue Rossetti the Man MA Boston Univ 1920
6064 SWANN Thomas B Wonder and Whimsy: The Fantastic World of
      Christina Rossetti MA Univ of Tennessee 1955 83 p
6065 VOGEL Joseph F Studies of Form and Meaning in the Poetry of
      Dante Gabriel Rossetti MA Univ of Florida 1965
6066 WOODWARD S F A Study of the Poetic Imagery of Dante Gabriel Rossetti
      BA Univ of British Columbia (Canada) 1951
See also 604, 697, 749, 894, 4550, 4608, 4609, 6123

JOHN RUSKIN

6067 AUSLANDER Charles Ruskin as a Literary Critic MA Columbia 1936
6068 BARBER Florence Ruskin's Ideas on Painting MA St Louis Univ 1930 50 p
6069 BEECHING Paul Q The Eighteenth Century Background of Ruskin's The
      Poetry of Architecture MA St Louis Univ 1956 143 p
6070 BERTOLOTTI David S John Ruskin's Concepts of Hypocrisy and Integrity
      MA Univ of Maine 1965 77 p
6071 BRILL Ernestine S Ruskin's Reputation (1900-1910) MA Univ of
      Maryland at College Park 1968 72 p
6072 CARLSON Samuel John Ruskin and the Evanescence of Life and Beauty
      MA Univ of Iowa 1964
6073 CART Elsie W Social and Economic Theories of John Ruskin MA Boston
      Univ 1929
6074 COLPITTS R A John Ruskin and His Social Message MA Boston Univ 1915
6075 CURTIN Frank D Ruskin's Place as an Art Critic MA Univ of Pittsburgh
      1929
6076 KACHER Russel E Nature, Society and the Self: Ruskin's Criticism
      of Wordsworth, 1843-1880 MA Univ of Maryland at College Park 1968
      95 p
6077 KOUNTZ Frederick J Perception and Some Bombast: The Heart of the
      New Criticism with a Thought on John Ruskin MA Univ of Toledo 1964
6078 McLEAN Robert S John Ruskin and the Renaissance MA Columbia 1952
      103 p
6079 McNEIL S M John Ruskin as a Disciple of Plato and a Social Reformer
      MA Boston Coll 1931
6080 MAGNANI Flavio Ruskin and the Religion of Beauty MA Ca Foscari
      (Italy) 1948
6081 MONTGOMERY Betty N John Ruskin's Criticism of The Heart of Midlothian
      MA Univ of Maryland at College Park 1968 126 p
6082 MOORE Nathan The Literary Friendship of John Ruskin (1819-1900)
      and Charles Eliot Norton (1827-1908) MA Carleton (Canada) 1965
6083 OTTO Edgar J Ruskin's Aesthetic-Religious Personality MA Univ of
      Iowa 1935
6084 POSTON Charles D John Ruskin and the Novel: A Study in Victorian
      Literary Criticism MA Univ of Oklahoma 1970
6085 ROGERS Ila An Evaluation of the Influence of the Bible in the Life
      and Work of John Ruskin MA Univ of Oklahoma 1938
6086 SAWIN Horace L John Ruskin and Elizabeth Siddal MA Univ of Kentucky

1948   104 p
6087 SMALLWOOD Osborne T The Attitude of John Ruskin toward Organized
      Religion of His Time MA Howard Univ 1939   57 p
6088 STEWART Donald M An Analysis of John Ruskin's Approach to Victorian
      Social Economy MA Univ of Maine 1936   82 p
6089 THOMAS Sara A Ruskin's Critical Estimate of Shakespeare MA Univ of
      Tennessee 1939
6090 UMPHLETT Wiley L Ruskin Versus Whistler: The Trial of Creative
      Vision MA Columbia 1960   77 p
6091 VAN TASSEL John E John Ruskin's Economic Thought MA Boston Coll 1953
6092 WOODALL James R Ruskin: The Women in His Life MA Univ of Kentucky
      1947   181 p
6093 WOODS Doran C Ruskin's Concept of the Relationship between the
      Government and the Worker MS Kansas St Coll at Pittsburg 1938
6094 WYATT Patricia L John Ruskin's Relationship to Evangelicalism
      MA Univ of Maryland at College Park 1966   72 p
See also 1240, 1298, 1817, 2090, 6123

                          GEORGE WILLIAM RUSSELL

6095 D'ESTE A M George William Russell's Orientalism MA Ca Foscari (Italy)
      1942
6096 GIANNONI B George W Russell and the Celtic Revival MA Ca Foscari
      (Italy) nd
6097 JORZICK Elizabeth The Ideas of AE, Mystic and Theosophist
      MA Columbia 1937
See also 6098

                          SIEGFRIED SASSOON

6098 ALLISON Alexander C II Pacifism as a Personal Response: Sassoon,
      Russell and MacDonald BA Amherst 1960
6099 COLA Anna M An Introduction to the Study of Siegfried Sassoon's
      Poetry MA Ca Foscari (Italy) 1947
6100 McDERMOTT F J Siegfried Sassoon: Realist and Rebel MA Boston Coll
      1941

                            WALTER SCOTT

6101 ACKERMAN Betty J Scott's Minor Characters: Image and Effect
      MA Bowling Green Univ 1962
6102 ALTMAN C O The Supernatural Element in Scott's Novels MA Ohio St
      Univ 1912
6103 ANDREW J The Novels of Sir Walter Scott as a Development of His
      Metrical Romances BA Univ of British Columbia (Canada) 1929
6104 APPLEGATE Patricia A Study of Scott MA Colorado St Coll 1962
6105 BACON Frances The Influence of Scott on the Early Novels of Balzac
      MA Univ of Oregon 1932
6106 BECKWITH John A Scott's Theory of the Novel as Expressed in His
      Critical Works and Practiced in His Novels MA Univ of Idaho 1929
6107 BELL Mineola B France and the Fiction of Sir Walter Scott MA Univ
      of Florida 1951
6108 BISHOP Barr B Sir Walter Scott: The Border-Raid Ballad Collector-
      Editor MA Brigham Young Univ 1967   99 p
6109 BLACK Jo A The Search of Sir Walter Scott MA Univ of Texas at
      El Paso 1968   118 p
6110 BLACK Louise A Study in Scott's Letters: An Examination of His
      Political, Social and Religious Views MA Univ of Texas at
      Austin 1941   122 p
6111 BOATRIGHT Mody C Plot Structure in the Novels of Sir Walter Scott

MA Univ of Texas at Austin 1923
6112 BOGNER Howard F Sir Walter Scott in New Orleans, 1818-1832
      MA Tulane Univ 1937
6113 BOLAND Sr M Loretto Ballad Influences in the Poetry of Scott
      MA St Louis Univ 1934 89 p
6114 CAMERON J H Scottish History in the Waverley Novels BA Univ of
      British Columbia (Canada) 1932
6115 CARTER Winnie M The Characterization of Men in the Novels of
      Sir Walter Scott MA Univ of Texas at Austin 1928
6116 COEN Sr Mary P Scott Uses Liturgy Abundantly but Fails to Secure
      Fullest Artistry MA Boston Coll 1934
6117 COLLINS Frank M The Witch in Sir Walter Scott's Novels MA Univ of
      Oklahoma 1939
6118 COLODNY Isidor Phases of Walter Scott's Influence upon the Historical
      Novel MA Univ of Vermont 1907 78 p
6119 CONNOR E J The Romantic Material in the Waverley Novels MA Ohio St
      Univ 1901
6120 COSBY Frank V The Interest in Spain of Sir Walter Scott,
      Walter Savage Landor and Robert Southey as Seen in Their "Roderick"
      Poems MA Columbia 1940
6121 DELANY Sr M Elenara Hawthorne's Indebtedness to Scott MA Boston
      Coll 1950
6122 DENNIS Eunice The Influence of the Popular Ballad on Scott the
      Romanticist MA Univ of Tennessee 1939
6123 DIGGLE Margaret The Treatment in Literature of the Ideal of Chivalry
      in the Nineteenth Century with Reference to Medieval Documents
      M Litt Cambridge Univ (England) 1928
6124 EAGAN Sr Mary C Rob Roy in History and in Sir Walter Scott MA Univ
      of Texas at Austin 1927
6125 ERNST Sr M Georgiana Literary Criticism ln the Letters of
      Sir Walter Scott MA St Louis Univ 1943 76 p
6126 FEENEY Mary E Comic Themes in the Waverley Novels MA Univ of Rhode
      Island 1965 121 p
6127 FRANSON John K The Narrator Frameworks in the Waverley Novels of
      Sir Walter Scott MA Brigham Young Univ 1969 92 p
6128 FRAZER M H Scott's Treatment of Folk-Song Material in His Scottish
      Novels MA Univ of North Carolina at Chapel Hill 1940
6129 GORSUCH Inez A Study of Representative Villains in Sir Walter Scott's
      Writings MA Bowling Green Univ 1942
6130 GRAHAM E V The Influence of Sir Walter Scott on Washington Irving
      MA Florida St Univ 1933
6131 GREEN Aubrey The Feminine Role in Sir Walter Scott's Novels
      MA Texas Technological Univ 1966 56 p
6132 HABER T B A Time Synopsis of the Waverley Novels MA Ohio St Univ 1925
6133 HAYWARD Grace History of Scott's Novels MA Univ of Kansas 1907
6134 HEBRON Mary D Sir Walter Scott in New Orleans, 1833-1850 MA Tulane
      Univ 1940
6135 HIRSCH Louise Walter Scott's Reputation as a Narrative Poet
      (1795-1832) MA Tulane Univ 1936
6136 HOLLOWAY M The Evolution of Scott's Idea of Romance BA Univ of
      British Columbia (Canada) 1931
6137 HOLTER Ethel E A Study of Scott's Critical Theory as Stated in His
      Prefaces and Illustrated in Waverley Novels MA Oklahoma St Univ
      1936
6138 HORN Ollie Literary Criticism of Scott's Character Portrayal in
      the Waverley Novels MA Univ of Iowa 1935
6139 HUNT James C The Nature of Sir Walter Scott's Interest in the Middle
      Ages MA Univ of Kentucky 1935
6140 JONES Dorothy W Indebtedness of the Southern Novel to the Waverley
      Novels MA Southern Methodist Univ 1939

6141 JONES O W Scott as a Romantic Poet MA Univ of North Carolina at
      Chapel Hill 1909
6142 KAHOE Margaret A Eighteenth Century Scotland as Reflected in the
      Works of Sir Walter Scott MA Univ of Chicago 1965
6143 KINDRED Lorena Citations on Sir Walter Scott in the *Edinburgh Review*
      from 1802-1829 MA Univ of Oklahoma 1938
6144 KLANCAR Anthony J Sir Walter Scott in Yugo-Slav Literature
      MA Columbia 1942
6145 LANCASTER Roger J The Community as a Social Unit in the Novels of
      Sir Walter Scott MA Ohio St Univ 1967 76 p
6146 LEDBETTER Homer M Realism in the Novels of Sir Walter Scott: A Study
      of Its Significance and Relation to Scott's Romanticism MA Oklahoma
      St Univ 1937
6147 LINDLEY Georgia French Criticism of Walter Scott MA Univ of Kansas
      1922
6148 LONG L G The Peasant Women in the Waverley Novels MA Ohio St Univ
      1931
6149 McATEE Irma V Gothic Elements in the Novels of Scott MA Univ of
      Iowa 1934
6150 McCRORY John D The Influence of the Waverley Novels upon Three Works
      by John Pendleton Kennedy MA Univ of Pittsburgh 1951
6151 MADSEN Lyle V The Medievalism in the Literature of Sir Walter Scott
      MA Mankato St Coll 1962 48 p
6152 MEAD R N Sir Walter Scott, the Historical Novelist MA Boston Coll
      1937
6153 MEEHAN Sr M Bernard Sir Walter Scott's Attitude toward Catholic
      Clergymen in *Ivanhoe* MA St Mary's at San Antonio 1945 140 p
6154 NELSON Donald A Sir Walter Scott and Sir Edward Bulwer-Lytton:
      Gothic Compromisers, Adapters and Expanders MA Ohio St Univ 1967
      120 p
6155 ODOM Keith C Aristotlelian Elements in Sir Walter Scott's *The Bride
      of Lammermoor* MA Oklahoma St Univ 1956 69 p
6156 PARRY William B Humor in the Waverley Novels MA Univ of Iowa 1934
6157 PIERCE M J The Development and Treatment of the Historical Romance
      from the Time of Scott to 1910 MA Boston Univ 1938
6158 POWELL Patricia K Some Non-Political Aspects of Scottish Nationalism
      in *The Lay of the Last Minstrel*, *Marmion* and *The Lady of the Lake*
      MA Lamar Technological Univ 1967 128 p
6159 RAGLAND Alice T Superstitions Found in Sir Walter Scott's Longer
      Poems Which Appeared Prior to the Publication of *Waverley* (1814)
      MA Univ of Kentucky 1931
6160 RAVANELLI Lidia Scottish Tradition and Folklore in Walter Scott's
      Novels MA Ca Foscari (Italy) 1946
6161 ROBB Anne J Sir Walter Scott's Interpretation of the Romantic Move-
      ment MA Univ of Pittsburgh 1939
6162 ROBERTS Frances The Supernatural in Scott MA Univ of North Carolina
      at Chapel Hill 1932
6163 ROTHWEILER Mary J Literary Criticism in the Letters of Sir Walter Scott
      MA St Louis Univ 1940 57 p
6164 RUSSELL David Scott's Methods of Creating Atmosphere, with Particular
      Reference to Foretelling MA Univ of Louisville 1961
6165 SAYRE Nellie M Scott's Attitude towards Catholicism MA Univ of Iowa
      1924
6166 SCALLY James J Sir Walter Scott's Use of the Gothic Tradition in
      Six Border Novels MA St Louis Univ 1970 75 p
6167 SCHENK Ralph H Sir Walter Scott's Treatment of Monasticism: A
      Critical Study MA St Louis Univ 1934 101 p
6168 SCHROEDER C M Scott's Conception of Womanhood as Revealed by a Study
      of His Heroines MA Boston Univ 1927
6169 SHANKLIN Agnes K Characterization of Women in the Waverley Novels

as Influenced by Romantic Elements in the Life of Sir Walter Scott
MA St Louis Univ 1952 114 p

6170 SHANNON E S The Use of Heraldry by Sir Walter Scott MA Univ of
New Mexico 1931

6171 SIMPSON Claude M Sir Walter Scott and His Publishers MA Southern
Methodist Univ 1931 129 p

6172 SMITH Robert G Comic Characters in the Major Novels of
Sir Walter Scott MA Montreal (Canada) 1966

6173 SMOOT Jane A Comparison of the Treatment of the Covenanters by
Scott and Galt MA Univ of Texas at Austin 1939 185 p

6174 STANDARD Lawrence E An Analysis of Scott's *The Lady of the Lake*
MA Western St Coll of Colorado 1963

6175 STERN Hannah A The Reflection of Scott in the Russian Historical
Novel of M N Zagoskin MA Columbia 1936

6176 STEVENSON A H A Study of the Roderick Legend in English Poetry
by Scott, Landor and Southey MA Rice 1926

6177 STEWART Clara M Witchcraft and Sorcery in the Writings of
Sir Walter Scott MA Univ of Iowa 1932

6178 TATUM Ola M Heroism and Devotion in Certain Characters of
Sir Walter Scott MS Kansas St Coll at Pittsburg 1941

6179 TOLMAN Helen L The Use of Superstitions in Scott's Longer Poems
Written after the Publication of Waverley in 1814 and in Selected
Shorter Poems Written prior to the Publication of *The Lay of the
Minstrel* in 1805 MA Univ of Kentucky 1937

6180 TOMASSO Theresa M The Humor in Sir Walter Scott MA Villanova Univ
1966

6181 TOYNE Ruth M Scott's Novelistic Technique in Theory and in Practice
MA Univ of Iowa 1934

6182 WALKER Clara R The Portrayal of Women in the Novels of Scott
MA Univ of Texas at Austin 1928

6183 WALKER Grady J Scott's Refinement of the Gothic in Certain of the
Waverley Novels MA Oklahoma St Univ 1959 57 p

6184 WALLIS Luther D Jr Medieval Elements in Sir Walter Scott's Novels:
Fact or Fiction? MA Columbia 1952 81 p

6185 WHALEY Grace W The Influence of Sir Walter Scott's Novels upon
Those of William Gilmore Simms MA Duke Univ 1929

6186 WILLIAMSON A C Historical Novelists: Scott and Dickens MA Boston
Coll 1937

6187 YEURY S W The Romance of the Scottish Border MA Austin Coll 1937
See also 972, 2106, 2416, 6081, 6913

THOMAS SHADWELL

6188 ALBERTSON Marguerite Thomas Shadwell and Restoration Comedy
MA Univ of Oklahoma 1939

6189 GEARY Edward A Thomas Shadwell as a Playwright MA Brigham Young
Univ 1963 85 p

6190 HUDSON Genevieve The Position of Thomas Shadwell in Restoration
Comedy MA Southern Methodist Univ 1933

6191 KUKUK Florence E Thomas Shadwell's Indebtedness to Moliere
MA Univ of Toledo 1931

6192 LOHN Jeannette Four Political Dramatists of the Restoration:
Mrs Behn, D'Urfey, Settle and Shadwell MA Columbia 1940

6193 PROFFITT Elma L The Comedies of Thomas Shadwell MA Univ of Oregon
1937

6194 SMITH Donald G Elements of Humour and Sentiment in the Comedies
of Thomas Shadwell MA Toronto (Canada) 1966

6195 STACHURA Rev Sylvester M The Meaning of "Humor" in Thomas Shadwell
and Restoration Comedy MA Boston Coll 1961

SHAFTESBURY

6196   FARLEY John J   The Background of Shaftesbury's *Letter Concerning
       Enthusiasm* and Its Place in the History of an Idea   MA Columbia 1950
6197   FLANNAGAN Mary A   The Philosophic Origin of Shaftesbury's Concepts
       of the True, the Good and the Beautiful   MA East Tennessee St Univ
       1957
6198   KEHRWALD Claire R   The Sentimental Deist: A Study of the Ethical
       Philosophy of the Third Earl of Shaftesbury   MA Syracuse Univ 1950
       139 p
6199   MILLER Myra G   Shaftesbury's Theory of Aesthetics in Its Relation
       to Eighteenth Century Literary Criticism   MA Texas Woman's Univ 1936
See also 18, 6601

SHAKESPEARE

6200   ACKERMANN Harry F   The Commonalty in the *Henry VI* Plays   MA Univ of
       Rhode Island 1969   95 p
6201   ADAMS Hazel P   Implications of Certain Christian Beliefs in Ten of
       Shakespeare's Plays   MA Univ of Texas at Austin 1948   103 p
6202   ADAMS Percy G   A Study of Voltaire's Attitude Towards Shakespeare
       MA Univ of Texas at Austin 1937   142 p
6203   AGNES Sr   The Dramatic Value of the Imagination in the Development
       of the Character of Macbeth   MA Boston Coll 1931
6204   AKIN Kathleen   An Analysis of the Imagery of *Antony and Cleopatra*
       and *All for Love*   MA Hardin-Simmons Univ 1960
6205   ALEXANDER A W   The Progress of the Cleopatra Fable in English Liter-
       ature   BA Univ of British Columbia (Canada) 1948
6206   ALEXANDER F M   The Reflection of Courtesy-Book Subjects in Shakespeare's
       Comedies with Subject Indices to *The Courtier, The Galateo* and
       Civile Conversation   MA Univ of North Carolina at Chapel Hill 1929
6207   ALEXANDER Ruth   Shakespeare's Use of His Source Material in *Measure
       for Measure*   MA Univ of Texas at Austin 1929
6208   ALLARD Francis X   Shakespeare's and Brecht's *Coriolanus*:   The Hero
       and the Masses and How They Relate to One Another   MA Stanford
       Univ 1966
6209   ALLEN Marguerite   A Study and Comparison of Certain Shakespearean
       Lovers with Bassanio Whom Dr C R Baskerville Has Proved to be the
       Ideal Elizabethan Lover   MA Oklahoma St Univ 1933   32 p
6210   ALLEN Rachelle L   Shakespeare's Use of His Sources in *Two Gentlemen
       of Verona*   MA Univ of Texas at Austin 1935
6211   ALLEN Roach V   Figurative Language in Shakespeare's Plays, *Romeo and
       Juliet, As You Like It, Hamlet* and *The Tempest*   MA West Texas St
       Univ 1940   175 p
6212   ALLISON Elizabeth D   Shakespeare's Military as Compared with the
       English Army of the Fifteenth and Sixteenth Centuries
       MA Louisiana St Univ 1938
6213   ALLISON Gladys M   Shakespeare's Treatment of Ghosts and Other Super-
       natural Elements   MA East Tennessee St Univ 1966
6214   ALPAR John J   Motivations of Self-Destruction in Some Shakespearean
       Characters   MA West Texas St Univ 1969   101 p
6215   ALPERN Fannie   Local Color in *The Merchant of Venice*   MA Univ of
       Pittsburgh 1933
6216   ALTHEIMER Lee M   Shakespeare's Use of His Source Material in *Othello*
       MA Univ of Texas at Austin 1928
6217   AMBACH Martha   The Introduction of Shakespeare to Germany by the
       English Strolling Players of the Seventeenth Century, with an
       Analysis of the German *Titus Andronicus* and the German *Hamlet*
       MA Ca Foscari (Italy) 1957
6218   AMBLER Elizabeth J   The Shylock Tradition   MA Washington Univ at

St Louis 1932   288 p

6219 AMBROSE R T   Comparison of *Hamlet* with *L'Aiglon* and *Richard III*
MA Boston Coll 1936

6220 ANDERSEN Austin   Modern Trends in *Hamlet* Criticism   BA Rutgers St
Univ 1964   143 p

6221 ANDERSON Leta A   Some of the Difficulties the Modern Reader Finds
When Reading Shakespeare and How to Overcome Them   MA Oklahoma
St Univ 1933   38 p

6222 ANDERSSON H O   The Study of Shakespeare's Sources from Langbaine
to Malone   B Litt Oxford Univ (England) 1949

6223 ANNE MARY Sr   Religion in the Plays of Shakespeare   MA Boston Univ 1951

6224 ARTHUR Malnor E   Parallelisms in *King Lear* and *Death of a Salesman*
MA West Texas St Univ 1964   141 p

6225 ASHBY Sylvia   Shakespeare: Versions of "The Golden World"
MA Texas Technological Univ 1966   72 p

6226 ATKINS Carl   Four Shakespearean Tragedies Since 1939   MA St Mary's
at San Antonio 1949   72 p

6227 ATWOOD Daniel M   A History of Shakespeare's *Measure for Measure*
Criticism   MA George Washington Univ 1967   98 p

6228 AYCOCK Wendell Shakespeare and Rodo: Recurring Themes and Characters
MA Texas Technological Univ 1965   57 p

6229 AYER Lucy E   Symbolism in Shakespeare   MA Boston Univ 1932

6230 BACHENKEIMER Myron S   Domestic Drama in the Time of Shakespeare
MA Univ of Pittsburgh 1932

6231 BAGLEY Mary M   The Supernatural in Shakespearean Tragedy   MA Boston
Univ 1932

6232 BAIER May V   *Two Gentlemen of Verona*: The Prologue to Shakespeare's
Romantic Comedies   MA St Louis Univ 1937   138 p

6233 BAKER Donald G   Shakespeare and the American West   MA Adams St Coll
1969

6234 BAKER John   Hotspur's Concept of Honor   MA Gonzaga Univ 1966

6235 BAKER Kathrin M   Hamlet and der Bestrafte Brudermord   MA Washington
Univ at St Louis 1917   59 p

6236 BAKER Samuel M Jr   Harley Granville-Barker and Modern Shakespearean
Stage Productions   MA Univ of North Carolina at Chapel Hill 1958
109 p

6237 BALDWIN R F   *Hamlet*: A Study in Reformation Orthodoxy   MA Boston
Coll 1941

6238 BALLARD Elizabeth L   A Questioning of Hotson's Hypothesis for
Shakespeare's *Love's Labour's Won*   MA Univ of Pittsburgh 1958

6239 BARKER Walter L   The Transparent Triviality of Shakespeare's Shylock
MA Univ of Rhode Island 1962   90 p

6240 BARNES John   The Biblical Diction, Imagery and Allusion of Shakespeare
MA Northwestern Univ 1905

6241 BARNETT Richard   Characterization of Macbeth: A Study of Macbeth's
Personality   MA Northeast Missouri St Coll 1959

6242 BARRETT Barbara T   A Moor, His Wife and His Ensign: A Study in
Contrasts between the *Novella* of Giraldi Cinthio, the *Othello*
of Shakespeare and the *Otello* of Boito and Verdi   MA San Jose St
Coll 1966

6243 BARRETT Lula M   Shakespeare's Use of Source Material in *Richard III*
MA Univ of Texas at Austin 1930

6244 BARRON Jewel   A Study of the Characters in *Richard III*   MA Baylor Univ
1940   171 p

6245 BARROW Lillian   A Study of Shakespeare's References to the Sea
MA Univ of Houston 1954   113 p

6246 BARRUS Ruth H   Three Worlds of Hamlet: Three Short Biographical
Stories; A Treatise on Organ Compositions Played in a Graduate
Recital   MA Brigham Young Univ 1966

6247 BARRY G T   A Study of Hamlet's Madness   MA Boston Coll 1935

6248 BARRY H L Cervantes and Shakespeare MA Boston Univ 1925
6249 BARRY J M Appreciation of Chivalry: Malory, Spenser and Shakespeare
      M Ed Boston Coll 1932
6250 BASS Leola I Shakespeare's Dramatic Use of Ghosts MA Oklahoma St
      Univ 1937 40 p
6251 BATEN Janie B Paternal Relations in Six of Shakespeare's Middle and
      Later Plays MA Univ of Texas at Austin 1931
6252 BAXTER Elizabeth War in Shakespeare's Plays MA Hardin-Simmons Univ
      1935
6253 BAYARD H R Certain Shakespearean Heroines MA Boston Univ 1926
6254 BEEBE Myra D The Use of Rhetorical Figures as a Guide to Character
      Development in *Othello* MA Texas Technological Univ 1960 178 p
6255 BELDEN Eldora Paternal Relations in Six of Shakespeare's Early Plays
      MA Univ of Texas at Austin 1928 111 p
6256 BELKIN Roslyn *Timon of Athens*: A Critic's Problem MA Montreal
      (Canada) 1964
6257 BELL Bessie P Shakespeare's Women BA Univ of Oklahoma 1903
6258 BELL Carole J A Study of Probable Sources for Shakespeare's Character-
      ization of Cleopatra MA East Tennessee St Univ 1965
6259 BENDER C P Shakespeare's *Richard III* MA North Texas St Univ 1968
6260 BENOIT Pauline E Proverb Lore in Shakespeare's Comedies MA Baylor
      Univ 1950 235 p
6261 BENSON John B Biographical Influences on the Writings of
      William Shakespeare M Ed Henderson St Coll nd
6262 BENT Larry W A Comparison of Verbal Ambiguity in *Romeo and Juliet*
      and *Hamlet* BA Acadia (Canada) 1966
6263 BERGMAN Jane A A Reinvestigation of Certain Textual Problems in
      Cymbeline, The Winter's Tale and *The Tempest*: Evidence for Revision
      and Dating MA Kansas St Teachers Coll 1966
6264 BERRY Claire A The Authorship of *Henry VI*, Parts II and III
      MA Washington Univ at St Louis 1917
6265 BERRY Elizabeth Shakespeare's Cleopatra MA Boston Univ 1929
6266 BICKER William D The Natural Perspective in *Measure for Measure*
      MA Univ of Santa Clara 1966
6267 BILLINGS Virginia P Shakespeare's Dramatic Method as Illustrated
      in *The Life and Death of King John* MA Butler Univ 1937
6268 BISHOP Curtis V A Study of the Source Material in *Taming of the
      Shrew* MA Univ of Texas at Austin 1928
6269 BLACK Lucia G Shakespeare's Misanthropes MA Louisiana St Univ 1941
6270 BLACKALLER George A Shakespeare's Imagery in the First Three Acts
      of *Julius Caesar* MA Univ of Texas at Austin 1950 81 p
6271 BLAINE Leota M Figures of Repetition in Shakespeare's History Plays
      MA Western St Coll of Colorado 1935 250 p
6272 BLAIR Bessie Figurative Language in Shakespeare's Plays MA West
      Texas St Univ 1940 251 p
6273 BLANCHE Evelyn K Shakespeare's Heroine, Lady Macbeth MA Boston
      Univ 1935
6274 BLATTY William P T S Eliot's Shakespearean Criticism MA George
      Washington Univ 1954 101 p
6275 BLOODGOOD Francis C Hamlet: The Man of Good Will MA Univ of Tulsa
      1962 96 p
6276 BLOODGOOD Jane C The Hidden Children of Shakespeare MA Univ of
      Tulsa 1958 87 p
6277 BLOUIN Gisele A Comparison of Racine's *Phedre* and Shakespeare's
      Othello MA Oklahoma St Univ 1948
6278 BOGGS Norma V Absolutists and the Development of Dramatic Action
      in *Love's Labour's Lost* MA Texas Technological Univ 1969 52 p
6279 BOGHOSIAN Thomas F Problems of Genre: Shakespeare and Melville
      MA Univ of Maine 1968 103 p
6280 BOICE Wilson S .Shakespeare as a Humorist MA Williams Coll 1907

6281 BOMAN Joseph *Timon of Athens* and Its Relation to Plutarch MA Univ
      of Iowa 1935
6282 BOSWELL F P Modern Trends in the Interpretation of Falstaff
      MA North Texas St Univ 1956
6283 BOULTON M A Study of William Richardson, with Special Reference to
      His Shakespearean Criticism B Litt Oxford Univ (England) 1948
6284 BOWERS Carolyn G Ghostlore in the Minds of the Shakespearean Audience,
      with Special Reference to the Dance of Death in *The Tragedy of
      King Richard III* MA Columbia 1937
6285 BOWLING William G Prince Hal: A Survey of the Life of Henry V While
      Prince of Wales, and a Study of His Character as Prince and King
      with Special Reference to the Plays of Shakespeare MA Washington
      Univ at St Louis 1925
6286 BOWMAN Benjamin C A Review of the Bibliographical Methods Employed
      by J Dover Wilson in the First Thirteen Volumes of the "New"
      Cambridge Shakespeare MA Univ of Oregon 1940
6287 BRACE Carl A Reconsideration of the Problems in Text, Source and
      Date of *Love's Labour's Lost* MA Kansas St Teachers Coll 1966
6288 BRACY William Jaques: A Study in Shakespearean Criticism MA Univ
      of North Carolina at Chapel Hill 1939
6289 BRANCH J W The Messenger in Shakespeare MA North Texas St Univ 1955
6290 BRANDON Lydia A Shakespeare's Influence on Tennyson MA Univ of
      Tennessee 1936
6291 BRASHEAR Lucy M Settings in Shakespeare's Plays: A Study in
      Shakespeare's Use of Sources MA Univ of Florida 1952
6292 BRASHEARS E The Authorship of *Henry VI*, Part I, Considered in Relation
      to the Sources of the Play MA North Texas St Univ 1940
6293 BRENNAN Sr Rose E The Development of the Chief Characters of the
      Troilus and Cressida Theme MA Univ of Southern California 1928
6294 BRERETON Margaret *The Merchant of Venice* MS Univ of Maryland at
      College Park 1942 89 p
6295 BRESTENSKY Dennis F The Textual Status of *King Lear* MA Duquesne
      Univ 1966
6296 BREWER Charles R Repeated Motifs in Shakespeare MA Hardin-Simmons
      Univ 1927
6297 BREWSTER·Paul G Shakespeare's Use of the *Palace of Pleasure*
      MA Univ of Oklahoma 1926
6298 BRIDGES Elizabeth D Shakespeare's Roman Plays: Source and Creation
      MA West Texas St Univ 1961 122 p
6299 BRIDGES Phyllis A Study of Parallelism in *King Lear* MA West Texas
      St Univ 1966 78 p
6300 BRITTAIN R L A Production Book of *King Lear* MA Columbia 1951
6301 BROADFOOT Mary A The Concept of the Fool in Renaissance Comedy,
      Tragic-Comedy and Tragedy: A Comparison and Contrast of Falstaff,
      Don Quixote and Hamlet MA Univ of Redlands 1966
6302 BROMBERG Lee C A Study of *Titus Andronicus* MA Cornell Univ 1966
6303 BROOKS Mildred L A Digest of Current Critical Material (1900-1935)
      Concerning *Macbeth* MA Univ of Tennessee 1937
6304 BROWN B L Woman, the Root of Man's Self-Destruction in Four
      Shakespearean Plays MA North Texas St Univ 1967
6305 BROWN Eric J The Influence of Social Disease upon the Imagery Found
      in Sixteen Plays of William Shakespeare MA Kent St Univ 1965
6306 BROWN James E Which *Hamlet* Shall We Teach? MS Kansas St Coll at
      Pittsburg 1949
6307 BROWN James F Hamlet and His Prototypes MA Univ of Nevada 1928
6308 BROWN Lloyd W The Troilus Figure in English Comedy MA Toronto
      (Canada) 1964
6309 BROWN Richard P *Antony and Cleopatra* and *All for Love*: A Comparison
      of Two Dramatic Methods MA Indiana Univ 1960
6310 BROWN Rosemary C Shakespeare and Montaigne MA Univ of Massachusetts

1952
6311 BROWN Sondra P   The Songs in the Restoration Alterations and
     Adaptations of the Shakespearean Plays, 1660-1710   MA Temple Univ
     1953   176 p
6312 BRUHN Gladys   Reactions of High School Seniors to Shakespeare's
     Plays with Suggested Methods for Teaching this Author's Work
     MS Ft Hays St Coll 1966
6313 BRUNER Davis K   Grand Opera and Shakespeare   MA Washington Univ at
     St Louis 1934   117 p
6314 BUECHMANN Claus-Peter   Some Problems of Shakespeare's Monmouth Plays
     MA Univ of Kansas 1965
6315 BULGREN Janis A   Reversals of Order in *King Lear*   MA Univ of Iowa 1965
6316 BULL Margaret G   Shakespeare's Use of History in the English Group
     of Plays   MA Univ of Richmond 1933   51 p
6317 BULLOCK Susan C   Another Melville-Shakespeare Relationship: Star-
     buck and Hamlet   MA Univ of North Carolina at Chapel Hill 1959   71 p
6318 BURCHAM John C   Shakespeare's Use of the Ghost in His Tragedies
     MA Univ of New Mexico 1938
6319 BURGESS Elanor H   Shakespeare's Treatment of Death in the Major
     Tragedies   MA Hardin-Simmons Univ 1958
6320 BURKE Mary F   Edward Capell, an Editor of Shakespeare   MA St Louis
     Univ 1938   79 p
6321 BURKHALTER Thelma K   Shakespeare Becomes a National Monument: An
     Attempt to Isolate and Describe the Point in English Literary
     and Social History When Shakespeare Was Popularly Recognized as
     the Greatest English Writer   MA George Washington Univ 1965   125 p
6322 BURLESON Shirley D   The Education of William Shakespeare   M Ed Hender-
     son St Coll nd
6323 BURNER Sandra A   Touchstone: The Complete Wise Fool   MA Hunter Coll 1961
6324 BURNESS Donald B   The Interaction of Multiple Plots in Shakespeare's
     Comedies   MA Trinity Coll 1965
6325 BURNETT Louis E   John Lyly's Influence on Four Plays of Shakespeare
     MA Univ of Texas at Austin 1931
6326 BURNHAM Margaret M   Stendhal's Theory of Romanticism as Expressed in
     His Essay *Racine and Shakespeare*   MA Univ of Oklahoma 1941
6237 BURNS J   Shakespeare's Elizabethan Public   MA Univ of Louisville 1926
6328 BURRIS Gladys T   Criteria of Gentility from Chaucer to Shakespeare
     MA Oklahoma St Univ 1932   47 p
6329 BURTON Mary E   Word Play in Shakespeare   MA Univ of Louisville 1925
6330 BUSAM W F   Similes and Metaphors in Shakespeare   MA Boston Coll 1928
6331 BUSHING Arthur S   Shakespeare's Concept of Time   MA Univ of Tennessee
     1948
6332 BUTLER Donald J   Shakespeare's "Sonnet 121": An Analysis of Its
     Meaning   MA Fresno St Coll 1966   79 p
6333 BUTLER Isabel   Shakespeare as a Conscious Dramatic Artist, as Shown
     by His Words in His Plays   MA Univ of Tennessee 1930
6334 BUTRICK Goldie E   A Reinvestigation of *The Troublesome Raigne*
     and Shakespeare's *King John*   MA Kansas St Teachers Coll 1964
6335 BYRD Samuel M   The Wit and Humor of Shakespeare as Revealed in His
     Comedies   MA Tulane Univ 1927
6336 CAHILL Sr Emily   Shakespeare's Use of the Supernatural in *Macbeth*
     and *Hamlet*   MA Boston Coll 1927
6337 CAHILL Sr Emmanuel   A Study of the Anonymous *True Tragedie of
     Richard III*   MA Univ of Texas at Austin 1944   156 p
6338 CAHILL Sr Helen M   The Adaptation of Shakespeare's Sources in *Henry VI*
     MA Villanova Univ 1964
6339 CALHOUN Emily M   Power, Will and Appetite in Shakespeare's *Troilus
     and Cressida*   MA Texas Technological Univ 1968
6340 CALHOUN Howell V   Sources of Shakespeare's Witchlore   MA Columbia 1942
6341 CALLAGHAN Sr Mary H   Character Study of Hamlet and Macbeth   MA Boston

Coll 1927
6342 CAMERON Kenneth W *Othello*: A Re-Examination of the Quarto of 1622;
      a Comparative Textual Study MA West Virginia Univ 1931 282 p
6343 CAMPBELL Irma E Characterization in Shakespeare's Roman Plays
      MA Univ of Texas at Austin 1928
6344 CAMPBELL Mary E Shakespeare's Tricks in Diction MA Austin Coll 1938
6345 CAMPION Frances R Gentle Ophelia MA Boston Coll 1929
6346 CANNAN Frederick F G Wilson Knight's Shakespeare Studies: An Expo-
      sition and Analysis of His Main Concepts and Their Applications
      MA Colorado St Coll 1962
6347 CAPRIO Carolyn M Conflict in Commitment: A Thematic Study of
      Shakespeare's *Coriolanus* and *Timon of Athens* MA Fairleigh Dickinson
      Univ 1966
6348 CARD Vivian R Shakespeare's Plays as Criticized by Englishmen and
      Americans of the Twentieth Century MA Boston Univ 1930
6349 CARGYLE John R An Analysis and Comparison of Shakespeare's *Othello*
      as the Basis for Verdi and Boito's Opera MA Hardin-Simmons Univ
      1962
6350 CARPENTER Sr Mary A The Text of Lewis Theobald's 1733 Edition of
      Shakespeare MA St Louis Univ 1938 77 p
6351 CARR Alden J Shakespeare's Kings MA Boston Univ 1931
6352 CARREY David R A Comparative Study of Analogous Elements in
      Shakespeare's *Othello* and Verdi's *Otello* MA Ohio Univ 1966
6353 CARROLL Sudie M Father-Daughter Relationship in Shakespeare MA Louis-
      iana St Univ 1939
6354 CARSWELL A I The Five Act Structure in the Thirty-Seven Plays of
      William Shakespeare MA Boston Univ 1920
6355 CARTER Alfred N *Hamlet*: A Study of Shakespeare's Sources MA Univ
      of Texas at Austin 1929
3656 CARTER Irene Shakespeare's Imagery in *The Tragedy of Hamlet, Prince
      of Denmark* MA Univ of Texas at Austin 1943 80 p
6357 CARTER Patricia M Shakespeare and Shaw as Writers of History:
      A Comparison of William Shakespeare's *Julius Caesar, Antony and
      Cleopatra* and *The First Part of King Henry VI* with Bernard Shaw's
      Caesar and Cleopatra and *Saint Joan* MA George Washington Univ
      1970 104 p
6358 CARTER Ronnie D Johnsonian and Hazlittian Criticism of Shakespeare's
      Plays MA Idaho St Univ 1966
6359 CASE Norman Shakespeare and the Tradition of Wordplay MA Hunter
      Coll 1966
6360 CHAMBLISS Ann M Contemporary Meanings of Light Images in *Romeo and
      Juliet* and *Othello* MA Univ of North Carolina at Chapel Hill 1958
      119 p
6361 CHAN M Aspects of Shakespeare's Use of Professional and Trade Jargon
      M Phil Univ of London (England) 1967
6362 CHANEY Mary L Recent Criticism of Shakespearean Stagecraft MA Univ
      of Pittsburgh 1931
6363 CHAUDHERY Sumita M Shakespeare and Plutarch's Moral Essays
      MA Howard Univ 1966 78 p
6364 CHENEY Elizabeth H The Costuming of Shakespearean Plays between 1590
      and 1760 MA Washington Univ at St Louis 1936 160 p
6365 CHERRY D H Personal Imagery in *Hamlet* BA Univ of British Columbia
      (Canada) 1951
6366 CHERRY Douglas The Courtly Love Theme in Shakespeare's Plays
      MA Univ of British Columbia (Canada) 1952 171 p
6367 CHIAVERINI Eileen M Plutarch and Shakespeare's Roman Plays MA Univ
      of Rhode Island nd
6368 CHILDRESS Jerrell P A Summary Bibliography of *Hamlet*, 1936-1940
      MA Univ of Tennessee 1950 63 p
6369 CHOI Young J Shakespeare's Use of the Melancholy Humor MA North

Texas St Univ 1968
6370 CLARK C A Dramatic Irony in Shakespeare BA Univ of British Columbia
      (Canada) 1922
6371 CLARK Edith J Shakespeare's Fools MA Boston Univ 1914
6372 CLARK Richard The Progress of Action in *Twelfth Night* MA Temple Univ
      1967 63 p
6373 CLARK Ruth E Elizabethan Animal Lore and Its Source: Illustrated
      from the Works of Spenser, Lyly and Shakespeare MA Univ of
      Arizona 1936
6374 CLASON Barbara E A Handbook to the *Merry Wives of Windsor* MA Univ
      of Oklahoma 1946
6375 CLAYTON Lillian P Stage Directions in the Early Texts of Shakespeare
      MA Univ of Oklahoma 1933
6376 CLAYTON O M Contemporary People in Shakespeare's Plays MA Univ of
      North Carolina at Chapel Hill 1927
6377 CLEOBURY A W The Shakespearean Criticism of Walter Whiter
      B Litt Oxford Univ (England) 1950
6378 CLIFFORD Harry R Shakespeare's Treatment of Courtly Love MA Oklahoma
      St Univ 1950
6379 CLINK Winifred C The Historicity of Shakespeare's English Queens
      MA Pacific Univ 1951 123 p
6380 COBB Marie An Analysis of the Second Act of Seven of Shakespeare's
      Comedies MA Univ of Texas at Austin 1940 131 p
6381 COCHRAN Ruth M Prospero: A Study in Shakespeare Character Criticism
      MA Univ of North Carolina at Chapel Hill 1946 100 p
6382 COCHRANE Dora G Shakespeare and Tapestry MA Alberta (Canada) 1966
6383 COE Daisy M A Comparison of Marlowe's *Edward II* and Shakespeare's
      Richard II with Special Reference to the *Chronicles of Holinshed*
      MA Univ of Texas at Austin 1939 156 p
6384 COHEN Eileen Z The Visible Solemnity: A Study of Concepts of
      Ceremony and Tradition in Richard Hooker and William Shakespeare
      MA Univ of Maryland at College Park 1958 86 p
6385 COHEN Eva M *Romeo and Juliet* on the Elizabethan Stage MA Univ of
      Pittsburgh 1915
6386 COHN William L The Malcontent in Early Shakespearean Drama
      MA Vanderbilt Univ 1965
6387 COKER E R Parental and Filial Relations in Shakespeare's Plays
      MA Univ of North Carolina at Chapel Hill 1930
6388 COLUZZI Ann C Shakespeare's Comedies and Histories: An Edition of
      Joseph Hunter's Unpublished Memoranda in Manuscript Addition 24495
      in the British Museum MA Georgetown Univ 1959 574 p
6389 CONCANNON D J Shakespeare's Lack of Spiritual Insight MA Boston Coll
      1936
6390 CONCHINE Vonda M A Study of Speech-Mannerisms Among Cruder Characters
      in Shakespeare's Dramas MA East Tennessee St Univ 1960
6391 CONLIN F S Shakespeare and Calderon MA Boston Coll 1927
6392 CONNER Theresa S A Comparison of the Chivalry Found in Shakespeare's
      Henry IV (Parts I and II) with the Noblest Traditions of Chivalry
      Before Shakespeare's Day as Found in English and Other Germanic
      Literature MA Oklahoma St Univ 1930 90 p
6393 CONNOLLY Margaret M Shakespeare and Milton in Their Last Major Works,
      The Tempest and *Samson Agonistes* MA Columbia 1951
6394 COOK Annie L Shakespeare's Use of His Source Material in *King John*
      MA Univ of Texas at Austin 1928
6395 COOK Charles H German Recognition and Criticism of Shakespeare from
      the Late Sixteenth Century through the Early Nineteenth Century
      MA Boston Univ 1945
6396 COOK Sidney M Jr Prisoners in Shakespeare's Plays MA Texas Christian
      Univ 1947 95 p
6397 COOKE K A C Bradley and His Influence in Twentieth Century

Shakespearean Criticism M Phil Univ of London (England) 1967
6398 COOMBER Melvin E A Study of the Limitations of Time and Space in
      Drama MA Toronto (Canada) 1964
6399 COPE Abigail J Enriching English Courses in Seventh and Eighth
      Grades by Using Materials from Shakespeare MA East Tennessee St
      Univ 1958
6400 CORSON Dorothy A Study of the Tragic Elements in Shakespeare's
      Comedies MA Pacific Univ 1930   53 p
6401 CORTRIGHT Mabel M Shakespeare Prefers "s": Shakespeare's Use of
      the "s" and the "th" forms of the Third Person Singular of the
      Present Tense MA Baylor Univ 1961   48 p
6402 COX Terrence C Dramatic Structure and Symbolic Patterns in
      The Winter's Tale MA Western (Canada) 1965
6403 CRABB Tommye L Shakespeare's Men of Wit in High Comedy MA Texas
      Arts and Industries Univ 1964
6404 CRABTREE Martha A Shakespeare's Romances: A Study of the Structure,
      the Inter-Relationships and the Medieval Conventions in the Late
      Comedies MA Univ of Texas at Austin 1958   87 p
6405 CRAWFORD Louise Shakespeare's Use of His Sources in Much Ado About
      Nothing MA Univ of Texas at Austin 1930
6406 CRENSHAW William T An Investigation of Iago's Use of the Sixteenth
      Century English Rhetorician's Schematization of the Topics of
      Invention MA Eastern New Mexico Univ 1969
6407 CREW Erman L Certain Shakespearean Old Men: A Study of Crafts-
      manship MA Auburn Univ 1959
6408 CROSSEN H J The Treatment of Death in the History Plays of Shakespeare
      MA Univ of North Carolina at Chapel Hill 1930
6409 CROWLEY A J A Comparison of Othello and Faust MA Boston Coll 1936
6410 CURTIS Dave L Hell is Murky: A Study of the Role of Darkness in
      Macbeth MA Univ of Delaware 1964   79 p
6411 CURTIS Eva Shakespeare's Treatment of the "Humorous" Character
      MA Univ of Oklahoma 1935
6412 CURTIS R E Tragic Potentialities of the Life of Shakespeare's
      Henry Bollingbroke MA Boston Coll 1939
6413 CUTRIGHT Frank The Sonnet-Lover in Shakespeare MA Univ of Richmond
      1935   52 p
6414 DALEY Arthur P The Influence of the Duelling Code on Three of
      Shakespeare's Plays: A Critical Study of Selected Plays MA Univ
      of Houston 1951   80 p
6415 DALL Dorothy Shakespeare and the Rival Poet: A Synthesis of Scholar-
      ship and Criticism MA Columbia 1940
6416 DAVIS Alma E The Bibliographical History of the Early Texts of Romeo
      and Juliet MA Univ of Maryland at College Park 1939   179 p
6417 DAVIS David G Shakespeare on War and Peace: A Study of These Subjects
      in Four of the History Plays MA Colorado St Coll 1964
6418 DAVIS Moita D Hamlet and the New Criticism MA Univ of Oklahoma 1954
6419 DAVIS Richard Jr Sir Tyrone Guthrie: His Theory and Practice of
      Directing Shakespeare MA Pennsylvania St Univ 1964
6420 DAY Sr Mary E Liturgical Imagery in Shakespeare's Tragedies
      MA Boston Coll 1958
6421 DEE Catherine A New Interpretation of Cleopatra in Shakespeare's
      Antony and Cleopatra MA St Louis Univ 1937   76 p
6422 DEELEY Sr M B Farewells in Shakespearean Drama MA Boston Coll 1934
6423 DeMARIA Robert Jr Reading The Tempest BA Amherst 1970
6424 DESAI Jagriti V Romeo and Juliet as a Tragedy of Fate and Character
      MA Oklahoma St Univ 1948   49 p
6425 DEVLIN B F Some Aspects of Death in Shakespeare MA Boston Coll 1931
6426 DEVLIN M M Gertrude of Denmark MA Boston Coll 1930
6427 DICKERSON Anne Instrumental and Vocal Music in England Preceding
      and During the Shakespearean Period, with Special Reference to the

Works of Shakespeare MA Boston Univ 1936
6428 DIELMAN Inez M Shakespeare's Iago in Aesthetic Criticism from
      Coleridge to Stoll MA St Mary's at San Antonio 1940 67 p
6429 DIMITSA Eleonora The Influence of Shakespeare on the Poetic Dramas
      of Shelley, Wordsworth and Coleridge MA Temple Univ 1964 52 p
6430 DIVINE Hugh W A Study of Some of the Problems in the Falstaff Plays
      MA Louisiana St Univ 1941
6431 DOBBS Jeannine Shakespeare's Fourth Dimension: An Afterlife of
      Love Restored MA Univ of New Hampshire 1969 50 p
6432 DONAGHUE Shirley Shakespeare's Reconciliation of Nature and Art in
      Selected Works BA Univ of British Columbia (Canada) 1970
6433 DONEGAN S E The Prose of Shakespeare and His Predecessors
      MA Boston Univ 1913
6434 DOREN Carol A A Study of the Relationship between the Poetic Imagery
      and the Dramatic Structure in William Shakespeare's *Antony and
      Cleopatra* MA Bowling Green Univ 1956
6435 DOSS Erma S Themes and Images in Shakespeare's *Venus and Adonis*
      MA Univ of Arkansas 1950
6436 DOTY Rebecca I Courtly Love in Shakespeare's Sonnets and Plays
      MA Univ of Louisville 1921
6437 DOW A J Critical Study of the *Menaechmi* and *The Comedy of Errors*
      MA Boston Univ 1912
6438 DOYLE E M Modern Interpretations of *Hamlet* MA Boston Univ 1940
6439 DRABECK Bernard A Shakespeare's *Othello* and Verdi's *Otello*: A Study
      MA Univ of Massachusetts 1956
6440 DRENNAN Marveline A Grammatical Analysis of *King Lear* MA Texas
      Southern Univ 1964
6441 DREW Hannah I History and Principles of Criticism: The Evidences
      that the Plays of Shakespeare Were Written by an Actor
      M Phil Northwestern Univ 1895
6442 DRISCOLL M A The Personality of Francis Bacon as Revealed in
      Shakespeare MA Boston Univ 1928
6443 DRISCOLL W J Problem of Localization in the Shakespearean Histories
      MA Boston Coll 1941
6444 DUBAY Sr Mary L Shakespeare's Prayers as a Device for Character
      Development MA Boston Coll 1949
6445 DUCLOS Albert J Actors of *King Lear*: Their Eras and Interpretations
      MA Univ of Maine 1965 158 p
6446 DUHMAEL Arthur P Shakespeare and the Whale: A Study of Shakespearean
      Echoes in *Moby Dick* MA Boston Coll 1952
6447 DUKE Lucille R Shakespeare's Use of Poetic Devices in Selected Plays
      MA Hardin-Simmons Univ 1949
6448 DUKES W J Shakespeare Criticism and *Richard II* MA Univ of North
      Carolina at Chapel Hill 1943
6449 DUNCAN Marlene V Shakespeare: The Alchemy of Iniquity or Shakespeare
      and Shylock MA Colorado St Coll 1968
6450 DUNFEY Sr Francesca Shakespeare's *Joan of Arc* MA Boston Coll 1957
6451 DUNLOY Dean A The Military Man in Shakespeare's Histories MA Texas
      Arts and Industries Univ 1964
6452 DUYKERS Elizabeth J The "Instant Tetter" of King Hamlet MA Univ
      of Texas at El Paso 1968 42 p
6453 DWIGHT Sheila D *Hamlet*: Some New Emendations and Explications
      MA Whittier Coll nd
6454 EARNHART Phyllis H Disease and Healing: A Pattern of Dramatic Imagery
      in Shakespeare's *Measure for Measure* MA Bowling Green Univ 1962
6455 EASTERDAY Beverly A The Stock Character of the Vice in Early
      Elizabethan Drama with Particular Reference to Shakespeare's Iago
      and Edmund MA Kent St Univ 1966
6456 EASTERLING Lorena B The Soliloquies of Shakespeare MA Tulane Univ
      1929

6457 EATON Elijah W A Psychological Study of Middle-Aged Lovers as Found
      in Certain of Shakespeare's Plays MA Oklahoma St Univ 1933 33 p
6458 ECHOLS C D The Curse in Shakespeare's Plays MA Univ of North Carolina
      at Chapel Hill 1942
6459 EDELMAN Marcia Man and King: A Comparison of the Morality Play's
      Mankind Figure and Shakespeare's Henry VI MA Hunter Coll 1964
6460 EDMUNDS W E The History of the Criticism of the Character of Richard II
      MA Univ of North Carolina at Chapel Hill 1945
6461 EDWARDS E L The Evolution of the Tragic Flaw, with Special Reference
      to Shakespeare's Chronicle History Plays MA Univ of North Carolina
      at Chapel Hill 1939
6462 EDWARDS J A The Conscience of Macbeth MA North Texas St Univ 1963
6463 EDWARDS Sarah H The Stage History of *Macbeth* MA Univ of Oklahoma 1938
6464 EGAN John J Thematic Unity in Shakespeare's *Troilus and Cressida*
      MA Duquesne Univ 1965
6465 EIDSON Donald R The Theme of *Henry IV*, Part I MA Oklahoma St Univ 196?
      50 p
6466 ELLIOT Elizabeth B Rosalind, Hermione, Perdita and Viola: A Study
      of Shakespeare's Characterization in the Light of His Sources
      MA Univ of Texas at Austin 1941 94 p
6467 ELMQUIST Karl E A Study of the Text of the First Quarto of Shakes-
      peare's *Merry Wives of Windsor* MA Univ of Texas at Austin 1939 87 p
6468 EMERSON Flora E Shakespeare's Prose MA Univ of Tennessee 1938
6469 EMERSON M I The Source and History of the Lyrics of Shakespeare's
      Plays MA Boston Univ 1910
6470 ENGLE Alan W Motivation in Shakespeare's Comedies MA Columbia 1951
6471 ENGLISH Rosemary J A Reinterpretation of Shakespeare's *Troilus and
      Cressida* in the Light of Modern Criticism MA Univ of Arizona 1942
6472 ERLICH Louise Literary Criticism as an Aid to the Theatrical Pro-
      duction of *King Lear* MA Indiana Univ 1966
6473 ERNEST Joseph M Jr Chorus Elements in Shakespeare MA Univ of Tennessee
      1942
6474 ESSARY Janet M A Comparison of the Tragedy Patterns in *King Lear* and
      Hamlet MA Texas Technological Univ 1969 63 p
6475 EVANS Charlotte S The Contribution of the Novella to Shakespeare
      MA Univ of California at Berkeley 1921
6476 EVANS Richard B The Place of Irony in Shakespearean Tragedy
      MA Univ of Oregon 1937
6477 EVANS William R Shakespeare's Gold and Jewel Imagery MA Columbia 1961
      80 p
6478 EVERETT Mary A Shakespeare's Use of His Source Material in *All's
      Well that Ends Well* MA Univ of Texas at Austin 1932
6479 EZELL Johanna A Most Pleasant Discourse on Renaissance Dreams in
      Which Is Included an Extensive Discussion of the Treatment of Dreams
      in Shakespearean Drama MA Temple Univ 1965 93 p
6480 FAGLES Robert Words Can Wield the Matter: A Study of Shakespearean
      English BA Amherst 1955
6481 FARRAND Margaret L The Sentimental Characters in Shakespeare's Plays
      MA Smith Coll 1926
6482 FAVERTY Frederick E Characterization, Humor and Realism: Their
      Development in Shakespeare's English History Plays MA Washington
      Univ at St Louis 1925
6483 FENG C M A Comparison of the Microcosm Analogy in Shakespeare and
      Chinese Thought MA Boston Coll 1959
6484 FERGUSON Frances R *Henry VI, Part II*: A Study in Play Revision
      MA Univ of Texas at Austin 1928
6485 FICHANDLER Zelda D Shakespeare in the Soviet Union MA George Wash-
      ington Univ 1950 224 p
6486 FIELD Carolyn C Textual Comparison of Four Shakespearean Plays in
      Pope and Theobald MA St Louis Univ 1940 92 p

6487 FINN Raymond J The Non-Dramatic Element in Shakespeare's Plays Aside
      from Lyrics and Soliloquies MA Univ of Iowa 1924
6488 FINNEGAN H A Shakespeare's Place and Influence in English Drama
      MA Boston Coll 1930
6489 FINNEGAN Virginia M Coriolanus: The Text and the Imagery MA Boston
      Coll 1965
6490 FISHER Sr Mary P Shakespeare's Personality MA Boston Coll 1927
6491 FISHER William J Measure for Measure and Shakespeare's "Dark Period"
      MA Univ of Arizona 1946
6492 FITZGERALD J T Shakespeare's Indebtedness to Marlowe MA Boston Coll
      1931
6493 FITZGERALD Sr Mary A Minor Characters in Shakespeare MA Boston Coll
      1934
6494 FLANNIGAN John G St Louis University Studies in the Text of Shakespeare
      MA St Louis Univ 1937 93 p
6495 FLYNN Br Borromeo The Honor Theme in Shakespeare's Parts 1, 2 of
      Henry IV and Henry V MA Boston Coll 1947
6496 FLYNN Margaret L A Study of the Aesthetics of the Songs in Shakespeare's
      Dramas MA Univ of Pittsburgh 1929
6497 FOLEY J Collins Shakespeare's Political Attitude toward the Common
      People as Portrayed in His History Plays MA Boston Univ 1949
6498 FOREMAN Jeanette A The Environmental Circumstances in Othello
      MA Univ of Delaware 1967 52 p
6499 FORSMAN Malcolm Verbal Echoes from North's Plutarch in Shakespeare's
      Roman Plays MA Univ of Texas at Austin 1934
6500 FORT B J The Concept of the Ennobling Power of Love in Shakespeare's
      Love Tragedies MA North Texas St Univ 1968
6501 FOWLER L G Shakespeare on the Influence of Music MA Boston Univ 1913
6502 FRAGALE F Bettina Shakespeare's Tragedy of Troilus and Cressida
      MA George Washington Univ 1964 105 p
6503 FREDERIKSEN Mildred E Oaths, Imprecations and Asseverations in
      Shakespeare with Particular Attention to Macbeth, Othello and Hamlet
      MA Washington Univ at St Louis 1960
6504 FREE Allene Shakespeare for Junior High Boys and Girls MA Hardin-
      Simmons Univ 1949
6505 FREEMAN Bernice Shakespeare's Changing Technique in Staging Love's
      Labour's Lost, Twelfth Night and The Tempest MA Univ of North
      Carolina at Chapel Hill 1932
6506 FREEMAN Ethel H The Significance of Shakespeare's Historical Plays
      in the Tragic Equation MA Smith Coll 1915
6507 FREEMAN Thomas G A Study of Television Adaptations of Shakespeare's
      Plays MS Kansas St Coll at Pittsburg 1956
6508 FREUND John R Dualism in Richard II: A Study in Thematic Structure
      MA Indiana Univ 1955
6509 FRIED Robert L Hamlet Paralyzed MA Univ of New Hampshire 1969 98 p
6510 FRIEDLAND Elias Shakespeare's Jack Cade MA Univ of North Carolina
      at Chapel Hill 1949 197 p
6511 FRIEDMAN Judith B A Study in the Verbal Consciousness of Shakespeare's
      Early Comedies MA Temple Univ 1964 73 p
6512 FRISCH Pearl The Disloyal Courtier in Shakespeare's Henry VI, Parts
      I, II and III and Richard III MA Hunter Coll 1967
6513 FROELICH Sr Mary G Alexander Dyce, Editor of Shakespeare MA St Louis
      Univ 1928 34 p
6514 FROMER Nancy E The World of Fortune and the World of Nature in
      Shakespeare's As You Like It MA Carnegie-Mellon Univ 1967
6515 FULLER Fleur Reflections of the Bible in Shakespeare's Richard III
      MA Oklahoma St Univ 1962 82 p
6516 FULLER Walter O A Quest for Order: Shakespeare and Machiavellianism
      MA Bemidji St Coll 1964
6517 GABBARD Agnes Child Characters in Shakespeare and His Predecessors

        MA Univ of Tennessee 1935
6518 GALLAHER Louvenia M Shakespeare's Imagery in *Much Ado about Nothing*
        MA Univ of Texas at Austin 1937 66 p
6519 GALLAHUE M L A Comparison of *Oedipus Rex* and *Macbeth* MA Boston Coll
        1929
6520 GALLEGLY J S Jr The Influence of Shakespeare's *I and II Henry IV* and
        Henry V on Succeeding Elizabethan Drama MA Rice 1926
6521 GALLIVAN Sr Teresa of St Charles The Dramatic Use of Death in *Henry VI*
        MA Boston Coll 1945
6522 GALT John R Shakespeare's Psycho-Pathological Knowledge as Manifested
        in *Hamlet* MA Boston Univ 1949
6523 GANN Myrtis Some Elizabethan Conceptions of the Honest Man as Revealed
        in Shakespeare's Two Tragedies: *Othello* and *King Lear* MA Oklahoma
        St Univ 1931 60 p
6524 GANSER Sr Mary J Emerson on Shakespeare MA Marquette Univ 1938 55 p
6525 GANZ Arthur F Shakespearean Productions on the New York Stage, 1925-
        1950 MA Univ of Tennessee 1950 104 p
6526 GAREN Margo "Policy Sits above Conscience": A Study of Shakespeare's
        Political Characters MA Windsor (Canada) 1965
6527 GARLINGTON Jack A Comparison of Shakespeare's *King John* with the
        Anonymous *The Troublesome Raigne* MA Texas Technological Univ 1938
        103 p
6528 GARRETT E L Shakespeare in the Work of John Keats BA Univ of British
        Columbia 1935
6529 GARRETT Ruth A Study of the Fourth Act in Shakespeare's Plays
        MA Univ of Texas at Austin 1934
6530 GARRIGUS Elizabeth S Psychopathological Factors Involved in the Main
        Characters of Williams Shakespeare's *King Lear* and *Macbeth*
        MA Boston Univ 1944
6531 GARRY Grace M The "Never Broken Chain": A Study of Blood Imagery
        as a Unifying Symbol of Shakespeare's Second Tetralogy MA Duke Univ
        1966
6532 GARTMAN Grace M A Comparison of the Nineteenth and Twentieth Century
        Criticism of Shakespeare's Heroines MA Pacific Univ 1950
6533 GASSNER Caroline Subversion of Character in Elizabethan Tragedy,
        with Special Reference to Shakespeare MA Columbia 1951
6534 GAVIN Norman J Dryden and Shakespeare: A Study in Creative Methods
        MA Marquette Univ 1950
6535 GAYLE Louise O *The Troublesome Reign of King John, Parts I and II*
        MA Univ of Texas at Austin 1925
6536 GEHRKE Ruth M Shakespeare's Use of His Sources in *Cymbeline*
        MA Univ of Texas at Austin 1931
6537 GENT C L Aspects of Technique in Some Elizabethan Shorter Narrative
        Poems, with Special Reference to Marlowe's *Hero and Leander*,
        Shakespeare's *Venus and Adonis* and *Lucrece*, and Drayton's *Endimion*
        and *Phoebe* M Phil Univ of London (England) 1969
6538 GEORGE Mary B A Study of the Authorship of the Songs in Shakespeare's
        Plays MA Univ of Oklahoma 1946
6539 GERLACH Ulrich H The Observations on *Hamlet* in *Wilhelm Meisters
        Lehrjahre* MA Cornell Univ 1966
6540 GIBSON John S Unity and Disease Imagery in *Henry IV*, Part II
        MA Texas Technological Univ 1965 61 p
6541 GIBSON Mary A Aspects of Shakespeare's Imagery MA Univ of Texas
        at Austin 1951 89 p
6542 GILBASPY Max M The Dramatic Functions of Letters in Shakespeare
        MA Texas Technological Univ 1968 50 p
6543 GILES Gerald W A Comparison and Contrast of *The Tempest* and *As You
        Like It* in Terms of Shakespeare's Use of Song MA Bowling Green
        Univ 1968
6544 GILL Elizabeth N The Changing Story of *Troilus and Cressida*

MA Univ of Richmond 1933   110 p
6545 GIORDANO Urania *The Taming of the Shrew*: A Study MA Columbia 1943
6546 GLEASON M K The Moor in Elizabethan Drama before and after *Othello*
      MA Univ of Iowa 1933
6547 GLOVER Allison A Study of the Criticism of Shakespeare's *Cleopatra*
      MA Univ of North Carolina at Chapel Hill 1946   127 p
6548 GNERRO Mark L The Influence of the *Commedia Dell'Arte* on the Subplot
      of *Love's Labour's Lost* MA George Washington Univ 1957   80 p
6549 GOCHBERG Donald S The Shylock Tradition: A Study in Popular Arch-
      types to 1596 MA Univ of Maryland at College Park 1960   125 p
6550 GOLDWASSER Robert The Serious Humor of *Measure for Measure* and
      Troilus and Cressida MA Brooklyn Coll 1966
6551 GOODLETT Mae B Shakespeare's Composition of His Source Material in
      Henry IV, Part II MA Univ of Texas at Austin 1934
6552 GOODMAN Alberta D The Contest in *Love's Labour's Lost* MA Emory Univ
      1966
6553 GORE Arabella The History of the Interpretation of Shylock in English
      and American Literary Criticism, 1796 to 1935 MA Univ of North
      Carolina at Chapel Hill 1938
6554 GORMICAN Sr Julia F .Shakespeare's *Julius Caesar* as a Problem Drama
      MA St Louis Univ 1946   131 p
6555 GOUGH Harry B A Study of the Crowd in *Julius Caesar* MA Northwestern
      Univ 1911
6556 GRAB Virginia Bertolt Brecht's Adaptation of Shakespeare's
      Coriolanus MA Columbia 1965   92 p
6557 GRABBE Mary L The Complex Humors of Corporal Sex in William
      Shakespeare's *The Merry Wives of Windsor* MA Emory Univ nd
6558 GRAF Dorothy A W Schlegel's Shakespeare Studies MA Columbia 1935
6559 GRAGG Donald B Shakespeare's *Julius Caesar* and Jonson's *Sejanus*:
      A Comparison MA Univ of Texas at Austin 1932
6560 GRAY Luther H Shakespeare's Use of His Material in *The Merry Wives
      of Windsor* MA Univ of Texas at Austin 1935
6561 GRAY M S The Occult as a Dramatic Device in Shakespearean Tragedy
      MA North Texas St Univ 1967
6562 GREEN Jo The Structure and Sources of *A Midsummer Night's Dream*
      MA Univ of Texas at Austin 1933
6563 GREEN Paula A The Meaning of the Metamorphic Scenes in *Othello*:
      City-State, Island Fortress and Barbaric Wasteland MA Emory Univ
      1965
6564 GREENSFELDER Blanche Y A Review of the *Hamlet* Theories MA Washington
      Univ at St Louis 1927   91 p
6565 GREER Clayton A Prototypes of Prince Hal and the "Irregular Humorists"
      in the Falstaffian Plays MA Univ of Texas at Austin 1927
6566 GREER Ina M The Use of Premonition in Shakespeare's Histories and
      Tragedies MA Univ of Iowa 1924
6567 GREGG William R Criticism of Shakespeare as a Dramatic Thinker
      MA Univ of Pittsburgh 1917
6568 GREGORY Marie C Characterizations of Troilus, Cressida and Pandarus
      in the Four English Versions of the Troilus Legend MA Univ of
      Redlands 1966
6569 GREGORY Pearle Interpretation of Shakespeare in America MA Austin
      Coll 1938
6570 GRETAR Betty Shakespeare's and Cinthio's *Othello*: A Source Study
      MA Kent St Univ 1966
6571 GRIMES Ralph E Shakespeare's War Against Time: A Study of His
      Sonnets MA Columbia 1950
6572 GROGAN Maryanne *Love's Labour's Lost, A Midsummer Night's Dream,
      Twelfth Night*: An Investigation of Love in View of Modern Theories
      MA Hunter Coll 1967
6573 GROOM Br Paul The Influence of the Morality Play upon the Tetralogy

Richard II, I and 2 Henry IV and Henry V of William Shakespeare
MA Boston Coll 1949

6574 GROSS Katherine   The Fool in Lear: Structural Relevance and Dramatic
Function MA Columbia 1964 202 p

6575 GROVES Roger L Certain Aspects of Kingship and the Commonwealth in
Shakespeare's Henry IV, Parts I and II MA Temple Univ 1966 56 p

6576 GUADNOLA Mary E The Treatment of Richard III in Historical Fiction
MA Univ of Colorado 1966

6577 GUEST Betty S The Political and Moral Significance of the Second
Tetralogy with Particular Reference to Sir John Falstaff MA Univ
of Oklahoma 1962

6578 GUICHARD Anne M Shakespeare's Julius Caesar and the French Drama
MA Smith Coll 1924

6579 GUTTMAN Selma The Sources of Shakespeare's Works: Contribution to
an Annotated Bibliography to Serve as a Supplement to Shakespeare's
Books by H R D Anders MA Columbia 1937

6580 HALL Norman G Richard III: A Production. A Director's Study of
William Shakespeare's Richard III (with Appendix, the Consummate
Villain) MA Columbia 1951

6581 HALLAHAN William Restoration Dramatic Tenets and Shakespearean
Adaptations MA Temple Univ 1952

6582 HALPERIN John Shakespeare's Richard II: A Tudor Textbook of Politics?
MA Univ of New Hampshire 1966 56 p

6583 HAMILTON Anne Shakespeare's Time Images and Ideas MA Columbia 1942

6584 HAMILTON Sr Elizabeth Ambition: A Recurrent Theme in Shakespearean
Tragedy MA Boston Coll 1958

6585 HAMILTON Grace L Manifestations of Mental Incompetency in Shakespeare
Dramatic Characters MA Oklahoma St Univ 1934

6586 HAMILTON Roberta M History of the Interpretation of Brutus, 1601-1948
MA Univ of North Carolina at Chapel Hill 1949 119 p

6587 HANEY Juanita B Changing Methods of Criticism in the Study of Hamlet
MA Hardin-Simmons Univ 1945

6588 HANKS Clifford O The Idea of Sin in Shakespearean Tragedy MA Oklahoma St Univ 1953

6589 HARDER Sarah Shakespeare's Henry V: Model or Machiavel MA Bowling
Green Univ 1967

6590 HARDWICK Charles S Macbeth: A Study in Appearance and Reality
MA Texas Technological Univ 1959 81 p

6591 HARPER Alice S The Portrayal of Shylock on the Stage MA Univ of
Pittsburgh 1916

6592 HARRELL Don W Order and Degree in the Possible Sources of
Shakespeare's Richard II MA George Washington Univ 1965 100 p

6593 HARRIS Elwin R Shakespeare's Coriolanus: Two Centuries of Critical
and Theatrical Tradition MA Univ of Maryland at College Park 1969
62 p

6594 HARRIS Thomas C Shakespeare's Debt to John Lyly MA Auburn Univ 1938

6595 HARRIS William O Honor and Ambition in Shakespeare, with Special
Reference to Julius Caesar MA Univ of North Carolina at Chapel Hil
1952 71 p

6596 HARROD Ann J The Opening Scenes of Shakespearean Tragedies MA Univ c
Oklahoma 1959

6597 HART Clyde E A Study of Shakespearean Tragedy in Relation to
Aristotle's Poetics MA Washington Univ at St Louis 1930 149 p

6598 HART Elizabeth H Shakespeare's Ghosts and Their Background in Folklore and Religious Belief MA Smith Coll 1925

6599 HART Era D Shakespeare's Use of His Sources in Macbeth MA Univ of
Texas at Austin 1929

6600 HART Stanley F Unity and Disunity in Antony and Cleopatra MA Columbi
1959 154 p

6601 HARTNETT Sr F M An Application of Ashley's Treatise of Honor to

Shakespeare's *Macbeth* MA Boston Coll 1954
6602 HARVEY Dianne Supernaturalism and Foreordination in Shakespeare
      MA Univ of Southern Mississippi 1966
6603 HATCHETT William R The Singing Fiction: Fact and Theory about
      Shakespeare's *Sonnets*; the Complete Story of Their Printing History
      MA Columbia 1951
6604 HAVENS Suzanne S A Study of Criticism of Shakespeare's Characters
      from 1660 to 1734 MA Univ of Kentucky 1965 64 p
6605 HAWKINS W Neil Shakespeare's *Comedy of Errors* Revised for High School
      and College Production MA North Texas St Univ 1964
6606 HAY Jolene Y Suggestions for Production, Implicit and Explicit, in
      Four Shakespearean Plays MA East Tennessee St Univ 1960
6607 HAY Sharon Character Development in *Edward II* and *Richard II*
      MA Bowling Green Univ 1967
6608 HAZELWOOD Saidee O Parent-Child Relationships in Certain of
      Shakespeare's Plays MA Oklahoma St Univ 1931
6609 HEADRICK Ineva Plot Structure in Shakespeare's Earliest Plays
      MA Univ of Texas at Austin 1924
6610 HEALY Sr Ann C The Convention of the Boy Action in the Tragedies
      of Shakespeare MA Boston Coll 1944
6611 HEARD Elma L *Cymbeline* and *Philaster*: A Complete Study MA Univ of
      Texas at Austin 1932
6612 HEEZEN Estelle E The Male Friendship Theme in Shakespeare MA Univ
      of Iowa 1931
6613 HEGBORN Lois A Shakespeare's Shylock: A Re-Evaluation MA North
      Texas St Univ 1966
6614 HENDERSON Marian E The Development of Shakespeare's Stage
      M Ed Henderson St Coll nd
6615 HENDON William S "I Am Not What I Am" *(Othello)* MA Univ of Oklahoma
      1957
6616 HENLEY Maria G Magnanimity and Liberality in *Coriolanus* and *Timon
      of Athens* MA Mount Saint Vincent (Canada) 1964
6617 HENSHAW Solomon O Political Thought in the Following of Shakespeare's
      Plays: *Richard III; Richard II; Henry V; Julius Caesar; King Lear;*
      and *The Tempest* MA Oklahoma St Univ 1932
6618 HERSCHEL Neil R Recent Textual Studies of *Hamlet* with an Examination
      of the States of the Major Soliloquies in the Quartos and First
      Folio MA Kansas St Teachers Coll 1965
6619 HERZMAN Ronald B An Analysis of Shakespeare's *Love's Labour's Lost*
      MA Univ of Delaware 1967 54 p
6620 HESS Marjorie E A Study of the Children in Shakespeare's Plays in
      Relationship to the Elizabethan Attitude toward Children
      M Ed Temple Univ 1953
6621 HESTER Martha E Death in Shakespeare and Webster: A Comparison of
      Antony and Cleopatra and *The White Devil* MA Columbia 1959 64 p
6622 HEYL Gladys E Theories on Hamlet's Reasons for Delay MA Boston Univ
      1930
6623 HICKEY Mary R A Study of the First Act of Four Shakespearean Tragedies
      MA Univ of Texas at Austin 1935 84 p
6624 HIEGEL Melanie A Twentieth Century Critical Views of the Villain-Hero
      in Shakespearean Tragedy as Illustrated by the Criticism of *Macbeth*
      MA Univ of Tennessee 1969 71 p
6625 HIGGINBOTTHAM Mary A Development of the Shakespearean Fool MA Univ of
      Tennessee 1941
6626 HIGGINS C J Shakespeare's Conception and Interpretation of Human
      Nature MA Boston Coll 1931
6627 HILDEBRAND M E Shakespeare's Troilus and the Critics: A Survey of
      Twentieth Century Criticism MA North Texas St Univ 1958
6628 HILL Lillia M Shakespeare's *Henry V*: A Critical Study of a Dramatic
      Character MA Boston Univ 1930

6629 HILTON Loyd H The Man of Thought Versus the Man of Action in Shake-
       speare's *Hamlet* and *Richard II* MA Texas Technological Univ 1957   82
6630 HINSHAW Lucille E The Shakespearean Tradition of Acting to the Nine-
       teenth Century MFA Univ of Oklahoma 1939
6631 HIRES Antoinette L An Analysis of Ducis' Adaptations of Shakespeare
       MA Univ of North Carolina at Raleigh 1949   164 p
6632 HOCH Mildred I Shakespeare's Use of His Sources in *Twelfth Night*
       MA Univ of Texas at Austin 1931
6633 HODGES Betsy L Shakespeare's Kings: A Study of Shakespeare's Use
       of Sir Thomas Elyot's *The Boke Named the Gouernour* MA George Wash-
       ington Univ 1956 106 p
6634 HOGAN J R Elements of Aristotlean Tragedy as Manifested in Shakes-
       peare's *Coriolanus* MA Boston Coll 1937
6635 HOGE Louise G Six of Shakespeare's Chronicle Plays Related to Modern
       Historical Studies MA East Tennessee St Univ 1959
6636 HOLE S S Angelic, Diabolic and Associated Imagery and Allusions
       in the Plays of Shakespeare, with Particular Reference to the
       Tragedies, the Problem Comedies and the Last Plays MA Univ of
       London (England) 1964
6637 HOLLOWELL Annabelle Shakespeare's Use of Comic Materials in Tragedy:
       A Survey of Criticism MA Univ of North Carolina at Chapel Hill 1940
6638 HOLT Albert H A Study of the Extra-Dramatic Scenes in Shakespeare
       MA Univ of North Carolina at Chapel Hill 1947   109 p
6639 HOLT Thomas Verbal Repetitions in the Plays of Shakespeare MA Howard
       Univ 1967   61 p
6640 HONIGMANN E A Studies in the Chronology of Shakespeare's Plays
       B Litt Oxford Univ (England) 1950
6641 HOPKINS Anthony D The Play Within a Play in Shakespeare MA Univ of
       British Columbia (Canada) 1965
6642 HOPKINS Violet E The Character of Banquo MA Hardin-Simmons Univ 1959
6643 HOSKINS Frank L Jr Master-Servant Relations in Shakespeare with Some
       Reference to the Same Relations in the Drama of the Elizabethan
       and Stuart Periods MA Univ of North Carolina at Chapel Hill 1947
       96 p
6644 HOUSTON B P The Dramatic Function of the Wise Fool in *Twelfth Night*
       MA North Texas St Univ 1962
6645 HOWE Alice E Thomistic Doctrines in Shakespeare's *The Tempest*
       MA Brigham Young Univ 1961 100 p
6646 HOWELL R M Romeo and Juliet: The Development of the Story up to
       Shakespeare's Day MA Ohio St Univ 1923
6647 HOWZE Bennett K Some Functional Uses of Puns in *Hamlet* MA East
       Tennessee St Univ 1957
6648 HUDDLESTON James L Three Women: A Study in Shakespeare's Dramatic
       Characterizations MA Univ of Colorado 1966
6649 HUDSON Sara L Shakespeare's Use of Imagery in *Troilus and Cressida*
       MA Univ of Texas at Austin 1949 102 p
6650 HUFF Frances T The Function of the Underplot in Shakespearean Comedy
       MA Southern Illinois Univ at Carbondale 1955   81 p
6651 HUFF J B Relation of the Shakespearean Drama to the English Romantic
       Movement of the Eighteenth Century MA Univ of North Carolina at
       Chapel Hill 1904
6652 HUFF Mildred S A Critical Analysis of Nahum Tate's Adaptation of
       King Lear MA Univ of Texas at Austin 1957 116 p
6653 HUGHES Geraldine A Study of Patriotism in Shakespeare MA Univ of
       Iowa 1935
6654 HUGHES Geraldine *Richard III* and Shakespeare's England MA Univ of
       Iowa 1935
6655 HUGHES Jerome W *Romeo and Juliet*: A Historical Study MA Univ of
       Iowa 1934
6656 HUGHES Thomas A The Relationship of Shakespeare's *Troilus and Cressid*

to the Main Earlier Treatments of the Trojan Story MA Toronto
(Canada) 1963
6657 HUME Thomas Jr Treatment of Roman Subjects by Shakespeare and
Pierre Corneille MA Univ of North Carolina at Chapel Hill 1900
6658 HUNDON Nancy R Elizabethan Domestic Affairs in the Plays of
William Shakespeare MA Rice 1958
6659 HURDIS Sara B The Problem of Political and Social Ideas in *Coriolanus*
MA George Washington Univ 1944 61 p
6660 HUSSON Chesley H The Use of Music and Musical Terms in the Plays of
Shakespeare MA Univ of Maine 1966 122 p
6661 IRVINE Virginia H The Compound Words of Shakespeare MA Univ of
Texas at Austin 1932
6662 IRWIN Elizabeth Antony and Cleopatra in English Drama MA Univ of
Pittsburgh 1929
6663 ISAACKS Eula M A Comparative Study of Hardy's and Shakespeare's
Peasant Characters MA Univ of Texas at Austin 1940 85 p
6664 ITZOE Linda V The Character and Role of Polonius in *Hamlet* MA Univ
of Wyoming 1965
6665 IWASAKI Soji The Sword and the Word: The Theme of Time in Three
Tragedies of Shakespeare M Litt Cambridge Univ (England) 1969
6666 JAARSMA Richard J The Great Doom's Image Theme, Structure and
Character in *Macbeth* MA Rutgers St Univ 1966 256 p
6667 JACKSON Kathleen L The Suffering-Redemption Theme as Presented in
Three Plays by William Shakespeare: *King Lear, The Winter's Tale*
and *The Tempest* BA Univ of British Columbia (Canada) 1965
6668 JACKSON Stella B Recent Trends in the Conception of Shakespeare's
Characters with Special Reference to Shylock, Falstaff, Hamlet and
Cleopatra MA Texas Technological Univ 1936 33 p
6669 JACOB Wilmer F Shakespeare's Influence on Some of the Early Romanti-
cists with Particular Reference to *Hamlet* MA Auburn Univ nd
6670 JACOBSEN Marietta Shakespeare's Use of Source Material in Writing
King Lear MA Univ of New Hampshire 1948 73 p
6671 JARA Patricia A The Christian Allegory in Shakespeare's *The Merchant
of Venice* MA Pacific Univ 1968 143 p
6672 JENKINS A S The Jealous Husband in the Plays of Chapman, Jonson,
Heywood and Shakespeare from 1597-1611 MA Univ of North Carolina
at Chapel Hill 1927
6673 JENKINS S F Figurative References to Nature in Shakespeare's Three
Earliest Comedies, His Earliest Tragedy, His Earliest Chronicle
History Play and in *Titus Andronicus* and *Henry VI* MA Univ of North
Carolina at Chapel Hill 1930
6674 JENKINS Vivian E Major Scholarship on the Identification of the
Mr W H in the Dedication of Sonnets of Shakespeare MA Howard Univ
1934 54 p
6675 JERNIGAN Osie C Jr *All for Love* and Shakespeare's Roman Plays
MA Univ of North Carolina at Chapel Hill 1950 60 p
6676 JOBE Phyllis G Shakespeare's Ideal Courtier MA Univ of Tulsa 1958
138 p
6677 JOHNSON Br Hilaire The Ideas and Images in Shakespeare's *Measure for
Measure* Which Are Derived from Palingenia's *Zodiacus Vitae*
MA Boston Coll 1958
6678 JOHNSON Lola V A Historical Survey and Evaluation of the Most Prom-
inent Theories that Shakespeare Did Not Write the Works Attributed
to Him MA Pacific Univ 1959 220 p
6679 JOHNSON Nora Fate, Fortune, Providence and the Stars: Forces of
Influence in Shakespeare's Dramas MA Washington St Univ at Pullman 1966
6680 JOHNSON Ruth W The Role of Functional Rhetoric in the Development
of Four Shakespearean Villains: Aaron, Richard III, Regan and
Iago MS Texas Technological Univ 1958 105 p
6681 JOHNSON Thomas P The Many Faces of Shakespeare: A Touring Production

of a Series of Scenes from Shakespeare's Plays MA St Coll of Iowa
        1966
6682 JONES Arthur E Colley Cibber's Alterations of Shakespeare's *Richard III*
        and *King John* MA Syracuse Univ 1941 93 p
6683 JONES B P A Consideration of Some Linguistic Phenomena in *Othello*
        and *King Lear* MA North Texas St Univ 1944
6684 JONES C W Reason Versus Passion in Shakespeare's Comedies MA Univ
        of North Carolina at Chapel Hill 1941
6685 JONES Carole A Study of Probable Sources for Shakespeare's Character-
        ization of Cleopatra MA East Tennessee St Univ 1964
6686 JONES Connie H Reformation Ideas in Shakespeare's Plays: A Study of
        The Merchant of Venice and *Hamlet* MA Texas Technological Univ
        1964 62 p
6687 JONES Jerry L Displaced Persons in the Plays of Shakespeare and Jonson
        MA Univ of Florida 1957˙
6688 JONES Robert The Problem of a Legitimate King in Shakespeare's *King
        John* MA Univ of California at Riverside 1958
6689 JONES Robert C Shakespeare's *King John*: The Problem of the Legitimate
        King MA Columbia 1959 54 p
6690 JONES Thelma L Classical Mythological References in Shakespeare's
        Tragedies MA Texas Christian Univ 1954 134 p
6691 JOSLIN Charlotte E The Technical Treatment of the Denouement in
        Shakespeare's Comedies Compared with that in the Tragedies
        MA Boston Univ 1899
6692 JUNKER Howard H What's Wrong with *Othello*? BA Amherst 1961
6693 KALMAY P P Shakespeare's Octavius: His Background and Significance
        MA Rice 1961
6694 KANZAKI Hisae N Kurosawa's *Throne of Blood*: A Japanese *Macbeth*
        MA Univ of Texas at Austin 1965 135 p
6695 KAVANAUGH M R Shakespeare's Influence on French Drama MA Boston Coll
        1936
6696 KEELER Katherine Three of the Doubtful Plays of Shakespeare:
        Henry VIII, The Two Noble Kinsmen, and *Edward II* MA Smith Coll 1904
6697 KEEN Nancy L The Problem of the Revision of *All's Well that Ends Well*
        MA Univ of North Carolina at Chapel Hill 1950 98 p
6698 KEISER A Shakespeare's Indication of Scenery through Descriptive
        Poetry MA Univ of Montana 1915 67 p
6699 KELLER Winnie B A Contrast of Chaucer's *Troilus and Criseyde* with
        Shakespeare's *Troilus and Cressida* MA Univ of Kentucky 1934
6700 KELLY Faye L Shakespeare's Use of Prayer in the History Plays
        MA Univ of Florida 1965
6701 KELLY Marie W Joan of Arc in Shakespeare MA Duquesne Univ 1966
6702 KELLY Mary L Villains in Shakespeare's Comedies MA Univ of North
        Carolina at Chapel Hill 1948 111 p
6703 KENT Ida L A Study of Othello as Shakespeare's Dominant Moorish
        Character MS Kansas St Coll at Pittsburg 1960
6704 KENT Maurice W *All's Well* and the Character of Helena BA Univ of
        British Columbia (Canada) 1967
6705 KERN John J The Time Scheme of *Othello* Reconsidered MA George Wash-
        ington Univ 1953 103 p
6706 KERR James L The Functions of Prose in Shakespearean Drama MA Whittier
        Coll nd
6707 KESTER Dorothy G A Study of *Macbeth* Based upon Seven Nineteenth
        Century Prompt Books MA Columbia 1940
6708 KIDD Dorothy A Stoicism in Shakespeare's Roman Plays MA Univ of
        Texas at Austin 1940 147 p
6709 KIDD Pansy I The Influence of Aristotle on Shakespeare MA Oklahoma
        St Univ 1934
6710 KIM Hye J Zen in Shakespeare MA Univ of Redlands 1965
6711 KIMBALL Harold M Jealousy in Shakespeare's Tragedies MA Pacific

Univ 1929 78 p
6712 KING Lucille Shakespeare's Use of His Source Material in *Antony and Cleopatra* MA Univ of Texas at Austin 1927
6713 KING M I A Survey of Shakespearean Productions in New York MA North Texas St Univ 1956
6714 KING Maude E *Richard II*: Shakespeare's Use of His Sources MA Univ of Texas at Austin 1929
6715 KISKADDEN Margaret Pedagogical Study of Shakespeare's Play *Julius Caesar* MA Univ of Pittsburgh 1922
6716 KITCHENS Edith P Shakespeare's Symphonic Alliteration MA Univ of Texas at Austin 1950 83 p
6717 KITCHENS Harvey C Shakespeare's Use of Fortune in His History Plays MA Texas Arts and Industries Univ 1964
6718 KLEIN Jenny The History of Johnson's *Preface to Shakespeare:* 1765-1934 MA McGill (Canada) 1936
6719 KLIEGMAN Benjamin Shakespeare's Dramatic Use of Music MA Columbia 1941
6720 KOLLERER Doret R Hamlet: Prince of Darkness MA Coll of the Holy Names at Oakland 1961
6721 KOON Beulah J Stage Directions in the Lines of Shakespeare's Tragedies MS Kansas St Coll at Pittsburg 1937
6722 KRESKY Ruth W The Love Theme in Shakespeare's *Troilus and Cressida* MA Sarah Lawrence Coll 1966
6723 KRIEGEL Rosemary Shakespeare for the Elementary School MA California St Coll at Long Beach 1965
6724 KUNST Arthur E Sanskrit Dramatic Theory and Shakespeare's *Othello* MA Indiana Univ 1956
6725 KUSHNER Sheila Heroic Rhetoric in Shakespeare's *Antony and Cleopatra* MA Columbia 1962 102 p
6726 LACKEY Allen D Evidence of Modern Slang Found in Shakespeare MA West Texas St Univ 1966 325 p
6727 LACKEY Dathel J The Relationship of Parents to Children in Shakespeare's *Romeo and Juliet, Hamlet, Othello* and *King Lear* MA Univ of Oklahoma 1947
6728 LACKEY Katherine Shakespeare's Political Philosophy MA Univ of North Carolina at Chapel Hill 1944
6729 LAKIN Barbara L Robert Heilman's Shakespearean Criticism: The Interpretative Web MA Colorado St Coll 1963
6730 LAMBERT John L Shakespeare's Groundlings: A Study of Some of the Humble Characters MA McMaster (Canada) 1966
6731 LAMEYER Gordon A The Elizabethan Tradition: Queen Elizabeth in the Poetry of Donne and in Marlowe, Marvell, Pope and Shakespeare MA Columbia 1959 191 p
6732 LAMONT Hayes C A Reading of *King Lear* BA Amherst 1957
6733 LANDAU Annette H Stoicism in Shakespeare's Plays MA Columbia 1943
6734 LANE Elsie M Treatment and Interpretation of Nature in Shakespeare MA Boston Univ 1931
6735 LANTOIN Paul M A Study in Shakespearean Criticism during the Seventeenth and Eighteenth Centuries MA Smith Coll 1931
6736 LAPPING Laura Elizabethan Prejudices as Reflected in *The Merchant of Venice* MA Long Island Univ 1965 101 p
6737 LARSEN Swen A The Dramatic Craftsmanship of the Opening Scenes of Shakespeare's Tragedies MA Boston Coll 1948
6738 LASHLEE Mary N The Musical Tone Quality of the Shakespearean Drama MA George Washington Univ 1933 26 p
6739 LATHAM Muriel The Seven Deadly Sins: Parallelism in Chaucer and Shakespeare MA Eastern New Mexico Univ 1964 69 p
6740 LATIMER Paula W A Study of the Idealism of Shakespeare's Troilus, Brutus and Coriolanus MA Univ of Houston 1965 132 p
6741 LAUGHLIN Mary R Oldcastle and Falstaff MA Louisiana St Univ 1936
6742 LAWELLIN Lois V Shakespeare's Treatment of the Common People

MS Kansas St Coll at Pittsburg 1932

6743 LAWRENCE Richard R *The Tempest*: Its Origin and Problems MA Williams Coll 1909

6744 LAWTON Esther C A Comparison of Some French and English Adaptations of Shakespeare's *Romeo and Juliet* MA George Washington Univ 1942 98 p

6745 LAXALT Peter D *Romeo and Juliet* as Tragedy MA Univ of Nevada 1956

6746 LAZENBY Ora The Anthony and Cleopatra Story in Eleven Versions MA Southern Methodist Univ 1933

6747 LAZENBY Walter *The Tempest*: A Study of Its Plot-Structure MA Univ of Texas at Austin 1938 120 p

6748 LEARNED Annabel F The Source Material of Shakespeare's *Titus Andronicus* MA Columbia 1936

6749 LEATH H L The Choric Element in Shakespeare's Second History Tetralogy MA North Texas St Univ 1958

6750 LEDERMAN Milton B The Significiance of Additions and Alterations in Shakespeare's *Coriolanus* MA Rutgers St Univ 1950 51 p

6751 LEE Anna C A Study of Shakespeare's Departures from Plutarch in the Characterizations of Caesar and Brutus in *Julius Caesar* MA Oklahoma St Univ 1968 66 p

6752 LEITNER Imogene B The Use of the Lyric in Shakespearean Drama MA Boston Univ 1929

6753 LELL Virgil G *Coriolanus* and the Philosopher King: A Comparative Study MA Colorado St Coll 1964

6754 LeMAITRE Darlene *As You Like It*: The Sum of the Parts. A Discussion of the Principal Elements of the Play BA Univ of British Columbia (Canada) 1968

6755 LEONARD Orel K Shakespeare and the Stage in Washington, D C, 1800-1835 MA George Washington Univ 1953 111 p

6756 LEWIS Anne M Courtship and Marriage in Shakespeare MA Columbia 1943

6757 LEWIS B B Shakespeare's Monarchical Views MA North Texas St Univ 1959

6758 LEWIS E D A Study of Shakespeare's Roman Plays in Their Relation to the Lives in North's *Plutarch* BA Univ of British Columbia (Canada) 1922

6759 LING Milton F Shakespeare's Use of His Sources in *As You Like It* MA Univ of Texas at Austin 1926

6760 LIPS Roger C A Critical History of Shakespearean Biography MA Univ of Louisville 1966

6761 L'ITALIEN Sr M Irene Shakespeare's Old Women MA Boston Coll 1948

6762 LITTLE Elizabeth A Implications of Social Justice in Thirteen of Shakespeare's Plays MA Univ of Texas at Austin 1943 192 p

6763 LITTLETON Taylor D Ghosts, Witches and Demons in Shakespearean Tragedy A Reflection of Renaissance Spiritualism MA Florida St Univ 1952

6764 LOCKE Sr Genevieve M Shakespeare's Use of the Underplot Illustrated from *Hamlet* and *Macbeth* MA Boston Coll 1927

6765 LOCKE Odeal Problems in the Text of Shakespeare's *Titus Andronicus* MA Univ of Oklahoma 1940

6766 LOLLOS John Love and Let Love: A Study of the Procedures Followed during the Writing and Directing of a New Musical Version of William Shakespeare's *Twelfth Night* at the Manhattan Campus of Hunter Coll MA Hunter Coll 1967

6767 LONG John H Shakespeare's Use of Music: A Study of the Music and Its Performance in the Original Performance of Seven Comedies MA Univ of Florida 1951

6768 LONG Mary F Death in Shakespeare's Last Plays MA Univ of Connecticut 1966

6769 LORD Mary E The Use of Realism in Comedies by Shakespeare and Jonson MA Syracuse Univ 1950 112 p

6770 LOVEALL James S The Function of Imagery in *Antony and Cleopatra* MA Pacific Univ 1949 58 p

6771 LOWE Thelma M Shakespeare's Possible Use of the Historic Sir John
        Falstolf in the Creation of Falstaff MA East Tennessee St Univ 1960
6772 LUCCHESI P G Tragic Satire in *Coriolanus* MA Boston Coll 1957
6773 LUCE A E Shakespeare in Nineteenth Century German Music MA Boston
        Univ 1915
6774 LUETCKE Mary E Philosophical Backgrounds for Shakespeare's *The Tempest*
        MA Univ of Texas at Austin 1931
6775 LURIE Cora *The Merchant of Venice* and *Measure for Measure* as Christian
        Plays MA Indiana Univ 1960
6776 LYNCH Barbara F Shakespeare's Comic Vision: The Fundamental Elements
        of Shakespearean Comedy MA Texas Technological Univ 1966   45 p
6777 LYON Rowland Nationalistic Implications in the Works of William
        Shakespeare MA George Washington Univ 1933   41 p
6778 McCANLESS Rosamond Shakespeare's Use of the Unfaithful Wife Motif
        MA Univ of North Carolina at Chapel Hill 1935
6779 McCARRON William E An Annotated Bibliography of *Othello* Criticism,
        1938-1963, with a Critical Introduction MA Boston Coll 1966
6780 McCARTHY M C Shakespeare's Theatre MA Boston Coll 1935
6781 McCARTHY Mother M E Shakespeare's Use of Wishes in *Richard III* and
        King Lear MA Boston Coll 1933
6782 McCHRISTY Cleo G Concerning the Syntax of the Infinitive in
        Shakespeare MA Univ of Texas at Austin 1919
6783 McCLENDON Mary J The Cleopatra Plays of William Shakespeare,
        John Dryden and George Bernard Shaw MA Lamar Technological Univ
        1965
6784 McCOLLUM Mary A Shakespeare's Use of the Messenger in *Titus Andronicus,
        Richard III, Hamlet* and *Macbeth* MA Univ of Texas at Austin 1951
        110 p
6785 McCOTTRY Mildred G Shakespeare's Treatment of Jealousy MA Boston Univ
        1943
6786 McCULLEN J T Jr The Use of Madness in Shakespearean Tragedy for
        Characterization and for Protection in Satire MA Univ of North
        Carolina at Chapel Hill 1939
6787 McDERMOTT Joseph T Famous Characterizations of *Richard III*
        MA Columbia 1951
6788 MacDONALD Jay D Boy-Actors in Shakespeare's Female Roles MA Cornell
        Univ 1966
6789 MacDOWELL The History of the Interpretation of Lady Macbeth in English
        and American Literary Criticism, 1747-1939 MA Univ of North
        Carolina at Chapel Hill 1939
6790 McELROY Marion P Shakespeare's Use of His Sources in *Troilus and
        Cressida* MA Univ of Texas at Austin 1936
6791 McFADDEN Alexander B Character Anachronisms in Shakespeare's History
        Plays MA Univ of North Carolina at Chapel Hill 1956   70 p
6792 McFARLAND Vera M Shakespeare's Dramatic Use of Plant and Garden Lore
        MA Univ of Florida 1954
6793 McGRARY J E Development of Shakespeare's Dramatic Powers as Shown
        in the Chronicle History Plays *King Henry VI, Richard III,
        Richard II* and *Macbeth* MA Boston Coll 1938
6794 McGRATH Sr Teresa G Character Portrayal in Shakespeare's and Jonson's
        Plays MA Boston Coll 1956
6795 McGREGOR Herman S Jr A History of the Criticism of the King in *Hamlet*
        MA Univ of North Carolina at Chapel Hill 1952   89 p
6796 McGUIRE Ralph L The Machiavellian Villain in Shakespeare MA Shippens-
        burg St Coll 1965
6797 McILWRAITH Clara B Shakespeare's Use of Letters in Twelve Represen-
        tative Plays MA Univ of Richmond 1965   187 p
6798 McKERCHER Leslie *Edward III*: A Shakespearean Play? BA Univ of
        British Columbia (Canada) 1967
6799 McKNIGHT George The Themes and Imagery in William Shakespeare's

Coriolanus BA Univ of British Columbia (Canada) 1964
6800 MacLAURIN J C The Dramatic Values of the Low-Life Characters in
       Shakespeare BA Univ of British Columbia (Canada) 1938
6801 McLEAN Annie T Shakespeare and Greene: A Study of Seven Plays
       MA Univ of Texas at Austin 1937 140 p
6802 McMILLAN Addie T The Ghost as a Medium of Revenge in the Elizabethan
       Drama outside Shakespeare's Works from 1585-1625 MA Univ of
       Oklahoma 1931
6803 McMILLIN Harvey S Jr The Soliloquies of Shakespeare's Major Tragedies
       MA George Washington Univ 1960 146 p
6804 McMULLEN Clara Characterizations in Shakespeare's Roman Plays
       MA Univ of Iowa 1931
6805 McNAMARA Sr Claire Some Psychology in Shakespeare MA Boston Coll 1927
6806 McNAMARA Robert J Classical Allusions in *Titus Andronicus* MA Univ of
       North Carolina at Chapel Hill 1954 58 p
6807 McNAMEE Virginia J Laurence Olivier's Film Productions of Shakespeare
       MA East Texas St Univ 1964
6808 McNULTY George J *All's Well that Ends Well* and the Late Romances
       MA Univ of Delaware 1967 58 p
6809 MacPHEDRON John D Application and Implication of Frye's Green World
       Theory to *Measure for Measure* MA Bowling Green St Univ 1966
6810 McPHERSON Mildred S A Historical Study of *The Merchant of Venice*
       M Ed Henderson St Coll nd
6811 McQUAID D C Generalizing Images in Shakespeare's Plays MA Boston Coll
       1933
6812 McREYNOLDS Finnis E A Study of the Sources of Certain of Shakespearean
       Tragedies BA Univ of Oklahoma 1908
6813 MADERER Margaret P An Exposition of the Theories on Shakespeare's
       Dark Lady from 1890 to the Present MA Columbia 1940
6814 MALARKEY Sally Aaron and Edmund: Examples of the Villain in Eliza-
       bethan Tragedy MA Columbia 1963 79 p
6815 MANLY William M King and Fools: A Study of the "King-Fool" Antithesis
       in *King Lear* and *Moby Dick* MA Columbia 1961 87 p
6816 MANNIX Helen E Shakespearean Tragedy: Disorder MA Boston Coll 1947
6817 MANRY Mary J Shakespeare's Sonnets: A Study of the Relationship of
       the Sonnets to the Narrative Poems and the Drama MA Univ of Texas
       at Austin 1955 103 p
6818 MAPLES B A Shakespeare's Use of Music MA North Texas St Univ 1962
6819 MARIOVITZ Eleanora D The Influence of Shakespeare on the Poetic Dramas
       of Shelley, Wordsworth and Coleridge MA Temple Univ 1965
6820 MARKWOOD Ruth The Falstaff Problem MA George Washington Univ 1942 11
6821 MARSH Robert T The Sources of *Richard II* MA Boston Univ 1947
6822 MARTIN Allen D Antony and Cleopatra in English Drama MA Louisiana
       St Univ 1939
6823 MARTIN Frances D Shakespeare's Italianate Villains MA Univ of Houston
       1961 65 p
6824 MARTIN James A The Artisans of Shakespeare's *Julius Caesar* MA Texas
       Technological Univ 1966 42 p
6825 MARTIN William F The Irony of *King Lear* MA Texas Technological Univ
       1966 52 p
6826 MARTINEAU Roger The Element of Time in the Sonnets of Shakespeare
       MA Montreal (Canada) 1965
6827 MASSEY Josephine B Classical Mythology in Shakespeare's Plays with
       a Dictionary of the Myths MS Kansas St Coll at Pittsburg 1933
6828 MATHESON P L The Convention of Disguise in Elizabethan Drama, Especial
       as Found in the Plays of William Shakespeare BA Univ of British
       Columbia (Canada) 1928
6829 MAULDIN Myrtle L Shakespeare's Use of His Sources in *The Winter's Tale*
       MA Univ of Texas at Austin 1926
6830 MAY Ellen D The Plot-Structure of Shakespeare's *Henry IV, Part II*

MA Univ of Texas at Austin 1926
6831 MEANS Bess M   The Comedy Element in Pre-Elizabethan Drama from the
	Beginnings to the Immediate Predecessors of Shakespeare MA Univ
	of Oklahoma 1932
6832 MEDICI Rosana   *The True Chronicle History of King Leir*   MA Ca Foscari
	(Italy) 1960
6833 MEERS Nola   A Study of Deterioration of Characters in Selected Plays
	of Shakespeare MA Hardin-Simmons Univ 1947
6834 MEEVEREN Arthur V   Shakespeare's Purpose in Portraying Shylock
	MA Univ of Iowa 1931
6835 MENARD Rita R   Shakespeare's Picture of Kingship and Rebellion
	MA Univ of Rhode Island 1957
6836 MENTO Joan   Love and Honor in Shakespeare's Comedies   MA Univ of New
	Hampshire 1968 116 p
6837 METCALFE Alvin C   A Tangle of Ivy: Representative Twentieth Century
	Criticism of *King Lear* MA Wagner Coll 1966
6838 METZ Zachary   Localization of Scenes in Shakespeare's Plays   MA Columbia
	1936
6839 MEYER Helen T   Fate, Fortune and Chance in Six of Shakespeare's
	Tragedies MA Univ of Texas at Austin 1946 84 p
6840 MEYERS Robert R   A Study of the Witches in *Macbeth*   MA Univ of Oklahoma
	1950
6841 MIHALKA Gwendolyn C   Shakespeare's Marriage and the Puritan Issue
	MA San Diego St Coll 1967 147 p
6842 MILAM Linda C   The Function of the Songs in Selected Shakespearean
	Tragedies: A Study of *Hamlet, Othello, Troilus and Cressida,
	Antony and Cleopatra* and *Macbeth* MA Univ of Texas at Austin 1962
6843 MILES Nelle A   Shakespeare's Use of Source Material in *Julius Caesar*
	MA Univ of Texas at Austin 1930
6844 MILEY Sr Elizabeth F   Ingratitude: The Basis of Shakespearean Tragedy
	MA Boston Coll 1927
6845 MILKMAN Cythnia R   The Commons in Shakespeare: A Reassessment
	MA Univ of Maryland at College Park 1968 94 p
6846 MILLER Barbara A   The Influence of the Physical Theatre and the Acting
	Company on the Composition of *Henry VI, Part I* MA Washington St
	Univ at Pullman 1966
6847 MILLER Lois M   Shakespeare and the Dance   BA Hunter Coll 1930
6848 MILLER Lois T   Stoic Themes in Selected Elizabethan Plays   MS Auburn
	Univ 1948 45 p
6849 MISENHEIMER James B Jr   The Literary and Historical Antecedents of
	the Hired Assassin in the Plays of Shakespeare MA Southern Illinois
	Univ at Carbondale 1954 97 p
6850 MITCHAM Mildred B   Political Implications of Shakespeare's Plays
	MA Oklahoma St Univ 1945 52 p
6851 MOCHEDLOVER Victor G   An Evaluation of the Critical Interpretations
	of the Character of Lady Macbeth MA Boston Univ 1947
6852 MONAGLE Mary W   Burlesque Elements in *A Midsummer Night's Dream*
	MA Boston Coll 1966
6853 MONCADA Ernest J   A Historical Assessment of Christian Evaluations
	of *Measure for Measure* MA Univ of Maryland at College Park 1960 91 p
6854 MONSKY Evalynn J   Nature, Nurture and Time in *The Tempest*   MA Cornell
	Univ 1966
6855 MONTGOMERY Dora E   The Influence of Travel on the Elizabethan Drama
	as Illustrated by Marlowe's *Tamburlaine*, Shakespeare's *Tempest*
	and Chapman's *Caesar and Pompey* MA Univ of Oklahoma 1936
6856 MONTGOMERY Roy F   Contemporary Allusion in Shakespeare's *King John,
	Merry Wives* and *King Lear* MA Univ of Tennessee 1954 143 p
6857 MOORE B   Shakespeare's Insight into Woman's Nature   BA Univ of British
	Columbia (Canada) nd
6858 MOORE Gertrude W   The Significance of Shakespeare's Use of Witches

in *Macbeth* MA Oklahoma St Univ 1937   41 p
6859 MORAN Harold M   A Source Unit in the Organization of Shakespeare's
      Tragedy of Macbeth for Senior High School M Ed Iowa St Teachers
      Coll 1952
6860 MORAN Helen A Guide to *Hamlet* Criticism MA Univ of Louisville 1937
6861 MORGAN Shirley U A Historical and Definitive Approach to
      Shakespearan Comedy MA West Texas St Univ 1958   211 p
6862 MORONEY Katherine E   The Letter as a Dramatic Device in Shakespearean
      Plays MA Univ of Oklahoma 1956   151 p
6863 MORTON L M Shakespeare's Attitude toward History MA Univ of North
      Carolina at Chapel Hill 1941
6864 MOSLE Paula M Shakespeare and the Sixteenth Century Judgment of
      Cleopatra MA Rice 1959
6865 MOTTA Isabelle An Essay on Shakespeare's *Coriolanus* MA Ca Foscari
      (Italy) 1926
6866 MOUNT Raymond I Jr Some Original Features of the Restoration Version
      of *The Tempest* MA Univ of North Carolina at Chapel Hill 1950   65 p
6867 MOYSE Jean H *Hamlet*: La Traduction de Gide MA Cornell Univ 1965
6868 MULARSKI Kenneth An Unpublished Anonymous Eighteenth Century Adapt-
      ation of Shakespeare's *The Two Gentlemen of Verona* MA Georgetown
      Univ 1968
6869 MULDROW Edna B An Edition of the Pre-Shakespearean Comedy or Inter-
      lude, *The Marriage of Wit* and *Science* MA Univ of Oklahoma 1927
6870 MURPHY Anne M Structural Distinctions between Shakespeare's Tragedies
      Based on Chthonic Myth and the History Plays in the Tetralogies
      MA Boston Coll 1968
6871 MURPHY Elby J Shakespeare and the Germanic Comitatus MA Texas Tech-
      nological Univ 1965   81 p
6872 MURPHY Kathleen A Three Studies in English: Shakespeare's *Troilus
      and Cressida*; Tennyson's *Idylls*; and Faulkner's Fiction
      MA Pennsylvania St Univ 1965
6873 MURPHY Lillian W A Study of Mark Antony and Octavius Caesar in
      Shakespeare's *Julius Caesar* and *Antony and Cleopatra* MA Univ of
      Tulsa 1941
6874 MUSSELWHITE Vergia M The Influence of William Painter's *Palace of
      Pleasure* on William Shakespeare MA Univ of Houston 1962   152 p
6875 MYERS Karen W The False Steward and the Magician: *Cupids Cautels*
      and Shakespeare's Plays, 1599-1607 MA Kansas St Teachers Coll 1965
6876 NAHRA Mathilda *Much Ado about Nothing*: A Critical Commentary
      MA Univ of Connecticut 1957
6877 NALL Margaret N A Comparison of the Social Attitudes of Thomas Dekker
      and William Shakespeare MA Texas Technological Univ 1965   84 p
6878 NAPPER Charlene A "Age Cannot Wither": A History of the Literary
      Criticism of the Character of Shakespeare's Cleopatra MA Univ of
      Wyoming 1964
6879 NARKIN Anthony P Shakespeare's *King Richard II:* Identity and
      Ritual MA West Texas St Univ 1969   79 p
6880 NASH Betsy B Shakespearean Tragedy and Aristotle MA Univ of Tulsa
      1956   75 p
6881 NATTSAS Albert C Development of the Jew in English Drama from the
      Liturgical Plays through Shakespeare's Shylock MA Boston Univ 1935
6882 NEGUELOUA Lillian M The Literary Reputation of Shakespeare's Cressida
      MA Univ of North Carolina at Chapel Hill 1948   76 p
6883 NELSON Donald E A Director's Study and Designs for the *Tragedy of
      Hamlet, Prince of Denmark* MA Mankato St Coll 1960   112 p
6884 NELSON Eda Sources and Relations of *Antony and Cleopatra* Dramas
      before 1607 MA Univ of Oklahoma 1934
6885 NELSON John R *As You Like It*: An Evaluative Study MA Univ of
      Oklahoma 1959
6886 NEWTON Cornelia A The Elizabethan Conception of Dramatic Structure:

According to Playwright, Producer and Critic with Special Reference
to Shakespeare   MA Smith Coll 1937
6887   NICHOLSON Catherine   The History of the Criticism of the Character of
Othello   MA Univ of North Carolina at Chapel Hill 1945
6888   NIELSEN Patricia J   Costume Design: *Romeo and Juliet*   MA Texas
Christian Univ 1968   137 p
6889   NOBLE Joe D   Foreshadowing in *Romeo and Juliet*, *Julius Caesar* and
Macbeth   MA Univ of Houston 1962   93 p
6890   NOLAN Joseph T   Shakespeare's Dramatic Method as a Guide for Radio
Writers Today   MA Boston Univ 1945
6891   NORWOOD Lillian S   A History of Criticism of King Hamlet's Ghost
MA Univ of North Carolina at Chapel Hill 1949   91 p
6892   NUCHOLS Mary   A Comparative Study of the Sonnets of Spenser and
Shakespeare   MA Univ of Tennessee 1938
6893   NYE Jerry G   Reflections of the Bible in Shakespeare's *Othello*
MA Oklahoma St Univ 1963   76 p
6894   NYGARD H O   Machiavelli and Shakespeare, Part I; Machiavelli and
Shakespeare, Part II   BA Univ of British Columbia (Canada) 1944
6895   OBERG Charlotte   Character and Theme in *Romeo and Juliet* and *Troilus
and Cressida:* A Comparative Critical Study   MA Univ of Richmond
1966   93 p
6896   O'BRIEN Sr Ruth M   A Comparative Study of the Tragedy of Seneca and
Shakespeare   MA Boston Coll 1963
6897   O'CONNOR Mother Philomena   Diversity of Characterization in
Shakespeare   MA Boston Coll 1929
6898   O'DONNELL Sr M Audrey   Shakespeare as an Elizabethan Sonneteer
MA Boston Coll 1947
6899   O'DONNELL William J   Shakespeare's Adaptation of Sources for *Measure
for Measure*   MA Villanova Univ 1966
6900   O'HALLORAN Sr Mary E   Joseph Quincy Adams: Shakespearean Editor
MA St Louis Univ 1945   128 p
6901   OLDANI Louis J   Elements of Pity in Comedies of Shakespeare: A Study
of Rhetorical Techniques   MA St Louis Univ 1962   119 p
6902   O'LEARY C J   Shakespeare's Heroines   MA Boston Coll 1936
6903   O'LEARY Maureen A   The Fate of the Aristotelian Canons of Eighteenth
Century English Criticism of Shakespeare   MA Washington Univ at
St Louis 1948
6904   OLIVE W J   Shakespeare in Relation to Literary Satire and Burlesque
in Elizabethan Drama   MA Univ of North Carolina at Chapel Hill 1929
6905   OLSTEAD Myra M   Shakespeare's Characterization of Historic Leaders:
A Study in the Dramatic Use of Sources   MA Univ of Florida 1954
6906   O'MALLEY Sr Esther M   The Seven Sacraments in Shakespeare's Works
MA Boston Coll 1945
6907   O'MALLEY Sr Judith   The Thomistic Concept of Justice in Four Shakespearean English History Plays   MA Boston Coll 1953
6908   OMANS Stuart E   Politics in Shakespeare's Roman Plays   MA Miami Univ
1964
6909   O'NEILL Sr M Agatha   Problems in the Play *Othello*   MA Univ of Oklahoma
1930
6910   OPPY Ivy   An Evaluation and Criticism of Shakespeare's Use of Historical Materials in a Selected Group of His History-Dramas
MS Ft Hays St Teachers Coll 1934   52 p
6911   ORCUTT H J   Cleopatra: A Comparative Critique   MA North Texas St Univ
1968
6912   ORR Gena H   The Use of Source Material in the Play of *Henry VIII*
MA Univ of Texas at Austin 1929
6913   ORR Ruth S   A Comparison of Shakespeare's *Henry IV* with Scott's *Fair
Maid of Perth*, Especially with Regard to Historical, Traditional
and Fictional Elements in Each   MA Oklahoma St Univ 1930   56 p
6914   ORTEGO Philip D   The Stamp of One Defect: A Study of *Hamlet*   MA Univ

of Texas at El Paso 1966   104 p

6915 OSBORNE A M   The Contribution of Shakespearean Actors to Shakespearean
      Criticism   MA Univ of North Carolina at Chapel Hill 1929
6916 OTTO Julia H   Women in Shakespeare's Time and in Shakespeare's Plays
      MA Washington Univ at St Louis 1943
6917 OTTO Mary K   Traditional and Contemporary Ideas in *The Tempest*
      MA Hunter Coll 1967
6918 OUTTEN Joyce W   Iago on the Stage and in Criticism: A Historical
      Survey   MA Univ of North Carolina at Chapel Hill 1958   87 p
6919 OWENS Esther W   Shakespeare's Roman Plays   MA Univ of Arizona 1942
6920 PACE C J   The Interest in Learning in Shakespeare's Plays   MA Univ of
      North Carolina at Chapel Hill 1942
6921 PANEK Leroy L   The First Quarto of *Henry V*   MA Lehigh Univ 1965
6922 PARKER Amy G   The Comedy of Manners as Exemplified in the Comedies
      of Shakespeare   MA Washington Univ at St Louis 1939   164 p
6923 PARKER Ann S   Tragedy in Arthur Miller in the Light of Greek and
      Shakespearean Tragedy   MA Texas Arts and Industries Univ 1968
      223 p
6924 PARKER M V   Shakespeare and the Idea of Justice   B Litt Oxford Univ
      (England) 1950
6925 PARKER Marlene F   Sound Devices in *I Henry IV, Macbeth* and *The Tempest*
      MA Univ of Texas at Austin 1965   115 p
6926 PARTEE Morriss H   A Study of Shakespeare's Child Characters in
      Richard III, King John and *Macbeth*   MA Univ of Texas at Austin 1964
6927 PATCH Shirley J   Shakespeare's Use of Disguise as an Instrument of
      Symbolic Initiation   MA Univ of Redlands 1966
6928 PATRICE Sr Mary   A Delineation of Shakespeare's Ophelia   MA Boston Coll
      1927
6929 PATTERSON Lorenzo J   Shakespeare and the Bible   MA Mankato St Coll 1958
      61 p
6930 PEARSALL Thomas E   The Use of Poison and Sleeping Potions in
      Shakespeare's Plays   MA Univ of Texas at Austin 1956   97 p
6931 PEDERSON Willard M   Setting as an Integral Part of the Text of the
      Shakespearean Play   MA Western St Coll of Colorado 1940   119 p
6932 PEMBERTON Nancy A   The Disguise Motif in Shakespeare's Romantic Comedies
      MA Univ of Tennessee 1965
6933 PENN Susan F   *Troilus and Cressida*: A Discussion of Value and the
      Challenge of Satire   MA Claremont Graduate School 1966
6934 PENNINO Mary   Falstaff and Old Age   MA Columbia 1953   76 p
6935 PERRYMAN Romie   Symbolism in *Macbeth*   MA Hardin-Simmons Univ 1960
6936 PETTIGREW Helen P   The Elizabethan Lover in Shakespeare's Comedies
      MA West Virginia Univ 1938   405 p
6937 PETZE Marlette   Job, Prometheus and King Lear: Three Voices in the
      Whirlwind   MA Univ of Delaware 1965   100 p
6938 PHARR Gladys W   Parental Relations in Six of Shakespeare's Plays
      MA Univ of Texas at Austin 1930
6939 PHILLIPS Allen C Jr   A Critical History of Marc Antony (In Shakespeare's
      Antony and Cleopatra)   MA Univ of North Carolina at Raleigh 1951   104
6940 PHILLIPS Eleanor   The Development of Shakespeare's Women Characters in
      Five of His Early Plays   MA Univ of Texas at Austin 1928
6941 PIERCE Richardia P   The Contrast between Reality and Appearance in
      Hamlet, Othello and *Macbeth*   MA Emory Univ 1964
6942 PIPER Margaret R   Friends and Friendship in Shakespeare's Plays
      MA Smith Coll 1910
6943 PITTMAN Philip M   This Little World of Man: A View of *King Lear*
      MA Vanderbilt Univ 1964
6944 PLAYER Marjorie M   Shakespeare's Wicked Uncles   MA Florida St Univ 1952
6945 POISSON Rodney P   The Heroic Couplet in the Plays of Shakespeare
      MA Univ of British Columbia (Canada) 1939
6946 POL Frances   Literary Criticism in Shakespeare   MA Univ of Maine 1909

149 p
6947 POLLARD Virginia B A Study of the Imagery of Shakespeare's Sonnets
     and Narrative Poems MA Oklahoma St Univ 1938 61 p
6948 POOL Hope Shakespeare's Use of His Sources in *Henry V* MA Univ of
     Texas at Austin 1927
6949 POSEY Nelda R Creative Instructional Aids for Motivating Interest
     in Shakespeare's *Macbeth* M Ed Howard Payne Coll 1963 116 p
6950 POTTER Carolyn F A Study of the Father Characters in Shakespeare's
     Plays MA Southern Methodist Univ 1965
6951 POWELL Edna F A Study of the Inherent and Environmental Causes of
     the Tragedy in *Macbeth, Othello* and *King Lear* MS Kansas St Coll
     at Pittsburg 1932
6952 POWERS Loretto F A Survey of the Oxford-Shakespeare Theory
     MA Columbia 1942
6953 PRICE John R Dramatic Function of the Fool in *King Lear* MA St Louis
     Univ 1948 152 p
6954 PRICE Joseph G Shakespeare's Comedies and Histories: An Edition of
     Joseph Hunter's Unpublished Memoranda in Manuscript Addition 24496
     in the British Museum MA Georgetown Univ 1958 190 p
6955 PROCTOR Perry M An Evaluation of Some of the Important Theories
     Concerning Shakespeare's Lost Years MA Southern Illinois Univ at
     Carbondale 1952 112 p
6956 PUTNAM Louis S "By Indirections Find Directions Out": Evidence of the
     Generative Paradox and Meaning of *Richard III* in Richard's Solil-
     oquies and Asides MA Univ of Delaware 1968 61 p
6957 QUICKSALL Carlyne Shakespeare's Use of the Mirror Emotion as
     Motivating Forces in *The Tempest* MA Texas Technological Univ 1931
     37 p
6958 QUINN Marlin R *Troilus and Cressida* and the New Criticism: Tragic
     and Satiric Elements in the Play as Reflected in Its Language,
     Imagery and Symbolism MA Univ of Maryland at College Park 1969 53 p
6959 RAFTER Sr Mary M Shakespeare: Product of the Catholic Middle Ages
     MA Boston Coll 1946
6960 RAINES Robert A The Spectator Motif in *The Taming of the Shrew* and
     The Knight of the Burning Pestle MA Univ of Delaware 1967 63 p
6961 RANDERSON John T Macbeth and Agamemnon: A Comparative Study
     MA George Washington Univ 1960 113 p
6962 RANKIN James M Voltaire's Criticisms of Shakespeare MA Texas Tech-
     nological Univ 1932 79 p
6963 RATLEDGE Wilbert H Jr The Problem of the Hero in Shakespeare's
     King John MA North Texas St Univ 1970
6964 READING E H Un Drama Nuevo with Special Reference to the Author's
     Treatment of Shakespeare MA Univ of Oklahoma 1923
6965 REDMAN Linda F Water Imagery in *The Tempest* MA Oklahoma St Univ 1965
     112 p
6966 REDWINE Lola L Restoration Versions of *King Lear* and *The Tempest*
     MA Austin Coll 1932
6967 REED Mitchel L A Critical Survey of *Measure for Measure*; Some Obser-
     vations on John Steinbeck's Writing; and *Troilus and Cressida*:
     Boccaccio and Chaucer MA Brigham Young Univ 1966
6968 REES Compton Jr English Renaissance Dream Theory and Its Use in
     Shakespeare MA Rice 1958
6969 REIBENSTEIN Alberta A A Study of the Principles of Poetic Justice in
     the Tragedies of the Age of Elizabeth Exclusive of Shakespeare
     MA Pacific Univ 1930 90 p
6970 REIGER George W *Macbeth* and the Medieval Tradition MA Columbia 1964
     73 p
6971 REILLY Agnes D Shakespeare's Use of Metaphor in the Historical Plays
     Richard II, Henry V and *Henry VI* MA Boston Coll 1940
6972 REUTER John R Delusion, Self-Realization and Renascence in *King Lear*

                    MA DePauw Univ 1964   29 p
6973 REYNOLDS Florence S Shakespeare and the Earl of Essex   MA Univ of
      Arizona 1944
6974 REYNOLDS Robert C   The Operation of Destiny in *Julius Caesar*   MA Univ
      of Florida 1965
6975 RHODES Rhoda F   Shakespeare's Use of Dance: An Analytical Study of
      All Dance Sequences in Shakespeare's Plays   MA Hunter Coll 1969
6976 RIBNER Irving   King Lear: A Study in Shakespearean Character Criticism,
      1710-1947   MA Univ of North Carolina at Chapel Hill 1947   142 p
6977 RICE Sr Mary B   George Steevens as an Editor of Shakespeare   MA St Louis
      Univ 1927   87 p
6978 RICHARD Sr Marie F   The Soliloquies of Shakespeare   MA Boston Coll 1959
6979 RICHARDSON John C   The Poetry of Shakespeare's *Antony and Cleopatra*
      MA Columbia 1942
6980 RICHESON Hazel   The Use of the Supernatural in Shakespeare   BA Univ
      of Oklahoma 1910
6981 RICKARD Anne M   The Role of Imagery in Revealing Disorder in
      Shakespeare's *Macbeth*   MA Ohio St Univ 1966   112 p
6982 RIESS M E   Essay-Types in Shakespeare's Drama   MA Univ of North Carolina
      at Chapel Hill 1929
6983 RILEY M Isabelle   Shakespeare's Use of Flowers in Poems and Plays
      MA Boston Coll 1933
6984 RILEY Sr Mary F   Shakespeare's Tragic Heroines   MA Boston Coll 1927
6985 RINGKAMP Henry C   Slander: A Motif in the Plays of Shakespeare
      MA St Louis Univ 1935   144 p
6986 RITCHIE J P   Christian Immortality in Shakespeare's Tragedies
      MA Boston Coll 1950
6987 RIVERA Sr Isabel M   An Analysis of Critical Opinion Linking Shake-
      speare and Calderon as Great Writers of Tragedy   MA Boston Coll 1950
6988 ROACH James V   *What Happens in Hamlet* and Its Reviewers   MA St Louis
      Univ 1938   56 p
6989 ROACH Mary J   Shakespearean Acting from Burbage to Garrick
      MA Washington Univ at St Louis 1931   178 p
6990 ROBERS Sr Mary B   Ambition in Shakespeare's Characters   MA St Louis
      Univ 1927   91 p
6991 ROBERTS Helen S   Character Development of the Kings in Shakespeare's
      History Plays   MA Texas Technological Univ 1969   93 p
6992 ROBERTS (Mrs) Luther G   A Comparative Study of Shakespeare's Sonnets
      and Six Plays   MA West Texas St Univ 1959   140 p
6993 ROBERTSON Helen S   The Rhetorical Humor of William Shakespeare
      MA Univ of Texas at El Paso 1968
6994 ROBINSON Anna F   A History of English Prosody from the Earliest Extant
      Beginnings until Shakespeare   MA Western St Coll of Colorado 1923
      102 p
6995 ROBINSON Herbert S   English Shakespearean Criticism in the Eighteenth
      Century   M Litt Cambridge Univ (England) 1930
6996 RODKIN David J   Shakespeare's Use of the Oath in the History Plays
      MA Columbia 1965   131 p
6997 ROGER Ethriah H   The Dramatic Fiction of Imagery in Shakespeare's
      The Winter's Tale   MA Texas Technological Univ 1967   59 p
6998 ROGERS Evelyn G   A Study in Shakespeare's *Troilus and Cressida*
      MA Univ of Massachusetts 1956
6999 ROMANOW Walter I   William Shakespeare: His Changing Dramaturgy
      in the Late Plays   MA Windsor (Canada) 1965
7000 ROMINE Carolina   Shakespeare's Contribution to the Comedy of Manners
      MA Washington St Univ at Pullman 1915
7001 ROSELLE Bessie L   A Study of Family Relations in Five Plays of
      Shakespeare   MA Univ of Texas at Austin 1940   191 p
7002 ROSENTHAL Lewis S   Shylock as a Puritan Usurer   MA Auburn Univ 1954
7003 ROSS Myrna   Mediaevalism and Humanism in Shakespeare   MA Univ of Iowa

1924
7004 ROWELL Garner R Literary Portrayals of Julius Caesar MA Univ of
     Louisville 1952
7005 RUBINSKY Blance Italian Parallels to Shakespeare's Early Comedies
     MA Columbia 1940
7006 RUBLE Minnie R Plutarch's Motivation of Character as Altered by
     Shakespeare in the Roman Plays MA Hardin-Simmons Univ 1958
7007 RUMBERGER William B The Functions of the Opening Scene in Twelve
     Shakespearean Plays MA Shippensburg St Coll 1965
7008 RUOFF Fred A The Influence of Shakespeare's Hamlet on Herman Melville's
     Pierre MA Rutgers St Univ 1949 60 l
7009 RUSHING James W A Study of the Spirits in Six Shakespeare Plays
     MA Univ of Texas at Austin 1949 78 p
7010 RUSSELL Dorothy A King Lear: A Study of Its Sources MA Univ of
     Texas at Austin 1929
7011 RUSSELL Mary C Shakespeare's Lonely Dragon MA Boston Coll 1960
7012 RUSSELL Sandra J "None Does Offend": A Study of Shakespeare's
     Conception of Justice and Grace MA Columbia 1958 149 p
7013 RUTGERS Gloria D A Study of the Nature of Kingship in King Lear as
     Related to the First and Second Tetralogies MA Temple Univ 1964
     68 p
7014 RUTHERFORD Vera R The Play of Edward III: Its Sources, Structure
     and Possible Authorship MA Univ of Texas at Austin 1927
7015 RYAN Frank J Jr Shakespeare's Richard II and William Carlos Williams'
     Poetry MA Pennsylvania St Univ 1965
7016 RYDOR Ella N Hamlet: Rhetoric and the Theme of Appearance and Reality
     MA Texas Technological Univ 1963 58 p
7017 RYTELL Georffry The Image of the Theatre in Shakespeare MA Univ of
     British Columbia (Canada) 1962 103 p
7018 SABISTON Elizabeth J The Function of the Fool in King Lear
     MA Indiana Univ 1960
7019 ST JOHN Rayward P Shakespeare's Use of Source Material in Henry IV,
     Part I MA Univ of Texas at Austin 1931
7020 SALAZAR Sabino Attitudes towards the Sea in Shakespeare's Plays
     MA Texas Arts and Industries Univ 1942
7021 SAMUELS Julius Shakespeare's Treatment of Class Conflicts in the
     English Historical Plays: A Comparison of the Plays with Their
     Historical Sources MA Columbia 1936
7022 SANDERS John T Musical Compositions Based on Shakespeare's Romeo
     and Juliet with Special Reference to Gounod's Opera MA Univ of
     Texas at Austin 1941 206 p
7023 SANDERS Lee C Shakespeare's Sentimentalists MA Univ of Tennessee 1950
     123 p
7024 SANDERS London A The Friendship Theme in Shakespeare MA Univ of
     Tennessee 1931
7025 SANDERS Sr Mary A Maternity in Shakespeare's Plays MA St Louis
     Univ 1936 80 p
7026 SANDERS Wiley B Shakespeare's Treatment of the Common People in
     His English and Roman Historical Plays MA Emory Univ 1918 51 p
7027 SANDISON J M Antony and Cleopatra and All for Love: A Comparative
     Study BA Univ of British Columbia (Canada) 1950
7028 SANZO Eileen B The Interplay of the Themes of Love and War in
     Shakespeare's Troilus and Cressida MA Columbia 1962 67 p
7029 SARGEANT H H The Study of the Pre-Shakespearean Drama before Malone
     B Litt Oxford Univ (England) 1940
7030 SAROOP Anthony Othello as Tragic Farce MA Alberta (Canada) 1966
7031 SARTAIN C P Realistic Characterization of the Minor Figures in
     Shakespeare's Chronicle Plays MA Univ of North Carolina at Chapel
     Hill 1931
7032 SCANLAN Thomas R Jr The Date of Timon of Athens and the Relationship

of the Play to *King Lear* MA George Washington Univ 1951 94 p
7033 SCANNELL L M Cleopatre MA Boston Coll 1931
7034 SCHACHT Harold T Christian Allegory in *The Merchant of Venice*
       MA Lehigh Univ 1965
7035 SCHARTLE Patty M Aristocratic *Coriolanus*: A Study in Shakespearean
       Criticism MA Univ of North Carolina at Chapel Hill 1946 73 p
7036 SCHOELLHORN Carmen S Shakespeare in the Neo-Classical Period
       MA St Mary's at San Antonio 1949 97 p
7037 SCHOEN Raymond G *Cymbeline* and the Idea of a Play MA Purdue Univ
       1965 92 p
7038 SCHUMACHER Paul J The Prophetic Use of Dreams in Shakespeare
       MA North Texas St Univ 1965
7039 SCHWARTZ Edwin J The Production History of *Romeo and Juliet* on the
       English Stage BA Rutgers St Univ 1955 76 p
7040 SCHWARTZ Ernest Elizabethan Music in Shakespeare M Ed Temple Univ
       1934 120 p
7041 SCHWARTZ Mabel M The Troilus-Cressida Tradition after Shakespeare
       MA Southern Illinois Univ at Carbondale 1961 145 p
7042 SCHWIENHER Lucy M Adaptations of Shakespeare during the Century
       Following the Restoration MA St Louis Univ 1928 55 p
7043 SCOGGINS Faye T Figurative Language in Shakespeare's Plays
       MA West Texas St Univ 1940 197 p
7044 SCOTT Loretta E Bradley on the Delay in *Hamlet* MA George Washington
       Univ 1951 93 p
7045 SCOUFOS Alice L Shakespeare and the Lords of Cobham MA Univ of
       Oklahoma 1963 247 p
7046 SEABORN H T *Hamlet*: The Search for a Basis of Moral Action
       MA Univ of California at Riverside 1958
7047 SEAMAN Richard L Blood Imagery in Shakespearean Tragedy MA Northeast
       Missouri St Coll 1964
7048 SEAMAN Venna F The Dramatic Effect of the Short Speeches in Three
       Shakespearean Tragedies: *Julius Caesar, Hamlet* and *Othello*
       MA Northeast Missouri St Coll 1965
7049 SEARCY Martha L Problems in the Text of *King Lear* MA Univ of
       Oklahoma 1930
7050 SECKINGER D L Political Ideas of Shakespeare MA Univ of North
       Carolina at Chapel Hill 1915
7051 SEELYE M A Nature in *King Lear* as a Basis for the Unity of Action
       MA Univ of North Carolina at Chapel Hill 1944
7052 SEELYE Muriel C A Measure of *Measure for Measure* MA George Wash-
       ington Univ 1964 80 p
7053 SEIBERT Loris E Shakespeare's Treatment of Elizabethan Ideas about
       Death MA Rice 1958
7054 SELLERS Lois C The Poison-Tongued Speaker in Shakespeare MA Oklahoma
       St Univ 1934 58 p
7055 SEMEL Jay M The Rejection of Falstaff: Three Centuries of Criticism
       MA Univ of Delaware 1968 121 p
7056 SESSIONS Barbara P Inconsistencies in the Character of King Lear
       MA Texas Technological Univ 1963 82 p
7057 SEVERSON Florence W A Study of the Oratory in Shakespeare MA Okla-
       homa St Univ 1930 105 p
7058 SHAFFER George B Shakespeare's Historical Sources for the Play
       Richard III MA Univ of Toledo 1947
7059 SHAMBLIN Rose Iago: The Instrument of War MA West Texas St Univ
       1966 79 p
7060 SHARP Alice V Shakespeare's Dramatic Examination of Commonplace
       Opinions MA Univ of Florida 1953
7061 SHAW Catherine M The Masque in Shakespeare MA Univ of British
       Columbia (Canada) 1963
7062 SHEEHAN Sr Mary A Shakespeare's Religion MA Boston Coll 1927

7063 SHELTON Elizabeth L   The Soldier in Shakespeare   MA Oklahoma St Univ
      1947 88 p
7064 SHELTON Trumanel   Parapsychology in Shakespeare   MA Univ of Texas
      at El Paso 1967 129 p
7065 SHERLEY Lorraine   A Study of Certain Character Types in Early Plays
      of Shakespeare   MA Univ of Texas at Austin 1930
7066 SHOENBERG Robert E   Mummery, Mythology and Misrule: A Study of
      Folk Ritual and Dramatic Tradition in the Festive Comedies of
      Shakespeare   BA Amherst 1957
7067 SHULTZ Dyson P   Three Studies in Poetry: Shakespeare's *Troilus*,
      Churchill's *Prophecy* and the Poetry of Robinson and Frost
      MA Pennsylvania St Univ 1966
7068 SIDER John W   "Heavenly Comforts of Despair": The Dark Elements
      in Shakespeare's Comedies   MA McMaster (Canada) 1966
7069 SILVERTHORNE E E   Medievalism in Shakespeare   MA North Texas St Univ
      1963
7070 SIMISON Barbara D   Shakespeare's *Henry V*: A Study of Its Textual
      Problem   MA Smith Coll 1931
7071 SIMMONS J D   A Study of the English Publications of 1623, Whereby
      Inferences Are Drawn Concerning Reading Tastes at the Time of
      the Publication of Shakespeare's First Folio   MA Univ of London
      (England) 1964
7072 SIMMONS Joseph P   The Function of the Fool in Shakespeare   MA Univ
      of Texas at Austin 1914
7073 SIMMONS Katherine P   Warwickshire Local Color in Shakespeare's Plays
      MA Univ of Oklahoma 1948
7074 SIMONINI Rinaldo C Jr   The Language Lesson Dialogue in Shakespearean
      Drama   MA Univ of North Carolina at Chapel Hill 1946 88 p
7075 SIMPSON William F   Nemesis in Classical Tragedy and in Elizabethan
      Tragedy through Shakespeare   MA Boston Univ 1936
7076 SIRMANS Sylvia L   Prospero's Journey: A Study of Order and Discourse
      in *The Tempest*   MA Emory Univ 1966
7077 SLOAN Harriett   A Study of the Fool in Shakespeare's Plays   MS Kansas
      St Coll at Pittsburg 1953
7078 SLOVER George W   A Comparative Study of the Symbolism in the Sources
      of *The Merchant of Venice*   MA Indiana Univ 1956
7079 SMALLWOOD Olivia   The Stage History of *The Merchant of Venice*
      MA Univ of Oklahoma 1936
7080 SMART Estella L   Shakespeare's Conception of the Ideal King as Revealed
      in *Henry V* and *Hamlet*   MA Oklahoma St Univ 1938 50 p
7081 SMITH Edgar L   Some Functions of Imagery in Shakespeare's *Richard II*
      MA Univ of Texas at Austin 1955 71 p
7082 SMITH Irene F   Reinterpretation of Character Traits and Values
      through Five of Shakespeare's Dramas: *Julius Caesar, Macbeth,
      Othello, King Lear* and *Hamlet*   MA St Coll at Fitchburg 1938
7083 SMITH John H   The Senecan Tradition from the Spanish Tragedy to
      Hamlet   MA Washington Univ at St Louis 1925 164 p
7084 SMITH Mary A   Metrical Analysis in Nineteenth Century English
      Criticism of Shakespeare   MA North Texas St Univ 1966
7085 SMITH Maurice A   The Development of Shakespeare's Tragic Villains
      MA Hunter Coll 1964
7086 SMITH R M   The Motivation of Characters in *Othello, King Lear* and
      Macbeth   MA North Texas St Univ 1942
7087 SMITH Sharon L   A New Look at Shakespeare's *The Tempest*: Sources
      and Date   MA Kansas St Teachers Coll 1964
7088 SNOOK Paul A   The "Mad" Hamlet: A Critical History   MA Columbia 1961
      288 p
7089 SNOW Nola J   Victor Hugo's William Shakespeare   MA Univ of Oklahoma 1925
7090 SPAKOWSKI Raymond   Shakespearean and Neo-Classical Influence in *The
      Prince of Parthia*   MA Illinois St Univ 1966

7091 SPARGO John W The Sources of Falstaff MA Washington Univ at St Louis
     1921 50 p
7092 SPAULDING Frances E Problem of the Date of *The Merry Wives of Windsor*
     MA Washington Univ at St Louis 1916 53 p
7093 SPEARS Alma E A Study of the First Act of Five Shakespearean Comedies
     MA Univ of Texas at Austin 1936
7094 SPECK Henry E The Complete Fool: A Study of Lear's Fool MA Univ
     of Texas at Austin 1961 103 p
7095 SPECKING Sr Mary de P Principles of Sound Morality in Shakespeare's
     Plays MA St Louis Univ 1933 91 p
7096 SPENCER Gloria B The Maturation of Romeo as Revealed in His Language
     MA Texas Technological Univ 1967 103 p
7097 SPENCER Selden P One of Shakespeare's Plays Compared with its Immediate
     Source as Regards the Characterization MA Washington Univ at
     St Louis 1916 27 p
7098 SPEYER Frances C Anger Has a Privilege: A Study of Comedy and Tragedy
     in *King Lear* MA Univ of Colorado 1966
7099 SPIKES Jean T A C Bradley at Mid-Century: A Survey of *King Lear*
     Criticism since 1945 MA Univ of Southern Mississippi 1966
7100 SPITZENBERGER Raymond D Shakespeare's *1 Henry IV, 2 Henry IV, Henry V*:
     Conceived as a Continuative Dramatic Epic in the Round MA Univ of
     Houston 1965 58 p
7101 SPOFFORD Edward W An Analysis of the Movement of Dialogue in *Julius
     Caesar* by Shakespeare and *Death of a Salesman* by Arthur Miller
     BA Amherst 1954
7102 STALLINGS Mary S The Elizabethan Stage and Its Influence on
     Shakespeare MA Washington Univ at St Louis 1925 122 p
7103 STAPLETON Ada B Shakespeare's Indebtedness to *The Troublesome Reign
     of King John* MA Washington Univ at St Louis 1916 29 p
7104 STARK Alice M The Water Images in *The Tempest* MA Columbia 1960 93 p
7105 STARK Edith M Machiavelli and Shakespeare MA Univ of Louisville 1930
7106 STARKS George A Late Elizabethan Dramatic Satire and Shakespeare's
     Measure for Measure MA Columbia 1941
7107 STARLING Betty R Biblical Allusions: Shakespeare's Tool for Character-
     ization MA Univ of Texas at Austin 1965 103 p
7108 STARR Gyndolyn N Shakespeare in Modern Mexico MA Univ of Texas at
     El Paso 1966 81 p
7109 STATON Eda P Dictionary of Shakespearean Characters MA Baylor Univ
     1924
7110 STEDMAN Helen A Shakespeare's Portia in *The Merchant of Venice*
     MA Boston Univ 1932
7111 STEPEHNSON Helen L Edmond Malone's 1790 Shakespeare MA St Louis Univ
     1935 72 p
7112 STEPHANY William A "The Surplice of Humility": A Study of *All's Well
     that Ends Well* MA Univ of Delaware 1967 64 p
7113 STEWART Josephine *Antony and Cleopatra* and *All for Love*: A Comparison
     MS Kansas St Coll at Pittsburg 1955
7114 STIEBEL Sidney A Related Essays on Plays of Marlowe and Shakespeare
     BA Rutgers St Univ 1968 42 p
7115 STOBAUGH Margaret H A Critical Study of Moratin's Translation of
     Hamlet MA Univ of Oklahoma 1939
7116 STONE Marjorie S The Comic Element in Shakespearean Tragedy
     MA Univ of Tennessee 1946
7117 STORM Julia H The Impasse of Action in the Development of Tone:
     A Study of Shakespeare's *Hamlet*, Chekhov's *The Sea Gull* and
     Pirandello's *Henry IV* MA Florida St Univ 1953
7118 STORY Lucille W The Revenge Motif in the *Oresteia*, *Hamlet* and *Winterse*
     MA East Tennessee St Univ 1961
7119 STOUTMIRE Frederick A Schoolisms in Shakespeare MA Univ of Richmond
     1937 166 p

7120 STROUP Joseph B The Problem of Staging in the Second Quarto of
     Romeo and Juliet MA Univ of North Carolina at Chapel Hill 1951 87 p
7121 SUTFIN Joe A The Imagery of Shakespeare's Clowns MA Southern Illinois
     Univ at Carbondale 1955 56 p
7122 SWEATT Frances A Critical Study of *Othello* MA Oklahoma St Univ 1939
     40 p
7123 SWEENEY H P A Critical Discussion of the Character of Hamlet
     MA Boston Univ 1939
7124 SWEET Mary W The Influence of Shakespeare upon Wordsworth MA Univ
     of Tennessee 1950
7125 SZLOSEK Joseph F Aspects of Jealousy as Treated by Shakespeare
     MA Boston Univ 1949
7126 TALBOT Barry W A Study of the Sources of the Shakespearean *Pericles*
     MA Univ of Texas at Austin 1934
7127 TAYLOR Anita G Shakespeare's Characterization of the Ingenue through
     Language: Juliet, Ophelia and Desdemona MA Univ of Texas at
     Austin 1967
7128 TEBBE Nancy L A Study of the Interpretation of the Character of
     Lady Macbeth MA Univ of Tennessee 1964
7129 TEETER Lillian B The Confidante in Classical Tradition Leading to
     the Confidante in Shakespeare MA Washington Univ at St Louis 1934
     169 p
7130 TEICHERT Edward A Jr Some Phases of the Changing Interpretation
     of William Shakespeare's Plays MA Univ of Pittsburgh 1960
7131 TERRY Louisa W The Developing Characters in Shakespeare's Plays
     MA Smith Coll 1929
7132 THOMAS Elizabeth Flower Lore from Shakespeare MA Austin Coll 1938
7133 THOMAS Katherine R Christian Patterns in *Cymbeline* MA Manitoba
     (Canada) 1966
7134 THOMAS M O A Study of the Criticism of Iago MA Univ of North Carolina
     at Chapel Hill 1944
7135 THOMAS Patricia T A Study of the Political Problems in *Richard II*
     MA Univ of Oklahoma 1965
7136 THOMASON Alton P Some Famous Hamlets: Their Place in the Progress
     of English Acting and Stagecraft MA Univ of Texas at Austin 1938
     133 p
7137 THOMPSON Bess H Herb Lore in Seven Plays of Shakespeare MA Univ of
     Texas at Austin 1949 84 p
7138 THOMPSON John W Emotional Imbalance in Shakespeare's *Coriolanus*
     MA Duke Univ 1965
7139 THOMPSON Larry W The Relationship of *1 and 2 Henry IV* MA Oklahoma
     St Univ 1962 64 p
7140 THORNE William B Folk Entertainment and Rituals in Shakespeare's
     Early Comedies MA Univ of British Columbia (Canada) 1961 181 p
7141 THROSSELL J L The Lovers of *Troilus and Cressida*: Ascending the
     Heights of Love and Honor MA Brigham Young Univ 1968 153 p
7142 TINSLEY Margaret H In the Mind's Eye: A Study of Shakespeare's
     Imaginative Use of Stage Properties in Six Representative Plays
     MA Univ of Richmond 1968 130 p
7143 TODD Mary E Shakespeare as an Individual MA Washington Univ at
     St Louis 1925
7144 TOMOWSKE Claire N Shakespeare's Use of Dance in His Plays MA Wash-
     ington St Univ at Pullman 1936
7145 TOOMEY Elizabeth The Problem of Revision in the First and Second
     Quartos of *Hamlet* MA Washington Univ at St Louis 1917 77 p
7146 TOWERS Ruth W A Comparison of Falstaff and Iago as Two of
     Shakespeare's Great Realists MA Univ of Tulsa 1941
7147 TOWNSEND Daniel D *Romeo and Juliet* in the Eighteenth Century
     MA Univ of Maryland at College Park 1968 61 p
7148 TOWNSEND Richard L The Influence of Shakespeare on the Poetry of

Lord Byron MA Univ of Maine 1966 93 p
7149 TREADWELL Thomas O Dark Shakespeare's Blotted Page: A Study of the
      Text of Shakespeare's Plays as Presented in the Editions of
      Alexander Pope and Lewis Theobald MA Columbia 1966 101 p
7150 TRIVEDI Sharti *Tempest* and *Shakuntala:* English and Sanskrit Dramatic
      Theory and Practice MA Boston Coll 1963
7151 TROYER Daryl E An Examination of the Travels and Tests of the
      Shakespearean Company MA Kansas St Teachers Coll 1965
7152 TRUEAX Mary C The Influence of William Shakespeare on Nathaniel Lee
      MA George Washington Univ 1941 101 p
7153 TRUESDELL Katherine A A Unit on the Teaching of *Romeo and Juliet*
      to Students in the Ninth Grade MA Cornell Univ 1966
7154 TUBELIS B A Shakespeare and O'Neill: An Evaluation of Technique
      in Tragedy MA Boston Univ 1940
7155 TUCK Marie T Some Legends in the Life of William Shakespeare
      MS Kansas St Coll at Pittsburg 1956
7156 TUCKER Beulah C Shakespeare's Use of His Source Material in *Merchant
      of Venice* MA Univ of Texas at Austin 1929
7157 TUCKER Ellie L Shakespeare's Use of His Source Material in *Timon of
      Athens* MA Univ of Texas at Austin 1933
7158 TUTTLE Gerda C Shakespeare Criticism in Germany in the First Quarter
      of the Twentieth Century MA Rivier Coll 1963
7159 TYRRELL Marcella S The Saga of Richard III with Special Stress upon
      the Literature of the Sixteenth and Seventeenth Centuries
      MA Columbia 1942
7160 UPSHAW Marion H The Function of the Elizabethan Lyric with Reference
      to the Plays of Shakespeare and Ben Jonson MA Univ of Arizona 1940
7161 USELTON B M Current Trends in the Interpretation of *Othello*
      MA North Texas St Univ 1962
7162 VAN Lindley W The Double-Repentance Morality and Shakespeare's *Henry IV*
      Plays: A Study of the Tradition of the Prodigal Son Dramas
      MA Duke Univ 1966
7163 VAN MEEVERN Arthur Shakespeare's Purpose in Portraying Shylock
      MA Univ of Iowa 1931
7164 VENABLE Eva Shakespeare's Use of Omens MA Univ of Tennessee 1931
7165 VIANELLO Angelina The Character of Hamlet MA Ca Foscari (Italy) 1954
7166 VINSON Bertha E The Significance of Shakespeare's References to
      Animals MA Univ of Texas at Austin 1947 140 p
7167 WALDO Myrtice R A Study of Characteristics in Ten of Shakespeare's
      Heroines and Influences Which Helped to Shape Them MA Auburn Univ
      1952
7168 WALDO Tommy R Musical Imagery in *The Taming of the Shrew*: Evidence
      of Single Authorship MA Univ of Florida 1955
7169 WALKER Melissa C The Ironic Use of Animals in Shakespeare's *As You
      Like It* MA Emory Univ 1966
7170 WALKER Richard S *Hamlet* and the "To Be or Not To Be" Soliloquy
      MA Clark Univ 1969
7171 WALL Janet Natural Order in *King Lear* MA Texas Technological Univ
      1961 65 p
7172 WALTER Elsa L Shakespeare's *Antony and Cleopatra* Compared with Shaw's
      Caesar and Cleopatra MA Univ of Iowa 1931
7173 WALTER John A John Wilson ("Christopher North"): Critic of
      Shakespeare MA Texas Technological Univ 1937 72 p
7174 WALWARK James H Jr The Development of the Plain Clowns in Shakespeare's
      Comedies MA Southern Illinois Univ at Carbondale 1960 59 p
7175 WARE Eunice L Shakespeare's Use of His Source Material in *Coriolanus*
      MA Univ of Texas at Austin 1928
7176 WARREN Carolyn What Has Happened to the Comedy of Manners?
      Shakespeare's Mark Antony; Longfellow: A Defense MA Brigham
      Young Univ 1958 84 p

7177 WARREN Ruth The Popularity and Influence of Shakespeare's English
      and Roman Historical Plays in America from the Beginnings to 1950
      MA Pacific Univ 1955 526 p
7178 WASSERMAN George R A Study of *All's Well that Ends Well* MA Univ
      of Pittsburgh 1953
7179 WATKINS Olive Shakespeare in Emerson's Prose MA Univ of Tennessee 1933
7180 WATSON Joe F A Study of Shakespeare's Departures from Plutarch in
      the Characterization of Antony in *Antony and Cleopatra* MA Oklahoma
      St Univ 1960 114 p
7181 WAY T J Shakespeare's Treatment of Source Material in *Julius Caesar*
      MA North Texas St Univ 1956
7182 WAYNE Don E Self-Consciousness in Shakespearean Drama MA Hunter Coll
      1969
7183 WEAVER Hildred Stage Business Implied in Dialogue of Shakespeare's
      Plays MA Texas Technological Univ 1939 75 p
7184 WEAVER Virginia B The Fifth Act in Six Shakespearean Tragedies
      MA Univ of Texas at Austin 1936
7185 WEBB Morrison D Shakespeare and Words: Language in the Comedies
      BA Amherst 1969
7186 WEBBER Jean P *Timon of Athens*: Its Relationship to Other Plays of
      Shakespeare Canon; A Study of the Play with Special Reference to
      Themes Related to Judaeo-Christian Thought and Expressed through
      the Plot, Characterization and Images of the Drama MA Univ of
      British Columbia (Canada) 1968 191 p
7187 WEIR John B A Study of *Richard III* with Especial Reference to Its
      Source MA Univ of Pittsburgh 1918
7188 WEIRICK Margaret C Three Studies in Characterization and Symbolism:
      Shakespeare's Enobarbus; Myth and Symbol in Eliot; and Hawthorne's
      Miriam MA Pennsylvania St Univ 1966
7189 WELCH Rev J E Character Study of Lady Macbeth MA Boston Coll 1931
7190 WELCH Margaret M The Influence of Shakespeare on Voltaire
      MA George Washington Univ 1940
7191 WELDON Marie L English and French Criticism of the Tragedies of
      Shakespeare in the Age of Voltaire MA Boston Univ 1931
7192 WELSH Andrew A Reading of *Coriolanus* MA Univ of Pittsburgh 1962
7193 WEST Gladys E A Prompt Book and Production Thesis of William
      Shakespeare's *The Winter's Tale* MA Washington St Univ at Pullman 1940
7194 WEST Sr Marie D The Exile Figure in Shakespeare's Plays MA Boston
      Coll 1967
7195 WEST Mary M Great Bible Nouns in Shakespeare M Ed Temple Univ 1935
      609 p
7196 WEST Mildred E A Study of the Third Act of Eight Plays of Shakes-
      peare MA Univ of Texas at Austin 1935
7197 WESTERGREN Mary Y Order and Degree in Shakespeare's Lancastrian
      Tetralogy MA Texas Arts and Industries Univ 1961
7198 WHITAKER Dorothy F Shakespeare's Religion MA Univ of Tennessee 1937
7199 WHITE Chick Existentialism in *King Lear* MA West Texas St Univ 1962
      74 p
7200 WHITE David B An Analysis and Comparison of the Villainy in
      Shakespearean and Non-Shakespearean Elizabethan Drama MA Oklahoma
      St Univ 1939 52 p
7201 WHITE Dovie M Great Interpreters of Shakespearean Tragedy MA Austin
      Coll 1932
7202 WHITE Georgie Shakespeare's Geography MA Univ of Tennessee 1938
7203 WHITE Marion Shakespeare's Use of Nature Description MA Univ of
      Pittsburgh 1929
7204 WHITE Natalie E *Hamlet* on the New York Stage, 1900-1910 MA George
      Washington Univ 1941 88 p
7205 WHITNEY Gordon C Cleopatra: A Model for Dido? MA John Carroll Univ
      1965

7206 WHITNEY Marcia The Cleopatra of Plutarch, Shakespeare and Dryden;
      Tone in Willa Cather; "The Maelstrom": An Original Short Story
      MA Brigham Young Univ 1959 83 p
7207 WHITSON Bobbie C Proverb Lore in Shakespeare's Tragedies MA Baylor
      Univ 1957 161 p
7208 WIESNER Sharon M A Critical Survey of Ancient and Modern Criticisms,
      Both English and American, of Iago's Motivation MA Univ of Omaha
      1965
7209 WILKINSON Elizabeth H The Oedipus of Sophocles as the Prototype of
      Lear MA Univ of Pittsburgh 1928
7210 WILLIAMS Frances E Some Technical Features of Shakespeare's Sonnets
      MA Univ of Texas at Austin 1954 120 p
7211 WILLIAMS Jeane M Dramatic Malapropisms in Shakespeare with Special
      Reference to Dogberry and Mistress Quickly MA Univ of Oklahoma 1961
7212 WILLIAMS John K Four Modern Hamlets: A Comparative Study of the
      Interpretations of Adams, Wilson, Schucking and Granville-Barker
      MA Georgetown Univ 1966 475 p
7213 WILLIAMS Mary L Shakespeare's Characterization of English Kings as
      Shown in His Early History Plays MA Univ of Texas at Austin 1926
7214 WILLIAMS Mina Shakespeare's Use of Rhetoric in *Julius Caesar*
      MA Texas Arts and Industries Univ 1958
7215 WILLIAMS Richard L Proverb Lore in Shakespeare's History Plays
      MA Baylor Univ 1960 176 p
7216 WILLIG Alan B A Study of Shakespeare's Puritan Characters: Malvolio
      in *Twelfth Night* and Angelo in *Measure for Measure* MA Villanova
      Univ 1965
7217 WILSON Albert W Tragedy and Satire in Shakespeare's *Timon of Athens*
      MA Whittier Coll nd
7218 WILSON Shirley H A Study of the Development of Shakespearean Festivals
      MA East Tennessee St Univ 1963
7219 WINDEATT Mary F Motherhood in Shakespeare's Plays MA Columbia 1941
7220 WINDSOR Lucinda B Iago: A Study in the Application of Rhetoric
      to the Problem of Appearance and Reality MA Texas Technological
      Univ 1963 75 p
7221 WINDSOR Prentiss C The Commoner in Shakespeare MA Univ of Texas
      at Austin 1947 220 p
7222 WOLPER Roy S Areas of Agreement in the Prefaces to Six Eighteenth
      Century Editions of Shakespeare MA Univ of Pittsburgh 1959
7223 WOMACK Mary B *King Richard II* MA Washington Univ at St Louis nd 176 p
7224 WOMACK Sonya T *Macbeth*: A Study of the Analogy between Macbeth and
      Satan MA Auburn Univ 1969
7225 WOMELSDORFF Carole J Recent Critical Studies of Shakespeare's *Troilus
      and Cressida* MA Hardin-Simmons Univ 1965
7226 WOOD David E Religious Beliefs of Shakespeare MA Univ of Richmond
      1926 59 p
7227 WOOD Frederick A Falstaff's Critics: Dryden to Bradley MA Univ
      of Tennessee 1970 83 p
7228 WOOD Teresa W The Application of Bradley's Theory of Reconciliation
      to Certain of Shakespeare's Plays MA Univ of Arizona 1936
7229 WOODMAN David *Measure for Measure*: An Investigation of the Three
      Major Characters MA Columbia 1964 95 p
7230 WOODRUFF Gertrude M Points of Similarity between the Earlier Drama
      and the Plays of Shakespeare MA Smith Coll 1936
7231 WOODS Julia N Shaw and Shakespeare MA Univ of Tennessee 1945
7232 WOOSTER Jean E The Problem of Evil in Shakespeare's Plays MA Oklahoma
      St Univ 1942 53 p
7233 WRIGHT E P The Tragedy of Shakespeare's Hotspur MA North Texas St
      Univ 1961
7234 WYATT Gayle D Resemblances and Differences in Three Plays of
      Shakespeare MA Univ of Texas at Austin 1957

7235 YARASHUS Albert L Granville-Barker and Other Producers of
      Shakespeare's *Twelfth Night* MA George Washington Univ 1969 123 p
7236 YEO Emsley L The Characterization of Othello and Iago in the Light
      of Comparative Idiom MA Univ of British Columbia (Canada) 1930
7237 YOUNG Beatrice K Health Imagery in *Richard II* MA Texas Technological
      Univ 1965 63 p
7238 YOUNG Carrie M A Comparison of the Plot-Structure of *Twelfth Night,
      Much Ado about Nothing* and *As You Like It* MA Univ of Texas at
      Austin 1931
7239 YOUNG Dora J Cotton Mather, Leader in the American Enlightenment;
      Gide and His Counterfeiters and Shakespeare and Fletcher, Eliza-
      bethan Collaborators MS Brigham Young Univ 1959 118 p
7240 YOUNG Eleanor P Teaching Shakespeare in High School MA Southern
      Illinois Univ at Carbondale 1950 282 p
7241 YOUNG Howard W A Study of the Functional Uses of Music in
      Shakespeare's Plays MA East Tennessee St Univ 1962
7242 YOUNGER Winifred M The Historicity of Shakespeare's Tragedy of
      King Henry VI, Part III and the *Tragedy of King Richard III*
      MS Kansas St Coll at Pittsburg 1952
7243 ZAAL J The Concept of Kingship in Shakespeare's History Plays
      MA Univ of London (England) 1950
7244 ZAHN Mildred L The Relationship between Husbands and Wives in
      Certain of Shakespeare's Plays MA Oklahoma St Univ 1932 48 p
7245 ZARET Paul The Clowns and Fools of Shakespeare M Ed Temple Univ
      1936 124 p
7246 ZIMMERMAN Rosalind L The Relation of Character and Function in Some
      Principal Shakespearean Women MA Auburn Univ 1967
See also 1065, 1384, 1485, 1600, 1627, 1697, 1792, 1813, 1850, 2756, 2870,
      2894, 2910, 2912, 2914, 2918, 2944, 3766, 3919, 4325, 4379, 4391,
      4698, 4931, 4949, 5035, 5046, 5067, 5102, 5148, 5156, 5674, 6049,
      6089, 7285, 7287, 7297

GEORGE BERNARD SHAW

7247 ADAMS Elsie B Bernard Shaw and the Aesthetes MA Univ of Oklahoma 1966
7248 BAKER Burton Capitalism in Three Plays by George Bernard Shaw
      MA Columbia 1962 52 p
7249 BARKELL Helen J George Bernard Shaw's Use of Woman in His Plays
      MS Kansas St Coll at Pittsburg 1933
7250 BARNETT Walter M Jr Constructive Views in the Dramas of
      George Bernard Shaw MA Tulane Univ 1925
7251 BARR Wendy M A Study of the Character and Significance of Cleopatra
      in George Bernard Shaw's *Caesar and Cleopatra* BA Univ of British
      Columbia (Canada) 1961
7252 BEBEY Francis A A Record of the Development of Set and Costume Designs
      for Bernard Shaw's *Misalliance* MA Pennsylvania St Univ 1966
7253 BELL Anna M Of George Bernard Shaw on Women MA Syracuse Univ 1949 90 p
7254 BELL Lucile K Joan of Arc BA Univ of Oklahoma 1912
7255 BEST Brian S Dramatic Applications of George Bernard Shaw's Religion
      of Creative Evolution MA Brigham Young Univ 1962 119 p
7256 BIGHAM J Kyle The Predicament of Reason in Two Plays by
      George Bernard Shaw MA Bowling Green Univ 1959
7257 BLONDIN Arsenne A Comparison of the Joans of Arc of George Bernard Shaw
      and Maxwell Anderson MA St Mary's at San Antonio 1949 65 p
7258 BRITCH Carrol P Socialist Realism: An Examination of the Success
      Formula of Two Shaw Plays on Love MA Indiana Univ 1964
7259 BROWN Bazil W Shavianism and Poverty BA Amherst 1953
7260 BUCK William A The Dramatic Criticism of George Bernard Shaw
      MA Univ of Pittsburgh 1930
7261 CALDWELL Michael S A Critical Analysis of *Candida* M Ed Henderson

St Coll nd
7262 CARDEN William F The Selection, Design and Production of
     George Bernard Shaw's *Candida* MA Whittier Coll nd
7263 CHRYSOSTOMOU Nikitas George Bernard Shaw and the Idea of Progress
     MA Columbia 1951
7264 CLIFFORD Ann T A Study of George Bernard Shaw the Reformer
     MA Univ of Houston 1948 107 p
7265 COLLIER Val J Too Shavian to be Women: A Study of Seven Shavian
     Women Characters MA Arkansas St Coll 1966
7266 COOK L J Shaw's Economic Theories as Found in His Plays MA North
     Texas St Univ 1951
7267 CORPORON Lewis L George Bernard Shaw's Religion as Reflected in Five
     of His Plays and Prefaces MS Kansas St Coll at Pittsburg 1939
7268 COSTRELL Edwin The Conventionality of Bernard Shaw MA Univ of Maine
     1938 115 p
7269 COUCOUVITIS Elinore J George Bernard Shaw: Reformer and Artist.
     The Evolutionary States in the World of the Dramatic Artist
     MA Univ of New Hampshire 1965 88 p
7270 COVEY Jewyl Joan of Arc in History and in Shaw MA Univ of Arizona
     1958 99 p
7271 COYKENDALL Duane Creative Evolution in the Early Plays of
     George Bernard Shaw MA Wayne St Univ 1965
7272 CRAIG Frank E The Hero of George Bernard Shaw MA Columbia 1941
7273 CSUPECZ Andrea M A Correlation of the Nietzschean Ubermensch Concept
     with the Shavian Superman Concept Found in *Man and Superman* and
     Caesar and Cleopatra MA Univ of Maine 1969 80 p
7274 DARDANO Patricia J A Comparative Study of the Women Characters of
     George Bernard Shaw and Oscar Wilde MA Univ of Rhode Island 1964
     99 p
7275 DAVID Virginia A Study of the Character of Joan of Arc as Interpreted
     in Three Selected Plays MA East Tennessee St Univ 1965
7276 DAVIS Sr Mary F An Analytical Study of Bernard Shaw's *Saint Joan*
     by Comparison with the Historical Records of Her Trial MA Univ
     of Maine 1955 118 p
7277 DENNY Reon L George Bernard Shaw as an Artist: A Study in the Com-
     parison of His Prefaces and His Plays MA Univ of Oklahoma 1930
7278 DERRICK Maureen The Heroines of Bernard Shaw: A Study in Balance
     MA Brigham Young Univ 1965 87 p
7279 DICKERSON Paul E A Prompt Book for an Actual Production of
     George Bernard Shaw's *Saint Joan* MA Western St Coll of Colorado
     1966 154 p
7280 DIETRICH Richard F The Ethic of the Shavian Hero as Developed in
     Three Plays by Bernard Shaw MA Bowling Green Univ 1960
7281 DODSON Robert G A Comparative Study of Three Dramatic Versions of
     Don Juan MA Univ of Oklahoma 1948
7282 EDDY Alice L The Literary Aspects of Fabianism in the Plays and
     Prefaces of George Bernard Shaw MA Washington St Univ at Pullman
     1926
7283 EIKEL Frederick Hauptmann and Shaw: A Comparative Study MA Univ of
     Texas at Austin 1936
7284 FARKAS Brooke B Shaw on Christianity: An Overview from Ten Works
     MA Indiana Univ of Pennsylvania 1962 58 p
7285 FELLOWS JoAnn H Shaving the Bard: Shaw on Shakespeare MA Univ of
     New Brunswick (Canada) 1965
7286 FERNALD Mary H The Literary Relationship between T E Lawrence and
     Mr and Mrs Bernard Shaw MA Univ of Maine 1962 160 p
7287 FISHER Martha L Cleopatra in Three English Dramas MA Univ of Texas
     at Austin 1941 113 p
7288 FLY Addie C The Basic Motivations of Shaw's Major Male Characters
     Widowers' Houses through *Heartbreak House* MA Univ of Mississippi

1954 112 p
7289 FOLCO Ricci F George Bernard Shaw as a Literary Critic MA Ca Foscari
     (Italy) 1938
7290 FOX John Bernard Shaw MA Washington Univ at St Louis 1932
7291 FRAZER Frances The Relationship between Theme and Form in the Plays
     of George Bernard Shaw MA Univ of British Columbia (Canada) 1960
     175 p
7292 GERTNER Elizabeth The Battle of the Sexes in the Plays of
     George Bernard Shaw MA Columbia 1950
7293 GLAZIER Priscilla The Influence of Samuel Butler on George Bernard Shaw
     MA Univ of New Hampshire 1937 65 p
7294 GOTTHELF Harold Bernard Shaw: The Reluctant Pessimist. A Survey of
     the Shavian Alternative from *Widowers' Houses* to *Heartbreak House*
     MA Columbia 1961 82 p
7295 GRADEL Ralph D The Critical Criteria of George Bernard Shaw as
     Applied to His Major Plays MA Kent St Univ 1964
7296 GRAVES Susan B George Bernard Shaw's Sources: Four Plays MA Columbia
     1963 68 p
7297 GUINEY Ellen C Shaw and Shakespeare's *Cymbeline*: A Discussion of
     Shavian Shakespearean Criticism MA Boston Coll 1966
7298 HACKETT Virginia M The Life Force in the Social Perspective in the
     Plays of George Bernard Shaw MA St John's Univ 1966
7299 HARPER Mary E The Critical Reception of Shaw in America, 1894-1906
     MA Univ of Oklahoma 1954
7300 HARRIS Merle E *Mrs Warren's Profession* by George Bernard Shaw
     M Ed Henderson St Coll nd
7301 HARRIS Richard H Bernard Shaw and the Economic Mind MA Columbia 1965
     122 p
7302 HICKS Thomas W The Dramatic Criticism of George Bernard Shaw MA Univ
     of Florida 1955
7303 HIPKE Judy A Angels Versus Men: Shaw's Conception of the Female
     Ideal as Seen in His Treatment of Teenage Women MA Univ of
     Massachusetts 1969 80 p
7304 HOPKINS Richard A Bernard Shaw's Views on Parents and Children
     MA Univ of North Carolina at Raleigh 1953 82 p
7305 HOWARD Patricia M The Socialist Critique of Bernard Shaw MA Univ
     of Louisville 1963
7306 HOYLE Mabel G The Religion of George Bernard Shaw MA Boston Univ 1936
7307 HUANG Tsokan Bernard Shaw as a Fabian Socialist MA Ottawa (Canada)
     1963
7308 HUFF Marcia Mr Shaw's Musical Profession MA Univ of Mississippi 1965
     124 p
7309 JAGUST Eugene The American Criticism of George Bernard Shaw, 1894-1940
     MA Columbia 1941
7310 JOHNS Harriet A Comparative Study of the Treatment of Joan of Arc in
     Selected Literary Works MA Univ of New Mexico 1949
7311 KIDDER Rushworth M Character and Convention in Shaw: The Development
     of Character in George Bernard Shaw's Drama from *Arms and the Man*
     to *Major Barbara* BA Amherst 1965
7312 KUPFERBERG Herbert Bernard Shaw: Music Critic MA Columbia 1941
7313 KUSHNER William An Analysis of George Bernard Shaw's *Arms and the Man*
     with Production Notes MA Temple Univ 1960
7314 LAWSON Alice K An Analysis of Women in George Bernard Shaw's Plays
     MA Univ of Tulsa 1951
7315 LEE Donna A Shaw's Rhetoric in the Disquisitory Plays MA Toronto
     (Canada) 1966
7316 LEVENSTEIN Alan P The Shavian Rogue BA Amherst 1957
7317 LIEBERMAN Leo The Influence of Samuel Butler on Bernard Shaw
     MA Univ of Maine 1938 98 p
7318 LYNCH Vernon E George Bernard Shaw: Socialist Playwright MA Univ

of Texas at Austin 1939   145 p
7319 McCANN Garth A   Bernard Shaw: A Study of His Satire   MA Miami Univ 196?
7320 McKINLEY Robert D   George Bernard Shaw: His Quarrel with Protestant
      Orthodoxy MA Toronto (Canada) 1966
7321 McMIKLE Barbara J   The Inviolable Maid from Lorraine: A Comparative
      Study of World Dramas Dealing with Joan of Arc   MA San Diego St Coll
      1964   112 p
7322 MAHAN Marie T   The Relevance of Bernard Shaw's Utopian Image   MA Univ
      of Connecticut 1969
7323 MANION Orville G   The Stage Directions of George Bernard Shaw
      MA Univ of Idaho 1948
7324 MARTIN Alice M   The Literary Relationship of Henrik Ibsen to
      George Bernard Shaw MA Univ of Oklahoma 1930
7325 MAZUR Ann P   Themes in the Late Plays of Bernard Shaw   MA Alberta
      (Canada) 1964
7326 MELAMED Judith T   The Comedy of George Bernard Shaw: A Theory and
      Its Application MA Columbia 1940
7327 MICHELMAN Cherry F   The Political Philosophy of George Bernard Shaw
      MA Boston Univ 1953
7328 MILLER Antoinette F   The Joan of Arc Theme in English and American
      Drama MA Univ of Tennessee 1950   149 p
7329 MORELLI Umberto George Bernard Shaw: The Realist and the Artist
      MA Ca Foscari (Italy) 1939
7330 MORRIS Norma J Shaw's Ideas on Artists and Art   MA Univ of Texas
      at Austin 1952   98 p
7331 NAIDOO Muthal   Form and Satire in Shaw's Widowers' Houses MA Indiana
      Univ 1967
7332 OARE William T Annie Besant Meets Mr Shaw: A Fabian Contrast
      MA Columbia 1937
7333 PATERSON Heather A George Bernard Shaw's Arms and the Man: A Director
      Production Book MA Univ of California at Davis 1967
7334 PAULEY Harry W George Bernard Shaw as a Drama Critic MA Columbia 1952
      74 p
7335 PERLIS Linda S Shaw's Theory of Tragedy: An Exploration MA Univ
      of Maryland at College Park 1968   72 p
7336 PERRY Sylvia Conflicting Responses to Shaw by Some of His Fellow
      Dramatists BA Univ of British Columbia (Canada) 1969
7337 POINDEXTER Mary R Shaw and Acting MA East Carolina Univ 1959
7338 PORTER Patricia E The Figure of the "Idealistic Realist" in Five
      Plays of George Bernard Shaw MA Bowling Green Univ 1957
7339 RADFORD Fred L The Political Extravaganzas of George Bernard Shaw
      BA Univ of British Columbia (Canada) 1966
7340 RAYBORN Claude H Shaw on War MA Univ of North Carolina at Raleigh
      1951   105 p
7341 REBENTISCH Will George Bernard Shaw: The Relations of the Prefaces
      with the Plays MA Louisiana St Univ 1938
7342 RENAUDIE Marie J Joan of Arc in Modern Drama: A Study and Comparison
      of George Bernard Shaw's Saint Joan, Maxwell Anderson's Joan of
      Lorraine and Jean Anouilh's L'Alouette MA Southern Illinois Univ
      at Carbondale 1958 · 87 p
7343 REYNOLDS Gordon D Three Utilitarian Writers: Bentham, Mill and Shaw
      MA Texas Agricultural and Mechanical Univ 1962   61 p
7344 RIEG Faith F A Study of Significant Dramatic Treatments of the Joan
      of Arc Story from the Fifteenth Century until the Present
      MA Columbia 1959   138 p
7345 ROWER Ronald The Late Plays of Bernard Shaw MA Columbia 1958   127 p
7346 SALISBURY Rita L The Theme of Conversion and Salvation in the Plays
      of Bernard Shaw MA Saskatchewan (Canada) 1966
7347 SCHALLHORN David J A Scenic Design for Shaw's Man and Superman
      MFA Univ of Oklahoma 1970

7348 SCHILLINGER Olive M Shaw's Contribution to the Tradition of the
      Comedy of Manners MA Univ of Pittsburgh 1928
7349 SCHULTZE Edward W The Life of Mrs Patrick Campbell and Her Friendship
      with Bernard Shaw MA Columbia 1952 75 p
7350 SHINN Jeanne The Position of Women in the Plays of Bernard Shaw
      MA Univ of New Mexico 1949
7351 SIELEWICZ Bronia M Studies in the Portrait of Joan of Arc in Modern
      British and American Fiction and Drama MA Boston Univ 1948
7352 SOUCIE Robert M Dramatic Theory and Practice in George Bernard Shaw:
      Our Theatres in the Nineties and the Plays to *Caesar and Cleopatra*
      MA Toronto (Canada) 1966
7353 SOWERS Eleanor J George Bernard Shaw's Life Force MA Oklahoma St
      Univ 1939 32 p
7354 SPANOS William V Bernard Shaw and William Blake: A Relationship
      MA Columbia 1954 122 p
7355 SPENCER Lawrence F The Catholic Criticism of George Bernard Shaw's
      Philosophy MA Univ of Oklahoma 1945
7356 SPICER Ura J A Study of the Weakling in the Plays of George Bernard
      Shaw MS Kansas St Coll at Pittsburg 1935
7357 STATHAM Yolanda *Major Barbara*: Shaw's Use of Nietzschean Ideas
      MA Fresno St Coll 1968 56 p
7358 STEGALL Mary J Shaw on Art and Artists MA Texas Christian Univ 1966
      122 p
7359 STEIN Rita L The Late Political Plays of Bernard Shaw MA Columbia
      1966 86 p
7360 STUBBE Marilyn H Inversion of Current Theatrical Patterns in the
      Early Plays of George Bernard Shaw MA Bowling Green Univ 1956
7361 SULLIVAN Jane V The Unwomanly Woman in the Novels of George Bernard
      Shaw MA Shippensburg St Coll nd
7362 THOMPSON Nesta M The Philosophy of Ibsen and Shaw as Revealed by
      the Treatment of Truth and Falsehood in Their Social Dramas
      MA Washington Univ at St Louis 1919
7363 TILGHMAN Charles S The Life Force in the Plays of Shaw: A Study of
      the Philosophy of George Bernard Shaw as His Source of Dramatic
      Action MA Fresno St Coll 1964 67 p
7364 TRAPANI Domenico The Art and Thought of George Bernard Shaw
      MA Ca Foscari (Italy) 1928
7365 TURNER Almeda C Bernard Shaw: His Views on Marriage MA Howard Univ
      1940 66 p
7366 VITALI Esmeralda Samuel Butler's Influence on George Bernard Shaw
      MA Ca Foscari (Italy) 1942
7367 VONDERHEID Louis W Shaw and the Censor MA Univ of Pittsburgh 1952
7368 WADDILL Mary B Shaw's Feminism as Revealed in His Characterizations
      of Women MA Texas Christian Univ 1947 78 p
7369 WALACH Marilyn The Shavian Woman as an Expression of Creative Vitality
      BA Univ of British Columbia (Canada) 1967
7370 WALLACE Sr Rose C The Female Characters of James Matthew Barrie and
      George Bernard Shaw MA Boston Coll 1946
7371 WEILER Sr M Marguerite Feminism in the Plays of George Bernard Shaw
      MA Villanova Univ 1966
7372 WHITE Florence E Shaw's Characterization of Women MA Univ of Texas
      at Austin 1924
7373 WILLIAMS Avis R Shaw's Attitude toward Women MA Univ of Texas at
      Austin 1957
7374 WILLIAMS Jeffery A Theme and Structure in Bernard Shaw's Political
      Plays of the 1930's MA Univ of British Columbia (Canada) 1968 105 p
7375 WILLIAMS Peter N George Bernard Shaw's Use of Dialect in *Major Barbara*
      MA Univ of Delaware 1968 56 p
7376 WILLIAMS Thomas R George Bernard Shaw: The Man, His Methods and
      Message MA Univ of Arizona pre-1933

7377 WILSON Elizabeth A Modern Treatments of Saint Joan of Arc MA Boston
Coll 1949
7378 WYNN Virginia Q Significant Modern Interpretation of Joan of Arc
MA Univ of Louisville 1948
7379 YAGHMOUR Fakhry H Shaw's Exposure of Illusions in Conventional
Morality MA Kansas St Univ 1965
7380 YAP Tin S Shaw, Chesterton and Dickens: A Study in Critical Opinion
MA Univ of New Brunswick (Canada) 1965
See also 921, 1215, 6357, 6783, 7172, 7231, 7488

PERCY BYSSHE SHELLEY

7381 ADAMS Charles F Gothic Elements in Shelley's Poetry MA Univ of Texas
at Austin 1954 84 p
7382 ADELSHEIMER Ellen F Kings Over Themselves: A Study of the Influence
of Calderon's *La Vida es Sueno* on Shelley's *Prometheus Unbound*
MA Carnegie-Mellon Univ 1967
7383 ALBAUM Charlet P The Political Thought of Percy Bysshe Shelley
MA Long Island Univ 1969 94 p
7384 ANDERSON Barbara R An Examination of Shelley's Attitude toward
Christianity MA Brigham Young Univ 1960 97 p
7385 ANDERSON Emma H Shelley's Attitude toward the Social, Political and
Religious Institutions of His Time MS Purdue Univ 1899
7386 ASKEW Melvin W The Development of Shelley's Doctrine of Love
MA Univ of Oklahoma 1950
7387 AUCHINACHIE G Keats' and Shelley's Use of Myth BA Univ of British
Columbia (Canada) 1958
7388 BALBONI Diana Women in Shelley's Life and Poetry MA Ca Foscari
(Italy) 1941
7389 BARRETT Marjorie The Visionary and Practical Elements in the
Revolutionary Writings of Rousseau, Godwin and Shelley MA Smith
Coll 1917
7390 BASS Clarence S Jr Shelley's Idea of the Perfectability of Man
MA Texas Southern Univ 1965
7391 BAYLIS Evelyn The Nature of Shelley's Idealism in a Few Shorter Poems
BA Univ of British Columbia (Canada) 1964
7392 BELANGER Serge A Shelley and the Principles of Lyricism MA Columbia
1959 73 p
7393 BENNETT Dolly B Youth's Vision Once Made Perfect: A Study of the
Epipsyche Woman and the Natural Utopia in the Poetry of
Percy Bysshe Shelley MA Columbia 1966 104 p
7394 BENNINGHOFF Mary Platonism in Five of Shelley's Feminine Characters
MA Univ of Tulsa 1937
7395 BERRYMAN Charles B Percy Bysshe Shelley and *Prometheus Unbound*
BA Amherst 1961
7396 BISHOP R J The Influence of Godwin on Shelley BA Univ of British
Columbia (Canada) 1938
7397 BLACK Charles L Percy Bysshe Shelley as a Translator of Verse
MA Univ of Texas at Austin 1938 243 p
7398 BLACKERT Helen I Shelley's "Defense of Poetry": Its Meaning and
Its Sources MA Univ of Oklahoma 1925
7399 BOAZ O O The Gothic Element in Shelley's Writings MA North Texas
St Univ 1948
7400 BRANCOLI BUSDRAGHI Mariadele Mary and Percy Bysshe Shelley in
Tuscany MA Ca Foscari (Italy) nd
7401 BRAXTON Emily C Shelley's *Prometheus Unbound*: A Critical Analysis
and Interpretation MA Univ of Richmond 1967 95 p
7402 BROOKES Verdine M The Political Ideals of Shelley MA Univ of Texas
at Austin 1938 206 p
7403 BROTZE S A The Intellectual Development of Shelley as Reflected

in *Queen Mab, The Revolt of Islam* and *Prometheus Unbound*
MA North Texas St Univ 1944
7404 BROWN Hilary The "Defense of Poetry" and *Prometheus Unbound* BA Univ
of British Columbia (Canada) 1962
7405 BRUNI Anna Shelley and Romanticism MA Ca Foscari (Italy) 1950
7406 BRYAN Mary C In Indebtedness of Shelley in *Prometheus Unbound* to
Aeschylus in *Prometheus Bound* MA Boston Univ 1945
7407 CAMPBELL Mona B An Analysis of Shelley's "Hymn to Intellectual Beauty"
MA Univ of Louisville 1949
7408 CAPIZ Pascual The Ideal of Shelley MA Univ of Iowa 1933
7409 CARLTON Esther M Sense Imagery in the Poetry of Shelley MA Univ of
Iowa 1933
7410 CONNELY Harold B A Bibliography of Percy Bysshe Shelley's Writings
and Analysis from January 1, 1930 to December 31, 1934 MA Univ
of Kentucky 1944 148 p
7411 COX Estaline Shelley as Seen in the Centennial MA Baylor Univ 1931
69 p
7412 DARROW Esther L Shelley's Romantic Attitude towards Science
MA Univ of Hawaii 1930 41 p
7413 DAVIS Barbara J Egocentricity in the Works of Shelley MA St Mary's
at San Antonio 1967 76 p
7414 DAVIS Billy J Shelley's Imagery in *Queen Mab* and *The Triumph of Life*
MA Univ of Texas at Austin 1954 169 p
7415 DAVIS James R The Symbolism in Shelley's *The Revolt of Islam*
MA Washington St Univ at Pullman 1941
7416 DEVANEY Mary E Radical Tendencies in Shelley MA Boston Univ 1936
7417 DOWDY Dorothy The Reading Habits and Reading List of Percy Bysshe
Shelley MA Univ of Texas at Austin 1943 216 p
7418 EALY Ann J Shelley's Despondency Theme: The Short Lyrics from
1817 to 1822 MA Kansas St Teachers Coll 1965
7419 EDWARDS Octavia N Shelley's *Prometheus Unbound*: A Study MA Univ of
Texas at Austin 1932
7420 ELDREDGE Harrison C Shelley: Nautical Romantic MA Columbia 1962 74 p
7421 ESOLEN Gary A Beyond the Attack: An Analytic Reappraisal of Shelley
and His Critics MA Syracuse Univ 1967 94 p
7422 FABRIZIO Richard "Monk" Lewis and "Mad" Shelley: A Study in the
Development of the Unrestrained Individual MA Columbia 1962 106 p
7423 FARRELL C A The Language of Color in Shelley's *Prometheus Unbound*
MA North Texas St Univ 1969
7424 FINNEGAN Anne The Shelleyan Philosophy of Death: A Study of the
Death Motif in the *Esdaile Notebook* Poetry MA Univ of Texas at
El Paso 1965 96 p
7425 FORREST Louise M A Study of Shelley's Imagery in *Prometheus Unbound*
MA Univ of Texas at Austin 1939 192 p
7426 GOODRUM Sherry D The Love Affairs of Percy Bysshe Shelley
M Ed Henderson St Coll nd
7427 HILL Rowland M Shelley's Theory and Practice of Religion MA Boston
Univ 1929
7428 HILLHOUSE Joseph N The Religious Faith of Shelley MA Univ of
Richmond 1925 75 p
7429 HURLEY Clinton F Jr Like a Dome of Many-Colored Glass: A Study of
Shelley's Use of Color MA Univ of New Mexico 1954
7430 HUSSEY Maurice J Shelley in English Periodical Criticism, 1811-1824
MA St Louis Univ 1938 79 p
7431 IRBY Lucretia The Philosophy of Shelley MA Texas Christian Univ 1922
82 p
7432 JACOBSEN Sally A Shelley's Cave Image: The Structural Importance
of His Natural Imagery in Portraying Feeling and Thought
MA Purdue Univ 1964 104 p
7433 JEFFREY Lloyd N The Influence of Christianity upon Some of Shelley's

Ethical Principles: An Evaluative Study MA Univ of Texas at
Austin 1947

7434 JOHNSON Elinor H Mary Godwin: The Feminine Counterpart of Shelley
(A Refutation of Trelawny's Statement) MA Univ of Richmond 1931   25

7435 KAUL Lucille C The Dualism of Shelley's *Adonais* MA Univ of New Mexico
1952

7436 KEATING Peter M Shelley and Jesus MA Univ of Texas at Austin 1954   66

7437 KERR John A Discussion of Time in Shelley's *Queen Mab* and "The Sensi-
tive Plant" BA Univ of British Columbia (Canada) 1970

7438 LACOUR James L Shelley's Ideas of Immortality MA Univ of New Mexico
1948

7439 LANGFORD Dale H Shelley's Ideal World MA Univ of Texas at Austin 1947
86 p

7440 LAWSON Sammy G The Imageless Truth: A Study of Shelley's *Prometheus
Unbound* MA Auburn Univ 1961

7441 LEWIS Benjamin H The Celt and Shelley: A Study of Certain Contrasts
and Resemblances between Welsh Literature and Shelley's Poetry
MA Pacific Univ 1926   88 p

7442 LILL Margaret Shelley: The Idealist MS Kansas St Coll at Pittsburg 1!

7443 LIRETTE Sr Mary G The Significance of Color in Shelley's Poetry
MA Boston Coll 1961

7444 LISAUSKAS Giedre G The Significance of Death in Shelley's Poetry
MA Washington Univ at St Louis 1962

7445 LOHMANN Christoph K Shelley's Progress in the Communication of
Perception MA Columbia 1961   76 p

7446 LONG Ulman E The Early Criticisms of Shelley in England and America
MA North Texas St Univ 1949   118 p

7447 LOTZ David W Shelley's *Epipsychidion*: An Introduction, Explication
and Analysis MA Washington Univ at St Louis 1964

7448 LOUGHEED Gwendolyn The Lyre-Lute-Harp Image as Used by
Percy Bysshe Shelley MA Bowling Green Univ 1960

7449 McADOW Ruth T A Bibliography of Percy Bysshe Shelley's Writings and
Ana from January 1, 1935 to December 31, 1939 MA Univ of Kentucky
1941

7450 McCRORIE Edward P Four Levels of Style in the Poetry of
Percy Bysshe Shelley MA Villanova Univ 1964

7451 McINTOSH Jean Shelley: The Reformer MA Southern Methodist Univ 1931

7452 McKINNON Linda T Shelley's Concept of Harmony MA Baylor Univ 1962   14

7453 McKNEW Myrtle T Aeschylus and Shelley's *Prometheus Unbound* MA Univ of
Maryland at College Park 1970   95 p

7454 McNIECE G M Shelley's Practical Politics and Philosophical Opinions
Related to His Vision of Society B Litt Oxford Univ (England) 1951

7455 MATTHEWS Craig G A Study of the Origins and Sources of Shelley's
The Witch of Atlas MA Univ of Oklahoma 1938

7456 MAYES Mayme L Certain Aural Factors in Shelley and His Poetry
MA Texas Christian Univ 1939   146 p

7457 MEARS Kathleen B The Reputation of Shelley in American Periodicals,
1839-1889, as Indexed by Poole MA Columbia 1941

7458 MEINBERG Anita Percy Bysshe Shelley's *Hellas*: A Critical Study
MA Columbia 1966   60 p

7459 MOLLENHAUER Br Francis E The Development of Shelley's Political Creed
in His Political Prose, His Letters and His Poetry MA Univ of
Pittsburgh 1951

7460 MORRIS Alf Imagery in Shelley's Early Verse, 1800-1816 MA Univ of
Texas at Austin 1938   121 p

7461 MURPHY Ethel A Some Peculiarities of Shelley's Rhythm MA Univ of
Louisville 1911

7462 NALBANDIAN C R The Imagery of Shelley's *Prometheus Unbound*
M Phil Univ of London (England) 1968

7463 OLIVER James B Shelley's Critical Views on Religion as Expressed in

Queen Mab MA Boston Univ 1948
7464 O'NEILL John P A Study of Shelley's *Adonais* MA Univ of Oklahoma 1953
7465 PAGET E H Political Ideas of Shelley MA Univ of Pittsburgh 1926
7466 PATTERSON Carl E Shelley and Keats in Their Search for Ideal Beauty
     MA Texas Technological Univ 1932 71 p
7467 PELLETIER R R Shelley and Milton MA Boston Coll 1957
7468 PIVETTI Renzo The Dramatic Possibilities of Percy Bysshe Shelley's
     Genius MA Ca Foscari (Italy) 1935
7469 PIXTON William H After *Prometheus*: A Critical Study of Shelley's
     Later Poetry MA George Washington Univ 1964 122 p
7470 POPE Florence E The Religion of Shelley MA Sul Ross St Coll 1933
7471 PRUITT Elizabeth E Shelley in America: A Bibliographical Study
     MA Univ of Texas at Austin 1940 118 p
7472 PURDY Strother R Yeats and Shelley MA Columbia 1955 118 p
7473 RAPF Joanna E The Fading Coal: A Study of the *Witch of Atlas* in
     the Light of Shelley's Figure of Intellectual Beauty MA Columbia
     1966 160 p
7474 RHODE Robert D The Greek Element in the Poetic Works of Shelley
     MA Univ of Texas at Austin 1935
7475 ROESCH Richard J A Semantic Inquiry into the Word "Love" as Used in
     Ten Poems by Percy Bysshe Shelley MA Bowling Green Univ 1952
7476 ROESLER Elmo V Imagination and the Bardic Vision of Ultimate Reality
     in Shelley's Poetry MA Univ of Wyoming 1965
7477 ROSSY Charlotte A Music and Poetry in Settings of Shelley's Lyrics
     MA Univ of Texas at Austin 1938 100 p
7478 RUFF Walta J Shelley and Censorship MA Colorado St Univ 1965
7479 SALIN Harriet B How Effectual Was Shelley? A Study in Shelley
     Criticism MA Univ of Louisville 1940
7480 SASSCER Cora D *The Cenci*: Shelley's Sources, Acknowledged and
     Hypothetical MA Univ of Maryland at College Park 1943 70 p
7481 SCHULTZ Allen W Vision and Revision: A Study in Shelley's Manu-
     scripts MA Univ of Maryland at College Park 1954 48 p
7482 SHANE Marion L Shelley: Christ and Antichrist MA Syracuse Univ 1946
     85 p
7483 SKUTCHES Peter In the Chapel of Infinite Desire: A Study of Shelley's
     Concepts of Death and Immortality in Relation to His Poetic Imagery
     MA Columbia 1962 121 p
7484 SMALL Anna F A Study of the Nature Images in the Lyrics of Shelley
     MA Smith Coll 1927
7485 SPRADLIN Judith E Dantesque Sources in Shelley's *Epipsychidion*
     MA Midwestern Univ 1966 86 p
7486 SPURLOCK Fay M Shelley's Conception of Freedom MA Baylor Univ 1933
     107 p
7487 STALLINGS Frank L Jr Symbolism and Imagery in *Prometheus Unbound*
     MA West Texas St Univ 1955 112 p
7488 STOKES Elmore E Shelley and Bernard Shaw: A Study in Late Nineteenth
     Century Socialism MA Univ of Texas at Austin 1948 238 p
7489 STREIFER Ruth B A Study in Romantic Reality: "Ode to a Nightingale"
     and "To a Skylark" MA Columbia 1963 59 p
7490 STROUSS Lois A Comparative Study of the Uses of Nature in the
     Endymion and *Prometheus Unbound* M Ed Temple Univ 1963 47 p
7491 STUTZENBERGER Albert Shelley's God MA Univ of Louisville 1948
7492 TABB Mary Shelley the Social Idealist in Selections from His Prose
     Writings MA Midwestern Univ 1968 113 p
7493 TAFFAE Paul M Shelley's *Epipsychidion*: The Critical Interpretations
     MA Columbia 1950
7494 TATHAM Lewis C Jr Shelley and Perfectibility MA Univ of Florida 1952
7495 TEMPLETON E M Shelley's Quest for Beauty MA Ohio St Univ 1932
7496 THORNBERRY Marion A Study of the Relations between Godwin and Shelley
     MA Univ of Arkansas 1931

7497 UBOM Edet A , A Study of Percy Bysshe Shelley as a Critic of Art and
      Society MA Howard Univ 1963 139 p
7498 WAGNER Elizabeth Godwinian and Platonic Doctrines in the Poetry of
      Shelley MA Univ of Louisville 1934
7499 WALSH Patrick F The Psychology of Color in Shelley's Poetry
      MA Boston Coll 1969
7500 WEAKLEY Mae Shelley's Views of Freedom as Revealed in His Life
      MA Texas Technological Univ 1939 58 p
7501 WEEKS John T Shelley's *Oedipus Tyrannus or Swellfoot, the Tyrant*:
      An Edition with Notes and Commentary MA Univ of Texas at Austin
      1963 148 p
7502 WHITE Edna E Shelley as a Dramatist MA Baylor Univ 1931 90 p
7503 WHITMIRE Josephine V Shelley's Conception of God MA Boston Univ 1938
7504 WIESNER Sr Mary I Twentieth Century Criticism of Shelley in the
      Light of Christianity MA St Louis Univ 1936 79 p
7505 WILCOX Margaret L Music Imagery in Shelley's *Prometheus Unbound*
      MA Univ of Florida 1964
7506 WILSON Dwight H Shelley as Revolutionist MA Howard Univ 1933 93 p
7507 WOLFE Richard C Time in the Apocalypse of Shelley and Blake
      MA Kent St Univ 1966
7508 ZIMMER Karl E Shelley's *The Cenci*: A Re-Evaluation MA Columbia 1954
      85 p
See also 849, 1083, 1088, 1090, 1095, 1101, 1144, 1232, 1437, 1808, 1893,
      3463, 3746, 4521, 4524, 5432, 5497, 6429, 6819

                          RICHARD SHERIDAN

7509 BROWN Cherry F Sheridan's Ladies of the Eighteenth Century MA Univ
      of Texas at Austin 1966 85 p
7510 CAMP Paul A The Complete Design for a Production of Richard Brinsley
      Sheridan's *The School for Scandal* MA Whittier Coll nd
7511 CAREFOOT Carol J *The Rivals*: A Study in Influence MA Texas Woman's
      Univ 1966
7512 GIRARDEAU Helen F Sheridan's Social Portraits MA Univ of Texas at
      Austin 1938 81 p
7513 HELD Maxton C Appearance Versus Reality in *The School for Scandal*
      MA Univ of Hawaii 1962 128 p
7514 KNOTT Ronald Sheridan's Use of Elements of the Restoration and
      Sentimental Comic Traditions in *The Rivals* and *The School for Scandal*
      BA Univ of British Columbia (Canada) 1969
7515 McVICKER Alberta C Sheridan's Indebtedness to Moliere and Certain
      Restoration Dramatists MA West Virginia Univ 1901 172 p
7516 PERRY Carrie A Dramatic Types and the Sentimental Trend in the
      Comedies of Richard Brinsley Sheridan MA Boston Univ 1935
7517 SELIGMAN Kevin L The Research, Design and Execution of the Costumes
      for Richard Brinsley Sheridan's *The Rivals* MA San Jose St Coll 1966
7518 SNIDER Rose Satire in the Comedies of Congreve, Sheridan, Wilde and
      Coward MA Univ of Maine 1936 222 p
7519 VALENTE Francesca *The School for Scandal* by Richard Brinsley Sheridan
      MA Ca Foscari (Italy) 1968
7520 WHELAN Irene F The First Fifteen Years of *The School for Scandal*
      in London MA Columbia 1943
7521 WILLIAMS George W The Stage History of Sheridan's Less Known Plays:
      A Study of the Change in Dramatic Taste during the Period 1775-1809
      MA George Washington Univ 1949 161 p
7522 WILMSEN June A The Development of Satire in the Plays of
      Richard Brinsley Sheridan MA Syracuse Univ 1948 76 p
7523 ZUCCHI Maria R Richard Brinsley Sheridan as a Dramatist MA Ca Foscari
      (Italy) 1959
See also 334, 1935, 3512

JAMES SHIRLEY

7524 AHNER F E Courtesy-Book Subjects and Ideas in the Plays of James Shirley
     MA Univ of North Carolina at Chapel Hill 1930
7525 CONROY John T James Shirley: Prophet of the Restoration MA Columbia
     1959 88 p
7526 DURI' Maria *The Lady of Pleasure* by James Shirley MA Ca Foscari
     (Italy) 1968
7527 FIVES Raymond J The Rhetoric of James Shirley MA Boston Coll 1951
7528 GREENBLATT Raymond B James Shirley and the Puritans: An Exercise
     in Literary History MA Univ of New Hampshire 1969 40 p
7529 GREENWOOD Billie W Dramatic Devices in the Plays of James Shirley
     MA Texas Technological Univ 1935 162 p
7530 MA Villin H Disguise and Eavesdropping as Dramatic Devices in
     Ten Plays of James Shirley MA Texas Technological Univ 1949
7531 McCLAMROCH R P Attitude of the Restoration towards James Shirley
     MA Univ of North Carolina at Chapel Hill 1922
See also 3199

PHILIP SIDNEY

7532 ARNOLD June D Theory and Practice of Characterization in Sidney's
     Arcadia MA Rice 1958
7533 CHALLIS L M A Study of Sidney: *Arcadia* and *Astrophel and Stella*
     in the Light of Contemporary Rhetoric and Literary Convention
     MA Univ of London (England) 1962
7534 CYWINSKI Benjamin S A Study of Sir Philip Sidney's *Astrophel and
     Stella* MA Marquette Univ 1948 126 p
7535 DICKENS Anne S Sir Philip Sidney's *Astrophel and Stella*: A Review
     of the Autobiographical Interpretations MA Univ of Kentucky 1949
     66 p
7536 DONNELLY Dorothy F The Relation of Sidney's *Old Arcadia* to the Arcadian
     Tradition MA Brown Univ 1966
7537 DuPREE Nancy B Comedy in Sir Philip Sidney's New *Arcadia* MA Auburn
     Univ 1967
7538 FOLEY Brendan E A Reading of Sidney's *Astrophel and Stella* MA Toronto
     (Canada) 1966
7539 GLASSCOE M Sidney's Treatment of the Theme of Virtue in *Arcadia*
     MA Univ of London (England) 1964
7540 GOLMON Ara A Sidney's *Arcadia*: A Study of the Two Versions with
     Special Reference to the Use of Proverbs MA Baylor Univ 1943 111 p
7541 GROVE Roxy H Proverb Lore in Sidney MA Baylor Univ 1933 275 p
7542 HILL Kathryn F The *Song of Songs* and Sir Philip Sidney's *Defense of
     Poesie*: A Comparative Study of Sacred and Secular Elements in
     Literature MA Texas Technological Univ 1969 74 p
7543 HOUCHENS Mariam S Sir Philip Sidney MA Univ of Louisville 1932
7544 JOHNSON Arnold The Letter of Advice by Burghley, Raleigh and Sidney
     MA Univ of Nebraska 1966
7545 JOHNSON William C The Epithets of Sidney's *Astrophel and Stella*
     MA Univ of Iowa 1965
7546 JUNGJOHAN Barbara M Sidney Prefers "s": Sir Philip Sidney's Use of
     the "s" and the "th" Endings of the Third Person Singular of the
     Present Tense MA Baylor Univ 1969 43 p
7547 KUERSTEINER Agnes D Sir Philip Sidney as Revealed in the Languet-
     Sidney Correspondence MA Indiana Univ 1942
7548 LEHAN R D Political Ideas in Sir Philip Sidney's *Arcadia* MA Boston
     Coll 1954
7549 LEIDER Emily W Characterization in Sidney's *Arcadia*: A Study in
     Literary Obsolescence MA Columbia 1961 112 p
7550 LEWIS Josie Sir Philip Sidney and the Influence of Platonism upon

the *Arcadia*   MA Florida St Univ 1955
7551 McGOWAN Martha J   Music in the Life and Works of Sir Philip Sidney
      MA Boston Coll 1965
7552 MAGRI Noemi   Sir Philip Sidney: *Astrophel and Stella*   MA Ca Foscari
      (Italy) 1961
7553 MILAM Carl H   Sidney and the English Renaissance   BA Univ of Oklahoma
      1907
7554 MURPHY Lucille C   Sir Philip. Sidney's Concern with the Protestant
      Cause as Seen in the 1593 *Arcadia*   MA Mississippi St Univ 1966
7555 OLSSON Kurt O   Love Motifs in Sir Philip Sidney's *Arcadia*   MA Columbia
      1963   176 p
7556 PONTEDERA Claudio   The *Defence of Poesie* or *An Apology for Poetry*
      by Sir Philip Sidney   MA Ca Foscari (Italy) 1966
7557 ROBINSON Evelyn B   Sir Philip Sidney's Conception of the Ideal Gentle-
      man   MA Howard Univ 1938   62 p
7558 SARCINELLI Lavinia   Sir Philip Sidney   MA Ca Foscari (Italy) 1922
7559 SEAT Clyde   The Aphorisms of Sidney   MA Baylor Univ 1941   127 p
7560 SEIFER Bernard   Sidney's *Arcadia*:   The Conception of Character of
      Pyrocles and Philoclea in the "Old" and "New" Versions   MA Columbia
      1953   71 p
7561 SINCLAIR David P   Metamorphosis and Mimesis in Sir Philip Sidney's
      Arcadia   MA Toronto (Canada) 1966
7562 SPEER Diane P   The Unity of Critical Precept and Creative Practice
      in the Work of Sir Philip Sidney   MA Bowling Green Univ 1965
7563 SPINA Sebastiano   Parmgianino's and Sir Philip Sidney's Mannerisms
      MA Ca Foscari (Italy) 1940
7564 TRUCKS Theordore E   Sidney's Moving Power of Poetry as an Aesthetic
      Doctrine   MA Univ of Oklahoma 1949
7565 VETRICK Robert C   The Grotesque in Sidney's *Arcadia*   MA Univ of
      Delaware 1969   58 p
7566 WARKENTIN Germaine   A Lesson in Love: A Study of the Unity of Sidney's
      Astrophel and Stella   MA Manitoba (Canada) 1965
7567 WIGGINS Peter D   The Comic Spirit of Sir Philip Sidney: The *Defense*
      of Poesie and *Astrophel and Stella*   MA Columbia 1966   65 p
7568 WYLIE Louise E   Sidney's Idea of the Brave Courtier   MA Indiana Univ 19
See also 2818, 3684, 3964, 5117

THE SITWELLS

7569 BRITTON Henry C   Synaesthetic Imagery in the Poetry of Amy Lowell
      and Edith Sitwell   MA Boston Univ 1936
7570 DVORAK Wilfred P   The War Poetry of Osbert Sitwell   MA Kansas St Univ
      1965
7571 LANDA Daniel   Edith Sitwell and the Cult of Childhood   MA Columbia 1942
7572 MISKO M John   A Study of the Themes in the Later Poetry of
      Dame Edith Sitwell   MA Duquesne Univ 1966
7573 MORTON Murray K   The Short Stories of Osbert Sitwell   MA Columbia 1959
      260 p
7574 OWER John B   Thematic Imagery in the Poetry of Edith Sitwell   MA Albert
      (Canada) 1966
7575 ROBERSON Sandra A   A Study of Edith Sitwell as a Critic   MA Baylor
      Univ 1967   70 p
7576 VARVEL Ralph E   The Pillar of Fire: Image and Theme in Edith Sitwell's
      "The Shadow of Cain"   MA Texas Christian Univ 1955   69 p
7577 WHITESEL George E   The Literary Individualism of Sacheverell Sitwell
      MA Columbia 1959   154 p

JOHN SKELTON

7578 BARNUM Priscilla H   Skelton's *Magnificence* Reconsidered   MA Syracuse

Univ 1960   120 p
7579 CARMINATI Maria *Magnyfycence* by John Skelton MA Ca Foscari (Italy) 1960
7580 FOSS Michael   John Skelton MA Temple Univ 1963   59 p
7581 GORDON Gary D   Point of View in the Poetry of John Skelton MA Columbia
      1966   87 p
7582 GRIFFITH Kathleen F   The Influence of the Medieval Morality Play upon
      the Poetry of Sir John Skelton MA Long Island Univ nd   70 p
7583 HENRY C J   Skelton's Perspective: The Manner of the World MA Rice 1966
7584 KOZIKOWSKI Stanley J   The "Resydewe" of John Skelton's *Bowge of Courte*
      MA Univ of Massachusetts 1968   53 p
7585 McQUISTON James R   The Satire of John Skelton's Poems in Skeltonic
      Verse MA Univ of North Carolina at Chapel Hill 1951   221 p
7586 MARING Donald E   John Skelton's *Garland of Laurel* MA Temple Univ 1966
      51 p
7587 SPINA Elaine F   Skelton's Achievement in *The Tunnying of Eynour Rummyng*
      MA Columbia 1965   124 p
7588 WILLS Floreid   Skelton's Proverb Lore MA Baylor Univ 1956   105 p
7589 WOODCOCK John A   Feathers in the Wind: A Study of the Poetic Methods
      of John Skelton BA Amherst 1961

CHRISTOPHER SMART

7590 BADESSA Richard P   Critical Reception of Christopher Smart's *Song to
      David* MA Univ of British Columbia (Canada) 1960
7591 DAVIES Barbara R   A Study of the Language and Major Themes of
      Christopher Smart's Religious Poems MA Manitoba (Canada) 1966
7592 GORDON Ronald M   A Grace Beyond: A Study of Christopher Smart
      BA Amherst 1965
7593 HAUSER William R   The Criticism of Christopher Smart in the Twentieth
      Century MA Univ of Pittsburgh 1955
7594 LEVINE Jay A   Religious Feeling in the Poetry of Christopher Smart
      MA Columbia 1954   126 p
7595 LOWE Judith O   Christopher Smart's Changing Conception of David: An
      Examination of His Religious Poetry BA Univ of British Columbia
      (Canada) 1968
7596 MARKOWITT Gerson G   Elements of Mysticism in the Poetry of
      Christopher Smart MA Rutgers St Univ 1950   84 p
7597 MAYNARD Temple J   The Achievement of Christopher Smart's *Song to David*
      MA Univ of British Columbia (Canada) 1963
7598 NEWITT E   The History of Christopher Smart Criticism BA Univ of
      British Columbia (Canada) 1955
7599 PARISH Charles   Christopher Smart and *Song to David* MA Univ of New
      Mexico 1955
7600 RIZZO Betty   Christopher Smart as Mother Midnight: A Study of the
      Poet's Two Voices, Wit and Wisdom MA Hunter Coll 1968
7601 SHIVER Barbara J   A Consideration of Christopher Smart's Hymns and
      Spiritual Songs for the Fasts and Festivals of the Church of England
      as Liturgical Hymns MA Auburn Univ 1968
7602 SIMPSON C James   Christopher Smart and the *Midwife Magazine* MA Columbia
      1942

TOBIAS SMOLLETT

7603 BAXTER Charles   Romantic Tendencies in the Novels of Tobias Smollett
      MA Columbia 1950
7604 BENVENI Pietro   *The Expedition of Humphrey Clinker* by Tobias Smollett
      MA Ca Foscari (Italy) 1969
7605 CAHILL Anne   A Comparison of the First Part of the 1811 Edition of
      Smollett's Translation of *Don Quixote of La Mancha* with that of
      John Ormsby and a Spanish Text MA Univ of Maryland at College Park

1930 30 p
7606 CAMP Eula A Comparison of Richardson's and Smollett's Use of the
      Letter Form MA Univ of Oklahoma 1933
7607 CANAVAN Thomas L Tobias Smollett, Physician and Novelist: A Study
      of His Medical Career and Some Medical Characters in His Novels
      MA Columbia 1963 117 p
7608 CREDIFORD J W Life in Eighteenth Century England as Reflected in
      the Novels of Dr Tobias George Smollett, 1721-1771 MA Boston Univ
      1940
7609 DALLEINE Blanche La France Sociale (1763-1789) d'apres Les Oeuvres
      de Trois Voyageurs Anglais: Tobias Smollett, Arthur Young and
      Horace Walpole MA Hunter Coll 1926
7610 DAUM Arnold R The Literary Criticism of Tobias Smollett MA George
      Washington Univ 1933 146 p
7611 DETISCH Robert J A Study of Characterization in Smollett's *Peregrine
      Pickle* MA Columbia 1960 104 p
7612 HILL A J Jr The Novel of Fielding and Smollett MA Williams Coll 1909
7613 HUBBELL Frank F Satire in the Novels of Smollett MA George Wash-
      ington Univ 1964 152 p
7614 KITCHEN Herminie B Physicians and Medicine in the English Literature
      of the Eighteenth Century with Particular Reference to the Novels
      of Tobias Smollett MA Rutgers St Univ 1933 178 p
7615 McLAIN John H The Humor in Smollett's Novels MA Univ of Pittsburgh 19
7616 MEEK Jethro A The Picaresque Novels of Tobias Smollett MA Univ of
      Texas at Austin 1934
7617 SCOTT W A Smollett's Reputation and Influence in the Eighteenth
      Century, Chiefly as Novelist B Litt Oxford Univ (England) nd
7618 SHOCKLEY G R The Eccentrics of Tobias Smollett's Novels MA North
      Texas St Univ 1961
7619 SMITH K K A Study of the Women Characters in Smollett's Novels
      MA Univ of North Carolina at Chapel Hill 1932
7620 WILLIAMS Jeanne H Tobias Smollett and the Novel of Naval Episode
      MA Temple Univ 1953
See also 2172, 2434, 2516, 3105, 3185, 6015, 6017

                              C P SNOW

7621 BOYTINCK Paul W The Novels of C P Snow MA McGill (Canada) 1965
7622 GRACE Matthew S The Political Novels of C P Snow MA Columbia 1960 1
7623 KEEN Edith D C P Snow and the Stranger-Brother Complex MA Stephen F
      Austin St Coll 1965
7624 McBROOM Robert L The Novelist as Technician: A Study of the Works of
      C P Snow MA Midwestern Univ 1966 132 p
7625 STEINER Thomas R The *Strangers and Brothers* Series of C P Snow
      MA Columbia 1960 105 p
7626 UNSWORTH Marion F The Nature of Power in the Novels of C P Snow
      MA Boston Coll 1963
7627 WILEY Margo C P Snow's Political Theory and the Political Novels,
      The Masters, The New Men and *The Affair* MA Univ of Texas at Austin
      1962 119 p

                            ROBERT SOUTHEY

7628 BUTLER M H Robert Southey's Interest in Ballads and Romances
      MA Univ of North Carolina at Chapel Hill 1943
7629 CHOPPESKY John C The Obsoleteness of Southey's Poetry MA St Louis
      Univ 1939 68 p
7630 MONK J D Robert Southey as a Narrative Poet: A Study of His Five
      Long Poems MA North Texas St Univ 1942
7631 PRABHAKAR T A Critical Study of Robert Southey's *The Curse of Kehama*

MA Univ of London (England) 1964
7632 WHITNEY Paul W Robert Southey's Reviews of Poetry in the *Annual Review*
       MA Univ of Maryland at College Park 1952   87 p
See also 1059, 1832, 6120, 6176

ROBERT SOUTHWELL

7633 BOZANICH Robert A Nicholas Breton, Thomas Robinson and Giles Fletcher:
       A .Study of the Influence of Robert Southwell MA Columbia 1958   90 p
7634 FITZPATRICK Sr M Bernard The Mary Poems of Robert Southwell
       MA Boston Coll 1965
7635 HARKINS Sr Joseph M Robert Southwell MA Boston Coll 1945
7636 HURLEY E F Robert Southwell: Jesuit Martyr-Poet MA Boston Coll 1933
7637 PRIDGEN Rufus A The Influence of Saint Ignatius' Spiritual Exercises
       on the Poetry of Robert Southwell MA East Carolina Univ 1968
7638 REINSDORF Walter D The Baroque Solution and the Poetry of
       Robert Southwell MA Columbia 1959   78 p
7639 SHAPIRO Elizabeth K The Poetry of Robert Southwell and Medieval
       Religious Drama: A Study of Influences MA Columbia 1964   145 p
See also 2801

MURIEL SPARK

7640 CUNDIFF Lois Muriel Spark's Wit: A Study of Her Novels MA Univ of
       Louisville 1967   134 p
7641 DOBIE Ann B Muriel Spark: A Short Study of Demonology MA Univ of
       Southwestern Louisiana 1966   196 p
7642 HUNT Joseph A The Style of Muriel Spark MA Univ of Hawaii 1966   53 p
7643 LOUGHEED Ronald C To Catch the Conscience: The Demonic Element in
       the Novels of Muriel Spark MA Windsor (Canada) 1964
7644 PILLAI Nandini A Study of Muriel Spark MA Colorado St Coll 1969
7645 PULLEN Myrcyl G The Satiric Element in the Novels of Muriel Spark
       MA Windsor (Canada) 1964
7646 STUBBS P J A Comparative Study of the Fiction of Iris Murdoch and
       Muriel Spark M Phil Univ of London (England) 1969
7647 WATT Alexandra A The Novels of Muriel Spark Examined According to
       the Terms of C G Jung's Theory of Modernity MA Alberta (Canada) 1966

HERBERT SPENCER

7648 ABEGG Edmund The Evolutionary Ethics of Herbert Spencer BA Rutgers
       St Univ nd   115 p
7649 GRUBB Carol N The Influence of Herbert Spencer's Essays on Education
       on *The Ordeal of Richard Feverel* MA Syracuse Univ 1950   53 p
7650 MALLOY Richard T A Critical Study of the Norm of Morality of
       Herbert Spencer MA St Louis Univ 1933   53 p
See also 4188

STEPHEN SPENDER

7651 CASS Walter J The Relation of the Major Points of Stephen Spender's
       Criticism to His Short Stories and to Representative Poems from
       His Major Poetic Works MA Boston Univ 1947
7652 JASKOW Rosemary "Alas, All White Heads Look Alike": A Study of
       Stephen Spender BA Univ of British Columbia (Canada) 1970
7653 LINDEN Virginia C The Origin and Development of the Conflict between
       Politics and Art in the Poetry of Stephen Spender from 1932 to 1939
       MA George Washington Univ 1959   273 p
7654 SELPH Carl L The Poetry of Stephen Spender: Personal and Social
       MA Columbia 1953   108 p

EDMUND SPENSER

7655 ADAMS Billie Edmund Spenser's Theory of Poetry MA Wake Forest Coll 1*
7656 ADAMS Sarah P The Psychological Continuity within Discontinuity of
      Spenser's *Four Hymns* MA Univ of Rhode Island 1968 72 p
7657 AIMAN Henry The Friendship Theme in *The Faerie Queene*: Spenser's
      Indebtedness to Aristotle and Heliodorus MA Kansas St Teachers Col
      1964
7658 ALDRICH Nathane E The Controversial *Cantos of Mutabilitie* MA Syracuse
      Univ 1958 84 p
7659 ALLEN Willie Spenser, Lucretius and the New Science MA Univ of Texas
      at Austin 1935
7660 AMES Ruth M Amyntas and Amaryllis: The Earl and Countess of Derby
      MA Columbia 1943
7661 AMISS Margaret The Pageant in Literature with Particular Relation
      to *The Faerie Queene* MA Columbia 1917
7662 ANDERSON Hattie R Spenser's Ideal of Conduct as Exemplified in the
      Allegory of *The Faerie Queene* MA Univ of Colorado 1923
7663 ANDERSON V L *The Shepherdes Calendar*: A Study of Prosody and Style
      MA Univ of Oregon 1938
7664 ARIAIL James M Some Immediate English Influences upon Spenser's
      Faerie Queene MA Univ of North Carolina at Chapel Hill 1924
7665 ARMISTEAD Robert A Spenser's Theory of Loyalty MA Baylor Univ 1932
      91 p
7666 ARMSTRONG R J A Spenser Bibliography BA Univ of British Columbia
      (Canada) 1950
7667 ARMSTRONG Robert J A Study of the Popularity of Edmund Spenser as
      Revealed by Allusion and Criticism between the Years 1600 and 1850
      MA Univ of British Columbia (Canada) 1952 147 p
7668 AYER James R Spenser's Concept of Justice and Its Classical Precedent
      MA Columbia 1960 65 p
7669 BAMBER Juretta V The Renaissance Paradox in Spenser MA Univ of
      Louisville 1927
7670 BARBER Cora L Spenser's Influence on William Browne MA Columbia 1905*
7671 BARLOW Josephine M Edmund Spenser and the Pleiade: A Comparison
      Centering in the *Amoretti* and *Les Amours* MA Boston Univ 1934
7672 BARNHART William J Spenser's Lively Anatomie of Death MA Univ of
      Tennessee 1949
7673 BARNHILL Lou V Prince Arthur's Role in *The Faerie Queene* MA Univ
      of North Carolina at Chapel Hill 1954 127 p
7674 BARROW Sarah F Studies in the Language of Spenser with Special
      Attention to the Etymological Attempts MA Univ of Chicago 1902
7675 BATTLE Martha L An Analysis of Spenser's Use of the Complaint in
      The Faerie Queene MA Univ of Kentucky 1957 150 p
7676 BAUMGARTNER Frances A The Original and the Conventional in *The Faerie
      Queene*: Books III and IV MA Texas Christian Univ 1965 75 p
7677 BEATTY Elsie The Criticism of Spenser during the Eighteenth Century
      MA Univ of Illinois 1925
7678 BELL Edna F Imitations of Spenser from 1706 to 1774 MA Univ of
      Oklahoma 1928
7679 BENCHOFF Howard J The Political Element in Spenser's Poetry
      MA Columbia 1904
7680 BEREK Peter From the House of the Interpreter: The Transformation
      of Allegory from .Spenser to Hawthorne BA Amherst 1961
7681 BERRY Albert M *Colin Clouts Come Home Againe* by Edmund Spenser,
      Edited with Introduction and Notes MA Columbia 1932
7682 BEUTNER Sr Mary L Spenser and the Emblem Writers MA St Louis Univ
      1934 107 p
7683 BEVINS Lloyd E Spenser's Use of Proverbial Material in *The Faerie
      Queene* MA Univ of Virginia 1940

7684 BIALAS Anthony   A Critique of Spenser's Archaic Vocabulary in *The Faerie Queene: Book I*   MA Northern Illinois Univ 1966
7685 BIGOTTO Lelia   *Amoretti* by Edmund Spenser   MA Ca Foscari (Italy) 1960
7686 BIXLER Mary H   Edmund Spenser's *Cantos of Mutabilitie*   MA Columbia 1944
7687 BODDY Margaret P   Some Aspects of the Ovidian Elements in Spenser's Poetry   MA Univ of Minnesota 1932
7688 BOSS Judith E   The Relationship of Books VI and VII in Spenser's *Faerie Queene*   MA Texas Christian Univ 1969   65 p
7689 BRAFFETT Joe M   The Last Twenty Years of Spenserian Scholarship: A Bibliographical Study   MA Univ of Oklahoma 1956
7690 BROWN L A   The Moral Allegory of Book V of Spenser's *Faerie Queene*   MA Univ of Washington 1914
7691 BROWN Margaret   The Range and Trends of Vocabulary of *The Faerie Queene*   MA Univ of Washington 1938
7692 BROWN Peter F   The Influence of Edmund Spenser on the British Romantic Poets, 1800-1840   MA Univ of Chicago 1905
7693 BRYAN Charleyne   A High School Edition of Canto VIII of Book III of Spenser's *Faerie Queene*   MA Oklahoma St Univ 1932   30 p
7694 BUCKNER Zeak M Jr   Edmund Spenser's Philosophy of Mutability   MA Texas Christian Univ 1962   104 p
7695 CAMMACK Maud H   A Critical Study of *Mother Hubberds Tale*   MA Univ of Oklahoma 1946
7696 CENESI Felice   Platonism in Edmund Spenser's Poetry   MA Ca Foscari (Italy) 1947
7697 CERVONI Monserrate J   Spenser's Use of the Alexandrine in *The Faerie Queene*   MA St Louis Univ 1937   63 p
7698 CHARAS Sheila   The Epic Martial Maid: A Study of the Tradition, with Special Attention to Spenser's Britomart   MA Columbia 1963   96 p
7699 CLARK Darryl L   Some Functions of the Mottos in Spenser's *The Shepheardes Calendar*   MA Univ of Rhode Island 1966   55 p
7700 COLLIER Robert E   Spenser's Use of Rhetorical Figures of Repetition and Rime: A Comparison of a Canto from Book I, Book IV and the Mutabilitie from *The Faerie Queene*   MA Univ of Kentucky 1960   115 p
7701 CONNELL Jack J   Arms and Armour in Edmund Spenser's *Faerie Queene*   MA Rutgers St Univ 1932   178 p
7702 CONNELL Stella J   The Literary Relationships of Edmund Spenser   MA Baylor Univ 1935   179 p
7703 CONWAY Charles A   The Courtly Entertainment and the Epic of the Red Cross Knight   MA Toronto (Canada) 1965
7704 COONEY Thomas E Jr   The Topography of Spenser's Elfland: A Study of Some Allegorical Meanings in the Landscape of Spenser's *Faerie Queene*   MA Columbia 1953   56 p
7705 COOPER Laura T   Spenser's *Veue of the Present State of Ireland*: An Introduction, with Notes on the First Fifty-Five Pages of Grosart's Edition   MA Cornell Univ 1913
7706 CORRIGAN Marie C   Spenser and the Geraldine Earls   MA Case-Western Reserve Univ 1935
7707 CURRY John V   The Epic Similes in *The Faerie Queene*   MA St Louis Univ 1938   83 p
7708 CUTHBERTSON Frances A   The Relationship of Heredity and Action in Spenser's *Faerie Queene*   MA Univ of North Carolina at Chapel Hill 1947   96 p
7709 DAVIS C Pruitt   An Exploration of Values: *The Faerie Queene,* Book VI and *Comus*   MA Texas Christian Univ 1965   146 p
7710 DAVIS Ellen M   The Influence of Spenser's Irish Residence on *The Faerie Queene*   MA Univ of Louisville 1932
7711 DAVIS William H   Castiglione and Spenser: A Study in Comparative Literature   MA Columbia 1908
7712 DeLACY Hugh E   Astrology in the Poems of Edmund Spenser   MA Univ of Washington 1932

7713 DENOON M E The Diction and Imagery in Relation to the Allegory of
      The Faerie Queene MA Univ of London (England) 1964
7714 DEVINE Elizabeth C *The Faerie Queene*, Book I: Criticism and Inter-
      pretation since 1932 MA Univ of Tennessee 1949
7715 DEXTER Dorothy The Device of the House in the First Book of
      The Faerie Queene MA Univ of Oregon 1939
7716 DIERICKX Frank P Visual Imagery in *The Faerie Queene* MA Univ of
      Minnesota 1941
7717 DONNELLY Rev Henry E The Influence of *The Courtier* of Baldassare
      Castiglione on Spenser's *Fowre Hymnes* MA Univ of Detroit 1936
7718 DOUGHERTY Sr Ann G Edmund Spenser's *Calendar* MA Villanova Univ 1965
7719 DOW Sr M Harriet *The Faerie Queene*: An Elizabethan Courtesy Book
      MA Marquette Univ 1954 121 p
7720 DOWLER Burnette W The Biblical Concept of Holiness in Spenser's
      The Faerie Queene, Book I MA Univ of Houston 1969 126 p
7721 DRISKILL L L The Unifying Conceptions and the Implications of Cyclic
      Structure in *The Shepheardes Calendar* MA Rice 1968
7722 DRISKILL Willie H A Study of Imagery in a Cross Section of Spenser's
      Poetry MA Univ of Alabama 1940
7723 DUFF Clarissa J The Reputation of Edmund Spenser Among the Romantic
      Writers MA Columbia 1938
7724 DUNLAP Lennis C Spenser's Concept of Mutability and Its Classical
      Background MA Univ of Tennessee 1952 109 p
7725 DURKEE Cora L *Britannia's Pastorals* as a Spenserian Imitation
      MA Yale Univ 1926
7726 ECKERT Florence The Portrayal of Nature in Spenser MA Univ of
      Chicago 1912
7727 EDMUNDS James M A Study of the Amoret Story in the Third and Fourth
      Books of *The Faerie Queene* MA Johns Hopkins Univ 1927
7728 EKSTRAND Doris The Influence of DuBartas on Spenser MA Stanford Univ
      1935
7729 ELLIS Esther Spenser's Faery Land MA Univ of Tennessee 1933
7730 ENTWISTLE Gretchen S Spenser's Imagery MA Univ of Arizona 1940
7731 ETHERIDGE Margaret Spenser's Use of Classical Mythology in *The Faerie*
      Queene MA North Texas St Univ 1941
7732 EVANS Ova M An Analytical Study of Courtesy as Exemplified by
      Sir Calidore in the Sixth Book of *The Faerie Queene* MA Oklahoma
      St Univ 1936 92 p
7733 FARIES Mary L A Commentary on the *Fowre Hymnes* of Edmund Spenser
      MA Temple Univ 1964 66 p
7734 FASSLER Barbara E Thomistic Causes of Sin in *The Faerie Queene*
      MA Ohio St Univ 1964 109 p
7735 FAY Lillian W Spenser's Theory of Knowledge MA Smith Coll 1894
7736 FEARS Velma A Study of Edmund Spenser's *Shepheardes Calendar*
      MA Univ of Texas at Austin 1935
7737 FENNO Cheryl B Interpretations of Allegory in Book I of *The Faerie*
      Queene MA Northeast Missouri St Coll 1967
7738 FEURER Martin The Similes in *The Faerie Queene* of Edmund Spenser
      MA Rutgers St Univ 1931 49 p
7739 FIELDS Albert W Literary and Critical Background for the Moral
      Eclogues of *The Shepheardes Calendar* MA Univ of Kentucky 1952 10?
7740 FIFIELD Louise D The Extent of Virgil's Influence upon Spenser as
      Revealed from a Study of *The Shepheardes Calendar* and *The Faerie*
      Queene MA Boston Univ 1935
7741 FINLINSON Arline R Spenser's Handling of Nature in *The Faerie Queene*;
      Special Aspects of Characterization in the Works of Willa Cather;
      and Determinism in "George's Mother" MA Brigham Young Univ 1961
7742 FORD Mildred Spenser's Characterization in *The Faerie Queene*
      MA Univ of Colorado 1926
7743 FORD Patricia A Implication of Imagery and Allusion in *The Faerie*

Queene MA St Louis Univ 1952 204 p
7744 FORSTER Catherine A Art, Nature and Spenser's Pictorialism
      MA Univ of British Columbia (Canada) 1966 100 p
7745 FRANCIS Alice S The Adonis Myth in Book III of *The Faerie Queene*
      MA Duquesne Univ 1965
7746 FRASH Robert M The Influence of the Fairy Mistress Romances on
      Spenser's *Faerie Queene* MA Univ of Illinois 1941
7747 FRAZIER F E Spenser's Arthur: A Study in Allegorical Significance
      MA Univ of Oregon 1937
7748 FRITTS Katherine T Spenser and Platonism MA Columbia 1929
7749 GALLUP Jennifer J Spenser's Exposition of Courtesy in Book VI
      of *The Faerie Queene* MA McGill (Canada) 1964
7750 GARLAND Jasper V Dress in the Poetry of Edmund Spenser MA Indiana
      Univ 1935
7751 GAYLON Linda J Spenser and Puttenham: A Test Case of the Question,
      Is Elizabethan Criticism Divorced from the Poetry? MA Indiana
      Univ 1962
7752 GEORGAS Marilyn D Spenser's Despair Episode MA Lamar Technological
      Univ 1963 127 p
7753 GIBBS Lloyd G Primitivism in the Works of Edmund Spenser MA Wofford
      Coll 1948
7754 GIBBS Marion The Allegory in the Sixth Book of Spenser's *Faerie
      Queene* MA Univ of Oregon 1946
7755 GILLETTE Alletta M Political Allegory in the Second Book of *The
      Faerie Queene* MA Univ of Washington 1911
7756 GILMAN Madeline *Faerie Queene*, an Auden Poem and Twain and Kafka
      MA Pennsylvania St Univ 1965
7757 GRIFFIN Arthur J Edmund Spenser and the Conventions of Pastoral
      Elegy MA Columbia 1964 122 p
7758 GROGAN Flossie R Spenser's Mutabilitie Cantos MA Oklahoma East
      Central St Coll 1949
7759 GROSSHANS Robert D Archetypes in *The Faerie Queene* MA Syracuse
      Univ 1949 145 p
7760 GUENTER M E The Influence of the French Pleiade on Edmund Spenser
      MA Boston Univ 1941
7761 HAASE Gladys D The Orthography of Spenser's *Faerie Queene* in the
      Light of Sixteenth Century Theories of Spelling MA Columbia 1939
7762 HAGGETT Dorothy G Spenser's Original Contributions to the English
      Language, Adapted from Words of Romanic and Classical Tradition
      MA Univ of Washington 1928
7763 HALL Alma B Hawes' *Pastime of Pleasure* and Book I of Spenser's
      Faerie Queene: A Comparative Study in Purpose, Content, Form and
      Style MA East Carolina Univ 1965
7764 HARTNEY Thomas Sacred Fury: Suggestions toward an Interpretation
      of *The Faerie Queene* MA McMaster (Canada) 1963
7765 HATCHETT Una V A Critical Study of Spenser's *Mother Hubberds Tale*
      MA Oklahoma St Univ 1939 38 p
7766 HEFFNER Hubert C Mysticism in Spenser's *Fowre Hymnes* MA Univ of
      North Carolina at Chapel Hill 1922
7767 HEFFNER R L Spenser and the British Sea Power MA Univ of North
      Carolina at Chapel Hill 1925
7768 HENDRICKS Ira K The Use of the Spenserian Stanza before 1798
      MA Stanford Univ 1926
7769 HILL Iris T *The Faerie Queene, Book III*: Spenser's Use of Myth
      MA Brown Univ 1966
7770 HOLLAND Edwin V Wit, Satire and Humor in Spenser's Poetry MA Indiana
      Univ 1955
7771 HUDSON Charles M Jr Edmund Spenser: Background and Performance
      MA Vanderbilt Univ 1934
7772 HUNTER Madelyn C The Relations between Edmund Spenser and William Cecil,

Lord Burghley   MA St Coll of Iowa 1928
7773 INGRAM Gladys A   The Music of Spenser's *Faerie Queene*   MA Oklahoma
St Univ 1932
7774 IRVIN Helen D   The Allegory of *The Faerie Queene*:   Current Estimates
and Evaluations   MA Univ of Kentucky 1965   86 p
7775 IRVINE Magnus H   The Old and New Elements in Spenser's Poetry
M Litt Cambridge Univ (England) 1932
7776 JACKSON Blanche G   A Study of Spenser's *The Tears of the Muses*
MA Univ of Washington 1912
7777 JACKSON Ellen P   Monotony and Variety in *The Faerie Queene*   MA Univ
of Colorado 1936
7778 JACKSON Ivonel W   Spenser's Poetic Concept and Figure of Nature in
Two Cantos of Mutabilities and *The Faerie Queene*   MA Univ of
Houston 1965   97 p
7779 JACKSON Ruth M   A Comparison of the Neoplatonism of *The Courtier*
with that of Spenser's *Fowre Hymnes*   MA Univ of Oregon 1933
7780 JAYNE Sears   An Edition of Ficino's Commentary on Plato   MA Univ of
Missouri 1945
7781 JOBSON Sr Florence M   Dialogue in the Major Poetry of Edmund Spenser
MA St Louis Univ 1967   353 p
7782 JOHNSTON Mary A   Patterns of Imagery in Edmund Spenser's *Complaints*
MA Univ of Tennessee 1966
7783 JONES Mabel L   Recent Interest in Edmund Spenser (1910-1930)
MA Univ of Oklahoma 1930
7784 JORDAN Rosamond B   The Heroic Simile in *The Faerie Queene*   MA Marquette
Univ 1935
7785 JORGENSEN Ruth E   Cleopolis, a Paraphrase of Book I of Edmund Spenser'
The Faerie Queene   MA Univ of Tulsa 1949
7786 KEENE Frances E   Italian Neo-Platonic Influence on Spenser's *Fowre
Hymnes*   MA Columbia 1936
7787 KEITHLEY Lenora T   A Comparison of Spenser's *Faerie Queene*, Book VI,
with Castiglione's *The Courtier*   MA Oklahoma St Univ 1936
7788 KING Emma C   Rhetorical Elements in the Poetry of Edmund Spenser
MA Univ of Chicago 1912
7789 KITSON C E   Humanism in *The Faerie Queene*   BA Univ of British Columbia
(Canada) 1943
7790 KONNEKER Adele S   Folklore Motifs in Spenser's *Faerie Queene*
MA Southern Illinois Univ at Carbondale 1964   68 p
7791 KYLE M F   Study of the Problems in Spenser's *Fowre Hymnes*   MA Univ of
Colorado 1937
7792 LANDY Alice S   The Meaning of Marriage in Spenser's *Epithalamion*
MA Univ of Florida 1965
7793 LANGDON Ida   Materials for a Study of Spenser's Theory of Fine Art
MA Cornell Univ 1911
7794 LAWSON Charles F   The Allegory of *The Faerie Queene*   MA Columbia 1904
7795 LE BEL Eugene C   Christian and Medieval Theology in Spenser's "Hymne
of Heavenly Love" and "Hymne of Heavenly Beauty"   MA Univ of
Chicago 1931
7796 LEIBLE Arthur B   *Mother Hubberds Tale* Edited with Introduction, Notes
and Glossary   MA Indiana Univ 1925
7797 LEMMING Edith M   Spenser and His Relation with Elizabeth, Lady Carey
MA Columbia 1916
7798 LEWIS Lambert E   A Possible Influence on the Bowre of Blis Episodes
in *The Faerie Queene*:   "The Groac'h of the Isle of Lok"
MA Indiana Univ 1942
7799 LINDEROTH Leon W   A Bibliography of Spenser, 1937-1958   MA Florida
St Univ 1960
7800 LINTON Robert H   The Code of Arms in Spenser's *Faerie Queene*   MA Univ
of North Carolina at Chapel Hill 1939
7801 LITTLETON Jean C   Spenser's Use of Allegory as a Technique of Story-

telling in the *Complaints* Volume MA East Carolina Univ 1964
7802 LOGAN Gail E Classical Mythology in Spenser's *Mutabilitie Cantos*
     MA Univ of Rhode Island 1968 68 p
7803 LYALL Laurence H Plotinian Elements in the Third and Fourth Books
     of Spenser's *The Faerie Queene* MA Midwestern Univ 1966 236 p
7804 McCABE Sr Mary A Spenser's Use of Repetition in *The Faerie Queene*
     MA St Louis Univ 1933 91 p
7805 McCAFFREY Edward W Britomat's Development as a Three-Dimensional
     Character in Book III of *The Faerie Queene* by Edmund Spenser
     MA Univ of Rhode Island 1968 79 p
7806 McCALIB Clytie A The Influence of Aristotle's "Nichomachean Ethics"
     upon the Fourth Book of Spenser's *Faerie Queene* MA Oklahoma St
     Univ 1936
7807 McCALLION Margaret Spenser's *View of Ireland* in Book VI of *The Faerie
     Queene* MA Hunter Coll 1967
7808 McCRACKEN Mildred L The Plan and Conduct of *The Faerie Queene*
     MA Univ of Oklahoma 1934
7809 McGILL Winifred A Study of the Spirit of the Work of Edmund Spenser
     MA Univ of Washington 1924
7810 McGOWEN John W The Glossarist of Spenser's *The Shepherdes Calendar*:
     A Survey of the Scholarship on His Identity MA Univ of North
     Carolina at Chapel Hill 1949 99 p
7811 McKEE Louise The Homeric Simile in Spenser's *The Faerie Queene*
     MA Oklahoma St Univ 1933
7812 McMANUS Francis X The Corporal Works of Mercy in Book I of *The Faerie
     Queene*: A Study of Sources and Analogues MA Catholic Univ 1937
7813 McMILLEN Roberta A Heroines of Spenser MA Baylor Univ 1965 92 p
7814 MADIGAN Francis V Spenser's Use of Magic in *The Faerie Queene*
     MA Columbia 1961 122 p
7815 MALMSHEIMER Richard R Three Studies in English: Spenser's
     Epithalamion; Paradise Lost; and Melville's *Benito Cereno*
     MA Pennsylvania St Univ 1966
7816 MALTBY Jeannette E Spenser's Use of the Bible in *The Faerie Queene,
     Books I and II* MA Univ of Washington 1926
7817 MARSTON Mary A The Structure of *The Faerie Queene*: A Critical
     Analysis MA Univ of Kentucky 1956 75 p
7818 MARSYLA John A In Pursuit of Myth: A Study of Edmund Spenser's
     Faerie Queene MA Arizona St Univ 1965
7819 MAXWELL Annie A Non-Classical Proper Names in Spenser MA Cornell
     Univ 1904
7820 MAZUROWSKI Sr Marie C Platonism in Elizabethan Poetry with Particular
     Reference to Spenser's *Fowre Hymnes* MA Univ of Detroit 1945
7821 MELDRUM H S *The Pastime of Pleasure* by Stephen Hawes: A Probable
     Source of Spenser's *Faerie Queene* MA Univ of Washington 1922
7822 MILLER Aloysius The Cosmic Philosophy of Spenser's *Mutability Cantos*
     MA Fordham Univ 1938
7823 MILLIGAN C B Antiquarianism in Edmund Spenser MA Univ of North
     Carolina at Chapel Hill 1923
7824 MITCHELL Anna F *Colin Clouts Come Home Againe* Edited with Intro-
     duction, Notes and Glossary MA Indiana Univ 1925
7825 MITCHELL Eleanor D Proverbial Material in Spenser's *Faerie Queene*
     MA Columbia 1939
7826 MITCHELL Pearl B An Analysis of the Aesthetic Qualities of Spenser's
     Poetry MA Stanford Univ 1931
7827 MITCHELL Robert The Union of Primitivism and Spenserian Form in
     English Poetry MA Univ of Oregon 1942
7828 MOCK H B Influence of Ovid on Spenser MA Univ of North Carolina
     at Chapel Hill 1923
7829 MOLELLA Lynne The Myth of Hercules in *The Faerie Queene* MA Syracuse
     Univ 1962 68 p

7830 MOORE C A Cosmological Ideas in the Poetry of Edmund Spenser
      MA Univ of North Carolina at Chapel Hill 1937
7831 MOORE Laura D Spenser: The Poet and Teacher MA Univ of Montana 1921
      69 p
7832 MOORE Marjorie A Comparison of the Literature of France and England
      during the Sixteenth Century with Special Reference to the Works
      of Spenser and Ronsard MA Univ of North Dakota 1923 62 p
7833 MOORE Sarah B Spenser's Language in the Eighteenth Century
      MA Columbia 1949
7834 MOSS Mary H Primitivism in the Poetry of Edmund Spenser MA Univ of
      Texas at Austin 1940 143 p
7835 MUNCIE Nina B The Importance of Myth in The Faerie Queene as Exemplified
      by Spenser's Use of It in the Story of "Florimell the Fayre", with
      Special Attention to Myth Classification MA Oklahoma St Univ 1932
      88 p
7836 NETTLES Grace N A Study of Meaning Changes in Spenser's Translation
      of DuBellay's Songe MA Univ of Florida 1965
7837 NEUVILLE H Richmond The Sonnets of Pierre de Ronsard and Edmund Spenser:
      A Comparative Study MA Columbia 1964 59 p
7838 NIX Martha J A Study of the Influence of the Morality Plays on Spenser's
      Faerie Queene, Book I MA Univ of Washington 1925
7839 NOOE Mary A The Spenserian Stanza in Great Britain, 1798-1900: An
      Essay and a Checklist MA Univ of Kentucky 1953 131 p
7840 NORTON Nathaniel Christian Humanism as Reflected in Books I and
      II of The Faerie Queene MA Univ of Redlands 1965
7841 NUTTING Hazel D Spenserian Criticism in the Past Decade MA Univ of
      Colorado 1928
7842 O'CONNELL Elizabeth M The Role of Emblem Literature in the Creation
      of the Allegory in Book III of Edmund Spenser's The Faerie Queene
      MA Bowling Green Univ 1962
7843 O'CONNOR J M Spenser's Use of the Saint George Legend, "The Fair
      Unknown", and Other Medieval Romance Themes in Book I of The Faerie
      Queene MA Univ of Washington 1926
7844 O'CONNOR Mary E A Study of the Failure of Spenser's Mother Hubberds
      Tale MA St Louis Univ 1950 194 p
7845 O'GORMAN Edward C A Study of the Hero in the Second Book of The Faerie
      Queene MA Columbia 1959 76 p
7846 OSBORNE Mary H Studies in Spenser's Use of the Theory of Kinds
      MA Univ of North Carolina at Chapel Hill 1942
7847 PACKARD Eulalia M The Golden Age Theme in Book V of The Faerie Queene
      MA Colorado St Coll 1960
7848 PACKARD Faith E Spenser's Influence on the Pictorial Landscape of
      Certain Eighteenth Century Poets MA Wellesley Coll 1931
7849 PADEN John E The Influence of Ovid's Metamorphoses on Spenser's
      Faerie Queene MA Oklahoma St Univ 1933 20 p
7850 PARKER R E Archaisms in Spenser MA Univ of North Carolina at Chapel
      Hill 1915
7851 PATE Olen C A Study of Vernacular Style in Spenser's Proverbs and
      Wise Sayings MA East Tennessee St Univ 1961
7852 PAVELICH Joan L Teaching and Delighting in The Faerie Queene: An
      Analysis of Spenser's Use of the Two Renaissance Critical Ideals
      MA Univ of British Columbia (Canada) 1964
7853 PEIRCE Marjorie B Spenser Allusions (1579-1651) MA Univ of Chicago
      1927
7854 PELTON Nellie F Minor Poems of Edmund Spenser MA Johns Hopkins Univ
      1918
7855 PFAFF Martha Spenser as a Sensuous Poet in Book II of The Faerie
      Queene MA Texas Technological Univ 1931 70 p
7856 PHELAN T A Edmund Spenser: The Strength and Weakness of His Genius
      MA Boston Coll 1932

7857 PICKARD Leona M A Study of Spenser's Use of the Pastoral Convention
      MA Ohio Univ 1941
7858 PIERCE John Temperance in *The Faerie Queene*, Book II and in Bryskett's
      Civil Discourse MA Ohio St Univ 1949
7859 POE Pascal Mutations of Justice in Book V of *The Faerie Queene*
      MA Univ of Connecticut 1969
7860 PRICHARD Ethel I A Grammar of Spenser's *Amoretti* and *Epithalamion*
      MA Oklahoma St Univ 1943   44 p
7861 PROCTOR Leta G Some Parallel Motives in Spenser's *Faerie Queene*
      and Homer's *Iliad* MA Oklahoma St Univ 1934   43 p
7862 RAMANATHAN Suguna Figures of Defiance in *The Faerie Queene*
      MA Temple Univ 1963   82 p
7863 RISSE Robert G Some Problems of Narrative Technique in Books I and
      III of *The Faerie Queene* MA Washington Univ at St Louis 1953
7864 ROBERTS J Russell Spenser's Use of Classical Mythology MA Washington
      St Univ at Pullman 1931
7865 ROBERTSON Margaret J Structure in Book VI of *The Faerie Queene*
      MA McGill (Canada) 1966
7866 ROSENTHAL Willis M A Study of Spenser's "Muiopotmus" MA Univ of
      Oklahoma 1937
7867 ROSNER Beatrice Wild Men in *The Faerie Queene* MA Hunter Coll 1961
7868 ROUX Fredric A Edmund Spenser and Sixteenth Century Eschatology
      MA Univ of New Hampshire 1963   49 p
7869 ROWE K T Relations of Ovid to *The Faerie Queene* with Illustrations
      MA Rice 1924
7870 RUDMAN Leah R Platonic Platonism in Spenser, with Special Reference
      to *The Faerie Queene* and the *Fowre Hymnes* MA Washington Univ at
      St Louis 1923   85 p
7871 RUSSELL Isaac W The Sources of Spenser's *Mother Hubberds Tale*
      MA Johns Hopkins Univ 1929
7872 RUSSELL Ruth W Spenser's Use of the Bible in the First Two Books of
      The Faerie Queene MA Univ of Oklahoma 1936
7873 SALMAN Phillips C The King's Two Bodies in Book V of Spenser's
      Faerie Queene: A Study of Spenser's Use of the Political Theory
      of the Dual Capacities of the Sovereign MA Columbia 1962   85 p
7874 SAMMONS Eugene Spenser's Politics MA Univ of Kentucky 1929
7875 SAMS Virginia L The Legend of Britain in *The Faerie Queene*: Com-
      pliment to Queen Elizabeth MA Wake Forest Coll 1965
7876 SCHIVO Sr Mary of Nazareth Traditional Christian Elements in the
      Poetry of Edmund Spenser MA Catholic Univ of America 1948
7877 SCHMITT Gretchen Spenser's Imagery MA Univ of Arizona 1939
7878 SCOTT Myra E Problems Arising in the Interpretation of Spenser's
      Shepherdes Calendar in Relation to Contemporary Affairs
      MA Stanford Univ 1928
7879 SCRIBNER Dora A The History of Spenser's Literary Reputation
      MA Univ of Chicago 1906
7880 SELDON Annette P Musical Allusions in the Poetic Works of Spenser
      MA Indiana Univ 1950
7881 SEN D A Critical Study of Spenserian Imitations from 1700 to 1771
      MA Univ of London (England) 1952
7882 SENDON Mary K Spenser's Use of Proverbs MA Baylor Univ 1932   140 p
7883 SHERRICK Hazel L A Study of Edmund Spenser's *Mutability* MA Univ
      of Washington 1925
7884 SHORT William H Justice in *The Faerie Queene*, Book V and in *A Brief
      View* MA Ohio St Univ 1948
7885 SHULL Virginia M The Descriptive Background of *The Faerie Queene*
      MA Yale Univ 1932
7886 SIMMONS Erma The Calidore-Pastorella Story as an Example of Spenser's
      Narrative Art MA Univ of Texas at Austin 1929
7887 SIPES Marilyn P Spenser's Conception of Chastity in the Third Book of

The Faerie Queene MA Hunter Coll 1964
7888 SMITH William B Rhetoric and the Mechanics of Spenser's Versification
MA Toronto (Canada) 1966
7889 SORENSEN Judith V Amoret, Edmund Spenser's Paragon of Love MA Ohio
St Univ 1967 79 p
7890 SPERDUTO Sr Filomena C Italian Influence on *The Faerie Queene*
MA Columbia 1940
7891 SPRUILL Mary J Masque Elements in Spenser's *Faerie Queene* MA Univ
of North Carolina at Chapel Hill 1922
7892 STARR Kathyrn M Dress in Edmund Spenser's *Faerie Queene* MA Rutgers
St Univ 1932 98 p
7893 STEPHENS Robert F A Bibliography of Masters' Theses Concerning
Edmund Spenser MA Univ of Tennessee 1949
7894 STEVENS Helen C The Generalized Observation in Spenser's *Faerie Queene*
MA Univ of Colorado 1944
7895 STRABEL Audrey L Love and Change in Books III and IV of *The Faerie
Queene* and in the *Mutability Cantos* MA Univ of Buffalo 1949
7896 STRANGNATT Mabel V Blood Relationships in Spenser's *Faerie Queene*
MA Columbia 1914
7897 STREATOR G I The Influence of Early Medieval Allegory upon Spenser's
Faerie Queene MA Univ of Washington 1913
7898 STREET Helen K A Study of Spenser's *Mother Hubberds Tale* MA Tulane
Univ 1928
7899 SYDNER Helen W A Study of the Buildings in *The Faerie Queene* MA Univ
of Colorado 1937
7900 SYMONS Lorretta A The Grotesque in Spenser's *Faerie Queene*, Book I
MA Univ of Delaware 1968 71 p
7901 TAYLOR Eva The Influence of Ireland on the Poetry of Edmund Spenser
MA Univ of Kentucky 1932
7902 TEER Thomas W Spenser's Knowledge and Use of Magic as Evidenced in
His Poetry MA Duke Univ 1949
7903 THOMAS Brian H Venus in *The Faerie Queene* MA Toronto (Canada) 1963
7904 TIDWELL M Fred Aristotle's Influence on Spenser's Treatment of Justice
MA Oklahoma St Univ 1936 36 p
7905 TRUNAGE Maxine The Golden Age and Other Primitivistic Ideas in the
Poetry of Edmund Spenser MA Indiana Univ 1960
7906 TRYON Jane L A Topographical Study of *The Faerie Queene* BA Univ of
British Columbia (Canada) 1967
7907 TYLER Roland W The Pictorial Elements in Spenser's *Faerie Queene*
MA Boston Univ 1931
7908 VANEK Olga M Spenser's Interest in Medieval Romance as Illustrated
in the First Book of *The Faerie Queene* MA Univ of Illinois 1930
7909 VAN VACTOR William E The Influence of Spenser's Moral Eclogues on
John Milton's Minor Poems MA Univ of Oregon 1946
7910 VAUGHAN Mary F On Pageants and Processions in Spenser's Poetry
MA Univ of Oklahoma 1928
7911 VILLEGAS Natividad D Spenser's Use of Classical Mythology in
The Faerie Queene MA Univ of Illinois 1948
7912 VINSON James A The Venus of Regeneration: The Tradition and
The Faerie Queene MA Rice 1956
7913 VOORHEES E N The English Pastoral after Spenser MA Boston Univ 1917
7914 WALLACE Allie B A Study of Some of the Proper Names in Spenser's
Faerie Queene MA Oklahoma St Univ 1931 83 p
7915 WALLACE Calvin R A Comparative Study of Church's Glosses and
Annotations on Spenser's *Faerie Queene* MA Univ of Tennessee 1930
7916 WALLERMAN Ira D The Court in the Poetry of Edmund Spenser MA Indiana
Univ 1935
7917 WALSH Sr Mary J Spenser's Use of the Bible in Book I of *The Faerie
Queene* MA Boston Coll 1956
7918 WATSON Sara R Spenser and Sixteenth Century Chivalry MA Case-Western

Reserve Univ 1929
7919 WEBB W S Studies in the Renaissance Fable with Special Reference to
      Spenser MA Univ of North Carolina at Chapel Hill 1925
7920 WEIGHTMAN Franklin C Marsilio Ficino's *Commentary on Plato's Symposium*
      and Edmund Spenser's *Fowre Hymnes* MA East Tennessee St Univ 1969
7921 WIDDER William J The Tail of the Dragon: A Study of the Number
      Symbolism in Edmund Spenser's *Castle of the Soul* MA Columbia 1952
      80 p
7922 WILKIE Katherine E Spenser's Britomart and Her Sources MA Univ of
      Kentucky 1939
7923 WILLIAMS LuElla B Spenser's Use of the Supernatural in *The Faerie
      Queene* MA Univ of Colorado 1939
7924 WINKELMANN Sr Mary A Spenser's Modification of the Renaissance Idea
      of Glory as the Motivation of *The Faerie Queene* MA St Louis Univ
      1961 374 p
7925 WOLLERMAN Ira D The Court in the Poetry of Edmund Spenser MA Indiana
      Univ 1927
7926 YANARELLA Marie T Spenser's Idea of Temperance as It Appears in
      Book II of *The Faerie Queene* MA Columbia 1940
See also 1353, 1367, 1430, 1459, 2804, 3174, 4231, 4725, 4727, 4946, 4949,
      5076, 5336, 5390, 5516, 5572, 5980, 6249, 6373, 6892, 8145, 8291,
      8294, 8474

RICHARD STEELE

7927 DAVIDSON Carter Sir Richard Steele: Reformer MA Univ of Louisville
      1926
7928 DRAPER William A Richard Steele's Theory of Comedy MA George Wash-
      ington Univ 1961 48 p
7929 FISCHER Judith A The Minor Periodicals of Richard Steele: Mirror
      of Augustan England MA John Carroll Univ 1966
7930 HENDERSON June M Swift and Steele: A Study in Personal Controversy
      MA Univ of Texas at Austin 1961
7931 LANE Carolyn Characteristics of Richard Steele's Editorship of
      Eighteenth Century Periodicals from the *Tatler* to the *Lover*
      MA Smith Coll 1919
7932 LOGUE Joe M The Letters of Richard Steele MA Univ of Texas at
      Austin 1935
7933 MILLER Judith C Steele's *Tatler* and the Reformation of Manners
      MA North Texas St Univ 1964
7934 QUARLES Dorothy M The Spirit of Didacticism in the Works of
      Sir Richard Steele MA Washington Univ at St Louis 1943 245 p
7935 SLONE Gwen C Richard Steele as a Moral Reformer MA Univ of Kentucky
      1965 122 p
7936 TAYLOR Garland F Richard Steele and the Theatre MA Tulane Univ 1934
7937 WOLFSOHN Ida C The Influence of Richard Steele in the History of
      British Morals MA Texas Woman's Univ 1934
See also 7, 13, 15, 16

JAMES STEPHENS

7938 HARDY Molly The Portrayal of Humanity in the Poems of James Stephens
      MA Univ of Arizona 1944
7939 MARTIN Margaret E Aspects of Proletarianism in the Works of
      James Stephens MA Univ of Texas at Austin 1938 154 p
7940 PYLE Hilary A James Stephens: The Irish Temperament in English
      Literature M Litt Cambridge Univ (England) 1961
7941 SOLOMON Bonnie T The Prose Fantasy of James Stephens: An Aspect
      of the Irish Renaissance MA Univ of Pittsburgh 1954

LAURENCE STERNE

7942 ABEL Robert H *Tristram Shandy*: The Context of Event MS Kansas St
      Coll at Pittsburg 1967
7943 ARMSTRONG John H *Tristram Shandy* by Laurence Sterne: The Motley
      Novel of a Gentleman-Jester BA Amherst 1954
7944 BARRIER Robert C The Development of Sterne's Moral Philosophy
      MA Univ of Omaha 1965
7945 BOGER Hazel G A Bibliography of Laurence Sterne MA Columbia 1937
7946 BRIDGER Steve The Unorthodox Birth of *Tristram Shandy*: Sterne's Use
      of Synecdoche BA Univ of British Columbia (Canada) 1967
7947 COPELAND John A A Study of the Phases of Sentimentality in the Major
      Works of Laurence Sterne MA Texas Technological Univ 1933 68 p
7948 FEINBERG Elaine C "There Is no Disputing Against Hobby Horses":
      The Private Worlds in *Tristram Shandy* MA Columbia 1962 77 p
7949 FIORI Ombretta Laurence Sterne: The Man of Little Feeling
      MA Ça Foscari (Italy) 1951
7950 GIRAULT Norton R A Study of Laurence Sterne's Novels MA Louisiana
      St Univ 1940
7951 GUINA Nerea The Sentimentalism of Laurence Sterne MA Ca Foscari
      (Italy) 1948
7952 GULLIVER Antony F The Form and Thought of *Tristram Shandy* MA Univ
      of Vermont 1965
7953 HURLEY Donna W The Medical World of Tristram Shandy MA Columbia 1963
      98 p
7954 LOMBARD Lee R John Hall Stevenson: The Eugenius of Laurence Sterne
      MA Columbia 1935
7955 MARTIN Arlie M The Rhetoric of Sterne's Le Fever Story MA Colorado
      St Coll 1967
7956 MARTINEAU Marie J The Mainspring of *Tristram Shandy*: Sterne's
      Theology of Sex MA Columbia 1965 79 p
7957 MATHESON Janet M The Structure of Laurence Sterne's *Tristram Shandy*
      MA Univ of British Columbia (Canada) 1968 112 p
7958 MICHELESI Augusto The Distinguishing Features of Laurence Sterne's
      Fiction as Seen through His *Tristram Shandy* and *Sentimental Journey*
      MA Ca Foscari (Italy) 1934
7959 NEWMAN Patricia A In Tristram's Parlor: An Analysis of the Reader-
      Writer Dialogue in Sterne's *Tristram Shandy* MA Auburn Univ 1967
7960 ORCHARD Isobel The Influence of Sterne upon Modern Fiction MA Univ
      of Oregon 1932
7961 PARKER Stanley W Some Aspects of the Life and Work of Laurence Sterne
      MA Boston Univ 1931
7962 PARSONS Mildred L Laurence Sterne: The Modernist MA Howard Univ
      1935 89 p
7963 PETRAKIS Byron Sterne's Use of the Absurd in *A Sentimental Journey*
      MA Univ of Florida 1965
7964 SCHAWACKER Erwin W Jr Impotence and Potency as Structural Motifs
      in *Tristram Shandy* MA Wichita St Univ 1966
7965 TOBIAS Jo G Intellectual Isolation, Sympathetic Correspondence: A
      Study of Communication in Sterne's *Tristram Shandy* MA Hunter Coll 196ꞌ
7966 WAGONER Mary H Laurence Sterne's *Tristram Shandy* and the Philosophers
      MA Univ of Texas at Austin 1957 80 p
7967 WALLACE Ewen E The Time Structure of *Tristram Shandy* MA Dalhousie
      (Canada) 1967
7968 WELLER Philip Tristram-Sterne's Hobby Horse: Its Rationale and
      Function in Characterization and Humor MA Washington St Univ at
      Pullman 1966
See also 2446, 3185, 3192, 5997, 6015, 6017, 8075

ROBERT L STEVENSON

7969 ACEVEDO Christina G Robert Louis Stevenson and the Child Mind
      MA Texas Arts and Industries Univ 1950
7970 ANSARI Rahila A Study of Robert Louis Stevenson's Reputation as a
      Novelist down to 1900 MA Leeds Univ (England) 1957
7971 BALLINGER Richard H Some Literary Theories of Robert Louis Stevenson
      MA Univ of Texas at Austin 1936
7972 BAMBINI Lina Robert Louis Stevenson MA Ca Foscari (Italy) 1939
7973 BILLINGSLEY James G Moral Good and Evil in Three Works of
      Robert Louis Stevenson MA St Louis Univ 1938 44 p
7974 BROWN L A The Personal Essays of Robert Louis Stevenson MA Univ
      of North Carolina at Chapel Hill 1911
7975 CHUBBUCK F S The Creation of Atmosphere in the Stevenson Short Story
      MA Ohio St Univ 1925
7976 COOK Hugh L Robert Louis Stevenson's Theory and Practice of Prose
      Fiction MA Auburn Univ 1940
7977 DELANEY William T Influence of "Skeltery" on Stevenson MA St Louis
      Univ 1933 57 p
7978 EVANS Betty D The Dual Personality of Stevenson's Characters
      MA Univ of Oklahoma 1944
7979 FELBAUM Tillie C Robert Louis Stevenson's Art of Narration
      MS Purdue Univ 1902
7980 GAMBINO Angela Robert Louis Stevenson MA Ca Foscari (Italy) 1949
7981 GIORDANO Maria Robert Louis Stevenson MA Ca Foscari (Italy) 1930
7982 HOWARD Volney A Robert Louis Stevenson's Methods of Writing Short
      Stories: A Technical Analysis MA Louisiana St Univ 1939
7983 JEFFERSON Louise The Religious Views of Robert Louis Stevenson as
      Revealed in His Letters and Essays MA Univ of Kentucky 1932
7984 KELL Winona D Stevenson's Talent for Friendship as Revealed in the
      Poems Addressed to Him MA Univ of Kentucky 1948 107 p
7985 KUNTZ Joseph M The Metrics, Imagery and Philosophy of Robert Louis
      Stevenson as Shown in His Poetry MA Univ of New Mexico 1934
7986 LAYTON Leroy S Elements of Realism in the Novels of Robert Louis
      Stevenson M Ed Temple Univ 1940 94 p
7987 McCULLY Katherine W Robert Louis Stevenson's Philosophy of Life
      MA Washington St Univ at Pullman 1921
7988 MASSE Benjamin L The Religion of Robert Louis Stevenson as Revealed
      in His Letters and Essays MA St Louis Univ 1932 66 p
7989 METZ Cora I Stevenson's Art of Writing in Theory and Practice
      BA Univ of British Columbia (Canada) 1922
7990 RIZZI Valeria Robert Louis Stevenson: The Man and the Writer
      MA Ca Foscari (Italy) 1952
7991 ROBERTS Mildred C A Comparison of the Writings of Melville and
      Stevenson Relative to the South Seas MA Univ of Kentucky 1936
7992 ROGERS Ruth Y The Children's Poetry of Robert Louis Stevenson
      MA Texas Christian Univ 1953 138 p
7993 ROSS Robert H Jr Robert Louis Stevenson, Man and Author, with Special
      Emphasis upon His Theories of Fiction and the Manner in Which He
      Carried Them Out in His Major Works MA Columbia 1940
7994 SKINNER Helen The Development of Stevenson's Prose Style MA Univ
      of Texas at Austin 1933
7995 SMITH Joyce A The Spiritual Adventure and Moral Symbolism in
      Selected Works of Robert Louis Stevenson M Ed Henderson St Coll nd
7996 SUITS Harold The Pirate Lore in *Treasure Island* MA Univ of North
      Carolina at Chapel Hill 1956 130 p
7997 TUCKER Lucille H Robert Louis Stevenson: Poetic Interpreter for
      Children and Adults M Ed Henderson St Coll nd
7998 WALKER Helen O Stevenson the Storyteller MA Univ of Arizona pre-1933
7999 WESTLAKE Mary B Major Influences of the Works of Robert Louis Stevenson

M Ed Henderson St Coll nd
8000 WILSON Louise A A Study of the Paragraph Transitions in Stevenson's
      Novels, Short Stories, Essays, Letters and Poetry MA Smith Coll 1913
See also 1982, 2106

LYTTON STRACHEY

8001 ALEXANDER June E A Study of Biographical and Critical Essays of
      Lytton Strachey MA Univ of Texas at Austin 1935
8002 DWYER Mary I The Biographical Methods of Lytton Strachey MA Boston
      Univ 1934
8003 McCELVEY George E Lytton Strachey and Techniques in Modern Biography
      MA Univ of Houston 1957 114 p
See also 4228

JOHN SUCKLING

8004 HUBKA Ronald R Suckling and the Epithalamic Convention MA Univ of
      Maryland at College Park 1969 57 p
8005 RICHMAN T Lefoy A Critical Study of Four Plays by Sir John Suckling
      MA George Washington Univ 1941 116 p
8006 SULLIVAN Victoria Sir John Suckling: Poet and Cavalier MA Columbia
      1965 83 p
8007 WOODARD Carolyn H The Drama of Sir John Suckling MA Columbia 1941
See also 4890

ARTHUR SEYMOUR SULLIVAN

8008 HAMM Mary E High School Teaching Problems in Sullivan's *Pirates of
      Penzance* MA Univ of Iowa 1935
8009 HARKINS Kathleen H A Critical Analysis of the Gilbert and Sullivan
      Operas MA Boston Univ 1946
8010 SCOTT Nancy C Five Little Known Operas of Gilbert and Sullivan
      MA Univ of Kansas 1966
See also 3427, 3429, 3430, 3433, 3434

JONATHAN SWIFT

8011 ALEXANDER Gwendolyn M A Survey of Criticism on Jonathan Swift's
      Gulliver's Travels from 1930 to 1964 MA Howard Univ 1965 127 p
8012 ALLMAN Eileen J Jonathan Swift and the Form of Satire: Voyage III
      of *Gulliver's Travels* MA Syracuse Univ 1966 119 p
8013 ALSTON R C Jonathan Swift: A Guide to Biographical and Critical
      Studies 1750-1950 BA Univ of British Columbia (Canada) 1954
8014 BESTER Beatrice An Interpretation of *A Voyage to the Houyhnhnms*
      MA Washington St Univ at Pullman 1939
8015 BOSTROM Irene Swift and Society MA Univ of North Dakota 1927 48 p
8016 BOYD David R Jonathan Swift at the School at Kilkenny MA Columbia
      1941
8017 BREWER Rose S Literary and Bibliographical Allusions in Swift's
      Journal to Stella MA Univ of Texas at Austin 1924
8018 BRIDEN Earl F The Element of "Anti-" Poetry in Jonathan Swift's
      Verse Satires MA Brown Univ 1966
8019 BRISMAN Leslie The Internalization of the Hack: Satiric Persona
      from Melville to Swift MA Cornell Univ 1966
8020 BURNS Verna C Jonathan Swift's Use of the Proverb MA Indiana Univ 1940
8021 CALDER Robert L Women in the Writings of Jonathan Swift
      MA Saskatchewan (Canada) 1965
8022 CHAVIS Trisha P Jonathan Swift's Use of a Fictional Universe in Four
      Treatise Satires MA Auburn Univ 1969

8023 CLARK Richard D Unifying Devices in *A Tale of a Tub* MA Univ of
     British Columbia (Canada) 1961 164 p
8024 COHON Hortense The Political Writings of Jonathan Swift: 1710-1714
     MA Columbia 1960 133 p
8025 COLE Elmer *The Drapier's Letters*: A Study in Swift's Rhetorical
     and Satirical Methods MA Montana St Univ 1965
8026 COOK Richard A Rhetorical Analysis of Swift's *History of the Four
     Last Years of the Queen* MA Washington Univ at St Louis 1953
8027 COSHOW Betty G The Dramatic Method in Swift's Verse MA Univ of
     Oklahoma 1957
8028 COX Geraldine C Jonathan Swift: Humanitarian or Misanthrope
     MA Univ of Maryland at College Park 1968 87 p
8029 CRAMPTON Nancy The Influence of Cyrano de Bergerac's *Voyages to
     the Sun and the Moon* on Jonathan Swift's *Gulliver's Travels*
     MA Butler Univ 1935
8030 DeWOODY Florence H Treatment of Women in Swift's Poetical Works
     MA Hardin-Simmons Univ 1962
8031 DICKEY Alice K An Undismayed Flaying: Comment on Several Poems
     by Jonathan Swift MA Univ of Nebraska 1965
8032 DIEMER Jane Swift's Views on Religion as Revealed in His *Examiner*
     MA Univ of Houston 1966 100 p
8033 EDMAN John H Jonathan Swift and the Muse of Poetry: The Years of
     His Youth MA Syracuse Univ 1952 103 p
8034 ELLIOTT James N Critical Estimates of Jonathan Swift during the
     Victorian Era MA Oklahoma St Univ 1966
8035 ELSER Arthur G Swift's Use of Multiple Personae in *A Tale of a Tub*
     MA Oklahoma St Univ 1966 61 p
8036 FAVARO Cecilia *The Battle of the Books* in Its Historical Setting
     MA Ca Foscari (Italy) 1946
8037 FOGARTY Patricia E A Study of the Influence of Rabelais' "Royaulme
     de la Quinte Essence" upon Swift's Academy of Lagado MA Univ of
     North Carolina at Raleigh 1959 61 p
8038 FOWLER Doris A Comparison of Mark Twain and Jonathan Swift as
     Satirists MA North Texas St Univ 1946
8039 FRANKENBERGER Earl C Jr Digressive Unity in *A Tale of a Tub*
     MA Texas Christian Univ 1967 50 p
8040 FRIEDMAN Anabel H Delusion at Wit's End: Aspects of Jonathan Swift's
     Singularity as Revealed in His Poetry MA Univ of Maryland at
     College Park 1966 65 p
8041 FULLER Gerry W Twentieth Century Criticism of Swift's Poetry
     MA Univ of Maine 1969 129 p
8042 GARVICK John D Swift's Christian Idealism and the "Ethos of
     Irreverence" MA Univ of Delaware 1965 66 p
8043 GRAHAM Edward Examining Swift's *Examiner* MA Columbia 1960 122 p
8044 HANDLER Dorothy E Swift's "Voyage to Laputa" and Its Place in
     Gulliver's Travels MA Univ of New Mexico 1962
8045 HANSEN Richard E The Techniques of a Tory Propagandist:
     Jonathan Swift, 1710-1714 MA Duke Univ 1966
8046 HARMENING Louis W Religious Satire in Swift's *Gulliver's Travels*
     MA Northern Illinois Univ 1965
8047 HAYDEN Gloria H Jonathan Swift and Women M Ed Central Washington
     St Coll 1966 117 p
8048 HERSEY William R The Political Satire in Jonathan Swift's Poetry
     MA Boston Coll 1966
8049 HIATT John A The Fool as a Speaker in the Satire of Jonathan Swift
     BA Amherst 1955
8050 HOBAN Joseph P The Importance of Swift's Residence at Moor Park
     to His Early Writings MA Univ of Arizona 1958 85 p
8051 HOLCOMB S B Jonathan Swift as a Satirist MA North Texas St Univ 1939
8052 HOMIER Donald F Jonathan Swift and the Persona of Lemuel Gulliver:

A Study of Twentieth Century Criticism on *Gulliver's Travels*
MA Univ of Toledo 1970
8053 IZZO Carlo Jonathan Swift MA Ca Foscari (Italy) 1925
8054 JOHN Harrison W Jonathan Swift: His Political Satire in Ireland
after 1720 MA Univ of Maryland at College Park 1969 60 p
8055 JONES Ruth E The Sceptical Stripe in Swift's Common Sense Banner
MA George Washington Univ 1950 143 p
8056 JOSEPHINE Sr Mary Swift and Counter-Enthusiasm: Aspects of the
Religious Thought of Jonathan Swift MA Boston Coll nd
8057 JOSEPHSON Mundi I Politics and Government in Selected Writings
of Jonathan Swift after 1715 MA Saskatchewan (Canada) 1964
8058 KANE H F The Influence of French Authors on Jonathan Swift
MA Boston Univ 1939
8059 KELLY Constance M Swift and "Wood's Halfpence" MA Hunter Coll 1962
8060 KINGERY Lucille C Jonathan Swift's *Directions to Servants*
MA Columbia 1951
8061 KINNEEN Martha F Jonathan Swift's Idea of History MA Boston Coll 1960
8062 KIRCHMEIR Wolfe E The Major Themes of Swift's Satiric Verse
MA Alberta (Canada) 1965
8063 KNIGHTS Paul A Jonathan Swift: Propagandist MA Louisiana St Univ 1941
8064 LAKE A C An Interpretation of Swift's Political and Social Philosophy
BA Univ of British Columbia (Canada) 1938
8065 LAMB Alma R The Digressions Concerning Critics and Madness in *A Tale
of a Tub* and Their Relations to the Story M Ed Henderson St Coll nd
8066 LANIER Genevieve What the Travels Did to Lemuel Gulliver MA Auburn
Univ 1949 117 p
8067 LEONARD James B "It's a Mad World, My Masters": An Inquiry into the
Sources of Swift's Comedy and Satire in Relation to Their Artistic
Expression MA Queen's (Canada) 1965
8068 LEWIS Hunter C The Religious Beliefs of Dean Swift MA Univ of British
Columbia (Canada) 1928
8069 LIGHTFOOT John E Jr Jonathan Swift: Political Journalist MA Baylor
Univ 1967 114 p
8070 LINDERMAN Deborah Beyond Satire: Fantasy and Absurdity in Works of
Jonathan Swift and Francisco de Goya MA Columbia 1967 110 p
8071 LOFTON Thomas A The Background in Jonathan Swift's Yahoo Man
M Ed Henderson St Coll nd
8072 LUK Elizabeth The Imagery of *The Drapier's Letters* by Jonathan Swift
MA Hardin-Simmons Univ 1955
8073 McGOVERN B F Peculiar Greatness of Swift's Satire MA Boston Coll 1934
8074 MACKIN Mary M Jonathan Swift: His Last Ten Years MA John Carroll Univ
1966
8075 McMILLAN Theresa K The Hack in Swift's *A Tale of a Tub* Compared with
Tristram in Sterne's *Tristram Shandy* MA Univ of British Columbia
(Canada) 1967
8076 MASON Katherine J Jonathan Swift: The Whimsical Dean MA Texas
Christian Univ 1949 90 p
8077 MATHEWSON George A A Study of *Gulliver's Travels* BA Amherst 1957
8078 MOORE Robert M The Dissected Spirit: A Survey and Critical Evaluation
of the Psychoanalytical Studies and Interpretations of Jonathan Swift
MA Univ of Maryland at College Park 1966
8079 MORGAN Gussie C Swift as a Literary Critic MA Tulane Univ 1929
8080 MOUNT James R A Re-Evaluation of the Fourth Voyage of Lemuel Gulliver
MA Auburn Univ 1960
8081 MURRAY Donald M Swift's Attitude toward Women MA Univ of Kentucky 1940
8082 NUCKOLS Samuel C Swift and Religion MA Univ of Kentucky 1938
8083 OCHSNER Shirley M The Scriblerus Club: An Important Association
for Jonathan Swift MA Mankato St Coll 1968 76 p
8084 PIKE Frank Swift's Journeys between England and Ireland MA Boston
Coll 1957

8085 POULTRIDGE Richard H Jonathan Swift's Use of the Earl of Wharton
      in His Political Satire MA Syracuse Univ 1950 69 p
8086 POWELL Dorothy Jonathan Swift's Literary Criticism MA Louisiana St
      Univ 1937
8087 PUTMAN Alan D Literary and Rhetorical Techniques in Swift's
      Drapier's Letters MA Toronto (Canada) 1965
8088 RAHN Beverly J Gulliver's Travels: Imaginary Voyage or Utopia?
      MA Columbia 1961 232 p
8089 RODRIGUEZ Angelo An Analysis of the Fourth Voyage of Gulliver's
      Travels and Its Relevance to the Twentieth Century MA Pacific Univ
      1969 90 p
8090 RUTHERFORD Shelley H Jonathan Swift in the History of the English
      Novel MA Oklahoma St Univ 1969 209 p
8091 SACHS William C Elements of Structure in A Tale of a Tub MA Univ of
      Redlands 1966
8092 SCHAEFFER Neil J Fools Among Knaves: A Study of Swift's Tale of a
      Tub MA Columbia 1964 80 p
8093 SCHUBART William R Swift's Attitude toward His Own Writings
      MA Columbia 1941
8094 SENSEMANN Wilfred M Four Eighteenth Century Biographers of Swift
      MA Columbia 1935
8095 SEYMOUR Mary H "That Ridiculous Passion": A Commentary on Five
      Marriage Poems by Jonathan Swift MA Univ of Delaware 1967 54 p
8096 SIBLEY Homer Dean Swift and His Educational Program MA Univ of
      Oregon 1934
8097 SIMS James H Theological Implications in the Works of Jonathan Swift
      MA Univ of Florida nd
8098 SINGLETON Flossie R The Religious, Political, Social and Economic
      Concepts in the Sermons of Jonathan Swift MA Howard Univ 1955 167 p
8099 SISSON James E Satire in Gulliver's Travels: A Synthesis of Inter-
      pretations of Swift's Satire, with Particular Reference to Book IV
      MS Auburn Univ 1947 121 p
8100 SMITH Bedford D Swift's Allegorical Apologetics and the Interpretation
      of A Tale of a Tub MS Ft Hays Kansas St Coll 1966
8101 SNELLING Robert D A Rhetorical Analysis of The Drapier's Letters
      of Jonathan Swift MA Stanford Univ 1965
8102 SNYDER Philip J The Reputation of Jonathan Swift, 1883-1908
      MA Columbia 1952 222 p
8103 STEVENS Francis R Jr Vive la Bagatelle: A Study of Jonathan Swift's
      Literary Trivia MA Columbia 1967 75 p
8104 STONE Sarah C The Irony of Swift MA Univ of Texas at Austin 1949 69 p
8105 STRINGER Gary A Relativity as an Artistic Technique in Gulliver's
      Travels MA Univ of Oklahoma 1966
8106 SUTHERLAND Raymond C Jr The Religious Background of Swift's A Tale
      of a Tub MA Univ of Kentucky 1950 126 p
8107 TAFT William W The Experience of Satire: A Reading of Jonathan Swift
      BA Amherst 1954
8108 TANCO Francis B Anti-Intellectualism in Swift's Major Works MA Baylor
      Univ 1949 117 p
8109 TARRAVECHIA Richard A Comparison of the Types and Methods of Satire
      in Gulliver's Travels and Candide MA Univ of Tennessee 1951 81 p
8110 THOMASSON Mary N The Depravity of Man as Seen in Gulliver's Travels
      M Ed Henderson St Coll nd
8111 THOMSON P G The Polemical Writings of Jonathan Swift BA Univ of
      British Columbia (Canada) 1948
8112 TIMMONS Mary B The Criticism of Swift's "Voyage to the Houyhnhnms",
      1915-1955 MA Univ of Tennessee 1956 81 p
8113 TOOMEY Ned Lemuel Gulliver: A Character Study MA West Texas St Univ
      1958 93 p
8114 VADEN Lillie T The Scholarship of Jonathan Swift's Gulliver's Travels

                    MA Howard Univ 1941
8115 VIFIAN John L   An Examination of the Critical Reaction to Swift's
        Poetry   MA Washington St Univ at Pullman 1956
8116 VITZTHUM Richard C   The Voices of Jonathan Swift   BA Amherst 1957
8117 VIVION F W   Some Constructive Ideas in Swift's *Gulliver's Travels*
        MA North Texas St Univ 1937
8118 WADEN Gladys W   Jonathan Swift's Minor Irish Tracts: Their Purpose
        and Method   MA Baylor Univ 1964   181 p
8119 WELCH George W   Folly, the Grubstreet Hack and the Troglodyte Philo-
        sopher: Erasmus and Swift's Creation of a Satiric Character
        MA Temple Univ 1966   45 p
8120 WHITE John H   Swift's Trojan Horses: The Role of the Houyhnhnms in
        Gulliver's Fourth Voyage   MA Oklahoma St Univ 1957   91 p
8121 WILSON James R   The Narrators of Jonathan Swift   MA Univ of Oklahoma
        1953
8122 WILSON Norman W   Antipuritanism in the Satire of Jonathan Swift
        MA Univ of Oregon 1941
8123 WINNARD Winifred   Jonathan Swift: Apostle of Moral Reconstruction
        MA Univ of Oregon 1933
8124 WITKOWSKI Susan S   Criticism of Swift's "Voyage to the Houyhnhnms"
        MA North Texas St Univ 1966
8125 WOODRING C R   Swift's Opinions of Contemporary English Literary
        Figures   MA Rice 1942
8126 WRIGHT Marie   Influential Backgrounds on Jonathan Swift's Writings
        as Revealed in *Gulliver's Travels*   M Ed Henderson St Coll nd
8127 ZBAR Flora J   The Change in the Critical Approach to *Gulliver's
        Travels*, Book IV, from the Beginning through 1961   MA Florida
        St Univ 1961   53 p
8128 ZWEIG Joseph E   Jonathan Swift and Mark Twain: A Study in Methods
        of Satire   MA Univ of Pittsburgh 1962
See also 1035, 2437, 2893, 2923, 3111, 3495, 4269, 4409, 4767, 5915, 5922
        7930

                    ALGERNON CHARLES SWINBURNE

8129 ARMFIELD Frank   Influences of Gautier and Baudelaire upon Swinburne
        MA Univ of North Carolina at Chapel Hill 1934
8130 BECK Thaddeus E Jr   Swinburne's Holy Muse: A Study of His Use of
        the Bible in *Songs before Sunrise*   MA Columbia 1961   167 p
8131 BECKER Anne L   Swinburne and the Folk Ballad   MA Washington Univ at
        St Louis 1933   152 p
8132 BENEMAN Charles H   Three Crowns for a Queen: A Study of Swinburne's
        Trilogy on Mary Queen of Scots   MA George Washington Univ 1947   169
8133 BUTCHART Montgomery   The Concepts of Liberty of Algernon Charles
        Swinburne   MA Univ of Pittsburgh 1928
8134 EAKER J Gordan   Swinburne's Growth toward a Philosophy of Life
        MA Univ of Iowa 1931
8135 ELLISON Lee M   The Non-Dramatic Poems of Swinburne   MA Univ of Texas
        at Austin 1914
8136 EVANS Kennedy   Swinburne in Relation to the Radical Thought of His
        Age   MA Texas Woman's Univ 1936
8137 GARBE Paul F   Swinburne's Poetry of the Sea   MA Wayne St Univ 1965
8138 JOHNSON Florence M   Swinburne: The Critic   MA Univ of Pittsburgh 1927
8139 KNIGHT Richard H   Subjectivitiy in the Tragedies of Algernon Charles
        Swinburne   MA Washington Univ at St Louis 1937   106 p
8140 LINDSEY Martha   Swinburne's Dramatic Substance and Technique
        MA Washington St Univ at Pullman 1932
8141 LONGO Renata   Swinburne and Mazzini   MA Ca Foscari (Italy) 1938
8142 LYON Nanna M   The Paganism of Swinburne   MA Columbia 1942
8143 McCAIN Ida H   Swinburne's Mary Stuart Trilogy   MA Univ of Texas at
        Austin 1940   175 p

8144 MIRICH Mark Swinburne's Theory of Poetic Drama MA Washington St Univ
      at Pullman 1940
8145 PRIM Philip L Animal Symbolism in Book I of *The Faerie Queene*, An
      Explication of Swinburne's *Hertha* and the Nature Poetry of
      Emily Dickinson MA Pennsylvania St Univ 1965
8146 PULLMAN Leonard Swinburne and Sadism: The Influence of the
      Marquis de Sade in *Poems and Ballads* (First Series) MA Columbia
      1964 108 p
8147 RIDDENHOUGH G The Revolutionary Element in Swinburne's Poetry
      BA Univ of British Columbia (Canada) 1924
8148 RON CAGLIA Rosamaria The Drama of Algernon Charles Swinburne
      MA Ca Foscari (Italy) 1952
8149 SAXTON Susan M *The Poems and Ballads*, First Series, and *Songs before
      Sunrise* of Algernon Charles Swinburne: A Re-Evaluation MA Indiana
      Univ 1963
8150 SMITH Laura B The Significance of Swinburne in the History of British
      Prosody MA Texas Woman's Univ 1934
8151 SPIVEY G C Elizabethanisms in Swinburne's Tragedies MA Univ of
      North Carolina at Chapel Hill 1925
8152 STEWART D S A Critical Study of Algernon Charles Swinburne's
      Atalanta in Calydon, with Special Reference to the Hellenic
      Influence on Swinburne's Thought and to Its Effect on His Plot,
      Imagery, Symbolism and Language B Litt Oxford Univ (England) 1950
8153 THOMAS M P The Shadowless Soul: Parallel Ideas on Nietzsche and
      Swinburne MA North Texas St Univ 1968
8154 THOMPSON Thelma R Algernon Charles Swinburne: No Other God, a
      Vision of Life MA Univ of Oklahoma 1968 269 p
8155 WELLS Mary A The Dramatic Technique in Swinburne's Historical Trilogy
      MA Texas Technological Univ 1934
See also 849, 894, 1440, 4608, 4957, 5215, 8463

                         JOHN MILLINGTON SYNGE

8156 ALDRIDGE M J John Millington Synge as a Dramatist MA Boston Univ 1941
8157 ALLEN Pearl S Poetic Elements in the Irish Dramas of John Millington
      Synge MA Oklahoma St Univ 1930 67 p
8158 BANDLER David B Jr Synge's *Playboy of the Western World* as Seen
      through a Study of the *Playboy* Riots MA Columbia 1966 72 p
8159 BARATTA Parker Death and the Vision of Emptiness in the Plays of
      John Millington Synge MA Columbia 1961 77 p
8160 BARTON Maude M John Millington Synge and the Irish Renaissance
      MA Univ of Oklahoma 1931
8161 CASTNER Barbara A An Archetypal Pattern in the Plays of
      John Millington Synge MA Univ of Maine 1969 132 p
8162 CRYAN James F The Symphonic Structure of Synge's *Deidre of the
      Sorrows* MA Univ of Toledo 1970
8163 DUNPHY Rev James R Music in Synge's *Riders to the Sea* MA Boston
      Coll 1965
8164 FORDE Pamela J Synge's Anomaly Dramatic Theory and Practice in
      Deidre of the Sorrows MA Boston Coll 1968
8165 GOTTFRIED Ethel A Study of the Criticism of the Plays of
      John Millington Synge MA Columbia 1942
8166 GREIDERER Edith M The Irish Peasant in Representative Novels of
      Samuel Lover and Charles Lever and in Representative Plays of
      John Millington Synge MA Washington Univ at St Louis 1939 256 p
8167 GURRY Sr Mary R Imagery in the Plays of John Millington Synge
      MS Kansas St Coll at Pittsburg 1937
8168 HARRINGTON John F Death and Loneliness: The Central Forces in the
      Plays of John Millington Synge MA Washington St Univ at Pullman 1966
8169 HART Rev William E A Critical Text of John Millington Synge's

The Playboy of the Western World MA Boston Coll 1964
8170 HUDSON E Jean *The Playboy of the Western World:* A Thesis Production
      MA Univ of Southern Mississippi 1964
8171 JACOBS Willis D John M Synge in the Irish Literary Renaissance
      MA Univ of New Mexico 1937
8172 JAST Ilda John Millington Synge MA Ca Foscari (Italy) 1963
8173 JONES Jennye S The Celtic Temperament as Reflected in the Works of
      John Millington Synge MA Oklahoma St Univ 1938
8174 KELLY Susan S A Comparative Study of the Drama of John Millington Syng
      and Federico Garcia Lorca MA East Tennessee St Univ 1969
8175 KENNEDY C A Synge's Portrayal of the Irish MA Boston Coll 1933
8176 LANGPAP Karen R John Millington Synge: A Study in Dramatic Imagery
      MA Auburn Univ 1965 131 p
8177 LAWSON Jonathan M John M Synge: Regional Dramatist MA Texas Christia
      Univ 1966 103 p
8178 LEVENE Mark J Poet, Nature and Woman in the Plays of J M Synge
      MA Toronto (Canada) 1966
8179 McCARTHY William E The Natural World of John Millington Synge
      MA Univ of Massachusetts 1969 86 p
8180 McDERMOTT P J John Millington Synge and His Plays: Their Realism
      and Technique MA Boston Coll 1927
8181 MONDZAC Stephanie P The Theatrical Technique of John Millington Synge
      MA Univ of Vermont 1965
8182 NOLL Arthur J A Project in Stage Direction for the Production of
      John M Synge's *The Playboy of the Western World* MA San Diego St Col
      1964 217 p
8183 O'CONNOR J J John Millington Synge MA Boston Coll 1938
8184 O'DWYER Jeremiah A The Irish Temperament in the Plays of
      John Millington Synge MA Univ of Arizona 1961 94 p
8185 PARCELL Marjorie R Celtic Folklore in the Dramas of John Millington
      Synge MA Univ of Arizona 1944
8186 RAFFIN Lucia John Millington Synge: *In the Shadow of the Glen* and
      Riders to the Sea MA Ca Foscari (Italy) 1967
8187 RATZ Margaret S John Synge: Irish Dramatist MA Univ of Pittsburgh 1?
8188 SCHMELZER Diana M John Millington Synge's *Deidre of the Sorrows*
      MA Univ of Maryland at College Park 1968 108 p
8189 SCHRIMSHIRE Stephanie John Synge's Green World MA Brigham Young Univ
      1963 120 p
8190 SELVER Vasanti A Tagore and Synge and Their Common Denominator
      MA Columbia 1951
8191 SHEEHAN Joseph D The Anglo-Irish Medium Employed by John M Synge
      MA St Louis Univ 1946 86 p
8192 SIDDALL David V The Plays of John Millington Synge MA Columbia 1960
      109 p
8193 SIMMONS Robert M John Millington Synge's Development as a Poet MA Un:
      of Rhode Island 1966 61 p
8194 STOTT William John Millington Synge: The One-Act Play MA Columbia
      1963 67 p
8195 TURNER David M Word Patterns in the Drama of John Millington Synge
      MA Manitoba (Canada) 1967
8196 WANDERER Pauline W Death and Vagrancy in the Life and Works of
      John Millington Synge MA Univ of Colorado 1965

JEREMY TAYLOR

8197 FULLAM William F The Presentation of Death in Jeremy Taylor's
      Holy Dying MA Columbia 1953 61 p
8198 HAMILTON Inez C A Study of the Erudition of Jeremy Taylor MA Wash-
      ington St Univ at Pullman 1940
8199 HOLMES David L The Early Career of Father Taylor MA Columbia 1960 6

8200 LOGAN William M Jeremy Taylor: "The Chrysostom of the English Pulpit"
      MA Univ of Texas at Austin 1937 141 p
8201 WILSON Gladys I The Literary Aspects of the Sermons of Jeremy Taylor
      MA Howard Univ 1934 53 p

WILLIAM TEMPLE

8202 FANT Delanie B William Temple and Reinhold Niebuhr: A Study on
      Nature of Man MA Emory Univ 1965
8203 MacLEOD Bessie J The Moral Philosophy of Sir William Temple
      MA Univ of Oregon 1938
8204 OBERMEIER Ella B Uses of "Shall" and "Will" in the Letters of
      Sir William Temple MA Univ of Iowa 1931
See also 527

ALFRED TENNYSON

8205 ACKERMAN Robert *In Memoriam*: A Review of Criticism MA Columbia 1962
      82 p
8206 BAILEY Leslie G Illustrations of Tennyson's Scientific Sensibility
      MA Baylor Univ 1966 217 p
8207 BAKER William H The Structure of *In Memoriam* MA Univ of Oklahoma 1961
8208 BARTRAM William Unification of Imagery, Word Music, Mood or Tone,
      and Levels of Meaning for Poetic Effect as the Main Factor of
      Technique in the *Idylls*: "Gareth and Lynette", "Lancelot and Elaine",
      "Balin and Balan" and "The Passing of Arthur" MA Bowling Green Univ
      1959
8209 BELL Brenda H The Victorian Hero and Tennyson's *Idylls of the King*
      MA Texas Technological Univ 1967 39 p
8210 BENDER Sidney R Alfred Lord Tennyson's English Historical Trilogy
      of *Queen Mary*, *Harold* and *Becket* MA Texas Arts and Industries
      Univ 1965
8211 BISHOP John K The Women in Tennyson's Poetry MA Univ of Texas at
      Austin 1940 106 p
8212 BLUE Eliza The Common Folk in Tennyson MA Tulane Univ 1926
8213 BONIS Margaret E Tennyson as the Voice of Victorian England MA McGill
      (Canada) 1936
8214 BOWERMAN Elma M Tennyson as a Descriptive Artist MA Northwestern Univ
      1903
8215 BRANDT Mary J The Bible in Tennyson M Ed Temple Univ 1933 201 p
8216 BROWN D E The Poetry of Tennyson's Old Age, 1880-1892 MA Univ of
      London (England) 1964
8217 CAHILL Sr Mary A Tennyson in the Hands of Catholic Reviewers
      MA St Mary's at San Antonio 1949 93 p
8218 CARANDINI Alda The Sources of Tennyson's *Idylls of the King*
      MA Ca Foscari (Italy) 1948
8219 CARLSON Alma S The Influence of the English Bible on the Diction
      of Alfred Tennyson M Phil Northwestern Univ 1903
8220 CARROLL Br James A Study of the Criticism of Alfred Lord Tennyson
      in the Nineteenth Century *Quarterly Review* MA St Mary's at
      San Antonio 1945 103 p
8221 CHASE Jane A *Idylls of the King* MA Northwestern Univ 1900
8222 CHRISTENSEN Merton A Alfred Lord Tennyson's Attitude toward Roman
      Catholicism MA Univ of Maryland at College Park 1950 88 p
8223 COGSWELL B L Tennyson's *In Memoriam*: A Study MA Boston Univ 1895
8224 COMBS Cecil S The Optimism of Tennyson MA Indiana Univ 1942
8225 CURTIS Br George The Influence of Conscience in *The Idylls of the
      King* MA St Mary's at San Antonio 1940 69 p
8226 DAWSON Clarence W Auditory Imagery in Tennyson's Poetry MA Hardin-
      Simmons Univ 1940

8227 DERBYSHIRE Samuel H Tennyson's Interest in Three Phases of
      Victorian Literature: Poetry, Science and Theology MA Columbia 1937
8228 DEVAKUL Suraja The Development of the Theme of Death in the Work of
      Alfred Lord Tennyson up to and Including *In Memoriam* MA Univ of
      New Brunswick (Canada) 1965
8229 DONAHUE Sr Mary L Tennyson's Relation to the Scientific Thought of
      the Nineteenth Century MA Marquette Univ 1924   47 p
8230 DONAHUE Thomas S Voyage Imagery in the Poetry of Alfred Tennyson
      MA Miami Univ 1964
8231 DOUGHERTY Faye V Tennyson's Purpose in the Use of the Bible
      MA Univ of Tulsa 1950
8232 EISOLD Barbara Alfred Lord Tennyson: A Study of His Changing Self-
      Image MA Columbia 1960   64 p
8233 ELLIOTT Phillip L Jr Tennyson's Poet Laureate Poems MA Univ of
      North Carolina at Raleigh 1958   111 p
8234 ERICSON Eston E The Main Currents of Alfred Tennyson's Time: In
      Science, Theology and Philosophy MA Univ of Maryland at College
      Park 1925   83 p
8235 FAIRES R S Philosophy of Tennyson's *Idylls of the King* MA Univ of
      North Carolina at Chapel Hill 1909
8236 FALK Sr Francis B Artistic Unity in Tennyson's *Maud* MA Boston Coll 196
8237 FARMER James S *Maud* and Its Relation to Its Time MA Univ of North
      Carolina at Raleigh 1950   116 p
8238 FAULK Ruth T Robinson, Tennyson and the Arthurian Legend MA Auburn
      Univ 1948
8239 FINNERTY T T Tennyson MA Boston Coll 1932
8240 FOREMAN Charles W A Study of Alfred Tennyson's Cambridge Confusion
      MA Univ of Pittsburgh 1938
8241 FORESTER Ailsey The Psychology of Feminine Behavior in Tennyson's
      Dramas and Narrative Poems MA Texas Woman's Univ 1937
8242 FREUNDLICH Lawrence S Tennyson's Two Voices MA Columbia 1962   60 p
8243 GENTRY Elsie Tennyson: Literary Creator of Moods M Ed Henderson
      St Coll nd
8244 GIVSON Faye Alfred Lord Tennyson: Literary Symbol of His Era
      M Ed Henderson St Coll nd
8245 GRAVES James F Tennyson's Poems (1833): A Reproduction in Typescript
      with the Revisions of 1842 MA Univ of North Carolina at Chapel Hill
      1951   372 p
8246 GRAY Merle W Tennyson's Treatment of the Character of Women
      MS Kansas St Coll at Pittsburg 1933
8247 GREB Dorothy L Tennyson's Social Interests MA Washington Univ at
      St Louis 1938   162 p
8248 GREEN Carlanda Ulysses in Nineteenth Century Literature MA Auburn
      Univ 1969
8249 GUNTER Garland O Archetypal Patterns in the Poetry of Tennyson,
      1923-1950 MA Univ of Maryland at College Park 1966
8250 GUYER June L Tennyson's Use of Celestial Bodies in His History
      MA Hardin-Simmons Univ 1953
8251 HAFFEY Dorothy H Water Imagery in Tennyson's Major Poems MA Texas
      Arts and Industries Univ 1965
8252 HAGAN Sr Mary P Summary of Tennysonian Criticism: 1929-1939
      MA St Louis Univ 1944   203 p
8253 HAMNER John T A Study of Melancholia in Tennyson's Major Work to 1855
      MA Univ of Texas at Austin 1950   88 p
8254 HANCOCK J B Man-Made Structures in Tennyson's Poetry MA Hardin-
      Simmons Univ 1952
8255 HARRAL Eliza G Tennyson's *The Princess*: A Medley MA Tulane Univ 1896
8256 HARRIS Lela H The Use of Birds in Tennyson's Poetry MA Hardin-
      Simmons Univ 1953
8257 HARRISON Sarah W Color as a Poetic Device in the Poetry of Tennyson

MA Univ of Tennessee 1948

8258 HASKELL H B   Tennyson as a Religious Teacher   MA Univ of Maine 1906   25 p

8259 HAWICK Mildred   Types of Women Characters Portrayed in *The Idylls of the King*   MA St Mary's at San Antonio 1940   69 p

8260 HENDRICKSON Amanda E   Tennyson's Reaction to the New Scientific Knowledge   MA Univ of North Dakota 1933   34 p

8261 HIRASAWA Retsuko   Pictorial Presentation in Tennyson's Poetry   MA Univ of Florida 1965

8262 HORMACHEA Christine X   Critical Opinion on *The Princess*   MA St Mary's at San Antonio 1945   106 p

8263 HORSMAN Nancy C   A Phonological Approach to Tennyson's *Maud*   MA Univ of British Columbia (Canada) 1969   79 p

8264 HOUSE Faye S   Tennyson's Use of Classical Mythology   MA Univ of Tulsa 1949

8265 HOUSTON Percy H   Tennyson: The Representative Poet of His Age   MA Williams Coll 1904

8266 HURST Billie R   Tennyson and His Victorian Social Consciousness   MA Baylor Univ 1954   154 p

8267 IMMEL Betty   Religion in the Poetry of Alfred Lord Tennyson   MA North Texas St Univ 1947

8268 JOHNSON David D   Arthurian Romance in Tennyson and Other Victorian Poets   MA West Virginia Univ 1903   246 p

8269 JOHNSON Lee E   Symbolism in *The Idylls of the King*   MS Kansas St Coll at Pittsburg 1956

8270 JOHNSTON Bertha M   Identification of Biblical Allusions in Selected Writings of Tennyson   MA Univ of North Dakota 1932   59 p

8271 JUDGE Alice M   The Social Views of Alfred Tennyson   MA Tulane Univ 1926

8272 KAPLAN Susan S   A Motif Study of *The Foresters*: *Robin Hood and Maid Marion*, a Play by Alfred Lord Tennyson   MA Univ of Maryland at College Park 1965   85

8273 KARP Dorothy   The Influence of the Old Testament on the Poetry of Alfred Lord Tennyson   MA Columbia 1936

8274 KEE Grace J   Proverb Lore in Tennyson's Poetical Works   MA Baylor Univ 1955   99 p

8275 KEEFER Robert L   Tennyson's Sources for *Harold*   MA Univ of Maryland at College Park 1964   73 p

8276 KILLHAM E J   Tennyson's *The Princess*: A Study with Special Reference to the "Woman Question"   MA Univ of London (England) 1953

8277 KNIGHT Ella J   The Conflict between Good and Evil in *The Idylls of the King*   MA West Texas St Univ 1966   91 p

8278 KNOX Leona   Tennyson's *Idylls of the King*   MA Univ of Texas at Austin 1930

8279 KUMPFER Petronilla A   Contemporary English Criticism of Alfred Tennyson from 1830 to 1847   MA Tulane Univ 1933

8280 KYNOCK Kevin C   A Critical Examination of the Imagery in the Plays of Alfred Lord Tennyson   MA Boston Coll 1966

8281 LAIRD Robert G   From Image to Symbol: Water Imagery and Its Relation to the Theme of the Quest in Tennyson's Poetry   BA Univ of British Columbia (Canada) 1963

8282 LAURENT Martha L   Tennyson and the Poetry of *The Germ*: A Study of the Early Pre-Raphaelite Poets' Relation to Tennyson   MA Univ of Georgia 1965

8283 LEWIS Roger C   Modes of Statement in *In Memoriam*: Tennyson   MA Toronto (Canada) 1964

8284 LIU Hsiao C   Tennyson's Literary Friends   MA Baylor Univ 1949   215 p

8285 LOWE Florence C   A Comparison of the Versions of Certain of Tennyson's Poems before and after His Ten Years Period of Non-Productivity, 1832-1842   MA Oklahoma St Univ 1936   142 p

8286 McCALL Margaret   The Spirit of Compromise in Tennyson's Poetry   MA Univ of Oregon 1936

8287 MALACHIAS Nicholas Z Tennyson and the Theatre MA Columbia 1951
8288 MALOCSAY Jan P The Odyssean Tennyson: Some Aspects of Classical
      Artistry in Seven Poems MA Univ of Tulsa 1965   60 p
8289 MARKHAM Robert C A Study of Tennyson's Historical Trilogy MA Univ
      of Richmond 1954   102 p
8290 MITCHELL William R Theological Origins of the Christ-Image in
      Victorian Literature with Special Reference to *In Memoriam*
      MA Univ of Oklahoma 1970
8291 MOFFATT J S Tennyson, Spenser and the Renaissance MA Univ of North
      Carolina at Chapel Hill 1917
8292 MONTROY Barbara Tennyson and Science MA Univ of California at
      Riverside nd
8293 MORGAN Violet E Tennyson's *Idylls* and Their Sources MA Boston Univ
      1937
8294 MORRELL Minnie C A Comparative Study of Spenser's *The Faerie Queene*
      and Tennyson's *The Idylls of the King* MA Univ of Tennessee 1935
8295 MUKOYAMA Yoshihiko The Idea of Progress in Tennyson's Poetry
      MA Baylor Univ 1960   83 p
8296 MURRAY Sr Mary V *In Memoriam*: A Study of Tennyson's Ambivalence
      MA Boston Coll 1963
8297 NEUFELDT Jerry The Public and the Private Poet in Tennyson from
      Early Poems to *In Memoriam* BA Univ of British Columbia (Canada) 196
8298 NEWTON Lewis W The Portrayal of Common Life in Modern English Poetry
      with Special Reference to Tennyson MA Univ of Texas at Austin 1907
8299 NORMAN Elsie A Background and History of Tennyson's Plays
      MA Baylor Univ 1949   134 p
8300 NYBERG Benjamin Tennyson's *Becket*: A Critical Comparison of the
      Arrangement for the Stage by Henry Irving with the Original Version
      MA Univ of Arizona 1959   57 p
8301 OLIVAS Br Bonaventure L Queen Mary in the Drama of Tennyson and in
      the Light of History MA St Mary's at San Antonio 1940   84 p
8302 PAGE Trudie M Tennyson's Message to Mankind M Ed Henderson St Coll nd
8303 PAYNE Jamie J Tennyson's Treatment of Nature MA Tulane Univ 1926
8304 POWELL Everett G Tennyson's Changing Views on the Evolution-of-Man
      Theory as Reflected in His Poetry MA Texas Arts and Industries
      Univ 1961
8305 POWER Dorothy S The Role of Mystical Experiences in the Life and
      Works of Alfred Tennyson MA Mississippi St Univ 1966
8306 PRICE Lucy E Tennyson's Religious Doubt and Faith MA Univ of
      Tennessee 1925
8307 RAMSDELL Grace R Philosophical Implications in Tennyson's *In Memoriam*
      MA Boston Univ 1933
8308 REICHERT Cleta M The Spirit of Nationalism in the Poetry of Tennyson
      MA Washington Univ at St Louis 1940   120 p
8309 RICHARD Anita The Mabinogion Source of *The Idylls of the King*
      MA St Louis Univ 1941   67 p
8310 RIDDLE Bernice S The Dramas of Tennyson MA Univ of Iowa 1924
8311 RIGGS Sparta E A Study of Mediaevalism in Tennyson's *Idylls of the
      King* MA Univ of Texas at Austin 1934
8312 ROBINSON Nellie W The Development of the Arthurian Legend as Found
      in Tennyson's *Idylls of the King* BA Univ of Oklahoma 1909
8313 ROGERS Franklin R A Comparison of Tennyson's *In Memoriam* and Hugo's
      Pauca Meae MA Fresno St Coll 1951   148 p
8314 SCHREINER Sr Marie C A Comparative Study of the Grail Poems of
      Hawker and Tennyson MA Boston Coll 1938
8315 SCHWALBAUM Joan Tennyson's Use of Dream, Trance and Madness
      MA Columbia 1965   155 p
8316 SCOTT Mattie B A Story of Tennyson's Use of His Sources in Five
      Idylls of the King MA Univ of Louisville 1914
8317 SHERMAN Eva M A Comparative Study of the Treatment of the Arthurian

Legend by Alfred Tennyson and by Edwin Arlington Robinson
MA Boston Univ 1932
8318 SHIELDS Virginia   Tennyson and the Ulysses Theme   MA Univ of Georgia
1965
8319 SHIREMAN Julia H   The Ebb and Flow of Tennysonian Criticism
MA Univ of Texas at Austin 1940   118 p
8320 SINFIELD A J   The Style of Tennyson's *In Memoriam* and Its Bearing
on Meaning and Structure   MA Univ of London (England) 1967
8321 SKEWES Alice R   A Study of Metaphor and Simile in Tennyson's Poetry
MA Univ of California at Berkeley 1924
8322 SKLAVOUNOU Diana   Alfred Tennyson as a Writer of Dramatic Monologues
MA Montreal (Canada) 1966
8323 SLOAN Rollin P   Didacticism in the Art of Tennyson   MA Univ of Texas
at Austin 1931
8324 SMITH Elizabeth M   *The Idylls of the King*: Studies in Plot-Structure
and Characterization   MA Univ of Texas at Austin 1927
8325 SMITH Elton E   The Palace and the Grail: Tennyson and the Recessive
Tendency   MA Syracuse Univ 1959   113 p
8326 SMITH Frellsen   The Dramas of Tennyson   MA Univ of Texas at Austin 1930
8327 SMITH Marta M   Woman in Tennyson   MA Univ of Texas at Austin 1901
8328 SPANGENBERG Alice   Tennyson's Attitude toward Science   MA Boston Univ
1925
8329 SPEIRS James G   Social and Political Thought of Tennyson in Relation
to His Age   MA Toronto (Canada) 1966
8330 STEINBACH Georgianna   Tennyson: His Views on God and Immortality
MA Univ of Arkansas 1951
8331 STEVENS Beatrice L   Tennyson: An Interpreter of His Age   MA Boston
Univ 1949
8332 STEWART Pearl L   The Significance of Tennyson's "The Promise of Way"
and Its Relation to the Intellectual Currents of the Times
MA Univ of Arkansas 1933
8333 STOREY Kenneth E   An Analysis of the Songs in Tennyson's *The Princess*
MA Univ of Tennessee 1965
8334 SYPHER Francis J Jr   Pastoral Elements in the Poetry of Tennyson
MA Columbia 1964   51 p
8335 THOMAS Percy E   Tennyson's Philosophy of Life   MA Northwestern Univ 1901
8336 TIPTON Robert L   Tennyson's Use of Malory's *Le Morte D'Arthur* in
"The Coming of Arthur"   MA Texas Arts and Industries Univ 1964
8337 TURNER Mildred E   The Influence of Biological Science on Tennyson
from 1833 to 1850, as Shown in His Writings   MA Oklahoma St Univ
1932   47 p
8338 TUSSING Adeline C   Manifestations of the Puritan Spirit in the Works
of Alfred Tennyson   MA Univ of North Dakota 1923   65 p
8339 TYSON Frances E   Musical Allusions in Tennyson's Poetry   MA Hardin-
Simmons Univ 1954
8340 VAN DEN NOORT Judokus   Theology in Tennyson   MA Boston Univ 1923
8341 VERCHERE R   Tennyson's Self-Criticism as Exemplified in the Revisions
of the 1833 Volume   BA Univ of British Columbia (Canada) 1922
8342 VINING R H   Tennyson's *In Memoriam*: An Introduction and Analysis
MA Boston Univ 1917
8343 WARE Malcolm R   Tennyson and the Romantic Tradition   MA Univ of
Tennessee 1951   96 p
8344 WEARDEN Dorothy M   Alfred Lord Tennyson: Poet Laureate   MA Univ of
Texas at Austin 1948   103 p
8345 WELCH Michael J   Circumstances in the Lives of Tennyson and His
Friends as Reflected in His Poetry   MA Boston Univ 1937
8346 WELLBORN Grace P   Tennyson's Conception of the Soul   MA Hardin-Simmons
Univ 1934
8347 WILEY Margaret L   The Religious Poems of Tennyson with Especial
Reference to Present Day Unrest   MA Univ of Texas at Austin 1924

8348 WILSON Jean A The Indebtedness of T S Eliot to Alfred Lord Tennyson
      MA St Univ of New York at Buffalo 1966
8349 WITTENBERG Corrine H The Way of Two Souls: A Study of the Philosophic
      Explorations of *In Memoriam* by Alfred Tennyson and *Moby Dick* by
      Herman Melville MA Purdue Univ 1969 87 p
8350 WOOD Cecile S A Study of the Characters in *Queen Mary* MA Baylor Univ
      1940 167 p
8351 WORTHY Mary E A Study of Tennyson's Use of Nature in *In Memoriam*
      MA Hardin-Simmons Univ 1952
8352 WYMER Thomas L Romantic to Modern: Tennyson's Aesthetic and Religious
      Development MA Univ of Oklahoma 1967 142 p
8353 YOUNGS Marie Some Revisions in Tennyson (Based on the 1830, 1833 and
      1842 Volumes) MA Washington Univ at St Louis 1918 77 p
See also 636, 764, 805, 849, 1053, 1801, 4947, 4948, 4955, 4957, 4964,
      4967, 4969, 5241, 6123, 6290, 6872

WILLIAM THACKERAY

8354 BARSS Margaret L Thackeray and the Schools of His Time as Revealed
      in His Writings MA Columbia 1941
8355 BELL Ruby M Plot-Structure in the Novels of William Makepeace Thackera
      MA Univ of Texas at Austin 1917
8356 CHENEY Merlin G *Vanity Fair* and *Gone With the Wind*: A Critical
      Comparison MA Brigham Young Univ 1966
8357 COAINA Sr Mary The Chorus in the Novels of Thackeray MA Univ of
      Texas at Austin 1929
8358 DEAN Cecil H Thackeray and the Eighteenth Century MA Univ of
      Pittsburgh 1926
8359 DELMAN Alice Thackeray the Art Critic MA Columbia 1951
8360 ELLISON Gerald V Tone and Point and View in Thackeray's *Henry Esmond*
      MA Texas Agricultural and Mechanical Univ 1966 93 p
8361 GIDDINGS Thomas H Biblical References in Thackeray's Five Major
      Novels MA Univ of Texas at Austin 1937 183 p
8362 GRANT William A The Historical Accuracy of Thackeray in *Henry Esmond*
      and *The Virginians* MA Univ of Kentucky 1933
8363 HARRIS Victor I Thackeray in America MA Univ of Virginia 1932
8364 IRELAN Nancy L Fool, the Week-Day Historian: The Narrator of
      Vanity Fair MA Univ of Oklahoma 1970
8365 JENKS Mary H Thackeray's Reading MA Univ of Tennessee 1945
8366 KOSSOVSKY Celia Marriage and Divorce in Thackeray's Novels
      MA Columbia 1935
8367 LOGAN R Louise A Translation of Life into Archetype: The Character-
      ization of Women in Thackeray's Early Works MA Temple Univ 1967 4
8368 McBRIDE Mary E William Makepeace Thackeray and His Prose Contribution
      to *Punch* MA Univ of Pittsburgh 1959
8369 McGLOTHLIN Belle Thackeray's Portrayal of Woman MA Univ of Texas
      at Austin 1926
8370 McGREGOR Marietta American Piracies of the Writings of
      William Makepeace Thackeray, 1838-1863 MA Columbia 1937
8371 MARTIN Marne C Thackeray's *English Humorists* Studies as Compared
      with the *Quarterly Review's* Nineteenth Century Estimation of These
      Same Men MA Columbia 1950
8372 MAUSKOPF Charles G Thackeray's Narrative Technique in *Vanity Fair*
      MA Univ of North Carolina at Chapel Hill 1958 145 p
8373 MURCHISON John T Jr *Vanity Fair* as a Composite Novel MA Columbia 196
      124 p
8374 OLIVER Velma K Thackeray's Critiques of Upper Middle Class English
      Society MA Univ of Maine 1938 83 p
8375 PAYNE Evelyn P The Irish Characters in Thackeray's Fiction MA Rice 1
8376 PHILLIPS Julia Thackeray's Narrative Technique MA Washington Univ

at St Louis 1939
8377 PLUMKETT F W The Early Works of William Makepeace Thackeray: A Con-
      sideration of Thackeray as a Critic of Contemporary Life MA Rice 1926
8378 REED Ruth B Religious Characters in Thackeray's Novels MA Univ of
      Texas at Austin 1936
8379 RICHARDSON Barrett R Thackeray and The Cornhill Magazine MA Univ of
      North Carolina at Chapel Hill 1950 118 p
8380 SMITH Marion K American Echoes of Vanity Fair MA Brigham Young Univ
      1966 117 p
8381 SPAULDING Kenneth War and Peace Concepts in the Works of Thackeray
      MA Univ of Montana 1937 61 p
8382 STOKER Ray C Characterization in the Novels of Thackeray MA Univ
      of Texas at Austin 1923
8383 TANNER Orea B Thackeray's Portrait of the American MA Columbia 1953
      127 p
8384 TODARO Rosella Realism and Satire in the Works of William Makepeace
      Thackeray MA Ca Foscari (Italy) 1949
8385 WILBAND Hazel G Thackeray: A Study MA Univ of British Columbia
      (Canada) 1920
8366 WILEY Mary R The Bible in Thackeray M Ed Temple Univ 1936 97 p
8387 XAVIER Sr Mary T The Objects of Thackeray's Satire MA Univ of North
      Dakota 1934 100 p
8388 ZACCARELLI Liliana The Historical Novels of William Makepeace Thackeray:
      A Reconsideration MA Columbia 1953 83 p
See also 2559, 8545

                              DYLAN THOMAS

8389 AMABILE George N The Patchwork Ark: A Study of the Poetry of
      Dylan Thomas BA Amherst 1957
8390 ASTLEY Russell The Stations of the Breath: A Study of End-Rhyme
      in the Poetry of Dylan Thomas MA Temple Univ 1967 62 p
8391 ATKINSON William "The Mad Doctor's Bag": A Study of Dylan Thomas'
      "Altarwise by Owl-Light" BA Univ of British Columbia (Canada) 1970
8392 BODENSTEIN Beatrice E Concordance to Eighteen Poems by Dylan Thomas
      MA Columbia 1955 153 p
8393 BROWNING Grayson D The Poetry of Dylan Thomas MA Univ of Texas at
      Austin 1955 152 p
8394 CLAIBORNE Jay W The Rub of Love: A Study of Humor in the Writings
      of Dylan Thomas MA Univ of Texas at Austin 1965 123 p
8395 CUMMINGS David E The Language of Dylan Thomas MA Columbia 1954 82 p
8396 DANIELS John H The Legend of the Green Chapel: A Study in the Back-
      ground and Attitude of Dylan Thomas MA Syracuse Univ 1955 194 p
8397 DELAP Anne M The Development of Dylan Thomas' Use of Private
      Symbolism in Poetry MA Oklahoma St Univ 1967 81 p
8398 DICKSON Karen "Reminiscences of Childhood" in the Poetry of
      Dylan Thomas BA Univ of British Columbia (Canada) 1965
8399 GINGERICH Martin E The Intricate Image: Two Poems of Dylan Thomas
      MA Univ of Maine 1961 55 p
8400 HAGGARD Ann B A Morphological Study of the Process of Compounding
      in the Poetry of Dylan Thomas MA Auburn Univ 1969
8401 HALPEREN Max "Moonless Acre": The Poetry of Dylan Thomas MA Florida
      St Univ 1952
8402 HAVEMANN C P Obscurity and the Mythic Quest for Shape: A Discussion
      of Dylan Thomas' "Altarwise by Owl-Light" MA Rice 1968
8403 HERBISON Robert Dylan Thomas and the Art of the Short Story: A
      Critical Consideration of Some Early Short Stories BA Univ of
      British Columbia (Canada) 1964
8404 HOGGINS Carolyn The Nightmare World of Dylan Thomas MA Texas Tech-
      nological Univ 1964 97 p

8405 JASIECKI Dorothy The Preposition in the Poetry of Dylan Thomas
      MA Barry Coll 1966
8406 JO Sue-Jin M Dylan Thomas and the Tradition of the Romantic Journey
      MA Columbia 1966   79 p
8407 LANTHIER Philip J Nature, Time and Style in the Poetry of
      Dylan Thomas MA Toronto (Canada) 1963
8408 LAWNICZAK Donald The Recurrent Image: A Study of Dylan Thomas
      MA Univ of Toledo 1961
8409 LEWIS Ward B Jr The Struggle from Darkness to Light: A Study in
      Development of the Poetry of Dylan Thomas BA Amherst 1960
8410 LIGHTNER Barbara E Some Creative-Destructive Processes in
      Dylan Thomas' Poetry MA Univ of Idaho 1966
8411 McKAY Donald F Dylan Thomas' Cosmology MA Western (Canada) 1966
8412 MILLER Joseph J The Grammar of Dylan Thomas in *Collected Poems*
      MA Columbia 1959   44 p
8413 MOFFETT Ethel A Dylan Marlais Thomas: Man and Metaphor MA George
      Washington Univ 1954   171 p
8414 MONRO Colin J "The Existentialist Void and the Divine Image":
      The Poetry of Dylan Thomas MA Univ of British Columbia (Canada)
      1962   136 p
8415 MOYNIHAN William T Dylan Thomas and the Auditory Correlative
      MA Univ of Connecticut 1957
8416 OCHSHORN Myron The Poetry of Dylan Thomas MA Univ of New Mexico 1953
8417 PHILLIPS Louis J Jr The Screen Plays by Dylan Thomas MA Hunter Coll
      1968
8418 PIORKOWSKI Stephen Dylan Thomas: Poet and Dramatist MA Hunter Coll
      1964
8419 RAFFORD Robert I Dylan Thomas Speaks BA Rutgers St Univ 1957   80 p
8420 REESE Bette Dylan Thomas: A Discussion of Macabre and Humorous
      Elements in His Early Prose MA Utah St Univ at Logan 1967
8421 RONAN John J Jr Dylan Thomas' Use of the Bible MA Univ of Illinois
      at Chicago Circle 1969
8422 RUARK Henry G Death Is all Metaphors: A Study of the Death Theme
      in the Poetry of Dylan Thomas MA Univ of Massachusetts 1965
8423 SANDERS Charles Poetic Characteristics and Problems of Dylan Thomas
      MA Univ of North Carolina at Chapel Hill 1958   66 p
8424 SEAMAN Andrew T The Poetry of Dylan Thomas: Studies in Form and
      Meaning MA Dalhousie (Canada) 1966
8425 SMOOT George A Metamorphosis and Dylan Thomas' "Ballad of the Long-
      Legged Bait": The Poetics of Harmonious Conflict MA Syracuse Univ
      1967   122 p
8426 SPANGLER Donald R A Collection of Explications of the Poetry of
      Dylan Thomas MA Univ of Pittsburgh 1954
8427 STAFFORD Tony J Dylan Thomas: The Obscurant MA Univ of Texas at
      El Paso 1961   119 p
8428 THOMAS David E The Moral Vision of Dylan Thomas MA Montreal (Canada)
      1963
8429 TIMMONS Grace A A Study of the Welsh Influences on Dylan Thomas'
      Poetry MA West Texas St Univ 1967   73 p
8430 WILSON Jeanne The Inspiration and Craft of Dylan Thomas BA Univ of
      British Columbia (Canada) 1967
8431 ZIMAN Ann P *Eighteen Poems*: With Dylan Thomas' Accent on Death
      MA Columbia 1955   69 p
See also 514,

FRANCIS THOMPSON

8432 BURNS John J Imagery of Francis Thompson MA Boston Coll 1948
8433 CARTER G F Francis Thompson as a Myth-Maker MA North Texas St Univ 1
8434 COLLINS J F Thompson and Davidson MA Boston Coll 1930

8435 CONLON T E Francis Thompson MA Boston Coll 1932
8436 CONNOLLY Eileen E Francis Thompson: Poet of Mysticism MA Boston Univ
      1945
8437 DANEHY T F Thompson's Hierarchial Vision of Creation MA Boston Coll
      1934
8438 DOOLAN James R Francis Thompson: A Study in Imagery and Mysticism
      MA Columbia 1961 84 p
8439 DUNN Joseph F Francis Thompson: His Thought and Personality as
      Reflected in His Works MA Univ of Texas at Austin 1935
8440 FLYNN Sr M Saint Augustine Pagan Symbolism in the Poetry of
      Francis Thompson MA Boston Coll 1945
8441 GEORGE Joseph J Francis Thompson: The Poet Revealed in His Images
      MA Boston Coll 1949
8442 GRAHAM Phyllis Francis Thompson and the Franciscan Spirit MA Columbia
      1962 75 p
8443 GUINAN Sr Agnes C Francis Thompson: An Aristotelian Critic MA Boston
      Coll 1945
8444 HANSON Sr Mary B The Imagery in Certain Poems of Francis Thompson
      MA Univ of Hawaii 1945 299 p
8445 HAWKINS Seth C Cosmic Symbolism and Nature Imagery in the Poetry
      of Francis Thompson MA Boston Coll 1964
8446 HENLE Robert J Lucretius' and Francis Thompson's Poetic Interpretation
      of the Universe MA St Louis Univ 1932 105 p
8447 HERLIHY Sr Julie B Thompson: Magian of the Sun MA Boston Coll 1937
8448 KESSINGER Sr Mary D A Concordance to *The Man Has Wings* of
      Francis Thompson MA Boston Coll 1964
8449 KILEY F L Francis Thompson's Elements of Poetry MA Boston Coll 1936
8450 KING Sr Monessa Ignatian Humility in the Life and Works of
      Francis Thompson MA Boston Coll 1943
8451 KUNKEL Sr Mary N Francis Thompson MA Boston Coll 1940
8452 LANDRIGAN J J A Study of Francis Thompson's "Ode to the Setting Sun"
      MA Boston Coll 1930
8453 LEE G C A Comparison between Francis Thompson's Treatment of Nature
      in *Poems* and that in *New Poems* MA Boston Coll 1937
8454 LOGUE S M Influence of Francis Thompson on Plunkett M Ed Boston Coll
      1933
8455 McCARTHY M Josephine Latinisms in the Poems of Francis Thompson
      MA Boston Coll 1945
8456 MARY Sr Matilda Francis Thompson as a Mystical Poet MA Univ of
      Oregon 1936
8457 MULDOON Emily G The Mysticism of Francis Thompson MA Univ of
      Pittsburgh 1937
8458 NORTON Sr Elizabeth M Autobiographical Reflexes of Francis Thompson
      Inspired by the Motif of Childhood MA Boston Coll 1942
8459 O'HARE Sr James Spirituality of Francis Thompson's Poetry MA Boston
      Coll 1929
8460 PILKINGTON May The Glossary of the Vocabulary of Francis Thompson's
      Poetry MA Univ of Kansas 1928
8461 QUINN Sr Ellen Imagery in the Poetry of Francis Thompson MA Boston
      Univ 1949
8462 REX Helen M The Ritualistic Tendency of Francis Thompson MA St Louis
      Univ 1929 72 p
8463 SAVARIA Sr Madeline G A Comparative Study of the Philosophy of Pain
      of Algernon Charles Swinburne and Francis Thompson MA Boston Coll 1945
8464 WALKER Sr Helen C Death-to-Self Theory of Francis Thompson MA Boston
      Coll 1935
8465 ZAGST Sr Mary S Francis Thompson: His Mind and Art MA Univ of Texas
      at Austin 1925
See also 2350, 2359, 2363, 3844

JAMES THOMSON

8466   BURKETT Tommy R James Thomson's Tragedies and the New Oppositions
       to Walpole MA Rice 1960
8467   COUTURIER Marie P Structural Patterns in Thomson's *Seasons*
       MA Toronto (Canada) 1966
8468   ERICKSEN Kenneth J James Thomson ("B V") in Search of a Creed with
       Particular Emphasis on the Doom of a City MA Rice 1963
8469   GATES Barbara T A Critical Study of Unity of James Thomson's *Seasons*
       MA Univ of Delaware 1961   50 p
8470   GERINO Marie R The Poetry of James Thomson MA Univ of Pittsburgh 1939
8471   GREGORY Florence I James Thomson: The Relation of His Works to His
       Life MA Univ of Maryland at College Park 1940   63 p
8472   GREGORY Joseph F Circumlocutions in Thomson's *Seasons* MA St Louis
       Univ 1941   85 p
8473   HILL Nancy K James Thomson "B V" and the Pessimistic Tradition
       MA Columbia 1962   72 p
8474   KEENAN Anna M James Thomson as a Follower of Spenser MA Univ of
       Minnesota 1932
8475   McKELLEGET Barbara James Thomson's Tragedies MA Columbia 1942
8476   McLOUGHLIN James G The Prophetic Tradition in the Works of
       James Thomson, "B V" MA Columbia 1966   55 p
8477   MARRA Giulio *The Seasons* by James Thomson MA Ca Foscari (Italy) 1968
8478   MENON Mida James Thomson: His Poetical and Patriotic Soul
       MA Ca Foscari (Italy) 1929
8479   MONTGOMERY Katherine W A Concordance to James Thomson's *Spring*
       MA Univ of Texas at Austin 1936
8480   MUKHERJEE S C The Poetry of James Thomson ("B V"): A Study in
       Imagery and Diction MA Leeds Univ (England) 1964
8481   POTTER Gordon V James Thomson and His *City of Dreadful Night*
       MA George Washington Univ 1948   88 p
8482   RHEA Robert L James Thomson: Nature Poet MA Univ of Texas at Austin
       1931
8483   SAPIENZA Grace M L'Influence des *Saisons* de James Thomson sur les
       Saisons de Saint-Lambert MA Hunter Coll 1941
8484   STALLINGS Louise R The Darling Theme: James Thomson and the Tradition
       of Nature Poetry MA Texas Christian Univ 1960   118 p
8485   SUHADOLO Josef James Thomson, Poet of *The Seasons* MA Ca Foscari
       (Italy) 1953
8486   WOLFE M J James Thomson ("B V"): His Connection with Contemporary
       Fashions in Thought and Literature B Litt Oxford Univ (England) 194
See also 3844, 8855

J R R TOLKIEN

8487   ADAMS Sarah S The Role of Gandalf in J R Tolkien's *The Lord of the
       Rings* MA Univ of Maryland at College Park 1967   64 p
8488   CAINE William R A Comparison of the Major Works of J R Tolkien
       and E R Eddison MA Lamar Technological Univ 1969
8489   CHURCH Michael T The Poetic Novels of Kafka, Tolkien and Hawkes:
       Creating the Imagination of Mass Man MA Auburn Univ 1969
8490   ELGIN Don D The Romantic Imagination: A Study of Romantic Thought
       in the Critical Writings of J R Tolkien MA Texas Technological
       Univ 1967   85 p
8491   FOWLER Sigrid H Speech Patterns in J R Tolkien's Trilogy *The Lord
       of the Rings* MA Emory Univ 1966
8492   GARLING David Good and Evil in *Lord of the Rings* BA Univ of British
       Columbia (Canada) 1967
8493   KEMP Margaret A Study of *The Lord of the Rings* by J R Tolkien
       MA Dalhousie (Canada) 1966

8494 LEVITIN Alexis A   J R Tolkien's *The Lord of the Rings*   MA Columbia 1964
      109 p
8495 LLOYD Linda N *Lord of the Rings* and the Meaning of History   MA Univ
      of Houston 1967   67 p
8496 LYDAY Jo W   Sehnsucht in J R Tolkien's *The Hobbit* and *The Lord of*
      the Rings   MA Lamar Technological Univ 1967   109 p
8497 ST CLAIR Gloria A   Studies in the Sources of J R Tolkien's *The Lord*
      of the Rings   MA Univ of Oklahoma 1970
8498 STEPHENSON Carol A   Fantasy as an Art Form: An Analysis of J R Tolkien's
      The Lord of the Rings   BA Univ of British Columbia (Canada) 1967
8499 STONE M C   *The Lord of the Rings*: An Examination of Mythic Elements
      MA East Tennessee St Univ 1970
8500 STONER William W   The Relationship of *The Hobbit* and *The Lord of the*
      Rings   MA Univ of Maryland at College Park 1966   53 p
8501 TEDHAMS Richard W   An Annotated Glossary of the Proper Names in the
      Romances of J R Tolkien   MA Univ of Oklahoma 1966
8502 TUCK M P   Tolkien's Elvish   MA North Texas St Univ 1968

                        CYRIL TOURNEUR

8503 BOLTON Phyllis L   Cyril Tourneur: Dramatist   MA George Washington Univ
      1951   113 p
8504 CONTINI Tiziano   *The Revenger's Tragedy* Attributed to Cyril Tourneur
      MA Ca Foscari (Italy) 1967
8505 CORRINGTON John W   Cyril Tourneur's *The Revenger's Tragedy*: The Moral
      Content   MA Rice 1958
8506 DELISLE H F   The Satiric Voice of Cyril Tourneur   MA Boston Coll 1959
8507 LARSEN Judith R   Tourneur Over Again   MA Columbia 1967   85 p
8508 PINCISS Gerald M   Morality and Sex in the Plays of Cyril Tourneur
      MA Columbia 1960   46 p
8509 RUDOLFO Giovanni   *The Atheist's Tragedy* by Cyril Tourneur   MA Ca Foscari
      (Italy) 1965
8510 SCHNEIDER Jack W   *The Atheist's Tragedy*: The Atypical Revenge Tragedy
      MA Texas Technological Univ 1969   71 p
8511 SCHULTZ Stephen C   The Concept of Usury in the Plays of Cyril Tourneur
      MA Stanford Univ 1966
8512 ZELAZNY Roger J   Two Traditions and Cyril Tourneur: An Examination
      of Morality and Humor Comedy Conventions in *The Revenger's Tragedy*
      MA Columbia 1962   71 p
See also 6848

                        THOMAS TRAHERNE

8513 BLANKENSHIP Clifford W   A Critical Approach to the Poetry of
      Thomas Traherne   MA Univ of Tulsa 1958   93 p
8514 CABRINI Sesto   Thomas Traherne   MA Ca Foscari (Italy) 1950
8515 CARROLL C Edward   "Summer in December": Thomas Traherne and Some
      Seventeenth Century English Devotional Writers   MA Univ of Toledo 1950
8516 CONE Floyd M   Thomas Traherne and the Poetic Tradition of the
      Restoration   MA Univ of New Hampshire 1966   44 p
8517 CONLON Jon R   Thomas Traherne and Edward Taylor: Their Mystical
      Quest   MA Univ of Houston 1968   71 p
8518 DEMARAY Hannah D   Thomas Traherne, Poet of the Absolute: A Study of
      the Thought and Light Imagery of Thomas Traherne   MA Columbia 1962
      104 p
8519 DIXON Norma E   The Influence of Neoplatonic Idealism and Philosophic
      Realism in the Works of Thomas Traherne   MA Brooklyn Coll 1965
8520 EBERLY Joyce E   The Imagery of Thomas Traherne Based on a Study of
      His Poems   MA Georgetown Univ 1960   172 p
8521 ENOMOTO Randall   Thomas Traherne: The Interior Vision   BA Univ of

British Columbia (Canada) 1965
8522 FIELDS Joan L   The Symbolic Third Eye in the Poetry of Thomas Traherne
     MA Univ of Kentucky 1964   104 p
8523 FORBES Violet E   The Originality in Thomas Traherne   MA Univ of
     Pittsburgh 1957
8524 GUTHRIDGE Sue   An Analysis of Thomas Traherne's *Centuries of Meditation*
     MA Butler Univ 1949
8525 HUNTER Charles S   Prophet of Felicity: A Study of the Intellectual
     Background of Thomas Traherne   MA McMaster (Canada) 1965
8526 LEE Keunsup   Thomas Traherne's World of Imagination   MA DePauw Univ
     1963   31 p
8527 MAY E   A Study in the Mysticism of Thomas Traherne   MA Florida St Univ
     1947
8528 MOLCK-UDE Susan B   Thomas Traherne's Conception of Childhood   MA Hunter
     Coll 1966
8529 RANDOLPH Jamesena C   Thomas Traherne's Conception of Sin   MA Syracuse
     Univ 1963   57 p

                              ANTHONY TROLLOPE

8530 BALSLEY Eugenia L   Trends in the Criticisms of Anthony Trollope's
     Novels Since 1948   MA Univ of Pittsburgh nd
8531 BARRY Anna B   Characterization in *The Barsetshire Chronicles*
     MA Univ of Texas at Austin 1931
8532 BJORKMAN Lynn R   Anthony Trollope: A Re-Evaluation of the Barset
     Novels   MA Brigham Young Univ 1965
8533 BRIDGES Katherine F   Ireland and the Irish in the Works of
     Anthony Trollope   MA Univ of Texas at Austin 1955   290 p
8534 BURKETT Grace D   Trollope's Theory of the Novel as Seen in the
     Barsetshire Group   MA Univ of Texas at Austin 1934
8535 BUSNESS Clare H   The Heroine Pattern in Trollope's Barsetshire Novels
     MA Florida St Univ 1949   73 p
8536 CROMPTON Rosamond   The Role of the Villain in the Works of
     Anthony Trollope   MA Columbia 1966   123 p
8537 CROUCH William G   Anthony Trollope: An Estimate of His Art as a
     Novelist   MA Univ of Pittsburgh 1927
8538 DWYER Charles L   The Contemporary Criticism of Trollope's *Barchester
     Chronicles*   MA Univ of Texas at Austin 1951   90 p
8539 GALIN Saul   Anthony Trollope: A Study of His Reputation in Periodical
     Magazines, 1847-1884   MA Columbia 1950
8540 GILLIKIN Haywood W   Anthony Trollope's *The Warden*: A Study of Rhetoric
     MA East Carolina Univ 1968
8541 GOTTLIEB Manuel   The Development of the *Barset Chronicles*   MA Columbia
     1965   147 p
8542 GOUDIE Jean H   The Autobiographical Element in the Novels of
     Anthony Trollope   MA Columbia 1935
8543 GRANT Ella K   Anthony Trollope's Literary Reputation   MA Univ of
     British Columbia (Canada) 1950   94 p
8544 GROSSI Giorgia   A Victorian Novelist: Anthony Trollope   MA Ca Foscari
     (Italy) 1948
8545 HAWTHORNE Mark D   Trollope's *Thackeray*: One Phase of Victorian
     Biography   MA Univ of Florida 1964
8546 INNESS Lowell   Novels of Anthony Trollope: A Study of Changing Literary
     Taste   MA Univ of Pittsburgh 1925
8547 KNOX James C   The Civil Man: A Critical Study of Fictional Culture
     in the Novels of Anthony Trollope   BA Amherst 1970
8548 LEE James W   Clerical Types in the Novels of Anthony Trollope
     MA Auburn Univ 1957
8549 LONG Edna L   Archibald Marshall: The Reincarnation of Anthony Trollope
     MA Univ of Toledo 1922

8550 McKENNA Samuel N Trollope and Hippopotamus MA Univ of Louisville nd
8551 MILES Ted Trollope's Advice to Novelists as Illustrated in the
       Barsetshire Novels MA Washington St Univ at Pullman 1951
8552 MOORE Robert H Anthony Trollope's Treatment of the Novel MA Indiana
       Univ 1940
8553 REDDICK Bryan D Several Characteristics of the Omniscient Technique
       in Fiction by Trollope, George Eliot and Lawrence: A Beginning
       Study of the Aesthetics of Point of View MA Syracuse Univ 1966 86 p
8554 ROBINSON Helen V Realism as Shown in Anthony Trollope's Barsetshire
       Novels MA Univ of Texas at Austin 1937 119 p
8555 ROLLINS Sarah F Contemporary Criticism of Anthony Trollope MA Univ
       of Texas at Austin 1963 165 p
8556 SCHWEIGHAUSER Charles A Anthony Trollope: A Critical Discussion
       MA Williams Coll 1960
8557 SINKS Nellie M The Barsetshire of Trollope and His Continuators
       MS Kansas St Coll at Pittsburg 1954
8558 STOVER Frances M The Victorian Church as Shown in the Novels of
       Anthony Trollope MA Bowling Green Univ 1938
8559 TUOHY A L Individual Note in Trollope's Barchester Novels MA Boston
       Coll 1938
8560 VINCENTE Remigio The Tragic View of Life in the Barsetshire Novels
       BA Univ of British Columbia (Canada) 1967
8561 WALKER Isaac N Contemporary Criticism of Trollope's Parliamentary
       Novels MA Univ of Texas at Austin 1955
8562 WALLIN Elvira B Anthony Trollope: A Study of Social Satire in His
       Barsetshire Novels MA Oklahoma St Univ 1941 79 p
8563 WALTON Elizabeth C The Influence of the Cathedral Setting on the
       Characters in the Novels of Anthony Trollope and Hugh Walpole
       MA Boston Univ 1931
8564 WILLIAMS Zula W A Study of the Clergymen in the Novels of
       Anthony Trollope MA Univ of Texas at Austin 1935
8565 WILSON Helen V A Study of Feminine Characters in *The Chronicles
       of Barsetshire* MA Univ of Pittsburgh 1931

HENRY VAUGHAN

8566 ANKER Ruth C An Interpretation of the Child in the Poetry of
       Henry Vaughan MA Columbia 1961 79 p
8567 CALDWELL Mary L A Study of Selected Translations of Henry Vaughan
       MA Syracuse Univ 1949 93 p
8568 CAMPBELL Morag D Platonic Concepts of Man and Cosmos in the Poetry
       of Henry Vaughan MA Manitoba (Canada) 1967
8569 DUVALL Robert F Biblical Imagery in the Poetry of Henry Vaughan
       MA Claremont Graduate School 1965
8570 FALK Evelyn R Scriptural Basis of Henry Vaughan's Eschatology
       MA Bowling Green Univ 1962
8571 FOY Norma Henry Vaughan's Hermetic Imagery MA Columbia 1951
8572 FRUM Austin P Henry Vaughan: A Search for a New Language BA Amherst
       1955
8573 GALBRAITH James An Anatomy of Evil: A Study of the Imagery of
       Henry Vaughan MA St John's Univ 1965
8574 GAUDETTE Sr Rita Henry Vaughan and the "Circle of Perfection"
       MA Boston Coll 1954
8575 HEYEN James A Henry Vaughan, Biblicist: A Study of *Silex Scintillans*
       MA Univ of Iowa 1965
8576 KNUTSON Lucille M The Inner Life of Henry Vaughan as Revealed in
       His Religious Verse MA Washington St Univ at Pullman 1943
8577 LOONEY Robert F Henry Vaughan's Prosody MA Univ of North Carolina
       at Chapel Hill 1955 70 p
8578 LYONS John O Henry Vaughan: A Study in Seventeenth Century Poetic

Symbolism MA Univ of Florida 1954
8579 RIDDICK Joseph M Henry Vaughan and the Book of the Creatures
      MA Vanderbilt Univ 1965
8580 SANELLI Alfred Henry Vaughan: The Way to Innocence MA Columbia 1966
      96 p
8581 SELDEN Lynn Henry Vaughan and the Bible MA Columbia 1966 117 p
8582 SHORE Dave The Portrait of a Mystic: A Study of the Mystical
      Imagery of Vaughan's *Silex Scintillans* BA Univ of British Columbia
      (Canada) 1965
8583 SWAB Joseph N The Light Imagery of Henry Vaughan MA Univ of Delaware
      1969 94 p
8584 SWAIM Joan H Biblical Themes in Henry Vaughan's *Silex Scintillans*
      MA Texas Christian Univ 1968 87 p
8585 VINCENT James C Figure and Image in Henry Vaughan's *Silex Scintillans*
      MA Univ of Oregon 1941
See also 2738, 3946, 3947, 3951, 3972, 3979, 4525, 5121

HORACE WALPOLE

8586 BLAKELY Gladys F Horace Walpole: A Critic of Literature MA Univ of
      Iowa 1924
8587 CONKWRIGHT Nancy T The Literary Criticism of Horace Walpole as
      Contained in His Letters MA Washington Univ at St Louis 1940
8588 DUGDALE Grant The Background of Horace Walpole's *Historic Doubts
      on the Life and Reign of King Richard the Third* MA Columbia 1950
8589 HATCH Ronald B Horace Walpole and the New Taste for Gothic
      MA Univ of British Columbia (Canada) 1964
8590 JONES Edna F Literary Criticism in Horace Walpole's Letters
      MA Univ of Oklahoma 1935
8591 KIMELS Sophie B Horace Walpole as a Literary Critic MA Columbia 1935
8592 MILLER Florence E Horace Walpole the Literary Critic MA Howard Univ
      1945
8593 MILLER Harvey D A Study of Horace Walpole and His Relation to the
      Stage MA Univ of Maine 1927 171 p
8594 MILLER Phillip J The Art of Living: A Discussion of Horace Walpole's
      Correspondence with Special Emphasis on His Letters to George Montag
      MA Idaho St Univ 1964
8595 TUCKER Ruth W Horace Walpole and British Imperialism MA Univ of
      Maine 1928 216 p
8596 WENTWORTH Helen B A Study of Horace Walpole as a Critic of the
      Eighteenth Century English Literature MA Univ of Maine 1926
8597 WILSON Theressa B Horace Walpole: A Study of His Literary Taste
      MA Univ of Pittsburgh 1929
8598 YORK Katherine M Horace Walpole's Criticism of Comedy MA Univ of
      Oregon 1941
See also 5974, 5977, 7609

HUGH WALPOLE

8599 GOMMELLINI Natale Hugh Walpole the Novelist MA Ca Foscari (Italy) 193
8600 McCARTHY John T Hugh Walpole: *The Herries Chronicle* MA Toronto
      (Canada) 1967
8601 MANNING Ethel Characterization in Ten of Hugh Walpole's Novels
      MA Univ of Texas at Austin 1938 125 p
8602 PORTER J M Hugh Walpole: Formative Influences MA Boston Univ 1939
8603 VINCENZ Lilli M The Treatment of Rebirth in Walpole's *Fortitude,*
      Sartre's *La Nausee* and Hesse's *Der Steppenwolf* MA Columbia 1960
      153 p
See also 8563

IZAAK WALTON

8604 CERINA Angela *The Compleat Angler or the Contemplative Man's Recreation*
      of Izaak Walton MA Ca Foscari (Italy) 1962
8605 GRIMES Margaret E Walton's Contribution to Biographical Literature
      MA Univ of Texas at Austin 1937
8606 YOUNG Frederick H Jr Izaak Walton's Conception of Biography
      MA Columbia 1959 68 p

MRS HUMPHREY WARD

8607 DUNDAS Diane M An Examination of the Moral Code in Mrs Humphrey Ward's
      Early Novels MA Bowling Green Univ 1963
8608 HARRIS Katherine M Mrs Humphrey Ward's *Robert Elsmere* MA Univ of
      Maryland at College Park 1954 108 p
8609 KANNENBERG Mattie M The Religious Problem in the Novels of
      Mrs Humphrey Ward MA Texas Woman's Univ 1932
8610 LOLIVA Emilio An Essay on Mrs Humphrey Ward's Religious Novels
      in Relation to Her Feelings and Her Life MA Ca Foscari (Italy) 1925
See also 1240

ISAAC WATTS

8611 BULLARD John M Imagery in the Poetry of Isaac Watts MA Univ of North
      Carolina at Chapel Hill 1955 95 p
8612 CRAIN Aldena L Isaac Watts: Poet and Preacher MA Univ of North
      Dakota 1930 106 p
8613 HARDING E R A Selection from Isaac Watts' *Horae Lyricae*, Including
      the Preface with Introduction and Notes, Textual and Critical
      MA Univ of London (England) 1963
8614 McCARTHY Sr Rose C Isaac Watts: His Religious Ideas and Poetry from
      a Catholic Point of View MA Boston Coll 1939
8615 MASSOUD Mary M Isaac Watts: An "Enthusiastic" Poet MA Columbia 1959
      222 p
8616 SWEETLAND Richard C Calvinistic Elements in Isaac Watts' Hymns
      MA Univ of Texas at Austin 1959 66 p
8617 THOMAS Helen S The Religious Poetry of Isaac Watts MA Rice 1943
See also 2314

EVELYN WAUGH

8618 BAYLOR Essie B Evelyn Waugh: His Life and Works MA Howard Univ 1948
      120 p
8619 BOWER A W Underlying Conflicts in the Novels of Evelyn Waugh BA Univ
      of British Columbia (Canada) 1960
8620 BROWN Lloyd R Evelyn Waugh: The Development of a Novelist MA Memorial
      (Canada) 1966
8621 CLARKE Mary C The Novels of Evelyn Waugh Studied in Connection with
      His Life Until the Outbreak of War in 1939 MA Columbia 1943
8622 CUTTER Muriel C The Progress of Satire in the Development of
      Evelyn Waugh as a Novelist MA Oklahoma St Univ 1965 129 p
8623 DOLCE Rose V The Quest for Self-Esteem and Honour in Evelyn Waugh's
      Trilogy *Men at War* MA Univ of Rhode Island 1964 102 p
8624 HALLORAN Paul F The Changing Comedy of Evelyn Waugh (Through a Glass,
      Blackly) MA Mankato St Coll 1967 53 p
8625 HOLIHAN Br Rudolph Evelyn Waugh: His Return to the Satiric
      MA Boston Coll 1949
8626 HOLLANDER Steven D On the Waugh-Path: A Study of Evelyn Waugh
      BA Rutgers St Univ 1963 139 p
8627 KIRBY C Lawrence Jr Evelyn Waugh: Satirist MA Boston Coll 1948

8628 LOTTMAN Herbert R Evelyn Waugh and the New Hero MA Columbia 1951
8629 MARSH George R Jr The Multiple Background of Evelyn Waugh's Military
      Trilogy MA Columbia 1964 70 p
8630 MAZE Mary J Satire and Catholicism in Evelyn Waugh MA Univ of Houston
      1964 115 p
8631 OETGEN George R Character as a Vehicle of Satire in the Early Novels
      of Evelyn Waugh MA Bowling Green Univ 1962
8632 SLIPPER Anne The Satiric Hero in Evelyn Waugh's Novels BA Univ of
      British Columbia (Canada) 1969
8633 SPRINGER Felix J Satire, Beliefs and Reticence: Their Antagonism
      and Combination in the Novels of Arthur Evelyn St John Waugh
      BA Amherst 1968
8634 SULLIVAN Gerald J Comic Art in the First Four Novels of Evelyn Waugh
      MA Univ of Oklahoma 1959
8635 WALLIS David H A Reading of Evelyn Waugh's *Brideshead Revisited*:
      A Critical Survey and Thematic Analysis MA Univ of Tulsa 1968   63 p

JOHN WEBSTER

8636 ANDREADIS Harriette Webster's Use of Imagery: *The White Devil* and
      The Duchess of Malfi MA Temple Univ 1965
8637 BAXTER J S The Tragic Hero in the Plays of John Webster BA Univ of
      British Columbia (Canada) 1948
8638 BERRY Donald R Webster's Proverb Lore MA Baylor Univ 1955 142 p
8639 BUCHAN Moyra J The Hired Villain in the Plays of John Webster
      MA Alberta (Canada) 1966
8640 BUCKLE Reginald W Webster and the Theatre of Cruelty: A Theatrical
      Context for *The Duchess of Malfi* MA Univ of British Columbia
      (Canada) 1966
8641 COLLINS Priscilla S The Development of the Villain Character in
      English Drama to John Webster MA Boston Univ 1948
8642 ENGELSKIRCHEN Howard The Trial Scenes of John Webster MA Columbia 196
      87 p
8643 GEWIN Sr Cornelius J The Arts of Language in the Plays of John Webster
      MA Boston Coll 1956
8644 GREEN Nancy R Love-Melancholy in John Webster's Tragedies MA Univ of
      North Carolina at Chapel Hill 1959 77 p
8645 GREGORY Catherine W A Study of Seneca and Webster MA Univ of North
      Carolina at Chapel Hill 1950 60 p
8646 HATTON Beula M The Nature of Webster's Tragic Genius MA Texas Tech-
      nological Univ 1951
8647 HEYMSFELD Joan A Ludwig Tieck's *Vittoria Accorombona* and John Webster'
      White Devil: A Chapter in English and German Literary Relations
      MA Columbia 1936
8648 JANUS Lorraine A John Webster: The Mannerist Perspective MA Univ of
      Maryland at College Park 1968 103 p
8649 KEVER Delynn M *The Devil's Law Case* (John Webster) MA Univ of Oklahom
      1958
8650 LIVERANI Luciana John Webster MA Ca Foscari (Italy) 1944
8651 LUNDELL Marilyn H Implicit Characterization in John Webster's
      The Duchess of Malfi and *The White Devil* MA Bowling Green Univ 1956
8652 LYNCH Marion P Thematic Imagery in *The White Devil* and *The Duchess
      of Malfi* MA Univ of Texas at Austin 1962 90 p
8653 McDOUGALL R L The Elizabethan Melodrama and John Webster BA Univ of
      British Columbia (Canada) 1939
8654 MITCHELL Marvin O John Webster: A Study of His Literary Fame (1602-
      1927) MA Univ of North Carolina at Chapel Hill 1948 147 p
8655 MOODY Julia P *The Duchess*: John Webster's Prince of Amalfi MA Brigha
      Young Univ 1963 95 p
8656 MOONSCHEIN Henry C A Critical Study of John Webster's Borrowings

in *The Duchess of Malfi* MA Lehigh Univ 1966
8657 MOORE Marcia W A Study of Sources and Influences Which Shaped
Bussy d'Ambois, The Duchess of Malfi, Sophonisba and *The Picture*
MA Univ of Houston 1965 109 p
8658 MORTON Gloria I John Webster's Point of View toward Three Villains:
Flamineo, Bosola and Romelio MA Texas Agricultural and Mechanical
Univ 1965 210 p
8659 OLDENKAMP Joan L The Duchess and the Burlador: A Comparison of the
Seventeenth Century Dramas of John Webster in England and
Tirso de Molina in Spain with Emphasis on *The Duchess of Malfi* and
El Burlador de Sevilla MA DePauw Univ 1958 92 p
8660 O'NEAL Sandra L A Study of Three Villains in the Dramas of John Webster
MA Texas Technological Univ 1969 69 p
8661 ORCUTT Candace The Operation of John Webster's Animal Imagery
MA Columbia 1962 61 p
8662 RIVELSON Sophia J The Reputation of John Webster in the Nineteenth
Century MA Columbia 1936
8663 SCOUTEN Arthur H The Death Theme in the Tragedies of John Webster
MA Louisiana St Univ 1938
8664 SGOBBI Laura *The White Devil* by John Webster MA Ca Foscari (Italy) 1965
8665 SHAW Edward B Jr The Function of John Webster's Imagery MA Univ of
North Carolina at Chapel Hill 1950 87 p
8666 TSOW Fan M A Study of John Webster's Dramatic Technique MA Toronto
(Canada) 1967
8667 TUCKER Kenneth John Webster's Tragic Vision MA Univ of Louisville 1966
8668 WANG T L The Literary Reputation of John Webster to 1830 B Litt
Oxford Univ (England) nd
8669 WARREN John T Imagery as Cosmic Settings in John Webster's Tragedies
MS Auburn Univ 1949 72 p
8670 WARREN Michael J The Rhetorical Foundation of the Dramas of
John Webster MA Dalhousie (Canada) 1963
8671 WHITE A M Webster and Elizabethan Melodrama BA Univ of British
Columbia (Canada) 1929
8672 WHITMAN Frank H The Unity of *The Duchess of Malfi*: A New Apology
MA Univ of Idaho 1965
8673 WILLIAMS Mary Webster's Tragic Heroines: Their Response to Moral
Ambiguity MA Stanford Univ 1966
8674 WYKES Viva L Convention and Realism: John Webster's Characterization
in *The White Devil* and *The Duchess of Malfi* MA Miami Univ 1964
8675 ZENNARO Annalisa *The Duchess of Malfi* by John Webster MA Ca Foscari
(Italy) 1965
See also 6621

H G WELLS

8676 BAILEY J O Scientific Novel of H G Wells MA Univ of North Carolina
at Chapel Hill 1927
8677 BERTSCHLER Martha M The Art and Thought of H G Wells MA Univ of
Texas at Austin 1929
8678 BURT Donald H G Wells and the Future of Man MA Mankato St Coll 1965
8679 CHIORAZZO Mario H G Wells, His Art and Mind with a Special Essay on
Sexual Relations and Woman's Emancipation MA Ca Foscari (Italy) 1928
8680 HUEBNER Alice E Utopian Novels of H G Wells MA Univ of Toledo 1944
8681 HURLEY Barbara A The Dream and the Nightmare: E I Zamiatin, H G Wells
and Utopia; A Comparative Study MA Cornell Univ 1966
8682 MARINELLI Otello Some Aspects of H G Wells' Short Stories MA Ca Foscari
(Italy) 1947
8683 MATHER J E The Women of H G Wells MA Univ of Arkansas 1918
8684 PAINTER James W An Introduction to the Religions and Social Philosophy
of H G Wells MA Univ of Tennessee 1923

8685 RIGUCCI Libia H G Wells, Novelist and Social Reformer MA Ca Foscari
(Italy) 1941
8686 SMITH Eula P The Later Educational Theories of H G Wells MA Univ
of Texas at Austin 1936
8687 SUDRANN Jean H G Wells: Artist and Reformer MA Columbia 1940
8688 TER VEER Catherine L H G Wells and His Planned Society MA Univ of
Maryland at College Park 1935 90 p
8689 WEBB Esther A A Study of Relative Clauses with Special Reference
to the Language of H G Wells MA Univ of Iowa 1931
See also 1982, 5173

JOHN WESLEY

8690 DAUES Placide The Relation of John Wesley to the Romantic Movement
MA Washington Univ at St Louis 1934 122 p
8691 HERBERT Thomas W The Literary Abridgments and Editions by John Wesley
MA Emory Univ 1931 114 p
8692 STEPHENSON Lee W John Wesley's Philosophy of Literature MA West
Texas St Univ 1968 123 p
8693 WHITENER William J The Founders of Methodism: John Wesley and
George Whitefield (A Study of Eighteenth Century Religious
Enthusiasm) MA Columbia 1959 105 p
8694 YAGER Sudie E John Wesley and Romanticism MA Oklahoma St Univ 1942
69 p
See also 2314

WILLIAM HALE WHITE

8695 FOND David In Quest of Love: A Study of the Role of Women in the
Life and Art of William Hale White (Mark Rutherford) MA Columbia
1962 73 p
8696 GILES R M The Novels of William Hale White, Mark Rutherford
MA Boston Univ 1925
8697 GIORDANO Elena William Hale White (Mark Rutherford) MA Ca Foscari
(Italy) 1956
8698 MERTON E Stephen William Hale White (Mark Rutherford): The Man
and His Work MA Columbia 1936
See also 3866

OSCAR WILDE

8699 ANTHONY Karen S Oscar Wilde's Use of the Fabulous Illustrated in
The Picture of Dorian Gray, Salome and His Fairy Tales
MA Washington Univ at St Louis nd
8700 BARMETTLER Robert S The Dramatic Method of Oscar Wilde MA Texas
Christian Univ 1963 79 p
8701 BATTE Helen E The Aesthetics of Oscar Wilde MA Columbia 1935
8702 BEALL Elma The Aesthetic Theory of Oscar Wilde MA Toronto (Canada) 1
8703 BELSHAW Diana A Consideration of the Plays of Oscar Wilde in the
Light of His Aesthetic Doctrine BA Univ of British Columbia (Canad
1970
8704 CHUTE Virginia H Oscar Wilde's Theories of Art MA Univ of Maine 1949
97 p
8705 CLOUDMAN Harry H A Study of the Aesthetics of Oscar Wilde MA Univ of
Oklahoma 1941
8706 FERLUGA Vittorio Oscar Wilde's Tragedies MA Ca Foscari (Italy) 1955
8707 FRITZ Fay H Oscar Wilde: Versatile Genius MA Univ of Texas at Austi
1938 147 p
8708 FULLER Cythnia Oscar Wilde's Critical Dialogues MA Univ of Massachus
1967

8709 GONCALVES Raquel The Affirmation of Christian and Social Morality in
      Oscar Wilde's Fairy Tales BA Univ of British Columbia (Canada) 1970
8710 HENDERSON Marian A Critical Analysis of the Play *Lady Windermer's Fan*
      M Ed Henderson St Coll nd
8711 HINDMAN Jennie L The Revival of the Comedy of Manners in England in
      the Later Nineteenth Century MA Texas Woman's Univ 1937
8712 HUTCHINSON H A Oscar Wilde: Art, Artifice and Reality BA Univ of
      British Columbia (Canada) 1960
8713 JACCHIA Umberto Oscar Wilde: His Life and His Theatrical Production
      MA Ca Foscari (Italy) 1941
8714 LORRAINE Antony P *The Importance of Being Earnest:* Considered as an
      Intellectual Pastoral MA Stanford Univ 1965
8715 MANDEL Robert S The Language of Insincerity in the Plays of
      Oscar Wilde MA Columbia 1966 134 p
8716 MEACHAM Johnnie M Oscar Wilde and the Comic Tradition MA Univ of
      Oklahoma 1945
8717 MEYERS Ronald J The "Contamination" of *Earnest*: A Study of the
      Conventions of Classical Comedy in Oscar Wilde's *The Importance of
      Being Earnest* MA Columbia 1959 78 p
8718 PRADELLA Antonio Oscar Wilde MA Ca Foscari (Italy) 1930
8719 RECOULLEY Alfred L Dorian Gray: Une Fleur du Mal MA Duke Univ 1965
8720 ROLANDO Marta Oscar Wilde MA Ca Foscari (Italy) 1938
8721 RYAN Eleanor K The Comedies of Oscar Wilde MA Boston Univ 1933
8722 RYCKEBUSCH Jules R Blue China: The Philosophy of Oscar Wilde in
      Relationship to His Plays MA Univ of Massachusetts 1965
8723 SAWYER J P The Aesthetic Principles of Oscar Wilde BA Univ of British
      Columbia (Canada) 1953
8724 SHAFER Susan M The Aesthetic and the Didactic: Changes in Wilde's
      Theory of Art MA Temple Univ 1965 43 p
8725 TAYLOR Jane B Criticism on Oscar Wilde MA Univ of Pittsburgh 1933
8726 VAN DEN HOVEN Adrian T From Arcadia to Byzantium: A Study of *The
      Picture of Dorian Gray* in Light of Wilde's Changing Concept of
      Beauty MA Windsor (Canada) 1966
8727 WHEELER L Ray A Critical Analysis of Oscar Wilde's *The Picture of
      Dorian Gray* MS Kansas St Coll at Pittsburg nd
See also 5187, 5815, 7274, 7518

CHARLES WILLIAMS

8728 BAKER Janet E Themes and Characterization in Charles Williams'
      The Place of the Lion MA Queen's (Canada) 1967
8729 CAVANAUGH Philip G The Theological Romances of Charles Williams
      MA Columbia 1958 184 p
8730 GRAVES Barbara A Images in the Novels of Charles Williams MA Univ
      of Tulsa 1969 82 p
8731 HENDRY R J The Theology of Charles Williams MA North Texas St Univ
      1962
8732 HENSEL James The Novels of Charles Williams MA Univ of Maine 1958 111 p
8733 HUDDLESTONE L C The Arthurian Poems of Charles Williams: Their
      Development and Background MA Univ of London (England) 1953
8734 SAIT Jim Patterns of Character and Image in Charles Williams' Novel
      The Place of the Lion BA Univ of British Columbia (Canada) 1970
8735 SMITH William L The Development of the Concept of the Image of the
      City in the Critical Works of Charles Williams MA North Texas
      St Univ 1965
8736 THOMPSON Phyllis J The Use of Myth in the Novels of Charles Williams
      MA Univ of North Carolina at Chapel Hill 1954 67 p
8737 THRASH Lois G An Annotated, Enumerative Bibliography of Works by
      and about Charles Williams MA Texas Technological Univ 1966 77 p

JOHN WILMOT

8738 GARDINER Frank C The Lyrics of John Wilmot, Earl of Rochester
      MA Univ of Oklahoma 1959
8739 GARDNER J H The Literary Reputation of John Wilmot, Earl of Rochester
      MA Univ of North Carolina at Chapel Hill 1941
8740 McKEWIN Carole A Ambivalence and Accent: Rochester and the Pastoral,
      Lyric and Satiric Genres MA Univ of Maryland at College Park 1967
      17 p
8741 PALMER Melvin D The Earl of Rochester's Attitude toward Women
      MA Univ of Maryland at College Park 1959 81 p
8742 SHERMAN John The Poetry of John Wilmot, Earl of Rochester MA Univ of
      Denver 1965
8743 SILVERMAN Stuart Poetry of Flowers: A Study of Selected Poems by
      John Wilmot, Earl of Rochester MA Columbia 1961 96 p
8744 SPADE John A Wit in the Poetry of John Wilmot, Earl of Rochester
      MA Univ of Hawaii 1965 148 p
8745 YACOWAR Maurice The Earl of Rochester's Recasting of Other Writers
      MA Alberta (Canada) 1965

MARY WOLLSTONECRAFT

8746 BOSWELL Cora L Mary Wollstonecraft: A Chapter in the History of
      Radicalism in English Literature MA Texas Woman's Univ 1936
8747 DEMESTICHAS Rose M Mary Wollstonecraft and the Rights of Women
      MA Univ of Pittsburgh 1934
8748 HARE Robert R The Base Indian: A Vindication of the Rights of
      Mary Wollstonecraft MA Univ of Delaware 1957 107 p
8749 HOLT Hermoine H Mary Wollstonecraft: Feminist MA Southern Methodist
      Univ 1930
8750 MUSSELMAN Hazel Wollstonecraft, Foreshadower of the Romantic Revolt
      MA Southern Methodist Univ 1931
8751 TORMOLLAN Miriam A In the Shadow of Mary Wollstonecraft: A Study
      of Two of Her Pupils MA Univ of Texas at Austin 1950 117 p
8752 WATSON Pauline J Mary Wollstonecraft: Author and Woman MA Univ of
      Iowa 1935
See also 207, 460, 7400, 7434

VIRGINIA WOOLF

8753 BARTO Barbara J Virginia Woolf and the Quest for Mrs Brown MA Kent
      St Univ 1965
8754 BAUER Wilma C *Between the Acts*: A Discussion of Its Form and Content
      MA Columbia 1961 91 p
8755 BLOOM Jean C An Analysis of the Sources of Moments of Vision in
      Virginia Woolf's Novels MA Pacific Univ 1963 166 p
8756 BODNAR John P The Influence of the Bergsonian Theory in Three Major
      Works by Virginia Woolf MA Shippensburg St Coll 1965
8757 BURROUGHS Ada E Virginia Woolf's *Orlando* MA Columbia 1943
8758 CHAMBERLIN Mary W The "Single Vision": Unities of Style in
      Mrs Dalloway, *To the Lighthouse* and *The Waves* MA Columbia 1966 83 p
8759 CHERNIKOWSKI Stephanie From Formlessness to Order: Virginia Woolf's
      Portrait of the Artist MA Univ of Texas at Austin 1966 114 p
8760 COLLINS Sarah L Virginia Woolf and the Stream of Consciousness Novel
      MA Univ of Texas at Austin 1939 130 p
8761 COMSTOCK Nancy A Study of Virginia Woolf's *Between the Acts* MA Univ
      of Louisville 1967 95 p
8762 COOK Roselee Virginia Woolf as a Literary Critic MA Marquette Univ
      1948 77 p
8763 DELLADONNA Judith An Investigation of Virginia Woolf's Attempt at

the Intergration of Status and Creativity MA Central Connecticut
St Coll 1966
8764 ECONOMOU Georgia Virginia Woolf: *A Writer's Diary* in Relation to
Four Novels: *Jacob's Room, Mrs Dalloway, To the Lighthouse* and
The Waves MA Columbia 1954 102 p
8765 FORSYTH Donna The Woman's Offering: A Study of Women as Centers of
Stability in Two of Virginia Woolf's Novels BA Univ of British
Columbia (Canada) 1967
8766 FRAULEY Ronald F The Focus of Narration in the Novels of Virginia Woolf
MA Boston Coll 1952
8767 FREEDE Frederic L Communion and Identity in the Novels of Virginia Woolf
MA Kent St Univ 1965
8768 GAITHER Mary An Analysis of Virginia Woolf's *Mrs Dalloway* MA Univ of
Louisville 1949
8769 GILCHRIST Frances C The Narrative Method of Virginia Woolf's *To the
Lighthouse* MA Univ of North Carolina at Chapel Hill 1958 64 p
8770 GILLESPIE Patricia E Artist as Woman: Feminism and Femininity in
Virginia Woolf's Works MA Texas Christian Univ 1949 91 p
8771 GRIER David Virginia Woolf and Albert Camus: Philosophy of the Absurd
MA Indiana Univ 1956
8772 GROSSMAN Joan A The Garden Image in Three Novels by Virginia Woolf
MA Temple Univ 1965 75 p
8773 HAND Susan E Virginia Woolf's Self-Realization: A Comparison of
The Voyage Out and *To the Lighthouse* MA Columbia 1966 120 p
8774 HATHWELL David R Characterization in the Major Novels of Virginia Woolf
MA Columbia 1966 85 p
8775 HENDERSON Nancy D Virginia Woolf's Search for Woman's Place in
Scholarship and Art MA Florida St Univ 1964
8776 JOSEPH Mildred M Virginia Woolf's Use of Psychological States in
Achieving Literary Effects in Her Novels MA North Carolina Coll 1964
8777 KANE Roberta Sex Polarity in Mrs Woolf's Novels MA Univ of Rhode
Island 1963 81 p
8778 KAPLAN Meredith The Early Short Stories of Virginia Woolf: Development of Techniques for the Novel MA Claremont Graduate School 1965
8779 LANGE Marjorie T Critical Opinions of Virginia Woolf's Novels
M Ed Temple Univ 1943 178 p
8780 LAZZARA Margery N A Study of Spatial Symbolizations in the Major
Novels of Virginia Woolf MA Bowling Green Univ 1955
8781 LIBERTA Sarah "The Perpetual Pageant": Art and Life in the Novels
of Virginia Woolf MA Texas Christian Univ 1965 104 p
8782 LOPES Maria A Nature Imagery as Characterization in Proust and Woolf
MA Univ of Texas at Austin 1965 91 p
8783 LOUCKS I Marie *To the Lighthouse*: Virginia Woolf's Art and the Art
of Life MA Southern Illinois Univ at Carbondale 1960 84 p
8784 MACE Sr Agnes K An Inquiry into the Part Played by Images and Figures
of Speech in the Technique of the Novels of Virginia Woolf MA Univ
of Montana 1941 103 p
8785 McHUGH Marvis A Study of Virginia Woolf's *The Years* MA Columbia 1959
66 p
8786 MOLLACH Francis L Theme and Structure: Virginia Woolf's Method in
Mrs Dalloway MA Syracuse Univ 1968 62 p
8787 NELSON Kelly E A Concept of Time in the Novels of Virginia Woolf
MA Texas Technological Univ 1969 46 p
8788 OSTOW Estelle S The Louder Boom and the Smaller Chime: Concerning
Affinities in Thought between Henri Bergson and Virginia Woolf as
Seen in *To the Lighthouse* MA Columbia 1953 157 p
8789 PAYTON Pamela Time in the Novels of Virginia Woolf MA Univ of
California at Riverside 1956
8790 PEPIS Betty A Virginia Woolf in France MA Columbia 1937
8791 RABINOWITZ I James Virginia Woolf: Vision and Design BA Amherst 1955

8792 REID Virginia P A Study of Virginia Woolf MA Univ of Louisville 1948
8793 RIESER Mary A The Influence of Feminism upon the Novels of
      Virginia Woolf MA Washington Univ at St Louis 1949
8794 ROARK Bobbie J Point of View in *To the Lighthouse* MA Univ of Colorado
      1965
8795 ROBB Jacarol T Virginia Woolf: A Bibliography of English Criticisms
      and Commentary MA Univ of Houston 1966 128 p
8796 RUSHMORE Robert P Mrs Brown and Mrs Dalloway: Character as Significan⸱
      Form MA Columbia 1953 77 p
8797 SCHIFFER Jennifer *To the Lighthouse*: The Language of Fiction
      BA Univ of British Columbia (Canada) 1968
8798 STEPHENS Eileen Influence of Post Impressionism on *Mrs Dalloway*,
      To the Lighthouse and *The Waves* BA Univ of British Columbia
      (Canada) 1969
8799 TALLENTIRE David R Virginia Woolf's Short Fiction: A Study of Its
      Relation to the Story Genre; and an Explication of the Known Story
      Canon MA Univ of British Columbia (Canada) 1968 202 p
8800 THAMES Anna M The Significance of Time as a Thematic Device in the
      Novels of Virginia Woolf MA Univ of Houston 1967 88 p
8801 THOMAS Sara T Construction in Virginia Woolf's *Mrs Dalloway* MA Univ
      of North Carolina at Chapel Hill 1950 85 p
8802 TRUSHIN Miriam The Opposition of Texture and Form in *Jacob's Room*,
      Mrs Dalloway and *To the Lighthouse* MA Columbia 1963 73 p
8803 UBER Shirley R Virginia Woolf: The Early Novels and the Search for
      Form MA Univ of Rhode Island 1965 92 p
8804 VAGUE Maedythe J Light as a Metaphor for Life: Imagery in
      Virginia Woolf's *The Waves* BA Univ of British Columbia (Canada) 196⸱
8805 WALKER Martha Virginia Woolf: A Restless Experimenter MA Univ of
      Texas at Austin 1952 470 p
8806 WALKER Virginia B Virginia Woolf's Imagery MA Columbia 1959 159 p
8807 WEISS Nancy Roger Fry's Aesthetics in Virginia Woolf's *To the Light-*
      house MA Northern Illinois Univ 1965
8808 WEISSTEIN Allyn L A Shape of the Mind's Eye: The Work of
      Virginia Woolf and Willa Cather MA Indiana Univ 1956
8809 WILLIAMS Joyce E A Great Androgynous Mind: Virginia Woolf
      MA Louisiana St Univ 1966
8810 WILLIAMS Nicholas B Virginia Woolf: A Woman with a View MA George
      Washington Univ 1958 146 p
8811 WILLIS Harold A The Stream of Consciousness Method of Virginia Woolf
      MA Univ of Florida 1949
8812 YAROS June The Significance of Time in the Novels of Virginia Woolf
      MA Temple Univ 1957 57 p
8813 ZIEGLER Robert P Virginia Woolf: Withdrawal as Aesthetic Distance
      MA Bowling Green Univ 1967
See also 1088, 3268, 3276, 5634

                         WILLIAM WORDSWORTH

8814 ADAMS Adele Auditory Imagery of Nature in Wordsworth's Poetry
      MA Hardin-Simmons Univ 1953
8815 AKINS Pearl E An Investigation of Three Possible Literary Influences
      on Wordsworth's *Preface to the Lyrical Ballads* MS Kansas St Coll
      at Pittsburg 1957
8816 ALLEYNE Joyce H Wordsworth's Poetic Language MA Queen's (Canada) 1964
8817 APOLLONIO Nella The Creative Sensibility of William Wordsworth
      MA Ca Foscari (Italy) 1950
8818 APTERBACH Isidor Wordsworth's *The Excursion*: A Revaluation
      MA Columbia 1962 108 p
8819 ARANT Rozel H A Study of Wordsworth's Concept and Use of *Joy*
      MA Northeast Louisiana St Coll 1969 98 p

8820 ARDUNA Arthur   The Visionary Gleam of William Wordsworth   MA Columbia
     1964 66 p
8821 ARLUCK Arthur   Wordsworth and Science   MA Columbia 1951
8822 ARNOLD Mabel V   The New Elements in Wordsworth's Pastorals   MA Univ of
     Iowa 1934
8823 BALLARD Gertrude E   Wordsworth's Critical Power as Revealed by a Study
     of His Textual Revisions of the *Lyrical Ballads*   MA Columbia 1905
8824 BANKS T M   Wordsworth and the French Revolution   MA Williams Coll 1907
8825 BARNARD Mary C   Wordsworth's Journeys as a Source of Inspiration for
     His Poetry   MA Univ of Arkansas 1931
8826 BATSON Gladys   The Common Man in Wordsworth   MA Hardin-Simmons Univ 1949
8827 BAUER Neil S   Wordsworth and "Peter Bell"   MA Columbia 1966   71 p
8828 BAUMAN Marilyn A   Breton's "A Farewell to Fancie": A Critical Edition;
     Wordsworth and Frost on Cities; and the Woods in Robert Frost's
     Poetry   MA Pennsylvania St Univ 1965
8829 BEATTY Frederika   William Wordsworth: 1840-1845   MA Columbia 1922
8830 BINGMAN M L   The Wordsworths' Scottish Tour   MA North Texas St Univ 1956
8831 BLEEKER Betty J   William Wordsworth's Kinesthetic Experiences (1776-
     1798)   MA Texas Woman's Univ 1966
8832 BLOOMBERG Sanford   An Interpretation of William Wordsworth's
     Ecclesiastical Sonnets   MA Columbia 1951
8833 BOLDING Lois L   Wordsworth's Philosophy of Childhood   MA Univ of Texas
     at Austin 1950   81 p
8834 BOLENIUS Emma M   Wordsworth as a Sonneteer   MA Columbia 1905
8835 BRANDAO Madellie   Wordsworth and the French Revolution   MA Tulane Univ
     1928
8836 BRENNEMAN Naomi   The Use of Color in Wordsworth's Poetry   MA Univ of
     Chicago 1921
8837 BURCHFIEL Olive P   The History of Wordsworth's Literary Reputation
     up to 1815   MA Univ of Chicago 1918
8838 BURKE James V   Wordsworth's Escape   BA Rutgers St Univ 1962   98 p
8839 CALLAHAN Cathryn C   The Epic Characteristics in *The Prelude*   MA Texas
     Technological Univ 1968   65 p
8840 CALLAN Anne P   A Study in the Structure of the Wordsworthian Sonnet
     MA Marquette Univ 1945   45 p
8841 CAMPBELL Anna L   Contemporary Criticism of the Poetical Works of
     William Wordsworth from 1793 to 1833   MA Columbia 1912
8842 CAREW Sr M Johnette   The Mother Theme in Wordsworth   MA Boston Coll 1962
8843 CARPENTER James A   The Stages in the Development of Wordsworth's
     Interest in Man   MA Univ of Mississippi 1934   127 p
8844 CARRUTHERS Ellen D   The Power of *The Prelude*   MA Vanderbilt Univ 1965
8845 CATES Carolyn S   Wordsworth's Sonnets: Style, Technique and Content
     MA Texas Technological Univ 1967   192 p
8846 CAVALLETTO George A Jr   Wordsworth's *Home at Grasmere*   MA Columbia 1966
     85 p
8847 CHANG Tiang H   A Comparison of the Nature Philosophy of Wordsworth
     with Chinese Taoism   MA Illinois St Univ at Normal 1966
8848 CHIPMAN Doris   The Attitude of Hawthorne toward Science Compared with
     the Attitudes of Rousseau, Wordsworth, Goethe and Poe   MS Ft Hays
     St Teachers Coll 1958   95 p
8849 CLARK Katherine L   An Analysis and Estimate of Its Effects on
     Wordsworth of the Annette Episode from Its Beginning until His
     Marriage   MA Univ of Mississippi 1939   99 p
8850 CLARK N L   Thoreau's Theory of Nature as a Teacher, Compared with
     Wordsworth's   MA Univ of North Carolina at Chapel Hill 1944
8851 COBB Leon W   Wordsworth's Loyalty to His Theory of Poetic Diction
     MA Univ of Nebraska 1915
8852 COCHRAN Bessie   The People of Wordsworth's Poetry   MA Univ of Texas
     at Austin 1910
8853 COLLINS Rev William J   The Role of the Imagination in the Poetry of

William Wordsworth   MA Boston Coll 1951

8854   COOK Donald L   The Pain of Separation in Wordsworth's Narrative Poems
MA Univ of Texas at Austin 1963   79 p

8855   COURTRIGHT Veda E   Plant Life in English Poetry from Thomson to
Wordsworth   MS Kansas St Coll at Pittsburg 1939

8856   CRAVEY Jeannette J   A New Era of Wordsworthian Criticism   MA Univ of
Oklahoma 1937

8857   CRONIN Elizabeth A   Wordsworth: A Student of the Middle Ages
MA Univ of Arizona 1936

8858   DANN Joanne   Wordsworth's Attitudes toward Age   MA Columbia 1964   71 p

8859   DAVIS Dorotha B   Does Wordsworth Conform to His Own Theory of Poetry?
MS Kansas St Coll at Pittsburg 1939

8860   DAVIS Ellen M   Childhood in Wordsworth's Poetry   MA Univ of Maine 1916
31 p

8861   DEAN Marion B   Wordsworth's Use of Celestial Bodies in His Poetry
MA Hardin-Simmons Univ 1953

8862   DENNIS Janice E   Wordsworth's Interest in the Medieval and the Gothic
MA Univ of North Carolina at Chapel Hill 1959   97 p

8863   DICKERSON Mary L   A Study of the Form, Sources, Interpretations and
Significance of *The Borderers* by William Wordsworth   MA Univ of
Tulsa 1963   70 p

8864   DIVINE John J   Wordsworth in English Periodical Criticism, 1798-1855
MA St Louis Univ 1938   106 p

8865   DUDLEY Luther E   The Treatment of Nature in the Poetry of
William Wordsworth   MA Univ of Texas at Austin 1916

8866   DUNLAVEY Richard F   The City and the Art of Wordsworth   MA Columbia 1959
95 p

8867   EARP M J   The Domestic Life of the Wordsworths   MA Univ of North
Carolina at Chapel Hill 1943

8868   ELSE Robert C   Variations in Wordsworth's Style   MA Columbia 1966   98 p

8869   ESCHHOLZ Paul A   Wordsworth's View of the City   MA Univ of Vermont 1966

8870   EVANS Anna C   Wordsworth: The Genius Versus the Man   MA Southwestern
Univ at Georgetown 1926

8871   EVANS Elizabeth A   Sensibility and Sentimentality in Wordsworth's
Poetry, 1785-1805   MA Univ of Pittsburgh 1947

8872   FARRAR Charles P   The Growth and Development of William Wordsworth's
Political Thought to 1805   MA North Carolina Coll at Durham 1922

8873   FAULKNER Norma J   Did William Wordsworth Follow His Theory of Poetry?
M Ed Henderson St Coll nd

8874   FEIK William R   A Study of Poetic Tributes to William Wordsworth
MA Indiana Univ 1950

8875   FELBAUM Gusta W   Wordsworth's Sensuous Endowment as Shown by the Images
He Uses in *The Prelude*   MS Purdue Univ 1904

8876   FISHER Joseph P   Wordsworth and Childhood   MA Univ of Louisville 1939
143 p

8877   FOLEY Henry A   Recent Trends in the Criticism of William Wordsworth
MA Northern Arizona Univ 1969

8878   FORBES G H   "Peter Bell" by Wordsworth   BA Univ of British Columbia
(Canada) 1956

8879   FOSTER Lulu   The Influence of Wordsworth on Modern Poetry   BA Univ of
Oklahoma 1910

8880   FOSTER Milton P   The Democratic Ideals in the Poetry of William
Wordsworth   MA Univ of Pittsburgh 1947

8881   FREIS Susan R   The Glory of the Dream: The Theme of Loss in Wordsworth's
"Intimations Ode"   MA Univ of Maryland at College Park 1968   90 p

8882   FROBERG Lawrence O   The Significance of *The Borderers* in Wordsworth's
Recovery   MA Indiana Univ 1942

8883   GIBSON Mildred O   The Influence of Dorothy Wordsworth on William
Wordsworth   MA Univ of Mississippi 1931   81 p

8884   GLASS Merle H   Wordsworth as Seen by His Contemporaries   MA Baylor Univ

1939 129 p
8885 GOFF Minnie L Wordsworth: A Poet of Nature MA West Virginia Univ
      1906 50 p
8886 GOLDFARB William Capital Punishment in Nineteenth Century England:
      Wordsworth the Victorian MA Columbia 1966 88 p
8887 GOOZEE Harriete A Study of Wordsworth's *Prelude* MA Boston Univ 1923
8888 GREENBERG Shirley B William Wordsworth and the French Revolution
      MA Syracuse Univ 1946 138 p
8889 HALL Louise M Color in Wordsworth's Early Poetry MA Columbia 1916
8890 HANSEN Judith L The River Duddon: Wordsworth's Loss of Vision
      MA Northern Illinois Univ 1966
8891 HARDY Helen E Contemporary Criticism of Wordsworth MA Columbia 1908
8892 HARKIN Ruby M Wordsworth's Use of Birds in His Poetry MA Hardin-
      Simmons Univ 1949
8893 HARLOW May H Wordsworth's Use of the Natural Forms of Water in His
      Poetry MA Hardin-Simmons Univ 1950
8894 HARRINGTON Janette Wordsworth's Descriptive Sketches and *The Prelude*,
      Book VI MA Univ of Arkansas 1929
8895 HARTSELL E H Wordsworth's Problem of Loss and Recompense MA Univ
      of North Carolina at Chapel Hill 1935
8896 HASNER Edith K Wordsworth's Recent Reputation MA Washington Univ at
      St Louis 1935
8897 HATCHETT Elwyn The Development in the Critical Attitude towards
      William Wordsworth, 1793-1820 MA Univ of Oklahoma 1935
8898 HEAD Emory L A Study of the Year 1805 in William Wordsworth's Life
      and Work MA Univ of Georgia 1922
8899 HENLEY Elton F A Bibliography of Wordsworthian Criticism, 1945-1957
      MA Florida St Univ 1959
8900 HERBISON Michael R Wordsworth and the French Revolution MA Univ of
      Wyoming 1966
8901 HERNDON George C The Critical Opinions of William Wordsworth as
      They Are Reflected in His Correspondence MA Univ of Kentucky 1947
      81 p
8902 HILDEBRANDT Josephine E Wordsworth's Prose MA Tulane Univ 1928
8903 HILDENBRAND Mary D Wordsworth and Thoreau: On Viewing Nature as a
      Way of Life MS Ft Hays Kansas St Coll 1966
8904 HILL Viola J Wordsworth's Imagery and What It Tells Us MA Indiana Univ
      1950
8905 HOSKINS Elizabeth The Relation between Man and Nature in Wordsworth's
      Poetry MA Univ of Louisville 1921
8906 HOUSEHOLDER Annabel L William Wordsworth's Philosophy of Life as
      Reflected in His Poetry MS Kansas St Coll at Pittsburg 1941
8907 HOWE Fred A The Educational Theories of William Wordsworth MA Univ
      of Chicago 1899
8908 HUFFORD Mary Wordsworth's Doctrine of the Formation of Moral Character
      MA Univ of Texas at Austin 1929
8909 HUGHEY Ruth W Wordsworth, 1830-1840: A Biographical Study MA Columbia
      1922
8910 HUGUELET Theodore L Wordsworth's Criticism of Eighteenth Century
      Poetry MA Univ of Tennessee 1951 112 p
8911 HUNT Kellogg W Wordsworth's Doctrine of Imagination, Especially in
      The Prelude MA Univ of Iowa 1935
8912 ISON Henri G Wordsworth and His Use of Reminiscence MA Hardin-
      Simmons Univ 1959
8913 JABOUR J A A Survey of Wordsworthian Criticism from Victorian to
      Modern Times BA Univ of British Columbia (Canada) 1953
8914 JACKSON Sally F Sports, Games and Pastimes in the Life and Auto-
      biographical Poetry of William Wordsworth MA Univ of North Carolina
      at Chapel Hill 1951 84 p
8915 JAMERSON Betty A Humanity's Appointed Shroud: Wordsworth's Principle

of Pleasure in Pain MA Western Carolina Univ 1969
8916 KAHN Thekla Wordsworth's Theory of Diction MA Univ of Missouri 1902
8917 KEELING Jennie D Wordsworth and Painting: A Study of the Influence
      of Painting upon the Writing of William Wordsworth and of His
      Poems which Relate to that Art MA Univ of Tennessee 1951 79 p
8918 KENNEALLY Michael The Background of Wordsworth's "Ode to Duty"
      BA Univ of British Columbia (Canada) 1968
8919 KEYSTON Judith M A Study in Wordsworth's Early and Later Style
      MA Toronto (Canada) 1963
8920 KHAN Hamid A A Study of the Relationship between the Sensuous and
      the Mystical in Wordsworth, with Some Oriental Parallels
      M Litt Cambridge Univ (England) 1955
8921 KLEIN Hans J German Criticism of Wordsworth MA Indiana Univ 1955
8922 KLIMAN Bernice W Within Narrow Walls: A Study of Wordsworth's River
      Duddon Sonnets MA Hunter Coll 1963
8923 KLOSTER Mabel P Nature in Wordsworth and Emerson MA Univ of Iowa 1940
8924 LAMBRECHT Klaus Wordsworth's Sonnets Dedicated to National Indepen-
      dence and Liberty in the Light of His Political Beliefs MA Univ
      of Louisville 1953
8925 LANDIS Florence P The Disciplinary Value of Nature in Wordsworth's
      Poetry MA George Washington Univ 1933 42 p
8926 LAWALE John O Wordsworth's Doctrine of Nature in *The Prelude* and
      The White Doe of Rylstone MA Univ of Oklahoma 1964
8927 LAWRENCE Janice L Guilt and Redemption in Wordsworth's Poetry
      MA Columbia 1965
8928 LEE Annie Wordsworth's Theory of Natural Education MA Columbia 1917
8929 LEE Maude E The Development of Wordsworth's Genius and Political
      Opinions MA Univ of Tennessee 1917
8930 LEWIS Clara D Wordsworth the Man as Seen by His Contemporaries
      MA Tulane Univ 1925
8931 LIGGINS Essie S Wordsworth's Reaction to Contemporary Criticism
      MA Ohio St Univ 1947
8932 LITTRELL Mary P Wordsworth's *Prelude* and Rousseau's *Emile:* A Com-
      parative Study of Personal Philosophies MA East Carolina Univ 1941
8933 LIVINGSTONE S T Wordsworth and the Doctrine of the Return to Nature
      MA Williams Coll 1901
8934 LONG Martha M *Pearl* and the Apocalypse; Wordsworthian Parodies; and
      the Development and Dissemination of William Dean Howells' Theory
      of Equality MA Univ of Tennessee 1964
8935 LUCKHARDT Virginia E Dorothy Wordsworth: An Analysis of Her Mind
      and Art MA Univ of Pittsburgh 1945
8936 McCASLIN Davida Wordsworth's Theory of Poetic Diction MA Univ of
      Minnesota 1912
8937 McCLEARY Lila M Mysticism in the Poetry of William Wordsworth
      MA Univ of Delaware 1965 64 p
8938 McCUMMISKEY James V Was Wordsworth a Pantheist? MA St Louis Univ 1939
      82 p
See also 72, 88, 433, 508, 519, 677, 849, 968, 1531, 1667, 1803, 1835,
      1889, 1891, 1893, 2794, 4195, 4199, 4513, 4525, 5310, 5486, 5538,
      5907, 6076, 6429, 6819, 7124

WILLIAM BUTLER YEATS

8939 ABRAMS Jean H The Rose Symbol in the Poetry of Yeats MA Columbia 1953
      89 p
8940 ANDERSON Carol Christianity in the Poems and Plays of William Butler
      Yeats MA Columbia 1963 112 p
8941 BALLARD Charles G The Heroic Plays of William Butler Yeats
      MA Oklahoma St Univ 1966 118 p
8942 BANKERT Jerrold P A Study of the Dance Plays of Yeats MA West

Chester St Coll 1966
8943 BARKLEY Roy R Romantic Elements in the Poetry of Yeats MA Univ of
     Texas at Austin 1965 254 p
8944 BHARGAVA Harsh V Indian Philosophy in the Poetry of W B Yeats
     MA Queen's (Canada) 1965
8945 BICKAL Robert R *The Tower* of William Butler Yeats MA Columbia 1951
8946 BILLION Maria Patterns of Conflict in Some Poems of William Butler Yeats
     BA Univ of British Columbia (Canada) 1970
8947 BLACKBURN Thomas H Truth and Imagination: A Study of the Poetry of
     William Butler Yeats BA Amherst 1954
8948 BLAYNEY Anne A Discussion of Selected Bird and Tree Symbols Illus-
     trating the Importance of Symbols in the Poetry of William Butler
     Yeats BA Univ of British Columbia (Canada) 1960
8949 BORDOW Rita L Yeats and Music MA Columbia 1950
8950 BRIDGES Peggy J Yeats' Dramatic Theory MA Univ of North Carolina
     at Chapel Hill 1958 76 p
8951 BRYCE Joyce Dichotomy and Resolution in the Tree Image in the Shorter
     Poems of Yeats BA Univ of British Columbia (Canada) 1968
8952 BUTLER Jone L Yeats' Byzantium Poems: Some Versions of the Pastoral
     MA Wichita St Univ 1966
8953 CALARCO N Joseph Unity of Action in the Later Plays of William Butler
     Yeats MA Columbia 1962 65 p
8954 CHIN Pearl S The Symbolism of William Butler Yeats BA Acadia (Canada)
     1966
8955 COON Henry L W B Yeats and His Personal Speakers BA Amherst 1955
8956 CRAVEN Sr Mary A Nature Imagery in the Early Poetry of William Butler
     Yeats MA Boston Coll 1952
8957 CUFF Elizabeth L Existential Themes in the Poetry of William Butler
     Yeats MA Texas Christian Univ 1965 85 p
8958 CUMMINGS Irving P Changing Concepts of Ireland in the Poetry of
     William Butler Yeats MA Univ of New Hampshire 1949 95 p
8959 DENNENY Corinne M William Butler Yeats as a Dramatist MA St Louis Univ
     1930 59 p
8960 DIETZ John J The Influence of the Occult on Yeats' Early Poetry
     MA Temple Univ 1965 52 p
8961 FAIRBAIRN Patrick W Supernatural Themes in the Plays of Yeats
     MA Toronto (Canada) 1966
8962 FEHLBERG Joan S The Golden Chain: Relationships between the Early
     and Late Poetry of William Butler Yeats MA Brigham Young Univ 1965
8963 FELDMAN Irving Yeats and the Artistic Vocation MA Columbia 1953 107 p
8964 FINAN Ellen F The Relation of Yeats to the Heroic Literature of
     Ancient Ireland MA Marquette Univ 1925 44 p
8965 GILL J C Ideas of Magic of William Butler Yeats MA Boston Coll 1932
8966 GODFREY Michael E The Development of the Symbol of the Dancer in
     the Poetry of William Butler Yeats MA McGill (Canada) 1966
8967 GORDER Charles R An Approach to the Vision of William Butler Yeats
     MA Columbia 1953 90 p
8968 GRIFFITHS Edwin S Glory in One Inextricable Beam: Yeats and a Nine-
     teenth Century Problem of Style BA Amherst 1963
8969 GRIFI Maria William Butler Yeats as a Dramatist MA Ca Foscari (Italy)
     1956
8970 HATCHETT M Ruth The Relation of William Butler Yeats to the Celtic
     Revival MA Univ of Oklahoma 1940
8971 HAZLEY Richard A From Innisfree to the Rag Shop of the Heart: Voyages
     of William Butler Yeats MA Columbia 1959 82 p
8972 HEXTER George J The Aesthetic Philosophy of William Butler Yeats
     MA Univ of Texas at Austin 1916
8973 HIRTH Mary M A Study in the Work of William Butler Yeats MA Univ of
     Texas at Austin 1956 485 p
8974 HOON Barbara J The Concern of Self-Unity and the Concept of Anima

Mundi in the Poetry of William Butler Yeats   MA Florida St Univ 1966
8975 HORAN Dolores V   The Profane Perfection: Beatitude in *The Collected
      Poems* of William Butler Yeats   MA Columbia 1961   95 p
8976 HOWARD Alan   The Function of Poetry in the Drama: A Study of the Verse
      Plays of W B Yeats   BA Rutgers St Univ 1953   125 p
8977 HUGHES Richard E   A Criticism of the Poetry of William Butler Yeats
      MA Boston Coll 1950
8978 HYMAN Virginia R   An Analysis of Yeats' *Byzantium*   MA Columbia 1961   90 p
8979 ISLAM Shamsul   The Influence of Hindu, Buddhist and Muslim Thought
      on Yeats' Poetry   MA McGill (Canada) 1966
8980 JOHNSON Alan P   A Twentieth Century Religion: A Study of the Plays
      of W B Yeats   BA Amherst 1953
8981 JOHNSON Eulah J   Tenor of the Criticism of Yeats and His Works as
      Shown by the Periodicals since 1934   MA St Mary's at San Antonio
      1948   82 p
8982 JOHNSTON Helen J   A Study of the Irish Influence on the Poetry of Yeats
      with Some Consideration of the Poems of the Last Two Decades
      MA Pacific Univ 1953
8983 KAYLOR Mary A   William Butler Yeats and the Shadowy Waters
      MA Sacramento St Coll 1966
8984 KOBAYASHI Manji   A Study of *Supernatural Songs* of William Butler Yeats
      MA Columbia 1966   142 p
8985 KELLEHER John J   The Metaphysical Quality of Yeats' Later Poetry
      MA Boston Coll 1956
8986 KELLY Patrick W   Mysticism in the Poetry of William Butler Yeats
      MA St Louis Univ 1938   55 p
8987 KOLLARITSCH Martha J   A Study in Yeats' Early Verse   MA Univ of Texas
      at Austin 1955   125 p
8988 KORGES Erwin J   Yeats as Playwright   MA Rice 1955
8989 KREITHEN Linda   William Butler Yeats: A Poet in and out of Politics
      MA Temple Univ 1966   91 p
8990 LAMBERG Walter   Cultural Primitivism in the Early Poetry of
      William Butler Yeats   MA Univ of Houston 1966   76 p
8991 LEHMAN E   William Butler Yeats: The Development of His Poetical
      Style   BA Univ of British Columbia (Canada) 1934
8992 LIGHTCAP Jane S   William Butler Yeats' Reputation in Selected American
      Periodicals: 1895-1940   MA Univ of Florida 1964
8993 LURIA Maxwell   Yeats' System: A Study in Symbolism and Religion
      BA Rutgers St Univ 1953   78 p
8994 McMANUS June J   A Study of Symbols in the Myth Plays of William Butler
      Yeats   MA Midwestern Univ 1967   103 p
8995 MILLER Donald W   Fathers and Sons in the Life and Works of
      William Butler Yeats   MA Columbia 1959   74 p
8996 MIURA Tokhiro   Images and Symbols in William Butler Yeats' Poetry
      MA Northeast Missouri St Coll 1959
8997 MULKERN Jane I   Yeats' Aristocratic Ideal   MA Univ of Hawaii 1966   50 p
8998 MURPHY Muriel J   Old Age and the Old Man Image in Selected Poems of
      William Butler Yeats   MA Columbia 1955   96 p
8999 NAPIER Donna   Every Stick Has Two Ends: An Examination of William Butler
      Yeats' Concept and Practice of Unity of Being   BA Univ of British
      Columbia (Canada) 1964
9000 NAPOLI Joanne L   The Total Quest: Myth in the Poetry of Yeats
      MA Univ of Vermont 1965
See also 348, 5907, 7472

Abbey Theatre
5756
Adams
7212
Adams, Henry
52
Adams, Joseph Quincey
6900
Adventurer
4212, 4216
Aeneid
1606, 2897
Aeschylus
3742, 6008, 7406, 7453
Africa
2194
Agamemnon
6961
Akenside, Mark
18
Alcestis
639
Ambrose, Saint
5380
America
91, 101, 166, 466, 873, 981, 1022,
1046, 1280, 1536, 1814, 4675, 4840,
5451, 6569, 7177, 7299, 7441, 7471,
8363
American Revolution
4882
American Tragedy
1027
Amores
2834
Anders, H R D
6579
Anderson, Maxwell
7118, 7257, 7342
Andrewes, Lancelot
2712
Annales
2470
Annual Review
7632
Anouilh, Jean
3280, 3283, 7342
Arden, John
381
Aristotle
2898, 2907, 4227, 4365, 5412,
6155, 6597, 6634, 6709, 6880,
6903, 7657, 7806, 7904, 8443

Arnold, Thomas
5744
Arthurian Legend
2836, 3645, 4948, 4950, 4957,
4958, 4959, 4961, 4964, 4968,
4973, 4974, 7747, 8238, 8268,
8312, 8317, 8325, 8733
Auden, W H
3793, 7756
Augustine, Saint
1721, 2682, 2899, 5666
Aurelius, Marcus
92
Australia
2619
Aylmer, Rose
4710
Babbitt, Irving
146
Bagehot, Walter
3920
Balzac
2572, 6105
Barnes, William
3833
Barnfield
4171
Baroja, Pio
2623
Bartas, Seigneur du
5450, 7728
"Bartleby"
5542
Baskerville, C R
6209
Baudelaire, Charles
4593, 8129
Bayle
1049
Beautiful Losers
4902
Bellow, Saul
2194
Benito Cereno
2118, 7815
Benoit
1563, 2877
Bentham
7343
Bentley, Richard
3580
Bergerac, Cyrano de
8029

Bible, The
30, 62, 297, 441, 468, 480, 484,
718, 795, 892, 918, 922, 924, 928,
933, 940, 1106, 1207, 1221, 1231,
1376, 1382, 1401, 1445, 1669, 1674,
2323, 2781, 2811, 2816, 2858, 3067,
3078, 3336, 3538, 3688, 3705, 3730,
3735, 3761, 3781, 3809, 3868, 3872,
3938, 3971, 4003, 4119, 4651, 4671,
4703, 4727, 5301, 5369, 5393, 5431,
5450, 5458, 5459, 5463, 5520, 5523,
5618, 6085, 6240, 6515, 6893, 6929,
6937, 7107, 7195, 7542, 7720, 7816,
7872, 7917, 8130, 8215, 8219, 8231,
8270, 8273, 8361, 8386, 8421, 8569,
8570, 8575, 8581, 8584
Billy Budd
3267
Boadicea
2315
Boccacio
1459, 1555, 1563, 6967
Boehme, Jacob
498
Boethius
1375, 1454, 1511, 1593, 1719
Boke Named the Governour
6633
Boileau
5921
Boito
6242, 6349
Book of Common Prayer
4219, 4247
Book of Job
1669, 5377, 5458, 6937
Bowles
1044
Boyle, Robert
292
Bradley
6397, 7044, 7099, 7227, 7228
Brawne, Fanny
4507, 4510
Braybrooke, Patrick
3619
Brecht, Bertolt
6208, 6556
Breton, Nicholas
7633, 8828
Bridges, Robert
4084, 4088, 5521
Brittania's Pastorals
7725

Brome
4303, 4333
Brown, Charles Brockden
3458, 3459
Browne, William
7670
Brownson, Orestes A
1292, 1752
Bruyere, Jean de la
3146
Bryant, Jacob
506, 513
Bryskett
7858
Burbage
6989
Caedmon
5450
Calderon
3195, 6391, 6987, 7382
Call It Sleep
2693
Campanella
277
Campbell, Mrs Patrick
7349
Camus
3477, 4896, 4902, 8771
Candide
8109
Capell, Edward
6320
Carew, Thomas
4326
Carey, Lady Elizabeth
7797
Castiglione, Baldassare
6206, 7711, 7717, 7787
Catch 22
4891
Cather, Willa
4987, 7206, 7741, 8808
Catullus
978, 3999, 4715
Cavalier Poets
4318
Cecil, William (Lord Burghley)
7544, 7772
Centaur
1096
Cervantes
1020, 2704, 3138, 3203, 6248,
7605

Cervoni, Dominic
2154
Champion of Virtue
5972
Chanson de Roland
5526
Chateaubriand
1200, 5334
Cheever, John
3412
Chekov
4990, 4993, 5002, 5005, 7117
Chenier, Andre
4544
Chettle, Henry
2474
Church
7915
Churchill
7067
Cibber, Colley
5925, 6682
Cicero
4145, 5724
Cinthio, Giraldi
6242, 6570
Circe
5554
Civile Conversation
6206
Clemens, Samuel
(See Mark Twain)
Clermont
5972
Cleveland, John
3412
Cocteau
2920
Cohen, Leonard
2671, 4902
Colet, John
5679
Collier, Jeremy
5203
Commedia Dell'Arte
6548
Compendium Physicae
1365
Comte, Auguste
3093
Conti
5454
Cooke, Thomas
5934

Cooper, James Fenimore
1129
Corneille, Pierre
2863, 6657
Cornhill Magazine, The
8379
Courtier, The
6206, 7717, 7779, 7787
Coward, Noel
5187, 5189, 7518
Crane, Stephen
7741
Crime and Punishment
2265
Cromwell, Oliver
5125, 5129
Crozier, Eric
3267
Cruikshank, George
2577, 2611
Cuthbertson
5972
Danforth
5902
Dante
4985, 5288, 5559, 7485
Darwin, Charles
3754, 4188, 4190, 4194
David Simple
3149
Davidson
8434
Death Comes for the Archbishop
4987
Death of a Salesman
6224, 7101
De Casibus
1338, 1352
De Morgan, William
2569
Dennis, John
5899
Descartes
276, 4886
Deschamps
1584
Devils, The
4154
Dialogues of the Dead
4328
Dickinson, Emily
597, 617, 1440, 6025, 6033,
8145

Divine Comedy
5288

Doctor Zhivago
3721

Dona Perfecta
3791

Don Quixote
1020, 3185, 6301, 7605

Dostoevski
2005, 2265, 4455, 4896

Dreiser, Theodore
1027

DuBellay
7836

Ducis, Jean Francois
6631

Duns Scotus, John
4096

D'Urfrey
6192

Dyce, Alexander
6513

Ecclesiastes
795

Eddison, E R
8488

Edinburgh Review
4198, 6143

"Elegy on Madam Hannah Sewall"
5902

Eliot, T S
56, 58, 95, 165, 1282, 1873, 2797,
2810, 2855, 2967, 3283, 3287, 3295,
4288, 5281, 5519, 5576, 6274, 7188,
8348

Elizabeth, Queen
6731, 7875

Elyot, Thomas
290, 6633

Emerson, Ralph Waldo
278, 1253, 1255, 1264, 1314, 1786,
1822, 5467, 6524, 7179, 8923

Emile
8932

Empedocles of Akragas
85

England
873, 1022, 1280, 1609, 1982, 2443,
2683

England, John
1752

English Review
3220

Epicurus
4000, 4718

Erasmus
5679, 8119

Etherege, George
1919, 1931, 4371

Euripedes
639, 3471, 6008

Evans, Sebastian
4953

Everyman
5281

Ezekiel
441

Falstof, Sir John
6771, 7091

Family Reunion
3295

Farquhar
1931

Faulkner, William
4425, 6872

Faust
1190, 5038, 6409

Ferrier, Susan
182

Fichte
1309

Ficino, Marsilio
7780, 7920

Fielding, Sarah
3149

"First Travels of Max"
2794

Fitzgerald, F Scott
3301, 3844

Flaubert
3001

Fletcher, Giles
2801, 7633

Fontaine
4658

Forest of Montalbano
5972

Foxe, John
927

France
141, 717, 2224, 4679, 5545, 6003,
6107, 7832, 8790

Franceshini
692

Franklin, Benjamin
4217

Freeholder
16
French Revolution
519, 1278, 1294, 1296, 8824,
8835, 8888, 8900
Freud
2133, 4401
Froissart
1584
Frost, Robert
7067, 8828
Froude
1260
Fry, Roger
8807
Frye
6809
Galateo, The
6206
Galdos
2587, 3791
Galsworthy, Ada Cooper
3314, 3330
Galt, John
6173
Garrard, George
2772
Gauguin, Paul
5191
Gautier
8129
Genesis
5450
Genet
5884
Gentleman's Magazine
4201, 4240
George, Saint
7843
"George's Mother"
7741
Georgics
3851
Germany
856, 3810, 6217, 7158
Gide, Andre
719, 1999, 2270, 6867, 7239
Gifford, William
5164
Gill, Eric
1245
Ginsberg, Allen
490

Giraudoux, Jean
3285, 6008
Godfrey, Thomas
1603
Goethe
108, 899, 1190, 5024, 5038,
6409, 6539, 8848
Gone With the Wind
8356
Gongora, Don Luis de
2700
Gounod
7022
Goya, Francisco de
8070
Granville-Barker, Harley
6236, 7212, 7235
Graunson
1453
Greece
1068
Greek Drama
639, 3075, 3471, 3690, 5312,
6008, 6923
Grigia
4477
Grosart
7705
Guardian
16
Guiney, Louise Imogen
3906
Guthrie, Tyrone
6419
Handel
2880
Hankin
5189
Hardy, Emma
3754
Harris, Joel Chandler
4658
Harte, Bret
4666
Hauptmann
7283
Hawes, Stephen
7763, 7821
Hawker
8314
Hawkes
8489

Hawthorne
    853, 2232, 2759, 6121, 7188, 7680,
    8848
Heilman, Robert
    6729
Heliodorus
    7657
Hemingway, Ernest
    2291, 3797
Henderson the Rain King
    2194
Henryson
    1377, 1387
Herbert, Magdalen
    2766
Hercules
    5554, 7829
Hesse
    8603
High Wind in Jamaica
    3490
History of Britain, The
    5600
Holderlin, Friedrich
    85
Holinshed
    5090, 6383
Holme, Constance
    3406
Homer
    115, 1359, 4954, 7811, 7861
Hood, E P
    3911
Hooker, Richard
    6384
Horace
    21, 3131, 3999, 4007, 4547, 5886,
    5898, 5915, 5940, 5954
Horne, R H
    3911
Hotson
    6238
Houghton, William
    2474
Howells, William Dean
    8934
Howl
    490
Hugh of St Victor
    5380
Hughes, Richard
    3468, 3490
Hugo, Victor
    2518, 7089, 8313

Hunter, Joseph
    6388, 6954
Ibsen, Henrik
    3796, 4483, 7324, 7362
Idler
    4216
Ignatius, Saint
    4740, 7637, 8450
Iliad
    1359, 5526, 5923, 7861
India
    4649, 4662
Industrial Revolution
    520
Ionesco, Eugene
    366
Ireland
    7705, 7710, 7807, 7901, 8054,
    8084, 8533, 8958, 8964
Irving, Henry
    8300
Italy
    76, 1090, 1119, 1592, 1857,
    3044, 4156, 4309, 4490, 4806,
    4857, 5577
James, Henry
    748, 833, 836, 2053, 2100,
    2118, 2130, 2156, 2221, 2291,
    2991, 3008, 3020, 3082, 3642,
    5233, 5571
Jefferies, Richard
    4139
Jeffers, Robinson
    896
Jesus
    7436
Jewett, Sarah Orne
    4985
Joan of Arc
    6357, 6450, 6701, 7254, 7257,
    7270, 7275, 7279, 7310, 7321,
    7328, 7342, 7344, 7351, 7377,
    7378
Jocelin Chronicle
    1302
Jones, Henry Arthur
    105
Jones, Inigo
    4347, 4361
Jones, Isabella
    4581
Jung, Carl
    82, 457, 7647

Juvenal
1086, 4266
Kafka
7756, 8489
Kalidasa
7150
Kane, George
4738
Kant
1800, 1876
Keach, Benjamin
912
Kennedy, John Pendleton
6150
Kennedy, Margaret
4980
Khayyam, Omar
795
Kierkegaard
135
Knight, G Wilson
6346
Kocher, Paul H
5713
Koestler, Arthur
5780, 5790
Kreipe, C E
5337
Kurosawa
6694
Kyd
4325, 4922
Laclos, Pierre
6005
Lady Pecunis
4171
Lagerlof, Selma
1285
Lancasters
1408
Langbaine
6222
Languet
7547
Lee, Nathaniel
7152
Lehman, Rosamond
4980
Lermontov
1152
Lessing
1811
Lettres Persanes
3522, 3541

Lever, Charles
8166
Lewis, Matthew Gregory
7422
Liberal, The
1160
"Little Musgrave and Lady Barnard"
1660
Lodge
3647
Lollardy
4739
Longfellow
7176
Looking Glass for London and England
3647
Lorca, Federico Garcia
8174
Loti, Pierre
2117
Lover
7931
Lover, Samuel
8166
Lowell, Amy
7569
Lowell, James Russell
5474, 5536
Lucian
4328
Lucretius
2859, 7659, 8446
Mabinogion, The
4955, 8309
McCormack, John
4476
Machant
1584
Machiavelli
270, 4021, 4391, 5097, 6516,
6589, 6796, 6894, 7105
MacInnes, Colin
1387
Madame Bovary
3001
Malaysia
1939, 1996, 2195
Mallarme
4403, 4478
Mallock
1362
Malone
6222, 7029, 7111

Malraux
 2147, 5790
Malthus, Thomas Robert
 3899
Mandeville
 2426
Manly
 4722
Mann, Thomas
 5024
Manning, Anne
 5462
Mannyng, Robert
 1715
Manrique, Jorge
 2790
Marivaux, Pierre
 3532
Marshall, Archibald
 8549
Martial
 3999
Martin, Richard
 4304
Mary, Queen of Scots
 8132, 8143, 8301, 8350
Mather, Cotton
 7239
Mazzini
 8141
Meditations
 4171
Melville, Herman
 627, 1667, 1940, 1993, 2118, 2138,
 2218, 2257, 2261, 3267, 4179, 5542,
 5972, 6279, 6317, 6446, 6815, 7008,
 7815, 7991, 8019, 8349
Menaechmi
 6437
Mencken, H L
 1437
Mexico
 3590, 7108
Michangelo
 4079
Midwife Magazine
 7602
Miller, Arthur
 6224, 6923, 7101
Miracle Plays
 1608
Mitchell, Margaret
 8356
M'Lehose, Agnes
 998

Moby Dick
 627, 2138, 2213, 2257, 6446,
 6815, 8349
Moliere
 4371, 5236, 6191, 7515
Molina, Tirso de
 8659
Montague, George
 8594
Montaigne
 273, 294, 6310
Montalbert
 5972
Montesquieu
 3522, 3541, 4877
Morality Plays
 5281, 6459, 6573, 7582
Moratin
 7115
Morton
 1365
Morton, Charles
 2442
Morton, Thomas
 3174
Murder in the Cathedral
 5281, 5576
Murdoch, Iris
 7646
Musil, Robert
 4477
Musset, Alfred de
 1180
Nabokov
 1282
Napoleon
 1127, 1135, 3811, 3857
Newval
 4604
New England Primer, The
 3496
New Testament
 718, 3938
Newton
 1236, 2328
Niebuhr, Reinhold
 8202
Nietzsche
 1270, 1275, 7273, 7357, 8153
Norris, Frank
 3835
North
 6499, 6758
Norton, Charles Eliot
 6082

Novalis
  4523
Noyes, Alfred
  5154
O'Brien, Flann
  5777
O'Connor, Flannery
  3620
O'Connor, Frank
  5777
Oedipus Rex
  2920, 6519
O'Faolian, Sean
  5777
Ogilvy, Margaret
  303
Oldcastle, John
  6741, 7045
Old Testament
  62, 484, 924, 1207, 5301, 8273
Olivier, Laurence
  6807
O'Neill, Eugene
  508, 4764, 6008, 7154
Oresteia
  3742, 7118
Orestes Myth
  2083, 6008
Ormsby, John
  7605
Ossian
  5485
Otello
  6242, 6352, 6439
Ovid
  499, 1438, 1458, 1534, 2834,
  3555, 3556, 4474, 7687, 7828,
  7849, 7869
Paine, Thomas
  101
Painter, William
  6297, 6874
Palace of Pleasure
  6297, 6874
Palingenia
  6677
Parker, Samuel
  5443
Parmgianino
  7563
Pastime of Pleasure
  7763, 7821
Pauca Meae
  8313

Paul, Saint
  151, 4071
Pearl
  8934
Petrarch
  2356, 2665, 2720, 3995
Phedre
  6277
Phillips, Ambrose
  5950
Phillips, John
  5402
Phillips, Stephen
  745
Picture, The
  8657
Pierre
  4179
Pirandello
  7117
Pit, The
  3835
Plato
  171, 296, 1881, 2699, 3246,
  3746, 5665, 6079, 7394, 7498,
  7550, 7696, 7748, 7780, 7820,
  7870, 7920, 8568
Plautus
  6437
Pleiade Myth
  7671, 7760
Plotinus
  2669, 7803
Plunkett
  8454
Plutarch
  6281, 6363, 6367, 6499, 6751,
  6758, 7006, 7180, 7206
Plutchik
  3622
Poe, Edgar Allan
  1070, 1081, 1083, 1799, 1867,
  1897, 3903, 6048, 8848
Poetics
  5412, 6597
Poole
  7457
Porter, Katherine Anne
  3642
Portrait of a Lady, The
  2130, 5233
Pound, Ezra
  671, 838

Power, Eileen
1429
Prometheus
6937, 7406
Proserpina Myth
1685
Proust, Marcel
4163, 4401, 8782
Psalms
5369
Punch
8368
Purcell
2880
Puttenham
7751
Quarterly Review
5556, 8220, 8371
Rabelais, Francois
5678, 5711, 8037
Racine
6277, 6326
Rambler
4212, 4216
Ransom, John Crowe
2794
Read, T B
1387
Redburn
1667
Reeve, Clara
5972
Renan, Ernest
46, 68, 158, 159
Restoration Wits
4024
Revelation of St John
4727
Reynolds, John Hamilton
4567
Reynolds, Sir Joshua
427, 447
Richards, I A
1852
Richardson, William
6283
Richter, Jean Paul
1239
Riley
312
Rimbaud
3797, 4403
Robbe-Grillet
4446

Robertson
3355
Robinson, E A
758, 861, 3869, 4948, 4973
5154, 7067, 8238, 8317
Robinson, Thomas
7633
Rob Roy
6124
Roche, Regina
5972
Rodo, Jose
6228
Rojas, Fernando de
1523
Roman d'Eneas
1530
Roman de Troie
1563
Romaunt of the Rose
1447, 1478, 1556, 1724,
Ronsard, Pierre de
3981, 7832, 7837
Room With a View
1365
Roper
1337
Rostand, Edmond
6219
Roth, Henry
2693
Rousseau
1130, 2415, 6003, 6005, 7389,
8848, 8932
Rowley, Samuel
2468
Rowley, William
5258
Royal Society
3094
Russia
2044, 6485
Sade, Marquis de
8146
Saint-Lambert
8483
Sainte-Beuve
89, 128
Sales, Francois de
3974
Salinger, J D
3468
Santayana, George
833

Sappho
1440
Sartre
6008, 8603
Satan
1183, 7224
Savoy Operas
3427, 3430, 3433, 3434
Schiller, Friedrich
1307, 1821, 1863
Schlegel, A W
6558
Schopenhauer
3722, 3788, 3826
Schucking
7212
Scotland
534, 1136, 1184, 2443, 4202,
4224, 4513, 6142
Scriblerus Club
8083
Scudery, Mlle de
396
Sea Gull
7117
Senancour
53
Seneca
2920, 5084, 6896, 7083, 8645
Settle
6192
Shaffer
5883
Shakuntala
7150
Siddal, Elizabeth
6086
Simms, William Gilmore
6185
Simon, Saint
5263
Sinclair, May
550
Sir Gawain and the Green Knight
4737
Skinner, M L
4799
Smith, Charlotte
958, 5972
Songe
7836
Song of Songs
7542

Sophocles
115, 3798, 7209
Spain
1542, 1592, 4642, 6120, 8659
Spectator, The
5, 16, 29, 3186, 5566
Spinoza
44
Sponde, Jean de
2800
Stael, Madame de
1223
Stanley
537
Stedman, E C
5571
Steevens, George
6977
Steinbeck, John
2566, 6967
Stendhal
6326
Steppenwolf
8603
Stevens, Wallace
80, 1896
Stevenson, John Hall
7954
Stoll
6428
Stow
2470
Surrey
5070
Swamp Angel
4902
Swedenborg
643
Sylvester, Joshua
5450
Syrus, Pubilius
1559
Tagore
8190
Tasso
1126
Tate, Nahum
6652
Tatler
16, 3186, 7931, 7933
Taylor, Edward
3965, 4171, 8517
Teresa, Saint
2347, 2360

Theobald, Lewis
6350, 6486, 7149
Theseus
360, 1451
Thoreau
1264, 1362, 1606, 8850, 8903
Throne of Blood
6694
Tieck, Ludwig
8647
Tolstoy
3811, 3845
Tristram Legend
150
Trivet
1590
Troilus and Cressida Tradition
1377, 1537, 7041
Troublesome Reign of King John
6334, 6527, 6535, 7103
True Chronicle History of King Leir
6832
Turgenev, Ivan
3317, 3353
Turn of the Screw
2118
Twain, Mark
3138, 4656, 4666, 7756, 8038, 8128
Tyndale, William
5666
Ujejski, Jozef
2254
Ulysses
8248, 8318
Updike, John
1096
"Valentine"
5571
Vanbrugh
1931, 3207
Van der Moot
3174
Vasari
818
Vega, Lope de
3203
Verdi
6242, 6349, 6352, 6439
Vergil, Polydore
286
Vico, Giovanni
4410

Virgil
1438, 2897, 3414, 3848, 3851, 5286, 5336, 5472, 5474, 5488
7740
Vittoria Accorombona
8647
Voltaire
2920, 5605, 5894, 6202, 6962, 7190, 7191, 8109
Von Ense, Varnhagen
1246
Voyages to the Sun and the Moon
8029
Wagner
4964
Walden
1606
Wallenstein
1821, 1863
Warburton, William
5924
Waste Land
5519
We
5787
Wedgewood
854
Wesker, Arnold
381
"Western Wind"
3496
Wharton, Earl of
8085
Wharton, Edith
963
Wharton, Joseph
5959
Where Angels Fear to Tread
1365
Whistler
6090
White, T H
4948
White Herron
4985
Whitefield, George
8693
Whiter, Walter
6377
Whiting, John
4154
Whitman, Walt
768, 1238, 1480, 1999

Wilhelm Meisters Lehrjahre
  6539
Williams, Rev J D
  819
Williams, Tennessee
  3869
Williams, William Carlos
  7015
Williamson, Henry
  4139
Wilson
  . 7212
Wilson, Ethel
  4902
Wilson, J Dover
  6286
Wilson, John
  7173
Winchester Manuscript
  4970
Winstanley, Gerrard
  930
Winterset
  7118
Wolfe, Thomas
  1109, 5024
World War II
  8621
Wycherley, William
  1919, 1931
Wyclif, John
  1614
Xenophon
  171
Young, Arthur
  7609
Young, Edward
  5904
Zagoskin, M N
  6175
Zamyatin
  5787, 8681
Zen
  6710
Zodiacus Vitae
  6677
Zoroaster
  5238

Abbiatici E 2447
Abbott J F 5272
Abbott M E 6363
Abbott W H 4025
Abdou E M 4845
Abegg E 7648
Abel R H 7942
Abernethy C 4903
Abraham B B 4292
Abraham D H 5753
Abraham F 3687
Abrahams C 423
Abrams J H 8939
Abrams M H 2303
Acevedo C G 7969
Acheson D 3500
Ackerman B J 6101
Ackerman R 8205
Ackermann A M 4200
Ackermann H F 6200
Ackert M J 5273
Acton E R 3300
Adair J M 3688
Adam G 4904
Adam Sr M D 5826
Adams A 8814
Adams A C 1362
Adams A C 5274
Adams B 7655
Adams C F 7381
Adams D A 2973
Adams D E 5275
Adams E B 7247
Adams E E 5276
Adams E H 1937
Adams E V 1042
Adams G R 1363
Adams H P 6201
Adams J 1364
Adams N E 3098
Adams P G 6202
Adams R J 2311
Adams R M 1905
Adams R R 2508
Adams S P 7656
Adams S S 8487
Adamson M A 2509
Adelsheimer E F 7382
Adkins J M 5277
Adlam P J 1938
Adler T P 3250
Agnes Sr 6203

Agnew J K 4026
Agnew Sr P M 3689
Aharoni A A 3099
Ahern E M 3301
Ahner F E 7524
Aichinger C P 1319
Aiello A 5754
Aiken M S 5278
Aiman H 7657
Airoldi T 1341
Aker M E 4742
Akers D 5007
Akin K 6204
Akins D W 1911
Akins P E 8815
Akrigg G P 41
Albaum C P 7383
Albert G E 348
Albertson L 4135
Albertson M 6188
Alden H H 1939
Aldrich J R 637
Aldrich J S 1785
Aldrich N E 7658
Aldridge M J 8156
Alexander A W 6205
Alexander E S 5720
Alexander F M 6206
Alexander G M 3303
Alexander G M 8011
Alexander I 545
Alexander J E 8001
Alexander R 6207
Algarin M 1365
Alger R C 4027
Allard A 1043
Allard F X 6208
Allen A 4201
Allen A H 947
Allen B 3690
Allen D C 2984
Allen E D 2850
Allen M 3691
Allen M 6209
Allen M T 1366
Allen P L 1044
Allen P S 8157
Allen R E 5808
Allen R F 1367
Allen R L 6210
Allen R T 1940
Allen R V 6211

Allen S F 5192
Allen S M 173
Allen T C 1941
Allen W 7659
Allen W R 543
Allender B L 544
Alley J M 3427
Alleyne J H 8816
Allingham P 5279
Allison A C II 6098
Allison E D 6212
Allison F 174
Allison G M 6213
Allison H M 1045
Allman E J 8012
Alpar J J 6214
Alpern F 6215
Alsmeyer H 5778
Alsop E M 1942
Alston M E 2312
Alston R C 8013
Alsup V D 4492
Altaffer C B 4147
Althaus P 1786
Altheimer L M 6216
Altman C O 6102
Alvis L S 948
Amabile G N 8389
Amarasingham G M 2985
Ambach M 6217
Ambler E J 6218
Ambrose R T 6219
Ames R A 5710
Ames R M 7660
Amiel J J 4293
Amis G T 5280
Amiss M 7661
Amory H 3100
Amundson J D 299
Anand S 5281
Andersen A 6220
Anderson A M 6024
Anderson B 638
Anderson B R 7384
Anderson C 8940
Anderson C L 5008
Anderson E H 7385
Anderson E K 169
Anderson G 1943
Anderson H A 546
Anderson H O 6222
Anderson H R 7662

Anderson I P   5997
Anderson J   175
Anderson J   6103
Anderson J S   176
Anderson L A   6221
Anderson M D   1368
Anderson M J   1369
Anderson M M   1370
Anderson M R   4493
Anderson M T   5721
Anderson N J   1371
Anderson R A   2665
Anderson S E   639
Anderson V L   7663
Anderson W D   424
Andreadis H   8636
Andreoli M F   2974
Andrew J E   3101
Andrews M C   4202
Angell C E   2383
Angell R C   616
Angell S   967
Angelo A N   1046
Angelo B H   177
Angevine M J   4494
Anghera F   42
Anglin J C   3501
Angus D R   1372
Angus-Smith J   2510
Anker R C   8566
Anonby J A   5282
Ansari R   7970
Anthony H   3692
Anthony K S   8699
Antico P J   2986
Anttonen E J   6025
Apollonio N   8817
Apperson E B   1373
Applegate E H   371
Applegate P   6104
Appoloni S   1011
Apterbach I   8818
Arant R H   8819
Arbogast J J   1374
Arcari R   5886
Archibald R M   1375
Archer L B   1047
Archuleta Br A C   640
Arduna A   8820
Argent R H   5283
Ariail J M   7664
Arkin S E   4203
Arluck A   8821

Arm S S   4877
Armfield F   8129
Armistead R A   7665
Armitage C M   2666
Armstrong J H   7943
Armstrong R J   7666
Armstrong R J   7667
Armstrong T M   2987
Arndt I A   1376
Arney L J   4710
Arnold G   3551
Arnold G H   1944
Arnold J D   7532
Arnold M V   8822
Arnspiger P   4396
Arsham A H   4188
Arthur L R   3502
Arthur M E   6224
Arthur R L   3464
Ashby S   6225
Ashford G   1734
Ashmore C D   3102
Ashton A D   5755
Askew A C   2304
Askew M W   7386
Askins D H   1945
Asp W B   2988
Astley R   8390
Aston M B   1
Astor S L   1946
Atchley D O   642
Athey F E   178
Atkin R   1377
Atkins C   6226
Atkins J   4743
Atkins S E   4891
Atkinson W   8391
Attlee G G   325
Atwood D M   6227
Auchinachie G   7387
Audette R A   5711
Audlin D J   1787
Augburn G   2511
Auslander C   6067
Austin A J   2667
Austin S   641
Avendell B B   547
Avery K E   3213
Avinger J   1947
Avison A   6026
Avison M K   1048
Avner S   5167
Ayala A L   4294

Aycock L W   2384
Aycock R E   1049
Aycock W   6228
Ayer J R   7668
Ayer L E   6229
Ayre R S   6027
Azar D L   4744
Azzi C   4295

Baatz W H   900
Babington M   1378
Bachenkeimer M S   6230
Bacon F   6105
Bacot G R   4204
Badessa R P   7590
Badiali G   4008
Badiello L   5157
Bagby C   1379
Bagley M M   6231
Baier M V   6232
Bailey C   5168
Bailey D B   5876
Bailey D D   5193
Bailey G H   548
Bailey J M   3435
Bailey J M   5284
Bailey J O   8676
Bailey L   1235
Bailey L G   8206
Bailey M F   2989
Bailey R C   376
Bailey S   3923
Baird D G   1788
Baird E B   2668
Baker A K   1948
Baker A W   5194
Baker B   7248
Baker D G   6233
Baker E   5887
Baker E D   1380
Baker E M   2669
Baker J   6234
Baker J E   179
Baker J E   8728
Baker J M   949
Baker J R   5285
Baker K M   6235
Baker N R   3304
Baker R O   5286
Baker S M Jr   6236
Baker V M   5888
Baker W E   3199
Baker W H   8207

Balboni D 7388
Baldi I 4495
Baldini L 4976
Baldwin G D 1789
Baldwin H L 2670
Baldwin M E 3552
Baldwin M F 43
Baldwin R F 6237
Baldwin R G 5864
Balkan S M 1949
Ball D A 1381
Ball M E 4745
Ballard C G 8941
Ballard E L 6238
Ballard G E 8823
Ballardini V V 5998
Ballenger J W 1917
Ballew J F 3924
Ballin M G 4746
Ballinger R H 7971
Balsevick M 2671
Balsham J 3408
Balsley E L 8530
Bamber J V 7669
Bambini L 7972
Band M W 4205
Bandler D B Jr 8158
Bandy F M 425
Banfichi P 38
Banham D S 4892
Bankert J P 8942
Banks J P 1382
Banks P F 2512
Banks T M 8824
Baratta P 8159
Barbeau A 2851
Barber C L 7670
Barber F 6068
Barber M de N 1790
Barber S J 4154
Barbieri A 1342
Barbour B 6028
Barbour D F 4296
Barbour J F 44
Barbour M M 45
Barbour R B 523
Bardella M L 3503
Barkatt A 2930
Barkell H J 7249
Barker E L 3980
Barker M 2513
Barker W L 6239
Barkley R R 8943
Barlow J M 7671

Barmettler R S 8700
Barnard C K 3103
Barnard M C 8825
Barnaud E E 1791
Barnes F D 3981
Barnes G 3305
Barnes G A 2514
Barnes H P 2672
Barnes J 6240
Barnes M C 5877
Barnes N N 5999
Barnes S G 1236
Barnett A W 4397
Barnett F W 5287
Barnett R 6241
Barnett W M Jr 7250
Barnhart W J 7672
Barnhill H L 269
Barnhill L V 7673
Barnum P H 7578
Barolini A 300
Baron H 1320
Baron W R 5967
Barr W M 7251
Barratt H 3586
Barrett A E 4496
Barrett B A 2515
Barrett B T 6242
Barrett Sr E T 1383
Barrett L M 6243
Barrett M 7389
Barrett M J 46
Barrette Sr M E 549
Barrier R C 7944
Barrington Sybil 5980
Barron J 6244
Barrosso F 2990
Barrow L 6245
Barrow S F 7674
Barrus R H 6246
Barry A B 8531
Barry G M 1792
Barry G T 6247
Barry H L 6248
Barry H V 4028
Barry J M 6249
Barry L 326
Barry M E 301
Barry Sr M T 5654
Barsaglia D 5722
Barss M L 8354
Bartels S T 3214
Barth M D 3428
Barth M G 550

Bartholome M 1950
Bartholomew J H 5288
Bartlett D R 4858
Bartlett H C 912
Bartlett L W 2313
Barto B J 8753
Barton A F 2673
Barton E C 4859
Barton E C 6029
Barton J D 47
Barton M M 8160
Barton W E 5684
Bartram W 8208
Baseheart K A 5289
Bass C S Jr 7390
Bass L I 6250
Bass M B 1050
Bass R W 5655
Bass W A 4155
Bataille R R 524
Batchelor J B 3251
Baten J B 6251
Bates A L 644
Bates A W 643
Bates M C 4497
Bathaniel G 2385
Batson G 8826
Battaglia M J 3280
Batte H E 8701
Batten M 2931
Battin J 1951
Battle M L 7675
Batts B B 1321
Baudin M C 5169
Bauer N S 8827
Bauer W C 8754
Bauman C P 3104
Bauman M A 8828
Baumgartner F A 7676
Baumwoll D 3215
Bauso T M 1051
Bawoom B E 1742
Baxter B W 4647
Baxter C 7603
Baxter C E 3925
Baxter E 6252
Baxter F L 1384
Baxter J E 48
Baxter J S 8637
Baxter S G 950
Bayard H R 6253
Baylis E 7391
Baylor E B 8618
Bazzana A 5195

Beach E K 3895
Beach Sr M A 2649
Beagan R T 4206
Beal G 180
Beall E 8702
Beaman E A 2516
Beaman M F 2448
Beamish F M 1052
Beard E 2852
Beard J F 3452
Beard V L 2674
Bearden R R 1385
Beasley R 645
Beaton A E 2675
Beattie H M 646
Beattie S M 3377
Beatty E 7677
Beatty F 8829
Beatty K W 4498
Beaver D D 1793
Bebey F A 7252
Beck C H 647
Beck F E 5009
Beck N A 5010
Beck P G 3982
Beck R P 943
Beck T E Jr 8130
Becker A L 8131
Becker A W 648
Becker B E 3306
Becker D W 3645
Becker L A 49
Becker M G 3896
Becker R J 1952
Becker R W 5889
Beckler H 5196
Beckwith J A 6106
Bedell J F 381
Bednowicz Rev J S 1386
Bedogni E 3390
Beebe M D 6254
Beechhold H F 4399
Beeching P Q 6069
Beede H F 2447
Beede M A 50
Beesley E A 649
Behar J 5779
Behlen Mother W 1743
Behm C 3252
Belanger S A 7392
Belanger T 385
Belden E 6255
Belfiglio M E 4207

Belfiore A R 4156
Belk L 4648
Belkin R 6256
Bell A M 7253
Bell B H 8209
Bell B P 6257
Bell C J 6258
Bell E B 650
Bell E F 7678
Bell E S 1387
Bell I F 5290
Bell K 2676
Bell L C 3465
Bell L K 7254
Bell M B 6107
Bell M E 2517
Bell M F 3587
Bell P B 3105
Bell P J 5011
Bell R A 349
Bell R M 8355
Belli Sr A 5723
Belshaw D 8703
Belson A A 2991
Beltz D S 551
Belyea B J 4946
Benard C G 1744
Benchoff H J 7679
Bender B T 181
Bender C P 6259
Bender S R 8210
Beneman C H 8132
Bennett D B 7393
Bennett E R 3926
Bennett L 4398
Bennett M 4499
Bennett Sr M J 5724
Benninghoff M 7394
Bennis Sr M A 2346
Benoit P E 6260
Benson C F 51
Benson C R Jr 2677
Benson J A 1053
Benson J B 6261
Benson P F 4860
Bent L W 6262
Bentley B A 4157
Bentley B A 5291
Bentley J G 4158
Benveni P 7604
Berek P 7680
Bergbusch M L 3693
Berge M C 2518

Bergen G T 4297
Bergen J R 3307
Berger J 5012
Berger T S 2450
Bergman J A 6263
Berland E D 5101
Bermack R 52
Berman L 651
Bernard C M 4400
Bernat P L 3679
Bernet R E 2451
Bernstein D 2519
Berntson L 968
Berra E J 3927
Berrigan A 652
Berry A M 7681
Berry B J 2347
Berry C A 6264
Berry C E 913
Berry D R 8638
Berry E 6265
Berry G M Jr 5110
Berry W G 2375
Berryman C B 7395
Bertapelle G 4905
Bertolotti D S 6070
Bertschler M M 8677
Bespaloff A J 2678
Besse L 5292
Bessent B R 5293
Best B S 7255
Best E G 3409
Best L G 5013
Bester B 8014
Betti I 4208
Bettini L 4856
Betto S 5014
Beutner Sr M L 7682
Bevins L E 7683
Beyer B M 3106
Bhargava H V 8944
Bhatia C 3694
Bialas A 7684
Bibb J 653
Bickal R R 8945
Bicker W D 6266
Bicley N K 1054
Bier R S 1953
Biggs M H 5262
Bigham J K 7256
Bigotto L 7685
Biller J 182
Billings V P 6267

Billingslea C B 2679
Billingsley J G 7973
Billion M 8946
Bilsland J W 3504
Binder B 3928
Binder R K 53
Bingham F C 3308
Bingle B A 4029
Bingman M L 8830
Binnette Mother M C 3929
Bird J 5890
Birdwell L W 5268
Birge V L 5294
Birney A E 1388
Bischofberger G 2853
Bishop B B 6108
Bishop C J 1389
Bishop C V 6268
Bishop J K 8211
Bishop N N 5295
Bishop R J 7396
Bishop S L 654
Bissell B J 2365
Bisson L M 183
Bittick E F 3309
Bitting M E 5296
Bivens W P 4298
Bivins S A 1390
Bixler M H 7686
Bjorkman L R 8532
Black A D 655
Black C L 7397
Black E R 5865
Black J 2314
Black J A 6109
Black J S 426
Black L 6110
Black L G 6269
Black L N 1012
Black R 656
Blackaller G A 6270
Blackburn M C 3310
Blackburn T H 8947
Blackert H I 7398
Blackmon B A 2992
Blaess F J 1954
Blagg M E 4649
Blaine L M 6271
Blair B 6272
Blair C L 657
Blair E H 2
Blair T M 3311
Blake L B 3107

Blakely G F 8586
Blakeman W M 1391
Blakeney E K 5808
Blakey D 5685
Blakney P S 658
Blanche E K 6273
Blankenship C W 8513
Blassingame R 1392
Blatty W P 6274
Blau R 3930
Blayney A 8948
Blazic T M 4747
Bledsoe B G 3281
Bleeker B J 8831
Blidstein G J 4112
Blinco E M 4748
Block L F 2993
Blodgett J E 3253
Blodgett M E 659
Blondin A 7257
Blong B A 184
Bloodgood F C 6275
Bloom H A 3254
Bloom J C 8755
Bloom L 4030
Bloom P B 2650
Bloomberg S 8832
Bloomfield M W 4721
Blouin G 6277
Blount T J 2520
Blue E 8212
Blum Sr M L 4031
Blumenthal E H 4977
Blyth M D 185
Blythe D E 5297
Blythe W K 1055
Board D H 1955
Boatright M C 6111
Boaz O O 7399
Bocasky C C 2854
Boccato A 327
Boddy M P 7687
Bodenstein B E 8392
Bodnar J P 8756
Boebel C E 1956
Boersch A H 1957
Bogardus H L 951
Bogdonowitz J 3695
Boger H G 7945
Boger R B 1958
Bogg J M 1393
Boggs N V 6278
Boghosian T F 6279

Bogner H F 6112
Bogosta W 1056
Bohanan M 186
Bohannon J A 5298
Bohon E 401
Bohrer J 2932
Boice W S 6280
Boland J E 4195
Boland Sr M L 6113
Boland Z E 552
Bolding L L 8833
Bolenius E M 8834
Bollin G K 4401
Bolton F 1394
Bolton P L 8503
Boman J 6281
Bonaro G 5835
Bonati B 5853
Bond B C 4861
Bonfanti A 1918
Bonham E 3696
Bonis M E 8213
Bonnell J E 1395
Bonnell J F 2855
Bonner N L 2521
Bonte A S 5015
Booher M 1057
Booker N B 427
Boone L P 1396
Boothby E M 660
Borchers L H 428
Borck J S 429
Bordelon R B 5299
Bordner K E 5878
Bordow R L 8949
Bordwell C 4299
Boren E 2386
Borland D B 5300
Borland W S 3200
Borror D P 4300
Boss J E 7688
Bostrom I 8015
Boswell F P 6282
Boswell G M 661
Botsford H V 2994
Bottalla P 4032
Bottalla U 3697
Bottenfield E W 662
Boulton M 6283
Boulware M 663
Bourne L V 1397
Bourque D 2856
Bovette P E 3453

Bowden W W   5301
Bowen B A   187
Bowen V F   3588
Bower A W   8619
Bower M E   3391
Bower S J   54
Bowering P E   4159
Bowerman E M   8214
Bowers C G   6284
Bowers L   664
Bowers L   1774
Bowers W G   3560
Bowes Sr S M   3589
Bowie E   4160
Bowling W G   6285
Bowman B C   6286
Bowman R E   5016
Bowman V M   901
Bowman W   386
Bowmer W S   4749
Bowrou G L   1959
Box F A   3931
Box G   665
Boyd D R   8016
Boyd H H   5302
Boyer B   1398
Boyett A L   1960
Boyle Sr M E   666
Boyle M T   382
Boyle P M   3466
Boytinck P W   7621
Bozanich R A   7633
Bozzo S   5775
Brace C   6287
Brack D W   1399
Brack O M Jr   667
Brackenbury B J   1961
Bracy W   6288
Braddy K O   3698
Braden R C   5303
Bradford E R   553
Bradford J E   2348
Bradford M E   4500
Bradley C   1400
Bradley C D   3553
Bradley E   3312
Bradley P G   5017
Bradley Sr R   1401
Brady T   668
Braffett J M   7689
Bragg J   2387
Braglia N   2452

Brake L R   5809
Branan M E   3467
Branch B C   5891
Branch J W   6289
Brand E K   1058
Brandao M   8835
Brandon E J   188
Brandon L A   6290
Brandt M J   8215
Brandy E G   1962
Brannan R L   1794
Brannen D V   5836
Brashear L M   6291
Brashear M M   1963
Brashears E   6292
Brasted H E   3313
Braswell M   4501
Brauch L M   1964
Brawley G W   525
Braxton E C   7401
Brearley K W   3699
Breck C   189
Breithaupt T   669
Breitling W   4846
Brennan Sr A   617
Brennan H C   3700
Brennan Sr R E   6293
Brenneman N   8836
Brenner A J   4722
Brenner O L   5304
Brereton J   5197
Brereton M   6294
Breslin J E   4402
Brestensky D F   6295
Brett S M   5866
Breunig J E   5656
Brewer C R   6296
Brewer M S   2388
Brewer R S   8017
Brewster P G   6297
Breyer B   3701
Bricker D C   3216
Brickwood J D   4403
Briden E F   8018
Bridge T J   430
Bridger S   7946
Bridges E D   6298
Bridges K F   8533
Bridges M E   431
Bridges P   6299
Bridges P J   8950
Brigg P A   3282

Briggs A E   1965
Briggs F A   432
Briggs J A   3468
Brigham J A   2933
Brill E S   6071
Brillhart F C   6030
Brim P C   1795
Brinlee R W   4033
Brinton M R   55
Brinton P A   3702
Briscoe D C   2934
Briscoe M L   1402
Briscoe S   670
Brisman L   8019
Britch C P   7258
Brittain R L   6300
Britton H C   7569
Broadbent C R   2522
Broadfoot M A   6301
Broadwin V H   2680
Brock D H   4301
Brockington P L Jr   2523
Brody S N   1403
Brogan B E   3201
Bromberg L C   6302
Bronzini M   328
Brooke E H   302
Brooke F R   3202
Brookes G H   5837
Brookes V M   7402
Brooks E L   433
Brooks F C   2524
Brooks H   56
Brooks I P   5892
Brooks L J   190
Brooks M L   6303
Brooks S K   3590
Brooks V L   5810
Broomfield O R   3217
Brotze S A   7403
Broughton L   4161
Brown A   5305
Brown A C   3108
Brown A W   1796
Brown B J   1966
Brown B L   6304
Brown B M   4302
Brown B W   7259
Brown C   3255
Brown C C   2995
Brown C F   7509
Brown D A   2332
Brown D E   8216

Brown D N 4502	Brunetta M L 5981	Burger M M 2390
Brown E 671	Bruni A 7405	Burgess E H 6319
Brown E A 3314	Brunswick G A 5893	Burgess H F 970
Brown E J 191	Bruttomesso G 1906	Burgis N P 5726
Brown E J 2857	Bryan C 7693	Burjorjee D M 1411
Brown E J 6305	Bryan M C 674	Burke F G 435
Brown E L 969	Bryan M C 7406	Burke J V 8838
Brown E L 1967	Bryan M D 1059	Burke Sr M A 4210
Brown G A 2389	Bryan R A 2683	Burke M F 6320
Brown G L 1404	Bryarly E 3703	Burke V M 4979
Brown H 3203	Bryce J 8951	Burkett G D 8534
Brown H 7404	Bubba L A 6031	Burkett T R 8466
Brown H L 2996	Buchan M J 8639	Burkhalter T K 6321
Brown H O 4750	Buchanan A P 329	Burks R O Jr 5811
Brown J 2681	Buchanan C R 30	Burks W 2684
Brown J E 4751	Buchanan M E 5894	Burleson A W 3554
Brown J E 6306	Buck D T 3	Burleson J J 330
Brown J F 6307	Buck J R 1970	Burleson L E 4862
Brown L A 7690	Buck W A 7260	Burleson L M 3704
Brown L A 7974	Bucker H H 5111	Burleson S D 6322
Brown L R 8620	Buckle R W 8640	Burlison P B 676
Brown L S 1968	Buckley Sr M A 5725	Burner S A 6323
Brown L W 6308	Buckley P F 4209	Burness D B 6324
Brown M 554	Bucklin G A 5686	Burnett L E 6325
Brown M 3983	Buckmaster E M 2453	Burnett R O 3932
Brown M 7691	Buckner M D 1407	Burnham D C 1014
Brown M A 3315	Buckner Z M Jr 7694	Burnham M M 6326
Brown M G 5306	Budziak L M 1971	Burns C 5020
Brown M P 4034	Buechmann C P 6314	Burns C P 3218
Brown N H 4978	Buehrer B 5308	Burns J 6327
Brown N L 672	Buell L W 1013	Burns J J 8432
Brown P F 7692	Buescher J L 1408	Burns J S 5309
Brown R A 1406	Bugbee L E 4650	Burns M I 3933
Brown R C 6310	Buhl P E 675	Burns P J 1919
Brown Sr R M 673	Buikstra E 303	Burns R A 1412
Brown R M 1405	Bulgren J A 6315	Burns V C 8020
Brown R M 5018	Bull M G 6316	Burr C 4035
Brown R P 6309	Bullard J M 8611	Burris G T 6328
Brown S D 4503	Bullington C S 6032	Burroughs A E 8757
Brown S D 5307	Bullock M R 3410	Burroughs P A 5838
Brown S P 6311	Bullock S C 6317	Bursk J H 4303
Brown T M 4504	Bundenthal T K 57	Burson L 5310
Brown T T 4947	Bunge E F 1409	Burt D 8678
Brown W F 5170	Bunn J H 434	Burt F D 5727
Browning G D 8393	Bunn O S 1410	Burton J R 4036
Brubaker N E 2997	Bunner E J 5645	Burton M E 6329
Bruce G H 2682	Buntag E B 4404	Burton R H 677
Bruce H R 4752	Bunyan D E 914	Busam W F 6330
Bruckner P J 1237	Burcham J C 6318	Busdraghi M B 7400
Brudevold B 4162	Burchfiel O P 8837	Bush S M 6033
Bruecher W 1969	Burckhart R E 4505	Bushing A S 6331
Bruhn G 6312	Burdette F R 1060	Bushnell N S 5895
Bruner D K 6313	Burgamy N P 2525	Busness C H 8535

Bussell A 1413
Busza A 1972
Butchart M 8133
Butcher M 2685
Butler A D 3705
Butler A F 1797
Butler B M 555
Butler D J 6332
Butler E L 678
Butler G 4506
Butler G M 4906
Butler G R 1322
Butler I 6333
Butler J L 8952
Butler M H 7628
Butler T 3219
Butman R H 4304
Butrick G E 6334
Butterfield S 5311
Byars J A 58
Bybrand G L 2858
Byerly E C 3505
Byerly M J 1414
Byers J R Jr 556
Byers J W 3385
Byers V G 4723
Bynell H B 3109
Byrd F M 3706
Byrd J E 2315
Byrd N B 971
Byrd S M 6335
Byrne V C 4037
Byrnes W A 679
Byron K H 5687

Cabrini S 8514
Cade G A 3707
Cadogan R E 4724
Cady J L Jr 4038
Cafferata F 4039
Caffery B 3316
Cahaland C W 1745
Cahill A 7605
Cahill Sr E 6336
Cahill Sr E 6337
Cahill Sr H M 6338
Cahill Sr M A 8217
Cahill R J 2686
Caine J P 5728
Caine W R 8488
Cairns F I 4651
Calarco N J 8953
Calder J R 5780
Calder R L 8021

Caldiere J 4753
Caldon B E 1000
Caldwell A A 680
Caldwell M L 8567
Caldwell M S 7261
Caldwell R M 1238
Caldwell W H 5021
Calhoun E M 6339
Calhoun H V 6340
Calhoun R D Jr 4163
Calhoun R R 2526
Caliri Sr M E 4040
Call R M 1415
Callaghan Sr M H 6341
Callahan Sr A B 2349
Callahan C C 8839
Callahan E F Jr 4405
Callahan J R 4406
Callahan M P 1416
Callan A C 1746
Callan A P 8840
Callan L F 4507
Callanan J A 1417
Callender J T 1239
Calori E V 4907
Cameron A B 2687
Cameron J H 6114
Cameron J R 4948
Cameron K W 6342
Cammack M H 7695
Cammarata B C 2350
Cammarota R S 4407
Camp E 7606
Camp P A 7510
Campbell A L 8841
Campbell C F 2998
Campbell D G 3708
Campbell D M 1061
Campbell G 5827
Campbell I E 6343
Campbell J A 5657
Campbell J D 3317
Campbell J K 4508
Campbell K G 681
Campbell L Q 5022
Campbell M B 7407
Campbell M D 8568
Campbell M E 6344
Campbell M G 1240
Campbell M I 4652
Campbell M P 5312
Campbell M T 4305
Campbell P 2999
Campbell R N 5896

Campion F R 6345
Canaan H L 3934
Canavan T L 7607
Candiolo G 1015
Candler T T 682
Cann H E 6034
Cannan F F 6346
Canning P C 1973
Cannizzo F 2391
Cannon D E 270
Cannon S C 5313
Canton R 4908
Cantono A 4306
Cantor H 5244
Capiz P 7408
Capper V L 1418
Capri C M 6347
Caprini A M 5171
Caraccia A L 683
Caragonne J M 1798
Carandini A 8218
Carboni B 5646
Carboni N 4980
Carbonneau L 3318
Card V R 6348
Carden W F 7262
Cardinale V G 3591
Cardle M 1419
Cardon S P 6000
Carefoot C J 7511
Carew Sr M J 8842
Carey Mother B L 4878
Carey J L 4113
Carey R 1974
Carey R G 4509
Cargyle J R 6349
Caricato F S 3935
Carigan W E Jr 684
Carigg M E 4211
Carioni A M 5961
Carletti I 4
Carlin C J 3392
Carlock M S 1420
Carlson A S 8219
Carlson N 2454
Carlson S 6072
Carlton E M 7409
Carlton S T 952
Carlton W G 1062
Carmean H 1799
Carminati M 7579
Carnaghi R 1421
Carnell C S 4938
Carner F K 436

Carothers F B Jr 3897
Carothers M T 2859
Carpenter J A 8843
Carpenter J B 1063
Carpenter Sr M A 6350
Carpenter R L 5688
Carr A J 6351
Carr B C 1800
Carr D D 557
Carr Sr M C 685
Carr W 3110
Carr W I 59
Carrey D R 6352
Carrillo T 5964
Carroll B 4041
Carroll C E 8515
Carroll Br J 8220
Carroll J M 3709
Carroll M V 2860
Carroll S M 6353
Carroll W M 1064
Carruthers E D 8844
Carson J F 5023
Carswell A I 6354
Cart E W 6073
Carter A N 6355
Carter B J 60
Carter B S 5968
Carter G A 686
Carter G E 8433
Carter I 6356
Carter L R 4949
Carter N F 5024
Carter P M 6357
Carter R D 6358
Carter R N 2527
Carter W M 6115
Carter Z T 1801
Carver J E 1065
Carver M R 688
Case I P 5647
Case N 6359
Caselli R 972
Casey Sr E P 4711
Casey J W 2688
Casey Sr L 4307
Casey M E 1747
Cash J L 1975
Casini E 1343
Caskey J H 3411
Caskie G L 2689
Cass M C 3710
Cass W J 7651
Castelfranchi S 1748

Castillo F E 2690
Castner B A 8161
Castor S K 973
Caswell W B 5314
Catanach Rev 687
Cates C S 8845
Cates W F 2691
Catlett L S 3111
Caudle J E 5658
Cavalletto G A Jr 8846
Cavanaugh E M 1422
Cavanaugh E R 4212
Cavanaugh P G 8729
Cavanaugh W C 3561
Cavazzana M 3386
Cawood N M 689
Cawton D D 3592
Cazzato M 4653
Cecconi L 558
Cecotti L 4009
Cella N 4114
Cenesi F 7696
Center E P 4308
Ceolato C 402
Cerato Morassutti F 4309
Ceresola C 304
Cerini A 8604
Cerow M F 3393
Ceruti M 2455
Cervetti M A 559
Cervoni M J 7697
Chadwick E M 4688
Chadwick W R 1423
Chaland A 4042
Chaliff C 4510
Challis L M 7533
Chamberlain B D 1241
Chamberlain M Jr 1424
Chamberlain R L 2333
Chamberlin M W 8758
Chambers D 4939
Chambers K R 1425
Chambers P 1426
Chambers S R 5839
Chambliss A M 6360
Chamness M 5971
Chan M 6361
Chandler C M 690
Chandler J W 2861
Chandler N G 4115
Chandler W K 5897
Chaney M L 6362
Chaney W O 2692
Chang T H 8847

Chapman A 5659
Chapman C 4981
Chapman D V 691
Chapman K W 331
Charas S 7698
Charbonneau L H Jr 19
Charette L Q 4164
Charlton J E 2392
Charlton J L 2528
Charter H R 4630
Chase J A 8221
Chase J E 5781
Chatfield H S 3319
Chaudhery S M 6363
Chavis T P 8022
Cheek E R 2529
Chelabi S A 61
Cheney E H 6364
Cheney M G 8356
Cherniavsky F B 4213
Chernikowski S 8759
Cherry D 6366
Cherry D H 6365
Chetkin R D 2693
Chetkow B H 62
Chew A 5982
Chew L C 1427
Chiara L 974
Chiari G 2481
Chiaverini E M 6367
Chiddie G A 4863
Childress J P 6368
Childs K W 5898
Childs R W 1066
Chillman D 1920
Chimsky M 1001
Chin P S 8954
Chinn H B 1242
Chiorazzo M 8679
Chipman D 8848
Chippindale N K 1977
Chlouber C S 4754
Cho S K 3711
Choate M J 692
Choi Y J 6369
Chong S 3000
Choppesky J C 7629
Chouteau J 3536
Chrisman P C 2456
Christensen M A 8222
Christensen S L 437
Christian E 915
Christin R E 3454
Christina G 2460

Christofoli L B 5660
Christopher J R 4864
Christopher W M 1067
Chrysostomou N 7263
Chrystowski M 3001
Chubbuck F S 7975
Church M T 8489
Churchman A C 5315
Chute V H 8704
Cinquemani A M 3984
Ciocco L G 438
Cipriani B 5756
Citron L S 2694
Civan J 2975
Clack A G 3646
Claiborne J W 8394
Clancey R W 6001
Clapp S L 693
Clark A P 4725
Clark C A 6370
Clark D L 7699
Clark E J 6371
Clark E L 387
Clark Sr E M 2530
Clark G 1735
Clark H F Jr 2531
Clark K L 8849
Clark L D 4755
Clark N L 8850
Clark P A 3256
Clark R 6372
Clark R D 8023
Clark R E 1978
Clark R E 6373
Clark R N 3712
Clark T L 1428
Clark W 1980
Clark W L 1979
Clarke A B 1921
Clarke B C 2695
Clarke D D 1429
Clarke J C 439
Clarke K O 3506
Clarke K W 1981
Clarke L 3112
Clarke M C 8621
Clarke R D 3469
Clarke R W 3713
Clarkson M 1982
Clason B E 6374
Claus A E 3002
Clay R L 3714
Claypool E P 3715
Clayton L P 6375

Clayton O M 6376
Clear P F 902
Clee D 694
Clee D G 4408
Clelland F W 975
Clemens A B 1983
Clements R S Jr 4689
Cleobury A W 6377
Clever W G 5867
Clewell L A 695
Clifford A T 7264
Clifford H R 6378
Cline C L 2532
Cline D M 1430
Clines P 3593
Clink W C 6379
Clipper L J 63
Cloninger M S 3716
Clothier S V 1984
Cloudman H H 8705
Clough F C 440
Clougher R E 1431
Clover C A 2935
Clubbe J L 1068
Cluett R IV 271
Clutter F H 3378
Coaina Sr M 8357
Cobau W W 916
Cobau W W 917
Cobb L W 8851
Cobb M 6380
Cobb R H 3569
Cobrin A M 2366
Cochran B 8852
Cochran C 5757
Cochran G E 3717
Cochran J 560
Cochran J C 2862
Cochran R M 6381
Cochrane D G 6382
Cocke L M 1985
Coe D M 6383
Coen Sr M P 6116
Coen P 4310
Coffey A O 1986
Coffey M E 1432
Coffin C M 2696
Cogan S 4311
Cogswell B L 8223
Cohen A J 4409
Cohen E M 6385
Cohen E Z 6384
Cohen G L 1433

Cohen M A 3113
Cohen R 4756
Cohen S L 5316
Cohen W H 5317
Cohn P J 3936
Cohn W L 6386
Cohon H 8024
Cok P 3394
Coker E R 6387
Cola A M 6099
Colaco M M 611
Colaneri M E 4116
Colavecchio B M 4043
Cole E 8025
Cole J O 1987
Cole M G 1243
Cole R W Jr 5879
Coleman A 5318
Coleman C A 5319
Coleman H E 3194
Coleman H L 1434
Coleman P 1988
Coleman P E 5112
Colfer B J 1989
Colin C 3937
Colley M E 696
Collier D H 2533
Collier R E 7700
Collier V J 7265
Collins B L 4410
Collins D M 1244
Collins D S 5320
Collins F M 6117
Collins J A 1749
Collins J F 8434
Collins J J 5321
Collins P S 8641
Collins S L 8760
Collins Rev W J 8853
Collmer L M 5322
Collmer R G 1435
Collmer R G 2697
Collos A 1802
Colodny I 6118
Colpitts R A 6074
Colson J A 1990
Colson T D 4044
Colter L W 3470
Colton R M 1769
Colucci D M 5880
Coluzzi A C 6388
Colville E J 4411
Combs C S 8224

Combs J R 3003	Cook H L 7976	Cortelli P A 2457
Combs M L 5172	Cook K F 4412	Cortland P 6035
Comer D B III 3570	Cook L J 7266	Cortright M M 6401
Comfort H N 4690	Cook Sr M J 5323	Cosby F V 6120
Commager H S 1991	Cook M S 3204	Coshow B G 8027
Compton E W 3938	Cook R 8026	Coss D L 1071
Comstock N 8761	Cook R 8762	Cossio M G 5854
Concannon D J 6389	Cook S J 5900	Costa G B 2864
Conchine V M 6390	Cook S M Jr 6396	Costa Sr M E 4909
Conci F 5689	Cook W J Jr 1994	Costa P M 2700
Concolato M G 4010	Cook W W 1995	Costrell E 7268
Condit J H 4757	Cooke B M 5025	Cotham M M 3647
Condon M 5141	Cooke K 6397	Cotter D J 1750
Cone F M 8516	Cooke L M 1996	Cottingham W T 976
Conkwright N T 8587	Cooke P J 4982	Cotton E G 2701
Conley R J 1069	Cooley F D 5263	Cotton N C 4216
Conley W B 3718	Coomber M E 6398	Coucouvitis E J 7269
Conlin F S 6391	Coon H L 8955	Coulling S M III 68
Conlin M J 4045	Cooney Rev A J 2698	Coulter C M 1998
Conlin R E 3719	Cooney T E Jr 7704	Coulter H M 1439
Conlon J R 8517	Coope G 3720	Coulter J L Jr 1072
Conlon R M 1992	Cooper A 65	Cound F P 2316
Conlon T E 8435	Cooper E M 4512	Courtney E L 697
Conn E H 1016	Cooper E P 3114	Courtright V E 8855
Connell J J 7701	Cooper J C 2863	Couthlin M N 2534
Connell P L 1993	Cooper L T 7705	Couturier M P 8467
Connell S J 7702	Cooper M 5324	Covey J 7270
Connelly Sr A P 4511	Cooper R 1070	Cowan J M 5026
Connely H B 7410	Cooper T A 192	Cowan S E 2936
Connor E J 6119	Cooper U C 1438	Cowen M E 1803
Conner M 1436	Cope A J 6399	Cox C A 5812
Conner T S 6392	Copeland J A 7947	Cox D M 5840
Conners L A 1437	Copeland P F 4165	Cox D S 4046
Connihan M 1245	Copley P A 66	Cox E 7411
Connolly B W 3939	Copping A E 4513	Cox G C 8028
Connolly E E 8436	Corbett I T 4215	Cox H S 2317
Connolly E J 1246	Corbishley J S 3721	Cox J C 1999
Connolly M M 6393	Corcoran D 5782	Cox M 5901
Connors J E 64	Coreth J H 2699	Cox M N 2381
Conolly L W 4758	Corey V K 193	Cox P H 5326
Conrad P W 953	Corgiati L E 1997	Cox R C 5198
Conroy E A 3594	Corley F J 5325	Cox T C 6402
Conroy J T 7525	Cornelison F J 2501	Cox W E 2702
Contini T 8504	Cornelius P M 5479	Coy S C 5269
Conway C A 7703	Corner M N 67	Coykendall D 7271
Conway M G 3320	Cornish M 4759	Coyle W 3004
Conway W D 5899	Cornwell C H 4654	Coyne R L 1073
Coogan M 4214	Corona D 4631	Cozart D T 3985
Cook A L 6394	Corporon L L 7267	Crabb T L 6403
Cook C 4312	Corrigan H F 3722	Crabtree J H Jr 4315
Cook C H 6395	Corrigan J C Jr 4117	Crabtree M A 6404
Cook D L 8854	Corrigan M C 7706	Cragg E C 698
Cook E 4313	Corrington J W 8505	Craig C A 1440
Cook E W 4314	Corson D 6400	Craig F E 7272

Craig R N   3115
Crain A L   8612
Crain W B Jr   1804
Cramblett M L   2000
Cramer F I   2001
Crampton N   8029
Crane J K   3723
Craven L G   1922
Craven Sr M A   8956
Cravey J J   8856
Crawford J F   4413
Crawford L   6405
Crawford L R   3005
Crawford P   1074
Crawford R R   4166
Crawley T E   3986
Crediford J W   7608
Creel B H   4950
Crenshaw T H III   2535
Crenshaw W T   6406
Crescini A   2502
Crestana L   2651
Crew E L   6407
Crilly B L   5629
Cring C C   3724
Cripe G R   5729
Crissey C   4316
Cristina G   2458
Cristina L   69
Crockett D   3455
Crockett E P   5327
Crompton R   8536
Cromwell A F   2536
Cronin E A   8857
Cronin F C   2351
Crooks A F   2937
Crosman R T   5328
Crossen H J   6408
Crouch W G   8537
Crow B G   2703
Crow C R   305
Crow F G   5329
Crowe F C   4514
Crowley A J   6409
Crowther J D   1075
Crozier G L   2002
Crull M E   3595
Crutcher M L   1805
Cryan J F   8162
Csupecz A M   7273
Cubine M V   1806
Cuddy L A   4414
Cudlipp A V   4760
Cuff E L   8957

Cuff E P   70
Cukerbaum B L   3116
Cullen L F   3725
Cullinan M E   3117
Cullins R A   5828
Cullis T   4893
Cully E L   1441
Culp P M   5797
Culver M C   3507
Cummings D E   8395
Cummings D L   6036
Cummings I P   8958
Cummings J B   3726
Cummings M L   1442
Cundari V E   5113
Cundiff L   7640
Cundiff P A   699
Cundiff V E   1443
Cunningham E B   3006
Cunningham L   1444
Cunningham M L   5330
Cunnington L   4894
Curda P M   3898
Curran C B   5331
Curran P   4217
Curran T M   1445
Curry J V   7707
Curry L B   194
Curry M L   700
Curry T W   4951
Curtin F D   6075
Curtin P A   1247
Curtis A F   4515
Curtis C H   2393
Curtis D L   6410
Curtis E   6411
Curtis Br G   8225
Curtis R E   6412
Curtis T M   701
Curtis W J   702
Cusenza M S   1076
Cushman C S   1912
Cutbirth N   1344
Cuthbertson F A   7708
Cutler E J   2537
Cutright F   6413
Cutter M C   8622
Cutts R   2865
Cywinski B S   7534
Czubakowska H   2003

Daffron P V   1446
Dagg M H   4952
Dagley E M   1447

D'Agostine R C   5730
Daiker V A   3007
Dailey J F   71
Daily M M   4218
Dakin Sr M A   1751
Dal Cer Franco D H   4761
Dale L F   4317
Dales D B   3008
Daley A P   6414
Daley Sr J S   4655
Dall D   6415
Dalleine B   7609
Dal Maschio M   1907
Dalton J V   526
Dalton M E   72
Daluga R B   2004
Daly I F   561
Daly J P   6018
Daly L T   3412
D'Amico P T   3118
Damashek R   350
D'Ambrosio V M   4415
Dames A F   4318
Damon H C   2866
Dancer M   3009
Dandridge R B   1017
Danehy T F   8437
Daniel B A   5332
Daniel M J   1923
Daniels J H   8396
Danker F E   2704
Dann J   8858
Danner M F   2005
Danziger B B   420
Darco M A   6037
Dardano P J   7274
Dardis M M   441
Dargel G W   5333
Darling W   4983
Darrell N P   3010
Darrow E L   7412
Dasch R A   2938
Dater W F   1807
Daues P   8690
Daughety N M   5902
Daulton P A   2006
Daum A R   7610
D'Avango M L   2007
Davenport G M   4416
Davenport M R   5813
Davey F W   5903
Davey L M   2490
David V   7275
Davidson A C   3596

Davidson C 7927
Davidson D 2008
Davidson E I 4762
Davidson R B 1448
Davies B R 7591
Davies E O 3119
Davies M J 1323
Davies O M 4189
Davis A E 5690
Davis A E 6416
Davis A H 1077
Davis B 1078
Davis B J 3011
Davis B J 3321
Davis B J 7413
Davis B J 7414
Davis C I 1449
Davis C P 7709
Davis D B 1450
Davis D B 8859
Davis D G 6417
Davis D W 73
Davis E B 3012
Davis E M 7710
Davis E M 8860
Davis H C 4656
Davis J 74
Davis J R 7415
Davis L 612
Davis L E 3195
Davis M 2394
Davis M C 3429
Davis M D 6418
Davis M F 388
Davis M F 7276
Davis M S Jr 75
Davis R Jr 6419
Davis R B 2939
Davis R E 3899
Davis S I 1808
Davis S L 2009
Davis V W 977
Davis W C 1913
Davis W E 3727
Davis W H 7711
Dawson C 2010
Dawson C W 8226
Dawson F M 5334
Dawson J F 1451
Day C G 3728
Day E 2011
Day Sr M E 6420
Dayle Sr T A 2352

Dean C H 8358
Dean C T 3729
Dean M B 8861
Deane R H 3648
Deans E V Jr 618
Dearborn B W 5335
Deardorff A J 3730
Dearmas D W 2012
DeBaun V C 5758
DeBlase S T 5814
DeBonis C 4712
DeBruyn J 195
DeCamp D 5841
Dee C 6421
Deeley Sr M B 6422
Deering D J 703
Dees M C 2013
Defensor E B 196
DeFilippi B 76
DeFilippi B 5991
DeFiore Sr M C 1452
DeGaff R M 4047
DeGiusti L A 4417
DeGraffenried G 4910
Dehnick P C 2395
Dehnick P C 2396
Deines M 1248
Deiss J J 3731
Dekker T 2476
DeKorte R W 3120
DeLacy H E 7712
Delafield M L 1809
Delahunty K R 4048
Delaney Sr A C 4049
Delaney M A 562
Delaney W T 7977
DeLano D A 3322
Delany Sr M E 6121
Delap A M 8397
DeLaura D J 2352
DeLaurentis L 613
De La Vega Suacedo M 1453
Del Bel Belluz T 3235
Delisle H F 8506
DellaDonna J 8763
Delman A 8359
DeLong C D 5336
DeLorme E F 77
Deltour Rev S 2867
Demaray H D 8518
Demarest G S 2538
DeMaria R Jr 6423
DeMatteis M 5027

Demestichas R M 8747
Demos P G 272
DeMoss M S 4953
DeMuro P W 4418
Denham W E 1454
Denious R W 1455
Denneny C M 8959
Denner K 5337
Dennis E 6122
Dennis J E 8862
Denny M 3094
Denny R L 7277
Denoon M E 7713
Dent C L 3013
Dent R W 5338
Denti R 3323
Denvir R F 3732
Derby D L 1456
Derbyshire S H 8227
Derrick M 7278
Derrick M C 704
Derstine V 5842
Desai J V 6424
DeSaulniers L B 4021
DeSimone P A 1079
DeSouza F J 4050
D'Este A M 6095
DeStephani M 2539
Detisch R J 7611
Devakul S 8228
Devaney M E 7416
Devine E C 7714
Devitt B M 5339
Devlin B F 6425
Devlin J E 1080
Devlin J F 1079
Devlin M M 6426
Dewaide L 3674
Deweese J J 1458
Dewitt D A 4419
Dewitt P B 705
Dewitt R H 2014
DeWoody F H 8030
Dewsnap T F 5691
Dexter D 7715
Dexter P F 1459
Diamond A 1460
Diamond D A 3324
Dice J E 2540
DiCesare M A 4420
Dick J A 2541
Dickens A S 7535
Dickenson M A 2015

Dickerman E K 2542
Dickerson A 6427
Dickerson M L 8863
Dickerson P E 7279
Dickey A K 8031
Dickey F G 5661
Dickinson L E 1081
Dickison B O 706
Dickson H 1082
Dickson H H 2016
Dickson K 8398
Dieb R K 2705
Diebels A E 707
Diebert R 5904
Diehl M E 5028
Dielman I M 6428
Diemer J 8032
Dierickx F P 7716
Dietiker D W 2017
Dietrich R F 7280
Dietz J J 8960
DiFeo M F 2835
Diggle M 6123
Diggs D A 2018
Diggs E 4691
Dike D A 442
Dillard R L 2019
Dilligan R J 4516
Dillingham J R 2543
Dillman M M 2396
Dillon Sr M F 3675
Dilworth E N 5843
DiMartino M A 4911
Dimini L 5029
Dimitsa E 6429
DiNatale M L 3236
Dingfelder D R 197
Dinkle P P 3196
Dippold D 3283
Dirks B J 4932
Dishman B E 2020
Divine H W 6430
Divine J J 8864
Dix R C 4763
Dixon N E 8519
Dobbins A C 1461
Dobbs J 6431
Dobie A B 7641
Dobie B M 6019
Dobson W 918
Docherty H A 4912
Dockery R M 2544
Dodd D L 527
Dodds W E 4219

Dodson R G 7281
Doernenberg E 2545
Doggett F A 2706
Doherty S M 708
Dohse M 4657
Dolan E M 5030
Dolan M E 6038
Dolan W E 709
Dolce R V 8623
Dolton D E 78
Domke C F 443
Donaghue S 6432
Donahue Sr M L 8229
Donahue T S 8230
Donegan S E 6433
Donelin K 3325
Donnelly D F 7536
Donnelly D S 5905
Donnelly Rev H E 7717
Donohue J W 5759
Donohue Sr R 3940
Donovan J 5340
Doolan J R 8438
Dorais F M 4051
Doran L G 3723
Doran Rev W J 5341
Doren C A 6434
Dorsi E G 4143
Doss E S 6435
Dotson D A 2546
Doty D M 4726
Doty E 3734
Doty R I 6436
Dougherty Sr A G 7718
Dougherty F V 8231
Doughtie M E 5
Doughton L M 710
Douglas A J 5342
Douglas J A 444
Douglas L 5906
Dow A J 6437
Dow Sr M H 7719
Dowan J M 5031
Dowd C R 2021
Dowdy D 7417
Dowler B W 7720
Downes C V 198
Downing B F 5199
Downs O U 3379
Doyle E M 6438
Doyle G P 79
Doyle J R Jr 1083
Doyle Sr T A 2353
Drabeck B A 6439

Drake P E 563
Dramin E I 1084
Dramin E I 1810
Draper A G 5264
Draper W A 7928
Drennan M 6440
Drennan R E 1462
Drew H I 6441
Drexler R D 5907
Dreyer E P 4220
Drimmer F 5142
Driscoll E M 711
Driscoll M A 6442
Driscoll W J 6443
Driskill L L 7721
Driskill W H 7722
Drohan W M 306
Drolette W B 3987
Droll N R 712
Dromgold P L 1324
Drown H O 713
Drummond E J 1752
Drumwright C M 3413
Dryer L L 4954
Dubay M 6039
Dubay Sr M L 6444
DuBose F M 5343
Ducharme Mother S V 3941
Duchemin H P 1085
Ducker B 445
Duclos A J 6445
Dudley E J 2022
Dudley L E 8865
Duehlmeier R A 3735
Duff C J 7723
Duffey W A 1463
Duffy C J 3471
Duffy D V 2459
Duffy L D 4940
Duffy W B Jr 2023
Dugan J 1464
Dugdale C E 919
Dugdale G 8588
Duggan Sr M R 2024
Duhmael A P 6446
Duke L R 6447
Dukes W J 6448
Dumaresq W W 5344
Dumbaugh W 446
Dumlop M R 714
DuMoulin P 5844
Dunbar L L 1465
Duncan J A 4421
Duncan L F 3649

Duncan M E 5200
Duncan M V 6449
Dundas D M 8607
Dundas J 5345
Dunfey Sr F 6450
Dunham J E 5346
Dunkleberg R E 5347
Dunlap L C 7724
Dunlap P A 4517
Dunlap S R 3900
Dunlavey R F 8866
Dunloy D A 6451
Dunn C H 199
Dunn C M 1924
Dunn F D 2025
Dunn J F 8439
Dunn J P 4764
Dunn M T 1325
Dunn R 5348
Dunphy Rev J R 8163
Dunson D G 1086
Dupertuis G 1249
Dupont G L 2707
DuPree N B 7537
Dupuis M M 1466
Durayni M R 5349
Durgan J P 3736
Duri M 7526
Durk F L Jr 4765
Durkee C L 7725
Durrwachter C J 2708
Dusenbury J T 1467
Dustin D D 3901
Dutli M C 5692
Dutton R R 1250
Duvall R F 8569
Duykers E J 6452
Dvorak W P 7570
Dvorkin E 4658
Dwight S D 6453
Dwyer C L 8538
Dwyer J A 3988
Dwyer M I 8002
Dyer L L 1087
Dyer M 1468
Dykes S E 3942
Dyson E M 5350

Eagan Sr M C 6124
Eagar M M 715
Eager H 2026
Eaker J G 8134
Eaker J M 954
Ealy A J 7418

Eames R P 2027
Earnhart P H 6454
Earp M J 8867
Eason J L 716
Easterday B A 6455
Easterling L B 6456
Easterly H C 1469
Easton R 4895
Eaton A D 2547
Eaton E W 6457
Eaton R B Jr 2548
Eaton V T 5829
Ebbs J D 2868
Eberhard F L 2028
Eberly J E 8520
Echols C D 6458
Eckert F 7726
Eckman J S 447
Eckman M L 3326
Economou G 8764
Eddleman R E 2029
Eddy A L 7282
Edelin S M 6
Edelman J R 564
Edelman M 6459
Edelson A M 5632
Edelson M E 3508
Edelstein A 4422
Edens A 3014
Eder D L 80
Edey O B 5158
Edgar P 5881
Edge C E 4766
Edman J H 8033
Edmondson R W 5908
Edmunds J M 7727
Edmunds P A 5351
Edmunds W E 6460
Edson T H 1088
Edwards E L 6461
Edwards H 1089
Edwards J A 6462
Edwards M B 3943
Edwards M E 4011
Edwards O N 7419
Edwards P J 3121
Edwards S H 6463
Egan J J 6464
Ege R E 1811
Egelston M 200
Egg N 3122
Eggemeyer E 528
Eggers J P 3902
Eggleston M B 1090

Egleston H F 2976
Eibner G 2709
Eidmans K M 2869
Eidson D R 6465
Eidsvik C V 4221
Eikel F 7283
Eikenberry F J 3903
Einhorn M 5633
Eisold B 8232
Ekstrand D 7728
Eldredge H C 7420
Eldredge L M 3555
Eldridge E F 717
Elgin D D 8490
Elgin R S 5352
Elkins A C 1091
El-Knudairi N 2710
Ellegood D R 5353
Ellen D H 5354
Ellenwood W R 7
Elliot B 1092
Elliott E B 2870
Elliott E B 6466
Elliott J 1018
Elliott J N 8034
Elliott L 2030
Elliott P L Jr 8233
Elliott R C 4319
Ellis A P 3904
Ellis E 7729
Ellis H M 4955
Ellis J N 2031
Ellis S 2032
Ellis W P 5114
Ellison G V 8360
Ellison L M 8135
Ellzey D L 5760
Elmore E B 1470
Elmquist K E 6467
Else R C 8868
Elser A G 8035
Elson J T 3597
Elwood W A 2397
Emerson F E 6468
Emerson M I 6469
Emerson O M 3015
Emery C M 5909
Emery E 5032
Emery J K 4222
Emson M E 81
Enderby M E 2398
Enders A F 2033
Engelskirchen H 8642
Enger N L 448

England H A 1093
Engle A W 6470
Engle J D Jr 1812
Engler W H 1019
English H E 2549
English J P 5033
English R J 6471
English W H 718
Enomoto R 8521
Entwistle G S 7730
Eoyang E C 619
Epp A M 4984
Epp H B 2034
Erdman E F 5693
Ergun D K 3650
Ericksen K J 8468
Erickson E C 3509
Ericson E E 8234
Erlich L 6472
Ernest J M Jr 6473
Ernst Sr M G 6125
Ernst M P 2871
Errera L 1770
Ervin R A 6002
Eschholz P A 8869
Eskridge M L 6003
Eslick T W 2035
Esolen G A 7421
Espie S B 2036
Esposito P J 4767
Essary J M 6474
Essery E H 3237
Essex R 4768
Esterman M J 4518
Etheridge M 7731
Etherton L L 5355
Eubanks K L 3123
Evans A C 8870
Evans B D 2872
Evans B D 7978
Evans C J 720
Evans C S 6475
Evans D G 1471
Evans E A 8871
Evans K 8136
Evans K T 2318
Evans N D 2399
Evans O M 7732
Evans O W 3220
Evans R B 6476
Evans R O 5356
Evans W R 6477
Evarts P Jr 4052
Everett M A 6478

Eversole R L 2319
Evetts J 3944
Ewing M J 307
Ewing R P 2400
Ewton G S 5034
Eyford G A 719
Eyre D J 2401
Ezell J 6479

Fabrizio R 7422
Facen E 565
Fadem R 566
Fagg R J Jr 5357
Fagies R 6480
Fahy W L 4118
Fairbairn E B 4985
Fairbairn P W 8961
Faires R S 8235
Fairey F G 1472
Falcomer C M 6040
Falk E R 8570
Falk Sr F B 8236
Fallahay N M 5662
Fallon R T 5358
Falsey E A 2873
Falson O J 1813
Fanelli R B 449
Fang E K 1473
Fant D B 8202
Faries M L 7733
Faris M T 201
Farkas B B 7284
Farley J J 6196
Farley M I 2551
Farmer J R 5359
Farmer J S 8237
Farmer M 6020
Farquharson R 1251
Farr C J 2977
Farrand M L 6481
Farrar C B 3651
Farrar C P 8872
Farrell C A 7423
Farrington L D 82
Fasken J S 3124
Fassina G 2491
Fassler B E 7734
Fauley F E 1094
Faulk R T 8238
Faulkinberry J L 721
Faulkner N J 8873
Faulstich B G 1252
Faust S 83
Favaro C 8036

Favero V 5992
Faverty F E 6482
Fay J A 2037
Fay L E 5201
Fay L W 7735
Fay Mother M R 5360
Fears V 7736
Feaster J H 2038
Fedoruk R B 5361
Feeney M E 6126
Feeny V L 2552
Fehlberg J S 8962
Fehr J K 3125
Feik W R 8874
Feinberg E C 7948
Feinberg H 4320
Feinberg S E 2711
Feinstein N D 3472
Felbaum G W 8875
Felbaum T C 7979
Feldman B E 4423
Feldman I 8963
Feldman L B 4769
Feldman R 4321
Felix R L 3437
Felker K R 4519
Fellin Rev J H 3945
Fellowes F G 5362
Fellows J H 7285
Felps J I 5910
Felps S C 5911
Fels W C 377
Felts M P 1474
Feng C M 6483
Fenley V M 1475
Fenn D F 450
Fenno C B 7737
Ferguson B E 2039
Ferguson B L 2712
Ferguson B L 5845
Ferguson F R 6484
Ferguson L E 722
Ferguson R B 5663
Ferguson R M 1253
Ferland W 2553
Ferluga V 8706
Fernald M H 7286
Ferrarini M P 4713
Ferraris E 1476
Ferrell R B 1326
Ferrell W R 2040
Ferriter Sr M L 567
Ferry A M 5363
Feshbach S 4424

Feurer M 7738
Fiawoo G B 5364
Fichandler Z D 6485
Fichter R P 2041
Fiddes T M 4770
Fiderer G L 5783
Field C C 6486
Fields A W 7739
Fields E C 1020
Fields J L 8522
Fields S B 202
Fiffick A L 2940
Fifield L D 7740
Fike D J 3414
Finan E F 8964
Finan K B 1480
Fincke L O 1477
Findley M K 5365
Fine L 723
Finesso E 5648
Finger Rev J 2874
Fink A K 4223
Finlanson A R 7741
Finlay Sr M G 5664
Finn J M 955
Finn R J 6487
Finnegan A 7424
Finnegan H A 6488
Finnegan J 1095
Finnegan V M 6489
Finnerty T T 8239
Finningan M J 451
Fiock M L 3438
Fiori O 7949
Firsch R Jr 5868
Fischer G 3327
Fischer G R 4879
Fischer J A 7929
Fisher J H 5912
Fisher J H 1096
Fisher J P 8876
Fisher M L 7287
Fisher Sr M P 6490
Fisher R E 1481
Fisher W J 6491
Fisk V 3016
Fittabile L F 2875
Fitzgerald D J 5983
Fitzgerald E F 3598
Fitzgerald J M 4425
Fitzgerald J T 6492
Fitzgerald L C 6004
Fitzgerald L Y 1814

Fitzgerald Sr M A 6493
Fitzgerald P H 4692
Fitzhugh M H 6005
Fitzpatrick Sr M B 7634
Fitzpatrick W P 4771
Fives R J 7527
Fladlien J E 5649
Flake E M 3599
Flammang E M 3415
Flanagan Sr M M 1753
Flanagan T J 724
Flanders W A 351
Flannagan M A 6197
Flannigan J G 6494
Flattery G W 1478
Flatto E 452
Fleischauer W L 5913
Fleming E L 2042
Flemming R M 4224
Flesher L 1254
Fletcher D R 4322
Fletcher E W 1479
Fletcher J W 2043
Fletcher N M 1754
Fling J B 5173
Flinker N 5369
Flory D L 2402
Flower J 5202
Flowers R H 4632
Flox R E 4119
Fludas J 3430
Fly A C 7288
Flynn Br B 6495
Flynn M L 6496
Flynn Sr M R 3600
Flynn Sr M S 8440
Foelber E E 4225
Fogarty P E 8037
Fogel S H 5962
Fogle R H 4850
Folco R F 7289
Folda O 2044
Foley Sr A J 4136
Foley B E 7538
Foley H A 8877
Foley H B 2320
Foley J C 6497
Foley L 4323
Foley Sr M M 4986
Foley T F 5846
Foley Sr V F 1482
Folk B N 4426
Fonaroff B S 5784
Fong D 8695

Fontaine P D 2403
Foord P E 5203
Forbes G H 8878
Forbes J W 3328
Forbes M M 2503
Forbes V E 8523
Ford A M 4714
Ford C M 1483
Ford H L 5035
Ford J F 5366
Ford M 7742
Ford P A 7743
Ford Z 2876
Forde H E 2877
Forde P J 8164
Fordyce-Clark C A 1097
Foreman C W 8240
Foreman F B 5204
Foreman J A 6498
Forester A 8241
Forman G 4427
Fornaro U 956
Forrest L M 7425
Forrey L W 5731
Forsman M 6499
Forster C A 7744
Forsyth D 8765
Forsythe S 2334
Fort B J 6500
Fortney A E 4120
Fos Br J L 5367
Foss M 7580
Foster D L 2941
Foster L 8879
Foster M P 8880
Fothergill R A 352
Fowler C M 1484
Fowler D 8038
Fowler G L 2878
Fowler J C 1815
Fowler L G 6501
Fowler M E 1100
Fowler S H 8491
Fox A B 1925
Fox B L 725
Fox C F 1098
Fox G 726
Fox J 7290
Fox J W 5963
Fox M C 2482
Fox S D 3473
Foy A C 5368
Foy N 8571
Foy V H 5914

Fragale F B 6502
Fraher Sr M D 3676
Framarin S 3652
Frampton M L 4428
Francis A S 7745
Francis K W 2045
Francis W A 5036
Francke W T 203
Frankenberger E C Jr 8039
Franson J K 6127
Franzoni O J 2046
Fraser D M 353
Fraser K W 4772
Fraser R P 3737
Frash R M 7746
Fratti M 2321
Frauley R F 8766
Frayne J P 620
Frazer F 7291
Frazer J M 727
Frazer M H 6128
Frazier F E 7747
Fredeman P D 4324
Frederiksen M E 6503
Free A 6504
Freede F L 8767
Freedman F S 568
Freeland S L 621
Freeman A T 5370
Freeman B 6505
Freeman E H 6506
Freeman P J 3510
Freeman R 4325
Freeman T G 6507
Frei J H 3946
Freis S R 8881
Freis W H 3989
French W W 84
Freudenreich C J 5205
Freund H J 85
Freund J R 6508
Freundlich L S 8242
Fricke H W 1485
Fried R L 6504
Friedberg B C 4326
Friedland E 6510
Friedman A H 8040
Friedman D J 453
Friedman J B 6511
Friedman J H 2047
Friedman M N 2404
Friend E 4429
Frisch J J 3738
Frisch P 6512
Friskel R 1099

Fritts K T 7748
Fritz F H 8707
Froberg L O 8882
Froelich Sr M G 6513
Froese R J 4865
Fromer N E 6514
Frost W 3680
Fruen B P 454
Frum A P 8572
Fry P L 2942
Fry R J 2048
Fuchs C S 4773
Fullam W F 8197
Fuller B K 1486
Fuller B S 3739
Fuller C 8708
Fuller F 6515
Fuller G W 8041
Fuller N I 622
Fuller W O 6516
Fullmer P P 5115
Fulmer O B 1816
Fulton A 3017
Fulton E 4167
Fulton J D 2460
Fung K Y 1101
Fuqua L 1487
Furberg J 4430
Furniss J N 3740
Furphy A A 2049
Furst K W 5732
Furstenburg W L 2847
Furtwangler 86
Fusillo R J 3284
Fuson J R 623
Fussell M 4913
Futrell J C 2504

Gabbard A 6517
Gabelnick F 5245
Gaddis A G 1345
Gaddis R G 4520
Gaffney M J 5174
Gagnon P A 4226
Gahagan M K 273
Gahagan N 4148
Gainey Sr M S 5665
Gaither M 8768
Galbraith J 8573
Gale C R 87
Galen R E 3601
Galgreath K 2354
Galin S 8539
Galio M L 2462
Gallagher E F 3395

Gallaher L M 6518
Gallahue M L 6519
Gallegly J S Jr 6520
Gallivan Sr T S 6521
Gallo M L 2461
Gallotti L 4693
Galloway P H 2462
Gallup J J 7749
Galt J R 6522
Galuppo M E 1346
Gambi B M 1775
Gambigliani Zoccoli C 920
Gambino A 7980
Gangewere R J 2879
Gann M 6523
Gannon Sr D 2554
Ganser Sr M J 6524
Ganz A F 6525
Garbe P F 8137
Garcia E C 1488
Gard R A 4774
Gard R R 2050
Gardiner F C 8738
Gardner B B 728
Gardner E D 1489
Gardner G M 3905
Gardner H C 2555
Gardner J H 8739
Gardner W L 5694
Garen M 6526
Garland B B 729
Garland J F Jr 1490
Garland J V 7750
Garland M M 1491
Garland R 5915
Garland R E 4866
Garlanda F 2463
Garling D 8492
Garling K 3238
Garlington J 6527
Garmon G M 2335
Garner C 274
Garner L R 5916
Garner N 2051
Garo M T 4327
Garratt W 1817
Garrett E L 6528
Garrett R 6529
Garrett R S 3511
Garrigus C 2556
Garrigus E 6530
Garriott H M 730
Garrison M B 5917
Garruto J C 2052

Garry G M 6531
Garst T 2053
Gartman G M 6532
Garvey M M 2355
Garvick J D 8042
Gary B L 4775
Garzilli H F 354
Gaskins P A 3512
Gass M E 3513
Gassner C 6533
Gaston K C 455
Gates B T 8469
Gates M C 3741
Gattuso J 4431
Gatz M H 1102
Gaudette Sr R 8574
Gavin N J 6534
Gaydon M A 2557
Gayle L O 6535
Gaylon L J 7751
Gazzini B 3571
Gear Sr M C 3906
Gearin J J 275
Geary E A 6189
Geddes G R 2054
Gehrke R M 6536
Geibel J W 5206
Geibel M G 1492
Gelb H 355
Gelders M S 944
Gelletich A 3396
Gemmett R J 3514
Gent C L 6537
Gentile J K 3126
Gentry E 8243
Georgas M D 7752
George D I 4227
George J J 8441
George J M 5695
George M B 6538
George M E 1493
Gerard B M 5371
Gerchow W D 276
Gerino M R 8470
Gerlach U H 6539
Germack M 1103
German S K 5634
Gerow B K 1494
Gerstein D 5761
Gertner E 7292
Gesner C E 6021
Getman O L 3018
Gettmann L E 2652

Getty A K 1495
Gettys P R 5372
Gewin Sr C J 8643
Geyer A L 1104
Giacobelli F 2055
Giannakopoulos J 5037
Giannetti J A 5882
Giannoni B 6096
Gibau B P 356
Gibb P L 1105
Gibbons C B 4694
Gibbons E 4987
Gibbons Sr M 1347
Gibbons M L 4053
Gibbs L G 7753
Gibbs M 7754
Gibbs M L 2322
Gibson E M 2558
Gibson J S 6540
Gibson K A 3221
Gibson K R 3677
Gibson M A 6541
Gibson M K 903
Gibson M O 8883
Gibson R J 3239
Gibson S S 5373
Giddings T H 8361
Giebel N J 2405
Giel E 2056
Giffen L L 3127
Gigli G 5815
Gilbaspy M M 6542
Gilchrist F C 8769
Gilchrist M E 1496
Giles G W 6543
Giles R M 8696
Gill A E 88
Gill D A 6041
Gill E N 6544
Gill H V 731
Gill J C 8965
Gillespie P E 8770
Gillette A M 7755
Gilley I M 204
Gillham M M 1022
Gillikin H W 8540
Gillis L M 5374
Gillon A 2057
Gilman M 7756
Gilman W H 4054
Gilmer A B 3742
Gilmore Sr J 734
Gilmore M 3019
Gilmore N E 2058

Gimes R E 6571
Gingerich M E 8399
Gingles J R 357
Ginn R C 3602
Giordano E 8697
Giordano L 5175
Giordano M 7981
Giordano U 6545
Giori M L 4914
Girardeau H F 7512
Girault N R 7950
Gish C S 2559
Giugni G 5375
Givson F 8244
Glasgow H B 5376
Glass F 277
Glass M 3907
Glass M H 8884
Glasscoe M 7539
Glauberman L M 5377
Glazier P 7293
Gleason J 3285
Gleason K F 733
Gleason W D 978
Gleason W K 6546
Gleeson W F Jr 4055
Globe A V 4727
Glotfelter M 1497
Glotzer M 358
Glover A 6547
Glover R Y 4776
Glynn F T 5038
Glynn H A 308
Glynn M G 5378
Gnerro M L 6548
Gochberg D S 6549
Goddard E 89
Godfrey G A 5207
Godfrey M E 8966
Goedeker Sr M L 90
Goergen N J 2406
Goff M L 8885
Goff V R 1348
Goins L P 3743
Golay E K 2560
Gold E R 4633
Gold L L 3329
Goldberg A R 5208
Goldberg D R 5209
Goldberg E 2059
Goldberg J F 4777
Golden E J 1498
Golden S M 1327
Goldfarb R L 456

Goldfarb W 8886
Goldfarb W B 1106
Goldinger L 5785
Goldman I 3515
Goldrup L P 1499
Goldsberry J R 3474
Goldsmith D 91
Goldsmith R W 735
Goldstein S L 1107
Goldwasser R 6550
Goleman B A 4121
Goll M M 734
Golladay M L 5176
Golmon A A 7540
Golson J A 2060
Gommellini N 8599
Goncalves R 8709
Gooch B N 2880
Good J M 1818
Goodlett M B 6551
Goodman A D 6552
Goodman M M 1500
Goodridge D J 6042
Goodrum S D 7426
Goodson E H 3947
Goodwin A M 2407
Goody I 3020
Goodykoontz W F 921
Goolrick W K Jr 5379
Goozee H 8887
Gorder C R 8967
Gordon E G 4659
Gordon G D 7581
Gordon I 5143
Gordon J W 3744
Gordon L M 1819
Gordon M F 5855
Gordon R M 7592
Gordon V V 2061
Gordy J L 389
Gore A 6553
Gore D 2408
Goree R G 3653
Gormican Sr J F 6554
Gorsuch I 6129
Gosnell D K 1501
Goss L C 92
Gossman A M 5380
Gottfried E 8165
Gotthelf H 7294
Gottlieb M 8541
Gottschalk B O 4328
Gottschalk K D 1820
Goudie J H 8542
Gough H B 6555

Goulet C 1108
Gove L J 2653
Govett B M 5972
Gowan S C 1502
Gowen M S 569
Grab V 6556
Grabbe M L 6557
Grabczak E 2062
Grace M S 7622
Gracis G 2505
Gradel R D 7295
Grady Sr M P 5666
Graeffe L B 1821
Graf D 6558
Grafton B 457
Gragg D B 6559
Graham C O 3257
Graham E 8043
Graham E V 6130
Graham H R 4329
Graham H R 4330
Graham M H 4432
Graham P 8442
Graham P R 8
Graham R E 1337
Granger M B 1503
Grant C M 1504
Grant E K 8543
Grant J D 1023
Grant J R 5869
Grant M 5039
Grant W A 8362
Grattan R III 359
Gratz C 2464
Gratz E C 1505
Graves B 3745
Graves B A 8730
Graves J F 8245
Graves L V 1255
Graves S B 7296
Gray A L 5381
Gray J A 5382
Gray L H 6560
Gray M S 6561
Gray M W 8246
Grayburn W F 2336
Grayson N J 4778
Grayston D 3572
Graziosi M L 6043
Greb D L 8247
Greeley M J 4331
Green A 6131
Green C 8248
Green D J 3475
Green E A 205

Green H 2063
Green H 278
Green H E 279
Green J 6562
Green L 4332
Green M A 2561
Green M E 4695
Green N R 8644
Green P A 6563
Green R S 736
Greenberg E L 2064
Greenberg J S 458
Greenberg S B 8888
Greenblatt D L 4056
Greenblatt R B 7528
Greene E P 3948
Greene E S 4779
Greenfield R 5786
Greensfelder B Y 6564
Greenstein D M 3681
Greenwood B W 7529
Greenwood L B 4988
Greer A W 1506
Greer C A 6562
Greer I M 6566
Greet A H 1002
Gregg P L 93
Gregg W R 6567
Gregory C F 5177
Gregory C H 1507
Gregory C T 2562
Gregory C W 8645
Gregory E C 4867
Gregory F I 8471
Gregory H K 1109
Gregory J F 8472
Gregory L N 737
Gregory M C 6568
Gregory P 6569
Gregson J W 5383
Grehan E P 2483
Greiderer E M 8166
Grenzow D B 2065
Gretar B 6570
Grey S Y 4780
Grieco K 5116
Grier D 8771
Griffin A J 7757
Griffin B C 1822
Griffin C W 738
Griffin E A 2066
Griffin G R 4521
Griffin G R 5384
Griffin L B 5385
Griffin W B 3908

Griffiss J M   2067
Griffith K F   7582
Griffith R R   1508
Griffiths E S   8968
Grifi M   8969
Griggs V   1509
Grimes M   3746
Grimes M E   8605
Grimes V M   5762
Grindle R M   3128
Grinnell R E   2563
Grisman A E   5246
Groak S M   390
Grobe C   1110
Grogan F R   7758
Grogan M   6572
Grohskopf B A   4228
Grolla G   957
Groom Br P   6573
Gros Louis K R   1003
Gross J J   1256
Gross K   6574
Gross R V   459
Grosshans R D   7759
Grossi G   8544
Grossman J A   8772
Grossmann R M   3330
Grove R H   7541
Groven J O   3603
Groves A K   94
Groves R L   6575
Growall S   95
Grozier M M   3021
Grubb C R   7649
Grundmann E M   5918
Grunlund B E   2564
Guaragno G C   3258
Guardia C E   4333
Guariento S   5969
Guastella T   3654
Guazzo D B   5386
Guenter M E   7760
Guerin M F   3439
Guest B S   6577
Guest L A   3604
Guetti J L Jr   2068
Guichard A M   6578
Guidi V   614
Guiet P   2069
Guilford M A   1024
Guina N   7951
Guinan Sr A C   8443
Guiney E C   7297
Gulbrandson H R   96

Gulliver A F   7952
Gunderson E D   332
Gundnola M E   6576
Gunstead A   2565
Gunter G O   8249
Gunter M A   460
Gurry Sr M R   8167
Gurtoff S A   4781
Gutcheon J D   5387
Guthridge S   8524
Guthrie W B   2070
Guttman S   6579
Guy W C   3747
Guyer J L   8250
Gwyn M M   5856

Haase G D   7761
Haase-Dubosc D H   3129
Haavisti A H   1510
Haber T B   6132
Hache Mother I M   4057
Hack E M   3748
Hacker M S   2566
Hackett M   4334
Hackett V M   7298
Haden G   2505
Hadgson R G   2410
Hadley O R   4522
Hadlock A F   1511
Hadsell S R   97
Hafen M K   6044
Haffey D H   8251
Hafner M   170
Hagan Sr M P   8252
Hagans M T   3476
Hageman E   739
Haggard A B   8400
Haggett D G   7762
Hahn F E   4880
Hahn H G   5919
Hahn M S   3286
Hailes R P   3130
Hailey J D   4335
Haldeman L W   1823
Hale M N   3095
Hale R   5178
Hale T   2071
Hall A B   7763
Hall B E   2409
Hall E N   2881
Hall J P   3749
Hall L M   8889
Hall M   461
Hall N G   6580

Hall R S   171
Hall S G   5210
Hall T M   206
Hall W H   462
Hallahan W   6581
Haller R S   3516
Hallett C A   4336
Halley T A   2356
Hallie P P   4881
Halloran A   5667
Halloran P F   8624
Halperen M   8401
Halperin J   6582
Halpern M I   9
Halpert J   5040
Halsey C V   3750
Halsey J   5041
Halsey J E   2836
Halstead C H   3949
Halstead D   3751
Halton B M   8646
Hamilton A   6583
Hamilton A C   5042
Hamilton E   372
Hamilton Sr E   6584
Hamilton E C   2072
Hamilton G L   6585
Hamilton H W   740
Hamilton I C   8198
Hamilton R M   6516
Hamilton S C   4058
Hamm M E   8008
Hamm M L   98
Hammer J   4149
Hamner J T   8253
Hampton L   333
Hampton Sr M P   1512
Hamrock T A   5388
Hana N K   4956
Hanawalt M H   1257
Hancock F B   4782
Hancock J B   8254
Hancock J R   1258
Hancock L F   4433
Hancox P   2073
Hand C E   741
Hand S E   8773
Hand S T   3131
Handler D E   8044
Hands S   403
Handwick C S   6590
Haney J B   6587
Hanford J   979
Hanke A M   4523

Hankins E M 3909
Hanks C O 6588
Hanks H S 1111
Hann B F 3416
Hanna E B 280
Hanna R III 5389
Hannenkrat F T 4059
Hansen J L 8890
Hansen K R 4012
Hansen R E 8045
Hanshaw S O 6617
Hanson Sr M B 8444
Hanthorne C M 2882
Harber B D 5984
Harbeson G M 5390
Harbin K 2484
Harbison R D 5920
Hard C F 2492
Harden L J 570
Harder B D 4524
Harder S 6589
Hardin L 4915
Hardin N J 5763
Harding E R 8613
Harding L A 4229
Hardison O B Jr 5043
Hardwick D L 3287
Hardwick E B 4989
Hardy B G 1824
Hardy G B Jr 1825
Hardy H E 8891
Hardy M 7938
Hare R R 8748
Harkey B E 1259
Harkin R M 8892
Harkins Sr J M 7635
Harkins K H 8009
Harlow M H 8893
Harman R N 1514
Harmening L W 8046
Harmon J O 1515
Harper A S 6591
Harper G G 1004
Harper Sr M C 3950
Harper M E 7299
Harral E G 8255
Harrell D W 6592
Harrell J M 742
Harrell K P 5391
Harrer E V 3752
Harriman R E 3517
Harrington A 3132
Harrington J 8894

Harrington J F 8168
Harrington R C 2567
Harris C V 1260
Harris E R 6593
Harris F B 904
Harris J D 1826
Harris J F 2568
Harris J M 3753
Harris K M 8608
Harris L H 8256
Harris M 5044
Harris M E 1516
Harris M E 7300
Harris P A 1328
Harris R H 7301
Harris S 3477
Harris T C 6594
Harris V I 8363
Harris V M 281
Harris W O 6595
Harrison A A 5993
Harrison J L 5117
Harrison R L 360
Harrison S W 8257
Harrod A J 6596
Harrod H L 743
Harrod L V 3222
Harscheid F E 4122
Hart A F 1112
Hart C E 6597
Hart C W 3022
Hart E D 6599
Hart E H 6598
Hart J E 3440
Hart K A 1517
Hart L C 4060
Hart M A 31
Hart Sr S A 571
Hart S F 6600
Hart Rev W E 8169
Hartman E R 2337
Hartman M E 5045
Hartman N A 4783
Hartmann B H 4525
Hartmann M M 3573
Hartmann R L 3754
Hartnett Sr F M 6601
Hartney T 7764
Hartsell E H 8895
Hartsell R C 2883
Hartshorne D R 5392
Harvey D 6602

Harvey D D 2074
Harvey Sr G M 5733
Harvey I 2569
Harvey L H 744
Harvey M J 4190
Harvey R G 5970
Harvey W R 1518
Harwood P A 4230
Haselden S R 1519
Haskell H B 8258
Haskell M 745
Haskins L 4434
Hasner E K 8896
Hassler D M 1113
Hassler G J 3331
Hatch H N 4526
Hatch M C 4013
Hatch R 2410
Hatch R B 8589
Hatchett E 8897
Hatchett M R 8970
Hatchett U V 7765
Hatchett W R 6603
Hathwell D R 8774
Hatscher M H 1827
Hauer L F 3205
Haugen M E 1005
Haught E H 2323
Hauke K A 5734
Hauser W R 7593
Havemann C P 8402
Havens S S 6604
Hawick M 8259
Hawk R E 4435
Hawkes M 746
Hawkins M A 5393
Hawkins S C 8445
Hawkins W N 6605
Hawley M B 5046
Hawley M G 1513
Hawthorne M D 8545
Hawthorne R G 4942
Hawthorne W M 3755
Hawver C F 4168
Hay F R 99
Hay J Y 6606
Hay S 6607
Hayden E E 3951
Hayden G H 8047
Hayden J O 1115
Haydock J J 2493
Haydon F M 3518
Hayes E 4527

Haylett B C   3562
Haynes L L   32
Haynes M J   5047
Hays M   3133
Hays W M   3756
Hayward A L   5179
Hayward G   6133
Hayward M E   207
Hazelton V F   1520
Hazelwood S O   6608
Hazley R A   8971
Head E L   8898
Head J L   1521
Headrick A W   1116
Headrick I   6609
Heald E C   5211
Healey E C   1329
Healy Sr A C   6610
Healy M L   1828
Heard E B   6611
Heard L   2978
Heberlein G K   1522
Hebron M D   6134
Hecht D F   5712
Hecht F T   5048
Hecht H L   4784
Hedin C L   208
Heezen E E   6612
Hefferman D   747
Heffner H C   7766
Heffner R L   7767
Heffron M M   209
Hegborn L A   6613
Heigen J T   748
Heiken P M   361
Heindel L H   5144
Heiny L   5049
Held M C   7513
Helgeson J E   4436
Hellal F   5050
Helphinstine F L   4785
Helsel M G   5180
Helvey J   5394
Hemby J B Jr   5395
Hemmert Mother M   4728
Hench K   210
Henderson A Jr   3910
Henderson J M   7930
Henderson L L   3678
Henderson M   8710
Henderson M E   5847
Henderson M E   6614
Henderson N D   8775
Henderson R A   33

Henderson S C   4231
Hendley W C   2411
Hendon W S   6615
Hendren P L   4634
Hendricks I K   7768
Hendrickson A E   8260
Hendrickson M R   1523
Hendry R J   8731
Heninger W C   4528
Henisey S L   4529
Henle R J   8446
Henley E F   8899
Henley M G   6616
Hennell D J   4916
Hennessey Sr J P   3990
Hennessy B C   4729
Hennessy W G   100
Henney F A   3223
Henniger I   1829
Henry C J   7583
Henry J H   5396
Henry N H   5397
Henry N O   572
Henry R   3134
Hensel J   8732
Hensley C S   6045
Henson B J   5181
Hepler D K   5985
Herakly T G   1117
Herbert J   464
Herbert T W   8691
Herbison M R   8900
Herbison R   8403
Herlihy J B   1524
Herlihy Sr J B   8447
Herman J   10
Hermann N E   3757
Hermann R J   5051
Hernandez J M   2075
Herndl G C   1525
Herndon G C   8901
Herrin M B   2570
Herring C A   2305
Herring G M   334
Herring J J   5398
Herring M L   4061
Herron H   5102
Herron M L   4530
Herschel J A   465
Herschel N R   6618
Herseth E N   5212
Hersey W R   8048
Hershberg S   4437
Herzman R B   6619

Hesketh-Williams P R
Hess G E   5399
Hess M E   6620
Hess V F   3023
Hesselberg A K   5400
Hester E C Jr   2943
Hester K D   463
Hester M E   6621
Hester W E   6006
Heung C W   3758
Heusel B S   4438
Heuston E F   1526
Heventhal C R Jr   4786
Hewitt A M   5052
Hexter G J   8972
Heyl G E   6622
Heymsfeld J A   8647
Heynen J A   8575
Hiatt J A   8049
Hibbs E C   1830
Hickey G T   573
Hickey M R   6623
Hicks C I   1118
Hicks G   3478
Hicks M   3991
Hicks O L   1755
Hicks P M   1831
Hicks T W   7302
Hiegel M A   6624
Higashi Y   34
Higbie R G   3135
Higginbottham M A   6625
Higgins C E   211
Higgins C J   6626
Higgins D M   466
Higgins D S   4233
Higgins Sr M S   5735
Highfield E L   2571
Highley M P   749
Highsmith M J   750
Hightower M L   6007
Hildebrand M E   6627
Hildebrandt J E   8902
Hildenbrand M D   8903
Hileman E A   6046
Hill A G   4337
Hill A J Jr   7612
Hill B M   4338
Hill C A   3759
Hill C S   391
Hill E M   4531
Hill G M   1119
Hill H A   5145
Hill I T   7769

Hill J A 3224
Hill J D 5053
Hill K B 467
Hill K F 7542
Hill L M 6628
Hill L N 5401
Hill M 5402
Hill M C 751
Hill M L 2076
Hill N K 8473
Hill O G 2077
Hill R M 7427
Hill V J 468
Hill V J 8904
Hillhouse J N 7428
Hillhouse V C 5668
Hilliard B B 101
Hillman D W 4532
Hilmo M 5054
Hilton L H 6629
Himelick J R 2367
Hindman G 2572
Hindman J L 8711
Hinds D H 2573
Hines J M 2574
Hines M M 5403
Hines S P Jr 3519
Hinkel J J 2121
Hinkley A T 5055
Hinnant C H 3136
Hinshaw L E 6630
Hipke J A 7303
Hipps G M 1025
Hirasawa R 8261
Hires A L 6631
Hirsch L 6135
Hirsh J C 1527
Hirth M M 8973
Hitch L J 5213
Hitchcock M L 4533
Hitner J M 752
Hnatko E 213
Ho M Y 5404
Hoak B A 3259
Hoar L M 5056
Hoare A D 5696
Hoban J P 8050
Hoblitzelle H Jr 2078
Hobrock P M 3760
Hobson S P 3520
Hoch M I 6632
Hodge M A 5118
Hodges B L 6633
Hodges N L 469

Hodges T K 3024
Hodges T K 5214
Hodnett J A 4339
Hoefer J S 5713
Hoerr C E 5736
Hoerr W A 3431
Hoey Sr M A 574
Hoff M J 4534
Hoffman C 4535
Hoffman D A 4787
Hofman D 102
Hofmann S V 2079
Hogan J R 6634
Hogan M M 5405
Hogan P G 282
Hoge L G 6635
Hoggins C 8404
Hohman M J 2837
Holcomb S B 8051
Holcombe J L 1776
Holden C J 4439
Holden M E 5406
Holder R C 2080
Hole S S 6636
Holihan Br R 8625
Holland E V 7770
Holland R D 5119
Hollander S D 8626
Hollenbach J W 3655
Hollinger R E 2506
Hollingshead M P 1528
Hollingsworth J K 2081
Hollmig M 2761
Hollow J W 5635
Holloway J M 1756
Holloway L H 2082
Holloway M 6136
Hollowell A 6637
Holly P M 3556
Holman R 5407
Holmes D L 8199
Holmes D M 5247
Holmes F W 1529
Holmes R 4062
Holt A E 753
Holt A H 6638
Holt B F 2357
Holt D 4536
Holt H D 4537
Holt H H 8749
Holt H J 4933
Holt H J 4934
Holt J A 1908
Holt T 6639
Holter E E 6137

Holton E A 283
Holton O D 4635
Homier D F 8052
Honey D 4868
Honey G 214
Honigmann E A 6640
Hood L D 754
Hood L I 2083
Hood V L 2084
Hoodecheck D J 3605
Hoodley F 1832
Hoofman J D 4234
Hoogers E R 4896
Hooker B E 4440
Hooker E 1530
Hoon B J 8974
Hoopes R G 3952
Hoorneman E R 3762
Hooyboer J J 3025
Hopkins A D 6641
Hopkins R A 7304
Hopkins V E 6642
Hopper R 4235
Hopper W D 3606
Horan D V 8975
Horan T J 5921
Horgan G M 4236
Horlick B 35
Hormachea C X 8262
Horn F D 5057
Horn H K 4660
Horn J L 2368
Horn O 6138
Horn R L II 1833
Horne R 980
Horne S G 3607
Horner C W 1261
Horner R W 922
Horney W J 1531
Horrigan Sr M A 3521
Horsman N C 8263
Horton B A 3026
Horton L D 5857
Horton M 4990
Hoskins E 8905
Hoskins F L Jr 6643
Hoskins H W Jr 5058
Hostetter P A 755
Hostettler E 3763
Houchens M S 7543
Houdaille J A 3764
Hougham G 4441
House F S 8264
Householder A L 8906

356

Houser H B   3332
Houston B P   6644
Houston C G   6047
Houston P H   8265
Howard A   8976
Howard D R   5408
Howard E   756
Howard H C   2085
Howard J S   981
Howard K E   309
Howard P J   215
Howard P M   7305
Howard R G   3240
Howard V A   7982
Howard W F   5409
Howard W J   1120
Howard W J   1771
Howe A E   6645
Howe F A   8909
Howe J M   3137
Howe J M   4237
Howe W A   2324
Howell C M   2848
Howell E   529
Howell J   3656
Howell R   6048
Howell R M   6646
Howes R F   1834
Howlett T J   2086
Howze B K   6647
Hoyle M G   7306
Huang T   7307
Hubbard M P   5922
Hubbart M A   3765
Hubbell F F   7613
Hubka R R   8004
Huddleston J L   6648
Huddlestone L C   8733
Hudnall A A   11
Hudson C M Jr   7771
Hudson E J   8170
Hudson G   6190
Hudson G E   1835
Hudson L T   1836
Hudson M   3522
Hudson N W   4788
Hudson R   3766
Hudson S L   6649
Hudson S M   3138
Huebner A E   8680
Huff F T   6650
Huff J B   6651
Huff L D   1532
Huff M   7308

Huff M S   6652
Hufford M   8908
Huggett M A   4340
Huggins J S   4238
Hughes G   6653
Hughes G   6654
Hughes H H   2575
Hughes J M   2576
Hughes J W   6655
Hughes R E   8977
Hughes S J   3911
Hughes T A   6656
Hughey R W   8909
Huguelet E W   12
Huguelet T L   8910
Hull E H   4957
Hulley S E   4847
Hulme F P   4661
Humble J E   5848
Hume T Jr   6657
Humphrey D M   3027
Humphreys M   4538
Hundon N R   6658
Hunsaker O   4341
Hunsicker C   3028
Hunt J A   7642
Hunt J C   6139
Hunt K W   8911
Hunt W M   2944
Hunter C S   8525
Hunter J S   1262
Hunter M C   7772
Hunter R A   2087
Hunter W H   4539
Huntley B   3767
Huntress E J   2577
Huokonen R T   2945
Hurd C E   4540
Hurdis S B   6659
Hurley B A   8681
Hurley C F Jr   7429
Hurley C L   3768
Hurley D W   7953
Hurley E F   7636
Hurst B R   8266
Hurst D W   2946
Hurt E L   624
Hurt J R   5410
Hussey M J   7430
Hussey S S   4730
Husson C H   6660
Hutchings D E   1533
Hutchins P   103
Hutchinson H A   8712

Hutmacher W F   1534
Huttanus W D   5215
Hutton E F   3769
Huvane J J   3139
Hyde K   4442
Hyde L   1535
Hyde M A   3260
Hyman E C   216
Hyman R L   3479
Hyman V R   8978
Hynds R   3770
Hynes F C   2578
Hysham M   2494

Ice B E   5411
Ihle S N   6008
Illingworth E   2412
Immel B   8267
Ingalls I   2413
Ingleby P   1121
Inglis G   3523
Ingraham E B   5216
Ingram G A   7773
Inman S E   1536
Innes L   8546
Inniss K B   2088
Irby L   7431
Irelan N L   8364
Ireson C C   1537
Irmscher W F   2742
Irons D E   4789
Irrgang K E   5412
Irvin H D   7774
Irvine M H   7775
Irvine V H   6661
Irwin E   6662
Irwin H E   3771
Irwin M E   3772
Isaacks E M   6663
Isbell B L   4636
Ise H L   2414
Islam S   8979
Islam-Soeldner A U
Isle P   757
Isma'il M J   4662
Ison H G   8912
Isted S A   1538
Italia P G   1838
Itzoe L V   6664
Ivey E D   1539
Iwanicki C P   2306
Iwasaki S   6665
Izzo C   8053

Jaarsma R J 6666
Jab L 3333
Jablkowska R 4169
Jabour J A 8913
Jacchia U 8713
Jackel D A 3774
Jackson B G 7776
Jackson C 1839
Jackson E P 7777
Jackson I W 7778
Jackson J W 1540
Jackson K L 6667
Jackson N P 4663
Jackson P R 1006
Jackson R 7779
Jackson S B 6668
Jackson S F 8914
Jacob W F 6669
Jacobs A 1840
Jacobs A F 758
Jacobs A V 5103
Jacobs E M 1841
Jacobs W D 8171
Jacobsen M 6670
Jacobsen M C 759
Jacobsen S A 7432
Jacobson P A 3953
Jacobson S M 4790
Jacoby J B 470
Jaffers D L 761
Jagust E 7309
Jamerson B A 8915
James A E 3775
James A W Jr 5182
James D L 3029
Jamison E L 760
Jamison L 2089
Janes S 2579
Janosek J J 5764
Janson-LaPalme Sr M B 1842
Janus L A 8648
Janzen H D 2743
Jara P A 6671
Jardini A M 3334
Jarrett D L 4541
Jasiecki D 8405
Jaskow R 7652
Jast I 8172
Jaunzems J 1541
Jayne S 7780
Jean-de-la-Charity Sr 3608
Jefferson L 7983
Jeffrey L N 7433
Jellison P W 3030

Jenkins A S 6672
Jenkins J H 5120
Jenkins K A 762
Jenkins S F 6673
Jenkins V E 6674
Jenkinson I E 1122
Jenks M H 8365
Jenne E A 5413
Jennings B 3776
Jennings T J 763
Jensen A 5414
Jepperson S D 923
Jeric M 3140
Jernigan O C Jr 6675
Jessup B E 5265
Jewell D M 404
Jewell K J 3380
Jo S M 8406
Jobe P G 6676
Jobson Sr F M 7781
Joffe P H 4791
Johari G P 1777
John D R 3777
John H W 8054
Johns H 7310
Johns R E 4792
Johnson A 5798
Johnson A 7544
Johnson A P 8980
Johnson C 1542
Johnson C 4897
Johnson C E 3141
Johnson D D 8268
Johnson E 2090
Johnson E H 7434
Johnson E J 8981
Johnson F M 8138
Johnson F W 2091
Johnson G M 2092
Johnson Br H 6677
Johnson K 5415
Johnson L C 1543
Johnson L E 8269
Johnson L G 3778
Johnson L V 6678
Johnson M 764
Johnson M E 4239
Johnson M N 3779
Johnson N 6679
Johnson N S 1123
Johnson R G 4793
Johnson R W 4063
Johnson R W 6680
Johnson T P 6681

Johnson W C 7545
Johnson W J 5714
Johnson W M 765
Johnston A R 4170
Johnston A S Jr 2376
Johnston B M 8270
Johnston E M 5416
Johnston H J 8982
Johnston J W 766
Johnston J W 5417
Johnston M A 7782
Johnston N 5418
Johnston R A 767
Johnston T M 3456
Johnston W D 5217
Johnstone D B 2093
Joiner E C 768
Joiner R 3335
Jonaitis T P 4637
Jones A E 6682
Jones A K 3780
Jones B M 104
Jones B M 2884
Jones B P 6683
Jones C 6685
Jones C A 4342
Jones C H 6686
Jones C W 6684
Jones D L 4542
Jones D W 6140
Jones E F 8590
Jones F E 2744
Jones G C 6009
Jones H C 2094
Jones H E 530
Jones H G 2885
Jones I E 1263
Jones J A 1544
Jones J C 3031
Jones J E 6687
Jones J S 8173
Jones L M 1124
Jones M C 2745
Jones M D 5419
Jones M L 5420
Jones M I 7783
Jones M T 4343
Jones M W 310
Jones O W 6141
Jones P 4443
Jones R 6688
Jones R C 6689
Jones R E 8055

Jones R L 1843
Jones R P 5059
Jones S F 769
Jones S R 2095
Jones T L 6690
Jones V 3032
Jones V L 217
Jones W D 1125
Jonquet E M 13
Jordan M 105
Jordan R B 7784
Jorgensen R E 7785
Jorzick E 6097
Joseph J L 3524
Joseph M A 4444
Joseph M M 8776
Joseph R E 5421
Josephine Sr M 8056
Josephson M I 8057
Joslin C E 6691
Jouzeh C S 4543
Jowsey W H 5923
Joyner N C 770
Joyner W 1545
Jubb D E 3241
Judd A P 3781
Judge A M 8271
Jungjohan B M 7546
Junker H H 6692
Justice S 5422
Justman S 5423

Kabel M R 3525
Kacher R E 6076
Kadet S R 2096
Kadish D 2415
Kahn A D 2886
Kahn E P 2416
Kahn S J 1844
Kahn T 8916
Kahoe M A 6142
Kaimann M E 5994
Kajii J 2580
Kalberer E H 3197
Kalbfleisch W J 4958
Kallison F R 771
Kalmay P P 6693
Kalpakgian M A 3142
Kambeitz C G 3609
Kamienny J 2097
Kaminsky M 4064
Kammer M P 5060
Kane H F 8058
Kane R 8777

Kane R C 4794
Kane R J 2098
Kannapell L 4544
Kannel G J 1546
Kannenberg M M 8609
Kantz K S 4240
Kanzaki H N 6694
Kaplan F 2581
Kaplan J H 5104
Kaplan M 8778
Kaplan M M 5424
Kaplan M N 2947
Kaplan S S 8272
Karminski A S 3397
Karp D 8273
Karr M L 3782
Kaske R E 1349
Kass M 3783
Kastel E M 3480
Katsumura E 3784
Katz E L 4991
Katz J S 3441
Katz M S 2099
Kauffman W L 106
Kaufman C L 2100
Kaufman J A 2101
Kaul L C 7435
Kaula D C 3225
Kaur S 3785
Kavanaugh M R 6695
Kawanishi S 3954
Kay H A 2102
Kaylor E J 4917
Kaylor M A 8983
Kbera S B 3261
Kearney M 107
Kearns R A 575
Keating J L 2746
Keating P M 7436
Keber F 5159
Kee G J 8274
Keefee D J 2103
Keefer R L 8275
Keeler D S 392
Keeler K 6696
Keeler P F 3786
Keeling J D 8917
Keen E D 7623
Keen N L 6697
Keenan A M 8474
Keene F E 7786
Keep R A 1845
Keer K L 2582
Kehr G H 4992

Kehrwald C R 6198
Keightley D N 5061
Keir W A 3262
Keiser A 6698
Keiser M W 4664
Keith M L 1026
Keith P 2104
Keithley L T 7787
Kelius J S 3657
Kell W D 7984
Kelleher D J 3033
Kelleher J J 8985
Keller J R 4731
Keller N F 405
Keller W B 6699
Keller W L 2747
Kelley G L 1264
Kelley M S 3034
Kelley R G 5737
Kelley Sr R L 1778
Kelley W F 5924
Kellogg O B 1547
Kelly C A 4344
Kelly C M 8059
Kelly E P 3288
Kelly F L 6700
Kelly G R 3955
Kelly J I 5218
Kelly M L 6702
Kelly M W 6701
Kelly P W 8986
Kelly S S 8174
Kelly T E 284
Kelty J H 3336
Kemp M 8493
Kendall G J 4545
Kendall K E 4150
Kendall L H 5425
Kendel H M 5248
Keneipp L M 5636
Kenley P M 772
Kenneally M 8918
Kenneally P A 1548
Kennedy A E 3226
Kennedy C A 8175
Kennedy E C 773
Kennedy J L 982
Kennedy J P 6049
Kennedy M V 774
Kennedy N A 2105
Kennedy Y E 5062
Kennelly L B 2887
Kenney R A 983
Kenney T J 3787

Kenney W P 4888
Kenny M A 625
Kenny T J 4151
Kent C C 5121
Kent I L 6703
Kent M W 6704
Kenyon L F 218
Kerckhoff W E 1265
Kerig L E 924
Kern C C 4546
Kern J J 6705
Kerns J M 3263
Kerr B A 2583
Kerr J 7437
Kerr J K 775
Kerr J L 6706
Kerrigan W W 5986
Kershaw H N 3442
Kersnar W S 3242
Kessi M 1126
Kessinger Sr M D 8448
Kessler B C 5973
Kester D A 1350
Kester D G 6707
Kestler C B 108
Kestner J A 4547
Ketcham L 5426
Kever D M 8649
Keys J W 3788
Keyser E 5219
Keyston J M 8919
Khan H A 8920
Kidd D A 6708
Kidd P I 6709
Kidder R M 7311
Kiely R J 4445
Kiley F L 8449
Kiley Sr M L 1757
Kiley P J 4241
Killham E J 8276
Killian V 5427
Killingsworth R B Jr 2106
Killman G D 109
Killoren J J 5849
Killorin J I 4022
Kilng M E 6714
Kim H J 6710
Kimball A G 4242
Kimball F M 3337
Kimball H M 6711
Kimble R J Jr 3789
Kimbrough R A 1549
Kimels S B 8591
Kimuca T S 3264

Kincaid E 776
Kincaid W P Jr 219
Kindred L 6143
King B R 406
King E C 7788
King J P 1846
King L 2107
King L 6712
King Sr M 8450
King M E 2465
King M I 6713
King M P 1266
King R F 1847
King V A 4548
King W H 1550
Kingery L C 8060
Kingsland J M 3417
Kinneen M F 8061
Kint E L 4243
Kirby L Jr 8627
Kirby Sr L M 3526
Kirby M R 2466
Kirby-Smith S 4795
Kirchmeir W E 8062
Kirchmeyer W G 5830
Kirk F J 2417
Kirk G A 2584
Kirk M C 1551
Kirk R 285
Kirk S S 3956
Kirkaldy-Willis I D 3289
Kirkham J W 5925
Kirkham M C 3563
Kirkpatrick J E 5250
Kirsch D 4151
Kirschenbaum S I 220
Kirschner P 2108
Kiser D H 1909
Kiskadden M 6715
Kiss S H 1848
Kistler S F 4345
Kitchen H B 7614
Kitchens E P 6716
Kitchens H C 6717
Kitson C E 7789
Kittredge P M 5428
Kivanc N 4549
Klaeger I S 3035
Klancar A J 6144
Klein D T 2888
Klein H J 8921
Klein J 6718
Klein K W 1552
Klein L S 5249

Kleinke V L 777
Kleinman P D 5220
Klemm G P 1127
Kliegl H L 1128
Kliegman B 6719
Kliman B W 8922
Kline T J 4446
Klineberg B A 4023
Kloster M P 8923
Klutey A M 407
Klutz S 3957
Kmen A J 1553
Knapp E H 3338
Knaus B M 2585
Knecht C 408
Knetzger Sr M C 778
Knight D R 2748
Knight E J 8277
Knight P C 1129
Knight R H 8139
Knight V L 1849
Knights P A 8063
Knock M 1554
Knott B J 4796
Knott R 7514
Knowlton M 5429
Knowlton T A 1555
Knox J C 8547
Knox L 8278
Knuckles T C 1130
Knutson L M 8576
Koban C 3610
Kobayashi M 8984
Koch A W 626
Koch I L 2109
Kohen W J 362
Kohl J A 1556
Kolbert R S 2110
Kollaritsch M J 8987
Kollerer D R 6720
Kolodziejczyk J 2111
Kolupke J A 3481
Konneker A S 7790
Koon B J 6721
Koon G W 5430
Koonce B G 4732
Koper P T 471
Kopp M A 4346
Korges E J 8988
Korn B C 3143
Korn F B 2418
Kossovsky C 8366
Kostka E V 1267
Kountz F J 6077

Kourday R M 1339
Kovnick E E 5995
Kowalyshyn R 4882
Kozikowski S J 7584
Krahenbuhl K M 4347
Kral E M 1268
Kramer P 2382
Krass A C 5669
Kraus R L 1269
Krause L A 2948
Krebs M R 1557
Kreinheder A G 4144
Kreischer M 311
Kreithen L 8989
Kresky R W 6722
Kretsinger E 779
Krieckhaus R 2749
Kriegel R 6723
Krienke M D 5160
Kroeber K 221
Kroft E P 5630
Kroll A 2949
Krouse A N 4797
Krukowski J D 1131
Krupa G 286
Kruppa J E 2950
Kucznski A 2112
Kuebler A 6010
Kueker T 4869
Kuenstler H R 3790
Kuersteiner A D 7547
Kuhlmann H J 5431
Kuhre W W 2750
Kukuk F E 6191
Kumpfer P A 8279
Kunkel Sr M N 8451
Kunst A E 6724
Kuntz J M 7985
Kunz D R 5122
Kupferberg H 7312
Kureth Sr J 2113
Kurtinitis S L 2751
Kurtovich R 4848
Kurz M T 5432
Kushner S 6725
Kushner W 7313
Kussy B 1270
Kutch J N 4191
Kutny R 5433
Kwass W 4348
Kyle M F 7791
Kynock K C 8280

La Beaume N C 2114
Lachance L 3611

LaChance P R 3482
Lackey A D 6726
Lackey D J 6727
Lackey K 6728
Lacoste Br A 3483
Lacour J L 7438
Lacy R C 335
Ladner C H 2419
Lahey G 5738
Lahive A 4349
Lahr N E 312
Laino B A 4171
Laird R G 8281
Laitner I B 6752
Lakas R R 1558
Lake A C 8064
Lake F D Jr 576
Lakeland A A Jr 3339
Lakeman-Shaw J F 4550
Lakin B L 6729
Lakin C 3398
Lal R R 958
Lall D S 1132
Lally F J 1271
Lamarca J M 313
LaMattery J J 4798
Lamb A R 8065
Lamb R J Jr 1272
Lambdin M 1273
Lamberg W 8990
Lambert B G 780
Lambert F X 3574
Lambert J L 6730
Lambert S C 5063
Lambrecht K 8924
Lameyer G A 6731
Lamkin B D 1559
Lammoglia A M 1560
Lamont H C 6732
Lancaster R J 6145
Lance D M 3791
Landa D 7571
Landau A H 6733
Lander W A 5434
Landers M V 3340
Landieth V D 4733
Landis F P 8925
Landon H M 336
Landon R D II 3792
Landram W H 222
Landrigan J J 8452
Landry C J 1561
Landry R J 4137
Landy A S 7792
Lane C 7931

Lane E M 6734
Lane E S 1133
Lane S 2115
Langdon I 7793
Lange M T 8779
Langevin G R 409
Langford D H 7439
Langford T A 5816
Langford V L 781
Langley L K 1562
Langpap K R 8176
Langton L B 5435
Lanham L 5436
Lanier G 8066
Lanthier P J 8407
Lantoin P M 6735
LaPaz L J 782
Lapeyre J A 4551
Lapping L 6736
Lareau E A 4447
Larkin J J 4665
Larmour V A 1563
Laroche J N 3036
LaRocque Sr F M 223
Larsen J R 8507
Larsen S 1351
Larsen S A 6737
Lash M A 1564
Lashlee M N 6738
Lasiter H Z 110
Laskowsky H J 5437
Latham J A 224
Latham J C 1316
Latham J P 3265
Latham M 6739
Latimer P W 6740
Latour Mother H 5670
Lattin L L 4734
Laudner M L 4065
Laughlin M R 6741
Laura B 5019
Laurent M H 4941
Laurent M L 8282
Lavers N L 3958
Lavia J T 314
Lavine G R 1007
Lawale J O 8926
Lawellin L V 6742
Lawery R S 4244
Lawler D L 4066
Lawlor M B 3793
Lawniczak D 8408
Lawrence J L 8927
Lawrence R R 6743
Lawson A K 7314

Lawson C F   7794
Lawson J A   363
Lawson J M   8177
Lawson R A   3794
Lawson S G   7440
Lawton E   2325
Lawton E C   6744
Laxalt P D   6745
Lay D C   3341
Layton L S   7986
Lazenby A L   5266
Lazenby O   6746
Lazenby W   6747
Lazzara M N   8780
Lea D   5438
Lea G   4666
Leach Sr D   14
Leake M M   5439
Leam H S   2116
Leamon D   2117
Learned A F   6748
Leary Sr M M   2752
Leath H L   6749
Leathwood W H   3575
Leavitt B D   4735
Lebedinsky M H   2358
LeBel E C   7795
LeBlanc Sr M P   5440
LeBlanc R   2838
LeClair Sr M R   5671
LeComte E S   5441
Ledbetter H M   6146
Ledeboer L D   3612
Lederman M B   6750
Ledford F M   925
LeDoux L V   472
Lee A   8928
Lee A C   6751
Lee D A   7315
Lee G C   8453
Lee H G   5442
Lee J T   4448
Lee J W   8548
Lee K   8526
Lee M A   2118
Lee M C   4350
Lee M E   8929
Lee M G   4552
Lee M M   3037
Lee M V   783
Lee R A   4799
Lee R F   2119
Leeper R R   373
Leese M J   2120

Leff A A   4800
Leff L J   4172
Lefkowitz J J   2753
Leggett B J   4123
Legris M   2654
Lehan R D   7548
Lehman E   8991
Lehmann R P   1850
Lehr Sr A   4959
Leible A B   7796
Leider E W   7549
Leighman C R   4638
Leininger L J   1565
Lell V G   6753
LeMaitre D   6754
LeMasters M H   4245
Lemay T J   784
Lemfert W   4553
Lemieux Sr G   5831
Lemish G J   1851
Lemming E M   7797
Lenaz G   5965
Lenning A   627
Lenninger G   6050
Lennon J K   2420
Lenoski D S   111
Lenz B J   1566
Leoff E   4554
Leonard J B   8067
Leonard O K   6755
Leonard V R   1134
Leonard V R   1758
Leone D F   4124
Leoni F   3658
Leopold R E   3144
LePage P V   3145
LePelletier J A   4196
Lerew D M   2754
Leschetsko H   2889
Lesen R   2755
Leshan D J   2586
Lesok K P   4993
Lessard Sr M S   3146
Lester J A   3266
LeSueur J M   3267
Levene M J   8178
Levenstein A P   7316
Levey D K   287
Levine J A   7594
Levine R   5064
Levitas M   4801
Levitin A A   8494
Levy A R   4555
Levy D   5926

Levy G S   2121
Levy L S   2122
Levy L T   1567
Levy M   2587
Levy M P   785
Levy P J   4449
Lewis A M   6756
Lewis B B   6757
Lewis B H   7441
Lewis C D   8930
Lewis D J   2588
Lewis E D   6758
Lewis E H   1568
Lewis H C   8068
Lewis J   7550
Lewis J E   2123
Lewis J S   1569
Lewis L A   4351
Lewis L B   2124
Lewis L E   7798
Lewis R   3484
Lewis R C   8283
Lewis R H   3959
Lewis V M   15
Lewis W B Jr   8409
Lewis W H   2125
Leyden W H   5765
Liberta S   8781
Libowitz H M   2756
Lick M V   5637
Lieberman L   7317
Liggins E S   8931
Lightcap J S   8992
Lightfoot J E Jr   8069
Lightfoot O   1570
Lightner B E   8410
Lill M   7442
Lilliard R G   2126
Lima J   5123
Lin P   2589
Linch M A   3795
Lincoln J E   4173
Lind C B   2421
Lindaman R E   4870
Lindberg E M   786
Linden J H   3343
Linden V C   7653
Linderman D   8070
Linderoth L W   7799
Lindgren C H   3344
Lindley G   6147
Lindsay B N   4352
Lindsay L A   3147
Lindsey M   8140

Ling M F 6759
Linkous G K Jr 3796
Linn E L 1571
Linneman Sr R A 2757
Linney D C 5065
Linton R H 7800
Lippincott H R 5443
Lips R C 6760
Lipska J 2127
Lirette Sr M G 7443
Lirette Sr M L 4067
Lisauskas G G 7444
Lister R 5251
Liston P F 1572
L'Italien Sr M I 6761
Littell P P 2590
Little E A 6762
Little T A 926
Littlejohn J E 4918
Littleton J C 7801
Littleton T D 6763
Littrell M P 8932
Litzinger B A 787
Liu H C 8284
Liverani L 8650
Liverani P R 4667
Livingston S T 8933
Livinston O E 1852
Lloyd L N 8495
Lo W D 3527
Lobetti Bodini G 788
Locke Sr G M 6764
Locke J D 4556
Locke M S 1573
Locke O 6765
Lockhart J H 789
Lockridge R F Jr 1135
Lofton T A 8071
Logan A J 4557
Logan D M 4353
Logan G E 7802
Logan R L 8367
Logan W M 8200
Logotheti F 364
Logue J M 7932
Logue S M 8454
Lohman M M 1228
Lohman W J 4668
Lohmann C K 7445
Lohn J 6192
Loliva E 8610
Lollos J 6766
Lomax J A 5221
Lomba M L 4068
Lombard L R 7954

Lombardi R W 5817
Long A 4558
Long B 4125
Long E 2839
Long E L 8549
Long E M 984
Long J A 2129
Long J H 6767
Long K P 3797
Long L G 6148
Long M 577
Long M F 6768
Long M M 8934
Long U E 7446
Long W 790
Longo R 8141
Longquest J L 5222
Longree G A 3613
Loomis C C Jr 578
Looney R F 8577
Lopes M A 8782
Lopez C L 5927
Lord F M 1574
Lord M E 6769
Lordan Sr M A 1759
Lorenzetto M 315
Lorenzoni M 4919
Lorraine A P 8714
Losee V O 1575
Loss A K 2840
Lottman H R 8628
Lotz D W 7447
Loucks I M 8783
Lougheed G 7448
Lougheed R C 7643
Louton A S 2951
Love C E 4246
Love E S 2130
Love F A 3614
Love M J 4715
Loveall J S 6770
Lovejoy R B 927
Lovell J H Jr 4802
Lovick L D 5444
Low V B 3268
Lowe F C 8285
Lowe J O 7595
Lowe T M 6771
Lowery D C 791
Lowry L 4559
Lowther L M 2758
Lozano A M 5858
Lucchesi C 5650
Lucchesi P G 6772
Luce A E 6773

Luchi L 2467
Lucier Sr M D 3960
Luck L J 3992
Luckhardt V E 8935
Luddy T E 2131
Luetcke M E 6774
Luk E 8072
Lundell M H 8651
Lundgren B R 2591
Luranc E 3528
Luria M 8993
Lurie C 6775
Lurkis I B 4560
Luter D W 4960
Luxton D W 4247
Lyall L H 7803
Lyday J W 8496
Lynch B F 6776
Lynch J J 1112
Lynch Rev J W 531
Lynch M 5818
Lynch M P 8652
Lynch V E 7318
Lynch W J 316
Lyncker H 3798
Lynds R J 3799
Lynes C M 3615
Lynn H B 1136
Lyon J B 1576
Lyon N M 8142
Lyon P L 225
Lyon R 6777
Lyons J F 4248
Lyons J O 8558
Lyons K M 5445
Lyons Rev R J 2890
Lyttleton L A 792

Ma V H 7530
Mabusth M H 288
Maca S 1137
McAdow R T 7449
McAffee H F 5870
McAleer J J 226
McArravy G 3961
McAskie C 1138
McAtee 6149
MacBrayne D B 4696
McBride E B 3912
McBride H M 4561
McBride M E 8368
McBroom R L 7624
McBryan P J 5672
McCabe J E 579
McCabe Sr M A 7804

McCabe Sr M C 1577
McCaffrey E W 7805
McCain I H 8143
McCain L H 1578
McCalib C A 7806
McCall L J 5446
McCall M 8286
McCallion M 7807
McCandless L B 793
McCanless R 6778
McCann G A 7319
McCarron W E 6779
McCarthy C 2592
McCarthy D C 2132
McCarthy D R 3616
McCarthy J P 3913
McCarthy J T 8600
McCarthy K J 2759
McCarthy M C 6780
McCarthy Mother M E 6781
McCarthy Sr M J 1760
McCarthy M J 8455
McCarthy Sr R C 8614
McCarthy T A 794
McCarthy W E 8179
McCarty M E 4562
McCaslin D 8936
McCauley L C 5850
McCausland E 1579
McCawley D L 5447
McCawley K J 1139
McCelvey G E 8003
McChristy C G 6782
McClarin V 4354
McClamroch R P 7531
McCleary L M 8937
McClellan D 2133
McClendon M A 3617
McClendon M J 6783
McCloin J T 1274
McCloy B J 473
McCluney M M 985
McClurg F A 2134
McCluskey M L 6051
McCollum M A 6784
McConnell A L 113
McConnell J C 1027
McConnell R 2136
McConnell R B 5448
McConnochie J 2760
McCord B 1761
McCord H T 4014
McCorkle J N 2135
McCormick Sr M E 3038

McCottry M G 6785
McCracken K A 227
McCracken M L 7808
Macrorie K 1028
McCrory T E 4450
McCrossan Sr V E 6052
McCue E L 580
McCullen J T Jr 6786
McCulloch R W 3039
McCullough N V 3800
McCullough P W 4174
McCully K W 7987
McCummiskey J V 8938
McCune S 2137
MacCurdy B 289
McCurry R 5449
McCutcheon D 4138
McCutcheon H H 3914
McDaniel G 2339
McDaniel Sr M 2422
McDaniel S 3381
McDaniels J D 2761
McDavid G E 3801
McDermott F J 6100
McDermott J T 6787
McDermott P J 8180
McDill J M 5450
McDonald D R 2138
McDonald J B 2359
MacDonald J D 6788
McDonald J E 5697
MacDonald M B 4961
McDonald M M 3618
McDonald R F 3290
McDonald S V 3040
McDonough D P 3962
McDonough J M 16
McDonough M L 4069
McDougall R L 8653
McDowell C F 3041
Mace Sr A K 8784
Macedo C D 1580
McElligott T J 1581
McElroy M P 6790
McEwen F B 3529
McEwen M J 1779
McFad en A B 6791
McFarland M A 1140
McFarland V M 6792
McFetridge K L 114
McGalliard J C 4716
McGavran J H Jr 1853
McGechaen J 5996
McGee H C 3269

McGhee R D 1854
McGill 7809
McGilley Sr M J 2360
McGinnis C F 5673
McGinnis C L 3418
McGinnis P J 5355
McGlaun R A 2762
McGlothlin 8369
McGovern A F 4669
McGovern B F 8073
McGowan M 4070
McGowan M J 7551
McGowan P M 4451
McGowen J W 7810
McGrary J E 6793
McGrath M L 5451
McGrath Sr T G 6794
McGraw L E 4883
McGregor H S Jr 6705
McGregor M 8370
McGuffie H L 532
McGuire C H 1141
McGuire Mother D 1762
McGuire D S 115
McGuire J F 3802
McGuire P M 3803
McGuire R L 6796
McGuire S V 5223
McHale M J 1582
McHugh M 8785
McIlwraith C B 6797
McInnis M A 116
MacIntire F W 795
McIntire N E 796
McIntosh J 7451
McIssac P W 6011
McKay D F 8411
MacKay K 5224
McKay K M 5225
MacKay R M 581
McKee J 2423
McKee L 7811
McKellar J G 3804
McKelleget B 8475
McKelvin D J 4563
McKemy A 1142
McKenna M 5832
McKenna S W 8550
McKennon W C 4356
McKenzie A I 117
MacKenzie D 4564
MacKenzie E D 3148
MacKenzie N 4670
McKeon M 2891

McKeon M W 3992
McKercher L 6798
Mackery M L 3805
McKewin C A 8740
Mackey J D 118
McKie G M 5452
Mackin M M 8074
McKinley R D 7320
McKinney I M 228
MacKinnon A A 3485
McKinnon L T 7452
McKnew M T 7453
McKnight G 2763
McKnight G 6799
McKnight W L 628
McLain J H 7615
McLanahan F H 4565
McLaughlin E R 3345
McLaughlin Rev JJ 4071
MacLaurin J C **6800**
McLaurin N D 797
McLean A T 6801
MacLean J L 2764
McLean Sr M S 1855
McLean R S 6078
MacLennan J F 2140
MacLeod B J 8203
McLeod C 229
McLeod F R 5453
MacLeod Sr M C 2765
McLeod Sr M S 3619
McLoughlin J G 8476
McMahon Sr C B 1583
McManus A 4452
McManus F X 7812
McManus J J 8994
McManamin M E 2766
McMikle B J 7321
McMillan A T 6802
McMillan C B 3149
McMillan J B 3806
McMillan K M 17
McMillan T K 8075
McMillen R A 7813
McMillin H S Jr 6803
McMindes M F 4566
McMullen C 6804
McMurchie K R 2593
McMurry M 1584
McMurty L J 4357
McNamara Sr C 6805
McNamara R J 6806
McNamee V J 6807
McNary N A 383

McNeal F S 1330
McNeal F S 5226
McNeely S S Jr 1926
McNeese W J 959
McNeil S M 6079
McNelly C 1585
McNelly R J 5227
McNew L D 5454
McNiece G M 7454
McNiece M 4453
McNulty G J 6808
MacPhedron J D 6809
McPherson C L 2139
MacPherson F B 2767
McPherson M S 6810
McQuaid D C 6811
McQueeney K R 5871
McQuilkin D E 5455
McQuiston J R 7585
McReynolds F E 6812
McReynolds G 5928
McReynolds J A 393
McSorley B T 2768
McSwiney M C 5833
McUlwee S L 533
McVicker A C 7515
McWilliams D J 3150
Madambe A N 421
Madden E E 928
Madden F 4249
Maddocks L J 1352
Madek G A 4250
Maderer M P 6813
Madewell V D 1856
Madigan F V 7814
Madsen L V 6151
Magaw E L 4567
Magealson V A 5456
Magee D C 4803
Magee M 2952
Magid J 629
Magnani F 6080
Magni M L 374
Magowan C C 5252
Magri N 7552
Maguire M M 2326
Mahaffey L K 3807
Mahan M T 7322
Maher J A 4254
Maher R A 4454
Mahoney A L 6053
Mahoney B J 5739
Mahoney J L 18
Mahoney L 5674

Malaby I H 5851
Malachias N Z 8287
Maladorno E 39
Malarkey S 6814
Malcom J 3808
Malkoff K 4455
Malloy I M 384
Malloy R T 7650
Malmsheimer R R 7815
Malnig R L 1857
Malocsay J P 8288
Malone C A 2893
Malone J F 2594
Malone M G 5766
Maloney C F 2769
Maltby J E 7816
Mamas H 4804
Manan A 3530
Mancini A R 2468
Mancini G 3042
Mancini G 3576
Mancuso Sr M H 3043
Mandel R S 8715
Mandell J D 4697
Mane S 3809
Maner A S 3346
Maney F A 2595
Mangold C W 3810
Manheim L M 5457
Manion O G 7323
Manly W M 6815
Mann C C 5458
Mann C W 2141
Mann D D 5459
Mann E 5929
Mann J S 4072
Manna J K 290
Manni L 5161
Manning E 8601
Manning J J 5859
Mannix H E 6816
Mannucci E I 6054
Manry M J 6817
Mansfield J G 2424
Mansfield M H 582
Manson E G 1586
Manuel H 4073
Manzuk J K 4015
Maples B A 6818
Mara G 1029
Maras E B 2770
Marchalonis S L 1587
Marchetti G 3044
Marconi E 410

Marcus R 3811
Marcus S P 2596
Marinell J P 4805
Marinelli O 8682
Maring D E 7586
Mariovitz E D 6819
Mark E H 1275
Mark J 3812
Mark L T 2771
Mark M C 2142
Marken R N 4074
Markham R C 8289
Markidou A N 1143
Markley M S 2597
Markowitt G G 7596
Marks W 5767
Markwood R 6820
Marley A E 4568
Marlowe J A 3620
Marmo M 4639
Marotta J 5460
Marra G 8477
Marrs E W 1276
Marsden K 3813
Marsh G R Jr 8629
Marsh R T 6821
Marshall G 3151
Marshall M E 337
Marshall M J 798
Marston L G 1927
Marston M A 7817
Marsyla J A 7818
Martell C L 4871
Martell Sr M A 3531
Martella S L 2772
Martens M L 1030
Martien N 1588
Martin A D 6822
Martin A M 7955
Martin A M 7324
Martin C W 2143
Martin D M 2144
Martin D W 3963
Martin E B 1144
Martin E C 4698
Martin E F 5930
Martin F D 6823
Martin G 1589
Martin H R 2145
Martin J A 6824
Martin J E 4358
Martin L H 1590
Martin M C 8371

Martin M E 7939
Martin M G 5651
Martin P T 5461
Martin R B 4640
Martin V M 1277
Martin W F 6825
Martine L H 5146
Martineau M J 7956
Martineau R 6826
Martini M 4920
Marx R J 5801
Mary Sr A 6223
Mary Sr M 8456
Marzari F 986
Marzullo M T 3486
Mascia M 4806
Masdowell D A 6789
Masey C 1145
Masinton C G 5066
Mason K J 8076
Mason L M 2146
Mason M A 4139
Mason M E 1278
Mason M R 799
Masse B L 7988
Massey I L 1591
Massey J B 6827
Massey T W 1592
Massirer M R 1279
Massoon L J 5883
Massoud M M 8615
Mast D D 4252
Masterson M 3045
Mastro Sr M L 4075
Mastrogiacomo I 3915
Matera E C 800
Mather G V 474
Mather J E 8683
Matheson G M 4175
Matheson J M 7957
Matheson P L 6828
Mathews A M 1146
Mathews R D 119
Mathews W F 5974
Mathewson D 120
Mathewson G A 8077
Matlock M 4682
Matson C 338
Matson V L 4176
Matter W W 4177
Matteson J L 2953
Matthews C G 7455
Matthews D J 5802

Matthews G S 5228
Matthews J V 3152
Matthews R E 19
Matthews V V 4197
Matze M W 905
Matzen B A 801
Mauldin L L 5462
Mauldin M L 6829
Mauldin T H 5463
Mauskopf C G 8372
Mawdsley M D 5067
Maxie D L 121
Maxwell A A 7819
Maxwell S H 802
May E 8527
May E D 6830
May J 4699
May N A 2147
May W 2979
May Z E 5253
Mayall M L 803
Mayer F P 5229
Mayer O H 3577
Mayer Y S 1593
Mayes B S 4717
Mayes M J 4569
Mayes M L 7456
Mayhall P R 2425
Mayhew A L 5884
Maynard T J 7597
Mays M J 4253
Mays R G 3994
Mayse S I 4570
Maze M J 8630
Mazer C D 5787
Mazur A P 7325
Mazurowski Sr M C 7820
Mazzoleni L 1147
Meacham J M 8716
Mead J F 3557
Mead R N 6152
Meagher K J 3153
Meagher M H 4571
Means A 2148
Means B 3457
Means B M 6831
Means J A 5931
Mears K B 7457
Medeiros Sr L 1594
Medjuck J A 5799
Meehan Sr M B 6153
Meek J A 7616

Meers N 6833
Meeveren A V 6834
Megargel D 5464
Megee M E 3046
Meginnis F S 122
Mehok W J 5740
Meier T K 534
Meinberg A 7458
Melamed J T 7326
Melanson G A 3532
Melchner Sr M R 4076
Meldrum H S 7821
Mele J S 3291
Meleedy Sr M R 4994
Mellinger G L 3578
Meloncini C 3243
Melton J E 3814
Melvin M L 4807
Menard R R 6835
Mendelsohn J 5465
Mendelson E B 1763
Mendilow A A 2149
Mendoza J D 365
Menegazzi C 5254
Menn W L 4642
Menon M 8478
Mento J 6836
Mercanti E 5698
Mercer J E 1331
Mercer M M 2507
Mercer T E 2469
Mercier Sr R I 1764
Merdler T B 5068
Meredith J R 2894
Mergler E 945
Merkle C M 5466
Mermel A 123
Meroney H 804
Merrill F H 3487
Merritt J D 2655
Merrix R P 2150
Mers Sr M B 2773
Merton E S 8698
Mescall F P Jr 5467
Mescola E 2598
Meserole H T 1910
Messenger W E 2151
Messimer M I 5741
Messini M 4700
Meszban M P 4178
Metcalfe A C 6837
Metz C I 7989
Metz G K 4254
Metz G M 3227
Metz Z 6838

Metzgar J M 5803
Meuth G S 4077
Meyer E A 2152
Meyer F J 1280
Meyer H T 6839
Meyer V B 4808
Meyers A C 805
Meyers R J 8717
Meyers R R 6840
Meyerson M E 4457
Mezey F C 4456
Miatello M P 2369
Michalski R E 5742
Michelesi A 7958
Michelman C F 7327
Michie S 806
Middleton B L 4995
Middleton J A 2774
Middleton R N 5105
Midgett W R 535
Midgeley E G 5932
Mihalka G C 6841
Mihills M 124
Milam C H 7553
Milam L C 6842
Milan D 1031
Milan N M 2849
Milano F 2841
Miles A 125
Miles N A 6843
Miles R W Jr 1858
Miles S 583
Miles T 8551
Miley Sr E F 6844
Milford R T 411
Milkman C R 6845
Millard J 4078
Millard M J 4079
Miller A 7822
Miller A C 1281
Miller A F 7328
Miller A L 4359
Miller A M 1595
Miller A U 807
Miller B A 6846
Miller B J 3815
Miller C 987
Miller D J 3047
Miller D W 4360
Miller D W 8995
Miller E M 1596
Miller F E 8592
Miller G E 3488
Miller H D 8593

Miller H F 4962
Miller H M 3621
Miller J C 3489
Miller J C 7933
Miller J I 1597
Miller J J 8412
Miller J K 5715
Miller J S 3382
Miller K A 4458
Miller L 3048
Miller L H Jr 4255
Miller L M 6847
Miller L T 6848
Miller M A 1148
Miller M A 4459
Miller M G 5468
Miller M G 6199
Miller M P 3816
Miller P A 2600
Miller P J 8594
Miller P L 5469
Miller R F 5933
Miller R H 126
Miller R H 4872
Miller R R 2153
Miller S E 127
Miller V 1353
Miller W 5255
Millican C B 7823
Milliken R A 4361
Millikin E M 4671
Millman S L 6055
Millmann R H 2775
Mills C J 808
Mills H B 2154
Mills H J 1598
Mills J H 2954
Mills J L 3622
Mills M S 1599
Mills M W 4809
Milunas J G 4362
Minard R S 3995
Minter B 4572
Minter M E 128
Minton M M 1600
Mioni P 4016
Mirabelli L 3533
Miranda I 475
Mires C 2327
Mirich M 8144
Mirza Z 3400
Misenheimer J B Jr 6●
Misko M J 7572
Mitcham M B 6850

Mitchell A F	7824
Mitchell B H	5124
Mitchell C H	4996
Mitchell E D	7825
Mitchell J D	476
Mitchell J E	366
Mitchell J E	809
Mitchell J G	988
Mitchell J L	5776
Mitchell M B	1914
Mitchell M O	8654
Mitchell P	129
Mitchell P B	7826
Mitchell R	7827
Mitchell S H	2155
Mitchell W R	8290
Miura T	8996
Mizell L G	4921
Moakler K	4080
Moan M A	5804
Moberg G	5470
Mochedlover V G	6851
Mock H B	7828
Moffatt J S	8291
Moffett E A	8413
Molck-Ude S B	8528
Molella L	7829
Mollach F L	8786
Mollema P C	1601
Mollenhauer Br F E	7459
Mollenkott V R	2776
Molloy P A	3206
Molony A J	1602
Monagle M W	6852
Monahan J W	3154
Monahan Sr T M	810
Moncada E J	6853
Moncrief S B	1149
Mondzac S P	8181
Money D E	3049
Monk D E	2156
Monk J D	7630
Monoson A	6056
Monro C B	2157
Monro C J	8414
Monsky E J	6854
Montague G B	1603
Montalberti G	5230
Montgomery A P Jr	3270
Montgomery B N	6081
Montgomery D E	6855
Montgomery K W	8479
Montgomery R F	6856
Montgomery R M	5069

Montroy B	8292
Moody D	4810
Moody I A	3207
Moody J P	8655
Moody O M	1032
Moody W A	477
Moomaw S L	1604
Moon B A	1282
Moon H D	412
Moon N F	4081
Mooney Sr B M	4573
Mooney J J	130
Mooneyham J	989
Moonschein H C	8656
Moore A S	4963
Moore B	6857
Moore C	2158
Moore C A	7830
Moore C E	5256
Moore D	1605
Moore D E	230
Moore D J	4574
Moore D K	2470
Moore F D	5471
Moore G B	811
Moore G W	6858
Moore H J	3817
Moore H L	5472
Moore J A	4811
Moore J K	5106
Moore J T	2656
Moore L D	7831
Moore M	7832
Moore M A	2601
Moore M L	5070
Moore M W	8657
Moore N	6082
Moore P B	2159
Moore R H	8552
Moore R L	2777
Moore R M	8078
Moore S B	7833
Moore T I	3818
Moo-Young K T	1606
Moran B A	2160
Moran H	6860
Moran H M	6859
Moran L P	3659
Moran L W	3292
Moran R E	5768
Morehead E W	3050
Moreines H	2161
Morelli U	7329
Morey E K	2162

Morey J H	2163
Morgan E C	20
Morgan G C	8079
Morgan H	2896
Morgan H D	2895
Morgan I L	3534
Morgan J P	131
Morgan J T	2164
Morgan L B	1150
Morgan M E	1151
Morgan S U	6861
Morgan V E	8293
Morland M W	1859
Moro T R	5473
Moroney K E	6862
Morrell M C	8294
Morrill L M	4082
Morris A	7460
Morris B F	3660
Morris C M	5474
Morris D W	3347
Morris F J	1607
Morris G R	132
Morris L A	2165
Morris M	1608
Morris Sr M M	4964
Morris N J	7330
Morris R J	1736
Morris V A	906
Morris W E	5475
Morrison B	4812
Morrison G	4997
Morrison W N	5699
Morrissette R R	3155
Morrissey A J	21
Morton G I	8658
Morton J D	5476
Morton L M	6863
Morton M K	7573
Moscotto G	3244
Moseley J	3156
Moseley V D	5147
Moser A M	2778
Moser W C	5477
Moses E P	2166
Mosher M T	2377
Moskowitz H S	4813
Mosle P M	6864
Moss D B	1609
Moss E L	3348
Moss M H	7834
Moss R F	2167
Motsch C P	536
Mott B E	478
Motta I	6865

Motte Sr M 1860
Mount J R 8080
Mount R I Jr 6866
Mowat A M 2168
Moxley C F 5478
Moyer M P 1610
Moyle C 1611
Moynihan P V 5934
Moynihan W T 8415
Moyse J H 6867
Mozdzierz C A 4460
Muir R L 2426
Mukherjea S K 1152
Mukherjee S C 8480
Mukoyama A 812
Mukoyama Y 8295
Mularski K 6868
Muldoon E G 8457
Muldrow E B 6869
Mulkern J I 8997
Mulligan L E 2779
Mullin D L 813
Mullins J J 814
Mumbulo R E 4884
Muncie N B 7835
Munson E K 2897
Muntz H E 2169
Murchison J T Jr 8373
Murdoch R 1283
Murphree J D 5183
Murphy A M 6870
Murphy C M 1861
Murphy D J 2175
Murphy E 231
Murphy E A 7461
Murphy E J 6871
Murphy J L 4256
Murphy K A 6872
Murphy L B 1033
Murphy L C 7554
Murphy L W 6873
Murphy Sr M C 815
Murphy M I 2171
Murphy M J 2602
Murphy Sr M J 4083
Murphy M J 8998
Murphy Sr M N 5743
Murphy P 3819
Murphy R A 5480
Murphy S 479
Murphy V M 2780
Murray D M 8081
Murray J F 1612
Murray Sr M P 1613

Murray Sr M V 8296
Murray N A 4084
Murray N D 2427
Murray P M 2172
Murredo M 3661
Musgrave M E 1780
Musgrave R L Jr 4461
Musio G 2173
Musselman H 8750
Musselwhite V M 6874
Myers B J 4575
Myers E B 4363
Myers J P 2378
Myers J R 1153
Myers K W 6875
Myers S R 3157
Myers V L 2603
Myers W J 5481
Mylott M I 1614
Myrick E M 5482

Nadel I B 4814
Nagy D M 3051
Nahra M 6876
Naidoo M 7331
Nakamura C C 3052
Nalbandian C R 7462
Nalesso M 2174
Nall M N 6877
Nam K W 133
Napier D 8999
Napier E M 2175
Napoli J L 9000
Napper C A 6878
Narkin A P 6879
Nascimben A 1928
Nash B B 6880
Nash C C 2428
Nash O 3535
Nath B 1862
Nations C G 4024
Nattsas A C 6881
Naughton Rev E V 929
Nauragio Sr M A 4576
Nause J D 3228
Nead M 1154
Neagle R T 3996
Neal L H 930
Necarelli S 5716
Neckers J H 3536
Necomb M J 3053
Nee J M 3623
Neeson J F 537
Neeson Sr M F 4577

Negueloua L M 6882
Neil A C 3820
Neilan B I 2340
Neill M L 2781
Neill R L Jr 413
Neilson F W 2782
Nelligan F A 5231
Nelson B K 2604
Nelson C C 1615
Nelson C E 816
Nelson D A 6154
Nelson D E 6883
Nelson E 6884
Nelson J 1616
Nelson J R 6885
Nelson K E 8787
Nelson K G 2176
Nelson M 5483
Nelson M V 5484
Nelson P J 3158
Nelson S L 4257
Nesbit F E 6022
Nestor S R 5485
Netterville D G 2605
Nettles G N 7836
Neu L M 4017
Neufeldt J 8297
Neufeldt V A 5486
Neuhaus C H Jr 2429
Neuman S K 3419
Neuthaler P D 5125
Neuville H R 7837
Neville M 4462
Neville M E 3558
Nevin C A 584
Nevins L 134
Newbold H 4578
Newburn B R 1863
Newby R L 4815
Newcomb M E 1284
Newcomb R 2898
Newcum Mother M 5700
Newell A 4126
Newell E E 5805
Newell S W 5487
Newitt E 7598
Newlands P 2177
Newman P A 7959
Newsom F W 817
Newton C A 6886
Newton L W 8298
Newton M M 5744
Newton W R 1155
Nicholas E R 3458

Nicholson C 6887
Nicholson D H 232
Nicklin D L 4701
Nickson J R 1929
Nielsen M E 5101
Nielson E E 3821
Nielson L E 4702
Nielson P J 6888
Nieuwenhuis M 4816
Nigro V T 946
Niketas G 2178
Nix M J 7838
Nobbe G 1156
Noble F 6012
Noble J D 6889
Noble T A 2783
Nochimson R L 1008
Noftsker O 585
Nogami Y 960
Nolan J A 2179
Nolan J T 6890
Nolan R F 2657
Nolen J R 4579
Nolen J T 2180
Noll A J 8182
Nooe M A 7839
Noonan J F 3822
Noonan J J 4085
Norby B J 378
Nored G 4364
Norford D P 5126
Norman A M 1157
Norman C J 3208
Norman E A 8299
Norris H A 4580
North C L 4853
North D M 2181
North J S 1864
Northcroft D J 414
Northrup F W 818
Northup E B 4086
Norton Sr E M 8458
Norton N 7840
Norvell C A 3823
Norwood L S 6891
Notopoulos P J 4849
Novack P A 1737
Novak R L 5071
Novi T 4676
Novotny J 4581
Nozick M 5638
Nuchols M 6892
Nuchols S C 8082
Nunan J C 1617
Nurick E 931

Nutt C R 3824
Nutting H D 7841
Nuwayser R A 5788
Nyberg B M 8300
Nye J G 6893
Nygard H O 6894
Nylund L 586
Nystrom L G 1285

Oaklander L 2182
Oare W T 7332
Oberg C 6895
Obermeier E B 8204
O'Brien F M 1865
O'Brien J A 1340
O'Brien J E 1618
O'Brien J J 1158
O'Brien M E 4258
O'Brien M J 233
O'Brien P E 1866
O'Brien P F 1619
O'Brien P W 4582
O'Brien R D 4087
O'Brien Sr R M 6896
O'Brien T F 4736
Occari D 5966
Ochshorn M 8416
Ochsner S M 8082
O'Connell C A 3682
O'Connell D 4463
O'Connell D H 5935
O'Connell E M 7842
O'Connell Sr S C 3537
O'Connor C I 6013
O'Connor D 3538
O'Connor J H 1620
O'Connor J J 8183
O'Connor J M 7843
O'Connor M E 7844
O'Connor M J 2784
O'Connor Mother P 6897
O'Connor P F 5232
O'Connor V 3964
Odarenko D M 3683
Odden E S 2183
Odell M E 2184
Odom K C 6155
O'Donnell Sr M A 6898
O'Donnell Sr M M 4935
O'Donnell W J 6899
O'Dwyer J A 8184
Oefelein I I 234
Oehmson M 2606
Oemler M S 5233
Oetgen G R 8631

Offutt E A 2495
O'Flaherty J G 317
Ogata T 4583
O'Gorman E C 7845
O'Gorman I G 2899
O'Grady G L 4365
O'Grady W A 5936
O'Halloran F M 1765
O'Halloran Sr M E 6900
O'Hanlon Sr M K 2185
O'Hara C M 1621
O'Hara J B 4885
O'Hara S 1622
O'Hare Sr J 8459
Okamura S 2186
O'Kelley T A 4886
O'Kelly D 1034
Oldani L J 6901
Oldenburg G M 1867
Oldenkamp J L 8659
Oldfield D E 3055
Oldfield E L 4152
Oldham P D 4817
O'Leary C J 6902
O'Leary F L 2900
O'Leary M A 6903
Olefsky E R 4965
Olivas Br B L 8301
Olive W J 6904
Oliver J B 7463
Oliver R M 235
Oliver R T 4259
Oliver V K 8374
Oliver W E 3401
Olley F R 990
Ollivier A P 236
Olmert K M 1623
Olmini A 4857
Olmstead J H 819
Olmsted M 3564
Olney J L 4854
Olney W IV 1868
Olphert W J 4673
Olsen D A 2485
Olsen W A 291
Olson K L 1869
Olsson K O 7555
Olstead M M 6905
O'Malley Sr E M 6906
O'Malley Sr J 6907
Omans S E 6908
O'Meara K C 4922
Omibiyi A A 3624
Ommassini G 4923

Onafeko C O   5072
O'Neal E   3825
O'Neal S L   8660
O'Neil N J   1870
O'Neill J P   7464
O'Neill Sr M A   6909
Onion M K   932
Opperman C   1159
Oppy I   6910
Orchard I   7960
Orcutt C   8661
Orcutt H J   6911
Ordway J K   5488
O'Regan J D   5489
O'Riley M   5073
Ormond W C   480
Orner F H   367
O'Roak N V   3293
O'Rourke T E   5490
Orr G H   6912
Orr R F   3826
Orr R S   6913
Orrick A H   4127
Ortego P D   6914
Ortolani C   481
Orton H M   3096
Osborn W   482
Osborne A M   6915
Osborne D   1624
Osborne M H   7846
Osburn N J   3490
O'Shea J H   4088
O'Shea J V   2955
O'Shea M J   4260
Oster E   1160
Ostercamp J F   3965
Ostow E S   8788
Ostro L H   1871
Ostrowski P S   1161
O'Sullivan R J   630
Otis P J   2956
Otten T R   4936
Otto E J   6083
Otto J H   6916
Otto M K   6917
Outten J E   2957
Outten J W   6918
Overholser R V   1625
Overpeck S A   3827
Overton C M   2187
Overton L H   4703
Owen G Jr   2471
Owen I B   5975
Owen L B   2188

Owen L B   4140
Owens D C   5074
Owens E W   6919
Ower J B   7574
Ownsby J M   1286
Oyewale J O   5675
Ozolins A   3916

Pace C J   6920
Pace H E   1287
Pack I M   3056
Pack J T   5745
Packard E M   7847
Packard F E   7848
Packard G V Jr   2189
Packman R E   1626
Padberg M J   2901
Paden J E   7849
Padovan C   2980
Pafford J   3349
Pafford W   5652
Page L M   2785
Page T M   8302
Paget E H   7465
Paige M   5702
Paige M M   22
Painter J W   8684
Paisley E   3917
Palestin S J   2842
Palmer A R   2190
Palmer E N   2902
Palmer J J   2903
Palmer M D   8741
Palmer M H   3565
Palmer P F   3828
Palmer P R   4818
Palumbo R M   172
Panek L L   6921
Pantuso G   5491
Paolo Rev F E   5872
Papadopoulou K E   3159
Papenfuss E   237
Pappas A J   1627
Papps E M   991
Parcell M R   8185
Parchman M E   820
Parigi S   4153
Parish C   7599
Parisi P E   2843
Parker A G   6922
Parker A S   6923
Parker B M   3057
Parker G B   4674
Parker J H   1162

Parker M A   238
Parker M A   1628
Parker M F   6925
Parker M V   6924
Parker R E   7850
Parker R W   2191
Parker S W   7961
Parker W J   3209
Parkinson F C   1629
Parkis P K   2192
Parks A G   2341
Parks R A   4584
Parnell E F   1630
Parnell K D   821
Parola G J   368
Parrott H L   822
Parry W B   6156
Parsons L C   3966
Parsons M L   7962
Parsons R   4819
Parsons V M   3829
Partee M H   6926
Pasqualato G   823
Pasqualato R   2193
Pass M C   4675
Passel A W   587
Passmore B S   4585
Pasternak W P   824
Pastorello A   1354
Patch S J   6927
Pate O C   7851
Paterni A M   1317
Paterson G H   3058
Paterson H A   7333
Pathmann R B   4261
Patin M C   1163
Paton W C   5937
Patrice Sr M   6928
Patrick M D   4128
Patricolo M T   4998
Patten A M   2904
Patten M M   5717
Patterson C E   7466
Patterson C I   2607
Patterson C W   5492
Patterson D   5493
Patterson L J   6929
Patterson N S   3539
Patterson S W   3540
Patterson T M   4018
Pattison D   1164
Patton A L   2608
Patton D D   5494
Patton E S   5495

Pauley H W 7334	Perkins A M 2787	Phillips M E 832
Paulson A R 5127	Perkins J A 3060	Phillips M H 2201
Pavelich J L 7852	Perkins K S 5938	Phillips M J 1632
Pawlyk J E 588	Perkins M K 829	Phillips T H 3060
Paxton G B Jr 2472	Perlis L S 7335	Phipps P F 5988
Paxton M 825	Perlmutter E S 483	Phipps T M 1633
Paylore P P 5987	Perrault L M 239	Piaggi M W 4924
Payne B 826	Perry C A 7516	Piaggio A 4999
Payne E P 8375	Perry C H 5676	Piazza M L 5128
Payne J J 8303	Perry C P 1872	Piccini C 5860
Payton P 8789	Perry D J 1166	Picco U R 2790
Pearce H J 1288	Perry G G 2197	Pick A 5790
Pearce S C 1332	Perry J O 3443	Pickard L H 2905
Pearce S M 2307	Perry S 7336	Pickard L M 7857
Pearce T 827	Perry T P 3831	Pickel L C 933
Pearce T M 5819	Perryman R 6935	Pickens M M 3296
Pearsall T E 6930	Person A L 830	Pickett J R 833
Peaslee A R 40	Perzanowski D J 4820	Piepho E L 5129
Peattie E G 292	Peschel C C 1631	Pierce J 7858
Peck B C 3491	Pessolano F J Jr 4821	Pierce M J 6157
Peck E M 5075	Peters A D 2198	Pierce M L 4588
Peckham D R 5148	Peters G F 3967	Pierce R P 6941
Peckover S L 2786	Peters M 1167	Pierson E A 1634
Pedemonti A 5496	Peterson E H 5076	Pieschel J A 4366
Pederson W M 6931	Peterson L S 4179	Pigot D C 2308
Pefoza A 2844	Peterson M L 5873	Pike F 8084
Pegg B M 5107	Peterson R G 5839	Pilkington J 293
Peirce E C 828	Petrakis B 7963	Pilkington M 8460
Peirce M B 7853	Petree C G 23	Pilkinton A B 1168
Peirce W P 2194	Pettigrew E 2199	Pillai N 7644
Pelagati E 6057	Pettigrew H P 6936	Pinciss G M 8508
Pelfrey C J 2195	Pettis M L 2788	Piorkowski S 8418
Pell J 3294	Pettoelio L D 2361	Piovan A M 395
Pellet M 3541	Petty D 3295	Piper M R 6942
Pelletier R R 7467	Petze M 6937	Piperno A 3350
Pelletier R R 5497	Peyton H 5499	Pirani L 5000
Pelton N F 7854	Pezet M J 2200	Piretti A 240
Peltonen D F 4586	Pezzato G 339	Pirsig R A 2609
Pemberton N A 6932	Pezzini C 5077	Pisana R 3402
Pence A M 394	Pfaff M 7855	Pisanceschi J P 1169
Pence E C 3830	Pfaff W L 3059	Pitcuithly M S 3832
Pendergast C 2196	Pfatteicher P H 2789	Pitman N H 3542
Pengergast H C Jr 5789	Pharr G W 6938	Pittman C L 1170
Pendergast J E 5498	Phelan T A 7856	Pittman P M 6943
Penil M J 135	Phelps M G 831	Pitsch M F 340
Penn S F 6933	Phenix R 538	Pittola U 4676
Penn W 2981	Philbin R G 5677	Pitts C M 2430
Pennino M 6934	Philips J 4587	Pitts E J 5500
Pepin Sr L 3625	Phillips A C Jr 6939	Pivetti R 7468
Pepis B A 8790	Phillips E 6940	Pixton W H 7469
Peplow M W 4966	Phillips E C 318	Plancher M 2486
Perez C 1165	Phillips J 8376	Platt A E 1635
Peril W 3662	Phillips J K 4262	Player M M 6944
Perissutti M 2496	Phillips L J Jr 8417	Plotkin F S 2431

Plumb R J Jr 24	Potter G V 8481	Prindle R M 2791
Plunkett F W 8377	Potter R J 3492	Prins A S 5504
Plummer F S 341	Potts H M 2610	Prior R R 934
Plummer R B 5501	Potts I 834	Priour K A 2611
Plummer T S 5234	Potvin J H 4464	Pritchard E 5976
Pocs J A 4089	Poultridge R H 8085	Pritchard H C 5505
Poe P 7859	Pouncey L 4090	Pritchard M 4591
Poe P L 1171	Pound R E 4589	Pritchard R K 4465
Poggemiller M 5769	Pound S J 3835	Pritchard V G 3351
Pohl M E 5502	Powell D 8086	Prtichard W P 589
Pohl O 1289	Powell E F 6951	Pritchett E P III 55
Poindexter M R 7337	Powell E G 8304	Proctor L G 7861
Poisson R P 6945	Powell J A 4590	Proctor P M 6955
Pol F 6946	Powell P K 6158	Proebstel L 4368
Polacco P 3663	Power D S 8305	Profeta D 5001
Poland E 4677	Power J E 5940	Proffitt E L 4091
Polato L 4704	Power T E 1290	Proffitt E L 6193
Pole E H 5130	Powers A 1638	Profitt D L 2206
Policardi S 25	Powers A 1639	Prosser D A 3445
Polizzi A 4705	Powers E E 1640	Proudfit I B 836
Polk A C 3161	Powers L F 6952	Provence C 3062
Pollack M 1355	Powers Sr M P 4678	Provence J 3245
Pollard D A 3833	Powis M B 2204	Pruitt E E 7471
Pollard V B 6947	Prabhakar T 7631	Pruitt P R 3493
Polley P J 2202	Pradella A 8718	Pryde M J 935
Polo A 631	Pradl G M 3271	Pryor W D 3684
Poloni M 5078	Pratt A 4718	Publicover I F 590
Pomerleau C S 4320	Pratt A V 1873	Pucci R 3063
Pomerleau M F 2906	Pratt D J 3836	Puckett C M 837
Ponce A 4263	Pratt L S 1172	Puckett W E 838
Ponsford M E 5131	Pratt M 2205	Puckett W W 1642
Pontedera C 7556	Precious M V 6058	Pullen M G 7645
Ponzio H J 3997	Preda A 4643	Pulliam C V 5185
Pool H 6948	Predoehl L P 1641	Pullman L 8146
Pope D V 1636	Prescott A L 4367	Puntney A T 839
Pope F E 7470	Preston J J III 5941	Purcell Sr M J 1643
Pope Z 241	Preston T R 992	Purdy S R 7472
Popowski D J 5184	Preto-Rodas R A 5639	Purnell R B 5507
Popp C L 3834	Price C 5653	Purvis T D 136
Popyach J 1637	Price D 3837	Putman A D 8087
Porter J M 8602	Price E J 3838	Putnam L S 6956
Porter L C 3459	Price J G 6954	Putzel R 5508
Porter M A 5820	Price J R 6953	Puzon Mother M B 2207
Porter P A 242	Price J V 4145	Pyle H A 7940
Porter P E 7338	Price L E 8306	Pyszhowski R J 2208
Posey N R 6949	Price M G 1333	
Posmantur M K 3421	Price R 3061	
Pospisil R 2203	Prichard E I 7860	Quarles D M 7934
Possenti A 3444	Pridgen R A 7637	Quattlebaum M C 245
Post K M 2958	Priest L P 835	Queen L T 3064
Poston C D 6084	Priestley C S 1874	Quick D E 2209
Poteet L J 243	Prim P L 8145	Quick J R 4466
Pothier G 244	Prince H M 2907	Quicksall C 6957
Potter C F 6950	Prince L M 5503	Quigley E A 5509
		Quillevere H G 2959

Quinlan G A   5162
Quinn Sr E   8461
Quinn J A   3162
Quinn M R   6958
Quinn P S   1644
Quinn R K   3918
Quirk F B   3626
Quivey J R   4889

Rabey H R   2210
Rabinovitz R   484
Rabinowitz I J   8791
Racca I   2473
Rackin P F   4822
Radford F L   7339
Raff W S   3065
Raffin L   8186
Rafford R I   8419
Rafter Sr M M   6959
Ragazzini M G   5861
Ragland A T   6159
Ragow F T   1645
Ragsdale I T   591
Rahn B J   8088
Railston A G   4925
Raines R A   6960
Rainwater V B   5510
Ramanathan S   7862
Ramey S R   2982
Ramirez A O   2362
Ramirez E   1646
Ramonow W I   6999
Ramos L V   4592
Ramos M D   5511
Ramsdell G R   8307
Ramsey G   2658
Ramsey H E   6014
Ramsey J S   3998
Ramsey O F   1647
Ramsey P Jr   3968
Ramsey R V   1648
Randall B   3066
Randall H W   2792
Randerson J T   6961
Randolph J C   8529
Raniolo M   1930
Rankin H A Jr   2908
Rankin J M   6962
Rankin J S   3969
Ranne V A   246
Ranson N J   961
Rapf J E   7473
Rappaport L M   1173
Rarig F M   3067

Raschick R E   3163
Rasey M B   5512
Raskin S   3352
Raskopi N A   2342
Ratledge W H Jr   6963
Ratte E H   294
Ratz M S   8187
Ravaggi M T   5108
Ravanelli L   6160
Rawlings L M   4719
Rawlings M L   5513
Ray R   2793
Rayborn C H   7340
Raynal M   3164
Read D R   3627
Read J E   4180
Read J W   4369
Read K   3165
Read M   137
Reading E H   6964
Ready M E   2211
Reagh E M   1174
Reaves H M   295
Rebentisch W   7341
Reckley R   3166
Recoulley A L   8719
Reddick B D   8553
Redding Sr M A   5791
Redewill H M   415
Redman L F   6965
Redwine L L   6966
Reed D J   138
Reed J C   2845
Reed L T   632
Reed M L   6967
Reed M V   5079
Reed R A   3970
Reed R B   8378
Reedy L D   3353
Rees B A   5821
Rees C Jr   6968
Rees F H   2212
Reese B   8420
Reese J E   1356
Reese M M   2794
Reeve P M   2960
Reeves F   1875
Reeves G B   2795
Reeves J   1175
Reeves V E   5235
Regan D   3167
Regan M E   139
Regan Sr R E   2213
Regosa R T   3068

Reibenstein A A   6969
Reichardt Sr M A   840
Reichert C M   8308
Reichman R M   1035
Reid M R   1781
Reid V P   8792
Reidy J K   5942
Reiger G W   6970
Reigstad P M   592
Reilly A D   6971
Reilly M A   379
Reilly R T   2363
Reiner A G   1649
Reinholtz H G   2909
Reinsdorf W D   7638
Reisen D   4593
Reith H W   1291
Reitzel F X   5514
Remmel M R   2328
Renaudie M J   7342
Rendle J A   4467
Reno R H   3839
Reuter J R   6972
Reutinger O W   3354
Rewa M P   4264
Rewis H S   5515
Rex H M   8462
Reyder H A   3403
Reynolds A   2214
Reynolds C E   3971
Reynolds D S   2796
Reynolds F S   6973
Reynolds G D   7343
Reynolds I E   5236
Reynolds J S   5516
Reynolds R C   6974
Reynolds T E   247
Rhea R L   8482
Rhines H D   936
Rhode R D   7474
Rhodes J F   4468
Rhodes R F   6975
Ribner I   6976
Rice B D   994
Rice E E   3355
Rice K W   2431
Rice M   5132
Rice Sr M B   6977
Rich H   3840
Rich M R   841
Richard A   8309
Richard Sr M F   6978
Richards E J   3841
Richardson B R   8379

Richardson J C 6979
Richardson M C 3210
Richardson N 3972
Richardson S B 2797
Richeson H 6980
Richetti J J 3168
Richman T L 8005
Richmond G A 2910
Richter S 3229
Rickard A M 6981
Ricker E A 4092
Ricks B 5517
Ricks B 5080
Ridd J C 2215
Riddehough G 8147
Riddell C M 2612
Riddick J M 8579
Riddle B S 8310
Rieg F F 7344
Riehemann M M 5718
Rieker R A 248
Riel A P 5746
Riepe O 2613
Rieser M A 8793
Riess M E 6982
Rifkin M 4594
Riggs S E 8311
Righetti A 4370
Rightor E E 140
Rigucci L 8685
Riley M I 6983
Riley Sr M A 4595
Riley Sr M F 6984
Riley Sr M L 1650
Rimel R D 2798
Rimmer J L 5943
Riner R S Jr 5518
Ringkamp H C 6985
Ringo Sr M A 1292
Riotte J H 4371
Rippel S J 5267
Ripperda J M 5519
Rippy T L 1651
Risley H M 1357
Rispoli T 5149
Risse R G 7863
Risty M J 3842
Ritchie J P 6986
Rivelson S J 8662
Rivera C L 3843
Rivera Sr I M 6987
Rivers D E 4926
Rivers I 4372
Rizzi V 7990

Rizzo B 7600
Roach J G 1652
Roach J V 6988
Roach M J 6989
Roark B J 8794
Robb A J 6161
Robb J T 8795
Robberecht P A 4679
Robbins O M 2911
Robbins W 142
Robbins W 842
Roberge P I 3169
Robers Sr M B 6990
Roberson S A 7575
Roberts E E 3999
Roberts E G 3170
Roberts E W 843
Roberts F 6162
Roberts H 6059
Roberts H S 6991
Roberts I S 2216
Roberts J P 4823
Roberts J R 7864
Roberts L G 6992
Roberts L T 4596
Roberts M 3246
Roberts M C 7991
Roberts M R 2799
Roberts M Y 2614
Roberts O P 3973
Roberts T J 2800
Roberts W A 2217
Robertson A 4469
Robertson A 4898
Robertson C H 5520
Robertson G E 3844
Robertson G E 5521
Robertson H 2615
Robertson H S 6993
Robertson M H 141
Robertson M J 7865
Robertson P C 319
Robida Sr L 3974
Robins H F 5522
Robinson A F 6994
Robinson B L 4093
Robinson E B 7557
Robinson E D 844
Robinson E E 3356
Robinson F W 2801
Robinson H S 6995
Robinson H V 8554
Robinson H W 4373
Robinson J R 4265

Robinson L 3845
Robinson N W 8312
Robinson R 2616
Robinson R J 4824
Robinson S 3975
Robinson V L 3846
Robinson W A 3357
Robinson W R 4000
Roblyer P W 4266
Robnett A R 5081
Robson M S 6015
Roche K J 3664
Rock B 3665
Rockett H M 5523
Rodaro L M 4470
Roddie C B 2617
Rodenchuk E 1176
Roderick W J 4001
Rodes R M 2218
Rodger J C 845
Rodgers L D 1782
Rodkin D J 6996
Rodriguez A 8089
Roebuck W G 2961
Roehl B M 2219
Roesch R J 7475
Roesler 1177
Roesler E V 7476
Roger E H 6997
Rogers E G 6998
Rogers F 4471
Rogers F R 8313
Rogers I 6085
Rogers J 5852
Rogers J E 3543
Rogers L J 3494
Rogers M T 2802
Rogers N 1178
Rogers P W 3685
Rogers R D 1179
Rogers R E 3358
Rogers R Y 7992
Rogers W F 4472
Rogers W S 3069
Rohr M R 3387
Roiter H 2432
Rolando M 8720
Rolfs A R 4706
Rollick G E 1653
Rollins S F 8555
Roman J 2370
Romine C 7000
Ronan C J 5747
Ronan J J Jr 8421

Ron Caglia R 8148	Rowe A C 6060	Rutherford S H 8090
Roodhouse A C 2803	Rowe D W 5822	Rutherford V R 7014
Roody S I 5703	Rowe K T 7869	Rutherford W J 848
Rooney L F 2220	Rowe W H III 5133	Rutland R B 3446
Rosa E 249	Rowell G R 7004	Rutledge R C 4873
Rose Sr M C 5525	Rower R 7345	Ruyle B J 1181
Rose N V 5524	Rowland J N 5002	Ryan A C 849
Rose P A 5526	Rowlands H E 2223	Ryan A M 5944
Rose V 320	Rowley G K 2912	Ryan C J 4270
Rosebaugh C G 2804	Roxbrugh J W 2806	Ryan E K 8721
Rosecrance J 2371	Roxby R J 1180	Ryan F J Jr 7015
Roselle B L 7001	Roy J C 2224	Ryan G E 3297
Roselli Br A 2221	Royster B H 847	Ryan J C 5748
Roseme D 2222	Rozsnafszky J S 3629	Ryan M J 3848
Rosen B J 4943	Ruark H G 8422	Ryan R M 4601
Rosen L C 2618	Rubben J 4899	Ryckebusch J R 8722
Rosenbalm J O 3171	Rubin D S 3230	Ryczek M H 4680
Rosenbaum J W 1876	Rubin M P 250	Ryder E N 7016
Rosenberg J 4825	Rubinsky B 7005	Rytell G 7017
Rosenberg R S 3070	Ruble M R 7006	
Rosenberger L P 846	Ruble S B 251	Sabine F J 3631
Rosenblatt J P 5527	Rudd M 2225	Sabiston E J 7018
Rosenblood B N 3172	Rudman L R 7870	Sachs W C 8091
Rosenfeld J P 4599	Rudolfo G 8509	Sadowski C F 1182
Rosenfeld R 4473	Ruff J R 1294	Sager N C 4944
Rosenfelt D S 4598	Ruff W J 7478	Sagert L A 143
Rosengard R S 485	Ruhe E L 4267	Sahni C L 3272
Rosengarten F 1293	Rumberger W B 7007	St Clair D W 144
Rosenman J B 1036	Rumble E W 4268	St Clair G A 8497
Rosenthal L S 7002	Rundell W 3359	St John R P 7019
Rosenthal N W 4599	Rundle U 5082	Saint Wilfred Sr 2620
Rosenthal W M 7866	Ruoff F A 7008	Sait J 8734
Rosner B 7867	Rupp H R 1654	Sakai H C 3849
Ross J K 5977	Rusch F E 5531	Salazar S 7020
Ross J P 5528	Rushing J W 7009	Sale R B 145
Ross L M 2805	Rushing P B 4707	Salin H B 7479
Ross M 7003	Rushmore H 4002	Saling V 4375
Ross Sr M A 4474	Rushmore R P 8796	Salisbury R L 7346
Ross M I 1766	Russ J R 2913	Salkoff G B 3850
Ross R H Jr 7993	Russell B L 4269	Salman P C 7873
Rossignol L J 907	Russell D 6164	Saltman E 3851
Rossini M 5150	Russell D A 7010	Salvidio F A 1183
Rossy C A 7477	Russell E 3360	Sammarelli M 5640
Rota E 4129	Russell I W 7871	Sammons E 7874
Roth H J 5529	Russell M 3383	Sampey J R 252
Rothweiler M J 6163	Russell M C 7011	Sample E J 5151
Rothwein A F 2619	Russell N 1655	Sample V M 1656
Rottino J F 3628	Russell R 3847	Sampley A M 5862
Rouce H D 4374	Russell R W 7872	Sampson H X 146
Rouse R 5530	Russell S J 7012	Sampson M 486
Roush G C 1877	Rust J D 3071	Sams V E 1783
Rousseau J G 3422	Rusyn Br A S 3630	Sams V L 7875
Roux F A 7868	Rutgers G D 7013	Samsey P C 5083
Rovatti E 4600	Ruth M V 26	Samuels J N 487

Samuels J 7021
Samuelson R E 4475
Sanborn B I 3173
Sandefer M L 253
Sanders C 8423
Sanders F D 5532
Sanders H M 254
Sanders J T 7022
Sanders L A 7024
Sanders L C 7023
Sanders Sr M A 7025
Sanders M C 3632
Sanders P S 5163
Sanders S E 4602
Sanders W B 7026
Sanders W E 2433
Sandini A 5641
Sandison J 5533
Sandison J M 7027
Sandstrom G A 3460
Sandwell S 4900
Sanelli A 8580
Sanferrare J R 488
Sanford C 4603
Sanita' L 6061
Sansing J W 2434
Sanson B A 1878
Santangelo G A 3072
Sanzo E B 7028
Sapienza G M 8483
Sarcinelli L 7558
Saretti F 3423
Sargeant H H 7029
Sargent E H 1657
Sarick H 3579
Sarno R A 2807
Saroop A 7030
Sartain C P 7031
Sartin E L 5084
Sasscer C D 7480
Saucier E N 5534
Saunders J 5535
Saunders J K 2621
Savage D B 5945
Savant J 4094
Savaria Sr M G 8463
Sawin H L 6086
Sawyer J P 8723
Sawyer R M 2622
Sawyers C 3544
Saxton S M 8149
Sayles N L 5536
Saylors R D 1658
Sayre I C 2226

Sayre N M 6165
Scafidel J R 1358
Scally J J 6166
Scanlan Sr M B 1659
Scanlan T R Jr 7032
Scannell L M 7033
Scapin G 615
Scaramuzza De Marco A 2474
Scarry J M 4476
Schacht H T 7034
Schade F A 2914
Schaefer E H 2309
Schaefer E M 1660
Schaeffer J 1184
Schaeffer N J 8092
Schallhorn D J 7347
Schamberg R S 4376
Schartle P M 7035
Schaub O H 4737
Schawacker E W Jr 7964
Scheer R 2227
Schenk R H 6167
Schenkel T 5678
Schereschewsky E F 4377
Scherle P J 851
Schiff M 4604
Schiffer J 8797
Schiffhorst J 2475
Schileo L 2343
Schiller D J 633
Schillinger O M 7348
Schivo Sr M N 7876
Schlabach B 4198
Schlegel J E 3424
Schloss M 5537
Schlueter H V 1880
Schluetter M A 3073
Schmelzer D M 8188
Schmidt D J 3425
Schmidt E 4477
Schmidt M J 255
Schmiedendorf I M 2623
Schmitt G 7877
Schmitz E W 3247
Schnakenberg C S 2476
Schneider A 3074
Schneider J W 8510
Schneider M B 1295
Schoellhorn C S 7036
Schoen R G 7037
Schoner A A 2624
Schools M R 1186
Schotter R D 369
Schramm H B 5085

Schratz B W 5086
Schreiner Sr M C 8314
Schreiner W R 593
Schrier V B 5538
Schrimshire S 8189
Schroeder C M 6168
Schroth J F 1187
Schubart W F 8093
Schultz A W 7481
Schultz G 396
Schultz J H 2435
Schultz S C 8511
Schultze E W 7349
Schulze M M 852
Schumacher C J 4271
Schumacher P J 7038
Schumacher W A 3495
Schunk K 2228
Schupf H A 2659
Schwab R P 4852
Schwager M L 256
Schwalbaum J 8315
Schwalbe D J 4826
Schwartz E 2229
Schwartz E 7040
Schwartz E J 7039
Schwartz H E 489
Schwartz M H 3852
Schwartz M M 7041
Schwartz S M 4827
Schwarz M D 4644
Schweighauser C A 855(
Schweikert J J 1661
Schwertman M P 2230
Schwetmen J W 2962
Schwienher L M 7042
Schwitalla Sr M G 853
Scigliano A R 3580
Scoggins F T 7043
Scott A 490
Scott A E 1188
Scott A H 5539
Scott C 3361
Scott E A 147
Scott J S 5237
Scott L E 7044
Scott M B 8316
Scott M D 491
Scott M E 2497
Scott M E 7878
Scott M S 5540
Scott N 3198
Scott N C 8010
Scott R L 3545

Scott S E   4605
Scott W A   7617
Scoufos A L   7045
Scouten A H   8663
Scouten L M   5541
Schribner D A   7879
Scrittori A   4378
Scruggs V L   1662
Scrutchins J R   148
Scully V C Jr   5087
Seaborn H T   7046
Seaman A T   8424
Seaman R L   7047
Seaman V F   7048
Searcy M L   7049
Sears E   594
Sears F I   3853
Sears O H   850
Searles J C   5542
Seat C   7559
Seaver L F   2231
Seckinger D L   7050
Secor R A   2232
Seeff A F   1663
Seelye M A   7051
Seelye M C   7052
Seibert B A   1296
Seibert L E   7053
Seidel M C   5679
Seidell M M   1664
Seifer B   7560
Seigel J P   1297
Selby D L   3362
Selden L   8581
Selden L B Jr   1881
Selden N A   2233
Seldon A P   7880
Self J   5543
Selig D M   5544
Seligman K L   7517
Sellers L C   7054
Sellers P C   539
Sellers W E   3447
Sells L F   3174
Selman I P   3363
Selph C L   7654
Selver V A   8190
Semel J M   7055
Sen D   7881
Sen S   2436
Sendon M K   7882
Senn H B   4606
Sennehenn C B   2808
Sensemann W M   8094

Sepianu F C   5545
Sessions B P   7056
Sessions W A   5134
Sessums A C   2372
Setseck M A   4146
Seubert E E   4274
Severson F W   7057
Sevier M W   492
Sewall M   1665
Seward W W   5946
Sewell S W   4379
Sexton J   5792
Seymour E S   1666
Seymour M H   8095
Seymour T   2437
Sgorbi L   8664
Shafer S M   8724
Shaffer A A   854
Shaffer G B   7058
Shaker D   1667
Shamblin R   7059
Shandler A   493
Shane M L   7482
Shanker S   5257
Shanklin A K   6169
Shankman R   1334
Shannon C A   4967
Shannon E S   6170
Shannon P H   5546
Shapiro B   2234
Shapiro C   494
Shapiro E K   7639
Shapiro M   5088
Shapiro M E   1668
Sharkey K F   4607
Sharon A   2235
Sharp A V   7060
Sharp M H   4003
Sharpe A V   1931
Sharrock R I   937
Shaver R J   3175
Shaw C M   7061
Shaw E B Jr   8665
Shaw H B   1669
Shaw J T   3919
Shaw P   3231
Shaw R B   962
Shaw W F   2236
Shaw W R   3854
Shea E A   3176
Shea V   1670
Sheehan J D   8191
Sheehan L M   3177
Sheehan Sr M A   7062

Sheehan P M   5547
Sheehan T M   3633
Sheiner N F   2963
Sheldon G   3855
Sheldrick H M   5152
Shelston A J   3404
Shelton E L   7063
Shelton E L   2237
Shelton J A   855
Shelton T   7064
Shelton W H   6062
Shepherd D Y   2310
Shepherd E   4608
Sherley L   7065
Sherman E M   8317
Sherman G W   3856
Sherman J   8742
Sherrick H L   7883
Sherry W L   4890
Shields J C   5238
Shields M F   1671
Shields R A   1882
Shields V   8318
Shields V M   5135
Shine W H   4609
Shinn J   7350
Shipley H   1672
Shipp R L   4141
Shirakawa S H   1189
Shireman J H   8319
Shirley H B   5548
Shirley I R   2915
Shirley J   416
Shirley M   4968
Shiver B J   7601
Shkolnick S   4095
Shleffar J E   2625
Shockley G R   7618
Shoenberg R E   7066
Sholley S   2809
Shook B J   1883
Shorb E   1037
Shore D   8582
Shores D   6023
Short W H   7884
Shorter M D   1190
Shouse C F   856
Shovrek M V   4681
Shrake J R   4096
Shroyer R J   495
Shull V I   995
Shull V M   7885
Shultz D P   7067
Shultz W C   4969

Shunami G 595
Shutts K 1298
Shy Z M 4380
Sibley A M 2810
Sibley H 8096
Siciliano E A 149
Siddall D V 8192
Sider J W 7068
Sidwell S J 5947
Siebert D T 4273
Siegel J W 5136
Sielewicz B M 7351
Siemers K 5549
Siepi A 908
Sievers A M 4887
Siferd N K 3634
Sigal L 150
Signorelli S 5948
Sikes J R 2238
Silbaugh H R Jr 1191
Silbaugh M C 4381
Silbernagel R J 4274
Silbert E W 4610
Silcox D P 4275
Silliman W W Jr 4611
Silver Sr M 5749
Silverman S 8743
Silverthorne E E 7069
Silvestri S 5874
Silvia D S Jr 1673
Simison B D 7070
Simkin S 5186
Simko J 4970
Simmons E 7886
Simmons J D 7071
Simmons J P 7072
Simmons K P 7073
Simmons M L 857
Simmons M M 3496
Simmons R E 496
Simmons R M 8193
Simonidses H A 1192
Simonini R C Jr 7074
Simpler M P 3857
Simpson C J 7602
Simpson C M Jr 6171
Simpson H 2329
Simpson H U 2660
Simpson L P 5770
Simpson W J 3405
Simpson W T 7075
Sims J H 8097
Sims R L 5885
Simzig E A 5704

Sinclair D P 7561
Sinclair J 858
Sinclair L 2526
Sinfield A J 8320
Singer A D 27
Singer S W 1884
Singh R 3273
Singleton E M 2239
Singleton F R 8098
Singleton K L 5187
Sinks N M 8557
Sipes M P 7887
Sircy O C Jr 1193
Sirmans S L 7076
Sisson J E 8099
Skelly Rev L 1674
Skelton J W 1675
Skewes A R 8321
Skinner H 7994
Skinner M L 859
Skinner M L 1194
Skinner V K 3364
Sklar J S 2964
Sklavounou D 8322
Skretkowicz F E 497
Skretkowicz V 498
Skutches P 7483
Slater M M 2240
Slicer D H 4927
Slights W E 3248
Slipper A 8632
Sloan E H 2241
Sloan E L 5978
Sloan H 7077
Sloan J B 5631
Sloan R P 8323
Sloan T J 5089
Slone G C 7935
Slover G W 7078
Small A F 7484
Small C Y 5550
Small R 2242
Smallbone J A 151
Smalley D A 2438
Smallwood O 7079
Smallwood O T 6087
Smart E L 7080
Smialkowa A 2243
Smith A 1299
Smith A E 2244
Smith A T 4019
Smith B 5793
Smith B D 8100
Smith B E 3546

Smith B G 1676
Smith B L 5771
Smith C G 3365
Smith C H Jr 4276
Smith C M 3858
Smith C R 860
Smith D G 6194
Smith D M 3461
Smith E 1196
Smith E A 5153
Smith E D 1195
Smith E E 8325
Smith E F 2983
Smith E L 7081
Smith E M 8324
Smith E P 8686
Smith F 8326
Smith G B 1738
Smith G M 3859
Smith G Y 5090
Smith H C 499
Smith H E 5949
Smith H H 1932
Smith H R 3920
Smith I F 7082
Smith J 4478
Smith J A 257
Smith J A 500
Smith J A 7995
Smith J F 1197
Smith J G 3462
Smith J H 7983
Smith J M 3448
Smith J P 5551
Smith J W 2245
Smith K B 4708
Smith K E 3860
Smith K K 7619
Smith L B 8150
Smith L H 4004
Smith L P 1198
Smith M A 5794
Smith M A 7984
Smith M A 7985
Smith M K 8380
Smith M L 861
Smith M M 4130
Smith M M 8327
Smith Sr M P 321
Smith N J 862
Smith P E 2811
Smith P E 2812
Smith R G 6172
Smith R M 7086
Smith S J 5950

Smith S L 7087	Sowers E J 7353	Squires R C 5555
Smith S R 2813	Spade J A 8744	Stacey I 4277
Smith W B 7888	Spagnuolo G D 2965	Stachura Rev S M 6195
Smith W H 2916	Spain L G 3075	Stack C J 380
Smith W J 4612	Spakowski R 7090	Stack K E 3179
Smith W L 8735	Spalding B 2253	Stackhouse W J 3232
Smock G E 2246	Spangenberg A 8328	Stafford F P 5556
Smoller S J 2247	Spangler D R 8426	Stafford T J 8427
Smoot G A 8425	Spann M W 3862	Stagni A 2373
Smoot J 6173	Spanos W V 7354	Stahl E W 4937
Snavely R C 4097	Spargo J W 7091	Stahl N M 3635
Snell F M 2248	Spark D 5795	Stahl Q S 5557
Snelling R D 8101	Sparron W K 4131	Stahr W E 2815
Snider R 7518	Spateholz H G 1885	Stallard S 867
Snipes W C 996	Spatt B 6016	Stallings F L Jr 7487
Snoddy C E 5552	Spaulding F E 7092	Stallings L R 8484
Snook P A 7088	Spaulding K 8381	Stallings M S 7102
Snorek G M 4738	Speak G M 422	Stallman R L 4830
Snow N J 7089	Spears A E 7093	Stambler E 3976
Snowden J A 5772	Speck H E 7094	Standard L E 6174
Snyder H E 2249	Specking Sr M P 7095	Stanford E B 5642
Snyder M S 5109	Speer D P 7562	Stansell D 36
Snyder N F 4828	Speirs J G 8329	Stapleton A B 7103
Snyder O B 1677	Spelfogel B K 5554	Stark A 5270
Snyder P J 8102	Spence R 5188	Stark A M 7104
Snyder R C 1199	Spencer G B 7096	Stark E M 7105
Sobell G J 501	Spencer H A 4382	Stark S E 4099
Sodowsky R E 5553	Spencer L F 7355	Starke M R 4613
Sogliero A A 2439	Spencer S P 7097	Starks G A 7106
Sohngen M L 417	Spencer V C 866	Starling B R 7107
Sokoloff H C 1300	Sperduto Sr F C 7890	Starr G N 7108
Soldani Sr M V 3384	Spevack M L 4193	Starr J M 2966
Soleti I 3861	Speyer F C 7098	Starr K M 7892
Solimine J 863	Spicer U J 7356	Starrett A L 597
Soller M 4192	Spikes J T 7099	Stasko Sr M L 2254
Solomon B 2250	Spilka M 4829	Statham D P 1682
Solomon B T 7941	Spina E F 7587	Statham Y 7357
Solomon E F 3497	Spina S 7563	Staton E P 7109
Solomon M J 418	Spires G F 3178	Stauffer R M 2255
Solomon V 2251	Spires M A 4383	Stavros G 1887
Solon J J 4739	Spitzenberger R D 7100	Steadman J M 5558
Solt M J 4874	Spitzer E 596	Steakley P M 3366
Somermier C E 2252	Spivack J 502	Stedman H A 7110
Somerville W G Jr 1678	Spivey G C 8151	Steele A L 3865
Sommerville M 1679	Spofford E W 7101	Steele G R 4831
Sonino B 864	Spradlin J E 7485	Steele M A 503
Sonstroem D A 4098	Sprado E L 1681	Steele O L 5092
Sorensen J V 7889	Sprague R S 2814	Stefancich G 5258
Sorenson A F 5091	Spring A J 3863	Stegall M J 7358
Sornborger N W 1680	Springer F J 8633	Stein D L 1683
Sorrell E N 865	Spruce C 3864	Stein K F 4100
Sorrells S K 1200	Spruill M J 7891	Stein R 1888
Soucie R M 7352	Spurgeon G 1886	Stein R L 1684
Soukup K J 28	Spurlock F M 7486	Stein R L 7359

Steinbach G 8330
Steiner T R 7625
Steingass D H 5705
Steinhauer R K 4479
Stellini S J 1686
Stengel J M 1772
Stephany W A 7112
Stephens E 8798
Stephens E B 152
Stephens J C 2661
Stephens R F 7892
Stephens R J 2627
Stephenson C A 8498
Stephenson H L 7111
Stephenson L W 8692
Stephenson W A 1201
Stepp N T 2256
Sterling A C 504
Stern H A 6175
Stern H J 505
Sternberg S 2257
Stetson G 5239
Stevens B L 8331
Stevens F R Jr 8103
Stevens H C 7894
Stevens I N 5559
Stevens L R 868
Stevens R T 3866
Stevenson A H 6176
Stewart C E 4480
Stewart C M 6177
Stewart D C 3463
Stewart D M 6088
Stewart D S 8152
Stewart G O 5240
Stewart G S 1009
Stewart J 7113
Stewart P L 8332
Stickman B B 540
Stiebel S A 7114
Stifler M H 1687
Stiga P F 2917
Stigler E V 5003
Stiller J 2629
Stinchcomb L 3367
Stine L 5154
Stinson M C Jr 2918
Stobaugh M H 7115
Stobie H R 1688
Stockdale J C 419
Stoddard F G 4384
Stoddard H 5004
Stoddard M A 1301
Stoker R C 8382
Stokes D E 3867

Stokes E E 7488
Stokes T R 1689
Stokes W H 2919
Stolfa B 4928
Stollman S S 5560
Stone A Jr 3076
Stone A N 1338
Stone D O 1202
Stone E A 3388
Stone J A 4945
Stone J S 5241
Stone M C 8499
Stone M S 7116
Stone R R 3868
Stone S C 8104
Stoneman P M 3077
Stoner W W 8500
Stooke D W 4682
Storey K E 8333
Storey Sr M D 5834
Storey P S 4020
Storey W 4614
Stork G B 3449
Storm J H 7117
Storm M G 4101
Storti A 5093
Story J M 997
Story L W 7118
Story M L Jr 2258
Stott J C 1203
Stott W 8194
Stouk D H 2967
Stout J H 1690
Stout Rev O H 2477
Stout W M 2630
Stout W W 296
Stoutmire F A 7119
Stovall S T 1359
Stovall V 4615
Stover F M 8558
Stowe M L 3636
Stowel F S 1302
Strabel A L 7895
Strandberg E A 2259
Strang M J 1038
Strange R P 258
Strangnatt M V 7896
Strasser W C 1691
Stratman Sr M M 4616
Streator G I 7897
Street H K 7898
Strehle S A 2330
Streifer R B 7489
Stretcher J S 598

Stricker M 153
Strickland A L 4971
Strimple V 869
Stringer D H 1204
Stringer G A 2816
Stringer G A 8105
Stringfellow W M 3078
Stripling E H 1692
Strobel R E Jr 3869
Stronach E E 2260
Strother H B 4617
Stroup J B 7120
Stroup T B 5989
Strouss L 7490
Strunk S J 3249
Stuart F C 998
Stubbe M H 7360
Stubbs D C 4875
Stubbs G G 2631
Stubbs P J 7646
Stuckert F A 2261
Stumpf E C 2487
Stutzenberger A 7491
Suarez R P 3637
Such P D 4278
Sudrann J 8687
Sugg R S 2331
Sugimura K 6063
Suhadolo J 8485
Suhweil E S 1205
Suits H 7996
Sukenick L 3079
Sullivan E M 2817
Sullivan F E 3080
Sullivan G J 8634
Sullivan G J 4279
Sullivan J J 1693
Sullivan J J 5155
Sullivan J V 7361
Sullivan M E 5750
Sullivan M M 259
Sullivan M T 1739
Sullivan M T 5561
Sullivan R J 5951
Sullivan R W 1694
Sullivan V 8006
Sullivan V M 3638
Sumida S H 5562
Summerhays D 5563
Summers J L 1206
Summers M F 541
Summers R M 2818
Sun M 2819
Sunday A M 1207

Sundell R H 5564
Sundquist E L 2820
Surette P L 1889
Survant J W 342
Sutfin J A 7121
Sutherland J D 5565
Sutherland R C Jr 8106
Sutherland W O Jr 5566
Sutton C 1695
Sutton C M 5567
Suvajian G K 1208
Suwannabba S 260
Suzuki K 3274
Svatik S 506
Svendsen J K 5568
Swab J N 8583
Swaim J H 8584
Swain G J 870
Swain V C 2821
Swann T B 6064
Swanson A L 5569
Swanson M A 1209
Swartchild W G 2822
Swartley S S 5570
Swartz D L Jr 5571
Swaney M I 3081
Sweatt F 7122
Sweeney H P 7123
Sweet M W 7124
Sweetland R C 8616
Swenson J G 3581
Swetsky J 3870
Swim L B 871
Swor C E 3582
Sydner H W 7899
Syers B B 3871
Sylvester H E 4102
Symes M W 5572
Symons L A 7900
Synnott B J 4832
Synnott B J 4858
Sypher F J Jr 8334
Szlosek J F 7125

Tabb M 7492
Taber G 2968
Tabunar E G 1039
Taege A L 2262
Taffae P M 7493
Taft R W 3082
Taft W W 8107
Taggart M 2263
Tagliavini P 5573
Tague H N 5574

Tahmizan Z D 963
Talbot B W 7126
Talbot J H III 872
Talcott J H 5094
Tallentire D R 8799
Tallman M A 1210
Talotti M 3211
Tamplin J G 4103
Tanco F B 8108
Tandy M 3872
Tanner O B 8383
Taplin C A 3298
Tapp T L 4280
Tarbox W G 3083
Tarpley B 5575
Tarravechia R 8109
Tate A 507
Tate G L 5005
Tate M T 3873
Tatham C 2632
Tatham L C Jr 7494
Tatro C L 5576
Tatum O M 6178
Tauss B 5006
Tayler E W 5137
Taylor A 3874
Taylor A G 7127
Taylor C R 3875
Taylor E 3406
Taylor E 7901
Taylor E C 2264
Taylor E D 1212
Taylor E D 3232
Taylor E K 1303
Taylor G F 7936
Taylor G O 2265
Taylor G R 3084
Taylor H H 2266
Taylor I O 1767
Taylor J B 8725
Taylor K C 5773
Taylor K H 5952
Taylor L E 1696
Taylor L J 508
Taylor M 4281
Taylor M E 1697
Taylor O W 2267
Taylor R K 4618
Taylor S V 5577
Taylor W W 1211
Teachout P R 1213
Teague M B 4619
Teague P 5578
Teare R 2268

Tebbe N L 7128
Tedhams R W 8501
Tedlow R J 4833
Teer B A 1933
Teer T W 7902
Teeter L B 7129
Teich N 4620
Teichert E A Jr 7130
Temple E R 5579
Templeton E M 7495
Tener R 5259
Terino E O 5751
Terner S W 5806
Terrell T 1214
Terrill R K 542
Terry A H 3876
Terry L W 7131
Terry M H 343
Terry W M 5095
Ter Veer C L 8688
Tervo E F 5580
Tosh G L 344
Tether S 5581
Tetreault R 1304
Tew A G 4683
Thalinger T W 3433
Thaman J M 3299
Thames A M 8800
Thames N 5582
Thannikari Sr M G 154
Theresa Sr M 2892
Thibault L 3342
Thom C M 3275
Thomas A C 1305
Thomas B H 7903
Thomas B L 1010
Thomas C A 261
Thomas D E 8428
Thomas D S 3180
Thomas E 7132
Thomas F E 1890
Thomas G K 1215
Thomas H L 4901
Thomas H S 8617
Thomas K R 7133
Thomas M B 873
Thomas M B 3181
Thomas M B 4876
Thomas M O 7134
Thomas P H 8153
Thomas P E 8335
Thomas P T 7135
Thomas R L 1216
Thomas S A 6089

Thomas S T 8801
Thomas W W 2379
Thomason A P 7136
Thomason C W 874
Thomason J W 509
Thomasson M N 8110
Thomerson C B 2269
Thompson B H 7137
Thompson B S 875
Thompson D C 1306
Thompson D S 2270
Thompson E 5583
Thompson J W 7138
Thompson L W 7139
Thompson L Z 1740
Thompson M M Jr 1307
Thompson N M 7362
Thompson P J 8736
Thompson R F 938
Thompson R H Jr 3921
Thompson S A 4902
Thompson T R 8154
Thompson W R 4282
Thomson P G 8111
Thornberry M 7496
Thorne S P 4834
Thorne W B 7140
Thornton A G 3426
Thornton G J 2823
Thornton J D 262
Thornton K L 263
Thornton M 3085
Thornton R D 3666
Thorp A M Jr 1335
Thorpe D L 4481
Thorpe J E Jr 4621
Thorpe M R 5584
Thorsen L S 2930
Thrash L G 8737
Throssell J 7141
Thurley G J 2633
Thwaites M R 876
Tidwell M F 7904
Tiengo L 2478
Tierney R J 4283
Tietze P A 877
Tilghman C S 7363
Timmons G A 8429
Timmons M B 8112
Timothy H D 155
Tindall B M 5189
Tindall M 964
Tinder N 397
Tingle G E 4972
Tinsley M H 7142

Tipton M E 2271
Tipton R L 8336
Tischler C P 4482
Tivnan J R 5260
Tkaczecki B 2272
Tobias J G 7965
Tobin P H 5585
Todaro R 8384
Todd L 878
Todd M E 7143
Tolbert E O 3639
Tolbert J M 5586
Toliver H M 4385
Tollers V L 156
Tolman H L 6179
Tomasini I 345
Tomasso T M 6180
Tomei M 1891
Tomowske C N 7144
Tomshany R A 2969
Tonsmeire S G 1217
Toole J K 4929
Toombs E O 322
Toomey E 7145
Toomey N 8113
Topping D M 3877
Torline Sr M E 5953
Tormey G 4740
Tormollan M A 8751
Torossian A S 1698
Tosarello J 3368
Tousley M 5587
Towers R W 7146
Towles S B 599
Towns R M 2440
Townsend D D 7147
Townsend E M 3559
Townsend G 1699
Townsend J B 5588
Townsend M J 1700
Townsend R L 7148
Toyne R M 6181
Trachtman P 510
Trahan E R 1218
Train L 2921
Trammell R T 1219
Trapani D 7364
Trapnell J B 1308
Traubitz N L 4284
Traugott W H 4285
Traver A A 4386
Treadwell A 3667
Treadwell L W 3878
Treadwell M E 5589

Treadwell T O 7149
Treanor M T 2273
Trere S 2662
Trevisani L 600
Trippet M M 3977
Trivedi S 7150
Trout C H 2634
Troyer D E 7151
Trucks T E 7564
Trudeau Sr P A 4104
Trueax M C 7152
Truesdell K A 7153
Truesdell L G 157
Trunage M 7905
Trushin M 8802
Trussler G 601
Trussler S J 3182
Tryon J L 7906
Tsow F M 8666
Tsuchida B T 4835
Tubelis B A 7154
Tuchinsky J 3668
Tuck M P 8502
Tuck M T 7155
Tucker A A 1701
Tucker B C 7156
Tucker E L 7157
Tucker K 8667
Tucker L F 4286
Tucker L H 7997
Tucker R W 8595
Tucker V A 4387
Tudor J V 2635
Tudor K 4836
Tuhey J T 939
Tuller S S Jr 2824
Tully M J 158
Tung M 5096
Tunnicliffe S 5164
Tuohy A L 8559
Turco A 3369
Turcot Sr A E 4973
Turkington E E 3370
Turnbull I 2274
Turner A C 7365
Turner B C 264
Turner B R 4181
Turner D M 8195
Turner H A 940
Turner L H 2275
Turner L I 5590
Turner M E 8337
Turner R G 1892
Turner R R 5680

Turner S 4837
Turner S J 1220
Turner W H 3183
Tuskan R C 2922
Tussing A C 8338
Tuthill H G 5954
Tuttle G C 7158
Tuttle H I 999
Tweddle M C 2923
Twomey L J 5681
Tye C A 3547
Tyeryar G L 4838
Tyler R W 7907
Tyre N 3407
Tyrrell M S 7159
Tyson F E 8339

Uber S R 8803
Ubom E A 7497
Uebele R C 1221
Uhl B 2276
Ulbrich E V 5591
Ulen F E 5955
Ullery E S 5979
Ulrickson L W 879
Umphlett W L 6090
Underwood G N 3086
Underwood M H 29
Underwood R S 511
Unrue D H 4388
Unsworth M F 7626
Unwin G H 2277
Updike M A 1893
Upshaw M H 7160
Upton P S 4182
Uragani R N 2924
Urban O H 5592
Urban W H 5097
Uselton B M 7161
Ussery A W 5593
Utterback E I 3669

Vaden L T 8114
Vadnais H A 3548
Vague M J 8804
Vail B A 2825
Valente F 7519
Valenti P L 1894
Vallas B W 323
Valliant O M 4132
Valois E E 4389
Van L W 7162
Vance N J 1702
Vancos M J 4105

Van Den Hoven A T 8726
Van Den Noort J 8340
Vanderburg N 1703
Vanderhoof P R 1336
Vandiver E P Jr 4390
Vandover Sr M L 2826
Vanek O M 7908
Van Haitsma G A 1895
Van Hammersveld E W 3879
Van Horn B R 602
Van Kluyve R A 1704
Van Liere C P 1705
Van Loon N 3184
Van Meevern A 7163
Vann B W 880
Vannell N L 3880
Van Pelt L J 4684
Van Scyoc L L 5190
Van Tassel J E 6091
Vanture P S 3276
Van Vactor W E 7909
Varmus H E 2636
Varvel R E 7576
Vasbinder S M 3185
Vaughan M F 7910
Vaughan Sr M T 1706
Vaughan S O 1707
Vawter M S 3450
Vazzoler A M 603
Venable E 7164
Vendramin E 3670
Verchere R 8341
Verdoner J 2278
Vermeersch Sr M J 346
Vernon J K 5594
Vespignani A 965
Vessels Br W 1768
Vesterman W R 1708
Vetrick R C 7565
Vianello A 7165
Vicari E P 634
Vickers M H 5990
Vida E M 1308
Vifian J L 8115
Viglia L 4183
Vigneault J 159
Villanueva Rev R E 3640
Villegas N D 7911
Vince R W 4199
Vincent J C 8585
Vincente R 8560
Vincenz L M 8603
Vincenzi M T 881
Viner A E 3881

Vining I J 160
Vining R H 8342
Vinson B E 7166
Vinson J A 7912
Vitali E 909
Vitali E 7366
Vitali M 2498
Vittozzi A 5823
Vitzthum R C 8116
Vivion F W 8117
Vizzardelli V 3087
Vizzini E N 4391
Vogel J F 6065
Vonderheid L W 7367
Von Der Mehden A 5595
Von Ende F A 5596
Von Kohl M 4839
Von Kreisler N A 1709
Voorhees E N 7913
Vos S M 941
Vossler A E 512
Vuyanovich L J 1710

Waddill M B 7368
Waddle A 2479
Wade J A 5777
Wade J D 4287
Wade M K 910
Wade M W 1711
Waden G W 8118
Wadlinger M C 5597
Wadman J C 2827
Wadsworth M E 1222
Waggoner E H 3882
Wagner E 7498
Wagner J S 2279
Wagner Sr M I 604
Wagner N E 3641
Wagner R A 5598
Wagoner M H 7966
Waide H I 605
Waite R S 161
Wakefield-Richmond M 399
Walach M 7369
Waldauer J A 882
Waldenmaier E A 398
Waldo M R 7167
Waldo T R 7168
Waldrip L B 883
Waldron F H 5800
Walker A J 4106
Walker B B 2828
Walker C R 6182
Walker F A 2663

Walker G J 6183
Walker H 2280
Walker Sr H C 8464
Walker H D 3088
Walker H O 7998
Walker H S Jr 3883
Walker I N 8561
Walker J D 942
Walker J D 2281
Walker J L 5242
Walker K E 1896
Walker L A 3186
Walker L H 1309
Walker M 1311
Walker M 8805
Walker M C 7169
Walker M J 2344
Walker N J 4133
Walker R H 1223
Walker R S 7170
Walker V B 8806
Walker W D Jr 2380
Wall C A 4930
Wall J 7171
Wall P A 884
Wallace A B 7914
Wallace A D 2637
Wallace C R 7915
Wallace E E 7967
Wallace E T 5599
Wallace P E 3434
Wallace Sr R C 7370
Wallace R F 5706
Wallerman I D 7916
Wallin E B 8562
Wallins R P 5600
Wallis D H 8635
Wallis L D Jr 6184
Wallis M L 2441
Walsh J E 4184
Walsh J J 4392
Walsh M J 4622
Walsh Sr M J 7917
Walsh Sr M S 5682
Walsh P F 7499
Walsh T J 3566
Walter E L 7172
Walter J A 7173
Walters D J 3642
Walthall N 5707
Walton E C 8563
Walwark J H Jr 7174
Wanderer P W 8196

Wang H 1934
Wang T L 8668
Ward C B 4974
Ward C F 4645
Ward D F 4483
Ward E J 3671
Ward H S 1712
Ward H W 5824
Ward M E 606
Ward N B 966
Ward P A 5138
Ward R S 5956
Ware E L 7175
Ware M R 8343
Warfield M R 4484
Warkentin G 7566
Warner D M 4185
Warner F C 162
Warner J M 1224
Warner L W 4685
Warner P S 1773
Warnock J P 1713
Warren C 7176
Warren H F 2282
Warren J T 8669
Warren L E 5156
Warren M J 8670
Warren R 7177
Warren S 2283
Warschausky S 2284
Warshaw N R 513
Wasser F R 1360
Wasserman G R 7178
Wasson M 1225
Waterfield C B 3672
Waterhouse R M 1714
Waters L A 2364
Watkins O 7179
Watson A 4107
Watson B H 4623
Watson C N 4393
Watson E W 3371
Watson J C 1226
Watson J E 2442
Watson J F 7180
Watson M R 6017
Watson P J 8752
Watson S R 7918
Watson T L 4186
Watt A A 7647
Watt D J 4187
Watt F W 163
Watters E A 885
Way T J 7181

Wayland A 265
Wayman V 164
Wayne D E 7182
Weakley M 7500
Wear R 165
Wearden D M 8344
Weatherbee G B Jr 171
Weaver H 7183
Weaver J D 3187
Weaver K D 400
Weaver R B 2499
Weaver V B 7184
Webb E III 1915
Webb E A 8689
Webb J 4840
Webb J B 3212
Webb L J 1716
Webb M D 7185
Webb W S 7919
Webber B G 5875
Webber E P 266
Webber J P 7186
Weber G L 2285
Weber H F 1227
Weber R F 5601
Webster R G 3097
Wechsler L 3277
Weeks J F 3188
Weeks J R 5774
Weeks J T 7501
Weeks N W 2286
Weigel C L 297
Weightman F C 7920
Weihe E H 4485
Weiler Sr M M 7371
Weiman E A 5139
Weinhold M W 3189
Weinstein R J 166
Weir J B 7187
Weir R D 2480
Weirick M C 7188
Weiss A 1717
Weiss D A 4841
Weiss J H 3190
Weiss L S 3233
Weiss N 8807
Weiss R H 2829
Weiss T R 4108
Weisstein A L 8808
Welch G W 8119
Welch Rev J E 7189
Welch M J 8345
Welch M L 7191
Welch M M 7190

Wellborn G P 8346
Weller P 7968
Wells M A 8155
Wells M C 1784
Wellwarth G E 5098
Wels A 2287
Welsh A 7192
Welsh H 5796
Welsh J M 4486
Wen F T 5602
Wenck R W 347
Wentworth H B 8596
Werlein H E 5603
Werman G 5604
Wertheimer S 4288
Wesley I S 1916
Wesolowski F 2288
West G E 7193
West Sr M D 7194
West M D 3372
West M E 7196
West M M 7195
West P N 5825
Westergren M Y 7197
Westlake M B 1999
Weston J M 2488
Weston P R 4005
Wetter J A 4487
Weyer I I 1718
Whalen J F 2925
Whaley G W 6185
Wheat M A 1719
Wheeler B M 1720
Wheeler D W 5605
Wheeler F L 3922
Wheeler J H 3884
Wheeler L R 8727
Wheelock W 2970
Whelan I F 7520
Whelan R 2289
Whidden Sr M B 3643
Whitacre W J 3373
Whitaker D F 7198
White A M 8671
White C 7199
White D B 7200
White D M 3498
White D M 7201
White E E 7502
White F C 267
White F E 7372
White F L 5606
White G 7202
White J H 8120

White L I 3583
White M 4134
White M 7203
White M B 4289
White M C 1721
White M E 1897
White M M 1898
White N E 4109
White N E 7204
White P C 370
White P T 4488
White R B 2443
White R S 5607
White S A 3191
White S B 5957
White W D 3389
Whitefield T L 5608
Whitehead C U 607
Whitehead D E 1228
Whitehead G G 4975
Whitehouse A G 3374
White-Hurst B M 1899
Whiteley T S 2290
Whiteman R T 2291
Whitener W J 8693
Whitesel G E 7577
Whitley R 5958
Whitman F H 8672
Whitman Sr M E 5708
Whitmire J V 7503
Whitmore A P 1229
Whitmore N 1722
Whitney G C 7205
Whitney M 7206
Whitney P W 7632
Whitson B C 7207
Whittier H S 2292
Whittington P K 2926
Whitton E M 2638
Whitty E E 3192
Whitworth L D 1230
Wickens G 3885
Widder W J 7921
Wiegand R 4006
Wiese G J 3886
Wiesner Sr M I 7504
Wiesner S M 7208
Wietlishpach R J 3193
Wiggin D C 911
Wiggins M C 3978
Wiggins P D 7567
Wilband H G 8385
Wilberg M M 5271
Wilbern D P 4842

Wilcock E 2293
Wilcox J C 5643
Wilcox J H 886
Wilcox M L 7505
Wilcox R H 4709
Wilcox S W 1231
Wilde H E 1900
Wilder E C 5243
Wiley B U 887
Wiley E W 1723
Wiley L M 1232
Wiley M 7627
Wiley M L 8347
Wiley M R 8386
Wilhelm F O 2294
Wilkerson C J 5863
Wilkie K E 7922
Wilkins A C 888
Wilkins C T 1312
Wilkinson E H 7209
Will Sr M L 2639
Willard D D 1724
Willard E P Jr 4007
Willard F R 3979
Willging H M 1725
Williams A D 5609
Williams A F 3089
Williams A L 5099
Williams A R 7373
Williams E 2295
Williams F E 7210
Williams G G 5959
Williams G L 2640
Williams G L 5610
Williams G W 7521
Williams H L 5611
Williams H H 4843
Williams H M 3887
Williams H S 514
Williams J A 7374
Williams J E 8809
Williams J H 7620
Williams J M 4394
Williams J M 7211
Williams J K 7212
Williams L B 7923
Williams L N 3584
Williams M 8673
Williams M 7214
Williams M J 5709
Williams M L 7213
Williams M P 5612
Williams N 4686
Williams N B 8810

Williams P N 7375
Williams R L 7215
Williams S L 2641
Williams S L 2927
Williams S R 1935
Williams T R 7376
Williams Z W 8564
Williamson A C 6186
Williamson A N 3888
Williamson E C 2444
Williamson L A 3090
Willig A B 7216
Willis F B 4395
Willis H A 8811
Willis J H 4489
Wills F 7588
Wills J C 608
Wilmsen J A 7522
Wilpiszewski M 3091
Wilson A E 5613
Wilson A W 7217
Wilson C W 1901
Wilson D H 7506
Wilson D L 515
Wilson E A 7377
Wilson E S 889
Wilson G I 8201
Wilson H B 2846
Wilson H V 8565
Wilson J 1726
Wilson J 8430
Wilson J A 8348
Wilson J R 8121
Wilson L A 8000
Wilson L R 4931
Wilson M M 1727
Wilson M S 1728
Wilson N W 8122
Wilson O J 3673
Wilson R B 37
Wilson R E 5165
Wilson R R 516
Wilson R S 5614
Wilson S H 7218
Wilson T B 8597
Wilson W A 5191
Wilson W L 1233
Wiltgen D 3567
Windeatt M F 7219
Windsor L B 7220
Windsor P C 7221
Winehouse B I 2345
Winfrey D C 4646
Winkelmann Sr M A 7924

Winnard W 8123
Winne E 3889
Winser L 3686
Winslow G G 1729
Winter C A 3890
Winter K J 5615
Winter Sr M V 5752
Wintergalen E H 5166
Winton F E 4624
Wire H P 5960
Wirth J G 2928
Wise J N 635
Wiseman E W 1730
Wissler H L 3549
Witek J C 517
Witkowski S S 8124
Witmer M G 3568
Witt D V 2296
Wittenberg C H 8349
Wittmeyer H F 2297
Wittreich J A Jr 5616
Wohlschlaeger R 2929
Wolfe J 4290
Wolfe J E 2830
Wolfe M J 8486
Wolfe R C 7507
Wolff G A 518
Wolfsholl C J 1313
Wolfsohn I C 7937
Woll B L 2642
Wollerman I D 7925
Wolper R S 7222
Wolsey S 519
Wolski H W 2500
Womack D 890
Womack J L 4625
Womack L L 5617
Womack M B 7223
Womack S T 7224
Womelsdorff C J 7225
Wood B 891
Wood C A 2489
Wood C S 8350
Wood D E 7226
Wood D V 4844
Wood F A 7227
Wood G D 4626
Wood J H 892
Wood J P 1731
Wood L A 2831
Wood R W 3585
Wood S J 1936
Wood T W 7228

Wood V M 2832
Wood W P 2298
Woodall J R 6092
Woodard C H 8007
Woodcock J A 7589
Woodfield J 3891
Woodman D 7229
Woodring C R 8125
Woodruff G M 7230
Woodruff S G 5618
Woods D C 6093
Woods J N 7231
Woodtke F J 1741
Woodward S F 6066
Woodworth D 3278
Wooster J E 7232
Wooten C E 5619
Wooten L L 4194
Wordon J L Jr 2643
Workman C M 3375
Worthy M E 8351
Wortley M P 1732
Wortman W R 2445
Wray M M 893
Wright E 2299
Wright E P 7233
Wright G M 2971
Wright J E 3451
Wright L B 4627
Wright M 894
Wright M 1902
Wright M 8126
Wright N E 5100
Wright P 2300
Wright R G 5620
Wright S T 2644
Wright T 2446
Wright T E 5683
Wright W O III 2301
Wrona J B 3279
Wyant J L 2374
Wyatt G D 7234
Wyatt G R 1733
Wyatt L C 5644
Wyatt P L 6094
Wykes D 2645
Wykes V L 8674
Wylie L E 7568
Wylie P R 2664
Wymer T L 8352
Wynd C 3892
Wynkoop W M 3550
Wynn V F 5621
Wynn V Q 7378

Xausa G 1361
Xavier Sr M T 8387

Yacowar M 8745
Yager S E 8694
Yaghmour F H 7379
Yanarella M T 7926
Yano F 1903
Yantha P M 1040
Yap T S 7380
Yarashus A L 7235
Yarker R M 3092
Yaros J 8812
Yates F T 895
Yates L 5622
Yates M C 896
Yates M L 2833
Yeager F 3893
Yeager M L 167
Yeats A W 4687
Yeo E L 7236
Yetzer B E 4110
Yeury S W 6187
Yinger D W 168
Yoder L E 298
Yong G H 4628
Yonker D Y 4142
York E M 520
York K M 8598
Yoshimura R 5623
Yost A B 3093
Young B 521
Young B K 7237
Young C J 1904
Young C M 7238
Young D A 897
Young D J 7239
Young E P 7240
Young F H Jr 8606
Young H F 5624
Young H M 2646
Young H W 7241
Young M L 1314
Young S N 2647
Youngblood M A 4111
Younger W M 7242
Youngs M 8353
Yu H C 5625
Yurewicz J R 1041

Zaal J 7243
Zaborszky D E 3376
Zaccarelli L 8388
Zagst Sr M S 8465

Zahn L 4490
Zahn M L 7244
Zaitz A W 5626
Zajchowski R A 4741
Zalaski B 3499
Zamparutti A 375
Zanconato A M 609
Zanconato G 610
Zane E V 2648
Zanetto M 4720
Zanon M G 5261
Zanon Dal Bo M 324
Zaret P 7245
Zarin E 2972
Zasada A S 5140
Zbar F J 8127
Zelazny R J 8512
Zellar L E 2302
Zennaro A 8675
Zerman M B 3644
Ziegler R P 8813
Ziman A P 8431
Zimmer D L 898
Zimmer K E 7508
Zimmerman E 268
Zimmerman J E 5627
Zimmerman P D 1234
Zimmerman R L 7246
Zimmerman R M 4629
Zinger A 3894
Zingman B G 3234
Zink G 5719
Zins R M 1318
Zolbrod P G 1315
Zucchi M R 7523
Zucker D H 4291
Zunder W L 2834
Zweig J E 8128
Zwerling L S 522
Zwicky L B 5628
Zylstra H 899